A Barfly's Guide To Chicago's Drinking Establishments

by the staff of
Chicago's Barfly Newspaper
Edited and designed by Tony Gordon

First Edition

Chicago, Illinois

A Barfly's Guide To Chicago's Drinking Establishments
Edited by Tony Gordon

Cover design by Curtis Stenger

Published in 2000 by:
  Barfly, Inc.
  P.O. Box 416580
  Chicago, Il. 60641-6580
  www.barflynews.com

Manufactured in the United States of America

ISBN: 0-9663209-0-5

To Marie Wuczynski for taking a chance on a goofy guy with a crazy idea.

Under The Table of Contents

Pictured here is the front door to Barfly's expansive offices in Chicago's beautiful Logan Square neighborhood.

The Barfly Staff

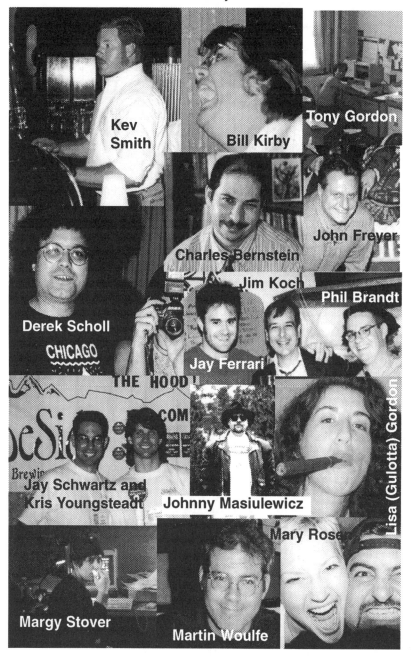

Kev Smith

Bill Kirby

Tony Gordon

Charles Bernstein

John Freyer

Jim Koch

Phil Brandt

Derek Scholl

CHICAGO

THE HOOD

Jay Ferrari

Jay Schwartz and Kris Youngsteadt

Johnny Masiulewicz

Lisa (Gulotta) Gordon

Mary Rose

Margy Stover

Martin Woulfe

Acknowledgements

This book is a culmination of five years of material published in Barfly Newspaper, a monthly periodical from January, 1994, to February, 1997; from March 1997 to the present, a bi-weekly in Chicago. Although my staff and I have worked our tails off these past six years to bring our readers Barfly Newspaper and now this book, none of it would have been possible without those who have advertised with us and those Chicagoans who answered our plea for help in exchange for a warm six-pack of Busch beer. Cheers to all.

-- *Tony Gordon*

The reviews in this book are written by:

Tony Gordon, Phil Brandt, Margy Stover, P. Geraghty, Holly Stevens, Marc Ruvolo, Eric Schnabel, W. Child, Kevin Smith, Anne Preshlock, Linda Abu-Shalback, Edward Marsh, Mary Waclaw, Andrea Sachs, Lisa Hofbauer, Roni Ambrister, Johnny Masiulewicz, Mike Curtin, Cynthia Grows, Michael Cotter, Jay Ferrari, Chris Handyside, June Hathaway Vigor, and Kristi Harrity.

Mark Kenseth, Paul Barile, Sean McKenna, Teri Gidwitz, Kevin Hayes, Dennis Mahoney, Bob Schertler, Pete Schmugge, Lisa Gulotta, Bruce McKenna, Kry, Bill Franz, Nicole Engebretson, Dave Carmody, Brian Diebold, Peter Axelrad, Bill Stephenson, Dan German, Patrick McAuley, Derek Scholl, M.A. Bell, and Darlene Saxon.

Sergio Barreto, Tim Dryer, Beth Gosnell, Jessesam Cramer, Stephanie Behne, Brendan O'Brien, Ron Slattery, Tom Luplow, Bart Schuster, David Hayes, Arunas Ingaunis, Brian Farrelly, Rich Webster, T. Wright Townsend, Melody Hendricks, Craig Greenfield, Nina Kokotis, Dan Tucci, Donna Donato, Jon Hermansen, Suzane Ruks, Jane Ignacio, and Chris Olvera.

Willy Laszlo, Joe Schweizer, Bud Naber, Roger Lonak, Jr.; T.M. Kornelsen, William Gleich, Aaron Baker, John W. Singer, Scott Terry, Lisa Kueng, David Dayen, Alice Bendig, Colleen O'Reilly, J. Quilter, Zach Paradis, Meg Rhem, George Rawlinson, Greg Dellinger, J. Quillian, Sean Deveney, Lee DiVita, Christy K. Rizzo, Kevin Toomajian, Dan Rafter, and Paul Dunk.

Photographs are by Tony Gordon, Phil Brandt, Simon Cygielski, Kevin Smith, Eugene Kimmons, Rick Barbee, Megan Miceli, Derek Scholl, Candace Brugger, Martin Woulfe, Paul Jersild, Bill Kirby, Tony Lunn, Paul Barile, Roy Koz, Tim Carroll, Paul Ristow, Mary Wisniewski, Arunas Ingaunis, and Ray Baruth.

Special thanks goes out to Sharon Woodhouse of Lake Claremont Press in Chicago who guided us through the book publishing process.

Introduction

Kim of Marie's Riptide Lounge, 1745 W. Armitage Ave.

*O*ne of the most common questions I am asked is: how did Barfly Newspaper begin? The idea for Barfly popped into my head in early 1990 while I was on an extended pub crawl of London, England. For nearly six months, I explored the pubs of London. Some places were fantastic others were rather scary. I got beat up, harassed, lost, and fat. It was in the scary places that I decided I needed some sort of guide — and the plans for Barfly began.

I originally thought to do Barfly Newspaper in London but later reconsidered and felt my homebase, Chicago, has just as many pubs and no guide either. At the end of 1990 I finished my journalism degree at the University of Arizona and headed home. I worked for several newspapers as a reporter, all the while planning for Barfly and looking for a partner. My plan was to create a guide as well as a community newspaper covering Chicago's bars. But I needed help, I couldn't do it myself.

Every time I thought I had a partner, they backed out when I mentioned that they would have to put up some money. I told everyone I knew about my plans for Barfly. After three years of searching, I finally found a partner when my friend Marc Ruvolo told me his roommate's brother Phil Brandt was looking to get into publishing. Marc gave me Phil's phone number and I called him up. I told Phil I was a friend of his brother and that I needed a partner to help create Barfly Newspaper.

On the phone, Phil sounded really interested, but he later told me he thought

Barfly's Guide to Chicago's Drinking Establishments

I was a quack (probably still does). Anyway, he agreed to meet with me in early 1993 at The Ginger Man, 3740 N. Clark St. I was living just down the street from the G-Man and this was my neighborhood tap.

Phil showed up with two of his friends and I told them of my plans for Barfly. They loved it. One of Phil's friends, P. Geraghty, even had an idea for a column that night called "Banned from the Pubs." We ran the column for about three years until P. Geraghty exhausted his tales of being thrown out of bars.

Back in the beginning, the summer of 1993, Phil and I laid concrete plans for the paper. We decided to do it monthly and our first issue would be January, 1994. The printing dates would coincide with those of Nadig Newspapers where I was working as assistant editor on Chicago's Northwest Side. Nadig puts out weekly newspapers and I often accompanied the flats (the raw layout for the paper) to the printer, Midwest Lithotype in Lansing, Ill. I told Dan Gouwens at the printing company of my plans for Barfly and he and the rest of the staff (thank you Carol!) were really helpful in all aspects.

Phil and I set up shop in the small bedroom of my Lake View apartment. We bought a computer and other publishing supplies. We went out and wrote a bunch of bar reviews and stories. I wrote under the name A. Brandon Gordon to conceal myself from the folks at Nadig. I didn't know if they would approve and I didn't want to lose my job. We spent November and December of 1993 putting together our first issue. It was a 12-page paper and rather crude. I had done quite a bit of cut-and-paste page design in college and at Nadig. But we really had no idea how much easier and more efficient computer design was.

Marc Ruvolo helped us get two advertisers, The Empty Bottle and The Wrigley Side Tavern. I bugged Marie over at the Riptide. Next to the Ginger Man, the Riptide was my favorite place and I spent quite a bit of time there. Marie liked the idea and took out the centerfold of the first and most every paper since then. We are incredibly indebted to her.

At the time, Phil was working at a construction company and every day after work we would meet at my apartment and work on Barfly. The first issue came out and our friends helped us distribute them. It wasn't very efficient, a large amount of papers never left our car trunks. It took us a few months to get distribution down.

But our immediate reception was great. Those that found the paper, loved it. We received a bunch of phone calls from people who wanted to write, do illustrations, take photos, and advertise.

By October, 1994, I felt I was crowding my two roommates with the production of Barfly. We pretty much took over the whole apartment. Though, my roommates Karl and Lisa never complained and I have to thank them. That month we moved to our first office shared with my friend Matt Fusello who was starting a record label — Anti-Gravity Records. We rented a rustic loft on Ravenswood and Grace.

The new office turned out to be a bust. There wasn't much heat in there that winter. We spent our evenings working on the computers (we had two computers at this point) wearing our coats and gloves and shivering. When the summer came, the place turned into a furnace. That was Chicago's record heatwave summer when hundreds of people died. We worked, stripped down to our shorts, pouring water over our heads to keep cool. Many days that summer, we just couldn't even work. It was just too hot.

In addition to the mice and roaches, we shared a wall with a karate studio. They were always slamming into the wall (just a thin piece of plywood) and knocking stuff over on our side. The rest of the building contained wood shops. The dust in our office was incredible. What a nightmare.

Yet the paper grew. We increased our circulation and gained more advertisers. Barfly even began to pay for itself. Basically, it had to, Phil and I were broke at this point. But as the paper grew, so did the work load. I couldn't cope with working all day at Nadig then going to Barfly's office and working all night. So I quit my job, borrowed a few thousand dollars and worked Barfly full-time. But the more I worked, the more it still began to mount. So I begged Phil to quit his job and help me out. It took months to convince Phil but eventually he came around.

We paid ourselves $125 a week and worked all day and all night solely on Barfly. When our lease ended in October, 1995, we moved into a building, 2823 N. Milwaukee Ave., owned by one of our advertiser's, Danny at Crown Liquor's and Tap Room. Danny was extremely kind and helpful to us. Unfortunately, he suffered a heart attack and died in April, 1998. What a terrible loss. We miss him. Our office is still located over his store. Hopefully his kids will let us stay in our office above Crown Liquor's for some time to come.

Barfly has been steadily growing since the beginning. All along we planned to do other projects like this book and our web page, www.barflynews.com. In March 1998, we increased our output to two papers a month. In early 1999, Phil left to pursue a career in computers, his real interest and is doing really well. Although I really miss working with Phil, my wife Lisa and local DJ Chris Waldbuesser have stepped in nicely. In 1999, we had our best year ever at the paper. We even added newspaper boxes to the streets of Chicago. The year 2000 should continue our success with a higher circulation and more newspaper boxes.

A big thank you goes out to all of our supporters, advertisers, writers, photographers, illustrators, and delivery crew who have given us an incredible amount of help.

The reviews in this book orignally ran in the paper and have been updated for this book. But one thing I've learned in five years, is that bars open and close with the wind. So some of these bars may have closed during press time and I know quite a few new ones have opened up and aren't in this book. So pick up the newest copy of Barfly Newspaper for the most up-to-date reviews. But use this book to find some Chicago classics. Chicago has more than three thousand drinking establishments. There are bars for everyone in Chicago. I hope you enjoy this book.

— Tony Gordon

Chapter One
The North Side

One of the many fine patrons at The Pumping Company, 6157 N. Broadway St.

The North Side traditionally begins at Madison Street. However, for our purposes, we're calling everything north and northwest of the Chicago River the North Side. There are approximately 25 neighborhoods on the North Side: Rogers Park, West Ridge, Uptown, Lincoln Square, North Center, Lake View, Lincoln Park, Near North Side, Edison Park, Norwood Park, Jefferson Park, Forest Glen, North Park, Albany Park, Portage Park, Irving Park, Dunning, Montclare, Belmont Cragin, Hermosa, Avondale, Logan Square, Humboldt Park, and West Town. The neighborhoods vary greatly. Uptown is a traditionally tough neighborhood with tough bars, Lincoln Square has many German bars, Lake View is quite diverse with Wrigley Field, sports bars and a strip of gay bars, Lincoln Park contains DePaul University and many college-type bars, Near North Side contains many fashionable bars and tourists, Jefferson Park, Portage Park, and Irving Park are working-class neighborhoods with typical Chicago tap rooms, Belmont Cragin has quite a few Polish bars, and West Town has the city's arts community and bars that cater to it. For a breakdown of North Side neighborhoods and the bars they hold see the index at the back of this book. The following reviews are in alphabetical order.

1

Abbey Pub
3420 W. Grace St.
773-478-4408
Hours: 11 a.m. to 2 a.m. Sunday to Friday,
11 a.m. to 3 a.m. Saturday

I thought I saw a leprechaun in the bathroom. I tried to grab it and say, "Gimme a Guinness!" But it got away.

This Northwest Side Irish bar offers a clean and comfortable atmosphere. It's great to hear the Irish accents of patrons and employees alike.

The Abbey is made up of two good-sized rooms. When entering, turn right for the restaurant/lounge area, or left for the bar.

Food is served in both rooms. The Abbey's menu consists of great Irish treats like Shepherd's pie, fish and chips, corned beef and cabbage, and an Irish breakfast with blood pudding, mmm-mmm good. The Abbey's Kelly Fitzgerald hinted recently that the menu will be expanding.

The big difference between the two rooms is that the restaurant offers live entertainment nearly every night. It has a large stage and a nice-sized balcony. The room is an excellent spot to catch a live band.

For dart players, there are cork boards in each room, no electronic boards here. The house has darts for the boards as well.

To drink the Abbey serves up some of the best pints of Guinness and Harp around. There is also an excellent selection of whiskeys.

This is just an excellent bar, a Chicago treasure.

Aftershocks Nightclub
(Now called Standing Room Only)
5405 W. Addison St.
773-202-9209
Hours: 7 a.m. to 2 a.m. Sunday to Friday,
open 7 a.m. to 3 a.m. Saturday

The crowd at Aftershocks is in their 30s, still living in the 1980s and having fun.

On a recent visit, I caught a ZZ Top tribute band called Eliminator. This three piece group did a fine job in handling the tunes from the boys of Texas. They covered all the hits ranging from "LaGrange" to "Sharp Dressed Man." I was disappointed when they played "Rough Boy" which is the least enjoyable song I think ZZ Top ever recorded.

The layout for this drinking establishment has a double bar at both ends. There is a dance floor which, in the 1970s, lit up for disco nights. If you get bored by the live band, which plays on a stage at the front, play some darts or pool.

On most nights, it's not hard to find a seat because there are plenty of tables

Barfly Aftershocks-aliveOne

throughout the bar. There are six TVs creating plenty of opportunity to watch your favorite sporting event.

To drink, tap selections are limited but reasonably priced. The three beers on draft are Miller Lite, Red and Genuine Draft, all for a $1.50 a glass, pitchers are $6.

— *Whiskeyhead*

aliveOne

2683 N. Halsted St.
773-348-9800
Hours: 6 p.m. to 2 a.m. Sunday to Friday,
6 p.m. to 3 a.m. Saturday

With 800 bootleg tapes, 100 live CDs, and live bands on weekends, aliveOne, 2683 N. Halsted St., is a live music lovers paradise.

The idea for aliveOne spawned at Miami University in Oxford, Ohio, where friends David Halpern and Benjamin Klopp were students in the early 1990s. After graduation, the friends settled in Chicago and turned their idea into a bar.

"We're both big fans of live music and big fans of bands of the past," said Halpern as a live Phish bootleg tape played in the background.

The list of bootleg tapes is huge. Some of the bands are the Grateful Dead, Pearl Jam, Dave Matthews Band, Pink Floyd and Jimi Hendrix. The live CD list is large as well with bands like the Doors, Miles Davis and Janice Joplin.

Stereo speakers are placed strategically throughout the bar to enhance the live tapes and CDs. The result is an excellent crisp sound. The bar is even decorated with photos of musicians performing live like Bob Dylan and Stevie Ray Vaughn. The photos were provided by rock and roll photographer Paul Natkin who has worked for bands like the Rolling Stones, Halpern said.

Patrons interested in hearing one of the bootlegs just need to pick a name and date out from shelves filled with tapes and let a bartender know.

"Just tell us what you want to hear like Stevie Ray Vaughn in 1982 at the Vic," Halpern said.

The bar that houses aliveOne was formerly the Dalmatian Lounge. Halpern, a native of New Jersey, and Klopp purchased the bar in Dec. 1996. They have completely erased any memories of the Dalmatian Lounge.

Gone are the black and white polka dots, dog photos, and an island bar that took up most of the center of the main room. In place are newly painted walls, new tile floors, rehabbed ceiling, a stage in front, a lounge room in back with couches, a bar and another area (formerly a theater) for live bands, and a beautiful new wavy-wood bar in the main room.

The construction took eight days of hard work, Halpern said. The transformation is really something. A painting of a psychedelic American flag with a woman's face barely visible in the piece takes center stage hanging over the main bar. The woman's fire orange hair jets out across the ceiling.

The improvements, the decor, live music sound, and patrons create an atmos-

The North Side aliveOne-Alumni Club

phere at aliveOne that is calm and inviting.

"I was here when it was the Dalmatian Lounge," said patron Steve Conrad. "It was awful. Now we come here once or twice a week for great music and to hang out. It is definitely a great place."

Open since Dec. 15, 1996, aliveOne is gaining in popularity. When interviewing Halpern on a Wednesday evening the crowds poured in. Halpern, working behind the bar, was almost too busy to talk because he was serving drinks to a thirsty 20-something crowd.

And drinks, aliveOne has aplenty with 18 tap beers such as Pike's Stout, Big Shoulder Porter, Slopeside Brewing Company's Bucktown Brown, Sam's Winter Lager, and their own Steely Tan. Pints cost $2 on Tuesdays and $3.50 the rest of the week. The bar stocks a complete list of wines and whiskies in addition to mixed delights. Specials include $3 martinis on Mondays, and $2.50 Jim Beam and Coke on Wednesdays.

This is the first bar the partners have owned, according to Halpern, age 25. He said he gained his experience working in East Coast bars and even patterned his back lounge after those in Manhattan.

And business has been good for aliveOne, Halpern said. Patrons seem to really enjoy the bar's pool table, Tommy pinball machine, and couches; aliveOne has lots of couches. The highlights at the bar so far have been live performances by bands such as the WrightWally's, Halpern said.

"The WrightWally's played opening night," Halpern said. "They were also on Jenny Jones at midnight. So when they were done playing we turned on the TV and saw them on the show."

— Tony Gordon

The Alumni Club
2251 N. Lincoln Ave.
773-348-5100
Hours: 5 p.m. to 2 a.m. Sunday to Friday,
5 p.m. to 3 a.m. Saturday

With two distinct rooms sporting two different atmospheres, the Alumni Club, 2251 N. Lincoln Ave., is definitely one of the most unique bars in Lincoln Park.

"We have a sports bar with a friendly atmosphere (first floor) and a party-in-the-living-room atmosphere with dancing and a fireplace (second floor)," said Alumni Club manager Todd Jurkuta.

When walking into the Alumni Club, the fourth such club operated by Chicago's Ala Carte Entertainment, patrons are greeted by friendly tie-toting staffers who offer up a seat in a dining or bar area.

The dining area has booths and tables all surrounded by televisions and sports memorabilia. Here, the Alumni Club really lives up to its name. This writer was seated directly under a University of Arizona football helmet, my alma mater.

Barfly Alumni Club

According to Ala Carte director of marketing Tim Borden, the company has made dining at the Alumni Club its main focus at the Lincoln site which opened in Jan. 1997, replacing Tippler's.

"We've been real happy with the menu," Borden said. "Every place that we own serves food."

Ala Carte oversees 16 establishments such as Magnum's Steak and Lobster, 225 W. Ontario, Moretti's Ristorante, 6727 N. Olmsted Ave. and at 1645 W. Jackson Blvd., and the Snuggery, located in Union Station at Canal and Adams Street. Other Alumni Clubs are located at 15 W. Division St., 871 E. Algonquin Road in Schaumburg and on 150 N. Michigan Ave.

Borden said the Alumni Club has 50 items on its menu and that each Ala Carte restaurant uses the same high quality food products.

"The Alumni Club has the same quality of meat as Magnum's," Borden said.

The menu at Alumni Club has 13 different appetizers including the VIP Platter made up of Buffalo wings, barbecue ribs, mozzarella sticks, chicken quesadillas and "Blooming Onion," a colossal onion battered with spices, fried and served in a chile-ancho sauce. There's also salads, specialties such as grilled herb chicken, steaks, burgers, sandwiches, wrappers and pizzas.

Borden said one of his favorites is Alumni's chicken Caesar wrap made up of marinated grilled chicken, Romaine lettuce, jack cheese, red onion, black olives, Caesar dressing and parmesan cheese wrapped in a thin whole wheat pita bread and served with fries and slaw.

"It is really great," Borden said. "I can tear through those things like crazy."

The pizza is special to this Alumni Club, the others do not carry it.

Pizza is available in pan and thin crust with 14 different toppings to choose from. In addition, the restaurant serves designer thin crust pizzas such as "Wild Mushrooms" made up of sliced portabello, shitake and button mushrooms, smoked provolone, garlic and herbs. After trying the "Margherita" pizza, made up of Roma tomatoes, mozzarella, basil, parsley, garlic and herbs, it is safe to say that these 8-inch dishes are excellent.

Service by the baseball-jersey-clad waitresses is attentive and friendly. Waitress Gwen Risbara, new to Chicago via Maine, said she enjoys working at the new Alumni Club.

"It's very interesting," Risbara said. "I like the people and the fact that it's laid back."

Across the room from the laid back dining area is a large rectangular bar. On the night of my visit, the soft stools were filled up with patrons drinking beer from one of the bar's 12 taps, 21 different bottled beers, five white wines, two blush wines, five red wines, six Champagnes and a variety of mixed drinks.

"If you want it, we can mix it," Borden said.

For beer drinkers, the Alumni Club offers "Micro Flights" which are samples of four different microbrews.

For patrons who want to sample a different atmosphere, simply walk up a short flight of stairs into a dimly-lit retro nightclub with a dance floor, DJ, sofas, lounge chairs, funky lamps, bar and pool tables.

The North Side Alumni Club-Andy's

"The second floor is the loft," Borden said. "It's a little more sophisticated with art on the walls (instead of sports jerseys) and '60s furniture."

Full menu is available upstairs as well, Jurkuta said.

Another item offered at the Alumni Club is cigars. The club's large wooden-humidor is located on the first floor and is stocked with 17 different types of cigars ranging in price from $6 to $15.

With lots to offer and two distinctly different rooms, the Alumni Club has been attracting a mesh of Lincoln Park denizens.

"We've been getting a nice wide variety of crowd," Jurkuta said adding that the age range of the clientele appears to be from age 20 to 40.

Borden concurred and said that the Alumni Club has something for everybody.

"You can watch sports and dine reasonably," Borden said.

— Tony Gordon

Andy's
11 E. Hubbard St.
312-642-6805
Hours: 11 a.m. to 1 a.m. Monday to Saturday,
6 p.m. to 1 a.m. Sunday

In the shadows of a Michigan Avenue overpass sits the place for jazz -- Andy's. This popular restaurant/bar is a bargain for those with a jazz and drinking appetite. On a budget? Spend a cover-charge-free lunchtime sipping a few drinks at a large U-shaped bar. The daily live performances draw a consistent and appreciative crowd. The prices for a meal at lunch have been rolled back to encourage more people to enjoy this place.

Saturday nights are special at Andy's. The opening act, John Regulus and his wife Rose Brady are first class. Their group of seasoned backup musicians paint a tapestry of traditional sounds upon which John and Rose place their own distinctive accents. The effect is like silk upon glass -- smooth, soft and elegant. Add your favorite drink, a comfortable chair and sit back and let the music fall down on you.

Andy's is a place where you set the mood for the rest of your evening. Stop in for a few drinks and enjoy the music, then move on, or stay awhile, and relax and enjoy dinner. You'll regain that mellow feeling you've been looking for all week.

Cover charges in the evenings range from $3 to $10, depending on the performance and, of course, increase the closer you get to the weekends.

-- Cupcake

Apple Pub

5737 W. Irving Park Road
733-202-6859
Hours: 3:30 p.m. to 2 a.m. weekdays, noon to 3 a.m. Saturday, noon to 2 a.m. Sunday

In my many travels down Irving Park Road, I hadn't noticed this neighborhood pub. It's tough to see because it's stuck between a clock store and a State Farm Insurance office.

On a recent Thursday night, I decided to make a stop at the Apple Pub which has been around for more than 10 years in the Portage Park neighborhood. Walking in, my first impression was, "God, this is a small bar." To my surprise, the pub has a lot to offer.

For recreation purposes, there is a pool table, a pinball machine, video poker, electronic darts and two cork dart boards in the back. An important note, the air conditioning actually works here. Another definite bonus, the jukebox here has a fine collection of the Rolling Stones, Stevie Ray Vaughn, and many others. For a buck, you, the bar consumer, have the privilege of picking five tunes. While listening to 'em, you can watch some baseball on one of three televisions positioned throughout the bar for viewing. On the night of my visit, it was noticeable that the Cubs are a popular item here.

The tap selection at this joint is very good and fairly priced. Some of the tasty brews include Guinness, Harp, Bass, Sierra Nevada, Pilsner, Woodpecker Cider, and BBK. For a cold tasty pint, the bar patron here pays $2.75. In addition, there are some tasty bottle selections such as DAB, Michael O'Sheas, and one of the most powerful beers ever produced, Elephant Malt Liquor.

Is the Apple Pub worth visiting? The answer would have to be yes. For a neighborhood bar, it has a lot to offer. This is not a pick-up joint, but it's a good place to just sit back and relax. If you are near Irving and Central, just go down another block and a half and you will be served with a cold brew.

— *Pete Schmugge*

Augenblick

3907 N. Damen Ave.
(Augenblick lost its lease in June, 1999, the owners are currently looking for a new site for their bar)

Three Chicago bar veterans teamed up in early 1994 to turn an old North Center mainstay tavern into a modern fun-filled bar. The three created a bar that draws on many North Side neighborhoods. The bar has incorporated the feel of Clark Street, Halsted Street and Wicker Park while maintaining a sense of the surrounding old German neighborhood.

"It's an easy-going place," said one of the owners Henri Borczwyk, who worked at Cabaret Metro/Smart Bar, 3730 N. Clark St., before opening

Augenblick.

"It's like having a party at your house," said a second owner David Butler, a former manager at Sheffield's, 3258 N. Sheffield Ave. The third owner Michael Hecker worked at Metro/Smart Bar for nine years before opening Augenblick.

From its exterior, Augenblick looks dark and unassuming with its small neon sign and blackened windows. Once inside, the bar opens up into a strolling sea of red and blue engulfing a shiney hardwood floor, candle-lit tables, a corner couch and a long bar.

Patrons won't find Miller, Bud or Coors beers at Augenblick, instead the bar serves eight different microbrews on tap and 40 microbrews available by the bottle. The bar also stocks 11 different brands of single-malt Scotch, six different wines and the bartenders are quite adept at mixing specialty drinks especially martinis.

Before the three owners took over, Augenblick, which is German for "In a blink of an eye," sat quietly under its former owner for about five years. All three owners were former patrons of the bar which is located just south of Irving Park Road on Damen Avenue.

While rehabbing the place, the owners learned a bit about the bar's sordid past. Apparently, sometime in the bar's past it was a house of ill repute where women could be purchased upstairs and in the basement of the bar. Butler said the bar's former owner told him that when he first purchased the bar in 1989 the basement was partitioned off into little rooms with a cot in each one.

The new Augenblick has created quite a different reputation for itself. With performances by the Waco Brothers, who wrote a song about the bar, impromptu jams from many Chicago musicians, beer tastings, Martini Soirees where patrons come dressed in tuxedos and evening gowns, Tuesday night Irish music, and charity events, Augenblick has become one of the best bars in Chicago.

Augies

1701 Wrightwood
773-296-0018
Hours: 11 a.m. to 2 a.m. Sunday to Friday,
11 a.m. to 3 a.m. Saturday

Don't step on the TVs upon entry. Multiple TVs on the floor can provide better hockey viewing than the average seat in the mezzanine section at the United Center. Augie's has seven TVs in all. With TVs in the floor, viewers can watch sports games from every angle. During football season, Augie's attracts quite a few Green Bay Packers' fans.

Augie's has an extremely pleasant atmosphere. It has lots of wood paneling, a long bar, stools and tables. Bartenders are rather cordial. There is an outdoor beach volleyball court (opened during the summer months) not an indoor version as the bartenders might have you believe.

Barfly Augies-Babe's

Ozzie, the owner, has been around forever at different locales. He will show you his silver shot award proudly displayed behind the bar for selling thousands of cases of VO throughout the millennia. He'll claim it was awarded because he only has 17 percent of his liver remaining.

Fine taps include Goose Island Honkers Ale, Oregon Pale Ale, BBK, Pilsner Urquell and Dab. A typical bar menu can be had at regular bar food prices, however, much to the dismay of my friend, not one strip of bacon could be found.

The bathrooms are unique in the fact that they have padded toilet seats — in case you find any bacon or visit the nearby Taco Bell. Until then, don't step on the TVs.

— Dave Carmody

Babe's
4416 N. Milwaukee Ave.
773-545-3137
Hours: 9 a.m. to 2 a.m. daily

In visiting Babe's on Milwaukee Avenue, I felt comfortable. This is a neighborhood bar without any hype or glitz. It is a drinking hole where you can drink a cold beer and shoot the breeze.

This tavern has been serving drinks for 10 years running. There is without a doubt that sports is one of the top draws here. As you walk into the establishment, a 60-inch screen lures patrons to watch the Bulls, Cubs, Bears or Hawks. Other recreational activities are darts, video poker, and a very good jukebox.

Babe's is not a pick-up joint. It is simply where you can drink and relax. It has many golden artifacts from the past. Like photos of the 1986 Bears team that won the Super Bowl.

The tap selection is limited to domestics. There is one thing that is certain, you can't beat the prices. A glass of Killian's Red is a mere $1.25. This price made me feel even more comfortable here. There are drinking specials which include a Vodka Lemonade for one buck on Monday, Bud and Red Wolf pitchers for $3.50 on Tuesday, all pitchers $3.75 for Wednesday, and Thursday a Kamikaze shot for $1.

What really shocked me about this bar? I actually received a free round. This is almost non-existent at most drinking holes anymore. Also, the bartenders here are friendly and quick, which is a definite plus for any business.

Besides these other plusses, the heating does work here. This is especially important for keeping the customers comfortable in the winter.

If you are tired of swinging trendy nightclubs and just simply went to relax with a cold drink with friends, check out Babe's on Milwaukee Avenue near Montrose.

— Pete Schmugge

Banana Joe's

940 W. Weed St.
312-337-3486
Hours: 11 a.m. to 2 a.m. Sunday to Friday,
11 a.m. to 3 a.m. Saturday

Near North and Sheffield avenues lies a cluster of concept bars and restaurants that set a rather odd scene. The cluster includes the dusty Southwest-concept of Bub City, the Louisiana swamps of Mudbug OTB (Off-Track Betting), the Italian-American cafe cuisine at Adagio, and an indoor beach party at North Beach.

The latest addition to this strange mix of establishments comes straight from the South Seas (actually Ohio). Banana Joe's has transformed a 22,000 square-foot warehouse into an entertainment complex with a remote tropical island flavor. Banana Joe, a fictional character with a wide-brimmed hat, sunglasses, and soul patch (a tiny goatee under the bottom lip) is according to part-owner Eric Schilder, "a take-off of myself and my brothers."

The concept restaurant and nightclub, which opened in September, 1996, was conceived, designed, constructed, decorated and owned entirely by brothers Jon, Joe, and Dave Field, brother-in-law Eric Schilder, and Paul Butler. Schilder said that they were involved in the construction and development of other restaurants and bars all over the country. From Morton's Steakhouse to Ala Carte Entertainment, "(We were) building for everyone else," Schilder shrugged his shoulders and said, "why not do it for ourselves?" So, they opened their first Banana Joe's in January, 1996, in a brewery district in Columbus, Ohio.

The attention that they have garnered on their home turf where "the concept has been well accepted," hardly seems to have taken them by surprise. "When you've got a line of several hundred people waiting to get in on a Thursday night," Schilder said adding, "we've got something here."

So, they decided to expand to some of the bigger cities throughout the nation. They opened a Banana Joe's in Buffalo, New York, at the former site of former Buffalo Bill's quarterback Jim Kelly's Sports City Bar and Grill followed by openings in areas such as St. Louis, Miami, and even possibly in Aruba.

Schilder said that he and his partners will be on hand themselves to open each location. To assist in the training of their enormous staff, about 40 people, they hired head chef Ron Francis and general manager Scott Schmidt. Francis, a graduate of the Culinary Institute of America, honed his skills in New Orleans under the wing of chef Paul Prudhomme (the guy who looks like Dom Deluise) and Schmidt was corporate opener for Cooker Bar and Grill, a chain of about 50 locations throughout the country.

The club Francis and Schmidt oversee is separated into two sections with five separate rooms; a restaurant, a nightclub, a billiards room, a mini video arcade, and an upstairs loft. The front section is a full service restaurant and bar with a

10

Barfly Banana Joe's-Bassi's

spicy island-inspired menu created by Francis. Schmidt said everything from the soups to the salsa is made from scratch. The gourmet selections carry medium range prices and offer many island flavorings such as Banana Joe's signature Tropical Caesar with Coconut Garlic dressing, Jamaican Jerk chicken skewers, and Grilled Mahi-Mahi with a special honey Macadamia nut crust. Appetizers like the Surf's Up Spinach and Artichoke Dip, which I had the opportunity to sample, are nearly a meal in itself.

The place is mostly decorated in raw, finished wood. Tin shanty roofing is used for its baseboard panels. The structural ceiling supports have been transformed into palm trees. The wall murals resemble the orange-red of the sun setting into a blue ocean and small tin pails are the lampshades of the dim light fixtures that hang low over the high restaurant tables and raised open booths.

A long walk down a short, narrow hallway leads patrons to the nightclub in the back half, which is a playground for grown-up girls and boys. Boasting 70 television sets throughout (including several 10-foot screens), Schmidt explained that there are 14 satellite dishes that can broadcast up to 15 different games from four different sound zones (front, back, pool room, and the upstairs space). The rooms are separated by thick walls and keep the sound from bleeding into the separate areas.

The billiards room, which is adjacent to the arcade, has five pool tables with a sixth one on the upper level, which also has the second of five bars. An island bar in between the two bars that line the opposite walls sits off-center on the main floor and together surround a three-level dance floor and cocktail table area complete with fog machine, state-of-the-art lighting and sound systems.

Live music can be heard in the front-section of Banana Joe's on Wednesday and Thursday with house bands The Generations (hits from 70s, 80s, and 90s) and The M80's ("from the creators of The Afrodisiacs" performing "New Wave" hits) respectively. Friday and Saturday nights will find a variety of local up-and-coming bands.

— Arunas Ingaunis

Bassi's

1200 W. Hubbard St.
312-243-9350
Hours: noon to 2 a.m. weekdays, noon to 3 a.m. Saturday, closed for private parties Sunday

You may never come across this bar accidentally. Its Martini-toasting sign seems to say "I've been here awhile without you chump."

In a seemingly quiet neighborhood, Bassi's, is located one block south of Grand on Racine. The bar lies in front of Hubbard Street's gallery of animal murals along the underbelly of Metra train tracks.

Bassi's is not a place to overhear the hypothetical fluff that congests most bars. There is a sanctity of drinking bottled beer out of little goblets. In little increments, your beer measures the depth of your stomach. It is immersed in glowing lights that make the bar appear to be floating, hiding corners and after a while you loose depth perception.

Bassi's is a place logged into some odd zone of history lag. Behind the lights, carefully put up in geometric diamond patterns, are photos and momentos. If you don't recognize any of these people or objects, you can peacefully reside in tranquil anonymity.

No taps, beer is cheap.

— Crumpey

Beachwood Inn
1415 N. Wood St.
773-486-9806
Hours: 1 p.m. to 2 a.m. daily

The Beachwood Inn is one of the few legendary bars in West Town and I recently had the pleasure of visiting there. Nothing fancy about this place that has been around for some thirty-odd years. Located just off of Milwaukee Avenue, the facade is faded and you can sense the serenity as you approach the landmark. I think the reason that it goes largely unnoticed is because most bar-goers in the area don't walk southeast of the Holiday Club. It's probably better that way.

I realize that as a bar owner, you don't want a quiet bar, but as a drinker it's a nice change of pace. According to the bartender, Richard (also affectionately known as 'Chooch'), they do get their share of busy nights, I just happened to be there when it wasn't.

If you head over there a little later in the evening, you can expect to get buzzed in. People sitting at the bar might throw a glance at an unfamiliar face that walks through the door, but that's only because it's one of the few things to do besides drink and watch TV. The folks are friendly, so conversation is likely if you are in the mood. The television set has got a few years on it, but medium-sized and adequate enough to satisfy those who are looking to watch da Bears or da Bulls.

Twenty seats with faux-fur-covered back rests run along the bar. There are a couple of booths and some big round tables that fill up the floor space. There is a jukebox that takes quarters and spins 45s, but unfortunately lacks creativity with a majority of pretty typical bar tunes. The back half of the bar is darkly lit and glows when the bowling video game or poker machine is on. The back wall is decorated with a variety of sports pennants. In between the bathrooms there is a small bookshelf that has a selection of books, mostly paperbacks, and an assortment of board games like Parker Brothers classics Sorry and Clue, as well as traditional games of strategy like Chess and Backgammon.

The taps seem to have been dry for some time so you get to choose from either a dozen bottled beers, half domestic, half imported or a modest selection of spirits of which you will not pay more than $3 for anything. The big bargain is $1 Watermelon and Jello shots. If the munchies are grumbling in your stomach, you can buy a bag of chips or go get some pizza slices from Big Tony's across the street and bring it back.

Word to the wise, if you head out there in the later part of the evening, call because they sometimes close early depending on the business. So if you find yourself taking the Blue Line home, get off at Division Street and walk a couple blocks up Milwaukee.

— Johnny Kesh

The Beat Kitchen
2100 W. Belmont Ave.
Hours: noon to 2 a.m. daily

What you do, what you drink, or how you say it often defines the mood of the moment, or may reflect the attitude of a generation. Where to be seen -- The Beat Kitchen. This bar gives up and coming musicians a place to perform. I would consider The Beat Kitchen one of the places musicians have to play at a few times while trying to cut their teeth into the really big, big music scene. I find that The Beat Kitchen is a place to be considered swank, while not pretentious, just a bit on the cool side.

I wouldn't consider an evening at The Beat Kitchen to be cheap. Covers can range from $6 to $8 with drinks costing between 3 to 5 bucks. However, it is one the best deals when viewing live music in the Chicago area. The place serves great food too!

Flexibility seems to key to many successful bars and clubs of the 1990s. The Beat Kitchen seems to be a quasi-alternative college bar of the 1990s. The location offers a live stage, a bar-type setting, and a room upstairs where you can play pool or break out checkers, chess, Scrabble, and stuff and have a game.

There are many bars with many themes in the Chicagoland area. I have to respect a place like The Beat Kitchen. It is a place to go and enjoy budding music talent in Chicago.

-- alt Ex gen

The Bend
5511 N. Lincoln

I don't have a telephone number or the hours of operation for The Bend. Asking for details like that could open me up to the question, "So what are you writing in that notebook?"

Nothing I'd want to show a regular.

The Bend sits in the elbow of that stretch of Lincoln infested with motels having nothing to do with travel. Guests share a room for an hour and leave in

The North Side Beat Kitchen

separate cabs.

When we walked in the bar, two men and a woman, all middle-aged to some degree, were the only customers. They seemed more like neighborhood lease holders than guests from the Apache, Summit, or Spa motels.

After giving Brian and me the necessary cold look, the woman and one of the guys got up to play the El Dorado slot machine.

On this Friday night, the bar never held more than eight customers at a time. At one point, the crowd included a child of about five. Down by the jumbo gumball machines, her mom was making a pay phone call under the leer of a man resembling a tabloid cover version of Burt Reynolds, only fatter.

Brian was distracted by a fart smell from the west. Was it the guy in fluorescent orange, hooded sweatshirt? His animated buddy with the good beard? Neither, Brian finally determined. The smell swelled every time the mom-of-a-woman bartender, Val, opened the cooler. Brian guessed at least one $2.75 bottle of Old Style lay broken inside.

"Interestingly enough, spilled beer thrives in a cold environment," Brian explained.

Other than the cooler's colonization problem, The Bend was tidy. The heart-shaped plastic trash can in the woman's room had been recently emptied. Only a dead-flat package of ketchup littered the floor around our stools. And waiting for its slots to fill with quarters, a Ziggy charity card faced the main aisle running along the bar.

Christmas garland ran parallel to a string of metallic dreidels across the bar back. A holly-draped Barbie-sized Church Lady guarded the register and Jack Daniels.

The focal decoration was the three-foot tree elevated behind the bar. The cardboard-and-fabric angel with her cottony swirl of hair would have been a sweet tree-topper except that the top foot of the tree was bent against the ceiling.

Angel was parallel to the floor. A sympathetic, pear-shaped elf (way too big for that tree) shot his brown eyes desperately heavenward.

Wedged in the branches, the elf was trapped. But Brian and I weren't.

Maybe it was the softer, younger, less-Mediterranean Robert DeNiro in the Venture sweater reciting, "Love is in the air, the cows go moo-moo, be careful not to step, in the doo-doo." Maybe it was Paula Abdul starting on the jukebox. We finally got up to leave.

And all the usual chatty Brian could say once the door closed behind us was "man, oh man."

— *Kathy Nilson*

Berlin
954 W. Belmont Ave.
773-348-4975
Hours: 7 p.m. to 4 a.m. Monday, 5 p.m. to 4 a.m.
Tuesday to Friday, 8 p.m. to 5 a.m. Saturday,
6 p.m. to 4 a.m. Sunday

One of the hippest clubs in the late night scene, Berlin offers the most diversity of any place in the city. Almost every night has a different theme, from New Wave nights to Gothic/Industrial music nights to drag queen nights. On the first and third Wednesdays of each month, Berlin features "Women Obsession," a popular lesbian night, and Thursdays feature male dancers.

Berlin was the brainchild of friends Tim Sullivan and Shirley Mooney in 1983. They opened the club because they felt Chicago needed a place where gay and straight men and women of all races could mingle comfortably. The club was also one of the first in the city to regularly feature video screens.

"It was all so fresh," Mooney said reflecting on the bar's early days.

In 1987, the club expanded and took on its present shape as one of the premier Chicago dance clubs.

What was once one small room is now one large room with art deco-filled light poles, a beautiful mural of scenes from a fictional musical show, wall candelabras like those in some old horror movie and thick draperies resembling those of the 1800s.

Tim died due to complications from AIDS in 1994 and Shirley and husband Julio Rosa moved to Puerto Rico in 1996 and now operate Casa Flamboyant bed and breakfast there.

Yet Tim and Shirley's legacy lives on at Berlin because one of their best friends Jim Schuman now owns the club and operates it with his partner Jo Webster.

Jim has incredible energy and seems to be really enjoying being at the helm of Berlin.

"We bought Berlin because we loved it," said Jim who left his post as American Hospital Association vice president to pursue Berlin. "I think what I appreciate most about Berlin is Tim and Shirley's philosophy when they started which is to create a place for everybody no matter who they are."

Jim is leaving his own mark on the club as well with many theme nights and funky fashion shows. Berlin is a must stop.

— Phil Brandt and Tony Gordon

Betty's

1600 W. Grand Ave.

312-243-8778.

**Hours: noon to 2 a.m. Sunday to Friday,
noon to 3 a.m. Saturday**

First impressions for this bar take a few moments, at least a quaff of a beer. Once that preliminary step is completed, the choice between staying and returning another day or heading straight for the door are more greatly divided than that "line in the sand."

Hell, I liked the place. I appreciate a bar where things are done right, especially those which one usually takes for granted. Whomever was putting in those little things patrons take for granted had a brain in his/her head. For example, I like a bar with a bar. Not a bar that fits like 15 to 20 people comfortably but has something like 50 stools tacked onto it.

And the stools have backs! Gadzooks, how long is it going to take every bar to figure out that they should have these stools? No patron should be subject to bar stools without backs, unless the place doesn't want patrons. They also put these backed stools at their raised tables too! It's such a simple concept — people are relaxing, they don't want to be practicing their best posture, especially after a few drinks.

Also, this bar is at an intersection of two busy streets. There is nothing worse than being at a bar in a location like this while that bland, orange light floods the majority of the bar along with the washed out white light of cars stopped at the intersection. Again, the people of Betty's have a clue and put up tinting on the windows to shade all that annoying light without taking away the view and preventing one on the outside from seeing what is going on inside.

All in all, this is a nice room. The decor is a happy medium; not overly exciting, nor completely drab. It's clean and well built. If any description were to fit it well it would probably be like a fern bar that never happened. They even have a beautiful stone, wood burning fireplace stuffed in the back.

Two pool tables, a jukebox and a couple dartboards make up the primary modes of entertainment. The pool tables aren't run consistently, the dartboards hardly used.

Near the end of 1998, a new generation took over Betty's. What was once a dive bar is now hip and cool. Betty's now has some of the best bartenders in the city like Rocco Webb, great DJs like Shon Dervis and live rockabilly. It's quite an amazing transformation.

— Phil Brandt

16

Big Chicks
5024 N. Sheridan Road
773-728-5511
Hours: noon to 2 a.m. daily

The first time I stopped at Big Chicks was on a Saturday night. The place was packed when we walked in. Music from the 1960s and 1970s intermingled strangely with New Wave from the 1980s and dance music of the 1990s. We crawled our way through to the bar which filled the front room leaving little if any room to walk. I couldn't even nudge my way through to the bar itself, it was so crowded. I eventually got a beer and had a great time, meeting lots of fantastic people.

I've been back many times since then. I've learned that afternoons at Big Chicks are peaceful, not very crowded. Great for a beer and conversation. Weekends at Big Chicks are a party. The clientele is a mixture of gay, lesbian and straight.

Drink prices are reasonable. Domestic beers cost $1.75, imports range $2.50 to $3.50. Big Chicks also has a wide variety of well drinks.

The layout features one long room and a side room with incredible art on the walls in each. The side room has a second bar which is key on crowded nights. There is no seating except the bar and in summer time a small beer garden filled with picnic benches.

Big Chicks has drink specials and theme nights throughout the year. It's a definate stop for any one in this Uptown vicinity.

Billy Goat Tavern
430 N. Michigan Ave.
312-222-1525
Hours: 7 a.m. to 2 a.m. Monday to Thursday,
7 a.m. to 3 a.m. Friday, 10 a.m. to 3 am. Saturday,
11 a.m. to 2 a.m. Sunday

Believe it or not, the Billy Goat Tavern was not created on the set of Saturday Night Live. It actually opened in 1934 near the Chicago Stadium (now the United Center), and 30 years later moved to its present home under Michigan Avenue in a sub-basement of crusty memories beneath a street of chrome and

17

The North Side Billy Goat Tavern

marble.

Of course, grudges are just memories with sharper edges, and few grudges have been held longer than the curse put on the Cubs by Billy Goat founder Billy Sianis. The curse was approaching its golden anniversary when the end of the hex coincided with the end of a brutal Wrigley Field losing streak during the 1994 strike-shortened baseball season. Coincidence? You decide.

The hub-bub began in 1945 when Billy tried to take his goat, Billy Goat III, to a World Series game at the Friendly Confines. Sianis and his goat were denied admission and the goat put a curse on the Cubs who went on to lose to Detroit in the World Series. The Cubs since never made it back to the World Series.

Billy's nephew Sam, now runs the tavern. In 1972 and again in 1983, Sam rented a limousine, showed up at Wrigley field with a red carpet and a sign that read, "All is forgiven. Let me lead the Cubs to the pennant. Billy Goat." Both times Sam and Billy Goat XII were stopped again.

Finally, in May of 1994, with the Cubs having dropped their first 12 home games, Sam and Billy Goat visited Wrigley. On that day the Cubs won their first home game of the all-to-brief season.

But the "Ghost of the Goat's Grudge" isn't the only legend lurking beneath Michigan Avenue. Behand a door that reads, "Butt in any time," is a passive class in Chicago history. Yellowed clippings of Chicago's greatest newspaper writers dot every wall. The offices of both the Chicago Tribune and Chicago Sun-Times are a short walk away. The largest wall clipping, is a blown-up copy of famed Chicago Barfly and Tribune columnist (who recently passed on to that big ole barroom in the sky) Mike Royko's farewell to Billy Sianis. Royko called Sianis the greatest inn keeper in Chicago.

The Billy Goat has the character every bar aspires to and an attitude that Ed DeBevic's wishes it could put on the menu, with one wall announcement suggesting that those who wish to tell the owner how to do things are welcome to buy him out.

There's also "Wise Guy's Corner" with a sign that reads, "If you're so darn smart, why ain't you rich?"

As for the menu, this is the place where Saturday Night Live based its skit, "Cheeseboiga, cheeseboiga, no Coke, Pepsi." Those cheeseboiga's cost $2.40 and prices go as high at $3.80 for the rib-eye steak. A bottle of Miller is $2 and this reviewer didn't have the courage to find out whetehr the taps with the Schlitz levers were telling the truth.

It was history before the "Not Ready for Prime Time Players" ever heard of it, and the Billy Goat Tavern, despite its dark and lowly location, remains a monument to the city's past.

-- Kev Smith

18

Bim Bom
5224 W. Belmont Ave.

Never having the opportunity to go to Europe, I've often wondered what it would be like to be in a hip club somewhere in Europe on a Friday night. I got my chance on a recent weekend when I walked into Bim Bom.

I always thought it was an interesting building for the area. This is Belmont, between Laramie and Central. Its not exactly where you would expect to find this kind of place. The front of the club has the appearance of heavy metal. Not the music, the material. Lots of screws and the entire front is painted sunset orange. A hand painted sign hangs reading Bim Bom. I have to admit, this looks pretty intriguing.

To satisfy my curiosity, I decided to see what this place was all about. The inside was more interesting than the outside. The inside walls were also lined with metal. Sheets of stainless steel, with what appeared to be photos screened on to them, hung as artwork. In fact the handmade lighting fixtures could also qualify as art. They really had a lot of cool stuff to look at.

It seemed to be mostly a younger crowd. Polish seemed to be the language of choice. They had a great jukebox. It was easy to drop ten bucks into. Everything from Miles Davis to The Clash. They had a pool table with tons of room to shoot. There was also a lot of action around the Foosball table.

Most of their beer selections were Polish imports both bottled and yap. They also had a good selection of Polish spirits. I asked the bartender if she could help me choose a beer. She gave me an Okocim. It was really good. I ended up drinking it the rest of the night.

I still hope someday I'll get to Europe, but I'll tell you what, after a few hours in Bim Bom, I started to forget I was on Belmont Ave.

— Tom Fisher

Bird's Nest
2500 N. Southport Ave.
773-472-1502
Hours: 5 p.m. to 2 a.m. weekdays, 11 a.m. to 3 a.m.
Saturday, 11:30 a.m. to 1 a.m. Sunday.

Bird's Nest opened Oct. 20., 1995. An estimated 500 people made their way through the bar that night with many of them waiting as long as 45 minutes to get in the door. The undeniably successful grand opening was a harbinger of things to come, as bar owner Matt Linder has created a casual atmosphere ready and willing to facilitate the masses.

The North Side Bird's Nest

Bird's Nest, 2500 N. Southport Ave., is a great bar. Pictured here are regulars Matt, Craig, and manager Sandi.

Formerly The Irish Anchor Club, Bird's Nest's newly diverse interior compliments a more diverse clientele. Not far from DePaul and in close proximity to rows of rehabbed houses, the opening night crowd was seemingly from all walks of Lincoln Park life. The front room has that "ye olde pub" type of atmosphere with a television at every glance. Set under a gold colored tin ceiling, the front room emanates that clean, austere, quasi-puritanical surrounding that is most desired when you want that "I could be at a bar on TV" type of feeling.

The back room could be a couch showroom as many couches are arranged in comfortable conversation-ready settings. The decor was somewhat inspired, Linder said, by other Southport Avenue bars such as the Schoolyard Tap and Southport City Saloon. Linder wanted to create a mellow back room with lots of artwork and a comfortable feeling. However, he said he wanted it free from that spill paranoia caused by a too "classy" surrounding.

To create a classy interior without having Murphy's Oil Soap on tap can be an expensive challenge. Fortunately, plastic slip covers were not used as a damage control option. There is also a small stage and back bar for nights with live acts. So with savings left from the furniture polish fund, there's free popcorn and pretzels daily, and chili on Sundays during football games.

Living with the nickname "Bird" since the seventh grade, Linder, just a mere hatchling at 24, decided to name his bar Bird's Nest. He or co-owner Mark Feitl are always on the premise. An owner occupied bar can sometimes either be a rarity or a scarcity, in this scenario, as Matt "Bird" Linder stated, "Some people just come to look at my hair."

Linder originally from Northbrook, recently returned home from Cincinnati

Barfly Bird's Nest-Bluebird Lounge

where he managed a sports bar. His main objective is to create a friendly surrounding where everyone just gets along and hangs out. Having crowded weekend-type nights is important, yet developing a diverse crowd of regulars is important for Linder who sees himself as just a regular.

Bird's Nest has 13 beers on tap. While there are always specials, regular prices are $2.50 Bud and Miller types; $3 micros including Sam Adams and Rhino Chaser; $3.50 gets you Guinness, Harp and Bass. Mixed drinks are $2.75 for well, $3.25 call and $3.75 premium. Some of the specials are Hops and Schnapps on Thursdays where $1.50 will get you a pint of Bud and $1.50 a shot of schnapps; $5 pitchers Bud/Bud light on Mondays. For bands on Wednesday and Saturdays the cover is about $3 and $4. In addition the back room is fully geared for private parties (75 to 100 guests).

To eat, Bird's Nest opened up its kitchen at the end of 1996 and offers all sorts of tasty appetizers like "Nest Eggs, otherwise known as jalapeno poppers filled with either cream cheese or cheddar cheese." Bird's Nest also serves up a bunch of yummy chicken sandwiches.

For college football fans, Bird's Nest is Chicago's home of Alabama games and all Mid-American Conference games.

Bluebird Lounge

1637 N. Clybourn Ave.
773-642-3449
Hours: 4 p.m. to 2 a.m. Sunday to Friday,
4 p.m. to 3 a.m. Saturday

I saw the Blatz sign and had to stop. But then again, who wouldn't?

I stepped in from the artificial sodium-lit night to a darkness I often missed in some of my bar trips. With the dim light glowing from the funky art-deco lamps at the booths and tables, I made out the bar to the immediate left and headed for a stool.

Resting my weary bones on the backed stool, I glanced over to my choices. There were bottles of Pilsner Urquel, Rolling Rock, Lite, Old Style, Bud, Point, Bell's Porter, and Amstel light. Checking the tap, I discovered Newcastle, Warsteiner, two types of Bell's, Leinenkugel's, Guinness, Sierra Nevada, Paulander, Legacy and Schlitz which claims the rights to the most attractive of the pull heads.

I noticed a lack of two common bar staples — a jukebox and a cigarette machine. But the owners of the place have compensated with a stereo system and packs of common-named smokes for sale behind the bar. The music is mainly alternative but it's not just the same old stuff played over and over on the radio. The sound itself is good. The music doesn't blare so you can have a conversation. The Bluebird sometimes has live music as well.

Patrons are a mix of folks from Paradox Parks — Lincoln Park and Wicker Park. That means some college types, artsy types, young professionals and musicians

Blue Chicago On Clark
536 N. Clark St.
312-661-0100
Hours 8 p.m. to 2 a.m. Sunday to Friday, 8 p.m. to 3 a.m. Saturday. Music starts nightly at 9 p.m.

Blue Chicago isn't a big place, so getting a seat at the bar or one of the seven or so tables along the wall can be difficult on the weekends. We, however, visited Blue Chicago during the middle of the week when the crowd was kind of thin which made getting a seat to watch some fine blues musicians that much easier.

The decor at Blue Chicago is pretty cool. If you've ever seen a Blue Chicago T-shirt, the paintings hanging on the walls of the bar will be very familiar. Blue Chicago has taken its paintings of "The Rambler" and "Mojo Mama" and put them on T-shirts for your wearing pleasure. The walls themselves at this Downtown blues haven are exposed brick which is the sort of look that a nice bar gives itself when it's trying to look old and run down. However, in this case, especially with the "Mojo Mama" staring down at you from above the bar, the look works. The ceiling at Blue Chicago is a whole bunch of Idaho Russet Potato sacks strung together which is an interesting touch albeit a little unusual. But who really cares about decoration when you are coming to see blues anyway?

The tap selection at this no-nonsense bar is nonexistent. If you want beer, you get it in a bottle. The selection is a little limited with imports such as Beck's and domestics such as Bud and Miller. A bottle of Beck's is $3.25 and, as always domestics are a little less.

The cover charge on my visit, a Wednesday night, was $5 which isn't too bad. Even on an off night as far as the crowd goes, if it's the blues you came to see at Blue Chicago you'll not be disappointed. The musicians come to play at Blue Chicago and play they do, crowd or no crowd.

— *Bill Stephenson*

Blue Frog
676 N. LaSalle St.
312-943-8900
11:30 a.m. to midnight weekdays
noon to 3 a.m. Saturday,
open for Bears/post game Sunday

A port hole window half filled with little plastic piggies, may seem an odd entrance way for a place called Blue Frog. However, having found this place after bailing a friend out of the Chicago police station around the corner, piggies seemed rather prophetic. Blue Frog with its neon sign and cute name, I figured it would be an up-beat type of place. Walking in, you feel as though you have been caught under the remains of a ship-wrecked toy box. Every board game and toy made before 1975, is suspended from the ceiling. The Patty Duke, Steve Canyon, and Vince Lombardi board games are a few that have been elevated to this sea grave. I guess you can say the decor is New Orleans' influenced.

Pigs, pigs, pigs. A little shelf of pig statues, pig plaques, a red pig logo, and a crock pot of weenies. I was there on the free hot dog Monday night football feast. Fortunately the crock pot had been fully gutted as my friend would have indulged in a gluttonous cathartic fantasy. As images from that famous pig movie, "Deliverance," undoubtedly pranced in my friend's head, I began to wonder about the quiet patrons. Except for one particular couple who were going through the board games available to play at a manic rate, every other person seemed rather low key. Between the football announcer's ramblings and the lone giggle and incessant tappings of a girl playing "Don't Break the Ice," it was very still. Did the other patrons eat too many weenies? Was the TV on too loud? Was every person there hiding out? Twilight Zone. I don't know?

The entire back wall of Blue Frog is a mirror, which would seem conducive to a person who wanted to talk with themself. I almost switched seats for this opportunity. Or I could have played one of the many available games located next to the refrigerator at the end of the bar. Mastermind would have been a good choice.

I started to think I was in a sinking ship. My friend had been far too traumatized for one evening to snap out of it. The bar was pretty cleared out. The frenzied game playing couple had switched to "Operation." Then the silent men next to me at the bar started to converse. As they discussed the tax ramifications of keeping men on death row, the diapered, bulb-nosed patient buzzed. I contemplated a mounted fish and the back-half of a stuffed Garfield sticking out of the wall. The goblets hanging over the bar could have been untouched relics from the Titanic. I then got an eerie feeling something was staring at me. Right in front of me, gaping all night had been a game called "The John." It was a smiling toilet with a large pipe coming from the bottom. I could instantly fabricate the rules. This summed up my evening, it was time for me to bail.

23

The North Side Blue Frog-Bootlegger's

At Blue Frog, students, Downtown business types and the average common-ers all harmoniously eat and drink and keep to themselves. A true testament of a bar's worthiness, is whether or not people go there by themselves. A testa-ment to the owners is when customers ask what they are doing for the holidays. It is also telling, if a customer returns after having a sufficiently surreal evening they ought not investigate. The only kind of place I would choose not to return, would be an establishment only decorated with permanently glued together puzzles.

No matter the circumstances that bring you there, finding a Downtown bar that is not all wood grain and sterile, or touristed and cardboard looking is a discovery. While the visual decor of Blue Frog is stimulus overboard, the atmosphere can be subtle. Perhaps appreciation comes slowly in time, like cooking a pig on a spit.

Blue Frog has exclusive drinks as well as weekly night specials that change monthly. The only mysteries remaining are: when my jail bait friend is going to pay me the $75 back and what exactly is Blue Frog's deal with pigs? I received one truthful answer. Supposedly, there was a mix up at the hospital. A little red pig has been deluded all his life into thinking he was a frog. Perhaps the pig isn't the only delusional mammal.

— Crumpey

Bootlegger's
13 W. Division St.
312-266-0944
Hours: 3 p.m. to 4 a.m. Sunday to Friday,
3 p.m. to 5 a.m. Saturday

This block-long section of Division Street is what Beale Street is to Memphis and what Bourbon Street is to New Orleans. Division street is Party-Central. Bootlegger's is one of the many wild drinking houses that line this street. It's a great place that packs 'em in on the weekends. It has a narrow bar but on weekend nights patrons need to just stop at the "tub-'o-beer" girl by the door for a beer.

A dance floor and some tables separate a front and back bar. It's so easy to get a drink in this place. There are waitresses all over as well. The clientele is often made up of tourists, suburbanites, conventioneers and college-age folks.

Music at Bootlegger's is spinned from a DJ who takes requests during the week. The music us usually Top 40 and classic party songs.

One last piece of advise. For those driving -- don't. Take a cab. There's no parking anywhere around there. And you shouldn't be drinking and driving anyway. Have fun, be safe.

The Boss Bar

420 N. Clark St.
312-527-1203
Hours: 11 a.m. to 4 a.m. weekdays,
11 a.m. to 5 a.m. Saturday, 2 p.m. to 2 p.m. Sunday

Downtown Chicago is filled with plenty of trendy, tourist bars for the fill of travelers to our big city, but the Boss Bar is one of those bars that is cool enough for city dwellers and visitors alike. Its placement is good, as it is near the Magnificent Mile, yet it is far enough away from many of the popular spots so that one is not caught in a slew of tourist traps.

The room is large with a huge island bar covering much of the floor space. There are some tables along the walls to escape staring at fellow patrons, and several tables also get set outside for a dining and drinking experience that offers a good view of Chicago's skyline. The bar's front wall on Clark Street is virtually a garage door, so one can still have that feeling of being in an "open" bar without actually having to sit out on the sidewalk. The entertainment is fair, with a pool table in the back and a couple video poker machines, however, the pool table doesn't offer much in players or competition until the late night hours.

The Boss serves food throughout the day and night, making it a cheaper spot amidst several pricey restaurants. The food is regular bar fare and is reasonably priced. An interesting twist on the food is that the "kitchen" is right at the front, however this does not distract one from drinking and having a good time with an abundance of smells.

The crowd is about as mixed as it gets due to its location. One thing to count on is plenty of men in this bar as "Bare Assets II," the strip club, is directly next door. However, the crowd is very relaxed and friendly, so the club next door should not be a deterrent at all. (I did have to wonder if that club does not help in finding female bartenders for the Boss, as they all look like they are straight out of Vogue magazine or something.)

The Boss is a bar dedicated to the late Mayor Daley and has a large painting with his likeness covering its south wall. I found this particularly ironic as his son continues to try to delete all the bars in his father's city. If there was only one reason to stop in here for a drink, besides all the other reasons discussed above, it would be so that one could dedicate their first swig to "The Boss" Daley and then turn towards City Hall while raising one's glass and the bird while screaming, "Respect thy father's wishes!" or any other pertinent phrase. But that's just my opinion.

Anyway, The Boss is a good place to hang out, drink or eat. The music is a good wide-range of songs that never get tiring, and the beer selection is alright as well. Domestics run $2.50 to $2.75 a bottle, including practically all the normal domestics, but there are a few imports running at $3.

— Phil Brandt

Boston Blackies
164 E. Grand Ave.
312-938-8700
Hours: 11 a.m. to 11 p.m. daily

Most of the customers at Boston Blackies come for the businessmen's lunch, or the 1993 Silver Plate award-winning hamburger. It's no wonder that owners Chris and Gus Maskaleris have prospered for 12 years with the same menu.

"We love the restaurant business," Gus said, "and would like to think of ourselves as a team of dedicated professionals—here to serve you in a clean and friendly atmosphere."

Boston Blackies got its name from designer Homer Tremelus, a friend of Chester Morris. Who's Morris? He played the character Boston Blackie in a 1950s detective series.

Blackies is small, seating about 75. Its design reminds one of a family's living-room. Pictures of the fictional Boston Blackie share wall space with shots of Chester Morris and his family. You could say that Boston Blackies belongs to another time. It even has a push-button cash register.

Gus said that when Boston Blackie entered a room or greeted a lady, he always removed his hat. This happens here, too, Gus said.

"The men wearing hats have to take them off," he said. "It's common courtesy."

Diners at Boston Blackies can order a half-pound Boston Blackie Burger, served plain or with a choice of toppings that include bleu cheese, cheddar cheese, olives or bacon. Potato skins are available as appetizers. Chili comes in a large and crispy tortilla topped with onions and cheddar cheese. Nachos garnish this dish.

The Mediterranean-style smelts come lightly breaded and fried. They cost $5.95. A "garbage salad" or a Caesar salad can be served along with a charbroiled hotdog. You can wolf down a ribeye steak sandwich. If you're a light eater, you can chomp on a breast of chicken sandwich.

Food prices range from $3.95 to $8.45. On the dinner side of the menu, you can order pork chops for $8.45, and 8-ounce prime filet for $12.45 or a New York steak for $13.95.

To wash down this great food, you can have a "frosty mug" of beer or soda. The brews start at $1.95 and runs to $2.95 for imported and domestic bottled beers. Wine is served by the bottle or glass.

Desserts! Yes, they have them. But it's a daily surprise for $3.

— Darlene Saxon

Breaktime

3635 N. Halsted St.
773-281-0095
Hours: 5 p.m. to 2 a.m. Sunday to Friday,
5 p.m. to 3 a.m. Saturday

A year after moving into my first Chicago residence on Irving Park, Larry Gianaris boldly opened a pool hall right around the corner. Primitive oil paintings stand tall throughout the remodeled room lined with 17 pool tables. For what seemed an eternity, Larry had no liquor license. He opened in mid-summer, and the place was less than comfortable.

After moving to the Lincoln Park area, I decided to visit Breaktime again. Wow!! and golly zukes! What a great place to sit and have a favorite cocktail or beer, or play pool. Larry, one of the more competent pool players I've seen, offers lessons to those who would like to improve or learn the discipline of pool.

The paintings, some mural size, are his work. Someone once said, do what you like and the money will come.

Larry now has a great staff working with him. Angel, Lisa and Sandra do a great job of making sure the drinks from Tim the barman are quickly available to customers trying their best to pocket the eight or nine ball.

Sitting at the bar can be an experience in itself. I have met some interesting people, including actor hopefuls, film producers and members of Chicago's finest. Breaktime is one of a kind. Those who like to play billiards or simply watch the game will be most comfortable here.

Breaktime offers ladies night from 6 to 10 p.m. on Thursdays, and half-price pool night on Tuesdays. Private parties can be arranged. Don't miss the American League pool night on Mondays.

The staff here really looks after you, and treats you like a good customer. Good going, Larry, and keep up the good work.

— J. Quillian

Brew and View at the Vic Theater

3145 N. Sheffield Ave.
773-618-8439
Movies are scheduled Thursday to Sunday nights.
Admission price is good for three movies

A few weeks ago an old chum and I really felt the urge to see a movie and as fate would have it, the movie we wanted see, "Wayne's World II," was only playing at the Brew and View.

We went to the Vic, paid $2.50 for admission, dropped another $7.50 for a neatly decorated plastic cup, found a couple of seats near the front of the theater and began to drink.

"Wayne's World" came on the screen which appeared a bit frail but after a few beers I was able to lose sight of the deformities and enjoyed the silly antics of Wayne and Garth.

To my most splendid surprise, as the movie went on a hardy stream of cocktail waitresses kept filling my cup of beer before I could drink half of it down. The waitresses also came around with pitchers of rum and Cokes. So I decided Brew and View was a piece of heaven.

It actually feels like you're sitting at a drive-in movie theater with the crowd drunk and sceaming in good fun. The drive-in theme is most apparent during the intermission when the house shows that old hot dog intermission film where a cartoon hot dog bun with arms is holding itself open trying to lure a ripe hot dog to jump inside. It's really important for all those in attendance to shout in drunken glee as the weiner finally jumps into the bun.

Brew and View has all kinds of specials from student nights to pizza nights. Movies are generally shown on nights when the theater isn't being used by a live band or other theatric performances.

-- Tony Gordon

The Brewery
3848 N. Harlem Ave.
773-625-7818
Hours: noon to 2 a.m. Sunday to Friday,
noon to 3 a.m. Saturday

It was a difficult task to find a beer garden on the Northwest Side of Chicago. The Brewery, however, has been serving up drinks in its beer garden for more than 11 years.

The Brewery's beer garden has six tables and a few trees to loom over drinkers' heads. It offers quaint sounds from Harlem Avenue, one of Chicago's busiest streets.

Within the bar, there are two bars that serve beers at reasonable rates. The beers on tap include Red Dog, Miller Genuine Draft, Old Style, Miller Lite, Icehouse and Molson Ice. The domestics cost $1 and imports cost $1.50 for a glass. For a pitcher, the domestics are $5, while imports are $7. In bottle beers, the domestics are $1.75 which include all the Miller and Bud products as well as Old Style. Imports include Labatt's, Beck's and Heineken for $2.25.

The Brewery is a sports bar. There are three televisions, two large screens, two foosball tables, two electronic dart boards and plenty of trophies. There are various beer signs hanging throughout the bar for decoration. It is a long narrow barroom, clean and a fine neighborhood drinking hole.

The crowd is mixed in ages from 25 to 35 with old timers thrown in to give the place a well-rounded crowd.

-- Pete Schmugge

Brigadoon
5748 W. Lawrence Ave.
773-777-2403
Hours: noon to 2 a.m. daily

Did you ever wonder how some bars remain open for business. In visiting this Jefferson Park establishment on Lawrence, east of Austin, there never seems to be any crowd in this drinking hole.

It is kind of baffling, because it is not a dump by any means. The beer prices are fair. There is a decent selection which includes BBK, a fine German beer for $4 every Saturday. There's a pool table and a couple of dart boards for recreation activities. The layout is welcoming and comfortable, but it doesn't seem too popular, at least not to the beer drinkers in this neighborhood. Maybe all the mirrors behind the bar are scaring the patrons out of the place.

Another problem for this establishment could be that the bar is in the middle of the block which is very residential. There are some businesses, but there are not very many. The result is that there is not much for this bar to feed off.

On the night I did this review, one of my friends joined me so he could listen to their selection of Beatles CDs. After all that trouble, guess what, no Beatles selections on the jukebox. After the first drink he started to fall asleep. The excitement of this place was too much for him to handle.

I listened to a number of selections and we decided to leave this quiet bar. If you like to drink alone, not be bothered and think of the glory days, this may be the place for you.

— Horslips

Brother Jimmy's
2909 N. Sheffield Ave.
773-528-0888
Hours: 5 to 11 p.m. Tuesday to Thursday, 5 p.m. to 1 a.m. Friday, 5 p.m. to 3 a.m. Saturday, 11 a.m. to 10 p.m. Sunday, closed Monday

It is the pride of the Carolinas. New York I suppose too. And now, Brother Jimmy's has invaded the Chicagoland area. The only problem that becomes instantly apparent is the decor. The pride of the Carolinas is fine, but do Chicagoans go for nothing but Tar Heel or Blue Devil paraphernalia? I think not.

The drinks are pricey, but once again this must have a lot to do with the neighborhood. The food is certainly a draw. Hot chicken wings and ribs seem to be what's on tap. There are weekly specials for the food that is worth trying out.

Why Brother Jimmy's? It's simple. The live bands are always a good bet here. Case in point, the regular appearance of Uncle John's Band. UJB always puts on a stellar Grateful Dead cover show. Unfortunately, I was in attendance for a Jerry Garcia tribute the Friday after his death last month. It was a touching tribute that brought tears to the eyes of many distraught Deadheads. I would not go so far as calling Brother Jimmy's a Dead bar. The waitresses all sport Brother Jimmy's shirts that depict dancing pigs in the traditional dancing bear fashion. A cheap rip off? Maybe, but you didn't hear it from me.

If you have the chance, look for UJB at Jimmy's. Jerry's death has not broken up one of the better cover bands in the Chicago area. If I may take a brief moment, we will miss you Jerry Garcia. Sometimes we live no particular way but our own.

— Brian Diebold

Brown Dog Tavern
531 N. Wells St.
773-645-1255
Kitchen hours: 11 a.m. to 10 p.m. Monday to Thursday, 11:30 a.m. to 11 p.m. Friday, 5 p.m. to 11 a.m. Saturday, 5 to 9 p.m. Sunday. Bar hours: are 11:30 a.m. to midnight Monday to Thursday, 5 p.m. to 1 a.m. Friday, 5 p.m. to 1 a.m. Saturday, 5 p.m. to 10 p.m. Sunday

Brown Dog Tavern is a relaxing, 30-something-ish bar. It's a good date bar, a great place to take people from out of town, and a solid option if you're looking to have a conversation with friends that you might actually want to hear.

Barfly Brown Dog Tavern-Bucktown Pub

The tavern is comfortable and well-designed, with golden-hued walls, a rich-looking 1940s-style bar, and a huge velvety sofa in the back. Attached to the bar area is a nice-sized restaurant and gallery kitchen. Brown Dog visitors can order food in either area. If you order from the bar the food will come out spread nicely on a white linen napkin.

The menu offers a great deal more than wings, potato skins, and other such bar staples. My mouth was watering as I perused the menu which described such delectables as a portabello mushroom sandwich, crab cakes, grilled pizza, and a tuna burger with shitake mushrooms. There is a full dinner selection including steaks, grilled fish, and pastas. And, if you have a taste for some old-fashioned drinking food, you can still get a full plate of nice, hot onion rings.

The purist among us will also be relieved to know that all the necessities for serious drinking are in place. The tavern carries a wide range of domestic and foreign beers which go for $3 to $5. Mixed drinks start at $4 and martinis are sold for $6 to $7.50. Interestingly the bar also carries an all-Australian wine list, about 50 in total, which start at $17.50.

Brown Dog carries its theme through the bar in a variety of ways. Bar patrons can choose from an array of "dog-themed" beers, including Old Brown Dog Ale, Sea Dog Blonde Ale, Two Dogs Lemon Brew, and their own private label brew, "Doggie Style Dark Lager" (nudge, nudge, wink, wink). Black T-shirts featuring the establishment's logo and a tag line that says "Sit, Speak, Eat," are for sale. And an entire collection of photographs depicting dogs wearing clothing while posing in people situations line the walls.

On a Tuesday evening around 10 p.m., there were a few couples engaged in conversation and a small group of women sipping wine, all sitting in the bar. There was no one in the restaurant area. But it picks up on weekend evenings.

"Things get kind of crazy around here on Friday nights," says manager Tad Edwards. "This is a great place for people between 25 and say, 40, to hang out with their friends and enjoy a few drinks in a modern tavern atmosphere."

— *Lisa Kueng*

Bucktown Pub
1658 W. Cortland St.
773-486-9086
Hours: noon to 2 a.m. Sunday to Friday,
noon to 3 a.m. Saturday

I think I should say right off that this is my favorite bar for relaxing. During the week you can always find a seat. "Sometimes you wanna go where nobody knows your name," as the old saying goes.

When you first walk into the Bucktown Pub, you are assaulted by a riot of posters and bric-a-brac stuck to the walls. It is basically a counter-culture shrine and underground comic museum. There's work by a variety of noted freak comic artists such as Skip Williamson and Dan Clowes, there's a pair of

One of the many drawings by famed comic book artist S. Clay Wilson that adorns the walls at The Bucktown Pub, 1658 W. Cortland St.

John Belushi's sneakers, a hand-written Charles Bukowski manuscript, movie posters, gig posters, and my favorite — the gig poster form a Jethro Tull/Sha-na-na gig. Imagine the people at that one.

The clientele is a mixture of old freaks, young post-punks, and neighborhood folks. No real pretension and everyone is quite friendly. Owner Krystyne Palmer is a Chicago bar veteran. There are few bar owners in the city who treat their customers as well as Krystyne.

Drink prices are affordable and Krystyne keeps a lot of beer on tap. My rec-ommendation is the 23-ounce "Bucktown Lager," a different cheapie every week at a great price. Other amenities at the Bucktown include free popcorn, pinball, a bowling game, and a classic rock jukebox.

The Bucktown Pub is an amazing bar, one that should not be missed.

-- Marc Ruvolo

The Bulls

1916 N. Lincoln Park West
773-337-3000
Hours: 8 p.m. to 4 a.m. daily

"Music until 4 a.m." is humbly advertised on the sign posted for The Bulls. The music that's played in this low basement-bar is jazz. In a city world renowned for live blues and jazz, the jazz at The Bulls is arguably some of the best live music performed in the City of Chicago.

The posters that adorn the walls of The Bulls are those of jazz greats including John Coltrane, Miles Davis, Billie Holiday and Thelonious Monk. But it's the stage that stands at the center of attention with a silhouetted Chicago Skyline as its backdrop, music pours forth in long jam sessions.

We found this to be true regardless of which night we went or whom was playing. In fact, in three nights that we visited The Bulls, we enjoyed three distinctly different styles of jazz. Wednesday night offered "Suenos," a Latino style quintet with strong percussion, bass, keyboard and sax. Thursday night was the "Tim Tobias Quintet" who seemed to have more of a new age jazz sound peppered with a little funk. (Side note: Anybody who knows anything about music has by now realized that I am not a music critic). Suffice to say, I liked what I heard. Sunday night was my personal favorite with the critically acclaimed Kenny Anderson Quartet wailing through what I consider the more traditional jazz sounds with drums, keyboard, stand-up bass and Mr. Kenny Anderson on trumpet.

Although we only went for the jazz and the drinks, The Bulls offers a short-order menu so your late night cravings won't go unheeded. The menu, though small, has a good variety of appetizers and sandwiches including calamari, peel and eat shrimp, chili and turkey burgers. Sandwiches generally run about five to six dollars whereas appetizers are a little less.

There are two taps to choose from at The Bulls, currently serving Leinenkugel's and Sierra Nevada Pale Ale. The bottled beer selection is a little more extensive, ranging from Lite to Heineken, with all beer prices hovering around three to four dollars.

It may seem anathema that in a town with a four-time world championship basketball team of the same name that The Bulls is quick to disassociate itself from any reference to basketball at all. However, legal disputes withstanding, this is the case. As best the bartender could figure, The Bulls takes its name instead from an archaeological site the original owner saw in France that involved a mural of some bulls in a cave. And lo and behold, the bartender then points out the fact that the walls and ceiling of the place are made to look like a cave and there's a mural of some bulls on the ceiling. Mere coincidence...I think not.

The Bulls, or as it is sometimes referred to, The Jazz Bulls is one of the stops on the Jazz Institute of Chicago's Jazz Tour. Ticket prices for the tour are $7

The North Side Bulls-Burwood Tap

which includes transportation and cover for 11 different stops between 6 and 11 p.m. that night. Truly a bargain worth looking into.

The Bulls is open seven days a week. Doors open at 8 p.m., music starts at 9 p.m. and, short breaks aside, goes until 4 a.m. Our cover was $5 per person which, considering the quality of the music performed is a good deal. There are calendars available inside. If you like a particular artist that you saw there one night, check the calendar, chances are they'll be back next week.

—Bill Stephenson

The Burwood Tap
724 W. Wrightwood Ave.
773-525-2593
Hours: 11 a.m. to 2 a.m. Monday to Thursday
10 a.m. to 4 a.m. Saturday, 10 a.m. to 2 a.m. Sunday

There's no great mystery to judging a good bar. Sometimes it's a simple matter of space: a) is there enough of it and b) what is done with it? While many find a cramped space exciting because of the perception of the room's incredible popularity, it has always served to remind me of the worst frat parties I ever attended, the ones where you're met with elbows inside fleece Patagonias with every step.

The Burwood Tap on the North Side is a roomy, sprawling tavern that has the look of just such a cramped bar from the outside. You can't tell that there's a back room upon approach; it just appears to be space on the corner.

The bar is assembled in three sections; a front room roughly the size of many other full rooms, complete with tables and a bar area; the pool table room, really just a point of passage between the two bigger areas (there's not too much space in here save for the pool table); and a huge back room, which has twice the tables as the front room. This allows for multiple kinds of experiences, be it chilling out at a quiet table, or mingling in a more convivial atmosphere.

We were greeted at the door by the waitress, who immediately began with a self-deprecating joke (seeing the size of our party, about 6 or 7, she remarked, "Everybody gets the same thing here. I can't remember too many orders.") While I don't know if I go for such an authoritarian manner of picking my beverage of choice, it set the tone for the evening. All of the waitresses were eager to please, willing to suggest specials or favorite drinks. The one shot special we did get, termed a MindRacer, did nothing for me, however. The only reason it seemed to be called a MindRacer was because it had three straws, thereby allowing for a faster finish. Well, whoever heard of drinking a shot with straws? Furthermore, this wasn't a shot; it was bigger than most Pepsis you can get in a stadium. I suppose that explains the $4 price, and the seeming lack of liquor.

Two large bars allow for quick ordering and virtually no lines. While there was so much flannel and plaid in the room (it resembled a series of Scottish family crests), the clientele may be more diverse during the week; one must allow for the inevitable dilution of a bar's true nature on the weekend. Just

34

Barfly Burwood Tap-Butch McGuire's Tavern

because of its sheer size, this place could accommodate so many people that seemingly anyone could come in and have a good time. It's not enormous, but big enough to be comfortable. And after all, that's exactly what we could hope to expect from a bar: that it provides the proper conditions for any kind of swell gathering to occur. Forget the old real estate mantra of location, location, location; folks, size does matter.

— Dave Dayen

Butch McGuire's Tavern
20 W. Division St.
312-337-9080
Hours: 10 a.m. to 4 a.m. weekdays,
9:30 a.m. to 5 a.m. Saturday, 9:30 a.m. to 4 a.m. Sunday

Butch McGuire's is famous for putting a stalk of celery in a Bloody Mary, it is the birth place of the Harvey Wallbanger and stands after 30 years as the traditional anchor of Division Street.

Little has changed about this simple cozy bar still owned and operated by the McGuire family. Patrons continue to be greeted outside by an old Irish-flag awning proudly showing the colors of the motherland. Inside this quaint pub, the walls and ceilings are decorated with Irish paraphernalia, hanging models and beer steins.

Butch McGuire's layout is surprisingly small for being "the granddaddy of them all" as singles bars go. The main bar is in the first and largest room with two small rooms adjoining it. The size adds to the neighborhood pub atmosphere which is accentuated by the wood-stained bar and stools.

Sporting events are shown on nine television sets nicely situated around the bar. Still Butch McGuire's isn't known as a sports bar but as a singles' hangout. The small but comfortable confines is a perfect setting for the pursuit of the opposite sex. Because of the size, pool tables cannot be found and only a few video games and dart boards are housed in the back portion of the pub.

At the bar itself, 20 beers including the great Irish Guinness are on tap and served in large heavy mugs. Bloody Marys are still a great bar treat as well as the famous Harvey Wallbangers. Besides Butch McGuire's famous standbys, a full bar is also served by a friendly and knowledgeable staff.

Complementing the full bar, Butch McGuire's offers a menu complete with burgers and appetizers. The kitchen also offers a sample of Ireland with its famous Irish whiskey loaf and corned beef sandwich. A brunch menu is served on Saturdays and Sundays with the specialties including an opportunity to build your own "O'omelet."

During the evening hours, Butch McGuire's traditionally hosts a packed house, with a crowd evenly divided between tourists and natives. Because Chicago is built on an Irish tradition, it makes perfect sense that Butch

McGuire's is Chicago's bar.

— Brendan O'Brien

BW-3

2464 N. Lincoln Ave.
773-868-9453
Hours: 11 a.m. to 2 a.m. Sunday to Friday,
11 a.m. to 3 a.m. Saturday

With two big rooms, a multitude of colors TVs, plenty of beer and a prime Lincoln Avenue location, BW-3 certainly has what it takes to be a fantastic bar. So it seems almost a shame that they decided to make it a fantastic restaurant. BW-3 (the "BW" stands for buffalo wing) is seen by many as a bar, and to a large extent it is just that. The front room offers a pool table, two color televisions and a big screen (invariably tuned to the ball game of the hour) and a jukebox that leans toward the modern. A solid selection of beers is rendered a virtual non-issue with great specials.

The atmosphere is generally upbeat, with a younger crowd generated in part by the close proximity of DePaul University. As a bar, BW-3 would be a unique drinking establishment were it not for a slightly cramped front room. There is more space, much more space in fact. That space comes complete with a second big screen and three other televisions, as well as tables, chairs and waitresses.

Don't knock the waitresses. They'll bring you both beer and wings, and it's the wings that makes the beer all the more desireable.

The menu features such staples as nachos, red hots, salads, sandwiches and hamburgers, referred to as "Weckburgers" because they come served on a kimmelweck roll, unless you opt for the kaiser or sesame bun. But it's the buffalo wings and buffalo chips that make BW-3 unique. Wings come in quantities ranging from lots of six or lots of 250 (bring your appetite and your high school graduating class). Besides the different qualities, patrons also can select from eight different temperatures for the wings barbecue sauce, which ranges from the temperate teriyaki to wild, which somewhat resembles a hangover; the taste will burn your mouth and stay with you for as long as it wants to, and there's nothing you can do about it but sweat it out.

With several franchises across the country, most of them in Ohio, BW-3 is the kind of place where dinner after work could lead someone to watch the ball game, shoot some pool and stumble home at 2 a.m. only to go back the next day.

Cafe Fresco
1202 W. Grand Ave.
312-733-6378
Hours: 11 a.m. to 2 p.m. weekdays,
noon to 3 a.m. Saturday, 11 a.m. to midnight Sunday

Steps from the Downtown grind there is a little spot where a handful of Loop workers head for beer and calimari.

This neat and clean bistro features all sorts of beers such as Leinenkugel's, Bud, Bud Light, Rolling Rock, Miller Genuine Draft, Lite, Zima, Red Stripe, Heineken, N.A. Hacken Bock, Paulander, and Mamba bottles. On tap there is Bass and Guinness. There is also a variety of wines and liquors to choose from.

Overall, this is an up-scale bar and calling this place a cafe is apt. Its layout consists of a brick wall, hanging plants, a long shelf holding brick-a-brack antiques, small yet comfortable bar with backed stools, and nice wooden round tables with candles on each.

Music in the Fresco is mellow and the jukebox features the sounds of such artists like Earth, Wind & Fire; Mariah Carey and Elton John.

To eat there is a wide variety to choose from for both lunch and dinner as well as appetizers.

Capitol Club
4244 N. Milwaukee Ave.
773-685-1194
Hours: 6 p.m. to 2 a.m. daily

In my many travels throughout ethnic Chicago, I have visited the Capitol Club several times. I always come away baffled by these visits to this popular Polish nightclub because I am not a Polish ethnic. The place is a getaway for recent Polish immigrants to separate from mainstream America. It's a one-night exodus from the rest of Chicago.

This night spot is especially popular on Saturday nights. There is a house band that offers a mixture of popular Polish pop and 1970s disco tunes and a large dance floor for those wishing to work up a sweat. The crowd, which runs from age 21 to 60 years old, is neither rowdy nor rude.

There are two rooms at this club. The first room has a small circular bar featuring two pool tables and a few video games. The second has ample tables for seating scattered around the room with a stage on the north side wall. The front of the room has a large dance floor and a bar that straddles one of the corners. In addition, it's dark enough so you can hide in the corner and whisper sweet-nothings into your date's ear. The blinking lights remind me of the 1970s and disco days.

The North Side Capitol Club-Cardinal Club

Capitol Club does not have drink specials. If you visit, be ready to pay three bucks a-beer. It's as expensive as Downtown, but where else can you go to experience another culture within the city. If you ever have the urge to visit Poland, go to the Capitol Club first. This is a Polish club, not your typical American bar.

— Herbert

Cardinal Club
5155 W. Belmont Ave.
773-685-1194
Hours: 8 p.m. to 4 a.m. daily

On a recent Saturday night I patronized a popular bar in my neighborhood and ordered a few round of my usual: two Rolling Rocks and a coke for $4.75 per. I decided to leave at about 11 p.m. and look for a little color. I was in high spirits.

I traveled about three or four miles to a popular Polish club to get myself ready for the Casimir Pulaski holiday held in March each year. The establishment I visited was the Cardinal Club, located for more than 20 years on the corner of Belmont and Laramie, in the Belmont-Cragin neighborhood.

The first thing I discovered was a $5 cover charge at the door for a house band called Wanderband. The group wasn't bad at playing popular covers, but I wasn't thrilled having to listen to their Polish disco tunes or Europo Tech. In between sets they had a comedian who was lamer than a dead duck. In addition to the aforementioned, the DJ tormented the crowd with more disco — yuck!!!

By this time, I was no longer in high spirits, to say the least. As the night went on, it didn't get any better.

The approach of the place is a nightclub theme. The club is very dark, which is good for the old timers. All the walls are black, with one wall (east side) sporting murals of nude women. The amazing thing is that this place starts to pack 'em in after midnight.

There are two rooms to the establishment, with one bar to a room. In the entrance room there are three video games, a pool table, a stage and a midsize dance floor. The back room holds an abundance of circular tables. In fact, there are too many of these objects throughout this establishment.

If you ever wonder what Polish night life is like, try going to one of these clubs. On most nights, there will not be native-born American in the place. The Cardinal Club is no exception. In addition, if you don't speak Polish at the Cardinal Club, you may have to pay an extra dollar for your beer.

— Lester

Carol's Pub
4659 N. Clark St.
773-334-2402
Hours: 9 a.m. to 2 a.m. Monday to Thursday, 9 a.m. to 4 a.m. Friday, 9 a.m. to 5 a.m. Saturday, 11 a.m. to 4 a.m. Sunday

Carol's Pub is a country bar. There's country music in the jukebox, country bands play on the weekends and many of the patrons are country folks.

During the week the bar isn't too crowded. But weekends bring in a good number of people. Especially when a band is playing. Folks dolled up in country garb, dance to the sweet sounds of Appalachia. The dancing is also conducive to a little singles scene where eager men approach the ladies for a dance — sometimes every lady in the bar. Anyway, there are plenty of couples out on the dance floor as well.

Carol's is one large room that is kept rather dark. One section has the stage and dance floor and the other contains a long bar, video slot machines and televisions.

They also offer hamburgers and French fries prepared the way you like them. And tap beer is only one dollar. I thought it was a fine deal.

I've always had a pleasant time at Carol's. However, it can get a bit rough at times. But, hey, so can most places.

— T.M. Kornelsen

Casey's
500 W. Diversey Parkway
773-871-5940
Hours: 11a.m. to 2 a.m. Sunday to Friday, 11 a.m. to 3 a.m. Saturday

Casey's is best described as a traditional neighborhood bar. Since 1985, this bar, a popular meeting place, has amassed a vast collection of sports memorabilia. Above the full circle bar is a shadow-box overhang filled with sports momentos including game balls, trophies and collector items. On brightly varnished, wooden walls are photos and artistic renderings autographed by such notables as Mike Singletary, Kareem Abdul-Jabaar, Billy Williams, Ernie Banks and Kevin Butler.

One of the popular traditions at Casey's is an annual celebration honoring legendary neighborhood bar owner/bartender Wally Ziegler. During his last years Wally was a Casey's regular. His unusual golf game is kept alive every August when Patron's attend the Smokin' 2 Iron Golf Tournament. The 24 competitors are armed with 2 irons and putters. Following the tournament the participants fill the bar to share golf stories and for some, their memories of Wally.

The North Side Casey's-Charleston

A group of neighborhood regulars maintain a tradition with their Wednesday evening gatherings at Casey's. Bartender Jeff Morris directly benefits from one of their traditions: When a group member travels he or she is required to return with and XXXXXXL polo shirts which advertises the city, golf course or other location on the pocket. In return Jeff delivers service with a snarl. But, they still love him.

Jeff, who has tended bar since Casey's opened in July, 1985, recently had the pleasure of serving Bull's Luc Longley and actor Tom Wopat.

A real sparkle comes to owner Terry Casey's eyes when he speaks of helping to sponsor the annual March of Dimes Snowball softball game. This marathon of mid-February games in which some 70 teams compete is played from Saturday until Sunday night. During the respective sports' seasons Casey's supports other softball and touch-football teams in city leagues.

On Dec. 7, Casey's fills for a celebration of Pearl Harbor Day. This tradition is complete with a huge Japanese flag and grows in numbers of participants each year. As can be imagined this day-long party is complete with appropriate titled shots and torpedo drinks.

The architecturally-minded might well enjoy the building which is a designated Chicago landmark. Numerous films including "Child's Play," "She's Having a Baby" and "Running Scared" have been filmed in and outside the landmark building.

When you feel the need to share the big game, drink, and nibble on complementary popcorn, visit Casey's. Casey's offers multiple televisions, darts, and various video games including Ms. Pac-Man.

— *J. Quillian*

The Charleston
2076 N. Hoyne Ave.
773-486-4757
Hours: 11 a.m. to 2 a.m. weekdays,
11 a.m. to 3 a.m. Saturday,
noon to 2 a.m. Sundays

The Charleston is typical of the new breed of Bucktown bars; sort of artsy in a coffee-house way, sort of a neighborhood tap. To most avid bar goers, they either love the Charleston or hate it. Like many places, the final decision of whether a bar is worthwhile or not is up to the patron. All I can say, is that the bartenders are friendly and drinks are reasonable.

Charlie's Chicago
3726 N. Broadway
773-871-8887
Hours: 3 p.m. to 2 a.m. daily

In my short career of writing reviews of drinking establishments, I am rarely taken aback by what I find. Most bars reviewed are in high-traffic areas with high-class clientele. Throughout the city, there are some terrific places to visit that are not considered to be among Chicago's hot spots. These places should be visited at least once. Hopefully, this review will give you a little push to venture outside the regular watering holes, to try a new neighborhood, a new bar and a new drink.

Here's an idea for a new hangout.

Charlie's Chicago could be that new hangout, but only if you like a bar with a large dance floor and a disc jockey. With the music and people spinning, the atmosphere is festive. On the particular night of my visit, country-western music was the flavor, and I enjoyed the taste. The lights were low, and the drinks plentiful. Prices are reasonable, so money is not a concern, unless you drink like a fish.

If two-stepping is not your style, there are plenty of things to do at Charlie's. The bar has a variety of pinball machines, dart boards and common video games. Most bars, of course, have these. But a bar would not be a bar without them.

Do not be fooled by Charlie's simple exterior. It's the friendly people, and the relaxed and comfortable interior that counts. So, for a new experience, which it will be, it is the place to try. If you can get yourself through the door, the people will lock you in.

— T.M. Kornelsen

Chicago 21 Nightclub
6020 W. Belmont Ave.
773-777-5208
Hours: 8 p.m. to 4 a.m. Sunday to Friday,
8 p.m. to 5 a.m. Saturday, open 365 days a year

With Chicago's rich ethnic tradition, it is hard not to find Polish bars on the Northwest Side of the city. Blessed with a sense of curiosity, I decided to make a stop at the Chicago 21 Nightclub, located just west of Austin Avenue on Belmont Avenue (6020 W.).

Walking in was a refreshing experience, because the air conditioning was working fine. On the night of this review, it was hot and sticky and the "air" was a life-saver. I found the decor of this nightclub appealing — all the walls

The North Side Chicago 21 Nightclub-City Limits Pub

were black. There is a long bar near the front entrance. Don't worry about finding a seat, plenty of seats are available. There's a dance floor for those with the energy to dance to the Euro-Tech tunes spun by a DJ every night.

It was an early weekday night when I arrived and I didn't expect a crowd. I was right, there wasn't a patron in the place. As with many late night bars, the crowds usually visit these establishments after midnight. This was confirmed by my friendly bartender, Carolina. The crowd, when it did arrive, was a good mix of women and men between the ages of 30 and 60.

The most popular drinks at Chicago 21 are the harder liquors which include vodka, Scotch, Jack Daniel's, and cognac. Specialties include frosted cocktails like Hot Tamale, Cupid's Kiss, Snowball, and Palm Beach, which can help cool you off on Chicago's hot summer nights.

The Chicago 21 Nightclub, opened in 1987, picks up on weekends and does get busy. To handle the crowd, there are six bouncers who work the front doors. Go there, check out the Polish heritage in Chicago. It is a lot cheaper to experience some culture right here in this fine town than visiting overseas.

— Pete Schmugge

City Limits Pub
7535 W. Belmont Ave.
773-237-2467
Hours: 11 a.m. to 2 a.m. weekdays,
11 a.m. to 3 a.m. Saturday, noon to 1 a.m. Sunday

In my latest voyage, I made a short trip to a local bar on Belmont called City Limits Pub which is three blocks west of Harlem Avenue. This is a no thrills comfortable pub on the Northwest Side of Chicago.

This is a good drinking establishment to go after work to get a cold brew. There are $3 pitchers every day of the week. All the beers on tap are Miller products which include Lite, Genuine Draft and Red Dog.

The decor of the bar is comfortable. There is a circular bar which sits about 30 patrons. There are also a few tables along the wall and in the back of the bar.

For entertainment for men, there are fashion shows at lunch and dinner times. Also, there are four TVs throughout the bar for your sports viewing. There is a pool table in the back along with two video games. Also, there is a jukebox with a fine mix of rocking tunes.

If you are hungry, there is plenty of tasty food offered at the pub. For sandwiches, there are burgers, meatball, Italian beef, sausage and bratwurst. Also, soup and salads are served. If you just want a snack, there are appetizers which include onion rings, shrimp, cheese sticks and chicken sticks.

If you are ever near Belmont and Harlem take a spin down to City Limits to get a cheap brew and good food at reasonable rates.

— Pete Schmugge

Clancy's Pub and Grill
4246 N. Lincoln Ave.
773-281-1007
Hours: 11 a.m. to 2 a.m. Sunday to Friday, 11 a.m. to 3 a.m. Saturday. Kitchen hours: 11:30 a.m. to 7 p.m. Monday and Thursday, 11:30 a.m. to 9 p.m. Tuesday and Wednesday, 11 a.m. to 10 p.m. Friday. Closed weekends

After a weekend of feeling down, stumbling in and out of several taverns and feeling no better than when I came, I found a bit of good old fashioned Irish cheer at Clancy's Pub and Grill. The lovely and attentive Nicola brought drink after drink as I soaked up atmosphere galore at this wonderful pub.

The first thing to greet me was the shillelagh, or the Irish attitude adjuster. It is, in short, a stick designed to hit people. It hangs intimidatingly over the bar, though it looks like it doesn't get much use.

The establishment is lit fantastically dim, providing my nocturnal ass a much needed break from the sunlight. The black marble Formica bar seats about 12 and comfortable high back chairs are in place of barstools. Should you fall off your chair, not to worry, the floor is carpeted. The walls are dark green around a plain white ceiling and dark wood paneling rides the rest of the way down. The bar back is also dark wood. Six or so booths accommodate drinkers and diners alike.

One of the biggest draws at Clancy's is Friday's all-you-can-eat fish fry. For $5.75 you receive homemade cole slaw and potato salad (or fries), lemon, a bread basket, and of course beer battered fish. Tuesday is all-you-can-eat pasta night and Wednesday you can get a four-piece chicken dinner with mashed potatoes.

Chef Tom is quick to point out the high standards he and co-chef Donna Hall keep for the kitchen. All fried food is cooked in pure vegetable oil that is changed regularly. The cole slaw is Tom's own recipe and almost everything is homemade.

"We use cod (for the fish fry), we don't (mess) around," Tom says. "And the mashed potatoes are real. I would not serve instant mashed potatoes." Though the rest of the menu is limited, it is rather refreshing to hear words of integrity from a bar kitchen.

The prices are right for the drinks as well as the food. Domestic bottles are $1.75 and tall call mixed drinks are under three bucks. Tap selections are limited to Old Style, Lite and Guinness. I knew that Guinness was served here even before seeing the tapper as the Irish accent I heard gave it away.

The crowd seems to be mostly regulars with a few newcomers (like my buddy Johnny C. and I) thrown in for good measure. Hand written signs on the walls advertise their many outings including an early September Cub game. A

The North Side Clancy's Pub-Clancy's Belmont

lighted sign denoted several birthdays scribed in grease pencil. I can only assume that these folks were patrons and or staff members. I forgot to ask, because as my pop would say, "It got a little drunk out that night."

Having never been to the other two taverns owned by the same individual: Clancy's Belmont Saloon and the Claddagh Ring on Foster Avenue, I can make no comparisons to them. But I can tell you that if the rest of the staff at this Clancy's is as great as Nicola and Tom, it is no wonder that a man they call "The Admiral" brings flowers to the girls behind the bar.

I would like to extend a personal debt of gratitude to the patrons and employees of Clancy's. Like I said in the opening, I was in a fucked-up state of mind that weekend but after leaving that joint I felt like myself again. It is a bar's purpose to make one feel good and thanks for doing the job.

— Bud

Clancy's Belmont Saloon
(Now called Seanachi)
2345 W. Belmont Ave.
773-549-4444
Hours: 2 p.m. to 2 a.m. weekdays,
10 a.m. to 3 a.m. Saturday, 11 a.m. to 2 a.m. Sunday

After yet another tiresome day of searching up and down West Belmont Avenue's famed "Antique Row" for Hummel Figurines and a black velvet painting of Hulk Hogan, I decided to wet my whistle at a nearby watering hole called Clancy's Belmont Saloon. Upon entering the bar, I was first struck by a prevalent, yet all-to-familiar faux Irish pub/sports bar decor permeating the room and then by my drinking buddy's fist because I was blocking the doorway in my quest to savor and soak in those precious first atmospheric impressions.

Saddling up to the bar, I was captivated by the flurry of activities taking place all around me in this lively, mid-size bar. There didn't seem to be a single person there who wasn't involved in or egging on some sort of competitive game, either for fun or profit. From the packed pool tables and video poker machines, to the in-house, computerized, remote-controlled Trivial Pursuit tournament, to the smattering of high-rolling regulars playing craps (or was it Backgammon) on the bar. I listened for any whispers of placing bets for cock-fighting matches I imagined held in some smoky back room but to no avail.

I did, however, spot a flyer announcing the qualifying round for a urinating contest to be held there and at other bars across the city in the coming weeks (call for the gruesome details and entry specifics).

My friend and I opted for the trivia game as our diversion of choice and ordered pints of Killians Red, reasonably priced at $2.25, instead of the Bud and Bud-light they had on tap. Domestic bottles went for $1.75 and a Heineken or Amstel Light will run ya $2.75. As far as my considering it an Irish bar, I've seen more authentic Gaelic flavor in a package of Thomas's English Muffins.

Barfly Clancy's Belmont Saloon-Clark Bar

They did have some U2 and Pogues in the jukebox, though, as well as the much ballyhooed "100 Irish Drinking Songs," but by and large it was predominately classic rock as far as the eye could see.

After talking with the woman at the bar, I learned of their daily occupation specials where, depending on your line of work and what day of the week it is, anyone from city workers to male nurses can enjoy $1 domestic beers all night (valid ID required). That deal sounded pretty cool. It's reassuring to see someone giving something back to the working class once in a while.

They're also sponsor a huge St. Paddy's Day pub crawl where a trolley takes participants, free of charge, on a tour of three participating Clancy's pubs. Smoked butt and cabbage are available. In a further effort to discourage drinking and driving, they distribute free mystery gifts to folks who produce a cab receipt or a CTA transfer at the bar that night.

Overall, a decent place to drink at, and there's even a great 24-hour diner next door where you can drink coffee, listen to old men argue about politics and eat egg-salad that's served all night for a mere 70-cents per serving.

— *Brian Farrelly*

Clark Bar
2116 N. Clark St.
773-327-3070
Hours: 2 p.m. to 2 a.m. weekdays; noon to 3 a.m. Saturday, noon to 2 a.m. Sunday

A friend of mine was the first to mention Clark Bar to me. Immediately, I thought of rich chocolate, creamy nougat and nuts. But no, she wasn't talking about the candy bar. She was talking about a bar on Clark Street.

Clark Bar is close to Lincoln Park Zoo, and directly across from Oven Grinders Pizza. If you blink, though, you may miss the bar completely.

It was a Sunday, the first time I frequented Clark Bar, slightly hung over from the previous night. I headed straight for the bar for that all important Bloody Mary. Sam the bartender makes a killer Bloody Mary. On this particular Sunday, only a handful of people sat in the bar. The Cubs game and the Masters Tournament played on the TV.

On tap is a selection of eight beers, anything from a Black and Tan to a Miller Lite. In the back is a pool table, dart board, pinball machine and video golf game. The bar is comfortable and homey, with well-worn wood floors that show only a hint of their once golden polished color.

The building was built in 1905, and was previously a shoe store and grocery store. Still in use today is an antique wooden color, dating from the bar's grocery store days. The building didn't become a bar until 1945, after Prohibition. It became Clark Bar in 1980.

Mark Powers, "The Hammer Powers," has been coming to Clark Bar for just about as long, and is considered somewhat of a barback who is always willing to help out at a moment's notice.

In the back, by the pool table, hangs a life-size picture of the St. Valentine's Day Massacre that appeared on the front cover of the Chicago Tribune on Feb. 14, 1929. The massacre took place only a few steps down from Clark Bar at the SMC Carriage Company on 2122 N. Clark St. The building where the massacre took place was demolished in 1967.

If you want to feel a little piece of Chicago history, and are fascinated by Al Capone, George "Bugs" Moran and "Machine Gun" Jack McGurn, this is the place for you. And don't forget the great folks behind the bar, especially Red, who enlightened me on the history of the bar and re-ignited my interest in Chicago's diverse history.

— Christy Rizzo

Clark Street Ale House
742 N. Clark St.
312-642-9253
Hours: 4 p.m. to 1:30 a.m. weekdays,
4 p.m. to 2:30 a.m. Saturday, 5 p.m. to 1:30 a.m. Sunday

As I turned off Chicago Avenue, walking south on Clark Street, a mocking Chicago wind followed me around the corner. Spring had come the week before, but this weather gave me doubts -- perhaps a Leinenkugels' Bock could convince me. Arriving at 742 N. Clark St., I shrugged off the cold, ducked into the doorway and entered.

The warmth of the room drew me in, the rich mahogany wood throughout, hanging ceiling lights and art-deco lamps lit the room featuring a tin stamped ceiling. Cocktail tables for two border both sides of a cherry wood bar. And behind the bar there are 24 taps of microbrews. A pretty, redheaded bartender greeted me and asked what my choice might be. Settling on a Golden Prairie Nut Brown Ale, I sat down and relished my first beer at the Clark Street Ale House.

Rich Wohn and Adam Ellis opened the bar in February 1995, even though the lease had been signed in June, 1993. Apparently, the opening was stalled by some good old fashioned politics. Someone else, with possible ties to government officials, wanted the place. So after a two year battle, Rich and Adam rightly got their liquor license.

The place was formerly the Stop & Drink, which was quite a dump. Rich and Adam did an amazing job cleaning this place up. From the remodeling to the drink and cigar selection -- Clark Street Ale House is excellent.

Those who enjoy it most are drinkers who know how to appreciate good beer, specifically microbrews. There are almost 50 microbrews available. About 85 percent of these are from Midwestern microbreweries with a few from across the country. Most of the draft choices are familiar names -- Bell's, Grant's, and Sierra Nevada amonth others. Some of the bottled brews are less recognizable, but just as noteworthy -- Anderson Valley, Rogue, Celis or Pyramid. But be

46

Barfly Clark Street Ale House-Claus's Tavern

forewarned, several of these brews are bottled in 21-ounce "bombers."

In addition to the beer selection, fine wines, single-malt Scotch whiskies, a port list (four are more than 60 years old) and other liqueurs are offered as well. If you don't imbibe, coffee, espresso and cappuccino are served.

Rich and Adam bring years of experience in the bar and restaurant trade to The Clark Street Ale House. They first worked together at Thunderbird's Bar and Grill in the mid-1980s. Adam went on to become assistant brewmaster at Golden Prairie while Rich opened The Fireside Restaurant in 1989, and later the Blue Iris. Both restaurants are known for eclectic menues. The Fireside has also become famous for its brewmaster dinners.

Back at The Clark Street Ale House, Rich and Adam offer a great deal for the selective drinker. Future events include visits from some of the brewers featured at the bar and possibly expanded hours to 4 a.m. during the week and 5 a.m. on Saturday.

-- Michael Cotter

Claus's Tavern
2159 W. Addison St.
773-472-6160
Hours: 2 p.m. to 1 a.m. weekdays, 1 p.m. to 3 a.m. Saturday, 1 p.m. to 1 a.m. Sunday

This little corner tavern offers no frills of design on first impression. Typical of small corner bars, the bar itself jets to the back parallel to the side street, while tables stand opposite it throughout its length. In the back is a pool table and a jukebox. One thing that's immediately noticeable about Claus's, is that it is so clean and orderly, making it a welcome sight over most corner bars I have visited.

Yet, there are some intricacies to the place, like the back bar, which is quite a sight. On top of the bar at the corners are a smattering of gray, ceramic mugs with logos of different German beers and German town crests. In the center of the top is another ceramic mug, but one that's more ornamental than practical. That one has to be about a foot-and-a-half high with intricate engravings on the mug. On the lid stands a ceramic 18th Century-style couple holding hands. It's quite amazing. Standing next to the ornamental mug, and contrasting its beauty with humor, is a giant pilsner glass with the words, "I bet you can't" printed with red letters.

Equally as amazing on top of the back bar is the amount of bottled beer this place offers. Forty-two bottles total, imported and domestic — for a corner tap, seemed just overwhelming for me. Claus's offers bottles of Beck's, Fransikaner, St. Pauli Girl Dark (or the golden-style in a 22-ounce bottle), Tennants, Bass, Dos Equis, Harp, Pilsner Urquell, Molson, Moosehead, Lowenbrau, Michelob, Spaten...whew! And to create a harmony of the overwhelming number of bottles and the handful of ceramic mugs, the wall behind has painted on it a nice little forested-mountain scene.

The North Side Claus's Tavern-Closet

Another little surprise on this back bar is that below the bottles and such, just above the cash register, is a couple of little translucent glass tiles with drawings on them. These drawings are Medieval-style scenes. On the far left is a tile of a woman cooking what I think are eggs. Next to that is a man and a woman sitting, with the man facing the woman smoking a pipe with a wry look on his face. All the while she has her back towards him and is knitting a stocking. At the base of the man and woman's feet are a dog and cat respectively. What the symbolic implications are, I have no idea. A third tile is a tavern scene which shows a man romancing (being romanced by?) a bar maid. Those are something unique I have never seen on a back bar before.

During my visit, I spoke with bartender Chris Benson who was a incredibly pleasant conversationalist. She gave me some background on the bar, explaining that the area was once a German stronghold, but has changed over the years with recent development.

"The clientele is still largely German," Benson said. "Very neighborhood German."

Claus, the bar's namesake, Benson explained, was the owner of the bar for many years. She said he had passed away a few years ago after which his wife took it over. Not having the stamina to continue on with the ownership, she sold it to the current owners who have run it for about the past three years.

"(The new owners) kept a lot of it the same," Benson said. "Though Claus had no jukebox, that's new, nothing really has changed."

She pointed out that all the ceramic mugs I was admiring, were all Claus's. Then she gave me a quick synapses on the history of the current owners. The current owners, though Polish, Benson said, got involved with the bar after becoming part of a rowdy group of mostly German guys that would frequent Claus's.

"Six or seven of (the original group) still come in here," Benson said. "The bartender on Saturday nights, Norbert Mueller, was part of that click."

Throughout the week the bar has drink specials. For Oktoberfest, expect to find Spaten Oktoberfest on tap. Other great German beers on tap are BBK Kaiser, Erdinger Weissbier, DAB and Bitburger. Choose from quarter or half liter glasses. For those that are American lager lovers, Old Style is also on tap. There are also a variety of handmade cigars available.

Claus's is a very friendly, clean corner tap room with its own unique German stylings and over-all feel. But whatever one's reason for stopping in Claus's Tavern, it's well worth it.

—*Phil Brandt*

The Closet

3325 N. Broadway St.
773-477-8533
Hours: 2 p.m. to 4 a.m. weekdays,
noon to 5 a.m. Saturday, noon to 4 a.m. Sunday

Barfly Closet-Club Foot

"The Closet's an odd place in a desert of people," said Audrey Rodriquez. "Different people flock to it for different reasons. It's got a little bit of everything and for those who don't fit into society — the avant garde — you are appreciated for being yourself."

One Monday a month on "Bang Your Head Night," the Closet swings like a Greek orgy. It's Xmas served up on blotter paper; Santa Claus has a nose ring, Mrs. Claus has a girlfriend and the elves are whiskey-hounds who tear into the kiddies' presents in an alcohol-fueled frenzy.

Amanda and I sat down at the bar, which was littered with suction-cup eye balls, plastic babies, fake noses and rub-on tattoos. It was a mannequin massacre. A flurry of tiny explosions hit the opposite wall. As snappers cracked on the floor, the bar and foreheads, the television was playing the Begotten, a grainy black and white film of corpses, strange robed figures and ghostly women.

We were given free jello shots to cut the edge of the night. Then we had four or five beers, a couple of shots and a few more beers. About that time a fog rolled into my brain, but I was prepared. I brought my prescription of Ritalin and after popping two, my mind kicked into gear and I regained focus.

You won't find any college sweatshirts or backwards baseball caps at the Closet. If you have a problem with lesbians or homosexuals, if you sleep with a picture of Pat Buchanan under your stained pillow, STAY THE HELL AWAY. It's sad when such statements have to be made, but the city streets teem with the bastard children of J. Edgar Hoover (he probably would have dug the Closet. After a hard day of persecuting the innocent he could have slipped into his finest doll outfit, smeared on some lipstick and strutted up to the bar in toeless high heels for a mimosa).

The point is, anyone so hell-bent on smacking a scarlet A on the public is hiding something. The Closet doesn't hide. People are free to be themselves without worrying what the punk next to them will say. It's glorious, especially at a time when our leaders get misty-eyed recalling the Salem witch burnings. Ah, those were the good old days. The righteous ruled with fire and brimstone and the weird ones shook with fear in the swamps.

But as I sat in the Closet, sucking on a Budweiser and taking in the crowd, I thought to myself, those swamps must have held fearsome parties that shook the chalice of God. And there's no place I would have rather been. Long live the weird.

— *Rich Webster*

Club Foot

1824 W. Augusta Blvd.
773-489-0379
Hours: 8 p.m. to 2 a.m. Sunday to Friday,
8 p.m. to 3 a.m. Saturday

When Chicago bar veterans Chuck Uchida and Lauree Rohrig became fed up

The North Side Club Foot

with Chicago's bar scene, the did something about it -- they bought their own bar Club Foot, formerly the Lizard Lounge.

Uchida, owner of Attica Recording Studio and former guitarist for local bands No Empathy and The Defoliants, got his start in Chicago bars by working the sound bard at the legendary Dreamerz (now Nick's), 1516 N. Milwaukee Ave., in Nov. 1987. He mixed the sound for many progressing bands like Gwar, Nirvana,m L7 and Fugazi. It was also at Dreamerz where he obtained most of his bartending experience.

"Dreamerz was the type of place where everyone (on staff) did everything," Uchida said.

Rohrig started in the bar scene as a disk jockey at Circuits (now defunct), 4355 N. Cicero Ave., the Artful Dodger, 1734 W. Wabansia Ave., and Dreamerz. She woorked at each of these clubs for a couple of years and was employed at Dreamerz, along with Uchida, until the bar closed on Nov. 14, 1993.

Uchida and Rohrig both said they enjoyed working at Dreamerz with its energy and that there just weren't any other bars around with the same vibe as Dreamerz.

"(Today) it is either go to a warehouse-sized dance hall or sit and stare at each other at a bar," Rohrig said.

"Every place just plays a set format, " Uchida added, "it's nothing but themes."

Rohrig remembers that when she and her friends used to go to the original Exit on Wells Street near North Avenue (now Tequila Roadhouse), the bar would play music ranging from AC/DC to Erasure within the course of the evening.

"I heard one person describe the selection of music there, 'if you don't like the music, wait 10 minutes.' And that's the way it was."

So fed up with what she calls "disappointing" bars, Rohrig said she asked Uchida to open a bar with her. Sharing her views on local bars, he jumped in. However, neither knew of the bureaucracy involved in opening a bar in Chicago.

"It was like having a baby," Uchida said. "It took us nine months to get the place open." They finally received a liquor license and Club Foot held its grand opening on Jan. 20, 1995.

It took months to find a suitable spot for the new bar, Rohrig said. She finally decided to make an offer to former Lizard Lounge owner Scott Gray.

Repairs to the old tavern, which has been a bar since the Turn of the Century, were minimal. The original tin ceiling is still in good condition. They added new paint throughout to "brighten up the place."

The layout of Club Foot is the same as the former Lizard Lounge. The bar is in front, the dance floor is in back with a DJ booth separating the two.

"It's a space like Dreamerz," Rohrig said. "We can crank it up in back, but people can still talk in front."

The bar has an excellent sound system. And for music, Rohrig brought in her

Barfly Club Foot-Club 950

record and CD collection started more than 20 years ago.

From bar patrons to bartenders to bar owners, Rohrig and Uchida have a firm understanding about what patrons are looking for. With a wide selction of music, a place to dance and a bar to down a few drinks, the duo is set to bring back the glorious scene they once enjoyed as barflies.

-- Phil Brandt

Club 950

950 W. Wrightwood
773-929-8955
Hours: 9 p.m. to 2 a.m. Tuesday to Friday,
9 p.m. to 3 a.m. Saturday

I did my review on Club 950. It's a great bar, and I like it. Did I mention that it is a great bar? They have drink specials. When I was there, on a Wednesday night they had $3.50 pitchers of Bud and Bud Light. Every night, they have $2 shots of Tequila, Blue Curacao, Keglevich, Fris Vodka, Royalty Vodka and others. I went with a couple of friends, and it is a great bar. If you're ever in the neighborhood, consider stopping at Club 950. Tell your friends, too!

OK, so let's stop the boring bullshit and reach into the mix of sentimental values that make up the atmosphere of a bar.

Club 950 lies just east of the intersection of Lincoln, Sheffield and Wrightwood, an intersection symbolizing the heart of yuppieville but possessing several signs of a Wicker Park/Bucktown mentality as well. I pass this intersection around 2 a.m. every day on my way home from work. At this time, an army of black leather pants, black leather jackets, black leather spiked bracelets, black hair, black eyebrows, black lip stick and tight black latex pants come pouring into the friendly neighborhood.

Who are these people? Where do they come from? What's going on in that bar? How do I meet these beautiful women dressed in radical clothing without feeling like an insecure geek?

What's with this black cow-hide frenzy? I can sum it up in one word, "Gothic." I never gave much more thought to the word until the bartender at Club 950, Theresa, began talking about the Gothic crowd. Then the disc jockey, Dave, talked extensively of the origins and meaning of the Gothic culture, upon my request.

Dave first told me about Gothic music.

"It's a mixture of a sort of dance rock. Rocky and guitary dance rock," he said. "R&R with heavy dancing, if done right."

But what are Goths?

"Gothic sprang out of a club in London called the Batcave," Dave said.

51

The North Side Club 950

OK, but what are Goths?

"Basically, Goths are people who read a lot and are vampire fans."

Bingo!

"They don't go out in the sun a lot and they have a fetish with bondage," Dave said. "Lots of latex. They're also fanatics of '50s B-rated horror films. But unlike popular belief, most Goths are not Satanic."

Why do Goths hang out at Club 950? On the outside, the club looks like an auto parts store. But a soothing aura of dim red, black and fluorescent lights mark its inside. A long oak bar trails along the west wall, while shelves of authentic genie bottles dot the rest of the entry room. This room, alone, is enough to make one forget that the other end opens onto a vast dance floor.

The second room also stuns. You would never guess a dance floor of such mammoth proportions could fit inside the small club. Opposite the entrance leading onto the dance floor stands the DJ booth. Behind that is the men's bathroom, consisting of a row of urinals with no door.

Off to the side of the dance floor, at least two dozen couches are hidden under a cloud of second-hand smoke. I love couches in a bar, and this is couch heaven.

Another doorway marks the same wall. This one leads to the pool room, filled by three tables. Dave the DJ said club management still has some work to do on this room. He didn't like the room, he said, because it was too bright. I agree. The room just doesn't fit the rest of the puzzle. Dave told me Club 950 has future plans to dim the room a bit and install a short bar. A perfect solution.

Thursday nights at Club 950 are 1980s theme song nights. For some reason, the Goths choose to converge here on these nights. The DJ has been trying to start a Gothic theme night on Wednesdays, but the Goths haven't showed up.

The club also gets occasional Goth bands. And management is testing different drink specials. For example, a brochure inside the bar announced a quarter beer night on a Wednesday, with a $3 cover. A message to all Goths from Dave the DJ: Go to Club 950 on Wednesday nights!

I don't mean to scare any mild-mannered, straight-looking yuppies. The night I stopped by Club 950, I wore a white T-shirt that glowed under the neon bulbs. Did a vampire come swooping down in defense of her territory? No. The bar features plenty of nooks and crannies, perfect for going unnoticed.

Oh, I almost forgot to mention the most important information about Club 950. Domestic beers available include Miller Genuine Draft, Miller Lite, Bud, Bud Light, Rolling Rock, Ice House and Sharps. Imported beers consist of Beck's, Heineken's, Bass, Guinness and Amstel Light.

— Willy Laszlo

CND Gyros Lounge
205 E. Grand Ave.
312-467-4195
Hours: 9:30 a.m. to 10 p.m. Monday to Saturday

No need to hunt for good Chicago-style food after tying one on at CND, it's a bar and a greasy spoon all in one. Entrants to CND will find on their left a full-service counter with gyro sandwiches, Italian beef, sausage, meatballs, burgers and every other traditional Chicago-style sandwich. A few paces south, and you're in the lounge. An adequate, well-appointed bar offers tap beer and a familiar selection of liquor. There's plenty of seating at the bar, and much more at the score of tables throughout the room. Darts and video slots are available, but what really sets CND apart is the fact that it's a licensed agent of the Illinois State Lottery. Play all your favorite games from the humblest scratch-and-win to Lotto.

CND's early hours make it a decidedly mid-day and after-work bar. Combined with the kitchen, it makes an ideal launching pad for a long night. What better way to fuel up than with a belly full of Old Style and a gyro plate? In addition to Old Style, CND's tap offerings include MGD and Miller Lite, as well as Bud and Killians. Bottled selections are more international, with Corona, Dos Equis representing Mexico; Molson and Moosehead from Canada; Heineken and Grolsch from Holland, Becks and Holsten from Germany, and Red Stripe from Jamaica. Add to that the bottled domestics and you have just about every taste covered.

CND patrons tend to fall into two categories: stopping in for a sandwich, or staying in to get slammed. That does not mean, however, that a well-lubricated guest won't hop around the corner to the food counter, then bring a Polish back to his spot at the bar. Prices might be a bit more than at a stand without a bar (the gyro sandwich is $4.15 without fries) but the value is more than made up by the convenience. And, if the season is right, CND sells deep-fried smelts, heaped in a basket with plenty of fries included for less than five bucks. One-stop shopping for an assault both the heart and the liver, CND is the total dining and drinking package.

— *Jay Ferrari*

Cocktail
3359 N. Halsted
773-477-1420
Hours: 4 p.m. to 2 a.m. weekdays,
1:30 p.m. to 3 a.m. Saturday,
1:30 p.m. to 2 a.m. Sunday

I walked into Cocktail at about 6:30 p.m. on a Saturday night and left an hour later hugging the patrons goodbye. And I'm really not an overly demon-

53

strative person.

I don't think I've experienced a warmer or friendlier bar anywhere in the city. Located in a primo position on Halsted's gay strip, Cocktail was established in April, 1996, by a group of four owners, two of whom also own Espial, a bistro at Sheffield and Armitage. The bar is tastefully decorated with beamed ceilings, exposed brick walls, funky, but subtle track lighting and a beautiful mahogany-colored antique bar.

"Cocktail is a place where people from all walks of life can interact," says owner Elizabeth Walker. "We're on the gay strip, but ethically and morally, we believe it's time for different types of people to mix it up."

Cocktail, 3359 N. Halsted St., is one of the warmest and friendliest bars in the city.

"This is a gay bar where straight people, lesbians, whoever can come in and feel comfortable," says Donny, a Cocktail regular.

"That's because it's the least pretentious," adds Todd, also a Cocktail regular.

That evening one group was drinking pints of beer and engaged in lively conversation. A few people were sitting at the bar chatting with the bartender. A group of five had ordered Chinese from Mark's Chop Suey, and were happily drinking and eating what appeared to be sweet and sour chicken. Very laid back. Donny and Todd even come into the bar on some Sundays wearing their flannel pajamas.

"It's comfortable," says Todd. "I could never go across the street wearing my PJs. They would take one look at me and say, 'I can't believe you came out in that...Girl, you're not dressed!'"

Apparently, though, things pick up quite a bit during prime time. The front wall of Cocktail is essentially one huge window with seats facing out onto Halsted. Patrons have been known, after enjoying a libation or two, to sit in the big window and rate passers-by on a scale of one to ten. They write their rat-

Barfly Cocktail-Congress Restaurant

ings down on cocktail napkins and hold them up to the window for display purposes. If anyone receives a seven or higher, they knock on the window to beckon the lucky pedestrian in and buy him or her a drink. Both men and women are rated — supporting the non-discriminatory theme of the bar.

Donny and Todd explained that the "Rating Game" led into the "Bag Game," which offers only three possible evaluations of the unsuspecting public. In the "Bag Game," people are judged on whether they should cover their head with a bag ("Bag"), their entire person with a bag ("Body Bag") or whether they are, in fact, attractive enough to go sans bag ("No Bag").

I asked whether the bag and rating games weren't just a wee bit harsh.

"Some people with low ratings have gotten really pissed off," admits Donny and Todd, though they don't seem overly concerned about this. Law of the jungle, I guess.

Cocktail offers a variety of musical options — a jukebox with selections ranging from Alanis to The Doors and, of course, a lot of disco. The bar also has a DJ spinning Acid Jazz on weekends and kicks the week off with "Opera Monday."

As you might imagine, martinis are very popular. (Donny, who is very passionate about the subject, pointed out that although he loves them, martinis are really nothing more than "three ounces of vodka in a fabulous glass.") Cocktail's martinis are served in 1940s-replica fabulous glasses and are a bargain at $4.50. Domestic beers are $2.50, imports are $3.50.

All in all, Cocktail has a lot to offer. Regardless of your "walk of life," I'm willing to bet that they'll show you a good time at Cocktail, and remember, you're probably a lot better off being in the bar than passing by the big front window.

— *Lisa Kueng*

Congress Restaurant & Lounge
3200 N. Milwaukee Avenue
773-286-5105
Hours: 7 a.m. to 4 a.m. daily

On a recent Friday evening, I visited the Congress Restaurant & Lounge. The bar offers good food and has a very good tap selection of beers which includes DAB, Okocim, Gosser, Pilsner Urquell and Bud. There is also a wide range of bottle selections. One of the beers is Trok which I never heard of.

The bar has two rooms. The front room is primarily a restaurant with a food counter and a bar setting on one side. There are plenty of food selections from Polish tasty treats to basic American fare. The prices are quite reasonable. For example, a ham & cheese omelet is only $2.85.

The back room has another bar. At the front, there is a stage where bands play the famous Polish tunes of the day. There is a sizable dance floor in front of the stage. The room sits more than 100 people, which is quite spacious.

The customers are primarily Polish. I have noticed recently that there has

The North Side Congress Restaurant-Corosh

been an influx of Czechs settling in Chicago and they do frequent Polish bars quite regularly. One of my friends was trying to talk to this guy and we thought he was Polish, but after a half an hour, we found out he was not.

One of the weirdest practices here is that they charge four bucks for beer on Friday in the back room. The reason is that it is dance night, but you can go to the front and get DAB in a 16-ounce glass for $2.25 or one of the other fine selections.

The service here is quite good, but be patient if you don't speak Polish. The bartenders are friendly, but they notice quickly if you are not one of the regulars.

The Congress is well worth a stop either for a good, tasty cheap meal or to get a cold tasty brew at Belmont and Milwaukee in the Avondale community.

— Herb

Corosh
1072 N. Milwaukee Ave.
773-235-0600
Hours: 11 a.m. to 2 a.m. Monday to Saturday,
11 a.m. to midnight Sunday

My visit to Corosh was troubled by a preliminary bout of schizophrenia -- is this a stylish bar or a solid restaurant? Fortunately, it's both. Corosh, named after its architect/sculptor owner, is an excellent place to start or finish an evening.

Appetites are well-served at Corosh (literally and figuratively, as both food and service are excellent). The menu reflects the split-personality, offering both bar food and entrees. The bar menu has burgers, quesedillas and the like in the five to seven-buck range. The restaurant menu, offering what the waiter described as "light Northern Italian" is at most $15 for an entree, with selections hovering around seven to 10 dollars. From the bar menu, I tried an especially good grilled chicken breast sandwich served with homemade honey bourbon sauce and curly fries. I chased it with a monster piece of chocolate moussse cake and some cinnamon dusted black coffee. Yum, yum.

Corosh has an inviting interior that reflects the owner's artistic inclinations. The long bar and restaurant area are upstairs and there is a cool view of the busy kitchen, so the cooked-in-sight truck-driver rule holds true. The upstairs has the feel of ancient Rome with beautiful columns along the bar and exposed brick walls. Downstairs, you'll find a pool table, Ms. Pac Man and (yes) Rollergames pinball. And there's a good selection of beer, with can't-miss favorites like Bass and Guinness on tap.

Corosh is not the place to go howl with the boys, smash bottles and trade shots. It's a trattoria that thinks it's a bar, or a bar that thinks it's a trattoria. In either case, it's done well.

-- Jay Ferrari

Courtesy Tap
1622 W. Belmont Ave.
773-477-9699
Hours: noon to 2 a.m. daily

I want to point out that I am the kind of writer that goes to great pains to find the good in every bar that I go into, whether for business or pleasure.

So don't expect me to focus on the fact that the urinal is chained to the wall in the men's room. I am also not going to dwell on the fact that the prices are a little too exorbitant for a place that offers as little as this place does.

But if bartender Tina likes the place, how bad can it be. She has worked there for three years and said she enjoys meeting the new people that walk in and teach her how to mix drinks she is unfamiliar with.

Now the backbar is a work of art. The beveled glass and high arching wood angles ache to tell stories of a happier (and cleaner) day when they saw a lot more action.

The place is actually quite big but the space is currently not being utilized very well. Tina says that the owner is going to move the pool table and bring in some dart machines which should attract a wider variety of clientele.

This will, hopefully, coincide with having beer taps installed so that the patron does not have to keep walking to the cooler to serve themselves.

For the Barfly who is strong at heart, you owe it to yourself to stop in the Courtesy Tap and get yourself a beer and chat with Tina. I would try to do it before they move the pool table. I just have this feeling that they will enlist the help of their self-service-trained patrons to hoist the heavy slate between beers.

Well, I guess this wasn't the nicest bar review that I have ever written. Perhaps we'll check back in a few months for an update on the progress of the Courtesy Tap.

— *Paul Barile*

Critters
3757 N. Cicero Ave.
773-545-8787
Hours: 3 p.m. to 2 a.m. Sunday to Friday,
3 p.m. to 3 a.m. Saturday

Chicago has just a few country bars. On a recent bar soirée, I decided to visit a Northwest Side country bar located just two blocks south of Irving Park on Cicero.

It has been a couple of years since my last visit to this club. There is still a long bar at the right of the entrance. On the night of my visit, a cold rainy night, there was about 30 patrons. Most in attendance seemed to have a good time, including me, in this larger than average club.

Critters has a stage up front, a pool table, video poker, and a dart league during the week. The lighting is dim, almost dark.

Holding court on that stage up front is the Johnny Rogers Band which plays every Friday and Saturday. The band plays plenty of Elvis, old rock classics and a mix of Country classics. There is never a cover charge and plenty of seats.

One of the drawbacks here is that there is no draft beer selections. Domestic bottles take reign here. But if you like Old Style, it's only one buck on Thursday nights.

A major point for my bar rating scale is service. Critters ranks high in quality, quickness, and courteous. Good service is what makes the distinction on good bars from bad bars.

Overall, if you like country and rock tunes, Critters is well worth a visit. So, if you are driving around the Portage Park neighborhood near Six Corners. You can experience a little country music in the city which seems rarer these days.

— *Pete Schmugge*

Crobar

1543 N. Kingsbury
312-413-7000
Hours 9 p.m. to 4 a.m. Sunday, Wednesday to Friday,
9 p.m. to 5 a.m. Saturday,
closed Monday and Tuesday

Every time my friend Kristen and I go to Crobar, she looks fierce. She always dresses to turn heads. By "turn heads" I mean more than just gaining attention through raw sexuality. Instead, she dresses in a way that shows her individuality, her comfort with and pride in her body, and a certain strength that results. Dressed in a fantastic-looking orange suit she found at a thrift store, an orange scarf and purple platforms, she gets your attention but also demands respect.

Thus begins our Sunday night. Each time we go to Crobar, we have the same talk. What "goodies" are we going to partake in that evening? E? K? G? Maybe talk to the big girl (She's a Methodist, you know)? We decide to play it by ear and see what happens. After a few early evening drinks at Empty Bottle, we hit Crobar around one, when the place really starts to kick.

Crobar is a nightclub that is part of the underground house music scene that Chicago gave birth to. On Sunday nights, the place booms with the sound of this in-your-face hybrid of disco-funk and R & B. House, while a subculture in America, has taken Europe by storm where it along with its cousin techno is constantly in the Top Ten. At concerts, this music can draw in excess of 30,000 people.

It's pretty hard to escape the music at Crobar. The propulsive thump of 808s and 909s (two vintage drum machines used to create much of house music's rhythm); echoing, warping, low-ended synthesizers; and the soulful, soaring

Barfly Crobar

vocals that can sound beautiful, sexy and angry all at the same time permeate every part of the club. Some places are louder than others — in front of the speakers, the music becomes a physical force you can feel hitting you — but overall this is not a quiet place.

Which is good. House music was meant to be loud. This space in which Crobar is located handles the high decibels well and is truly a trip. The design of the club brings to mind a combination science fiction movie and a velvety 1920s speakeasy. Metal catwalks and stairs cut through the cavernous warehouse space. On both ends of the club, rooms hang from the ceiling and look like the command decks of the space stations in "Battlestar Galactica." All this is combined with a row of large, arched, glowing purple windows and a chillout room with plush carpet and thick, soft chairs and sofas. The overall look of the club reminds me of Terry Gillam's "Brazil."

The look of Crobar is nothing compared to the people who go there on Sundays. It is one of the best places in Chicago to people watch. People dress from the ordinary (jeans and white undershirt) to the extreme (a goateed young man looking very Huggy Bear, wearing a snakeskin vest and pants, a thick white belt and boots, and a golfer's hat; another man with hair dyed the color of a highlighter, vinyl pants, a dog collar with three-inch spikes, and Frakenstein boots). What makes a lot of people great to watch is that they exude a certain confidence which comes from being able to pull off such outrageousness with comfort, ease and a wicked sense of humor. Rather than look at them and laugh, you look at them with a kind of admiration.

Kristen and I hook up with a friend of ours, one of these fierce people, selling rolls for $20. He says they're fantastic. Knowing the stuff he's gotten us in the past and looking at the two black pupils expanding over his eyes, we know he's telling the truth. Kristen and I decide to indulge, and 15 minutes later we KNOW he was telling the truth. After a few more drinks, we realize it's time to dance. We drank Budweiser and vodka tonics, by the way, Crobar is not really a connoisseur's place. Most of the beers, spirits and liquors they serve are standards gotten at any bar anywhere. Unfortunately, like most clubs, the drinks are expensive — $3.75 to $5.

DJs Terri Bristol and Ralph Rosario have worked the crowd into a frenzy. The kinetic mass of bodies is fierce. Some people's movements, whether it's a gyration of the hip, a kick of the leg, or an extension of the arm, are both fluid and jerky at the same time, yet all are done with an intensity that does not hold anything back. The fact that some people can get on the dance floor and move with such unselfconsciousness, graceful abandon shows a control of the human body that is fun to be a part of.

It's four a.m. and people are leaving Crobar. A lot of them covered in sweat but still fierce. A bunch of people we know are going to an after-hours. Kristen and I decide whether or not we want to go. I mention there might be a tank. Enough said.

— Joe Schweizer

59

Crystal Inn
Charlotte's Bar & Grill
6000 W. Gunnison St.
773-775-3616
Hours: noon to 2 a.m. Sunday to Friday,
noon to 3 a.m. Saturday

On a recent Wednesday, I visited a local sports bar in the Jefferson Park neighborhood. The Hawks were playing the Flames and the bar was filled with hockey fans.

When you walk into this place, you first notice the square shape of the bar, which seats at least 35. After finding a spot, I was startled by the reflection of a familiar round shape in front of me — me. This place has plenty of mirrors.

The crowd was mostly males who like to watch sports, but you have to remember this was Wednesday night. The atmosphere is laid back with good and friendly service. It is a clean neighborhood bar.

There are two large-screen TV sets as well as three additional sets placed throughout the bar. On one side of the room, there are tables that face one of the projection television sets and a large mirror. On another side of the room, there is a pool table which was in use the entire night.

There are no tap beer selections. Domestic bottles are $1.75 while import beers go for $2.50 and up.

If you are near Lawrence and Austin, stop in Crystal Inn, Charlotte's Bar & Grill, and get one of their delicious hamburgers and a cold brew. Don't worry about parking, there is a parking lot and plenty of street parking.

— *Pete Schmugge*

Cubby Bear
1059 W. Addison St.
773-327-1662
Hours 8 p.m. to 2 a.m. Wednesday to Friday,
11 a.m. to 3 a.m. Saturday, 11 a.m. to 2 a.m. Sunday,
open Monday nights during football season.

After many visits, I've come to the conclusion that Cubby Bear has a split personality. As a cornerstone of Wrigleyville nightlife, the bar depends on the adventures at and around Wrigley Field during baseball season.

It's sort of the unofficial second home of the Cubs. Some great post-game parties (win or lose) begin at the Cubby Bear and often continue down Clark Street until the morning hours. There is a general feeling of revelry as soon as you enter those comfortably air-conditioned confines on a hot summer day.

Watch out for tourists and high beer prices, though. While it's great fun to practice your drunken victory (or more accurately, loss) dance with people you meet from all over the country, Cubby Bear takes advantage of your drunken-

60

Barfly Cubby Bear-Cullen's

ness and charges the same for beers as the ballpark does. Maybe they think you get used to paying $3.75 a beer. Maybe you're from out of town and don't know better. Maybe you are simply too drunk to care. You do have the chance to buy overpriced shirts at the bar's growing souvenir stand even if you don't drink the beer. At least take advantage of the sound system and the three floors you can spread out in after being jammed in your seat at the game.

Which brings me to the off-season Cubby Bear. When there's no baseball, the bar is mostly a concert venue. As a longtime Wrigleyville resident and admittedly a summer patron, I have to confess to seeing a few concerts there. In fairness, I've heard good things about big-name acts like B.B. King and Eric Johnson who have appeared to sell-out crowds over the years.

Happily, Cubby Bear has an extensive menu of tasty bar food to choose from if you've forgotten to eat at the ball park. With that sound system and many screens, Cubby Bear is a great place to watch sports of all kinds. When this reporter thinks back to the day when she was at the Cubby Bear watching the first Dream Team (basketball) receive gold medals after the 1992 Summer Olympic Games, she just about gets a tear in her eye.

Coincidentally, we were at the Cubby Bear after a ball game and the place was packed. It was a gorgeous summer day, and the Cubs might have even won. The star Spangled Banner, booming through the speakers, cut through the partying and every single person in the place turned to the nearest TV. Together, friends and strangers, tourists and Chicagoans, Cub fans and realists, watched the camera move slowly along the proud faces of Jordan and Pippen and the rest. I tell you, you could hear a pin drop in the Cubby Bear that afternoon. It was one of my more exceptional moments in any bar. OK, I feel a little too much like Bob Green, but it really was a great thing.

— Stephanie Behne

Cullen's
3741 N. Southport Ave.
773-975-0600
Hours: 5 p.m. to 2 a.m. Sunday to Friday,
5 p.m. to 3 a.m. Saturday

At first glance, Cullen's Bar and Grill sits comfortably with the rest of the buildings on the 3700 block of Southport Avenue; then you realize that, not too long ago, it wasn't there at all. Formerly the site of a small department store and a rug cleaning service, Cullen's now shares the space with the new Mercury Theatre and Carlucci's Streganona. Michael Cullen, the proprietor of Cullen's and the Mercury Theatre, wants to give the impression that this bar, opened in 1996, is as comfortable and welcoming as your favorite old saloon. And with all the effort and passion that he has put into this project, he may have succeeded.

Upon entering the barroom, I found it hard to believe that this was a newly constructed bar. But Michael confirmed that before the first bar rail could be

61

The North Side Cullen's-Cut Rate Liquors

installed, the whole building had to be gutted. Only then were the extensive plans and minute detailing laid out.

The barroom has the look and feel of a drinking establishment from the earlier part of this century, with tin-stamped ceilings, Yorkshire brass handles and antique lighting. The bar, inspired by the Brunswick Del Monte designs of yesteryear, is constructed from birchwood, Honduras mahogany and bordered with marble. The walls are painted in the style of Cezanne, a 19th Century French painter. The overall effect is quite impressive.

Twelve taps offer up everything from standards like Budweiser to specialties and imports like Witmer and Guinness. A large selection of bottled beer, including many microbrews, is on hand and a full list of wine, Champagne and premium liquors is available.

Alan Katz, who hung his chef's hat at the Blue Mesa, 1729 N. Halsted St., from 1988 to 1996, presides over the kitchen. The menu features American standards like meatloaf and chicken pot pie, specialties like Irish stew, fish and chips (wrapped in Irish newspaper) and several tempting desserts like chocolate cake and assorted fruit cobblers.

In addition, the building next door houses the relatively new 350-seat Mercury Theatre. Michael Cullen, whose background is in theatre production, will also be active at the Mercury. Before becoming involved in the bar and restaurant industry (this is his first venture), Michael received a masters of fine arts from the Goodman School of Drama. In the 1970s, he was part of a theatre group and independent commercial theatre in the Midwest.

A plaque at the bar is inscribed with a quote that Michael learned from his mother; it reads "Never lose the common touch." This openness is reflected in the bar's approach to all who enter its doorway. Everyone is welcome and few will be disappointed.

-- Michael Cotter

Cut Rate Liquors & Package Goods
1687 Division St.
Don't Call At All!
Hours: 7 a.m. to 1 a.m. daily

Sometimes you want to go where nobody knows your name. And they couldn't give a crap if you came. You wanna drink where people think that life is going down the drain. You want some beer so you can wallow in your own pain.

If there were a clever situation comedy based on Cut Rate Liquors, that would have to be its theme song. Unlike "Cheers" however, this place serves up a frosty mug of cold, hard reality. It's sort of like what "Cheers" would be like if you replaced the cast with the clientele of your local methadone clinic and substituted the sound of audience laughter with the sound of human hope slowly dying.

There's no quick-quipping fat guy at the end of the bar with a good-natured

Barfly Cut Rate Liquors-Cy's Steak and Chop House

ribbing for everyone. Instead there's an old guy with a dent at the base of his head big enough to pour a bowl of Fruit Loops into. He regales you with the story of how he was imprisoned in Joliet for five years for shooting and killing the man who tried to cave in his skull with a hammer.

There's no hilarious sexual tension between the ex-pitcher bartender and (insert untalented actress here). Instead there's six guys huddled around the video poker machine, cheering their friend to get the computer-generated bikini babe's top off. And there's no overbearing postman boring everyone to tears with his verbal diarrhea. Instead we have a liquored-up fundamentalist Christian pounding his fists on the bar and yelling that "Christ is your Lord and mighty goddamn savior!!" Point of reference: never bait a drunk guy who's shouting about Jesus.

After several minutes of trying to ignore this guy, I gave in and attempted to communicate. Our conversation didn't go much further than his demanding we get down on our knees and "Pray for God's forgiveness!!"

I responded, "Well you first." After that he screamed and knocked over his bar stool. It got ugly. He began chanting some sort of curse and shaking his fingers at our beers. Thankfully a buddy of his quieted him down with a fishbowl-sized glass of Bud (a steal at 75 cents a pop). With that the owner announced they'd be closing in five minutes.

My drinking companion and I also checked out the "packaged goods" section of the place. Beer here is just as inexpensive as in any 7-11 cooler and a whole lot easier to buy. Whoever thought of selling beer-to-go in a bar is a genius.

— Brian Farrelly

Cy's Steak & Chop House
4138 N. Lincoln Ave.
773-404-5800
Hours: 11:30 a.m. to 11 p.m. weekdays,
11:30 a.m. to midnight weekends

Bam! Crack! A plate hit the floor a couple feet away. A waiter and bus boy whisked away the fallen dessert with military precision, skillfully wielding one of those industrial brooms with an attached dust bin. The waitress repeatedly apologized, as if she'd spilled coffee in the customer's lap.

I think she knew I was reviewing the place. Maybe that made the cleanup quicker, the staff more apologetic. But before anyone had a chance to whisk away the shattered plate, I saw the wreckage. Even though the plate landed face-down on the floor, those pear slices remained fanned, looking awfully tasty. Details such as that sold me on Cy's Steak & Chop House.

The pre-meal bread, for example, was too hot to touch. And for bread spread, we were given a plate of butter pads surrounding a head of baked garlic.

Kim, our waitress, warned my martini-loving friend Kathleen that the Hail Mary she ordered would be closer to a Bloody Mary than a martini. Maybe, she said, she'd consider having that on-the-rocks. Kathleen switched her order

The North Side Cy's Steak and Chop House

to an Absolut Pepper Martini, "executive" sized for a dollar more.

Our wood table sat in the center of the place. I noticed that the seating was generously spaced. One couple was able to keep their toddler in a full-blown stroller outside their booth without crowding the aisles.

The restaurant's over-all look is dark and rich, with exposed brick walls, taupe and burgundy drapery, and lighting covered with metal vines.

A small, television-equipped bar is available just inside the door to accommodate anyone waiting for a table.

Most diners wore summer-casual: T-shirts, Polos, shorts, skirts. The wait staff, though, was buttoned-up, wearing crisp, white long-sleeve shirts, black pants and black ties.

The mood was relaxed — so much so that at several moments I forgot I was doing a review and got caught up discussing fellow diner Steve's idea for a product that would, at the very least, delight the martini set, if not revolutionize the way the drink is prepared. (He would not be happy if I said more.)

Maybe my mood had something to do with my pre-dinner Columbia Crest Chardonnay. The wine list that runs the back side of the menu ranges from $3.25 Chardonnays to $5.50 Merlots. I don't know wine, so I really can't rate the flavor, but the two glasses got me adequately light-headed.

Not ravenous, I skipped on the appetizers but enjoyed watching my companions sample theirs.

"This is really, really, really good," Steve said over the skinned, grilled eggplant appetizer stuffed with cheese. "You can taste the different flavors of the ingredients."

Kathleen, a good cook herself, raved about her baked artichoke. She said it was well-done, but not overcooked. She analyzed the breading: "It's really light. You don't feel like you won't be able to eat the rest of your dinner."

But what she later discovered forced her to break out in a happy poem: "There are pine nuts. There are pine nuts. There are pine nuts in my artichoke!"

She was happy with her entree, though it couldn't live up to the artichoke. She rated her swordfish as "dry, but very flavorful." The rosemary "complements the fish well, and yet you can recognize the rosemary."

Steve's entree also had a hard time following his appetizer's performance.

"They spent all their time on the eggplant and they did a good job of it. The pasta-and-shrimp is just good."

Steve did clean his plate, though. Kathleen, his wife, explained that he has always been a member of the Clean Plate Club.

My 10-ounce filet mignon was labeled the "Best in the City" on the menu. I haven't eaten enough filet mignon to judge, but I did enjoy that chunk of meat.

"You wouldn't have to salt that," Kathleen remarked after sampling a bite.

The three of us shared a refreshing slice of key lime pie to finish the meal. We'd go back.

Prices on appetizers range from $4 to $6; on burgers and sandwiches from $4 to $7, and $8 to $29 for entrees.

— *Alice Bendig*

D Duck's

3555 N. Ashland Ave.
773-348-9087
Hours: 10 a.m. to 2 a.m. daily

More than likely, you've never heard of D Duck's place. This small bar on North Ashland has been around since 1962 (there was some debate between the customers on the actual date), but it serves mainly a local crowd. The owner, Don, named the place after his "handle" (CB radio name) as a truck driver — D Duck.

At D Duck's you'll find a nice neighborhood clientele who like to talk about the Cubs and who has been shooting good pool. Pool seems to be the main attraction and the table in back is a good one. Don't worry about not finding a suitable stick because you're sure to locate a winner out of the 30 or so that fill a corner in the back room.

If you're looking for a more competitive game of billiards, D Duck's sponsors a pool league on Mondays and Wednesdays during the fall and winter.

I recommend you stop in for a $1.75 Old Style and a game of stick.

— Aaron Baker

Deja Vu

2624 N. Lincoln Ave.
773-871-0205
Hours: 6 p.m. to 2 a.m. Sunday to Friday,
6 p.m. to 3 a.m. Saturday

A familiar feeling sweeps through you as you walk into the bar. Glance up, and the polished tin ceiling looks vaguely familiar. Look down, and the black-and-white tiled floor rings a bell. You just don't know why.

As you scan the rest of the bar, that same familiar feeling continues to charm you. It seems like you've been here before. But everything is too different.

A group of people begin cheering. You cruise over to see what's going on. Tonight is turtle racing night. Finally, you know what's happening. What you've been experiencing is Deja Vu, 2624 N. Lincoln Ave., which re-opened its doors to the public on May 22, 1997.

Deja Vu opened in 1983. If you've been there before May 22, 1997, and haven't returned since, you probably remember it as a run-down and rickety old bar that was nearly vacant until 2 a.m. when the Lincoln Park locals and DePaul students would finally roll in, long after other nearby bars had closed. Deja Vu, both old and new, has one of the few 4 a.m. licenses in Chicago. The structure itself is a city landmark. Built in 1881, the building has seen time as a brothel, taco stand and various other bars.

Recently, new owners Sean Fallmer and Jason Barker came across an opportunity they couldn't resist. They had a chance to breath life back into this

65

famous bar.

Due to the bar's condition, though, major changes were made. Almost everything inside was redone. The new owners added a deejay booth and stage. They redid the bathrooms, and installed an expensive new plumbing system. New paint lines the walls, and the decorative floor and tin ceiling have been polished.

Fallmer and Barker didn't change everything. Deja Vu traditions such as turtle racing, cheap beer specials ($1.50 Old Style), theme nights and the original tin ceiling and black-and-white floor live on. But aside from these traditions, you'd never guess it was the same bar.

This popular, yet beleaguered, bar has been transformed into a modern and inviting late-night lounge. A mammoth of a bar sits strongly at the side. Here, Deja Vu offers 12 kinds of draft and 15 bottled beers. There is also a large collection of liquors. Deja Vu offers a slew of signature drinks, including a "Wisconsin Lunch Bucket," a shot of Jim Beam dropped into a glass filled with Old Style beer and orange juice. This even comes with a wedge of cheese.

A wide variety of bands play at the bar weekly. The stage, which sits just a few feet above the main floor, is home to Cassius Clay, Denise La Grassa and other big-time local bands. Every Sunday is jazz night, while the first Thursday of every month will feature rock-a-billy.

Because Deja Vu is one of the few places open until 5 a.m. on Saturdays, hunger will definitely strike. Not to worry. A variety of "pub grub" is served, including jalapeño poppers, mozzarella sticks, French fries and taquitos.

Deja Vu is well known in Chicago, of course. But a few years back, it even made national news. Once, during one of the turtle races, a turtle fell off a table onto the floor. A woman accused the bar of animal abuse. The Wall Street Journal covered the story, and David Letterman even mentioned it on his show.

If you were once a regular at the "Vu," you must come in and see the changes. And if you've never been here before, it's a great place to enjoy a beer or mixed drink, listen to great live music and enjoy yourself in a relaxing atmosphere. And, most important, it's open extremely late on weekends.

— Kevin Toomajian

Demo's Pub
3843 W. Fullerton Ave.
Hours: noon to 2 a.m. Sunday to Friday, noon to 3 a.m. Saturday

"Everybody needs a little place they can hide. Somewhere to call their own, don't let nobody inside. Every now and then we all need to let go..."

Tom Keifer from the band Cinderella belted out these lyrics all over MTV a few short years ago, probably not even knowing that he was describing Demo's Pub on Fullerton Avenue.

"It's a hideaway," Tony says from behind the bar. With a smile he adds, "Guys come in here, not with their girlfriends."

Barfly Demo's Pub

By and large that seemed to be true, although I was sitting right next to a man and his wife. Everyone however, was having a good time and didn't appear to be hiding from anyone, but you can never tell.

Even though Demo's is just one of about a dozen bars in a mile long stretch, it has a few things that make it truly unique. A really excellent paneling hangs from the walls. It gives the place kind of a lodge-y feel. Two huge swords await behind the bar for the beheading of unruly patrons. At least that's the way they look — medieval and menacing. Between the two suspended swords is a fish tank that houses piranhas, in case you really piss them off.

Amusements are the same as just about any other bar in Chicago: two poker machines, electronic darts and a pool table. The table, however is covered in this really cool red felt and is still only 50 cents per game. If you're brave, you can challenge the regulars to a game, but I wouldn't recommend it. I'm a pretty fair shot, and they embarrassed me all over the place. The jukebox has everything from Kansas to Metallica and some Snoop Doggy Dogg thrown in for good measure. When no one is playing it, local radio stations are piped through the stereo system. It was WGCI when I was there, unfortunately.

"It depends on the crowd," Tony says.

Tony, who is the son of the owner, made it clear that he is not just a bartender, he is *the* bartender. He is an excellent one at that. And Nitza, who takes the reigns when he is not there, is fantastic as well. Let's face it, it is the person behind the bar that makes a place what it is. If you want a real treat, stop in during the day when Tony's father, John, is doing the pouring. He is one of the nicest, most insightful men I know. With the crew they have, not only do you leave with a good buzz, but a little more insight on the life that God gave you.

"Pappa John and Tony are two of the greatest people on earth," one female regular said. Even though she also said the earth was spinning for her then, it was a point well made.

Pictures of half-naked ladies line the walls, as well as a Red Dog border across the ceiling. Domestic bottles are only a buck and a half (when was the last time you saw that?), and shots of Jack Daniels are $1.75. This is one of the reasons I have never left Demo's Pub sober. They also serve glasses of beer called "fishbowls" for $1.50. They get the name from the fact that they look like, well, fishbowls. No need to worry what will come in the aforementioned glass, as Budweiser is the only beer on tap.

All in all, Demo's is a nice little neighborhood bar. A bit clique-ish perhaps, but after a few stops, you'll become part of the clique. Painted on the front window beneath the name are the words, "where the fun starts," and that could very well be for some. When I asked Tony where the saying came from, I got a story that started like so many others I've told and heard, "One drunken evening..."

— *Bud*

Dick's Last Resort

North Pier
435 E. Illinois St.
312-836-7870
Hours: 11 a.m. to 4 a.m. weekdays,
11 a.m. to 5 a.m. Saturday, 11 a.m. to 3 a.m. Sunday

How's your self-esteem? Make sure it's real healthy when you walk into this joint. Located in the basement of the touristy North Pier Market, you'll be greeted by rude and funny folks who really don't give a shit if you're having a nice day. Immediately you get the sense that there are few rules here. Tables are crammed together in long rows and mismatched chairs are stuffed around them. If you're looking for a place to have a nice quiet drink and conversation -- this ain't the place. By the end of your adventure, you'll know the people sitting around you.

Butcher paper serves as your placemat. The wait staff, on a whim, will toss handfuls of paper napkins into rotating ceiling fans just to see them fly. When the place really gets jumpin', you'll see rolls of toilet paper fly by as they're tossed from waiter to waitress as they TP your section. At the bar, you'll notice a vast selection of bras suspended from the ceiling, all sizes and shapes. Have you formed a mental picture of the place yet?

Since this indoor/outdoor "resort" can be reached by foot or boat, the patrons are usually fun loving a raucous. The music, live or piped in, is loud and the crowd can get rowdy. So why come here? 'Cause it's fun!!!

The most notorious drink isn't on the menu. You have to ask for it by name -- the Condom Cocktail. A thankfully fresh condom is stretched across a glass of 7-Up (or any carbonated beverage) and shaken vigorously. Like a science project, a few seconds later, the "condom at rest" becomes fully erect!!

But seriously folks, the booze and food here are worth the trip. The bar sports a selection of more than 70 beers with Killian's Red, Fosters and Coors Lite on tap. If you're real thirsty, you can order a special 24-ounce "Big Ass Glass" of beer and keep the glass. Cost of this monstroxity is $7.50.

On Sunday mornings, along with a fabulous brunch, is a Bloody Mary bar. A glass of straight vodka is plunked down and the garnish is up to you. Vodka, however, is not the only spirit Dick's serves on Sunday. Gospel music accompanies your feast. So at last, a place that simultaneously fills your tummy and your soul.

Dinners can be a bit pricey, but the portions are plentiful. Buckets of ribs, chicken, beef bones, pork and catfish range from $10 to $16. Appetizers are large portioned and appealing.

With long hours, a vast range of drinks, plentiful food and wild and crazy mood, Dick's Last Resort is a place that will guarantee a good time -- one you'll remember for a long time.

-- *Cupcake*

68

Diversey River Bowl

2211 W. Diversey Parkway
773-227-5800
Hours: noon to 2 a.m. Monday to Thursday,
noon to 4ish a.m. Friday, 9 a.m. to 4 a.m. Saturday,
9 a.m. to midnight Sunday

Pardon me, but there seems to be something missing from every Chicago entertainment guide book that does not have Diversey River Bowl — better known as The Diversey Rock-n-Bowl, either on the front page or under the heading "Must Go." Why is this establishment not touted as much as Billy Goat Tavern or Mothers? Why, when conjuring up images of Chicago, do we see copper felines or metal mutations in and around Daley Plaza? Planet Hollycrap and its surrounding sickness is a disparagement for this city. Perhaps it is time to reassess. There's nothing like putting on a freshly sanitized pair of bowling slippers, finding that perfect ball, requesting some goodly RUSH and just knocking those pins down.

Therapeutic? Athletic? Even Mathmatic! The din of pins going down is more harmonious than a den of hibernating bears. It's the perfect activity for the cold season.

Skeptics beware, upon entering Diversey River Bowl you may see bowlers rockin-out in their perspective lanes. You may posses displaced shame for them. You may think, it's only Led Zeppelin that WCKG plays once an hour, what's the deal? While your getting your shoes you may hear a B-96 party radio ditty. While you are picking out your ball, you may recognize a Q101 alternative hit and think, "all these balls look the same."

Upon arriving at your lane, you realize the group next to you are all wearing bowling gloves, and the ones next to them don't even seem to be playing. After completion of the first round of drinks and practice throws, you may start thinking some other worldly energy is beginning to posses you. If you don't mind Old Style and you start craving Styx, the bowling specter may be waiting in your next frame.

The Diversey Rock-n-Bowl possession has several characteristics. Bowling out of turn or just throwing ball after ball after ball ignoring your friends is one sign. Not bowling at all and spending your time visiting the bar or plaguing the DJ is another indication. If you are dancing on the ledge between lanes to "Baby Got Back" or simulating sex with the ball return, chances are it is too late for an exorcism. There are other minor afflictions such as the spiritual displacement achieved when you believe in the Zen of bowling. This is apparent if you start bowling with you eyes closed or are completing each throw in a "Karate Kid" type stance. You may want time to sit and meditate before you come down from the mountain. When you realize your game is improving as your speech skills dwindle and those arrows on the lane is what your aiming for, it may be time to stick your face over the hand blower. If you start hypoth-

69

esizing about the machine that drills holes in balls, it may be time to go count the lockers in the bathrooms.

You pay for your lane at a $10 hourly rate. There are open lanes every night. Shoes are $1.75. Domestic beer is $2 while Heineken is $3. If someone on the staff takes pity on your group, trays of strange shots in plastic medicine cups may be delivered on the house. It is rumored that certain Chicago celebrity types are known to frequent the rock-n-bowl. Don't go out and buy an autograph book though. The Diversey River Bowl is the perfect late night or early afternoon spot to go, get out that aggression and reintroduce the phrases "rock," "rad" and even "twenty-two skidoo" to your vocabulary. Be sure to throw your ball towards the pins.

— Crumpy

Dome Room
(Now called Aura)
632 N. Dearborn
312-266-2114
Hours: 10 p.m. to 4 a.m. Sunday,
8 p.m. to 4 a.m. weekdays, 10 p.m. to 5 a.m. Saturday

When I mentioned to a friend that I would be writing a review of Dome Room, he suggested that the best way to convey its atmosphere would be to simply leave a blank space. That pretty much sums the place up. The Dome room is akin to a fancily-wrapped box with nothing inside.

The potential is there. The interior of the club is quite attractive. It rises three-floors atrium style and is capped off by its namesake dome, which sports a rather impressive painting of a Zeus-like figure on its surface. The sound system is excellent and the band stage is large with good sight lines. The second and third floors are very dim and offer a variety of chairs and couches for lounging or, I suppose, making-out. The walls are lined with paintings by local artists. Sounds decent enough, eh? The only problem is the place was probably designed this way in response to a survey conducted among twenty-something, suburban office workers. There's absolutely no trace of uniqueness.

Another problem is the price of beer. I know the joint is in a tourist area and mainly caters to people with plenty of money, but getting charged $3.25 for a bottle of Budweiser isn't only excessive, but intelligence-insulting. Contrary to what I expected, the people who work there are all nice enough and the vibe of the crowd was friendly and open rather than pretentious and annoying, but somehow I just couldn't get into the place.

The reason I was there in the first place was to see a band. For live music, the Dome Room is certainly an adequate venue. As mentioned before, the sound system is great. Even better, however, is the fact that the bands are off the stage by midnight, giving you enough time to go to a real bar in a real neighborhood. So if you too find yourself having to go there to see a friend's band, take heart,

Don't Worry

3938 N. Central Ave.
773-202-9618
Hours: 4 p.m. to 2 a.m. Sunday to Friday,
4 p.m. to 3 a.m. Saturday

We didn't. Worry that is, during our stay at this Northwest Side tavern. Approaching the place, we smiled at the sign in the front window that said, "YES, WE'RE OPEN," kind of like something you might see in the local pharmacist's window. Others had apparently read the sign as well, because the bar was just about full on a Sunday night, and you don't see much of that in this area.

I was told by the bartender that prior to the opening of this bar, this site used to be a Chinese restaurant. Well, someone put a lot of thought and money into the decor of Don't Worry. Aside from the pink Formica bar, they have a bunch of small round tables along the perimeter for those who prefer a more intimate seating arrangement. Every wall in the establishment is painted black, multicolored spheres as well as a mirror ball hang from the ceiling in the front, and there are mirrors everywhere. They have just enough beer and liquor signs to let you know that you are in a bar, but not so many that it seems tacky, as so many Chicagoland taverns do. Even the overhead sign outside the front door doesn't say "Budweiser," or "Old Style," it says, "Don't Worry."

Refreshing, huh?

While so many of the bars in the Portage Park neighborhood have forgotten what soap and sponge look like, this place is immaculate. If we were authorized to award a Good Housekeeping seal of approval, one would certainly hang from the walls of Don't Worry. We mean to say that this place is so clean that the glasses hung on the racks behind the bar do not even have spots on them! We are by no means neat freaks, but when an ashtray is emptied as soon as a cigarette is put out, that's impressive.

On our recent visit, the crowd consisted completely of classy, mellow Polish-Americans who all seemed to know each other. There was very little Polish blood in the veins of our group, and we were by no means classy, but we seemed to fit in anyway, as when an establishment truly has class, no one is out of place. And although nearly everyone was smoking, one could barely tell, because Don't Worry is so well ventilated that it doesn't even have that "bar smell."

We counted over 120 bottles of liquor behind the bar, including three different kinds of sloe gin. They are well-stocked to say the least. A friend ordered a vodka martini and although the bartender was unfamiliar with the drink, with a little coaching, the end result was an excellent concoction. As soon as the friend said "vodka," however, she grabbed a bottle of Absolut, assuming that we wouldn't want some bottom-shelf swill. This added a touch of class where there already was plenty. Two beers are on tap — Okocim and Pilsner Urquell

71

— both are tasty and smooth. They are served in a large round mug for $2.50. The cooler is filled with a large selection of European imports, including a wonderful brew called Zywiec, and if you can't pronounce it, just point to the sign as we did. Nothing is outrageously priced, as you would think by looking at the almost "nightclub" atmosphere, domestic bottles are under two dollars.

If you are hungry, there is food to complement your cold brew. For four bucks, you can get some Pierogi, Bigos, Kielbasa, or Golabki.

For recreation activities, there are three video poker games and a pool table available for the patron's enjoyment. In addition, you can watch a Polish news show or an old movie on TBS on one of two TVs. The jukebox has everything from Polish folk music to heavy metal, and would be quite good if they took out the Ace of Base CD.

Don't Worry in Polish means "Always be happy." This is good advice for anybody. If you feel happy, make a stop at this comfortable, clean neighborhood drinking establishment.

— Bud and Pete Schmugge

Dublin's

1050 N. State St.
312-266-6340
Hours: 11:30 a.m. to 4 a.m. daily,
11:30 a.m. to 5 a.m. Saturday

Dublin's, an old Irish-style pub, has a welcoming ambiance, if you can get a seat. The bar top, lined with stylish trinkets from the old country helps set an out-of-the-country but not out-of-the-town mood. Dublin's is not a tall Irish tale, but a real bar that attracts more than just the locals.

Sitting at the bar is convenient for quick refills: there's always a pleasant bartender around to fill your glass, and you can also order from a full service menu. The appetizers are popular, but don't ignore the dinner offerings.

It doesn't matter if you're coming in for just a drink or dinner, the staff is friendly and well trained. In this establishment you can take a spot at the bar or wait for the candle-lit table of your choice.

Attracting customers of all ages, Dublin's is a place for anyone. After hours, the place fills with many business people looking to unwind and on the weekend with the twenty or thirty "somethings."

The jukebox in the back offers a nice selection of tunes, however the music is usually drowned out by the crowd. If the conversation is lacking and you need some distraction, you can fixate on one of several TVs mounted on the wall.

Dublin's isn't just a drop-by sort of bar but a place where anyone can come for a drink or catch a game on TV.

— T.M. Kornelsen

The Duke of Perth

2913 N. Clark St.
773-477-1741
Hours: noon to 1 a.m. Sunday, 5 p.m. to 1 a.m. Monday,
11:30 a.m. to 2 a.m. Tuesday to Friday,
11:30 a.m. to 3 a.m. Saturday

When you think of the Chicago bar scene, the first thing that generally comes to mind is the incredible number of Scottish pubs that dot this fair city. Indeed, is there anyone in Chicago that hasn't spent a night out with a few friends drinking Bunnahabhain 12 year-old and eating Scotch eggs? I shouldn't think so.

Okay, so maybe you're not aware of Chicago's Scottish bar scene and maybe your taste for those things Scottish could use some familiarization. But then, I suppose that's understandable being that one of two distinctions that Chicago's The Duke of Perth claims is that it's the city's only Scottish pub. The other distinction is that it carries one of the world's largest collections of single-malt Scotch. And, with some 60 different bottles, varying through years and distilleries (the oldest being a Springbank — vintage 1958), who's to argue?

The Duke of Perth is a cozy bar that has more places to sit than it has room to stand. Sort of an anomaly for many Chicago bars where the general rule of thumb is standing room only, and then a few more on top of that. The decor in the bar contributes greatly to the cozy feeling that the place has. There are pencil sketches and old photographs lining the walls as well as a random airplane propeller lying in the corner (which I'm told doesn't really mean anything). There's also a beer garden to the rear of the bar that's very well done, with painted walls surrounding large picnic tables and several small garden plots, all under the shade of a few trees.

The menu at The Duke of Perth is made up both of Scottish fare with offerings such as Scotch eggs and Steak and Kidney Pie, as well as more traditional wings and sandwiches that are given names like Haggis Wings and the MacPoulet Sandwich (chicken breast with sautéed mushrooms and onion covered in Swiss cheese). All of which are very good and fairly priced. The Duke's lunch specials will get you a salad, sandwich and fries for $6. Although it is more famous for its all-you-can-eat-fish fries every Wednesday and Friday for $6.95.

The Duke does not offer a vast selection of beers to choose from, but what they do have both on draught and bottled is good. Excepting the random Miller product, all other beers available are either from Scotland or England. On draught, from Scotland is McEwan's Export Ale and Tenent's Lager. From England is Fuller's ESB, Watney's Cream Stout, Newcastle Brown Ale, Dry Blackthorn Cider, and Woodpecker Cider. In bottles, options include Theakston's Old Peculiar, Guinness (warm or cool), and Mackeson Triple Stout among others. A pint of draught beer is reasonably priced at $3 whereas bottles

73

are $3.50 and up.

Of course the real story in a bar that has one of the world's largest collections of single malt Scotch is just that, the Scotch. There is a separate menu at the bar for Scotch that's broken up into the separate and distinctive malt producing regions of Scotland. We tried Scotch from the Island region and the Highland region of Scotland. Both were excellent, although priced on the high end of the scale at $4.50 per glass. A bit steep? Perhaps. Good Scotch? Definitely.

— Bill Stephenson

Ed and Jeans

2032 W. Armitage Ave.
Hours: 11 a.m. to 10:30 a.m. daily

With the current onslaught of yuppiedom™, true neighborhood haunts are dropping like flies under gibbering waves of 708ers and the Daley administration's practice of assassinating taverns at will. Finding a bar where you can sit down where the owner serves you and treats you like family is becoming a thing of the past.

Enter Ed and Jeans to the rescue. You've probably driven by on Armitage and wondered what the hell was up with that place. Being one of the last true family owned and operated taverns in Bucktown is what makes Ed and Jeans truly a gem amongst all the poser bars in the area. The only bartenders you'll find here are Jean and her son Larry (Ed passed on some seven years ago) dispensing dollar cans of Busch or buck-seventy-five bottles of Old Style to a mostly local crowd of regulars from 11:00 a.m. to 10:30 p.m. nightly. The prices can't be beat. Sheer value alone demands a visit here. Ed and Jeans only has about a dozen barstools and standing room for another 30 or so. Crowding is never a factor.

The amenities are as follows; mixed drinks? Vodka tonics or screwdrivers that's about it. Jean refuses to make anything else. Food? Forget it. Jukebox? Unplugged in the corner, reserved for "special occasions." Pooltable? Takes up half the bar and God help you if Ma catches anyone betting on games. Tap beer? Nope. Microbrews? Hahahahahaha, have a can of Busch. Bartenders? Jean, the warmest and most friendly barkeep in the city. Jean is known as "Ma" to all of her regulars as well as the kids in the neighborhood. We saw two people stick their heads in the door just to say hi to Ma when we were there.

Ma has had many offers to buy her bar but she looks upon it as her home and refuses to sell. After all, she lives in the back half of the building and if she ever closes she says she will turn the bar portion into her living room. The weird part of it all is the bar feels as though she already has done just that. It's got that comfortable, clean, welcome feeling you just don't see around any more.

You won't get a dance floor or pints of Bells Prune Stout at Ed and Jeans.

74

Barfly Ed and Jeans-Edgewater Lounge

What you will get is a feel for how bars used to be in Chicago. It's a throwback to the times when a bar was the cornerstone of the neighborhood, a meeting place for friends to get out of the cold and trade some lively talk, a few jokes and maybe kick your brothers ass at a game of pool. It's the kind of place where bullshit isn't tolerated and you'll be asked to leave if you decide to be a jerk. Leave your attitude at the door, it just won't work here.

Stop in to see Ma, she's a Chicago original.

— Ron Slattery

Edgewater Lounge
5600 N. Ashland Ave.
773-878-4403
Hours: 9 a.m. to approximately 11 p.m.

The Edgewater Lounge is among the best neighborhood hideouts I have seen. With virtually no crowds, service comes quick and easy. You'll be waited on not by a waitress, but by the owner, Mary.

Mary has owned and operated the Edgewater Lounge for years. She greets most customers by name, and chats with strangers too. Her quick smile and desire to include me in the conversation surprised me. At first, I made no effort to speak to the strangers sitting at the bar. However, they did with me. It was nice to be greeted, rather than ignored or hit on. It all made me stay a little longer than I had planned.

The lounge is also a restaurant. It offers a full menu and has a dining area in the rear. Among the many choices are cheeseburgers, soup, fries, barbecue beef and grilled cheese sandwiches.

The bar takes up the full length of the front room. Trust me, it's big. There's plenty of room for everyone and all the stools are within an eye-shot of the TV screen. This, of course, is very important during the Bulls season.

Edgewater Lounge is definitely not for everyone. It is a wonderful place to kick back, but the crowd is older than some may desire. This is not the place for getting drunk, getting lucky or acting the fool. The crowd is mature, so make sure you are too.

The place has seen its share of trouble. Mary found a way to fix that, though. The bar's entrance is a glass door and door bell. Yes, a bar with a door bell. You can make the door go ding-dong, but it's up to Mary to make it buzz. This seemed to be the answer to Mary's prayers after being held up a few years ago.

— T.M. Kornelsen

El Jardin

3407 N. Clark St.
773-327-4646
Hours: 5 p.m. to 2 a.m. Sunday to Friday,
11 a.m. to 3 a.m. Saturday

Need a margarita? Got a bra? This is one of the splendid features for women. A margarita will be awarded for any size bra. This from a drinking establishment that advertises having "Chicago's most infamous Margarita." El Jardin has braziers littering the ceiling from the free margaritas awarded to any daring young miss who cares to relinquish her chest support. Women used to give a T-shirt for a free shot. I was told that the bra donations started to appear (two in one night) when a young lady inquired as to what she would get for her bra. And so the tradition began.

But that's not why the margarita is "infamous." The taste and almost immediate inebriation is the attraction. Wayne Wagner, one of the maintenance crew, told me that they went from selling 20 gallons of the "most mind-altering margaritas" when the place opened in 1989 to 250 gallons per-week these days.

With three bars, one of the first floor and two on the second, there's a world for anyone. About 1,000 people manage to make El Jardin their place of pleasure on weekend nights.

Having 1,000 people filling their bellies plump full of the infamous margarita specialty, there's bound to be some sort of ruckus, even in the usually sage and congenial atmosphere of El Jardin. Frank Prochaska is head of security, and the bartender on Sundays. He, along with the maintenacne crew, tell me that if a fight breaks out, someone will always be on your side. Good news.

Enough about margaritas. El Jardin, the bar with a sombrero for an entrance, pleases many of the senses. Besides the full spectrum of bras to fixate upon, there is an array of sports memorabilia like a gigantic picture of George Halas. There is also one of three original documents given to the Halas family honoring the founder of the Bears and his contributions signed by late mayor Harold Washington. The document, now propped up behind the first floor bar, was discovered in the garbage by the Halas plumber. Appearing on the second page, Halas is quoted as sayinig, "Never go to bed a loser."

A different special awaits every party-goer during weeknights at El Jardin. Plus, there are always free nachos.

-- *Mark Kenseth*

El-kees
4500 N. Elston Ave.
773-282-0813
Hours: 7 a.m. to 2 a.m. daily

El-kees doesn't have much of a beer garden. In fact, I was convinced they didn't have one at all after I'd glanced about the place.

"You have a beer garden, don't you?" I had to ask the bartender.

"If you wanna call it that," she snickered back at me.

It turned out the beer garden was hidden behind a closed, unmarked door near the men's bathroom. And, as I said, it's not much of a beer garden. Set up along the side of the building, three wooden, hexagonal tables and benches sit out on the concrete. Without any sort of fence or enclosure around you, you get a good view of the neighboring back yards and could even lumber right into them if you so desired. While this might cause a huge problem in a neighborhood like Wrigleyville, the quiet area in which El-kees sits doesn't seem to lend itself to rowdy beer bashes in the great outdoors.

And though the evening was quite pleasant after the recent heat wave, we were the only ones sitting outside. From what the bartender implied, I don't think El-kees' beer garden gets all that much use. Which is kind of nice. After sitting out there for awhile you almost forget the fact that you're drinking at a bar rather than a friend's back yard.

Inside, the place is pretty non-descript. A typical low-key neighborhood sports bar, it features a pool table and some arcade games, as well as a few TVs. It was Sunday night and not many people were around, but as all the patrons were in their mid-to-late twenties, I imagine the place draws a pretty good local crowd on Friday and Saturday nights.

In the matter of prices, El-kees deserves a thumbs-up. We drank DAB beer on tap for only $2 a pint. One big drawback however, is that during the one round we drank inside, the patrons all sang along with that annoying song about looking up at the sky and getting real high by 4 Non-Blondes. The song came on the jukebox not once, but twice within 10 minutes.

Outside of this, El-kees is one of those average, mundane watering-holes where, though you'll probably never have a great time, you certainly won't have a bad one either.

— Creepdoggy

Elliots Nesst
20 E. Bellevue Place
312-664-7010
Hours: 6 p.m. to 4 a.m. Sunday to Friday,
6 p.m. to 5 a.m. Saturday

Our mission to find one of Chicago's best beer gardens was easily completed

77

The North Side Elliots Nesst-Emerald Isle

when we strolled by Elliots Nesst in Chicago's Gold Coast. We could not have picked a better outdoor patio to spend time at on a Saturday afternoon-turned-evening. The weather was a balming 85 degrees with a cascading breeze blowing off Oak Street Beach to cool us down. Of course the Coronas helped too.

We sat amongst enormous buildings and weekend shoppers rushing by wishing they too, could sit down for a drink. Elliots Nesst offers perfect spirits for all occasions; from hanging out with friends to going on that first date. This bar does not only offer great outdoor fun, but also includes a huge indoor bar for those rainy days. Either way, folks are guaranteed a great time.

Everybody at Elliots Nesst was talking, smiling and laughing. The outdoor garden provided plenty of opportunity to people-watch. We sat drinking a variety of imported beers and before we knew it, time flew by, which only made us appreciate Elliots more.

Entertainment was all around us. From the hustling traffic on Rush and Bellevue to a young boy thrilling customers with his karate stunts. Everyone had started a night of drinking. Soon enough the beer garden of weekend warriors became engulfed in the Chicago-summer-partying-atmosphere. The mood was accompanied by cold beer and body-chilling shots ordered by all from the enthusiastic wait staff.

The waitresses, such as Diane De-Alva, worked hard to get all the orders up as quickly as possible. They too looked as though they were enjoying the weather, the bar and the customers.

Elliots started off our long summer on an exciting beat. It would be impossible to have an uneventful time at the Nesst. Relaxing with friends at a place that offers an incredible social scene, spontaneous entertainment and cool drinks reassures us that we are, indeed, living in the best city!

—Suzane Ruks and Jane Ignacio

Emerald Isle

6686 N. Northwest Hwy.
773-775-2848
Hours: 2:30 p.m. to 2 a.m. Sunday to Friday,
2:30 p.m. to 3 a.m. Saturday

While driving down Northwest Highway on the Far Northwest Side, you will notice a large green awning on the 6600 block. Guess, what? This is Emerald Isle bar. I have been visiting this drinking establishment for the past seven years. In that time span it has swithched owners once. The bar recently received a facelift which included new booths, new ceiling, new lights, new bar, and new seats. There are two rooms at the Isle. One room has booths, dart boards, video games and a foosball table. The main room has a large bar with padded seats with a stage up at the front of the room. There is live music Thursdays through Saturdays. The music ranges anything from alternative rock to traditional Chicago blues.

One of Emerald Isle's trademarks is its availability of fine import beers on

Barfly Emerald Isle-Emmit's

tap. Of the 12 beers on tap, there are eight imports inlcuding Bass, Harp, Woodpecker Cider, Guinness, Newcastle, McEwans, Double Diamond and Dusseldorfer. Pints of imports cost $3 each. While domestic pints are $2. Pitchers of imports are $9 and pitchers of domestics are $6. The variety of domestic beers isn't as great. Most of the domestic beers are Miller and Bud products.

Almost all the clientele are in their 20s. There are not many customers older than age 30. Some nights, I feel like an old man on teen night. This is expecially true on Thursday night which seems to be college night. Though the crowd is young, it is not rowdy. Most of the clientele drink Miller Lite and Budweiser.

In addition to the fine brews and atmosphere, the Isle has a kitchen which opens for lunch and closes late. The menu includes burgers, fish, Polish sausage, and a variety of appetizers.

-- Pete Schmugge

Emmit's
495 N. Milwaukee Ave.
312-563-9631
Hours: 11 a.m. to 2 a.m. Sunday to Friday,
11 a.m. to 3 a.m. Saturday.

"When you lie, you lie with a beautiful person; when you cheat, you cheat death; when you think you need a drink, stop by Emmit's," is the establishment's house toast that whispers in your ear as you walk into this historic 100 year-old building at the corner of Grand, Halsted and Milwaukee.

A bank during Prohibition, it has since operated as a tavern under one name or another. In the 1980s it was known as O'Sullivan's Irish Bar, a hangout for Chicago Tribune pressmen, police and legendary St. Patrick's Day celebrations.

After closing down in 1989, the site stood vacant for a number of years providing a location where many commercials and motion pictures were shot including "Uncle Buck" and "Backdraft." In 1990, Ron Halvorsen noticed the property was for sale but didn't think much of it. Halvorsen, who has been in construction since 1970, had been to O'Sullivan's a few times.

"Only for St. Patrick's Day," he said.

In 1993, together with brother Gary and partner Kevin Doherty they set out to invest in something that they could redo and rent out. He saw O'Sullivan's on his way to look at another property.

"I was driving down Halsted to look at another building on Green," Halvorsen recalled. "I went to Milwaukee to turn around and saw that it was still for sale." A quick trip to city hall to do a title search disclosed the building was in foreclosure. A call to the attorneys revealed it was going on auction. Two weeks later he had gotten his dream property at a great price.

It took two and a half years, every day (sometimes 24-hours-a-day) to rebuild the place from top to bottom (9 months alone to do the bar). Half way through, they decided they would run the place themselves. Now you can find Ron

Halvorsen, a little more relaxed, smiling and greeting patrons, making conversation while overseeing his professionally trained staff. But who is Emmit?

"Robert Emmet," Halvorsen told me, "was one of the first men exiled from Ireland for his beliefs. He's someone you want to pay tribute to."

The proper spelling had already been used so they changed the "E" to an "I" and cleverly dotted it with a shamrock.

Emmit's is huge with lots of exposed brick and high ceilings, so it's well ventilated to accommodate all kinds of smokers (they are proudly cigar friendly). It's lightly decorated with knick-knacks, not only with an Irish flavor, but expressing the history of that location itself (including a framed article from an old issue of Barfly).

The deep, dark wood that was used for the bar and trim is Cherry, Mahogany, and Oak lending authenticity to the Irish atmosphere that they boast. The friendly, attentive wait staff is also authentic as they have hired employees that are Irish, some of them actually straight from Ireland.

"I've been to other Irish bars in the city," said Kathryn Hanley, who was born in Birmingham, England, and grew up in Ireland, "and this is pretty authentic." Some of the other Irish natives that work there got the job through a J1 visa program that allows adults between the ages of 22 and 47 to live and work in America.

"We've made it fun for them," said Halvorsen, who has helped them experience Chicago by sponsoring various outings to events and sights that make Chicago unique.

The great advantage that Emmit's has is that it is a restaurant as well as a pub, thus allowing for a much more diverse patronage. When you can offer food (and I'm not just talking about burgers and hot wings) as well as drinks in such a classy setting you will get families, you will get business lunches, you will get the Downtown after-work crowd, and you will get your average barflies looking for an interesting place to drink.

If the large seating capacity, which includes a second floor, doesn't give you a clue to the heavy emphasis on the restaurant aspect of Emmit's, then the menu just might impress you. They offer corned beef with cabbage, hearty stews, steaks, soups, appetizers, ostrich burgers, and a variety of shrimp dishes (featuring a 24-count peel-and-eat for a mere $4.95). From authentic to exotic, no entree costs over $15 and most are no more than half that price. Sundays are open for brunch and at 2 p.m. they kicks off their Country Fried Chicken Night. The kitchen serves a full menu daily until 2 a.m.

The menu also conveniently lists the 11 brews they have on tap including Goose Island, State Street, Blue Moon, and Devil's Mountain. One interesting note here, while there are many places that serve Guinness (a personal favorite of mine), I have yet to experience anyone else that takes it so seriously.

"Our goal is to be the number one Guinness in town," Halversen said. "You build a Guinness, you don't pull a Guinness."

I have to admit, the one that was poured for me had a distinct flavor that I'd not tasted before. Also listed are a modest wine selection, a classic Scotch selection, not to mention the cigars that are displayed on the left side of the backbar, ranging in price from $3 to $12.

When I asked if Halvorsen had a final quote he'd like to give me, he told me quite on the contrary, "Cead Mule Failte" which in Gaelic means, "100,000 welcomes."

— Arunas Ingaunis

The Empty Bottle
1035 N. Western Ave.
773-276-3600
Hours: 6 p.m. to 2 a.m. daily

When Bruce opened this place up in 1993, it was a hip, quiet bar with cheap prices. Soon the crowds arrived and Bruce moved to a bigger place at 1035 N. Western Ave. and opened neighborhing Bite restaurant. Now Empty Bottle is an alternative rock and jazz emporium. There are bands scheduled most every night. It is a good space to catch an up-and-coming band, play some pool, pinball, electonic darts, and to check out cool art on the walls by local artists.

Eva's Lounge
3502 N. Cicero Ave.
773-545-4409
Hours: 11 a.m. to 2 p.m. Sunday to Friday,
11 a.m. to 3 p.m. Saturday

Yeah, I know it's an unusual line of work walking around bars in my underwear. But somebody's gotta do it, and modeling lingerie for Sheer Madness is a great way to find new bars because I have to talk to all the customers. I really get a feel for (and from) the crowd. There is something about lingerie that seems to bring out both the best and worst in folks. People will say anything to a women in a fishnet teddy.

One of the best experiences I've had recently was at Eva's Lounge on Cicero just south of Addison. The place itself is huge, with a giant island-type bar, pool tables, and a jukebox stocked with three decades of rock-n-roll.

Eva, a pretty blonde who with a word can put her rowdiest customers in their place, is not above working the bar when it's busy or drinking with the customers when it's slow.

The crowd is a diverse mix: the sales guys from the car dealership across the street, a free-lance photographer, a couple of Harley-riders, a few who fancy themselves as young studs, and of course not one but two of those older fellows who appear at the same time daily, drink the same drink always and seem to speak to no one.

The North Side Eva's Lounge-Exit

The women patrons are a down-to-earth bunch who are comfortable with me in costume, talking to their men, and who have great senses of humor. The finance manager from the car dealership won a whip from me with which she said she'll use to keep the sales guys in line. Then there's Shirly, a tattooed biker-mama who wants to fix me up with her son, who needs a "nice girl" (if she only knew!) and who brags she could give any of those young studs a run for their money.

Last time I was there, Eva told me, "It's a zoo out there." She does have quite a menagerie including a sheep dog named Budweiser. But most of the customers don't bite and they're really only wild in a good way.

— *Colleen O'Reilly*

Exit

1315 W. North Ave.
773-395-2700
Hours: 8 p.m. to 4 a.m. Sunday to Friday,
8 p.m. to 5 a.m. Saturday

After ruling Chicago's alternative club empire during the 1980s from its original Wells Street location, Exit elected to take a hiatus from 1992 to 1995 for motives that to this day remain undivulged. Whatever those reasons may have been, after nearly three years, the powers that be regrouped, refinanced and hunted down a site unique enough to edify the Exit's resurrection. They found it in a site of what once was a leather gay bar, channeling the locations lingering weirdness into a venue with their own inherent weirdness. The result is an establishment that can most aptly be characterized by the collective portrait of Exit's "pseudo-patron saints" -- John Gacy, Sid Vicious, Adolph Hitler, and Frank Booth, which hang in a place of prominence above the club's bathrooms.

Providing a home for this bizarre centerpiece is a structure and decor that lends itself to a trite thematical dichotomy, for while the club's reopening was nothing but a symbol of renewal and rebirth, entering the environment of Exit resembles nothing short of death.

Rusted doors open through an obliquely windowed facade into an interior festooned with enough skulls, gasmasks and other macabre gee-gaws to make even Alice Cooper feel right at home. Designed by Ray Paseka of the Hospitality Design Group, Exit's interior is a musty cocoon of surfaces not unlike the sprayed-on insulation of most grade school heating pipes. Gothic chandeliers, strange mechanical configurations and the infamous go-go cages from the original site help add to the zitgeist developed during Exit's early salad days on Wells.

The layout is much different than the original Exit except for the original bar that lines the east wall on the first floor. Across the bar is one of the most unique seating arrangements ever installed in a club; a set of six antique, full-sized motor bikes, bolted solidly to the floor and lined up as if they were just waiting for Pee Wee Herman to knock them over. Toward the rear of the first

Barfly Exit-Extra Innings

floor, what looks like the empty shell of a huge fireplace, shelters more seating, and the way back holds pay phones, a few electronic games and a $1 pool table.

Exit's industrially-oriented jukebox is stocked with a wide variety of prime "Headbangers' Ball" and "Alternative Nation" CDs and teems with selections both new, (Killing Joke, Nine Inch Nails, Smashing Pumpkins) and of the classic genre (Doors, Motorhead, KISS).

A fitting compliment to this music, and to the Exit's atmosphere in general, is a plethora of video screens that adorn the walls and bar. The three separate systems can be seen broadcasting at any given time classic techno-odd films such as "Blade Runner," "Brazil," the local news, "America's Most Wanted," and Exit's theater, a tape of ancient B-quality Arnold Schwarzenegger film clips montaged with various porno snippets.

A few months after the opening of the new Exit, the bar opened its second floor. The space features another bar and a good-size dance floor.

Despite all of these entertaining distractions, in the end Exit does not forget the fact that it is first and foremost a bar, and in that sense is first and foremost a dispenser of fine spirits. With a full stable of import and domestic beers, 16 brands of tequila, more than 40 bourbons, and various frozen shots including, but not limited to, Black Sambuca and Baren Jager, Exit is fully armed to satisfy even the wildest tastes. Tap and bottled beer range in prices from $1 up to $3.25, and mixed drinks in any number of configurations, (including their signature Star War Martini), go no higher than $4.

-- Johnny Masiulewicz

Extra Innings Sports Bar
6801 W. Addison St.
773-282-8669
Hours: 7 a.m. to 2 a.m. Sunday to Friday,
7 a.m. to 3 a.m. Saturday

In the dark corners of the Northwest Side, perched menacing over Mount Olive Cemetery, stands Extra Innings Sports Bar at Addison Street and Oak Park Avenue. Was this drinking establishment a welcoming watering hole or was it a horror domain of the walking dead?

To my recollection of the night, the bar was quiet with the exception of one screaming college football fan. I was unable to determine if his team had just lost an important game or if an evil specter from Mount Olive had suddenly materialized before him. At that moment, I almost ran out of the bar in fear.

What does Extra Innings have to offer? The best deal here is the cheap beer prices. It's $4 for a pitcher of Old Style or Miller Genuine Draft. Weinhardt's Ale is $5. Domestic bottles are $1.50 and imports are $2.50. There are four dart boards available, a pool table and two poker video games. Not surprisingly, watching sports takes precedence at Extra Innings.

It's a neighborhood bar, not a party bar or a pickup joint, as its patrons average age range is well over 25. The decor is mostly wood-panel walls. It has a small disco ball in the back. At the bar, there is a very large clock, so you can't miss the time. Throughout the establishment there are beer advertisements. Tables line the wall next to the bar and offer more than enough seating for a small place. In many ways, it reminds one of small-town bars in Wisconsin. It has the same look and feel.

Though the prices are reasonable, the tap offers no specials, not even for Bear games. This seems strange, especially for a local sports bar.

This is a bar to start the night, not to end one. If you're somewhat young, I recommend you come here during the week for some cheap brew, or come early but go somewhere else later.

— Pete Schmugge

Fado`

100 W. Grand Ave.
312-836-0066
Hours: 11:30 a.m. to 2 a.m. Sunday to Friday,
11:30 a.m. to 3 a.m. Saturday

Fado` (pronounced f'doe) is Gaelic for "long ago," and that's the feel the Dublin-based Irish pub company was striving for when they designed the new pub at Grand Avenue and Clark Street. They spared no expense, as was evidenced by this reporter during a two hour visit recently.

On entering the premises, one is immersed in a world of timber, stone, and glass, hand-crafted and imported directly from Ireland. Assembled over nine months beginning last April, the pub is spread over three floors, with large and small bars respectively on the first and third levels. There is also a seating area on the second floor that is serviced by a waitress. Though over 3500 square feet, the designers have subdivided the space in such a way as to create several distinct areas, compromising volume for intimacy.

This beautiful oasis for Irish pub lovers is owned by Fado` Holdings LLC, a group comprised of Irish and American businessmen. They also have outlets in Austin and Atlanta.

I met with general manager Mike Gallagher early on a Wednesday evening and was surprised to find the bar and seating areas already pretty full.

"Food sales have gone surprisingly well, often accounting for 40 percent of our business," Gallagher said.

The other 60 percent of Fado`'s business is draft beer, of which Guinness is by far the best seller. Citing the folks at Guinness, Gallagher said Fado` was their ninth biggest account in the state for 1997, based on just a month's worth of business. That's an awful lot of Guinness, but they also offer Harp, Bass, Woodpecker Cider, Boddington's, Leinenkugel's Creamy, and local brew Golden Prairie.

The later three are "hydrogenated" beers, like Guinness, where the brew is pushed with a combination of CO_2 and nitrogen through specific pourers to

Barfly Fado-Family Bar

produce a less filling, creamier textured and flavored beer. This is a very costly and time-consuming process, and Fado` prides itself on following the brewers serving instructions to the letter.

They also carry a full compliment of well and premium liquors. Particularly impressive is their selection of Irish Whiskeys, including Middleton Very Rare, Jameson 1780, Bushmills 10 year-old, Powers, Black Bush and Tullamore Dew.

Like many Irish pubs that strive for authenticity, Fado` avoids the use of soda guns and pours strictly from cans and bottles. They even brought in a couple sodas from the old country to make customers feel like they'd just waltzed in from picking four-leaf-clovers. From a bartenders standpoint, this no-gun policy is a real pain. Opening a can or bottle adds an unnecessary step when you're slammed.

Similarly, they've installed a gravity-pour system which turns the liquor bottles upside-down in tapped holders. Though common in Europe, this system is used mainly in airports and tourist traps in the states, and leaves customers with a feeling they're getting ripped off. From my opinion as a bartender, it also inhibits speed pouring, or making a "good" drink.

Speaking of bartenders, those at Fado` are very professional and friendly.

Back to the design, Fado` is a visually striking example of Irish pub design. They've spent gobs of money creating this slice of Dublin in the heart of the Midwest, and the little touches that I might find gimmicky or annoying are the very details that make Fado` what it is, an authentic Irish pub. Anyone can put green food coloring in their beer on St. Patrick's Day, but these guys walk the walk and talk the talk. If Irish food and drink is what you crave, then you're in good hands at Fado`.

-- Paul Dunk

The Family Bar
6340 W. Irving Park Road
773-685-8134
Hours: 7 a.m. to 2 a.m. Sunday to Friday,
7 a.m. to 3 a.m. Saturday

Going to bars by yourself is a trip. You get to be a fly on the wall for the craziest conversations. The night I went to The Family Bar was no exception. I was there on a Wednesday night around 9 p.m. and the place was pretty empty. I was one of seven people inside, not to mention the youngest person to set foot in the place.

You have to be curious who hangs out at a bar that opens at 7 a.m. I sat next to a woman who was telling Leah, the bartender, about another women in the bar who was prone to smashing beer bottles over people's heads. She noticed I was listening when I laughed under my breath and she ended up buying me a shot. I listened in on an old man's conversation about why he doesn't like to go to church anymore since they no longer offer altar wine in the service. I figured

The North Side Family Bar-Farragut's

it wouldn't be such a good idea to accept a drink from him.

Everybody at The Family Bar drinks either Old Style or Miller Lite because that's all they have on tap for 75 cents a glass. The beer selection is extremely limited, no imports. Everything is very cheap though — the beer, the food and the Grenadier cigars they sell for 65 cents. The menu offers chili, hot dogs, and other standard sandwiches and munchies. But if you're really hungry, I recommend stopping in Mr. Zee's across the street who serve up excellent Greek chicken, ribs and gyros.

The Family Bar has a vintage cherry wood bar covered with cooler doors. Other than that, there is nothing really interesting to look at inside. They have the basic pool table, jukebox and darts. They also have a long cooler stocked with six-packs, cases and mixers to go.

The Family Bar is a local bar typical in many Chicago neighborhoods. So for those who enjoy drinking Miller or Old Style in a local tap room, this is your place.

— Lee DiVita

Farragut's

5240 N. Clark St.
773-728-4903
Hours: 3 p.m. to 2 a.m. Sunday to Friday,
3 p.m. to 3 a.m. Saturday

My friend and I walked into a packed Farragut's on a Thursday night with every intention of having one beer and calling it a night.

Ha!

Not a stool was without a butt, so we made our way through a group of guys who'd obviously just finished playing softball (I won't mention how I came to that conclusion), and ordered a couple of beers. An average $2 each. Good sign.

Giving my friend her beer, we decided to check the front tables again for an empty seat. Nope. So we stood at the end of the bar and slugged from our bottles. Before I got half through, a girl named Tammy, who sat about four seats away, raised her beer to toast me. I have to admit I was a little weirded out at first. But as it turned out, she was just toasting my good taste in beer. We clicked our Bud Lights (yeah, yeah, I know) and my friend laughed as she gulped her Miller Lite. Tammy's friend, Jim, then bought us a round. So much for one beer!

Matt, the bartender, was quick with the beers and even quicker with a friendly smile. Onna, whom I later found out was part owner with her mother, sat behind the bar masterfully pouring a patron a Weisse.

Farragut's opened in mid-1997 replacing a place called Soul Jam. Floor-to-ceiling windows trimmed in wood beautify the building from the inside out. When open, they give the bar a fresh, airy appearance. Four small tables sit at the entrance, followed by the typical bar decor: a golf game, poker machine,

Barfly Farragut's-Fieldhouse

pool table, cigarette machine, dart machine and a laser disc jukebox belting out the hits.

Farragut's does feature some original decor, such as a tree stump cut into a chair and an 8-foot or so mirror surrounded by thick wood and lights.

I was very impressed by the bar itself. It was not only exceptionally clean, but it offered a lot. Nine tap beers are available: Miller Lite, Harp, Leinenkugel, Goose Island, Summit Heaven, Summit Weisse, Summit IPA, Bells Amber Ale and Schell Pilsner, to be exact. And the prices? Very reasonable.

Numerous wines and bottled water stocked the bottom shelves. Domestic beers were displayed above.

As Matt opened us another beer, we watched two dogs playfully frolic about the bar. Baseball caps one by one started leaving, and by 11 p.m., the windows were open, making it harder and harder for us to leave.

Only one special is offered so far, Hefe Weizer Wheat Ale for $2.50. But Onna says plenty more will follow. She also sponsors two softball teams during the week, on Thursdays and Sundays.

As I caught Matt grab a quick pinch of chew, I laughed out loud. What a great neighborhood bar...

"The neighborhood's everything," Onna said. "And we need to get some art on the walls."

— Kristi Harrity

The Fieldhouse

2455 N. Clark St.
773-348-6489
Hours: 4 p.m. to 2 a.m. weekdays,
1 a.m. to 3 a.m. Saturday, noon to 2 a.m. Sunday

For a good taste of what the Fieldhosue looks, or even feels like, sit down in front of your TV set about 6:30 p.m. and flip on WGN. The opening of "Coach," it seems, may well have been filmed at this North Clark Street Tavern.

If you're looking for color, you'll get a stiff neck. The tavern's walls from seven-feet down, feature a range of black-and-white photographs, most of them of baseball scenes. Color is located one floor up, where five color screens share space with a range of college banners. None of the screens are oversized, but the bar's relatively small size and the placement of the screens ensures that none of the Fieldhouse's patrons are completely out of position.

The Fieldhouse was smaller a few years ago, before a remodeling in the rear half allowed the installation of a pool table (before the work, the bar's dart board combined with a narrow walkway created a Beirut-like free-fire zone). Nevertheless, The Fieldhouse isn't going to make anyone forget about the Astrodome, as it's a bar and some tables crammed into a standard 12-foot-by-60-foot space. On busy nights, some extra space is created along the north wall through the removal of tables; once attendance pushes past 70 people, that extra space is mightily appreciated. One warning: if you think the bar can be small, wait until you see the bathrooms. Claustrophobes will be better off in a glove compartment.

You can count on pretty decent drink specials but no menu, although one bartender said that the establishment isn't completely adverse to patrons to pick up a sandwich along the way and bring it in with them.

The bar's character is somewhat misrepresented by the "We're insured by Smith & Wesson" bumper sticker on the cash register. More in keeping with the college banner and sports memorabilia are such T-shirts that say, "Beer is Food," "Take me drunk, I'm home," and "It's not a small world, it's a big bar." The wall-mounted shot wheel offers, for $2.50 a spin, a chance at one of nine shots of 100 percent hard liquor.

Still, perhaps the most endering trait of the Fieldhouse is its matchbook. Adorned with the standard logos, addresses and phone numbers on the outside, the matchbooks open to reveal not merely matches but a space reading "WE met at The Fieldhouse" along with a blank for a name and phone number.

What can I say? I've gotta like a bar that thinks I've got a chance.

-- Kev Smith

Finley Dunne's Tavern
3458 N. Lincoln Ave.
773-477-7311
Hours: 5 p.m. to 2 a.m. weekdays,
11 a.m. to 3 a.m. Saturday, 11 a.m. to midnight Sunday

What is it about the average, friendly, meat-and-potatoes tavern that gets the heart pumping? Maybe it's that average, friendly, meat-and-potatoes taverns no longer exist in the vast number they once did. It's a relief to trip over one every so often.

The tavern has evolved from the neighborhood pub it once was into the martini clubs we now inhabit in droves. And for that reason, the average, friendly, meat-and-potatoes tavern, when we do stumble upon one, gives off a comfortable sense of the past, a sense of security also found in grand motherly kitchens and ivy-strewn baseball parks.

They're also good, of course, because you can get shit-faced for cheap.

Finley Dunne's Tavern is such a place. What was once a brightly lit Yak-Zies Fish Shack and Grill has been renovated, restored and refurbished by partners Joe Kenny, Tim Quinn and Jim Roth, all Chicago bar industry veterans. And although you can still feel hints of the light yellow, varnished and glazed wood that is signature Yak-Zies, you can also tell the new owners are slowly sprinting away from that look.

The trio's first order of business upon purchasing the space late in 1996 was to pilfer the bar top and old-time telephone booth from another great tavern, the Amazing Grace Tap — now sadly departed from its post at the corner of Grace and Paulina.

Barfly Finley Dunne's

"This is such a great neighborhood," says Kenny. "And such a great city for tavern history. We really set out to focus on the history of Lake View, Ravenswood and Chicago in general in the design and atmosphere of the place, so we were thrilled when we were able to borrow the bar top from the Amazing Grace. We were happy to keep it in the neighborhood."

Indeed, the history of the tavern's namesake is worthy of a paragraph or two. Finley Peter Dunne was a columnist for the Chicago Evening Post at the end of the last century. Dunne, in an attempt to cater to the Irish immigrants filtering into Chicago, wrote his column for the Post with a brogue vernacular to better relate to the average Joe — or Seamus.

But even more pertinent, Dunne wrote his columns from the perspective of a bartender, Mr. Dooley, whose fictional tavern was on Archer Avenue. At the Turn of the Century, Mr. Dooley's views, philosophies and opinions on the welfare of the nation and the state of the world were widely read, and immediately thereafter widely discussed in the actual taverns of Chicago's neighborhoods.

The Chicago Tribune recently called Dunne "one of the pioneers of the newspaper column" and described his alter-ego, Mr. Dooley — a literary ancestor of Mike Royko's Slats Grobnik — as "an every-man philosopher and saloon keeper."

Kenny and his partners have recognized the interest Chicagoans have in the city's history and have gone in search of documents relevant to their bar, the neighborhood in which it stands and the Chicago tavern in general. They are now in the process of decorating their pub with these monuments to the city's cultural past.

"I think every time you walk into a bar you should see something new. That's one of our goals. It should always be interesting to sit down with a pint in front of you and just look around," says Kenny.

But Finley Dunne's is not a museum, it's a neighborhood bar paying homage to bar ancestors that paved the way. In that spirit, Finley Dunne's hosts neighborhood baby christenings, pipes in legendary Green Bay radio color man Max McGee on Milwaukee's AM 620 for Packer games and donates fridge space when its neighbors suffer a power outage and need somewhere to throw their gallon of milk and left-over cold-cuts.

If, for some reason, the neighborhood cold-cuts do spoil, Finley Dunne's will provide sustenance for the hungry. A menu that includes items like Roasted Red Peppers with Chihuahua Cheese ($4.75); Wings in batches of 10 ($4.25), 20 ($7.50), 50 ($19) and 100 ($38), and in mild, medium, hot and Chicago Fire flavors — "One of the benefits of buying a bar from Yak-Zies," says Kenny. "They threw in the cook with the chicken wing magic touch."

Also, there is Chicken Tang Pizza ("tang" refers to the wing sauce.) ($8 for a 12" pie); Veggie Burger ($5.50); and various chicken and turkey sandwiches (from $5.75 to $6.75). Finley Dunne's puts out free food from 5 to 8 p.m. on Fridays, and has a fried chicken and mashed potatoes dinner every Sunday evening ($5.95 for a single serving, $9.95 for all-you-can-eat).

The North Side Finley Dunne's-Fireside Restaurant

The beer selection is impressive. Kenny lists about 32 beers at press time and is installing a new line system that will accommodate more. In a month or so he hopes to have between 40 to 60 beers available on any given night. The whiskey selection is wanting, but will shortly be updated and supplemented, we were told.

With a managing and bartending resume that includes places like the original House of Beer on Division Street and many years at Gamekeepers on Armitage and Lincoln, Kenny knows the sports bar universe well and recognizes its importance on the Chicago landscape. He's counting on a big football season.

"We are by no means a sports bar, but having said that, we will find any game people want to see," he says. "I have a background working complicated satellite systems at sports bars, and we understand that when a game is on, it's on, people don't want to wait around for the bartender to find the right channel while minutes are ticking off the clock. They'll go to the next place where the game's already playing. In this city, the allegiance, on game day at least, is to the game, not the bar. So if the game is floating around out there in space, we'll find it and bring it down to your barstool."

Additional entertainment in the bar includes a pool table, a video golf game and a jukebox with the standard range of CDs from Chuck Berry and Dean Martin to The Wallflowers and Dave Matthews Band to Lovin' Spoonful and the Violent Femmes with a smattering of the Beatles and some local bands thrown in. (I also spied The Who's Meaty Beaty Big and Bouncy — a rare, if silly, jukebox treasure.)

Finley Peter Dunne made a name for himself in Chicago by penning opinions about controversial topics of the day in a way people could understand and relate to. It is exactly this spirit of controversy and debate that has made the American tavern such a lively and entertaining institution through time. Nowhere in America has the culture of the neighborhood tavern been more lively and entertaining than in Chicago. Mr. Dunne would be proud to see his name on such a worthy descendant of this American tradition, plopped in the middle of the city he loved.

— T. Wright Townsend

Fireside Restaurant and Lounge
5739 N. Ravenswood Ave.
773-878-5942
Hours: 11 a.m. to 4 a.m. daily

Peter Eberhart built this roadhouse in 1904 to accommodate the farmers from the surrounding areas en route to the city market. In 1940 a barfly would have been winging it to the edge of Chicago to enjoy a libation there, then known as Sturveant's Roadhouse. These days the Ravenswood area is well within the boundaries of the city and easily accessible. Since 1990, when Rich Wohn opened his Fireside Restaurant at this location, it has gained a reputation as one of the best restaurants on the North Side. Many people come here to eat, never

Barfly Fireside Restaurant and Lounge-Foley's

realizing that around the doorway to the restaurant lurks a most comfortable and well-stocked bar. In addition to that, a spacious, split-level beer garden awaits, too.

In 1992, Bob Jones came on as general manager, bringing his years of experience managing The Canoe Club with him. He brought a new level of visibility to the Fireside bar, presenting events such as the many memorable Brewmasters' Dinners. Faced with the challenge of a relatively small cooler, he has still managed to stock it with 50 different beers, many of them regional microbrews. Ten beers on tap are always available, and throughout the year, seasonal brews are offered. Some of the choices currently on tap include Paulaner Mai-Bock, Leinenkugel's Honey Weiss and Golden Prairie Blonde Ale. Thirty wines by the glass are served and an impressive selection of single malt Scotch, port, Cognac and other fine liquors are stocked, too.

The Brewmasters' Dinners are a fine dining and drinking experience combined. Scheduled several times throughout the year, the dining room and beer garden are reserved for an afternoon of good food and drink. Hosted by the Fireside and presided over by four visiting brewmasters, a menu featuring their brews as part of all the recipes prepared is served. Of course, Rich and Bob make sure that all of the beers are sampled by everyone.

Food is served at the bar until 3 a.m. everyday, 4 a.m. on Sunday. All of the food is prepared from scratch using only fresh ingredients, including the herbs and spices grown on the patio in the beer garden. Daily, four entrees specials are offered, including one from sister restaurant The Blue Iris. Also, soup, appetizer and dessert specials are listed. On Sundays, brunch is served from 11 a.m. to 3 p.m. This is where you can experience the infamous "Build your Own" Bloody Mary bar, complete with 110 ingredient choices (everything from veggies to Liquid Smoke).

In late 1996, Bob Jones headed back to his native South Side and opened up a Fireside Restaurant at 10730 S. Western Ave. Now Chicagoans at both ends of the city can enjoy the fine food and drink at the Fireside.

— Michael Cotter

Foley's Bar and Grill
1841 W. Irving Park Road
773-929-1210
Hours: 10 a.m. to midnight Sunday to Thursday, 10 a.m. to 2 a.m. Friday and Saturday

The facade of Foley's has all the tell-tale signs of your typical neighborhood pub, but once inside you are overcome with a strange feeling that you have just walked downstairs into you uncle's rec room. Expecting the stacked washer and dryer to be just around the corner, your first question is, "Where are the dogs playing poker?" The main difference between Foley's and your uncle's rec room is that your uncles rec room is probably a bit bigger.

With the bar taking up most of the floor space, the remaining space has enough room for electronic poker, electronic darts, and of course patrons. The wall-mounted jukebox has an excellent mix of tunes ranging from Irish folk music to Patsy Cline.

The beer selection is the typical line of domestic and imported beers with domestic bottles priced at $2.25.

As the impression in your bar stool deepens, a subtle transformation happens, you begin to feel at home. You can almost see your Uncle Larry with a can of beer in his hand ready to launch into his war story for the tenth time (even though he never left stateside).

Foley's, like your uncle, is endearing and, after the booze sinks in, you might even describe it as intimate. It is a little bar with a lot of charm. A place well suited to the needs of those who seek to enjoy their beer without the usual annoyances; that is crowds, college kids and goatees.

-- Bob Schertler

Four Farthings Tavern & Grill
2060 N. Cleveland Ave.
773-935-2060
Hours: 11:30 to 2 a.m. daily

As a bar/restaurant, the Four Farthings has two personalities: a white table-cloth, servers-in-ties side, and a narrower bar area. Up until 10 p.m., full menu and service is available in both, with everything from a $7 burger to veal, Cajun shrimp and andouille, and New York strip. The entrees run from $11 to $23, but appetizers could certainly stand as a meal, especially with such delicacies as gorgonzola ravioli, hearts of palm and artichoke salad, or chicken tortellini in basil, garlic and olive oil.

A product of its Lincoln Park location, even on the bar side the Four Farthings feels bright and new, with the appropriate atmosphere touches of wood trims and vintage Chicago photographs. Points for a pool table which has its own room but can see and be seen from the bar. Also for a wine list which covers the entire menu back in small font: the basics, sparklings, desserts, grenache, mourverde, tenpranillo... From Germans, a Washington Hills gewerztraminer, a Scharffenberger, Blanc de Blancs from Mendocino, Calif., and a dessert Beernauslese, Binger Bubenstuck.

The other two divisions of Four Farthings have less to do with its geography than its prices. Understandable, the more exotic wine list costs are not for the light of heart, but for the seekers of specials in the line of strawberry white chocolate creme brulee (which goes surprisingly well with Warsteiner, by the way). Cigars are available for $7.

Beer, however, comes in a comfortable variety, and April features Rolling Rock at $5/10 bottles or $2.25 each. Sam Adams Spring Ale at $3.50, and Grant's Winter Ale at $3. Warsteiner clocks in at $4.

On the whole, the Four Farthings is quiet, formal but friendly. There is a warm wood-feel throughout giving it that welcoming English-pub feel. And if you find yourself in New Buffalo, Michigan, look for Farthings' sister locale, Casey's Bar and Grill.

— Jen N. Tonic

Four Treys

3333 N. Damen Ave.
773-549-8845
Hours: noon to 2 a.m. daily, noon to 3 a.m. Saturday

With all the great places to drink in Roscoe Village, this corner tavern seems to be sometimes overlooked.

Warm is the best way to describe the feel of the bar. Drinking here is like drinking at someone's house, and not in the basement. Just the layout gives the illusion to an apartment and automatically creating more of a party atmosphere than a bar atmosphere. Even the bar looks as it could have been hand-made. What better place for a tap than coming out of the back wall and through a fake barrel cover?

But the most amazing thing is the fact that the lights are turned up. Not blinding, but just enough so there are really no shadows. At first I did not know what to think of this, but after being back, I actually preferred it. I have always enjoyed the darkness of a bar, and have actually refused to stay in a bar if I feel the lighting is too bright. But this place just doesn't need that darkness. In fact, if the lights were any dimmer, I think it would ruin the whole house-party feel. I also had the feeling that the lighting kept my spirits as well as others in the bar turned up.

The crowd is good too. It is, not surprisingly, mainly neighborhood people. Many come to play pool while others to drink and relax. During the day it is more of an older crowd, with a good mix in the evenings. Pool players are serious about their game, but serious as in having a good time. League pool players take up one of the two tables from 7 to 10 p.m. Monday through Thursday, but there is free pool on Saturday. The mix of the crowd really extends through the jukebox which is very diverse. While one moment one may hear the latest grunge hit, soon it will blend into a R & B track and some good down-home Southern Rock may kick in. Who knows?

As far as drinks are concerned, beer is bottled except for Miller Genuine Draft and Lite on tap. The bottles include a few common domestics up to a good selection of imports. Beer prices are in the lower to average realm, while drink specials such as the $4 pitchers on Monday and buck drafts on Wednesday make this place a good choice for low dough. In the liquor category this place comes well stocked; mixed and neat drinks are the norm here.

— Phil Brandt

Frank's

2503 N. Clark St.
773-549-2700
Hours: 11 a.m. to 4 a.m. Sunday to Friday,
11 a.m. to 5 a.m. Saturday

"What the hell is this place?"

"Look at the guy in the flannel shirt with the baseball cap. I think it's one of those brief-case-by-day, baseball-cap-by-night guys."

"What about that guy in the black leather jacket and the Caesar cut?"

Feeling flustered with sobriety, we decided to venture inward for a peep (and a drink). We were amazed: Frank's was a hip, swingin', funky bar with enough potential to make two beautiful, single, club-loving, party-starting, bodacious babes happy on a Saturday night.

Subsequent to taking a seat we looked around. We first stumbled into a boomerang-shaped table that is only an itsy-bitsy teeny-weeny bit of their 1950s decor. Before we knew it, the two of us were standing right in front of an astonishingly nice, long, hard . . . BAR. Our conversation was limited as we listened to both new and oldies music. We became engulfed in multi-colored lava lamps and had a larger-than-life black-and-white photograph of "Old Blue Eyes" himself staring down at us.

Our party was clearly getting started. We sat sipping away at drinks served in cobalt-blue martini glasses, and enjoyed a cold specialty shot from the bartender. The bartenders were especially attentive to not only us, but to the fun-seeking crowd around us. Mixed drinks, unique beers and mind-altering martini's were being ordered and served to elevate everybody's already happening moods.

Frank's offers good conversation (which we won't disclose), potent drinks and a unique atmosphere. What began a place to pre-game, provided more than just a fever on a Saturday night.

— Suzane Ruks & Jane Ignacio
Not just another Siskel and Ebert of Chicago Bars!

Friar Tucks
3010 N. Broadway
773-327-5101
Hours: 2 p.m. to 2 a.m. Sunday to Friday,
2 p.m. to 3 a.m. Saturday

Ever wondered what it would be like to enjoy a warm, cozy bar inside of a whiskey keg? Friar Tucks' facade is shaped like the top of a cask and the interior is dark wood.

While it may look like a whiskey keg, Friar Tucks feels more like a certain bar popularized on television during the 1980s.

"This is a Cheers bar," says owner Angelo Como. "One of the things I am most proud of is that this is a place where a lady can come in alone, have a drink and not feel intimidated."

The clientele is more than a little interesting and strongly interconnected. An example is a courteous character called Star Trek John. His nickname has become so well known that some no longer remember his first name. The range of occupations represented include a graphic artist; professional dancer; contractors, media types, accountants, financial consultants, cops, realtors, caterers and outside salespersons. You need something done? Hey, talk to that guy over there.

When I met Julie and her husband Pat, I was very surprised that Julie and I shared former service in the U.S. Coast Guard.

"I will have been coming here 10 years in May," Julie confirmed. "This is the most fun I've ever had. I just hate it."

Julie isn't the only one who raves about the place.

"Before I came to Friar Tucks, I thought of it as a vortex," said Mary Jo. "I'm really glad I gave it a chance. People care about each other here. When someone is gone for a period they are asked about. This is a great heterosexual bar in a gay area. I just love this bar."

I assume that because of her attractiveness, Mary Jo has earned the nickname HMMJ (High Maintenance Mary Jo). She is delightfully amused by it and a number of versions have spun off from it.

No one knows for sure the origin of Mary Jo's moniker but it sounds suspiciously like a contribution from Rick "The Cop." Rick has been a customer of Friar Tucks since it opened.

"I come here for the show," Rick says caustically. "This is a gold mine for a student of human moves."

Rick has a set schedule at Friar Tucks on Friday and Saturday evenings. He enjoys two mini-pitchers of Busch between eightish and 10:30 p.m. He and I were introduced by former bartender Kenny Miller and we have met there ever since. We have been compared to the two old men in the Muppets balcony. We vent criticism, compare stocks and in general stay safely in our own "no fly zone."

Rick lives by two favorite sayings, "You gotta be a little patient," and "Be brief, be blunt, be gone."

One thing that has changed recently is that the Saturday night group has grown significantly. Just like the Cheers theme song..."where everybody knows your name." Friar Tucks is a bar of mostly regulars who have known each other for a lot of years. This does not preclude the new regulars like myself from feeling right at home.

This is certainly an establishment where you can grab a place at the bar or a table and be left alone if you want. During winter months one of the more enjoyable features is a large brass canopy fireplace which is welcome when the hawk is bearing down with 30 mph breath. The ambiance is further enhanced by a large range of music from a CD player when the jukebox is not being played.

"This is a people type bar," says Angelo. "We send flowers to people who are sick and the customers here care about each other."

I have witnessed this a number of times when acquaintances from Friar Tucks were in the hospital or sick at home. On the cork announcement board there is a volunteer notice for those interested in working with my charity, the National Runaway Switchboard.

On Thursday nights Friar Tucks has karaoke night. This is well attended by regulars and those who are just fans of karaoke. Most evening, groups will send out for pizza or wings and a tradition of sharing is the norm.

An enormous collection of photographs appear on the south wall. These photos span the entire history of the bar. Long time bartender John Wong appears in a number of these pictures.

Occasionally Tucks, as regulars call it, offers road trips to casinos and the horse races. You can see evidence of the customers' camaraderie by a large grease pencil board where the dates of patrons' birthdays are listed each month. Recently, Angelo's daughter, nicknamed Cricket, took over management of the bar after extensive travels to South American countries. She is now in the Caribbean no doubt picking up new drink recipes to challenge John Wong. So, while she's away getting that all important viva Macarana tattoo we will be thinking about her.

Last but most certainly not least is the fact that Friar Tucks is a great place for holidays. The winner of the 1996 Halloween contest was W.C. Fields himself. On other holidays there are cookouts, buffets and such to make whatever holiday a great celebration. Want to join a group? It may take you while but try Friar Tucks. For a Cheers bar, Tucks gets four wings.

(Note — don't park your car next door in the grocery store's lot. You will be towed.)

— *J. Quillian*

Fumatore

1705 N. Halsted St.
773-266-9521
Hours: noon to 2 a.m. Sunday to Thursday,
noon to 4 a.m. Friday and Saturday

The cigar boom has given rise to another form of yuppie entertainment, the cigar box, a space where smokers can congregate without hearing the bitter remonstrations of the politically correct. You won't be hearing, "Those things take years off your life, you know," at a cigar bar.

Fumatore, hidden away on the second floor of a building across from the Steppenwolf Theatre on Halsted, is a perfect example of the benefits of a cigar bar, and also the clientele they attract. The look of the place is downbeat 1950s jazz; when the focus of your attention is held in your hand and inches from your mouth, lighting issues are not foregrounded. The bar is across the room from the walk-up entrance, and it extends generously on both sides. On the right is the lounging (Read: smoking) area, complete with couches, a wall of TV monitors, and (of course) dim lighting. On the other side of the dimly-lit room is the dimly-lit dance floor, a decent sized hardwood bounded by a full length window that looks out onto Halsted. Flanking that is a "private" room, made increasingly less private by the transparent glass that separates it from the dance floor. Several items of interest to cigar aficionados (old boxes, humidors, photographs) are sprinkled liberally throughout the bar.

Even when I was there, on a Tuesday night, and with a $15 cover, the place was jumping. While the supposed "event" that night was a good cause (a bene-fit for one of the bar regulars who is fighting cancer), it's likely none of the finely dressed, somewhat fearsome-looking crowd knew about it. For all the talk of the cigar bar being a Generation X affiliation, this place had none of that. These were Italian suit-wearing, money-in-the-pocket-to-burn, possibly "well-connected" professionals. (If I elaborate any more on that I'll probably have my legs broken, so I'll go no further. Good thing those editors at Barfly printed this article under a pseudonym. You did do that, right? Guys?)

Whatever the crowd, the mood of the bar is Italian. The greeter at the entrance welcomed us with an offering of cannolis. What can I say? They don't go with beer, but I was captivated. If you go to Fumatore, which you should at least once, be sure to bring your matching gold cufflinks and the best recipe for a martini (and calzone) you can find. And bring cigars. Lots of cigars.

— Dave Dayen

The North Side G&L's-Gallagher's Tavern and Grill
G&L's Fire Escape
2157 W. Grace St.
773-472-1138
Hours: 8 a.m. to 2 a.m. Monday to Saturday,
11 a.m. to 2 a.m. Sunday

A garage band once wrote a song, dedicated to those fearless fighters of flames, called "Fireman," but as that was a fine tribute so is this bar on the corner of Grace and Leavitt. Fire helmets and helmet plates litter the space above the bar and sleeve patches are framed for display.

I've seen some quality jukebox selections in my wanderings but this place has one I can't get enough of. The box has probably every volume of "Oldies But Goodies." About 20 volumes in all. Also, the box contains some of the best Irish songs and bands like the Clancy Brothers. Sure there are the basic pop 1960s and 1970s classics, and some 1990s and country for the unadventurous. Although Neil Diamond does have disc space here, "America" is not on the play list.

The Fire Escape is a roomy, neighborhood bar with plenty of seating at the bar, space to move between there and the tables, and a few tables to sit with friends. On the corner of the bar is a brass pole extending from the ceiling to the bar. I'm sure it has been asked before but I couldn't help but ask my date to spin around on it, but she was bogus and slapped me instead. So with that response, I got her one of the select beers they have in the cooler.

Hamm's in cans and Stroh's in bottles! I was in heaven until I saw the special they have with Busch cans for a buck! This was such a choice selection, I couldn't help but quaff just a few until I went on to get a few Jello shots. Then there's the tap -- Old Style, Harp, Guinness, Miller Light, Killian's Red. Yes!

-- Phil Brandt

Gallagher's Grill and Tavern
2426 N. Racine Ave.
773-929-7759
Hours: 7 a.m. to 2 a.m. Sunday to Friday,
7 a.m. to 3 a.m. Saturday

If you're looking for that one bar that feels like home, search no more. When I walked in, I was greeted with an air of cheeriness and familiarity. I had just come from another bar that made me feel unwanted, rejected. So this was like a breath of fresh air, and I proceeded to make myself comfortable in front of an inviting fire place.

An outstanding oval shaped bar encompasses half the room, giving the bar an elegant flair, but this does not detract form the neighborhood feel of the bar. A great variety of people are attracted to Gallagher's for various reasons. The owner Kevin Gallagher took over the former Chase Tavern in October 1994. He

Barfly Gallagher's-Gallery Cabaret

said he does not want to exclude anyone from his bar.

"For me to interface with that many walks of life is probably why I own this bar," Gallagher said.

One can't help but notice the framed pictures that decorate the pristine walls, plus an assortment of plants that accentuate the homey surroundings. A big picture window makes for great people watching and situated by the window are two dart boards.

One one finds their way past the glorious marble bar, there's a raised level with a pool table and more of a sports atmosphere than the living room-type ambiance feeling of the entrance room.

Once can't help but notice the great deal of effort that Gallagher has put into making his bar a special place. He caters to a wide scope of the community and is a sincere person who wants to make people feel welcomed. He has daily drink specials and a full service kitchen open from 10 a.m. to 10 p.m. Sunday to Thursday, 10 a.m. to 11 p.m. Friday and Saturday.

This bar just oozes with good vibrations and holiday cheer especially around St. Patrick's Day. Gallagher is the grandson of an Irish fiddle player.

The one thing that really stands out in my mind is a smoke eating machine Gallagher has installed so you don't go home reeking of smoke -- groovy.

-- Lisa Gulotta

Gallery Cabaret
2020 N. Oakley Ave.
773-489-5471
Hours: 5 p.m. to 2 a.m. Sunday to Friday,
4 p.m. to 3 a.m. Saturday

In 1988, artist Kenny Strandberg had a vision. He wanted to open a bar that would be a springboard for local artists of all types. His vision was shared by fellow artist Darlene Mehegan, and together they brought to life the Gallery Cabaret.

"We wanted to give artists an avenue, a place to show their work," says Kenny from behind the bar. In this they have succeeded. You need only walk through the door on any night of the week to find a wealth of creativity.

The walls of the Gallery are crowded with the work of local artists. The bar continually hosts shows featuring the work of fledgling artists, and new works are displayed every couple of weeks.

"Most of these people have never had a show before," Kenny said. I ask if any of the work is his, and he points out several paintings, most notably the ever-present green nudes.

Musicians, too, can get their first shot on stage here, whether they come in on one of the several diverse open mic nights, or get booked to play on a weekend. Susan "Grammy" Simon, bartender and booker of bands, tells me that before anyone heard of the Smashing Pumpkins, Liz Phair,

Open mike jams are a great time at Gallery Cabaret, 2020 N. Oakley Ave.

Urge Overkill, Red Red Meat, and the Wesley Willis Fiasco, they were rocking the stage at the Gallery.

Friday and Saturday nights are saved for bands, but every other night of the week you will find something interesting going on, from open mic to comedy improv to performance art. One of the my favorite nights is Tuesday, the open blues jam with Fish and the Bluefins, a very tight and talented trio comprised of Fish on guitar, Greg K. on bass, and Uncle Steve on drums. The band has a wide repertoire of traditional and modern blues, and are more than capable of backing up anyone who might decide to join them on stage. Their identities are shrouded in mystery, and you never know when a bigshot on the local blues scene might put in a guest appearance.

Behind the stage is a full-wall mural, and weekend bartender Josh "Weasel" Verdon gives me the bigger picture on the big picture. The mural was painted by the nephew of Darlene Mehegan, a guy named Casper. Casper is going to be featured in an upcoming independent film about Chicago muralists called Sketches. I want to know more, so Weasel puts me in touch with Tony "The Fly," a Chicago performance poet and the assistant director of the film. The Fly tells me that Sketches is centered around a competition that is sponsored by the CTA every year, and that it utilizes only Chicago talent. It seems that not only does everyone here have a nickname, but nearly everyone you talk to will likely have some kind of artistic connection.

The Gallery crowd is an eclectic, eccentric mix of artists, musicians,

Barfly Gallery Cabaret-Gamblers

and neighborhood regulars. I ask Grammy if the clientele has changed to reflect the changing Bucktown neighborhood. "Not really," she says, "the crowd has pretty much stayed the same." Essentially, though, the Gallery is a corner bar, with the homey, comfortable feel of a corner bar.

Some of the regulars are quick to tell me about Kenny "Swede" Strandberg's homemade Gloog, and I know from experience that they serve the best Bravissimo Pizza in town. The building has housed a bar for many, many years. Before it became a haven for local artists, it was a Hispanic bar, and 15 years prior to that it was a Polish bar. As I sit and eat my Bravissimo, Kenny tells a story of a woman who recently came in and told him that she had her wedding reception on the site in 1947. Even more than 50 years ago, 2020 North Oakley was a place of great beginnings.

— Donna Donato

Gamblers
4908 N. Pulaski Road
773-545-3566
Hours: noon to 2 a.m. Sunday to Friday,
noon to 3 a.m. Saturday

Laura, a peroxide Patti Smith, has had enough of Michelle, who sits across the table. Stone-silent, Michelle is thinking about everything but Laura's tantrum. Why, for example, does the top of the table keep inching closer to Michelle's face? Will she be able to get a divorce in time to get married this Valentines Day? Where did she leave her glasses last night?

Fed up with the silence, Laura stands, leans in, and screams, shut up! Shut up! Shut the fuck up! The shouts put the doorman on alarm. An arms length from Laura, he's ready.

Jackie, a fortyish woman who just minutes before had been a blur of frosted hair and royal blue knit as she stocked and wiped and stocked and wiped the bar, has stopped to monitor the situation. She keeps an unblinking eye on the scene as the doorman confers with her. She's directing this intervention. She owns this place.

Finally tired, Laura jerks on her fringed, black leather. Not so drunk that she is without manners, she leans over the bar and says a few words to Jackie and the bartender, a pleasant young man with seriously-thick glasses. They smile back at her.

The warm fuzzies end with the "Fuck you!" Laura barks to the doorman as she blasts out the front door. Good, good the doorman responds, meaning it.

Steps behind her is Michelle's fiancee. When he returns, he delivers his report: I found her on the landing. Got her to crawl into bed, though.

In addition to a couple dozen strangers who paid the $3 cover to support the evenings bands, the remaining half of the Gamblers crowd are local folk. These

101

regulars live their Fridays and Saturdays against the background music the bands supply.

And for the most part, on most evenings, the customers get along. Jackie has never had to call 911. She catches trouble before it gets troublesome. She will call wives and take keys. She wants the bar to be comfortable enough that a lady can walk in alone.

In many ways, Gamblers is all-bar: Meatloaf CDs in the jukebox; televisions tuned to ESPN; a clip frame holding bags of chips; dartboards; Tiffany-style lamps courtesy of Old Style; a cigarette machine; a selection of $1 and $2.50 beers, $5 pitchers, and $2.25 and $2.75 liquor; a Protex condom machine with the porn-o-plenty novelty pack option; a pinball machine; and a sideroom complete with stage and stackable chairs for band nights.

But there's a little more thought to this bar. Three live plants sit on the table closest to the window. A bag of Tootsie Rolls waits in a plastic pumpkin for trick-or-treaters. The large mirror painting of Errol Flynn's face wears a happy skull mask. A full-length mirror hangs in the women's room.

A Crock Watcher crockpot stands ready for the next Guest Chef night, when patrons cook for patrons (word is a few patrons are real chef-guys who work Downtown). Jackie has a long list of events planned: Hobo Stew nights, 17-pound turkey raffles, day-long barbecues, ballroom dancing taught by Shriners, and an annual scavenger hunt with a photocopied sheet of rules that include, if we ask for an animal, it must be alive.

It might have been the Scotch and Jack Daniels, respectively, talking when my friend Kathleen and I agreed: if either of us were solo some evening and had a hankering for Scotch or Jack, we'd go to Gamblers.

— Alice Bendig

The Gin Mill

2462 N. Lincoln Ave.
773-549-3232
Hours: 11 a.m. to 2 a.m. Sunday to Friday,
11 a.m. to 3 a.m. Saturday

Hospitality is the theme at The Gine Mill located in Lincoln Park.

"We're just enthusiastic," sad owner David Haslinger. "I'm at the door Thursday through Sturday thanking people for coming."

The Gin Mill opened July 8, 1994, in a site formerly occupied by a bar called Kasey's. Haslinger said he rehabbed the 3,200 square-foot bar to give it a classic look which includes open-brick walls, a varnished old-time wood bar, railings, new furniture and a new paint job. He also opened large front windows facing Lincoln Avenue.

A major feature that separates The Gin Mill from Kasey's and other bars in the area is that Haslinger, a native of Detroit and a major Motor City sports fan, shows Detroit, Michigan University and Michigan State University sporting events on satellite televisions.

Barfly Gin Mill-Ginger Man

Haslinger, a 1990 graduate of Michigan State University, said he set a goal for himself to own a bar within five years of his graduation. While a student, he worked at a bar in East Lansing, Mich., called the Land Shark. He and his friends referred to the bar as The Gin Mill, thus he carried the name to his own bar. He also brought along his closest college friends to work at the bar.

Haslinger's other bar experience inlcudes stints at Mother's, 26 W. Division St., and the Waterloo Tavern, 2270 N. Lincoln Ave. His college buddies/employees have worked in popular bars around the city as well like Hi-Tops, 3551 N. Sheffield Ave.

The Gin Mill caters to a young upwardly mobile crowd; those in their late 20s and early 30s. The jukebox features music from the 1970s to 1990s and the bar has unplugged live blues on Thursdays.

-- Tony Gordon

The Ginger Man
3740 N. Clark St.
773-549-2050
Hours: 3 p.m. to 2 a.m. Monday to Thursday, noon to 2 a.m. Friday and Sunday, and noon to 3 a.m. Saturday

The "G-Man," as affectionately known by regulars, has been a fixture on this corner of Clark Street for about 20 years. This reviewer has been going there for the past 13 years. It's definitely a home-away-from-home for many folks. It has a comfortable wood decor and one of the best bottled-beer selections around.

It has the feel of an English Pub and a diverse crowd. It is a prime place for conversation, has an excellent jukebox with old blues and jazz, three pooltables and two pinball machines.

The Ginger Man is usually pretty crowded on weekends; especially if the Cabaret Metro next door has a popular band playing. During the week, the atmosphere is relaxed and the pool tables are open or have a short wait. One of the best features of this bar is that it has two bathrooms for both men and women so you never have to wait too long to relieve a heavy bladder.

The second best feature is that those who work at the G-Man hate Cubs' fans. The G-Man is just a stone's throw from Wrigley Field and when the *flubs* are in town, this surrounding neighborhood is nothing short of a nightmare. Drunken Cub fans take over the area with little regard for those who live there. But the G-Man attempts to ward off these little devils with a blast of loud classical music after all baseball games.

"How 'bout some Aerosmith, man," a disappointed Cub fan can often be heard saying.

But the bartenders usually throw a shrug as they crank a little Mozart.

103

The North Side Ginger Man-Ginger's Ale House

One final note, Bobby the Harley bouncer stood guard at the door on weekends for many years. Unfortunately, Bobby died in May, 1998. This man was the best bouncer in the city. He was stout, had a handlebar mustache, often wore a beret and was an extremely kind fellow -- unless you did something wrong. For years I started and ended my evenings at the Ginger Man. I've had some wonderful times there and Bobby was a big part of the fun. I'll never forget him and I'll surely miss him.

-- Tony Gordon

Ginger's Ale House
3801 N. Ashland Ave.
773-348-2767
Hours: 11 a.m. to 2 a.m. Sunday to Friday,
11 a.m. to 3 a.m. Saturday

Hi gang, Barfly's roaming photo-geek here with another review. As I sit in Gamblers enjoying a cold one, the band Southhaven approaches. They recommend I try Ginger's Ale House. They realize I have no life to get in the way of this venture, I agree.

Going south on Ashland from Irving Park, a plain wooden sign tells me I'm here. It doesn't look like much from the outside but as I open the door, I'm pleasantly surprised. A line from an old "Fireside Theater" comes to mind, "Wow what a groove." It's not as dramatic as opening the gates to Oz but it's pretty cool, nothing flashy just a real nice bar with etched mirrors, old fashion wood tables and booth and my favorite feature of any bar; a high ceiling.

Ginger's Ale House is owned by Tony Griffin and Jamie Hale. Tonight Tony is working the bar, he describes the crowd as young professionals. "Oh shit, yuppies," I think to myself. But after a few minutes I notice these people have personalities and an open friendly, non-pretentious manner about them.

The first patrons I meet are three Irish lads named Greg, George and Rory. They say they love this place and visit often. Rory is a screenwriter who talks in length about his writing and latest project "The Ultimate Patriot."

I move to a table of regulars and ask what they like about this place. The ladies say loudly "Tony." The men respond with location and atmosphere. Elle and December like the bartenders and the food. Sandy, a former bartender comes here for fun after tending bar elsewhere. She shows me the jukebox and boasts proudly it has the most diverse selection she has ever seen.

I strongly agree with all the above. Tony and Jamie have done a great job of creating a comfortable friendly atmosphere. They have 16 beers on tap (nine are ales) and bands perform on Fridays and Saturdays. I didn't try the food but it looked and smelled great. I guess I'll have to go back.

— Derek Scholl

Gio's Sports Bar
4857 N. Damen Ave.
773-334-0345
Hours: noon to 2 a.m. daily

The jukebox at Gio's Sports Bar is as diverse as any in the city, featuring offerings from the Beatles to the Cranberries. And next to albums from K.D. Lang and the Police, sits "Eterno Navidad," a CD filled, of course, with Spanish Christmas songs.

The selection fits the bar. Sitting on the corner of Damen Avenue and Ainslie Street, Gio's attracts a diverse crowd, something that's fitting for the Ravenswood neighborhood.

"This neighborhood really is changing," said Adrian Camacho, general manager of the bar. "We're seeing a lot of rehabs going up. Everywhere you look, people are rehabbing apartment buildings. A lot of people are moving in. The neighborhood is getting more and more popular."

But that doesn't mean the Camacho family is doing anything different.

Gio's operates these days pretty much the same as it has for more than 15 years. It's a family business, owned by Camacho's brother, Humberto. Friendliness and a laid-back atmosphere have long been the mainstays of this neighborhood establishment, Adrian said. And that isn't about to change.

"This is a nice place to stop by," he said. "We have a real friendly crowd, a lot of regulars. No problems are allowed."

That explains the somewhat menacing sign on the front door, which tells patrons they must have two picture IDs to get in. That policy, Camacho said, helps keep away the "bad crowd."

"It's important to have a nice crowd," he said. "That's what we want here."

Cleanliness, too, is another of Camacho's selling points. And on a recent Saturday afternoon, it was easy to see why. Gio's was as spotless as a bar could be.

Unlike many areas of the city, the Ravenswood neighborhood isn't known for its bars, and Gio's may be one of the best-kept secrets in the area. It features a pool table, dart boards and foosball machine. The television shows non-stop sporting events, and beer is cheap. Tecate beer bottles were selling for $1.75 recently, while all Miller bottles cost $1.50.

A quiet crowd gathered at Gio's that afternoon, watching college basketball on the television. Pedro Vega was among them. He's been coming to Gio's for about a year-and-a-half now. Most weeks, he stops in three to four times.

"You appreciate having a nice, friendly place to come to," he said, taking a break from the video poker machine against the front wall. "You get a chance to unwind. You don't have to kick the dog when you get home."

Like Camacho, Vega also appreciates the crowd and the cleanliness of the bar.

"It really is a friendly crowd," he said. "And when he says it's clean, he

105

means it. That's really important. You don't want to spend much time in a bar that isn't clean."

Gio's holds two dart leagues. And it's a favorite of several teams of neighborhood basketball players, who celebrate victory, or lament defeat, after their games. These patrons mix easily with the neighborhood regulars, giving Gio's its relaxed atmosphere.

"We've had a pretty consistent crowd in here, even with the neighborhood getting more popular and well-known," Camacho said. "It's good to see things happening around here. It's good to see the new people coming in."

Of course, these people are going to need a place to drink. Gio's wouldn't be a bad place to start. There's just one problem: the jukebox features the "Macarena," too.

— Dan Rafter

Girlbar

2625 N. Halsted St.
773-871-4210
Hours: 6 p.m. to 2 a.m. Tuesday to Thursday,
3 p.m. to 2 a.m. Friday, 6 p.m. to 3 a.m. Saturday,
noon to 2 a.m. Sunday

The name speaks for itself. Girlbar is the latest dance club to open its doors to the lesbian community.

Formerly the Zodiac Lounge, Girlbar co-owners Jennifer Murphy and Lynn Malec opened in June, 1996. Murphy's experience encompasses such jobs as tending bar at another popular woman's club, a waitress in fine dining, and even some time spent mixing drinks on the ships down at Navy Pier. Malec was previously the owner of Winner's Sports Bar and Grill, 4530 N. Lincoln Ave., which still operates as a gay club known as the Rainbow Bar.

"We have been friends for 10 to 12 years and just decided (we) wanted to open our own business," Murphy said. "Chicago needed a nice new club for women."

"We looked at quite a few places and this really fit what we visualized." According to Murphy, the place was a shambles but they "really liked the space and could do two different atmospheres."

"Lynn and I are both perfectionists and wouldn't sleep until it was right," Murphy said. So they worked "night and day" along with a contractor, renovating the dilapidated space for three weeks. "(We were) under pressure because opening weekend was Gay Pride Weekend," Murphy said.

Because Gay Pride is such a big attraction, Murphy said they hyped the bar during the time they were working on it through word-of-mouth and advertising in the gay press.

"Opening weekend was crazy," Murphy recalled. "We saw driver's licenses from every state, there were mobs of people."

Barfly Girlbar

Other than the crunch to open on time, there were virtually no problems in getting started. Murphy admitted that they were a little worried about opening a club in Lincoln Park but were set at ease as the neighborhood has apparently made them feel very welcome.

"The first day we got here we went to the alderman's office, introduced ourselves, told them what we're doing and they've been very supportive," Murphy said.

"This is the first lesbian bar in an upper class neighborhood," Malec said. "The women are really glad they have a nice place to go in a nice area."

Although it's predominantly a lesbian bar, Murphy made it clear that, "we're always boy friendly."

"Wednesday night (Girlbar) becomes Boybar with an all male staff," Murphy said. "The boys seem to love it just as much as the girls do."

Murphy said that they are pleased and have been pleasantly surprised with all the positive response and support from everyone.

"We get between five and six hundred people that go through here on a Saturday night."

It seems that the reason for their success lies in the fact that it really is two different places in one. Downstairs is the nightclub and upstairs is the neighborhood tavern.

The front entrance is a hallway separated by a windowed partition. The first level has a long, full service bar with cocktail tables running parallel along the opposite partition, and when it's crowded the pathways become narrow and cozy.

There is a nice-sized dance area, surrounded by cocktail tables, that has a variety of upbeat, DJ-spun tunes. Quality lights and sound system keeps the energy level going all night. There is only a short walk to the sublevel leading to the bathrooms and a quiet place to use the pay phone.

There are two, separate flights of stairs opposite of one another to get to the second level. You can find a small bar in a furthermost corner that serves limited mixed drinks and a single tap selection, featuring their very own Girlbar Brew, all served in plastic cups. Two pool tables are centered in the middle of the red-painted room that seems to be occupied most of the night. A large stained glass decoration blocks most of the view of the small outdoor deck that overlooks Halsted Street.

On tap, choices are Sam Adams, Guinness, Widmer Weiss and Girlbar Brew, an amber ale. Draught selections run from $3.50 to $5. In bottles, they carry such selections as all Miller products, Corona, Rolling Rock, Amstel Light, Beck's, and Hacker-Pschorr Weiss. Domestic and import bottles cost $2.50 and $3.50, respectively. Mixed drinks are in the range of $3 to $5.

"This is not my first business, but it is my first bar," Murphy said. "Although it takes a lot of time and money, what makes it all worthwhile is all the women enjoying it and coming back. We really appreciate (that) support."

— Arunas Ingaunis

Glascott's Saloon
2158 N. Halsted St.
773-281-1205
Hours: 11 a.m. to 2 a.m. Sunday to Friday,
11 a.m. to 3 a.m. Saturday

Records are scarce, recollections are foggy, but what we do know is that Chicago's Glascott family has owned a saloon in this city for more than 100 years.

Patrick Glascott, who emigrated to Chicago from Ireland, opened a saloon in the late 1800s on Ashland Avenue between Lake and Madison streets, according to his grandson Dennis Glascott.

"We don't know when," Dennis said. "It could be in the 1880s or 1870s or even the 1860s."

An old photo of the place shows some of the regulars dressed nice and wearing derbies. The bartenders wore ties and the bar had gas lamps and spittoons.

Patrick Glascott died in 1904. He had five children. Two of his sons continued on in the saloon business. His son Bill owned a bar at 2519 N. Lincoln Ave., now known as Irish Eyes. Bill let his brother Larry tend bar on occasion and Larry eventually opened up his own place at 2158 N. Halsted St. in 1937, according to Dennis, one Larry's seven sons. Larry also had a single daughter.

"The whole area was Irish so he moved over here," said Larry's grandson Tim, age 31, who now manages Glascott's Saloon at 2158 N. Halsted St. "The only other bar here as long is Kelly's (949 W. Webster St.)."

Tim said his grandfather was quite a character.

"He was a short, mean old guy," Tim said. "He was about five-foot-five and he always had a cigar."

He purchased his saloon from the O'Gara family and named it "Larry's," Dennis said. He discovered that the third floor of the building had been a speakeasy during Prohibition. There was a hidden entryway and a typical speakeasy door with a peep hole.

However, Larry's Saloon, was nothing like those speakeasies of the Roaring Twenties. Larry's catered to working men.

"Back then, women didn't go to taverns," Tim said. "It was a shot and a beer place. Both of my grandfathers never drank a pint of beer. They always had a shot glass."

The clientele at the bar was mostly Irish and Larry knew most of the patrons.

"You had mostly in that area all tradesmen," said Dennis, age 54, who would scrub glasses at the bar when he was a kid. "It was open at 7 a.m. and workers lined up to get a shot than catch a bus and go to work."

All of Larry's sons helped out at the bar.

"I remember chipping the ice on Sunday mornings," said Bob Glascott, age 51, who is also Dennis' brother and Tim's uncle. He said big blocks of ice were delivered to the bar regularly from a company in the neighborhood. He and his

Barfly Glascott's Saloon

brothers would regularly chop the ice up. The chipped ice would then be dropped into the beer tap system and onto coils to keep the beer cold.

When Bob, Dennis and their brothers were kids, the bar looked much different than it does today. It had a 42-foot long bar, a drop ceiling, and just two windows looking out on Halsted Street.

The long bar, Dennis said, created a few problems for his father. In order to handle customers on a busy day, Larry wore a changer instead of going to the cash register after every transaction.

"Sometimes he'd set a bottle up and ask a guy what he had," Dennis said. "He worked on the honor system."

Dennis said he even heard a story where his father wore roller skates to slide up and down the long bar.

The bar was a real meeting place for lots of neighborhood folks, especially to watch television, Bob said. Friday night boxing matches on television were real popular at the bar in the 1940s, he said.

"Taverns were the first places to have TVs," Bob said. "Families didn't have TVs until the 1950s. If (your tavern) had a TV it was a real business go-getter."

Bob, Dennis and their brother Tim (there's quite a few guys named Tim in the Glascott family) took over the running the bar from their father in 1970. Larry Glascott died in 1975 and they renamed the bar Glascott's Saloon.

Bob said the neighborhood was run down when he and his brothers took over the bar.

"The bar was pretty rough," said Bob who was working as a school teacher at the time. "I remember people I taught with thought I was crazy going over there. They wouldn't go over there."

It's hard to imagine Halsted Street in Lincoln Park run down. Today it is one of the nicest stretches in the city. But for much of this century it was a high-crime area. Bob said he remembers when the area across the bar on Halsted Street was a vacant lot.

"Guys would drink beer and set up card tables out there," Bob said.

The seeds for modern Lincoln Park were planted in 1965, Bob said, when Mayor Richard J. Daley named the area Park West and announced an improvement plan.

"It was pretty neat to see it (the neighborhood) get built up," Bob said. "Some parts are now unrecognizable."

The Glascott's joined the rehab frenzy and completely fixed up the bar in 1979. They really brightened up the place. Old photos of the facade show an unattractive neighborhood tap. In 1979, the Glascott's created an aesthetically pleasing tavern both inside and out. The north wall of the bar was all brick. They cut in large windows overseeing Webster Street. The front of the bar had two small windows. Now it's practically all one large window overlooking Halsted Street. The old drop-ceiling was taken out and the original tin-ceiling was patched up. The long bar was cut down in size and tables were added.

In the 1980s, a fourth generation of Chicago Glascott's began working at the

The North Side Glascott's Saloon-Gloria's Sports Bar

bar. Tim started in 1987 as a doorman.

"I worked a few years as a bartender, then I became assistant manager then manager," said Tim noting that 10 other Glascott's work at the bar as well.

Few bars in Chicago can claim the type of family legacy like Glascott's.

"I find it funny that my father had it, we worked it, now they have it," said Bob who has children working at the bar.

The 1980s, when this new group of Glascott's came, there was a regeneration for the saloon and the neighborhood. In the late 1980s, there were lines around the corner to get into Glascott's.

"We were so busy in the 1980s," Tim said. "(Bar patrons) had either Rush Street or us. Now there is a lot of competition from Bucktown and Wrigleyville. We're still a busy place but we don't have lines around the corner."

As manager, Tim has helped bring Glascott's into the 1990s by expanding the tap beer selection to 14 and adding a cash station among other amenities.

The Glascott's celebrated their 60th anniversary at the Halsted Street location in April 1997. It was a huge party with old and new patrons and employees toasting a Chicago legacy. But you don't have to have a special occasion to stop in the legendary Glascott's. Any time is a great time to stop by Glascott's and share a Chicago treasure.

— Tony Gordon

Gloria's Sports Bar
5663 N. Clark St.
773-728-0603
Hours: 3 p.m. to 2 a.m. daily

Gloria's, named for the owner's sister, is a delightful little pub. It's been in operation for since 1995.

On the night I visited, the bar had wonderful Valentine's Day decor. Hanging from the ceiling was cut-out Cupids. Red balloons were covering the support poles and draping the walls.

Another piece of decor was a huge head of a deer. In my opinion, I don't appreciate dead animal heads when I'm trying to have a good time. But that's just my opinion.

Anyway, the folks who work at Gloria's are very nice and speak both English and Spanish. Also, the jukebox is stocked with Spanish rock music.

Other stuff in the bar includes pool tables, game machines, a band stand and dance floor. Two people were playing pool, the evening I was there. The bar was a bit slow that evening, but with the bandstand and dance floor, it appears that there are nights when the crowds come in.

So, if you're ever up this far north on Clark Street, stop by Gloria's.

— T.M. Kornelson

Gold Star Lounge
1755 W. Division St.
773-227-8700
Hours: 4 p.m. to 2 a.m. weekdays,
3 p.m. to 3 a.m. Saturday

The Gold Star is one of the few remaining landmarks from the old "Polish Broadway," which during the time since Prohibition made Division Street, between Milwaukee and Western avenues, famous.

Legendary Chicago author Nelson Algren roamed these streets after World War II and forever memorialized the history of the area in compelling books like "The Man With The Golden Arm," which later became a movie starring Frank Sinatra, and "Never Come Morning."

Around the corner from the Gold Star is Frankie Machine Park, named after the main character in "The Man With The Golden Arm."

For the first 50 years of the 20th Century, much of West Division Street was settled by Polish immigrants. The area west of Damen was settled by East European Jews. During Prohibition, Division Street was known for speakeasies, whorehouses and gambling dens. After Prohibition, many of the speakeasies turned into Polish Polka bars and the whorehouses and gambling dens continued on.

Gold Star was a major part of the "Polish Broadway." Its outside marquee still maintains the appearance from the bar's former "hotel" days. A Polish woman ran the bar from the 1930s until 1990. She lived in a small room in the back of the bar. The wall is now knocked out and a pool table resides there currently.

An antique key rack to the left of the front door once held keys to the rooms upstairs. While bartending, the old owner would rent the upstairs rooms and 15-year-old Polish girls to the regulars.

During Prohibition, the bar operated as a speakeasy and is equipped with tunnels in the basement that exit to Division Street. The original bar is still in place and is beautiful. There is a lot of open space behind the bar where formerly stood an open beer closet and a grand piano.

Today, the bar is owned by two women who have tried to maintain much of the bar's history with their current incarnation (except for the prostitution) of the bar. New additions include the owners love of sports and art. One owner is an avid Green Bay Packers fan, and I'm told that Superbowl Sunday, or any game days are excuses for great parties. Gold Star is often in cahoots with Phyllis' Musical Inn, another relic from the "Polish Broadway," for pool tournaments and bus trips to sporting events.

In addition, the walls are covered with work from local artists. Once a month, anyone who feels like contributing can be a part of their showings.

To best describe Gold Star, here is what one of the regulars had to say: "(Gold Star is) kind of like your first apartment, nothing fancy, but you'll always feel a certain nostalgia for it."

He went on to explain that the atmosphere has really changed over the past year with the addition of Liquid Kitty (during the "Polish Broadway" days, the bar housed one of the biggest Polka bars called the Orange Lantern) down the street. He said that even the owners are a little annoyed with the gentrification of the neighborhood and the attraction of youngsters to the area.

"I hate to use the word 'yuppie,'" said bartender Janelle, "but that's what they are."

Many patrons said that even with the crowds getting younger, it's really no big deal.

"This place is no-beef, there are never any fights," said another regular. "I think it's good that people feel safe here, the more the merrier."

Other amenities include domestic bottles at $1.50, a great crowd and free pizza on big game days. And on top of all that, the place is haunted. Another bartender, Ian, told me of a few fascinating sightings.

There is a pay phone to the right of the front door where the owners have seen a man walk by from time to time. Later, a Chicago ghost hunter and his psychic girlfriend did a walk-though and felt a presence near the phone. After some research, they found out that in the 1940s, a robbery was attempted at the bar. The robber was standing near the phone when the owner shot and killed him. There also have been footsteps heard in the upstairs apartments and a woman in a green dress has been spotted wandering around.

The ghost hunter also said there were presences in the corner of the bar where the piano was and in the basement. True or not, I thought that was pretty cool. Unfortunately, I didn't get to meet the spirits.

One person told me simply that the Gold Star is a blast — I agree.

— Lee DiVita

Goofy's Hock Shop
4355 N. Elston Ave.
773-282-9458
Hours: 8 a.m. to 2 a.m. weekdays,
8 a.m. to 3 a.m. Saturday, 11 a.m. to 2 a.m. Sunday

Goofy's Hock Shop is a very nice neighborhood bar where a lot of retired firemen hang out along with a nice group of guys, mostly blue-collar tradesmen, and a few females.

Goofy (Don the owner) is goofy about the Disney cartoon dog Goofy and the entire place is Goofified with pictures, items, etc.

Don took the place over a little more than a year ago and completely renovated it, opening up two rooms. One room is for games like pinball and pool, and for events. It's a great place to catch a sporting event on TV. The other room, which is smaller, is for parties and events.

The bar has been around for many, many years and was formerly the Hock Shop. On the dark side, this is a bar where the notorious John Wayne Gacy, of

Barfly Goofy's Hock Shop-Goose Island Brewpub

happy memory, used to stop in to drink.

Today, Goofy's Hock Shop is a great place. Don hosts several nice events for St. Pat's Day, New Year's Eve, and other holidays. In April he held a birthday party for the house parakeet, Sly (Sylvester), who just got a new condo behind the bar.

Fun stuff goes on all the time at Goofy's. It is a terrific place to go and there are $1 drafts — great!

— Tom Gilmartin

Goose Island Brewing Company
1800 N. Clybourn
773-915-0071
Hours: 11 a.m. to 10:30 p.m. (last call) Sunday,
11 a.m. to 12:30 a.m. (last call) Monday to Thursday,
11 a.m. to 1:30 a.m. (last call) Friday and Saturday

Sick and tired of watching colleagues with more education move ahead of you in the workplace? Have you ever considered going for your advanced degree? At Goose Island Brewing Company it's never been easier to obtain your MBA (Master of Beer Appreciation) than right now!

Dive right into Goose Island's core requirements, currently including Extra Special Bitter and Honest Stout. Receive extra credit throughout your year-long program in such subjects as Winter Warmer, Rotweizen, and Demolition Ale. Finally, at the end of just one short year, you could be proudly displaying your Goose Island MBA T-shirt to envious co-workers as you cruise by them with this prestigious degree on your way to corporate infamy. For those of you already holding your degrees, or for those who wish nothing more than to enjoy a Honker's Ale every now and then, Goose Island will accommodate you as well.

Throughout the year Goose Island offers a wide variety of English, American, and German style ales as well as several lagers. Goose Island also boasts cask-conditioned ales, sometimes referred to as "hand pumped" ales on a regular basis. However, should you order a cask-conditioned ale, don't be surprised when you're served a tall glass of warm, flat beer. To be honest though, the cask-conditioned ales alone are worth the trip. Besides, they're not really warm or flat, just cool and lightly carbonated which reflects the way the way these beers have been served for centuries throughout England.

At any one time, Goose Island has six draft beers available as well as two cask-conditioned ales. Prices for these beers may vary, usually depending on the amount of alcohol in the beer which will be a reflection of the amount of ingredients used in making the beer. We paid $4 for a hand pumped E.S.B., and $3 for other draft beers.

If you don't choose to eat, you may, with beer in hand, wander throughout the rooms of "the Goose" checking out old pictures and memorabilia of

The North Side Goose Island Brewpub

Goose Island, 1800 N. Clybourn Ave., is Chicago's best brewpub featuring excellent food, amazing beers, and great rooms for pool and partying.

Chicago as well as several awards prominently displayed from the Great American Beer Festival that Goose Island beers have earned over the years. You also have the option of shooting a few rounds of pool on one of the new championship-size pool tables. Rental is $10 per hour in the evenings, cheaper during the day.

After all this wandering and drinking, you may decide that you will eat after all. Good choice. Goose Island's menu is nothing if not interesting. Wherever you choose to sit, you'll find a basket of seasoned potato chips and a jar of sweet/hot mustard. The chips are a definite must try, especially if you're trying to work your way through the entire selection of beers on a single night. Appetizers can be traditional, however, if you're getting bored with mozzarella sticks, etc., I recommend the garlic, shrimp and pesto pizza. The beef burger is a good and traditional offering, but again, I'd suggest the unusual Garlic Lamb Burger for those seeking something different. Lunch or dinner should run about $12 with appetizer and sandwich.

Having met a few people who hold a Goose Island MBA, I must confess that I am envious. Pick up a listing for yourself of the year-round selection of 40 Goose Island beers and you too may feel compelled towards higher education.

I plan to start my fall/winter term immediately.

— *Bill Stephenson*

Sean Banaszkiewicz and Heather Kaminski enjoy the famous 'Boot' at The Great Beer Palace, 4128 N. Lincoln.

The Great Beer Palace

4128 N. Lincoln Ave.
773-525-4906
Hours: 1 p.m. to 2 a.m. Monday to Thursday, noon to 2 a.m. Friday and Sunday, noon to 3 a.m. Saturday

The bar that is "Open for Beer" is a nice place to sample beers from Germany in authentic German mugs while eating pretzels and hot mustard. This part of Lincoln Avenue is very German. The native tounge can be heard for blocks and The Great Beer Palace is no exception.

What really separates this place from the others is the "Viking Raid," where patrons can earn a Viking helmet for conquering a set number of German beers. Another great drinking game here is the boot where patrons order a glass boot filled with beer and pass it around. The person who finishes the boot off, has to buy the next one. We encourage folks to take a cab here.

Beer prices range from $2.50 for a quarter liter to $7.50 for one liter. Domestic beers cost $1.75.

Taps include Woodchuck Cider, Chapeau, Spaten, Newcastle Brown Ale, Bass Ale, Guinness Stout, Gosser Pilsner, Bitburger, Pilsner Urquell, Gosser Dark, Kostritzer Black Beer, Beck's Dark, Erdinger Weiss, Pschorr Weiss, Kutcher Alt, BBK Kaiser Pilsner, BBK Marzen, and Konig Pilsner. In the spring look for Maifest beers and in the fall look for Oktoberfest beers.

Food is served all day and night.

In the summer, the bar opens its beer garden which is really nice. Vines wrap up and down the neighboring buildings and even crawl above the seats forming an awesome effect of a natural roof. During the day, the vines and umbrellas offer protection from the sun. At night, the garden is well lit with lights at the door.

The Great Beer Palace is just a really fun place to go and barflies shouldn't miss it.

Green Mill

4802 N. Broadway Ave.
773-878-5552
Hours: noon to 4 a.m. Sunday to Friday,
noon to 5 a.m. Saturday

Chicago ruefully has progress to thank for the systematic razing of some of its most historic organized-crime-related landmarks including Dion O'Banion's flower shop, the garage at 2122 N. Clark St. where the St. Valentine's Day Massacre occurred, and the alley where Dillinger was killed.

Maybe Chicago thusly has the tortured spirits of these places to thank for the resilience and the lasting popularity that has kept standing one of the most colorful relics from the scurrilous yet ultimately history-shaping chapter in the city's history: The Green Mill.

According to old newspaper articles, The Green Mill opened in 1907 as a roadhouse diner and restop for the parades of mourners traveling to and from St. Bonaventure Cemetery and steadily grew in size, clientele and popularity to the point where in the mid-1920s, it was the largest and most notable nightclub in the nation and became the anchor, along with the Aragon Ballroom, the Uptown Theatre and the Riviera, of the world's most popular entertainment complex.

With a series of roaring dance floors on a second floor that encompassed most of the corner of Broadway and Lawrence avenues, the promise of the finest of liquor and women and music below, and a huge private garden in the building's courtyard, the Green Mill served as the perfect escape from the puritanical rigors of the religious and prohibitionist right. Attracting the white-gloved and tuxedoed "haves" of the underworld, entertainment and political circles, the Green Mill also was a bastion against the tremors of the impending Depression that was soon to rock the country.

"Machine Gun" Jack McGurn, notorious as the principle gunman in the St. Valentine's Day Massacre, was a part-owner of the club in the 1920s and 1930s and subsequently brought in his clan of heavies including dubious names such as Anthony "Big Tuna" Accardo, Mickey Cohen and Fred "Shotgun Ziegler" Goetz, as regular patrons. Also attracting a dubious crowd was infamous moll Texas Guinan, who acquired the Green Mill's sublet as a ghost payroller of sorts and grew to become the country's most famous and sought-after late-night hostess.

This olio of nightly and oftentimes night-like characters gave itself to an atmosphere that was uneasy as it was festive. And like a constantly-run pressure cooker, this atmosphere occasionally blew. The most notable of these releases involved legendary entertainer Joe E. Lewis, who unfortunately got involved in a war between underground factions arguing over performing rights and who, on Nov. 10, 1927, was subsequently beaten, slashed and de-toungued him in his Uptown hotel room.

Barfly Green Mill-Griffins Public House

The perpetrators who ordered this attack were never fully determined, but a truckload of both evidence and common sense indicated strongly that the main perpetrator was none other than the Green Mill's most famous regular, Al Capone. Although the club that he owned was across the intersection at the spot now occupied by Equator Club in the historic Broadway-Lawrence Building, Capone preferred to hold court nightly at The Green Mill.

An authentic autographed photo of him sits on top of the Mill's baby grand and serves as a constant homage to his presence as does the private right-front booth where he and his cohorts always sat. Covered in green velvet and specially situated in order to accomodate a clear view of both the front and back doors, the booth was recently reintroduced in its original glory during a massive restoration in 1986.

This restoration, a successful attempt to return the existing Green Mill to its heyday splendor, also fully uncovered and retreated the origianl mahogany bar and the intricate art-deco wall appointments. Most exciting, however, was the discovery of a vast network of underground tunnels connecting various Uptown establishments to each other and to Lake Michigan. Thought to have been originally used for coal transport, the recent findings of impromptu bulwarks and barricades, trap doors that open up into key places in the various buildings (Including one on the floor behind the aforementioned mahogany bar), and even an ancient wooden coffin stuffed with a plethora of old financial records and slips, lends credence to the theory that these tunnels were used for much more than simply fuel conveyance.

These days The Green Mill no longer relies on coal, but it does rely on the legends that the tunnels and the other Prohibition-era relics symbolize to keep its visitors coming in and to keep its regular patrons entertained. There are a multitude of other clubs in the city where one can go to hear some of the world's hottest jazz, or to be enlightened by some fo the most innovative poets and writers that the city has to offer. But at no other place can one so vividly hearken past to the Windy City's by-gone days by sitting in the very seat from which Capone ruled Chicago, treading the same floors that played host to a veritable "Who's Who" of the FBI's classic most wanted list, or even getting a pilsner glass filled to the brim with Schlitz on tap for a mere 75 cents, as one can get at The Green Mill.

-- Johnny Masiulewicz

Griffins Public House
2710 N. Halsted St.
773-525-7313
Hours: 4 p.m. to 2 a.m. Monday to Friday,
4 p.m. to 3 a.m. Saturday

Upon first entering Griffins Public House one of the first thoughts that crept to mind was that this will make for a great hideout. Griffins is a great bar to go to if you want to avoid the day. It is dark and comfortable with plenty of char-

117

The North Side Griffins Public House-Grizzly's Lodge

acter.

The dimly lit bar is long and narrow with a smattering of tables. There is a constant game of pool or darts available. There is a small beer garden in the back that should be taken advantage of whenever possible. They also have a pretty good selection on the jukebox.

When I first sat down, I was greeted warmly by an affable bartender. He came complete with his own Irish brogue. The beer selection is pretty well varied. They have the regular selection you would expect on tap, while also having a cooler full of microbrews for those of us who like to mix up or enjoy beer sampling.

If you want to get serious about drinking, there is an outlet for you. Infused vodka shots are an excellent way to get tanked and not even notice. These are shots of Finlandia vodka that have been filtered through different fruits which allows for each shot to go down quickly. I recommend the strawberry. There is also an infused tequila shot, but I couldn't tell what it was being soaked in and wasn't feeling that brave.

If you want something to eat you can get it from upstairs. Bearboy Gourmet Subs is located directly above Griffins. They have a decent menu and you don't have to leave your barstool to get at it. The subs are dropped from above through a convenient plastic tube that runs between the two establishments. It's worth ordering food just to watch the novel delivery.

The clientele is a friendly one. There is a mix of young and old with good humor being a common trait. The bar is neighbor to a Chicago Firehouse, so good story telling is available on a regular basis.

Griffins Public House is a treat. Time seems to go by at a more reasonable pace there. It proved to be a shady place for sunny people.

— *J. Quilter*

Grizzly's Lodge
3832 N. Lincoln
773-281-5112
Hours: 11a.m. to 2 a.m. daily,
11a.m. to 3 p.m. for Sunday brunch

Family fun with sustenance, sports, and swill. The Great White North meets the North Side with the lodge theme done up to the extreme. The front offers a small, rectangular bar seperate from the dining area. Yes, this place offers meals and plenty of them to choose from.

There are tables as well as booths to sit at and try one of the specialties. Plus, the booths along the wall have personal TVs set up to watch what ever game you, or your group, prefer. The tables in the middle are center stage to either a large-screen TV or a small stage on the reverse side where a band drops in to play.

If not eating or watching the game, head to the back where there is a small room with both a pool table and an even smaller bar. Directly outside the

118

The good folks at Grizzly's Lodge, 3832 N. Lincoln Ave., winners of Barfly's 1997 Best Bar and Best Bartender contest.

windows of this room is a beer garden.

The garden is set up with 10 tables many with parasols to shade the table from the sun. Eat, drink or do both out here. The garden stays pretty quiet being set back far enough off of Lincoln Avenue, but the sound of the "el" in the background ruins the Northern lodge-type atmosphere experienced walking through the place.

It's a good sports bar-type restaurant. Definately a good family restaurant/bar. It's a fairly calm crowd. Ages range from mainly 30s on up and the main type of music is country/western, but no cowboys with attitudes.

Beers run $1.75 for domestic pints and on up for more premium beers like Bass or Guinness. If you're tired of beer, toss one of Grizzly's specialty drinks back. They have great names like Yukon Slush, Hair of the Bear, Log Splitter, and Klondike Mary.

Gunther Murphy's
1638 W. Belmont Ave.
773-472-5139
Hours: 2 p.m. to 2 a.m. Sunday to Friday,
2 p.m. to 3 a.m. Saturday

The North Side Gunther Murphy's-Guthries

My friend Dawn and I wandered down Belmont Avenue and found ourselves in Gunther Murphy's where we were greeted by Eamonn Stafford, who is probably the friendliest bartender in Chicago.

Stafford said he has been bartending at Gunther Murphy's for about four years and considers himself a part of the furniture.

Gunther Murphy's is a dimly lit comfortable little pub that is a local mecca for Irish exchange students as well as a growing clientele of non-Irish patrons who are discovering the place as a venue for live music.

Bands perform in a backroom so that patrons who want to relax and have a drink, have a choice as to whether they want to hear the band or not. If live music is your thing, it is imperative that you stop in and grab a schedule of the upcoming bands which includes perennial favorites New Duncan Imperials as well as the band that has got to have the coolest name — Torturing Elvis.

To drink, Gunther Murphy's has an excellent selection of beers. The tappers look as busy as a call girl at a Shriner's convention. All of the best beers are represented here like Harp, Guinness, Woodpecker Cider. Stafford is very adept at serving them properly to his patrons. His rapport with folks his quite a site, even the pretty young girls who twist his arm and force him to do shots with them.

There is the obligatory fireplace in the middle room which makes Gunther's very popular in the winter. The middle room has a lack of jukebox speakers which makes conversation very relaxing.

"It's very cozy," Dawn said.

I had to agree. I relished my thick dark beer and looked at all of the people around me drinking and talking in the inimitable brogue.

The backbar is pretty standard issue with a variation of green lights (what color did you expect) behind the beveled glass which lent authenticity to the pub feel. Another cool component is mile markers posted in the bar that are straight from Ireland. Stafford wasn't clear on why they don't use these particular signs in Ireland anymore but I had to wonder that maybe it has something to do with the fact that they are hanging in a bar in Chicago.

Anyway, Dawn and I agree (again) that this place is highly recommended for the serious drinker as well as someone who just wants to have a good time and be treated well by the friendliest bartender in the city.

We will definitely see you there.

— Paul Barile

Guthries

1300 WAddison St.
773-477-2900
Hours: 4 p.m. to 2 a.m. weekdays,
2 p.m. to 3 a.m. Saturday̦noon to 2 a.m. Sunday

When a building has been in existence in the Wrigleyville neighborhood for

Barfly Guthries-Ham Tree Inn

more than 100 years, it's bound to have at least one ghost. It seems that Guthries is no exception.

Normally an unobtrusive "Cheers"-like corner bar , even during the baseball season when it's inundated with suburbanites, stories of ghostly activity have been reported by both employees and patrons alike since the bar moved into the building in 1986.

Whoever the ghost is, it most often times has manifested itself with ghostly footsteps across the floor, usually after closing and usually when the remaining employees are working in the basement. The last time it happened, upon hearing the footsteps a bartender rushed up these basement stairs and the steps immediately stopped when he reached the top. The bartender saw no one.

The owner of the bar, however , has seen the ghost: it was standing in an upstairs window and was dressed in what appeared to be a 19th Century-style military uniform.

There have also been witnessed reports of televisions turning themselves mysteriously on and off, enough so as to put a real scare into the staff.

Not too long ago, a woman who is known to have a special sensitivity to the realm of the undead came into the bar . Upon entering she immediately knew that there was some kind of presence in the bar. But she could also sense that it was a benevolent one.

Having a quaff with this friendly ghost, (the staff does actually leave libations for it at times) can be done every day. Guthrie's offers up for both the physical and the ethereal world a wide selection of domestic and imported beer and also serves a menu of typical bar fare including specials during the Bears games.

-- Johnny Masiulewicz

Ham Tree Inn
5333 N. Milwaukee Ave.
773-792-2072
Hours: noon to 2 p.m. Sunday to Friday, noon to 3 p.m. Saturday

Without a doubt, the Ham Tree is one of the best neighborhood bars located on the Northwest Side of Chicago. Not only does it have a cool name but the Ham Tree features 101 different bottled beers at reasonable prices.

The bar keeps its beer mugs and large glasses in an old-time refrigerator. There are not many bars around that keep its glasses cold.

The cost, $2 for Miller and Bud products, $2.75 for specialty beers like Samuel Adams and other micros, $2.25 for imports like Molson, and $3.75 for Tucher Weiss. There are six beers on tap, Killians Red, Old Style, Leinenkugel's, Miller Lite, Honey Brown Lager, and Gemutlichkeit. The prices for the cold and clean-tasting tap brews is quite reasonable. A 10-ounce mug for domestics is $1.25 and for imports $1.75. For an 18-ounce glass, domestics are $1.75 and imports are $2.50. In addition, pitchers are $5 for domestics and

The North Side Ham Tree Inn-Harp and Shamrock

$8 for the imports.

The crowd that frequents the Ham Tree is mixed. In the day time, there are the old regulars while at night there is usually a mix of blue- and white-collar workers. As the night progresses, the crowd can get younger with college students and softball teams.

Besides drinking, the bar has two television sets and a large screen for the viewing pleasure of patrons. Sport programs are mostly shown. There is a pool table in the back of the bar, two dart boards, a video game, a foosball table and a jukebox which ranges from the Gin Blossoms to the Beatles.

If you want to get away from the crowd, the Ham Tree does have a small beer garden in the back of its establishment. But you better hurry, there is only three picnic tables. This spot is usually the first to be taken.

To eat, there are chips, peanuts and popcorn. If you want to get adventurous, there are frozen pizzas available.

If you are ever in the Jefferson Park area, the Ham Tree is without a doubt worth a stop and many more. There are great cold beers available with good friendly service. This drinking hole is located just north of Foster on Milwaukee Avenue.

— Pete Schmugge

Harp and Shamrock
1641 W. Fullerton Ave.
773-248-0123
Hours: 1 p.m. to 2 a.m. Monday to Thursday,
11 a.m. to 2 a.m. Friday and Sunday,
11 a.m. to 3 a.m. Saturday

Wanna know where all the hard-core Irish dart competitors disappear to after tiring of the dart season? This is the place, with a couple of dart boards, and plenty of plaques. The bar is a total of two rooms, but mainly everything is up front. There is a bar, three Draw Poker machines, a couple tables, a dart board, and a jukebox. The bar offers the main beers in domestics, along with Heineken. There are also imports, like Harp in bottles and Guinness in those groovy cans with CO_2 catridges which give the beer that tap feel.

There is a dart board up front between the bar and the windows overlooking Fullerton Avenue. The other board is in the back in a more spacious room. The boards are both cork, of course, and they do sell flights and other dart accessories, in case some repair is needed. If playing in teams, head to the back where there is more room to move around, instead of cramming into the corner. In the back there is only the cigarette machine, bathrooms (located in the front of this room, not near the board), and a television to keep tabs on the game.

The jukebox has a handful of Irish CDs, and even an Irish drinking songs CD. There are also the old standbys and some latest hits. Usually, a range of these will be flowing from the speakers.

122

Barfly Harp and Shamrock-Harry's On Elston

The bartenders are extremely nice folks and patrons get treated well at the Harp and Shamrock. It's definitely worth a visit.

Harry's On Elston
5943 N. Elston Ave.
773-774-4166
Hours: 8 a.m. to 2 a.m. Sunday to Friday, Saturday until 3 a.m.

Nothing beats an air-conditioned bar in the middle of a brutal Chicago summer. Harry's On Elston is no exception.

The outside looks welcoming, a few beer signs glowing in the window. The inside doesn't lack charm, either. Wood paneling rides halfway up the walls, meeting a field of green at its tops. The tiled drop ceiling is typical of the Northwest Side, as are the tile floors. The bar, with blond wood grain along its length and darker veneer in the corner, seats about 24.

The back bar is beautiful dark wood, and above the liquor sits a wonderful collection of Elvis and old car booze decanters. Track lighting showcases this collection. And mirrors along the wall opposite the bar will help you figure out what kind of shape you're in at 2 a.m., after the many beer signs have had their marketing way with you.

Has this ever happened to you? You've got the munchies and you ask the individual behind the bar for that beckoning ounce bag of Doritos. This otherwise wonderful bartender then sodomizes you for $1.50 or more for that bag. This blows. Harry's, however, has the prices right on the rack. Chips and peanuts costs 50 cents, while cashews come in at 75 cents. This is the only food Harry's serves, but for about $2.50 you can have all the saturated fat the USDA requires for an entire day.

The crowd seemed made up of a mixture of ages and occupations. The owner, Brian, confirmed this.

"We get a lot of tradesmen," he said. "I thought it might be hard to mix the younger crowd with the older, but they blended well."

Everyone at Harry's seemed not only to know each other, but talk to each other, as well. Brian added, "This is a great neighborhood tavern."

I hope he didn't think I was going to argue with that.

Here's a tip from your fellow barfly, Bud. If you need work done — construction, plumbing, electrical or tile work — hang out in the Northwest Side taverns like the contractors do. If someone is not involved in the type of work you need, odds are they know someone who is. Hang out in my neighborhood if you want to support some crack-headed thief and buy stolen tools to do the job yourself.

As typical as Harry's is for this part of the city, one thing struck me as odd. These people play some pretty glum music. The jukebox spits out Van

The North Side Harry's On Elston-Hidden Shamrock

Morrison, Simon and Garfunkle, Springsteen at his most depressing and some country. When Elton John's "Rocket Man" came on, it sounded uplifting.

Even odder was the way the regulars stood around the machine, as if to prevent anyone from playing a few notes of happiness. Hell, they seemed upbeat enough. "Sympathy for the Devil" did come through the speakers after all that negative stuff. That made me feel better. Perhaps it was a lone sad soul in the joint with a $5 bill. I even heard some REO Speedwagon.

The prices are right, sad music aside. Domestic bottles are $1.75, and a game of pool runs 50 cents. Tap selections are limited to Lite and Genuine Draft, but the bottled liquor selection is fantastic.

Harry's is a nice community tavern. It even sponsors sports teams. People bring their dogs to this bar, and their kids (just don't let them bite the dogs). While it may seem like just a regular gin mill to the untrained eye, remember that there is no such thing as a typical bar. I believe they all have living, breathing souls. That's especially so with one as community- and family-oriented as Harry's.

The only thing on which I can fault Harry's is the one news clipping hanging from a wall. It appears that some jackass named Bill Granger likes to denounce Cubs fans and print it in the Daily Herald newspaper. Fuck him.

Why does someone named Brian own a place named Harry's on Elston? I don't know. I didn't get a chance to ask. I was too busy soaking up the peaceful atmosphere at one of my new regular stops.

— Bud

Hidden Shamrock
2723 N. Halsted St.
773-883-0304
Hours: 1 a.m. to 2 a.m. Sunday to Friday
11 a.m. to 3 a.m. Saturday

When you go to most bars in Chicago and say to the bartender: "I'll have a pint of Guinness," it usually doesn't feel quite right. However, at the Hidden Shamrock, with its Downtown Dublin feel, it would seem rather awkward to say to the bartender: "Budlight please."

The Hidden Shamrock has two rooms each with a bar and fireplace. The front room has tables where you can sit and order Irish food or listen to live entertainment and the back room has pool tables and a big screen television for sports. The bar has lots of stained wood and brass to emphasize the Irish pub feel. In addition, this place is one of the only bars in the city where you can purchase an Irish World Cup victory T-shirt.

The patrons represent the Lincoln Park/Lakeview area. They are well-dressed, groomed and perfumed. Yet, one gets the feeling that all is welcome here. Hey, they let me in.

Higgins Tavern
3259 N. Racine
773-281-7637
Hours: 7 a.m. to 2 a.m. Sunday to Friday
7 a.m. to 3 a.m. Saturday

Hungry for some bratwurst, hambur gers and the like and want to wash it down with an imported or domestic? Then Higgins is the place to do so between the hours of 10 a.m. to 10 p.m. when, as the sign reads, the "ITCHEN" is open, serving "RATS" instead of "BRATS." There are other witty signs like, "The 10 Stages of Drunkeness," to measure how the evening is progressing.

Choose from the bar, from protruding wall tables, or one of the round tables which seats about six to enjoy a meal at. Have a drink and take a breath of cigar-flavored air. The menu offers a variety of bar-food delights such as a $2 hot dog and a $6.50 ribeye steak sandwich. Watch the game on a wide-screen television, bask in the glory of great football moments especially those of the Michigan State Spartans, or toss a few coins into the jukebox to hear some popular music or movie soundtracks.

Domestic beers are $2.25 up to $3.25 for bottles, or you can grab a can of selected brews for $2. There is a choice of Bud and Miller products, as well as San Francisco's Anchor Steam. Imports go from $2.75 to $3.25. Selections also include Molson, Bass and Harp and pints of Guinness for $3.50 and domestic glasses for a buck and a half. They also have pitchers for $6.50 of domestic taps. The popcorn is free. Canned brew , when applicable, is the default, so ask for a bottle if you want a bottle.

The crowd is mainly locals, regulars and male. It is a close knit bar, as the bartender will shoot a friendly game of dice with the boys. The age range is 30ish on up, but during prime eating times, the crowd varies more.

The Hob-Nob Tavern
3932 W. Irving Park Rd.
773-588-2385
Hours: 2 p.m. to 2 a.m. weekdays,
11 a.m. to 3 a.m. Saturday,
11 a.m. to 2 a.m. Sunday

"It's the large assortment of beers and the pretty waitresses that keeps people coming back," said manager Rich Stacho.

The bar opened in spring 1996. On the night I visited, the crowd of mostly younger happy people sat around the bar or under the impressive collection of beer mirrors. The feeling was very relaxed and easy.

The North Side Hob-Nob Tavern

The bar itself, and all of the tables look very noirish with very slick black marbelite finish, like the kind of bar Mickey Spillane would slam his drink on. As a matter of fact, the whole interior seems very slick and polished which, frankly, is not the hallmark for that neighborhood.

The walls are unfinished brick which adds to the mystique but even they suggest an affectation rather than simply being "under construction." The walls that face the street are glass which would allow for contemplative moments with your drink watching the traffic glide down Irving Park Road.

The beer cooler adds to the whole picture with an inviting red light which actually makes the beer look sexy. I am not kidding. The sight of that Bass Pale Ale bathed in a deep-red light gave me unnatural yearnings.

"It's got a corner bar attitude with a downtown look," said regular Alex Eliades. "Really friendly, but very classy."

George and Bill, the owners of the Hob-Nob are also very interested in catering to their customers needs. On Sundays and Monday nights, they put out a free buffet. I'm not talking finger food here. These guys put out roasted chicken and sub sandwiches. On Thanksgiving there was turkey.

The bar pizza that they serve is Taylor Street which, I did not have a chance to taste, but it is nice to see someone serving something other than the (once great) Home Run Inn frozen pizzas.

They also try to stock beers that their regular customers drink, as if the current array of bottled beers wasn't impressive enough.

"If you'll drink it, they'll try to get it for you," Stacho said.

If you are interested in playing pool, they are in a league and they are working toward getting in a dart league. These are two staples for the bar game crowd. This is one of the few bars that I have seen that actually has room around the table to shoot.

They have three TV sets and a rack for a fourth which, on a late Friday night, was playing a college basketball game. I am sure if you are there on a Sunday afternoon or a Monday night, you will have no trouble seeing the football game.

As if all this wasn't enough, they are currently preparing to open an addition which would give the bar a horseshoe effect as well as increase the good spirits that they are providing for North Side drinkers. They are also planning a holiday dance to break in the new space.

So if you are ready for a change of pace in your "corner" bar experience, rush on down to Hob-Nob and check out the pretty waitresses and the wide assortment of bottled beers such as Hacker Pschorr, Sado Creak, and Guinness Stout.

— Paul Barile

Hog Head McDunna's
1505 W. Fullerton Ave.
773-929-0944
Hours: 11 a.m. to 2 a.m. Sunday to Friday,
11 a.m. to 3 p.m. Saturday

A tavern that balances lots while sacrificing little, Hog Head McDunna's biggest drawback is most likely its location. Off the beaten track that is Lincoln or Halsted avenues, this tavern resides further west to offer most of what bar patrons seek as they venture into the night.

Like a good soundtrack to carry you to the bottom of your libations? Live music is scheduled two to three nights a week with cover charges between $3 and $6, and the jukebox has Elvis, Sinatra and Bell Biv Devoe, with plenty more to supplement that variety.

Two pool tables and four English dart boards are spread between the two main rooms, with the dart boards placed out of the way enough that no one will go home with an unexpectedly pierced ear. The large fireplace, with openings to both rooms, adds warmth along with a cozy ski chalet effect.

The three regular television monitors, combined with the single projection screen, make Hog Head McDunna's more than adequate for watching sports, and if you get tired go to the back of the front room and crash; it looks like a basement back there what with the sofas and total lack of lighting.

Both tap beer and bottles cost $2.75 or $3, while mixed drinks go no higher than $4.50. Dedicated samplers can choose from 11 beers on tap, including the bar's own Hog Head Ale.

The tavern is big on specials like wings, chili and bloody Mary's. The menu is not extravagant, but the food is reliable and the prices range from $4 to $6.

The bar's location is away from other city bars, which makes cabs rarer than they should be, although Hog Head's popularity is slowly improving that situation. The truth is that while this tavern does require somewhat of a special effort to visit, enjoying it requires no effort at all.

Holiday Club
1471 N. Milwaukee
773-486-0686
Hours: 6 p.m. to 2 a.m. Sunday to Friday
6 p.m. to 3 a.m. Saturday

Spicing up that Sunday night drink-fest became one bar easier when Holiday Club premiered its "Bamboo Lounge" night on Sunday April 14, 1996. For this evening, this Wicker Park bar is transformed into a tiki bar.

"There's no real good tiki bars in the area," said owner Tim Juliusson.

Juliusson, an enthusiast of 1940s and 1950s retro club atmosphere, wanted to

Don't miss the Bamboo Lounge on Sundays at Holiday Club, 1471 N. Milwaukee Ave.

experiment with a new feel to his place while still keeping "period correct." Realizing that the area was lacking in such a treat as a tiki bar, Juliusson decided to give it a try

Opting to give his regulars a choice of atmosphere, Juliusson decorated only the back room for the Sunday evening trip. He covered the walls with bamboo mats, tiki masks and palm leaves while placing artificial palm trees throughout the room. Keeping with the usually dark tiki bar lighting scheme, he replaced the normal soft, white lighting with red, blue and green bulbs, a string of garden lamps and candles. The evening drink menu features a selection of blender drinks, such as Coladas and Margaritas complete with special glasses shaped as tiki statues, coconuts and volcanos with a little bamboo drink umbrella.

The host of the evening is DJ Dickie Davenport, a lounge aficionado who really gets the atmosphere going.

On every other day, the Holiday is completely covered in early 1960s, art-deco-type paint and neat knick knacks like the ceiling lamps. There is a pool table in the back and a good amount of seating, including window ledge padded seats. The best thing about the inside has to be the jukebox with a barrage of great tunes from great bands throughout the selection list. If there is one particular reason to go here, the jukebox is definitely the reason.

In the summer, the Holiday has a beer garden located on the side street Honore. The seats and tables are both plastic. The "garden" really is more like that of an outdoor cafe. It's an excellent spot for a summer drink.

-- Phil Brandt

Hollywood East
5650 N. Broadway
773-271-4711
Hours: roughly 10 p.m. to 4 a.m. daily

At tourist traps all over the island of Jamaica, you can buy T-shirts emblazoned with the word "irie." The word, which loosely translates to "way cool," conjures images of ganja-smoking Rastafarians, even though the wearer of the shirt is more likely a CPA from Dayton.

"Irie" isn't the true byword of the islands, though. That would be "soon come" — it will happen when it happens. Hey, relax, you're on vacation.

Like that greenhorn tourist from Dayton on his first night in Negril, I was a little worried when we showed up at Hollywood East at 9:30 p.m. on a recent Saturday to find the doors locked. The club is supposed to open at 7 p.m. Owner Pierre Bingue promptly let us in, though.

"I guess we're early," I said, surveying the empty tables.

"Yeah, you're early," Bingue said. "The action starts around 10:30."

Palm trees and beach scenes brightened the walls of the hangar-like room. Colored lights strung around the bar and dance floor, while tinsel garlands completed the illusion that we'd stepped off a dreary stretch of Broadway and into a dreadlock holiday. I understood: Soon come.

Since we had some time to kill before the natives got restless, my husband and I grabbed a couple of stools at the bar and ordered two bottles of Heineken. It turns out, we were in good company. Bingue told us that Heineken is his biggest mover, closely followed by Guinness Stout.

"It depends on the crowd, though," he said. "Some nights it's a lot of rum and coke."

Hollywood East first opened its doors in the summer of 1986. Haitian-born Bingue described the experience as a "dream that went wild." Four years later, he added a restaurant specializing in Jamaican "jerk" barbecue and soul food.

He soon found, though, that the money is in the drinks. Now, he limits the menu to a couple of nightly specials available until 3 a.m. My husband and I split an order of curried chicken, one of the evening's specials. It turned out to be a delicious combination of spicy-sweet stewed chicken with beans and rice.

As we finished picking our chicken bones clean, couples and small groups dressed for a serious night out began to fill the tables at the room's edges. I started to wish I'd put more effort into my appearance, instead of just throwing on my big-shirt-and-leggings uniform. By now it was a little after 10 p.m., and the reggae band was going through its sound check.

This band, Charles "Organaire" Cameron and the Sunshine Festival, plays frequently at Hollywood East on Saturdays. Thursday nights showcase Latin bands, while Fridays feature a deejay spinning house music.

Cameron, who played harmonica with Bob Marley in the '60s, led his tight band through a set of upbeat original songs. Folks grooving on the music, both in pairs and on their own, filled the dance floor. Even the most rhythm-impaired couldn't miss this beat.

By midnight, the place was standing-room-only, and the crowd at the bar was three deep. We stopped at the booth near the door to buy the band's CD before stepping back into that cold, dreary stretch of Broadway, fighting the deflated feeling that it was fun while it lasted, but vacation's over and tomorrow will come too soon.

So stop by Hollywood East for a rum and coke. Pretend that muggy lake-effect breeze is a cool tropical zephyr.

Visitors to Hollywood East should call the bar before arriving to check on opening time. It's also wise to check beforehand for a cover charge.

— June Hathaway Vigor

Home Tavern
2828 N. Lincoln Ave.
no phone
Hours: 4 p.m. to 2 a.m. daily

Looking for a classy bar filled with attractive, well-dressed, pleasant-smelling hipsters and exotic beers and spirits? Don't go to the Home Tavern. Nestled on Lincoln Avenue between Thurston's and Elbo Room to the north and Delilah's to the south, Home Tavern is anything but hip.

When you sit under the bright, fluorescent lights beaming down on the bar and take in the dusty collection of bottles on the shelves, the atmosphere is much more Franklin Park than Lincoln Park.

What Home Tavern does have, however, is cheap tap beer and plenty of available bar stools. I first found the place after squeezing my way out of Elbo Room one crowded Friday night. Though I'd paid good money to see the featured band, the packed-cattle atmosphere and half-hour wait for a beer had led me to abandon my friends and hit the street. Figuring I'd meet them out front after the show, I then wondered just where the hell I could go that would be any better. Practically every bar within walking distance was sure to be just as crowded and expensive.

Then I saw the Old Style sign only a short walk away. The only such sign on Lincoln for at least a dozen or more blocks. As I hoped, the bar was neither crowded or expensive. I was one of four patrons in there and at the age of 28 was a good 20 years younger than any of them. We all sat apart and paid no attention to each other.

The elderly lady behind the bar was curt and nothing more. I drank some beer and whiled away an hour watching a bad cop drama on the TV atop the old fridge in the corner. There was no line at the bathroom, no mass of bodies to be jostled by, no women to have ridiculous fantasies over, no strapping, healthy lads able to afford better beer than me, no need to try to come off as anything other than the gone-to-seed, burgeoning young alky I like to pretend I'm not becoming. For that particular evening, it was perfect.

Barfly Home Tavern-Howard's Bar and Grill

So when you're on Lincoln near Elbo Room and need a few drinks but can't stomach the place, give Home Tavern a chance. It ain't fun, it ain't hip, it ain't a place to get laid or even a place to talk. It's a place to drink, period. And we can all use a joint like that once in awhile.

— *Bill Franz*

Hopleaf
5145 N. Clark St.
773-334-9857
Hours: noon to 2 p.m. weekdays,
noon to 3 a.m. Saturday
11 a.m. to 2 p.m. Sunday

Up in Andersonville is the "Friendliest bar on the North Side." This "friendly" crowd comprised mainly of neighborhood folks are prepared to defend their bar from carloads of suburbanites or cab loads of city idiots.

If you are able to sneak in you may find a huge beer selection ranging from $1 Huber bottles to $6 Pumpkin or Oatmeal stout. Tap beers such as Bass, Guinness, Berghoff and Pilsner start at $1.50 a pint. Leine bottles are $1.50, Weiss bier is $3.50 and wine is $2 for a glass. In addition, there's a different cheap beer available in pitchers for $5 each month as well as bags of peanuts and spinach pie for sale and free pretzels and chips. On Sunday mornings the bar offers coffee and bagels with lox and cream cheese.

The Hopleaf consists of one room containing a horseshoe-shape bar , a television, and the bartenders crank out from their stereo classic old 45-inch record-type music. The place is well ventilated with ceiling fans and open windows so non-smokers aren't overcome with tobacco fumes. There's also some comfortable stools, booths, tables and chairs that are pretty much occupado whether its noon on Monday or midnight on Friday or Saturday.

Howard's Bar and Grill
152 E. Ontario St.
312-787-5269
Hours: 11 a.m. to 1 a.m. Monday to Saturday,
11 a.m. to 7 p.m. Sunday

As long-time patrons and new customers alike will agree, it is a pretty nice place to hang out and have a beer or two. Although seating is a little limited without the outdoor patio open, there is usually room enough for a couple or a small group. If you are into a quiet pub for an after-work drink, or a peaceful dinner, this is the place for you.

Howard's patronage is mainly the post-work crowd, or Downtown shoppers on the way home. This, and the inevitable playing of Frank Sinatra on the juke-box, allows you to relax and put a couple down without the hustle and bustle of

The North Side Howard's Bar and Grill-Hudson Club

a large club or tavern.

Howard's has a limited selection of tap beer and drinks, and the menu consists mainly of "bar food" (cheeseburgers, fries, chicken wings, etc.); but the prices are reasonable, they are open for lunch, and the service is always cheerful. Just like any respectable bar, though, "The customer is seldom right."

— *David Hayes*

The Hudson Club

504 N. Wells St.
312-467-1947
Hours: 2 to 10:30 p.m. Monday to Thursday,
2 to 11 p.m. Friday, and from 5:30 to 11 p.m. Saturday.
The Hudson Club is currently closed on Sunday.
Valet parking is available for $6.

My first revelation as I walked into the Hudson Club was the mere reality that I don't get out enough. I was in complete awe as I took in the view just past the huge brushed aluminum door.

Inspired by the supper clubs of the 1940s, and the Hudson car of that era, Steve Soble and Howard Natinsky joined together with designer Jordan Mozer to create River North's hottest new restaurant and bar.

The "old" 1940s supper clubs had everything facing in the same direction in order to see the big-name entertainers who took the stage.

"Our stage is the bar," said manager Larry Dwyer. "It's where most of our energy and activity goes on."

He wasn't kidding. The bar takes up 50 feet, and seats up to 60 patrons. Underneath a large silver-lined mirror rests a striking display of 100 or more top-shelf liquors. The bar's centerpiece is its Winekeeper system, which allows it to maintain 100 wines by displacing oxygen with nitrogen.

You can purchase the wines by the bottle, glass or flight. A flight is a taste of four wines that are related to one another by grape, varietal, geographic region or style. The flights range from white to red, starting at $9.25 and going as high as $36.25.

The beer selection is just as majestic, with 20 different draft choices and 50 bottled. The choices range from Miller to Blue Fin Stout. If beer-tasting is your thing, there are three flight seven-ounce portions from which to choose.

Viewing the rather large, 175-guest dining room, my eyes were as inquisitive as a child's. Maroon velvet draped the two- and four-person booths and funky Star Trek-like chairs. Small white candles sit burning in the ashtrays.

"We took the big space that we had and looked to achieve intimacy," Dwyer said.

And a job well done. The customers appear serene under the silver aluminum replicas of the Hudson car tail-lights.

The menu of eclectic American cuisine with French and Asian influences was

Barfly Hudson Club-Huettenbar

created by Hudson's executive chef Paul Larson.

The hors d'oeuvres are plentiful, 26 to be exact. They range from assorted caviar and oyster shooters to tuna rolls.

The appetizers are smaller in number, five cold and five hot. They're all under $9. Things like chicken wings and potato skins are missing. They're replaced by corn-flack crusted shrimp and ahi tuna carpaccio. Salads, wood-fired pizzas and fruit and cheese plates are also available.

The 12 entrees range in price from $13.95 to $25.95, and come with sides of potatoes and vegetables. Numerous choices of Scotches, bourbons, ports and brandies accompany the dessert and coffee menu.

The Hudson Club also features a 25-guest lounge with sofas and armchairs for cigar and pipe smokers. A separate party room that will hold up to 65 people is coming this month.

Waitress Staci said that the Hudson Club has a good thing going. It's more a word-of-mouth place, because they don't advertise.

Customer Paula agreed, saying that she heard about the club through friends at work. She brought along her friend from out of town, Tina.

"I'd come back," they both said at the same time. "The food was very, very good," Paula added.

So, if you're looking for impressive food, a variety of liquor, unique and exciting decor and friendly staff, the Hudson Club is the new place you don't want to miss.

— *Kristi Harrity*

The Huettenbar
4721 N. Lincoln Ave.
773-561-2507
Hours: 11 a.m. to 2 a.m. Sunday to Friday,
11 a.m. to 3 a.m. Saturday

A bit of the old world still lives on in Chicago's Lincoln Square neighborhood. Along this stretch of Lincoln Avenue can be found the Meyer Delicatessen, Chicago Brauhaus, Merz Apothecary (established in 1875), Cafe Selmarie and other storefronts with a European flavor. Nestled among them is the Huettenbar, a cozy place with the look and feel of an Alpine Hideaway.

Upon entering the barroom, the chandeliers and wood-work lend the room a welcoming warmth. A long bar runs the length of the room; several tables and a couple of booths offer ample seating. Behind the bar, a pastoral scene is painted on the wall, showing a lone lodge amidst the vastness of the Alps (loosely translated Huettenbar means "mountain hut"). Next to this, a portrait of a smiling fräulein beckoning with full mugs of beer is displayed. As you order your first round, you may recognize the woman serving you as the same one in the picture. She is Irma Frolich, owner and hostess of this establishment.

Austrian-born Irma has operated the Huettenbar for 11 years. The space has been a tavern since 1959. Chicago Brauhaus owned it prior to 1985; Irma's

The kind folks at Huettenbar, 4721 N. Lincoln Ave.

mother was a cook at the Brauhaus. When Irma found out that the bar was for sale, she decided to try her hand at the business. Formerly a production artist, she knew little about running a bar.

"My customers were the ones who taught me how to run my own place," she says, with a laugh. "I learned the trade day by day. Louie, the bartender, was here before me, and he helped greatly." Her relaxed and light-hearted attitude serve to make the place a friendly environment.

Indeed, if you're interested in sampling one of the many German liqueurs offered, you might require Irma's or Louie's assistance. Besides the familiar Jagermeister (available on tap—beware!), Westfalen Jager or Kabanes are variations of the herbal based liquid, slightly smoother and more mellow. In addition, flavorful liqueurs such as Edel-Kirlch (cherry), Echte-Kroatzbeere (blackberry) or Crazy Ananas (pineapple) can be savored.

Of course, there is beer! Ten draft selections and many more bottled brands available. On draft, some of the choices include Konig Pilsener, Spaten Lager, BBK Marzen and Kostritzer Double Dark, Boulevard Stout, a Kansas City microbrew, even makes a surprise appearance. Bottled selections are just as varied, including Dortmunder Union, Franziskaner Dark Weiss and Aventinus Dopplebock.

The beer list has expanded to include microbrews and some select domestics because the customer base has grown to new neighborhood residents and another generation of patrons, as well as the long time regulars.

The jukebox reflects the diversity of musical tastes here. Local faves like the Mighty Blue Kings, classic rock and Motown, Sinatra and Bennett and yes, German music — all are played. One selection, "Bombenstarke Fussball-und," is a nod to the soccer teams that come to drink after their games. Traditional titles, like "Das grosse Schlager Wunsch-Konzert" are listed too. During daytime hours, the Huettenbar is decidedly mellow. Classical music is played and espresso and cappuccino are served.

A regular who's been coming to the Huettenbar since it opened, summed it up.

"This place has a civility not found in most barrooms. People are friendlier, more laid back here. That's a rarity these days."

Fortunately, for Chicago barflies, they need only traverse to Lincoln Square for the same atmosphere found in that mountain hut.

— *Mickey Cotter*

The Hungry Brain
2319 W. Belmont Ave.
773-935-2118
Hours: 8 p.m. to 2 a.m. Sunday to Friday,
8 p.m. to 3 a.m. Saturday

The Hungry Brain is simply put — a really cool place to hang out. Hatched in April 1997, The Hungry Brain has nothing to prove since owners Luz Cordova and Janis White have proven that nothing will stop them from creating the type of establishment that they have desired to open for nearly a decade.

It was only appropriate that I enjoyed an ice cold bottle of Schlitz, quaffed out of a Pilsner glass, as I listened to the owners story of near failure, yet triumphant success. The Hungry Brian story is pure Chicago. A tale of tenacity and resiliency, a chronicle of never giving up.

Luz and Janis met each other in the 1980s while working together. Spending their evenings in the clubs, the two decided to attend bartending school together. This way they could not only enjoy the social atmosphere of a bar, but also make a couple of nickels, dimes, and quarters. After working for other bar owners, the two decided to take the plunge and open their own establishment. Easier said than done.

After scouring the city for a location, the two purchased the old Improv Institute building and quickly brought the place up to code. One super cool thing about The Hungry Brain is that many of the Improv features are still present including the stage and the sound booth. Just think, you can enjoy your cocktail "on stage" while relaxing on a couch. Speaking of furniture, most of the tables and chairs were either donated by customers or purchased at thrift stores. This unique collection truly enhances the charm of the entire bar.

After passing the different code inspections, the two owners completed the necessary paperwork in order to obtain a liquor license. Of course, liquor licenses are pretty tough to come by here in the city and the process takes some time. Much to their dismay, Luz and Janis were denied. Nevertheless, they reapplied, yet this time with aid of an attorney and presto, the pair was granted their license. Chalk one up for the little guy!

If you're hungry for food, you won't find it at the Hungry Brain, at least for now. Food requires another license. But if you are looking for a location that offers a somewhat eclectic atmosphere, this is the place. I would say that the place is subdued, since it has an energy all its own.

Decor consists of different art pieces sprinkled throughout the bar room, while the actual bar is something to behold. Nearly 44 feet in length, this Formica monster is a must see. Of course, you'll find a full service bar and some great beers on tap including Sierra Nevada and Bass. The musical entertainment is provided by a trusty CD jukebox and you'll find some tricky games of skill to eat up your quarters.

The Hungry Brain is a neighborhood tap room with some real urban flavor. Quite a few customers are from the immediate Roscoe Village area. In fact, if you love the art of poetry, check out Wednesday nights. Look for live music to be added sometime down the road along with some other surprises.

The next time you need a beverage and a story of perseverance, coupled with some real charm, head to The Hungry Brain.

— Greg Dellinger

Iggy's
700 N. Milwaukee Ave.
312-829-4449
Hours: 7:30 p.m. to 2 a.m. Sunday to Wednesday, 7:30 p.m. to 4 a.m. Thursday and Friday, 7:30 p.m. to 5 a.m. Saturday

The only cool place left in Chicago to see an outdoor movie is Iggy's, 700 N. Milwaukee Ave. You can't sit on the hood of your car and watch a movie there but you can dine on some Pesto Chicken Fussili, drink a martini, smoke a cigar, and watch an offbeat film outdoors in Iggy's beer garden.

The movie selections range from Polyester to Goodfellas to special theme nights. The movies are shown on a large 10 foot by 10 foot screen. There's even hot buttered popcorn and surround sound.

"It's like being at a mini-movie theater where you can smoke and talk," said Iggy's owner Dion Antic who has been showing outdoor movies since he opened the place in 1992.

"I always thought of doing a movie theater with second or third run films and where you can smoke," Antic said. "This is an offshoot."

Antic's basic philosophy for Iggy's is to always try and do things a little different, he said.

Iggy's is definitely a little different. It's one of the only places where a patron can order a gourmet pasta dinner at 4 a.m. on a Saturday night.

Actually, food is served late every night at Iggy's. Meals are served until 2 a.m. Sundays through Wednesdays, until 4 a.m. on Fridays and until 5 a.m. on Saturdays.

Eating and watching a film on a cool summer night is the way to go. The out-

Barfly Iggy's-Inner Town Pub

door movies begin in July. Antic said he shows outdoor movies until Nov. 15 and installs heaters for the fall.

There's usually two features shown and the show begins around 9:30 p.m. or sunset and goes until 2 or 2:30 a.m. There is never a cover charge.

Inner Town Pub
1935 W Thomas St.
773-235-9795
Hours: 3 p.m. to 2 a.m. Sunday to Friday
3 p.m. to 3 a.m. Saturday

I first walked into the Inner Town Pub in 1992. Having just moved back to Chicago from a crazed New Orleans, I'd been instantly charmed by the relaxed, quiet, sort of "bohemian-rural" atmosphere of the place. From the stuf fed moose head keeping watch over the bar to the Christmas light-strewn American flag tacked up on a wall. It was like stepping into some remote, vaguely-hip roadhouse in the middle of the woods.

Having sat for some 30 years now just a block east of Damen at Winchester and Thomas, the Inner Town Pub has become a part of the booming Wicker Park bar scene, yet despite the usual attitude and stiff prices that have begun to surface in most of the establishments in the area, the Inner Town Pub remains one of the cheapest, most laid-back taverns I've yet to come across in the city.

Unless you're an out-of-control letch or something, I can't imagine anyone ever feeling unwelcome here. The general clientele ranges over a pretty wide field; the only common denominator being that everyone is low-key and friendly. I've yet to have ever feel any sort of bad vibes in the place. And though several established Wicker-Parkian joints have had their atmospheres both subtly and abruptly changed in just the past couple of years, the Inner Town Pub has remained a constant for as long as I've gone there.

As for special events, there's a largely acoustic, musical open mike every Thursday. Keep in mind though that the music comes second to the pool playing. Pool is taken very seriously here, with a long wait most nights on the two tables. There's also two video poker machines for you more solitary gambler sorts, and when you're on a losing streak both materially and emotionally, you can take solace in the decent amount of old country-and-western music selections on the jukebox. There's also music as diverse as The Flaming Lips and Sade on it as well.

What really makes the Inner Town Pub dear to my heart, though, is the fact that it's the perfect place to get drunk on a lazy afternoon. There's only three small windows up in the front, and when you slip into the dimness, the outside world quickly ceases to have any real importance. The pool tables and jukebox are easily accessible, and muted light from the large, stained glass window up over the small stage in back fills the place with a warm, comfortable glow. Ah, it's heaven. I swear back a couple of years ago it seemed as if my friends and I

The North Side Inner Town-Irish American Heritage

spent every damn afternoon in the joint. Declining health and sanity forced us to ease up on the practice, but there's still those occasional weekday afternoons when I've got the day off and plan to spend it accomplishing something productive, only to finally say the hell with it, make a few phone calls, and off I go, parking my ass on an Inner Town Pub barstool awaiting a couple of buddies. It's like a mini-vacation for the small sum of 20 bucks or so. Highly recommended. Beer prices start at only 75 cents for a Schlitz on tap and prices table off at $3 for a pint of Guinness.

Oh, by the way, if you're wondering who runs the place, all you've got to do is wander in there with a woman or two in your group. It's a pretty safe bet that before too long an older fella in a bolo tie and leather vest will come up and introduce himself to them. This is Mike, the owner, who's always hobnobbing about the place. He's got an eye for the lasses, you might say. But don't worry, he's a perfect gentleman. And so is the rest of the crowd. You ladies won't find any meat-market tactics going on in here, but then it's not as if a romance or two can't be struck up either, for the place can get pretty filled up at times.

-- Bill Franz

The Irish American Heritage Center (IAHC)
4626 N. Knox Ave.
773-282-7035
Hours: 9 a.m. to 10 p.m. Monday to Thursday, 9 a.m. to 1 a.m. Friday and Saturday, hours vary on Sunday. Pub hours: 4 p.m. to 1 a.m. on Fridays and Saturdays.

The IAHC was founded a decade ago to preserve Irish Heritage and to create a community social center.

The building itself had previously housed a high school and college before lying dormant for several years. So it was in disrepair when the IAHC moved in. Paint had peeled of the walls, punk kids broke in and smashed windows and turned the building into their personal sty.

According to IAHC spokesman Frank Kilker, a vast array of craftsmen and artisans from the city's Irish community banded together to rehabilitate the building. Strict attention was paid to detail which is evident by the paintings on the walls upon entry. An artist recreated drawings taken from the Book of Kells by duplicating them on the walls in paint. The Book of Kells is the Celtic Bible created by Irish monks and is one of the oldest preserved documents in the world. The book resides in a museum at Trinity College in Dublin.

But getting back to the IAHC and its detail, even its bathrooms are labeled in Gaelic: Fir (men) and MNÅ (women).

The IAHC houses a museum on its second floor featuring classic Beleek

138

Barfly Irish American Heritage Center

Porcelain, traditional lace and artistry, and even a rare exact duplicate of the Book of Kells. The building also has a 680-seat auditorium used for plays written by Irish authors and for traditional musical performances. The auditorium was restored through donations. For a $100 donation, donors receive a memorial seat engraved with their name. Mayor Richard M. Daley's inscribed seat is in the front row and center — go figure.

A variety of classes are held at the center and include everything from Celtic music and dancing lessons to Gaelic language courses, to golf, soccer and even Alcohol Anonymous meetings.

One of the key features of the center and one of its continual fundraisers is its 5th Province Room — a traditional Irish Pub. Its name is derived from a comment made by current president of Ireland Mary Robinson when she said that the original four provinces of Ireland are indeed in Ireland but the fifth province is the Irish People in America.

"The pub is one of about six or seven fundraisers that we have but it is our bread and butter," said IAHC spokeswoman Sue Hogan. "It is one of the few places you can drink and feel good about it because it all goes to charity. All profits from the bar go directly to the IAHC."

To construct this pub, walls from four adjacent rooms were knocked out. Customary slate flooring was installed and an Irish Stone fireplace was built including a crane and black metal cooking pot. An oil painting above the fireplace and mantle depicts three Irish musicians on a wheel cart at a country crossroads.

A fully stocked horseshoe shaped bar features Irish Whiskeys: Jameson, Bushmills, Powers, and Tullamore Dew. Brews on tap include Harp, Guinness, McEwans, Tenants, and a few domestics. Imports run $3 and domestics go for $2.25. Irish sodas such as Cidnoa (apple), Club Lemon and Orange and Lucozade (similar to Gatorade and an Irish favorite for hangovers) are also available.

To eat, the 5th Province Room serves traditional Irish fare such as corned beef sandwiches, fish and chips, and Irish Sausage and chips. All are served with fries, slaw, pickle and a roll for under $4.

Another pleasant feature at the 5th Province Room is its low, circular, lead-footed tables near the fireplace situated perfectly for viewing two and three piece bands which perform every Friday and Saturday night. These are mostly traditional acts but will occasionally break out with something from the 20th Century.

While you are sitting back with your friends in the 5th Province Room knocking back a pint or two, maybe you could impress others in the room with your newly found Irish knowledge acquired here: Erin Go Braugh means Ireland forever. The patron saint of Ireland, St. Patrick, was actually an Englishman captured by Irish pirates who escaped to France where he became a Catholic priest. He had a vision that he should return to Ireland to preach Christianity. He became very popular in certain circles and was even given credit for driving all the snakes out of Ireland.

The North Side Irish American Heritage-Irish Eyes

"I don't think that there were any snakes in Ireland to begin with, but somebody can take credit for it," added Kilker.

There is also a patroness saint of Ireland, Saint Bridget who followed the teachings of Saint Patrick and led women to become nuns.

But here's some deeper history: the Celts are a broad range of ancient people from West and Central Europe. The Gaels are Celts but a much smaller group consisting of the Irish and Scottish. Celtic refers to the groups of languages spoken by the Celts and its the name of 12 large, usually non-Irish, men from Boston. Gaelic refers to the traditional Scottish and Irish languages.

The Irish have taken a bum rap when it comes to alcohol. Stigmatized as lushes, the Irish actually are the fourth biggest bunch of lushes in Europe. Rating above them are the Germans, French and Spanish, according to Kilker. In addition, there is a large Irish Catholic group called the Pioneers that willingly take a pledge to abstain from alcohol for life.

The IAHC is a result of 150 years of Irish immigrants coming to the U.S. The majority of Irish immigrants arrived in America in the 1840s during the Great Potato Famine. They generally settled in Boston, New York and Chicago. Most Irish settlers in Chicago originally settled in the Bridgeport neighborhood on the city's near Southwest Side.

— Dave Carmody

Irish Eyes
2519 N. Lincoln Ave.
773-348-9548
Hours: 3 p.m. to 2 a.m. weekdays,
noon to 3 a.m. Saturday, 6 p.m. to 2 a.m. Sunday

Gerry O'Connell is probably the closest thing to a modern-day leprechaun that you can get. Tall, with strawberry blond hair, bright eyes and a pronounced Irish brogue, O'Connell certainly looks the part. And after as little as two minutes of conversation with him, the deal is sealed.

If you've been to Irish Eyes, 2519 N. Lincoln Ave., you're sure to recognize O'Connell, who is the bar's owner as well as its entertainer on some weekends. He sings and plays the guitar, performing a rousing repertoire of drinking music with an Irish-American flair. All of his songs are performed with crowd participation in mind.

"If it wasn't for the crowd, I wouldn't have an act," comments O'Connell, with an ear-to-ear smile on his face. "People love to experience that unity...they come here with their friends, put their arms around each other's shoulders and sing along."

And sing along they do. A typical night's work for O'Connell includes performing such universal classics such as "Pack Up Your Troubles" and "Drunken Sailor," a song everyone remembers their father singing during their childhood. Or maybe that was just my father. Anyway, O'Connell also performs a broad

Barfly Irish Eyes

Irish Eyes, 2519 N. Lincoln Ave., owner Gerry O'Connell keeps his patrons entertained with drinking music that has an Irish-American flair.

range of Irish songs. A big crowd pleaser is the called "The Unicorn," during which the entire crowd sings and does accompanying hand motions to the camp-song like lyrics... "There were green alligators and long-neck geese, humpty-back camels and chimpanzees...there were cats and rats as sure as you're born, but loveliest of all was the unicorn." The crowd gets really excited about this one. Honest.

More than half of O'Connell's act is humorous in nature. He does a lot of folksy music which sounds really wholesome at first, like something from an Irish Spring commercial. Then you start to listen to the lyrics and realize it's actually about some Irish maiden who's slept with half the village or something. It's a lot of fun, especially after you've had a few Harps.

And fun is what O'Connell is all about. During the hour that I talked with him, I don't think he ever stopped smiling. You have to figure that dealing, night after night, with a drunken crowd which insists on singing loudly and off-key, grabbing your microphone, grabbing each other, etc...has to get annoying after awhile. Especially over the 20-plus years that O'Connell's been performing. But he's completely unfazed.

"I can laugh at the worst," says O'Connell. "And as long as it's not too crowded or the person's not too drunk, I don't mind them getting up on stage with me."

And he really means it. I wouldn't be anywhere near as cheerful if some

141

goon with beer breath tried to sit behind my desk with me and sing while I was working.

But O'Connell takes it all in stride. He was born and raised in Dublin and began his career by acting in school plays when he was 9 years old. He came to the U.S. in 1978 and the way he makes it sound, he got his start here almost by accident.

"Some friends of mine had a Dixieland band," he says. "They were playing a party and asked me if I would go along and sing some Irish songs. I told them I didn't know any Irish songs and that I didn't sing, but they made me come anyway. We got there and they played for awhile and then all of the sudden they made this big announcement... 'And now straight from Ireland, Gerry O'Connell, singing his Irish favorites...'"

"I had no idea what I was doing," he continued. "I didn't have anything prepared, I didn't know the words to any of the songs, so I did what I do now, I made it up."

And so it seems O'Connell's U.S. career just took off from there. He continued with the Dixie band, first playing washboard and then progressing to guitar. Eventually people started asking the band if they could "just get the Irish guy" to play for their events. He started doing a solo act and one day he stumbled upon Irish Eyes while visiting his sister, who lived around the corner.

"I loved to hang out here," O'Connell says. "So I asked if I could play and the owner said he wasn't really sure, it was really hard to fit in."

But Whitey, also a regular performer at Irish Eyes, asked O'Connell if he wanted to sing a few songs with him one night. The performance went over well and earned O'Connell his first actual gig there on the Fourth of July in 1982. O'Connell had been out drinking all night the evening prior. And when O'Connell says all night, you can be assured that he means all night.

After his sleep-deprived, alcohol-rich evening, he went to a picnic where he continued drinking and did another performance. And then he headed to Irish Eyes for his first official performance at the venue. Apparently the events leading up to the performance only enhanced it. And the rest, as they say, is history.

O'Connell performed at Irish Eyes, as well as various other locations in Chicago and nationally, before buying the bar a few years ago. Now he keeps the bar and performs there on weekends "as a hobby." He also runs another (undisclosed) business and has just opened a second bar in St. Petersburg, Florida, called The Bayside Irish Pub.

In his free time, which I'm guessing has to amount to about 17 minutes per week, Gerry enjoys his wife and two daughters, Maggie, 7, and Casey, 3. Both girls periodically perform with O'Connell at the bar.

O'Connell performs at Irish Eyes about four months out of the year on Saturday and Sunday nights. So clear your throat, get your singing voice tuned, practice your Unicorn synchronized dance movements, and head over to Irish Eyes for a few brews and an evening with Gerry. Top o' the evening to ya!

-- Lisa Kueng

Irish Village

6215 W. Diversey Ave.
773-237-7555
Hours: 11:30 a.m. to 2 a.m. Tuesday to Friday,
4 p.m. to 2 a.m. Saturday, 4 p.m. to 2 a.m. Sunday

The Irish Village is the sort of place one can go and really experience traditional Irish everything. The music is all Irish. The dancing is all Irish. This bar prides itself on the Irish food served, which is some of the best in the city. This place will bring a tear to any Irishman's soul, and convert any non-Irish into Irishmen for a night. The atmosphere is not pretentious. The bar is interesting to sit and watch the entertainment provided nightly. The bar features Guinness, Harp, and Miller Lite on tap. There are about eight different bottled beers to choose from.

The Irish Village is always jam packed on St. Patrick's Day. I recommend reservations, if you can get them.

-- Gen eX ault

Irish Wolfhound

3734 N. Milwaukee Ave.
773-736-1010
Hours: 11 a.m. to 2 a.m. Sunday, 10 a.m. to 2 a.m.
weekdays, 10 a.m. to 3 a.m. Saturday

Your opinion on the Irish Wolfhound depends on your larger view of the world, whether you see the glass as being half empty or half full. I, being an optimist, felt that the Irish Wolfhound was a welcome way-station on the urban landscape. A place where your libation is served by an angelic bartender with a slight brogue, translucent behind the bar. Others would see it as a neighborhood dive.

The bar is located on Milwaukee Avenue, just north of Addison. Although located close to a busy intersection and across from Schurz HIgh School, at night it feels a bit desolate. The surrounding buildings, small industrial shops, add to the feeling of entering some sort of industrial hinterland.

Inside, the bar's kelly-green walls have the immediate affect of bringing about inner harmony. The layout is long and narrow, so the ergonomics of the situation forces one to immediately belly up to the bar. A wise use of limited space. If one is inclined to start the festivities at a slower pace, one can retreat to the far end of the bar and shoot a game of stick.

The mood is best described as down to earth. Populated by mostly Irishmen and Mexicans, one will quickly feel like one of the boys, being that the domestic beer is a $1.50 a bottle. Two televisions, a jukebox, and the cast of characters are the primary sources of entertainment.

The Irish Wolfhound is a definite stopover when traveling down Milwaukee

The North Side Irish Wolfhound-J.T. Collins Pub

Avenue. Down to earth, cheap beer prices, and decorated with posters of your favorite soccer clubs, the Irish Wolfhound offers much. Any bar where Kenny Rogers' "The Gambler," is played back-to-back deserves much respect.

-- R. Schertler

J.T. Collins Pub
3358 N. Paulina St.
773-327-7467
Hours: 4 p.m. to 2 a.m. weekdays,
11 a.m. to 3 a.m. Saturday, noon to 2 a.m. Sunday

The classic cocktail is back! I made this happy discovery recently on a snowy Sunday afternoon at J.T. Collins Pub, opened in early 1995. Stopping in with the promise of a pint of Guinness and a brief respite from the Chicago chill, I ended up spending the entire afternoon exploring the wonderful world of the J.T. Collins cocktail menu (more on the later). After hours of gazing into a martini glass in front of me, a foolish grin on my face, owner Tam Magee was able to get me to listen as he told me about his bar.

Located at the intersection of Lincoln Avenue, Paulina and Roscoe streets, J.T. Collins is in the heart of the Roscoe Village neighborhood. Formerly the Torchlight Cafe, which was originally a coffeehouse, later becoming a bar. Tom had more definite ideas about what he wanted J.T. Collins to be.

"Roscoe Village has a neighborhood feel to it and I wanted this bar to reflect that," Tom said. "Whether people come in for a drink or to eat, I want them to be comfortable here."

If J.T. Collins only served drinks, it would still have the potential to be a worthwhile stop on the Chicago watering hole trail. What J.T. Collins does offer -- the afrementioned cocktails, a good selection of beers, including some notable microbrews, and an appetizing and inventive menu -- gives it all the points of a great spot to check out.

While many bars serve food, typically good but not exceptional, Tom offers a menu that is more than you would expect.

"I wanted to serve good food, food with a flair, but keep it at pub-grub cost," Tom said.

The menu is designed by chef Jody Denton of The Eccentric, 159 W. Erie St. Other chefs cooking at The Eccentric are also on board here. The menu is impressive while the prices are very reasonable. Appetizers, soups, salads, sandwiches and entrees are offered; homemade pizza is available, even after the kitchen has closed (10 p.m. weeknights, 11 p.m. weekends). The flatbread with Santa Fe chicken sausage, parmesan and vegetables or the stuffed Gorgonzola burger are highly recommended. A dessert menu is available as well.

A variety of liqueurs, whiskies, a hot drink menu, 17 bottled brands and nine tap brews are on hand to enjoy. Microbrews include Wit and Otter Creek Copper Ale; on draft, Belll's and Golden Prairie Nut Brown Ale are standouts.

144

Barfly J.T. Collins-Jack Sullivan's Public House

Copper Ale; on draft, Bell's and Golden Prairie Nut Brown Ale are standouts.

And now for those cocktails! The "classic" drinker might enjoy The Vesper (007 Dry Martini) -- three measures gin, one measure vodka, one-half measure of Lillet, lemon twist and, of course, shaken not stirred. The adventurous might try the No Hangover, The Chocolate Martini (Nutty Chocolate, too) or the PB&J Martini. I found the Tangerini to be pleasurably addicting.

With its art-deco bar, panoramic windows and comfortable atmosphere, this is a place that invites you to enjoy the pleasures of the classic tavern.

-- Michael Cotter

Jack Sullivan's Public House
2142 N. Clybourn Ave.
773-549-9009
Hours: 10 a.m. to 1:30 a.m. Sunday, 10 a.m. to 2:30 a.m. Saturday, 11 a.m. to 1:30 a.m. Monday to Friday. Food is served until 10 p.m. Sunday to Wednesday and until midnight Thursday to Saturday

Jack Sullivan's opened on Jan. 1, 1996. The owners are Mike Roberts, Brendan Costello and Phil and Tom Piazza, who also own McGees and the Wrightwood Tap. Needless to say, they have been in the business quite a long time.

"I've got to admit, I'm getting older. We all are," Roberts said. "You can only hang out in the clubs or in trendy places for so long. We set out to open the kind of place that we would like to hang out in ourselves."

It's a sports-oriented bar with a twist.

"We're shooting for an older crowd," Roberts said. "An adult bar with patrons closer to our age."

Sullivan's is very appealing visually. Being bi-level, the first floor offers a bar along with pool tables and dart boards. The second level offers a bigger bar with a good sized dining area. Seventeen, soon to be 18, TV screens, cover both floors for game viewing pleasure. The second floor also offers a high ceiling with a domed glass window.

"This was probably the biggest waste of space I've ever seen," Mike said. "We wanted to take advantage and make it visually appealing."

Sullivan's offers a wide variety of drinks. Guinness and Oregon are on tap, complimented by a wide variety of bottled domestics and imports. They also offer a wide choice of top-shelf liquors and the prices are all moderate.

To eat, all you have to do is say the word and a huge menu is set before you. Not your typical bar food, Sullivan's offers a wide assortment of gastronomic delicacies. The pork chops are about as thick as my arm, and the chicken-kabobs appetizer are served to perfection. Entrees are all served dinner style with potatoes and veggies.

— Brian Diebold

Jagiellonia

3636 Belmont Ave.

773-583-9554

Hours: noon to 2 a.m. weekdays,

11 a.m. to 2 a.m. Saturday, 11 a.m. to 1 a.m. Sunday

Eastern Europe meets "South of the Border" in one of the more bizarre, but in a good way, bar atmospheres I've ever come across in this town. After hitting a few other joints in the Belmont/Milwaukee area in my hazy wanderlust to find a cool spot to park my butt and drink my fill, a drinking buddy and I stumbled upon an unassuming corner bar in a seemingly condemned building and decided to try our luck.

Stepping into this mysterious tavern, we were met by the sweet sounds of "The End" just as a small fracas between some old Mexican men was starting to heat up. Not wanting to stare, or get punched in the face for that matter, we quickly took a seat at the bar and pretended not to notice as the men escalated their shouting match into a shoving one and finally drunkenly dragged each other outside.

Strangely enough, no one else in the place seemed too interested in the event, so I gathered the two guys were just regulars involved in a little friendly dispute.

Turning our attention to more important matters, we ordered two drafts of Old Style ($1 each) from an exotically pretty Polish woman behind the bar and gave the place the once over. The bar is decorated with an endearing mixture of soccer balls trophies won by the patrons and cones of fly paper hanging from the liquor mantles. The house diversions are your standard triumvirate of pool table, dart board, and smutty electronic poker machines, but they somehow seem boldly interesting in this strange setting.

Whereas the other Belmont bars we stopped into that night were filled with depressing locals drowning their sorrows in Jack Daniel's and Guns N' Roses, this place had some real flavor. Maybe it was the warm feeling of witnessing Polish and Mexican Americans throwing darts with each other instead of at each other, or the wonderful melting pot of classic rock, flamenco, new age and Depeche Mode that's in the jukebox. Maybe I was just full of the beer of human kindness from all the drinking that evening, but I really enjoyed the night there.

The staff is very friendly, though not entirely English speaking, the beer is reasonably priced (domestic bottles are $1.50, imports around $2.50) and the bathrooms have nifty shower curtains around the toilets instead of stalls. It's a great place to go on a weekend to soak in the ethnic crossroads of Chicago because beer really is the universal language of man.

— *Brian Farrelly*

Jake's Pub
2932 N. Clark St.
773-248-3318
Hours: noon to 2 a.m. daily

I was having a hard time finding Jake's until I spotted Scott the owner's 1970 GTO convertible on Clark Street and knew we were getting close. We were pretty damn anxious to get to any bar which is known for its "economy sized" shot glasses. No thick walled pseudo shot glasses at Jake's, your money is well spent. The 70 or so beers (at last count) Scott carries had Dan (our beer geek) patting his Buddha in anticipation.

Jake's has been Jake's since 1933, which is surprising considering that such longevity is a rarity in a world of mall bars. The current Bloody Mary recipe is the same one used opening day 1933. Scott bought the bar in 1993 and turned what was a dive into a damn good corner bar (with what our group discovered was one of the best selections of beer, booze, cigars and crowd in the city). As Scott puts it, "I said to myself, I should buy this place so I went and fucking bought the place."

Before 1933 Jake's was a candy store which was a front for a speakeasy next door. The building has been granted landmark status which means hanging a sign requires approval from the landmark commission. Needless to say, you won't be seeing a "Jake's" neon sign blinking on Clark Street anytime this century. Not that the lack of neon is hurting business, as Jake's has a great mix of artists, advertising people, bands staying at Days Inn (nearby on Diversey Avenue) and neighbors. The word of mouth on Jake's is that it's a damn cool bar to hang out in. Forget the sign Scott, you don't need it.

Scott rotates his beer selection constantly. There is always something new. He has a great selection of imports as well as some of the finest micros. He is also one of the few bars in the city deemed worthy enough to have Bells Solsun on a regular basis. Jake's also carries three kinds of cider (wheee). He has 10 taps currently and is adding more each month. For the budget minded, Schlitz in the can is always available. Jake's also sells beer to go. The bottom line is, beer is spoken here.

Jake's is cigar friendly offering a fine selection for sale at the front counter as well as cigar "tastings." Current selection: AVO XO, Fonseca, P.G. and Davidoff.

Jake's has more than 200 CDs behind the bar and a damn good jukebox (which we fed regularly). Any given night you'll hear Morphine, Uncle Tupelo, Rage Against the Machine or Hank Williams Jr. They also have darts, pinball and a kick-ass back area for pool. Beware though, the regulars are not hacks on the pool table.

Overall, on a 10-point rating system Jake's gets a solid 10. These people know how to take care of you as well as give you a damn fun room to get liquored up in. The music, beer and bartenders (go on a night when Heidi

147

works... never shy cocktails) make this one kick-ass corner bar. Oh, did we forget to mention the sub-zero Jager and Rumpleminz cooler. Get in here!

-- Dan German

Jay's
933 N. State St.
312-649-9188
Hours: 11 a.m. to 4 a.m. Sunday to Friday,
11 a.m. to 5 a.m. Saturday

I first became familiar with Jay's in 1993 when the bar's location was the present Hunt Club on Maple and State. In the spring of 1995, one of Willie Nelson's buddies, Carl, introduced me to Jay. Little did I know that Jay is Chicago bar legend Jay Emerich. When I lived in New York City, I frequently ran into Leroy Neiman. Jay is surely his Chicago twin.

Since 1965, there has always been a Jay's. The original operated at Bellvue and Rush. Jay felt the itch to expand, though, and opened other places. The Rally Ally opened in 1965; The Store in 1967 and Store Antics also in 1967. The world famous Faces (1971-1979) was often featured in "Playboy" magazine and other commercial literature. One has to wonder if Hugh's Playboy Clubs didn't get their ideas from this "member key club."

The list of Jay bars goes on ... The Sitzmark (1967), The Sting (1978), Mr. E's (1983), Jay's on the Park (1993), Jay's Mountain View California (1985-1992) and the current Jay's, which opened in January, 1995.

The very attractive manager, Darleen Lee, says that the Jay's of today is the most sophisticated of all Jay's operations. With 3,000 square feet, Jay's offers two full bars, satellite televisions with projection screens, state-of-the-art sound system, a DJ booth, pool tables, a relaxing outdoor cafe and a kitchen serving up those famous half-pound burgers until 3 a.m. every night.

With all this experience, Jay continues his success by offering such events as his reunion party, held in May, and his Reggae music nights held on Sunday evenings in June and July.

I love history, and Jay is a large part of Chicago's recent past. So, for those afraid of loud music, bring your ear plugs, or at least your sense of humor. You'll enjoy yourself with Jay.

— J. Quillian

Jefferson Inn
4874 N. Milwaukee Ave.
773-283-5522
Hours: 11 a.m. to 2 a.m. daily

In transit to the Jefferson Inn, I felt a strange sense of apprehension. I was taking the exact route I took every day in high school: the Addison bus to the Addison el stop on the O'Hare line, to Jefferson Park terminal for a connecting

Barfly Jefferson Inn-Joe's on Broadway

bus. It was with this strange sense of flash back funk, that I swung open the inn's door. Perhaps if I had noticed the inn's large white Old Style sign hanging over Milwaukee Avenue while in high school, I would have never made it to college. Then again college was four years too long.

Once inside, I quickly assumed my rightful place at the bar. Accompanying me at the bar, positioned at the corner stool, was a dead ringer for my friend's dad. My friend Tim discovered this bar at the end of an all-day drinking binge. All this leads to the fact, that the only reason the Jefferson Inn stuck in my memory, is that Tim stumbled in while a lingerie show was in progress. For my arrival, there was just a sign announcing that the show, cleverly named Sheer Madness, was every Thursday and Saturday, from 8 to 10 p.m.

My heart heavy with disappointment, I ordered a beer. The low price of $1.50 for my bottled Bud boosted my spirits. With no models to view, I quickly absorbed my surroundings. Booths lined the wall opposite the bar, and a small back room held additional booths and an electronic dart board. After scanning the posters of movie stars from a bygone era, my eyes fell on the television. Amazed that a few Budweisers could make "Grace Under Fire" enjoyable, I ordered another one and stayed for "Coach."

-- Bob Schertler

Joe's On Broadway

3563 N. Broadway St.
773-528-1054
Hours 11 a.m. to 2 a.m. Sunday to Friday,
11 a.m. to 3 a.m. Saturday

For the life of me, I can't quite put a finger on Joe's On Broadway. This would definitely be a location to gather with friends when the Cubs, Hawks, Bears, etc. are playing.

The beer selection is average and the prices tend to be a bit high. But this in not surprising when you consider the neighborhood. Imports can go anywhere near $4 a pop, with drink specials that vary from night to night. While I have not witnessed it for myself, I hear that on certain nights free food such as pizza is offered. Do not take my word for this, you may want to call.

The air conditioning is average and the decor is somewhat interesting. From inflatable deer heads to 1970s bathroom floor tile, Joe's On Broadway provides a cheesy yet often homey feel. There is a funny carved wooden sign behind the bar for the regulars. It gives a specific price list for excuses when someone calls the bar looking for you. For example, if the bartender says he hasn't seen you, it will cost a quarter. If he says you stepped out to the Jewel food store next door, that will cost 50 cents. Of course the always popular, "I thought I saw him going to the Church across the street" will cost you a whopping $2.

Besides watching sports games, Joe's has a ledge you can sit at that look directly out on to Broadway. This at times can offer one hell of a show. Men

The North Side Joe's on Broadway-John Barleycorn

can try to entice women to come in as well as the other way around but the women don't seem to fall for it as often as men do. Gee, I wonder why? Anyhow there are plenty of characters in this neighborhood that can make for an interesting time. Case in point, the Vietnam vet that tried to impress my girlfriend by saying that if I or my friend Mike would only feel his bicep, we would go running out the door. Then he and Erin would be left to enjoy a night of drinking and old war stories. Thank God she didn't fall for it.

— *Brian Diebold*

John Barleycorn
658 W. Belden Ave.
773-348-8899
Hours: 11 a.m. to 2 a.m. Sunday to Friday,
11 a.m. to 3 a.m. Saturday

If the giant moosehead hanging to the left of the dark-wooden bar could talk, he would probably weave a tale enshrouded in urban excitement. John Barleycorn, a Lincoln Park bar/restaurant is not only famous for its hamburgers and chili, but also for its jaded past.

Taverns of various names have stood on this site since 1890, when the building itstelf was completed. During the Prohibition era, the building housed a successful saloon where the famous bank robber John Dillinger was a regular. During the 1920s, the present-day rear dining room of the restaurant was a Chinese laundry that served as a front for bootleggers to bring liquor in. Once inside, the liquor was transported to the basement, providing easy transportation of liquor to the saloon by means of a small elevator to the upstairs saloon.

Patrons at this speakeasy also entered throught he Chinese laundry like the bootleggers so as not to be noticed by authorities. Currently at the front of John Barleycorn are large picture windows, but at the time these windows were not installed or bordered up so the saloon appeard to be closed.

Dillinger himself was famous for buying the house a round of booze, which didn't last for too many years, as Dillinger was gunned down in front of the Biograph Theater just two blocks away.

After those sinister and dangerous times, the saloon passed hands for many years until the early 1960s when a Dutch proprietor bought the saloon and named it John Barleycorn Memorial Pub. Today it is a nautical lovers dream.

Surrounding the bar and two dining rooms is an extensive display of handmade model ships, which date as far back as 1800, and gives a feeling that Columbus could be going over navigation charts in the next room. With subtle classical music being played in the background and the rear dining room's fireplace as well as the life-sized crest above the mantel, you almost want to stoke up the fire, sit in an easy chair and order a snifter of brandy. Overall, you might feel as if you were in a ship's dining cabin with dark lighting from yellow-colored round lamps on the stucco and dark wood walls, the hardwood floors as

Barfly John Barleycorn-Joy Blue

well as the round-bulbed chandeliers.

Everyone can feel comfortable at John Barleycorn. During my outing, young families, older couples and typical Lincoln Park-types, filled the restaurant's tables and burgundy chairs.

You'll find no success in asking the bartender to play your favorite song or have no luck hoping the CD jukebox takes your wrinkled dollar bill because all the music John Barleycorn plays is classical. The bar also shows a continuous display of 5,000 art slides from different periods on its three screens which is a pleasant distraction to look at if your dining partner is less than exciting. Also the art slides will make you appear intellectual if you can recognize a few of those Van Gogh's falshing by on the screen, not to mention that you'll be thankful you passed Art 101 freshman year.

The restaurant's menu has a large variety of sandwiches, salads, entrees, and appetizers that could go way beyond typical bar fare. John Barleycorn offers nightly dinner specials which are more than reasonably priced. The "famous" half-pound burger makes my list of one of the top three places in Chicago to get a great burger. Each time I have trekked to John Barleycorn for a burger, I have been treated great by the staff and there is usually little or no wait for a table.

While it seems more of a restaurant than a bar during the winter months, wait until summertime when a large patio opens up on the backside of the rear diningroom. The "outdoor cafe" fills up during the afternoon and evening with bar-goers who like to throw back a few while sitting out in the much-needed warm weather.

And liquor is no stranger to John Barleycorn. With more than 15 domestic and 17 imported beers, John Barleycorn has the barley and hops for you. Of course, beer is not the only intoxicating beverage available, just check out the liquor and spirit display behind the bar.

A large red and green neon sign hanging in one of the front windows paying homage to John Barleycorn -- the proverbial red-nosed drunken Irishman -- welcomes the hungry and thirsty looking for a history lesson, fantastic model-ship viewing as well as great food, not to mention mugs full of frosty beer.

-- Dennis Mahoney

Joy Blue
3998 N. Southport Ave.
773-477-3330
Hours: 4 p.m. to 2 a.m. Sunday to Friday,
4 p.m. to 3 a.m. Saturday

On a random Saturday night, buddies Mark Kwiatkowski, Chris Krubert and Christian Sikorski couldn't figure out where to go. After complaining amongst themselves about the bar scene and how unoriginal it was, Kwiatkowski suggested that they, "start their own place." Like a married couple that talks about

The Joy Blue family located at 3998 N. Southport Ave.

having a child, they sat and discussed what they were going to name it (without knowing if it was going to be a boy or girl).

When the deal closed on their new place in the spring of 1996, they settled on a name; actually about a dozen names, all of which had satisfied them until a better one came up. Whatever the name, it had to have Blue in there somewhere, apart from liking the color itself, Kwiatkowski liked the way it sounded in a bar name. No sooner were they ready to open when the oxymoron hit them as the catchy title they needed, people drink when they are sad, but they mostly drink when they are happy.

So now you can find Kwiatkowski and his fellow co-owners who, incidentally, have been friends since childhood, hanging out on the corner of Irving Park Road and Southport Avenue at their Joy Blue. The new bar replaced Austin City Limits, an old neighborhood tap.

At first appearance, Joy Blue seems smaller than it actually is because of the focus on the corner entrance and its sterile, gallery-like quality. Upon further investigation, you find a lot more on the inside. In addition to the City Limits space, they acquired the space next to it which was a Mexican restaurant called La Vallita. In fact, it was the same owner, and the restaurant had preceded the bar. However, as the owner got older and had no one to continue on with the business, he decided to sell at a time when the Joy Blue owners were looking for a location.

According to Sikorski, they had been looking around for some time; they knew what they wanted, saw what they liked, and took advantage of the opportunity. While the functional design and creative inspiration comes from

Barfly Joy Blue

Kwiatkowski, it took the craftsmanship of City Limits regular Matt Reilly to make this dream a reality. Reilly, a carpenter by trade, already had the floor plans drawn up when he introduced himself to Kwiatkowski and told him what he could do for him.

Kwiatkowski was not only skeptical, but he had another carpenter already lined up. Now whether it was fate or intuition, he changed his mind at the last minute and gave the job to Reilly the day before construction was to start.

Joy Blue is made up of three rooms. The main room containing the street entrance has been completely redone. The floors are new; the barback, extending almost the entire length of the east wall, is new and the long L-shaped bar is new.

Incorporating everything they liked about bars into one place, the owners have made the most of the space, resulting in three entirely different atmospheres to relax and enjoy. The middle room connecting the three is the Martini Room and has a small bar that serves up an extensive Martini menu, after dinner drinks, and will most likely see in the near future a variety of fine wines for Friday night tastings and connoisseur appetites.

The third room is a lounge featuring velvet couches and a pool table. This is the most relaxing room and provides an intimate setting where one can socialize without having the actual hustle and bustle of a busy bar near by. The wall of this furthermost room has a mural depicting Impressionist characters in an American saloon reminiscent of the early 1900s. Art is a major focus of this establishment and it has a lot to do with Reilly's love of fine art.

Although the focus is on art, it is the kind of space that is functional on many levels. Live acoustic music is done on an occasional basis, Joy Blue can accommodate a wide range of private party needs and is almost certainly open to the idea of doing open mike poetry.

First and foremost, Joy Blue is a bar and serves a wide selection of unique beers and spirits. Nine taps pour local and national micros as well as imports, and a listing of 38 bottled beers is bound to have something you like. Featured are Belgian beers, regarded by some as the best in the world, such as Saison Dupont and Chimay Ale, unless, of course, you prefer a lemon brew like One-Eyed Jack or perhaps Red Hook's Double Black Stout.

There is no shortage of single malts or small batch bourbons including favorites such as Glenfiddich and Maker's Mark. Interesting to note is a healthy selection of rum and tequila including Captain Morgan's private stock and Patron XO Cafe which is a coffee liqueur made with tequila. The aforementioned martini menu serves up a wide range of flavored martinis. There is a small list of Napa Valley wines available to those whose preference lies therein, and whether you like it or not, a signature shot called the Blue Joy.

Bar policy is to please you. The service is friendly and helpful (if you're not sure what something tastes like, you'll probably get a sample; if you've got a question they always have a minute to stop and answer). According to Kwiatkowski, "Joy Blue is acceptably decadent."

So there is no pretense at Joy Blue; what you see is what you get. You get a crowd that ranges from Armani to flannel and everyone in-between. There's "something for everyone," says Reilly.

— *Arunas Ingaunis*

Jub Jub Club

2447 N. Halsted St.

773-665-7557

Hours: 8 p.m. to 2 a.m. Sunday to Friday,

8 p.m. to 3 a.m. Saturday

I really didn't feel like going out on the Wednesday evening I was scheduled to cover "Swing Night" at The Jub Jub Club. Not at all. I spent a good 15 minutes coming up with creative ways I could get around it, postpone it, write the story without going, whatever. Finally I sucked it up and forced myself out the door, into my car, and drove to the club where I found a parking spot right out front. Already, I felt better.

I walked in and immediately found the smallish room intriguing. It's very dark and heavy velvet drapes hang in the front, completely covering all the windows. Candles are placed on the bar and most of the tables and there are these funky little circular booths to sit in with low knee-high tables in the middle of them. The music hits you right away — it's unusual, authentic swing, sung with smoky voices, and foot-tapping qualities. The whole thing feels like an escape...sort of "Hernando's Hideaway-ish."

Wednesdays at Jub Jub are a special occurrence. I haven't been there on any other night, but I'm told by friends who have, that it attracts mostly a late-20s to early-30s Lincoln Park crowd, lots of grad students, with maybe some eclectic bar-goers mixed in. Not true on Wednesday. On this particular night, I saw groups of women decked out with pretty cool-looking strappy dresses, spiky shoes, and pouffy hair. I saw groups of men wearing off-beat looking clothing and make-up, guys outfitted in "swing-wear" such as suspenders and hats, and girls in 1940s-style garb. But don't be put off if you want to check out the scene but don't feel like wearing spiked heels or suspenders to it — there were also people there in plain old jeans and T-shirts, and even one guy in his, "I'm an investment banker and I didn't have time to change before I came here," suit.

More important than the way these people looked is that they were all very very nice and a lot of fun. I was told that a lot of Wednesday-nighters are industry people who work at other clubs and bars, and indeed I met a few of them. I talked to people that work at Shelter, Red Dog, Roscoe's...and were out kicking back and enjoying themselves.

When I sat down at the bar I was immediately greeted by Krystal, one of Jub Jub's special Wednesday night bartenders. She and two other bartenders, both named Rob, come in on Wednesdays only, just to "run the Swing Show." And run it they do. All of them are extremely outgoing and sociable, spending almost as much time in front of the bar chatting with patrons as they do behind

Barfly Jub Jub Club-Jury's

it. Their charm sets the stage for the whole experience and almost immediately made me feel as though I were at a private cocktail party given by three great hosts and hostesses whom I didn't know very well.

And they also look the part. Krystal was wearing a sequined cocktail dress and Rob Number One was wearing a ruffled tuxedo shirt and a red velvet jacket. (Just for the record, he was wearing pants too.) The three of them bring in all sorts of props and toys to provide added zest over the course of the evening. For example, Rob Number Two told me he usually brings in fresh berries to use as garnish for drinks like The Cosmopolitan. They have a camera there, to take pictures of patrons, and keep an album of all their photographs at the bar. They keep a book called the "Notorious Book," filled with patron names, addresses, notes and graffiti. And they have all these funny little books which they pass around for people to peruse with titles like "How to Avoid Love and Marriage" and "Love and Sex Questions." Krystal even gave me a hairstyle magazine. The whole thing is pretty wacky and a lot of fun.

If you're not into hairstyles or sex questions, you can dance. I was there around midnight, which was just a little early for the floor to start hopping. A few couples, who seemed to be pretty accomplished swing dancers, got out there, but it apparently doesn't kick in until later. The DJ herself dances and gives lessons upon request. And the bartenders also make it a point to dance with their guests.

The whole thing was a blast. I can't think of any other time when I was so not in the going-out mode and had such a damn good time. Check it out.

-- Lisa Kueng

Jury's
4337 N. Lincoln Ave.
773-935-2255
Hours: 11:30 a.m. to 2 a.m. Sunday to Thursday, 11:30 a.m. to 11 p.m. Friday and Saturday.
Kitchen open from 11:30 a.m. to 10 p.m. daily

Jury's is named after a famous hotel in Dublin, Ireland, but does not pose itself as an Irish bar. It's a classy neighborhood restaurant and bar that boasts an elegant luncheon and dinner menu with linen tablecloths and napkins decorating a modest seating area.

Depending on your mood, you can go for a cheeseburger and fries or, if you've got the spare change burning a hole in your pocket, you may opt for a fancy appetizer such as mushrooms sautéed in red wine and a tender filet mignon. Considering the gourmet menu, it is quite reasonably priced (even the starving artist can afford a bowl of soup).

Even though Jury's opened in April 1996, it has been around since 1979, known as The Jury Room and formerly located at 2432 N. Lincoln Ave. The

155

kitchen and dining room have been scaled down, but owners Peter Borkman and Dan Borchers want everyone to know that not much else has changed. "The key to success," said Borkman, "is consistency with service." And customers do keep coming back, he said. Jury's regulars have had no problem making the connection with the slight name change, and the new location is just a short distance north of the former Jury Room.

Among the regulars are neighborhood pubsters who have been going to what ever bar has been at the new location, which has evolved from a hangout for baseball and softball players, to the Mediterranean restaurant Spice, to its current manifestation. At Jury's you'll find family and friends looking for something good to eat and a relaxing atmosphere where you can enjoy a jukebox of jazz and country classics.

You won't find a karaoke night, weekly darts tournaments or some local band blaring their greatest garage hits. Not that there is a special dislike to that crowd, it just doesn't fit in with Jury's program (snaggletooth beware, this is not your standard shot-and-beer tap room).

Jury's new look and upscale menu, which includes a selection of fine wine and port, is inspired by Borkman's experience as a waiter in a fine-dining restaurant. Combined with Borchers' expertise in beer, you know that you're in store for quality consumption. Beers offered include a variety of specially priced microbrews, along with popular choices including Bass, Guinness and Pilsner Urquell. If you're not in the mood for beer, you may want to try a French red wine such as Cotes Du Rhone, or a vintage Portuguese port such as Cockburn's. Fine Scotch and bourbon are also always in store. If you're at a complete loss, ask the bartender to pour his favorite, the Borkman Martini.

I asked Peter Borkman what was an important factor in making this business successful. He replied, "The owner being here. Customers appreciate that, and prefer it."

In an industry that has an average life expectancy of three to five years, their record speaks for itself.

— Arunas Ingaunis

Justins

3358 N. Southport Ave.
773-929-4844
Hours: 11 a.m. to 2 a.m. Sunday to Friday,
11 a.m. to 3 a.m. Saturday

This was my first time at Justins. I have heard good things about the place and had to check it out for myself. I was amazed at the size of Justins. With the bar placed in the center of the room, there is still a lot of room to get comfortable. The night I was there, you could find someone at every table, yet you still felt you had room to breathe.

I was lucky enough to get a mini tour of Justins latest addition from manager

Barfly Justins-Kasey's

Michel Drape. This is a new party room, or should I say party floor, that opened in May, 1998. They have spent a lot of time and effort working on the details like the fully restored hardwood floors, and the giant windows overlooking Southport. They also have a back deck that gives you a great view of the beer garden. I could go on and on about the new party room, but that could be a whole other story.

The first thing that hits you when you enter the Justins beer garden is a huge tree that sits smack dab in the middle. Michel told me it's a male Mulberry tree, and I'll take his word for it. All I know is, this thing is big. This is great for the summer, because it provides a lot of shade. The garden is also surrounded by large bushes that give you great privacy. They have two cool lamps that, according to Michel, are from the Chicago World's Fair of 1933. One winter someone had the balls to climb the fence and steel one of the lamps. They never did recover the missing lamp, and eventually had to have a replica made to fill the spot, you would never know the difference.

They also have a great little shack at the back end of the garden which is used to serve cold bottled beer in the summer. The shack is decorated with some odd things including a golf club, a ski, and a table and chairs. Michel told me that they have plans to tear the shack down. They plan to have a bar that would span the length of the garden. This would open a lot of space at the back end of the beer garden.

Justins is a cool place whether inside or out. It's really no surprise that Justins has been in business for 14 years. Some people argue, they are the reason the Southport strip is what it is today.

— *Tom Fisher*

Kasey's
6261 W. Montrose Ave.
773-725-9754
Hours: 7 a.m. to 2 a.m. daily

It is rather dark down that particular stretch of Montrose, a few blocks east of Wilbur Wright College's new campus. Kasey's light emanates in the distance, as only a tavern's shingle can when you are as thirsty as I was that Sunday evening. I honed in on it like a heatseeker.

The nearly full bar on a Sunday night was the first clue that this was a pretty decent place. No one goes to a shitty bar, right? Especially on the Sabbath day. The vibe in Kasey's that night was great, as I wasn't greeted with leers as I entered, but no one was falsely friendly and annoying either. It was as if the whole crowd had silently said in unison, "You're here and that's cool, but if you weren't, that would be cool too."

It seemed like a mellow joint and I like mellow joints on a Sunday. It looks like a tavern that you might find further north in this state, like it could be a

157

refuge for hunters and fishermen. The wood paneling, tile drop ceiling with white Christmas lights strung around the perimeter gives this bar a cozy, woodsy feel.

A regular household refrigerator behind the bar always makes me feel more at home. Kasey's has its share of the big brewing company's paraphernalia including four neat mirrors from Miller that depict bears and wolves and such natural scenery. The bar itself runs the length of the west wall and seats about two dozen. It is a laminate, white marbled with gold and a woodgrain outer border.

This has got to be the only tavern in Chicago (or anywhere, for that matter), that has a Bear's helmet hanging next to a Packer's helmet side by side as if they weren't rivals at all but sister teams.

Actually, after last season, I should have no trouble at all believing that the Bears were really the sisters of the Green Bay's team in disguise. They need to realign the divisions so that the Bears could play a team of their own skill level such as high schools or convalescent homes.

Kasey's has a separate room for a pool table and two dart boards hang on either side of it. The table is as level as bar tables get, and its distance from the bar insures plenty of room to shoot.

This offset room also has a ledge and some stools along one wall so patrons have something to set their drinks on as they play or watch the games. Two video slot machines and four televisions are also part of the establishment. And the jukebox is outstanding having everything from Willie Nelson to Seger to Cypress Hill. Guns and Roses and AC/DC made my day.

Genuine Draught and Old Style are the only two tap beers and 14 ounces of either are only an even dollar on Mondays. Domestic bottles are a dollar Wednesdays and only a buck-seventy-five the rest of the time. A short call mixed drink was two and a quarter and the dude knew how to mix a drink. I love microbrews as much as anyone, but getting a big buzz for a little money is also one of my favorite things.

I imagine Kasey's draws a neighborhood crowd for the most part. The Plumber's Local 130 banner hanging on the wall beneath a Leinenkugel's oar was another indication of the type of crowd they draw.

They have a set up behind the bar called "toss a coin for the widows and orphans of police officers," and a flyer for the 10th anniversary run for the Little Angels. That showed me that the bar was charitable and involved in the community.

They also have hard boiled eggs for 50 cents. I don't know who in the hell eats those things in a bar but it is nice to know that they are available should I ever develop a taste for them while sucking down a brew.

Kasey's is a good bar. It is not a hip bar, a trendy bar or an overly-classy bar but it is a good bar. If I lived closer, I would be a regular. Kasey's has everything you could ask for, a good crowd, a good feel and good amusements. It is not uptight and it is not fake. I mean, people were talking to each other about their families and things, not just the superficial jabber I'm accustomed to hear-

Barfly Kasey's-Kat Klub

ing in overpriced, overdone taverns. I can't wait to see Kasey's on a Friday or Saturday night, I'll bet it rocks.

By the way, even the mens' room was immaculate.

— Bud

The Kat Klub

6920 W. North Ave.
773-589-9334
Hours: noon to 2 a.m. Sunday to Friday,
noon to 3 a.m. Saturday

Do you remember bars? Before we all got caught up in microbrews, tropical bars, blues clubs, and sports clubs, there were places that were just bars. Just like the ones my dad used to prop me up to, order me a Coke, and teach me to drink and just be one of the guys. The kind of place where people of every social class meet, and are equal, for the individual with the fullest drink is the richest. This describes The Kat Klub to the very letter.

The horseshoe-shaped bar holds at least six people at any time of the day. Electric "candle-lit" lanterns hang from the ceiling to give the place that "pub" type of atmosphere. The mirrors behind the bar are spotless (something I always look for, I don't know why), and football slogans a-plenty hang from the walls. There's a ledge along the front window to accommodate more drinkers in case the bar is full, which it often is, or to hold the more reclusive type.

This is the kind of place that houses mostly regulars, but they are certainly friendly to newcomers as well. It's really nice to see a barstaff that makes an effort to know everyone. Some people just sit at the bar and read. The bartenders drink here on their days off. Maybe it's things like that that make the place so comfortable. Everyone leaves on a Sunday morning not mildly buzzed, but usually stumbling, with another great time at The Kat Klub behind them.

Amusements are typical, two video slot machines, pub darts and a small pool table squeezed into the corner. One of the best parts of the entire establishment is the shuffleboard bowling machine, complete with a can of shuffleboard wax on top. I missed those so much, as when I was too young to see over, much less drink in bars, that was the only game my small hands could manage. They also hold fashion shows every Wednesday and Friday, which my dad still won't let me see.

Domestic bottles are under two dollars, Beck's two and two bits, and the three taps consist of Old Style, Bud Light and Berghoff Red. There is a regular cornucopia of hard stuff behind the bar. A sign on the wall denotes that they may even serve pizza, but who in the hell goes to a bar to eat anyway? Tall call mixed drinks are two seventy-five, and I had too many.

Star and Joanne, bartenders both agree that "it's like family."

"I think it's great," yelled an older patron from the corner, and the rest of the

159

The North Side Kat Klub-Kelly's on the Green

crowd seemed to have coinciding opinions about the bar. This is a place where you can't stop in just once, as it is too friendly to forget. Perhaps it's the Eve Arnold print from "The Misfits," or the Boulevard of Broken Dreams enlightened in neon, or maybe it's just because it is a nice, clean place.

In summary, it's nice to get out of Bucktown once in a while to find an establishment that isn't a theme bar, a microbrew haven, or a hot pick-up spot. The Kat Klub is just a spot where people gather, talk and relate, get to know each other, play some games and become close. Like family. Like it should be. So you go to the newest 1970s retro disco dance club and smoke your latest selection from the cigar of the month club. I'll be at "the bar" with a pack of Marlboros.

— Bud

Kelly's on the Green
2664 N. Greenview Ave.
773-871-7309
Hours: noon to 1:30 a.m. Sunday, 2:30 p.m. to 1:30 a.m. weekdays, noon to 2:30 a.m. Saturday.

Hidden amongst new town homes and rehabbed houses in the northwest corner of Lincoln Park is the area's best kept secret — Kelly's on the Green. Kelly's is a cozy neighborhood bar with loads of beers, televisions for the sports fan, a pool table, a cork dart board, pinball and a friendly atmosphere.

In March 1998, Tim Vaughan purchased the bar. Vaughan has maintained Kelly's on the Green's specialness. The site has housed a bar for years. In 1989, a group of bar veterans led by Dave Amado, purchased what was an old rundown tavern and turned it into an upscale neighborhood bar. They kept the original back bar and ceiling and added vintage 1920s light fixtures, new tables and stools, rehabbed the walls and put up a pictorial of Chicago history featuring Al Capone, Richard J. (The Boss) Daley, old Cubs, Sox, Bears and Bulls photos and pennants, beer company memorabilia and a shelf full of 100 year-old bottles dug up from across the street when new townhouses were being built.

Kelly's on the Green has created quite a name for itself among folks in the neighborhood. "Bad Bad" Leroy Brown, the actual guy from the Jim Croce song of the same name, stops in occasionally to play pool with the regulars. But most come into the bar to drink beer. Kelly's has 21 beers on tap. A few years ago, this was the most in the city. But now a few places have more taps. But the selection at Kelly's is still awesome — from micros, macros, and imports.

I've spent many-a-evening in Kelly's on the Green. I like the bartenders, the crowd, the location. It's just a good place to go.

— Tony Gordon

Kelly's Pub

949 W WebsterAve.
773-281-0656
Hours: 7 a.m. to 2 a.m. Sunday to Friday
7 a.m. to 3 a.m. Saturday

Kelly's Pub is a neighborhood Irish bar, catering to neighborhood residents as well as DePaul students. The bar is often filled to the brim on weekends.

Kelly's has an urban feel enhanced by the roar of the "el" trains going by, as well as a wall full of DePaul and Chicago memorabilia. It has a full bar, they carry Guinness, Harp, and Bass on tap, as well as a few other imports. For those who like Jagermeister, they offer it on tap.

Kelly's carries the predictable American brews, including Bud, Bud Light, Miller, Miller Genuine Draft, Rolling Rock and Old Style. Sam Adams and Leinenkugel Red were two interesting domestics on the menu. Prices are reasonable; domestic drafts are $2; imports $3.25. Pitchers of both are $5.50 and $9.50 respectively.

Want something to munch along with your drink? Pick from a selection of salty snacks, like chips, pretzels, etc., or order something more substantial, from burgers to mostaccioli. Food prices are reasonable too; prices range from $1 for soup to just under $5 for one of Kelly's sandwiches.

The bartender told me that Kelly's offers daily food and drink specials. They offered an Italian sausage special the day I stopped in.

Entertainment at Kelly's includes seven or eight televisions in strategic locations, two video games, including video darts. The jukebox features soundtracks, classic rock and Irish music CDs, along with the occasional hipster album like Urge Overkill, Tom Waits and Patsy Cline.

Expect Kelly's to packed on St. Patrick's Day. The overflow will be contained by a large heated tent just behind the bar itself.

-- Alexis

Kerouac Jack's

3407 N. Paulina St.
773-348-4321
Hours: 4 p.m. to 2 a.m. Sunday to Friday
4 p.m. to 3 a.m. Saturday

This unique bar at the corner of Lincoln, Paulina and Roscoe touts itself as a "beatnik restaurant and bongo bar." If that alone doesn't give you an idea of what to expect, the word "eclectic" comes to mind. Aside from vintage furniture and knick knacks, there's some funky hand-painted art which looks as

The North Side Kerouac Jack's-Keysters

The first floor has a full service restaurant and a 30-foot walnut wrap-around bar. Table tents along the bar include a beatnik dictionary so you can finally learn just what is a "riff" or a "Jim." There is also a decent but slightly above average priced beer selection which includes Bongo Beer (a Leinenkugel product). On Tuesdays and Thursdays you can get jumbo margaritas for $3.50. Upstairs is the "Party Pad" which is decorated in true beatnik-apartment fashion. This consists of vintage sofas, psychedelic lighting and entertainment in the form of a quarter -a-game pool table, and old-fashioned baseball and bowling games.

Outside is a charming but rather urban sidewalk cafe where you can sit and listen to trains from the Paulina station next door and watch traffic as you munch on the somewhat pricey but excellent eclectic cuisine which includes satay and unusual variations on Italian favorites.

Strangely enough, a must-see at this bar is the bathrooms. Although at first glance they seem typical, any place that has Kerouac readings piped in over a loudspeaker is worth checking out. The bathroom also boasts some "Wise words from Nordine" painted on the wall. It reads, "Don't try to be what you're not...The island you have is the island you've got." Whatever that means, if you're looking for something different in a neighborhood-type bar , a true "hipster" should check out this place.

--Paris

Keysters
4155 N. Pulaski Road
773-539-7837
Hours: 2 p.m. to 2 a.m. weekdays,
2 p.m. to 3 a.m. Saturday, 11 a.m. to 2 a.m. Sunday

What makes a good bar? The attributes of quality establishments include good atmosphere, decor, selection and prices. On a recent trip, I visited Keysters, a neighborhood pub on Pulaski Road just two blocks north of Irving Park Road. This drinking hole passes the grade for providing drinks, service, and atmosphere with flying colors.

Keysters has been in business since 1983 serving cold drinks in the Old Irving Park neighborhood. It is a small comfortable and clean establishment. The bar does cater to sports fans and makes it easy with TVs spread throughout. There is a circular bar which takes up most of the space in this joint. In addition, it has a pub feel, because of the wood trim throughout. It felt like I was drinking overseas.

For recreational activities, there are dart boards and a foosball table to test your competitive skills. After working up a thirst, Keysters offers many specials. Some of the specials rotate month by month. The current bargains include 50-cent drafts on Mondays, free pizza for all Bulls games, $1 domestic bottles on Wednesdays, Guinness and Bass pints for $2 on Thursday, and drinks for women are $1 on Saturdays.

Sometimes I wonder why women get drink specials anymore. I have met some lady bar patrons who have drunk me under the table. So much so that every time I'd get up to go to the washroom, their pints were gone by the time I got back.

Anyway, this was the first time I visited Keysters and I intend to visit this drinking hole in the near future again. So if you are on Pulaski Road heading north, stop in and get some good brew with quality service without any hassle.

— *Pete Schmugge*

Kincades Bar and Grill

950 W. Armitage Ave.
773-348-0010
Hours: 11 a.m. to 2 a.m. Sunday to Friday,
11 a.m. until 3 a.m. Saturday

Kincades is a maze disguised as a Lincoln Park sports bar. After a few drinks, when this bar is packed on a weekend night, walking around can be quite confusing. Nevertheless, there's much to do and drink at this place. There are large televisions in many of the rooms. There's electronic darts on one level, pool tables on another level and plenty of seating throughout the bar.

Kincades has a kitchen with many food stuffs to dine upon during Bulls and Blackhawk games. The bar also has a shuttle service to the games so stadium-goers can enjoy a draft at Kincades such as Killians, Bass, Bud and Miller before the games.

Fridays are big at Kincades so get there early for pool or darts. The crowds are largely college students and young professionals.

Kingston Mines

2548 N. Halsted
773-477-4646
Hours: 8 p.m. to 4 a.m. Sunday to Friday
8 p.m. to 5 a.m. Saturday

Let's face it, you can go anywhere to get a drink. When you're ready for something more than just a fast beer, when you want an experience or to be part of history in the making, head for the Kingston Mines. Located in the 2500 block of North Halsted for the past 12 years, the Mines has been a Chicago landmark since the late 1960s.

On any given night you will find the first quality blues that made Chicago famous. Don't get me wrong, the Mines is not a high-class, high cover-charge spot. In fact, the atmosphere is sort of pleasingly dull. No interior decorator went wild in here. Plain wood tables, rickety chairs and stools, long wood bars in two of the three rooms are backdrop to main focus; two stages that host two bands every night. Each band alternates playing for an hour each while the

The North Side Kingston Mines-Konak

patrons move back and forth from room to room to see the live music. Quite a bargain for the $8 to $10 average cover charge.

Name performers such as Eddie Clearwater, Son Seals, Charlie Love, and Chick Rogers are regulars. The former Valerie Wellington got her start at the Mines. Lesser known bands are also showcased and still deliver that feel-good, real-good, sometimes down and dirty blues.

As for the clientele, they range from young to yuppie, old to older, anonymous to famous. On any given evening you may find famous faces such as Mick Jagger, Michael Jordan, Harrison Ford or Michael J. Fox tucked in a corner. The night before his tragic helicopter crash, Stevie Ray Vaughan was at the Mines.

Why do so many celebs show up at the Mines when there are lots of Blues bars to chose from?

"We have a long-standing reputation of a friendly, wholesome place. People are treated well here, and we always deliver good music," said Doc Pelligrino, owner and operator. Doc shares the responsibility of running the place with four of his five children, but he is the final word on the choice of music. "I have always loved people, and I know what music will appeal."

Recently retired from the medical profession, Doc is quick to point out he did not make his fortune from the medical profession or the Mines.

"It was the stock market that supplied the capital to keep the Mines afloat over the past 25 years," Doc said. "I was recently asked to speak at the annual meeting of the Bar and Nightclub Owners conference in Chicago. I advised newcomers to the business to work for someone else for three to five years and to listen and learn all you can."

Sort of an eye opener when you realize how much goes into making the surroundings great when you want to go out for an evening and come away with an experience. Any night you spend at the Mines will be just that -- an experience.

Mixed drinks range from $3.50 to $5. Bottled beers go for $2.75 to $3.25. Pizza is available for those who get hungry. Plans are in the works for a full-service kitchen in the near future.

--Cupcake

Konak
5150 N. Clark St.
773-271-6688
Hours: noon to 1 a.m. Sundays, 3 p.m. to 1 a.m. Monday to Thursday, 3 p.m. to 2 a.m. Friday, noon to 2 a.m. Saturdays

Friendly patrons and friendly bartenders are my criteria for making a bar a special place. Upon visiting Konak, I was lucky enough to find a new bar to add to my small list of special bars. One of the main things which makes Konak special is owner Art Akova, a native of Turkey who has been running

164

Barfly Kokopelli-Konak

Konak, 5150 N. Clark St., owner Art Akova is a former professional soccer player.

Konak for two years. Akova, an avid soccer fan and former professional player, said he came to the U.S. in 1971 passing up a chance to play soccer professionally in Turkey. He said he was far more intrigued with the prospect of coming to the U.S. than to play soccer. However, soon after he arrived in Chicago he joined on the Chicago Mustangs, the city's first professional soccer team as a midfielder in 1972. He said he played for the Mustangs for a year than went on to pursue other interests.

Konak reflects Akova's love for soccer and sports. He has two autographed soccer balls from the German National Team perched on shelves behind the bar. He said he acquired the soccer balls at the World Cup here in Chicago during the summer of 1994. Akova also shows sports on televisions throughout the bar including a big-screen TV in the bar's "Living Room" — a cozy room with couches and carpeting near the back of the bar.

Konak is a great place to watch a game. Its diverse crowd is attentive to the games and cheers on our Chicago teams with a kind vigor. Akova also serves a variety of good food. His specialty is homemade pizza of which he makes the whole thing from scratch including the dough. He also serves a tasty batch of fish and chips on Fridays.

The bar is located in Andersonville, a North Side neighborhood known for its Swedish heritage but is currently a diverse, friendly mix of Chicagoans. Akova is well aware of the area's heritage and serves Glögg, a traditional Swedish winter wine.

Konak is situated about 10 feet south of Foster Avenue on Clark Street. It is a clean, long and loosely divided three-room establishment. Depending on where you are situated in Konak, it can feel like a pizzeria, a bar or a cozy living room. Adding to the overall pleasure of the place is a pool table and three video slot machines.

Draft beers include Bass, Harp, Bitburger and Red Wolf costing $2 a pint. The assorted list of domestic bottled beers includes the usuals such as Leinenkugel's, Miller and Rolling Rock for $2 a bottle. Konak has a small selection of quality wines available for $2.25 a glass.

Akova said he has not yet developed a specialty drink to call his own but on the night of my visit to Konak, many patrons were ordering "Dirty Mothers" which is made up of Kahlua, tequila and cream.

Akova said he likes to greet patrons and he knows many of them by name. He said he wants visitors to Konak to leave the bar knowing they had a good time. Well, I had a good time and will be back for sure.

— Tony Gordon

Kronies
18 E. Belview Place
312-649-6500
Hours: 3 p.m. to 4 a.m. weekdays, 3 p.m. to 5 a.m.
Saturday, 11 a.m. to 4 a.m. Sunday

One year ago I stopped into Kronies in hopes of getting out of the cold and knocking back a few. One year later I returned to really pay attention to detail and see if anything had changed. Nothing had.

Kronies is a comfortable pub just north of the Loop off of Rush Street. It is a no-frills bar in the midst of the beautiful Oak Street area. The inside decor reminds me of walking into a half-finished basement. The place is about 20 years old and is very cold. The walls are covered in freehand writing and beer posters, with the occasional license plate and old-time photograph. There are dart boards and a jukebox, but the night I was there the patrons (and the bartenders) seemed to be more interested in the Bulls game playing on the four TVs and one big screen inside.

The bar is owned by Gary and Daria Kron. About 11 years ago, Kronies bought Eliot's Nesst, the bar next door at 20 E. Belview (312-664-7010). The purchase added two more bars to the place, including a cozy one upstairs used for private parties and busy weekends.

Bartender Mike Bloem explained the bar is frequented by lots of Loyola and Northwestern students. Thursday night is popular at Kronies due to its 32-ounce Miller Lites for $2. Wednesday features $3 yards of Bud Lite while on Friday and Saturday pints of Bud and Miler Lite are $2. Bottled beer is of lim-

Barfly Kronies-La Cita Lounge

ited variety but Kronies does carry imports on tap such as Murphy's Irish Stout and New Castle Brown Ale. On slow evenings you can catch patrons dining on carry out from Ranalli's off Rush. They will deliver acclaimed favorites from pizza to pasta to Mexican dishes until 2 a.m.

Kronies can be a quiet place to hang during the week and a busy, crowded mess on the weekends. Either way, the crowd is friendly and the atmosphere is casual. Kronies never charges a cover and is cigar-friendly. It is a good option in a neighborhood of window shoppers and valet parking.

— Lee DiVita

La Cita Lounge

5975 N. Clark St.
773-506-7051
Hours: 2 p.m. to 2 a.m. Sunday to Friday,
2 p.m. to 3 a.m. Saturday

The bar is obscure with only two lit signs visible from the outside. The exterior looks gloomy and shadowy, but beyond the double doors of 5975 N. Clark St. is La Cita Lounge.

Upon entering the bar it's difficult to miss its beautifully exposed-brick walls. And once you're in, the bar is located on the left with a long row of stools. Tables are set up in the front window. However, you wouldn't know it from the outside because drapes are hung in the window, making it impossible to see inside. This gives the feeling, from the outside, that the place is a bit dismal. But from the inside this isn't true.

La Cita Lounge is a small, local bar with a bit of Spanish and Mexican flair. Most of the employees speak Spanish and when I was there it was the only language spoken by the young bartender. If you don't speak Spanish, it can be difficult to order a drink.

The bar is managed by Rosa. She has worked at the bar since it opened in May of 1996. And by her side sits security. Rosa said the bar has never had a fight, but it still has security. She said security is usually checking IDs at the door.

"Who are they going to respect more?" Rosa asked while pointing to a husky security guard.

The bar had a reasonable number of patrons for a Thursday night. It has a laid back environment and everyone seems to have a good time.

In the rear of the bar are two pool tables and a pinball machine. There is plenty of entertainment while you're throwing a couple back. Face it, how much outside entertainment do you need while sitting in front of a bar filled with liquor? And passing the time with snacking isn't an option. La Cita Lounge doesn't have a kitchen. So if you're hungry, BYOF. Television is out too unless you can understand the Spanish station. However, drinking is what

The North Side La Cita Lounge-La Flor De Acapulco

seems to be in.

So if you feel like running south of the border for a night, La Cita Lounge is the place to go.

— T.M. Kornelsen

La Flor De Acapulco
6021-23 W. Grand Ave.
773-637-8737
Hours: 10 a.m. to 11 p.m. Monday to Thursday,
10 a.m. to 1 a.m. Friday and Saturday,
11 a.m. to 11 p.m. Sunday

Underneath a huge green, white and red canopy on Grand Avenue lies a little touch of Mexico.

Host extrodinaire Javier translated the name for me as "The Acapulco Flower." I thought it meant "The Floor of Acapulco," but then again, my Spanish sucks rather badly.

Before the food or the margaritas, the first thing you notice is Javier. Host, waiter, and bartender, he is extremely charming, and always makes one feel at home.

The bar seats about 12 and seems to have every kind of booze imaginable behind it. Margaritas come in several sizes including a single for $1.95, a double for $2.95, the grande is $3.95, and the super grande goes for $8.95 and should only be ordered if you are incredibly thirsty. They also have several kinds of beer, but I strongly recommend the margarita. We're not talking run-of-the-mill, weak-as-hell, sterile, yuppified, watered down, made for 10 year-old children drinks, these are quite strong as well as tasty.

La Flor De Acapulco has an interior that is quite strange and very Mexican. Stucco walls display everything from sombreros to fishing nets. Accented with wood, it makes one feel at home and relaxed. A large garage door faces the street and can be opened on nice days. The Mexican flag and an American flag hang from the ceiling.

Speaking of nice days, bartender Juan says that on warm days, they open up their beer garden. This garden is way cool. From the cobblestone-type ground to the shack-like structure coming off the garage, it is one of the nicest I have seen. Old street lamps illuminate the garden and it is enclosed in brick. I cannot wait for it to open.

The food is out-fucking-standing. La Flor De Acapulco is without question one of the top three or four places in the city. It really stands out in that area because the place a few doors down serves what tastes like dog food. From the burritos to the shrimp cocktail, everything I have tried is of very high quality and tastes wonderful. The portions are huge for the price.

Barfly La Flor De Acapulco-Lake Breeze Lounge

New friends Rodger and Doll and old friends Steve, Theresa and Jeff agree. Doll even goes so far as to say, "I know it is good because it tastes like the food I would have at home." Being of Spanish descent, she knows its authenticity.

One of the reasons I like to eat Mexican so often is the fact that you are greeted with food as soon as you enter in the form of chips and salsa. La Flor De Acapulco has excellent salsa. The green is not quite as good as the red, but it is still better than about 75 percent of the salsas out there.

As with the margaritas, the food or the salsa aren't made for the squeamish. This is the real thing and it's pretty god-damn good. There are thousands of Mexican joints that serve Americanized food in this city. The Acapulco Flower is not one of these places. Please don't even come here if your idea of great Mexican food and margies is Pepe's. I don't want to have to wait for a table just because you stopped in an establishment that you're not going to be able to handle. This place is so Mexican that I was afraid to drink the water.

I don't mean to attack Pepe's. I like the place and eat there myself sometimes. But La Flor De Acapulco is the real thing. Hell, it's even family owned. This is a serious time for margarita lovers and unfortunately, there are only a few serious places.

— Bud

Lake Breeze Lounge
5401 N. Broadway St.
773-275-3604
Hours: 10 a.m. to 2 a.m. daily

The Lake Breeze Lounge is a little bar in a dark, little, out-of-the-way part of the city.

Upon entering the bar, I took a quick survey of the establishment. I noticed instantly there were no cliques of people, only individuals sitting at the bar and a few others scattered about the premises.

I walked up to the bar, placed my order with the bartender, and was pleasantly carded. I took a step back, smiled, and pulled out my driver's license. The Lake Breeze Lounge is off the beaten path and surprised me with its cautiousness. However, we must applaud them.

The Lake Breeze Lounge does not seem to be a popular hang out for young people, but a quiet place that serves mostly locals. The music was country and the chatter was kept to a low roar. Customers were still able to hear one of the two television sets. The news was on.

The lounge has a few poker game machines and a mini-bowling ball machine. A beer is a $1.25 for tap and you do get what you pay for.

The lounge's aesthetics are not exquisite, but holiday decorations are up and they are prepared for business.

— Tanya M. Kornelsen

The Lakeview East Bar and Grill, 3110 N. Broadway, is open 21-hours a day.

The Lakeview East Bar and Grill
3110 N. Broadway Ave.
773-281-5997
Hours: 7 a.m. to 4 a.m. daily

Some things never change. Some things never should. The Lakeview East Bar and Grill is such a place. A true microcosm of what makes Chicago, well, Chicago! Young, old, yuppies, theater people, street people, rebel and regulars; they're all welcome here. Open 21 hours every day, all varieties drift in and out, some like clockwork. Regulars perch on their favorite stools, sip a drink and comment on life as they see it. The theme song from the television program "Cheers" comes to mind, "...a place where everyone knows your name...." You can be as friendly or as anonymous as you choose.

It's a place where you can stop in and grab a drink then move on or you can stay awhile, shoot a game of pool, play a video game or get lost in the music. A large CD jukebox is the focal point midway down a long wall. The music selection is as diverse as the patrons. From Sinatra to B.B. King, Pearl Jam to Andrew Lloyd Weber, a couple of dollars sets the music mood to drink, think, talk or shoot some pool. One thing for sure, the sound system is superb.

Owner Alan Segal says he opened the place 12 years ago with a definite philosophy in mind.

170

Barfly Lakeview East-LAMA

"I wanted a place where everyone, and I mean *everyone*, would feel welcome," Segal said. "After all, that's what America is made up of -- all kinds of people."

The decor, (if you can call it that) reflects his attitude. Red, white, and blue are the predominate colors which reflects his armed service background.

"I'm a Vietnam Vet, combat duty," Segal said. "When I came home, I didn't feel welcomed."

A sign hanging in the bar says "The Lakeview always welcomes all Vets." I wanted to get as far away from stereotyped bars as possible. No ferns hang in the place. No waiters say, "Hi, my name's Bob." The staff is as diverse as the patrons. Segal practices what he philosophizes. His manager is Hispanic, Segal is Jewish, as is one of his bartenders, his wife is Afro-American, other employees range from Italian to Irish. This harmonious blend of staff and patrons creates an atmosphere where everyone is welcome and Segal proudly says, "We all get along."

A 25 foot-long bar dominates the room. Behind it is the traditional mirror and carved oak surround. During the summer months, patrons sit next to the open windows and feast their eyes on the street circus of Broadway. Guaranteed, there's always something or someone to look at on Broadway.

On tap, you'll find Heineken, Miller Genuine Draft and MGD Light. A full range of hard liquors and mixed drinks are available at a sliding scale. The time of day you drink determines the price. Stay away from the house wines. Check the daily schedule for specials, as they vary each day.

During sports events two televisions at both ends of the bar draw a big crowd. Drink specials during the games always encourage an appetite. So, when you've yelled yourself hungry rooting for your favorite team, yell for Mac, the resident chef. With a full kitchen in the back he can whip up a knockout snack or meal before the next commercial. His plump chicken wings are enough to make the Colonel hang his head in shame. And the hamburgers? They're juicy and enormous. Be real hungry when you order one. Mac is on call from 4 p.m. to 4 a.m. to satisfy any appetite any time of the night.

Don't have time to stay and visit? Drop into the adjoining packaged goods store, it's perfect for the quick stop and shop customer.

To sum it up, the Lakeview East is a place that can be counted on for drinks you know, music you recognize, friends to meet and food that satisfies.

-- Cupcake

Latin American
Motorcycle Association
2619 W. Division St.
773-278-6362

Celebrities have a way of finding things that real people do and make it fashionable for a while. Specifically things that groups of people have been doing for a long time and will continue to do when the stars get bored with them.

One of the groups that was riding motorcycles (Harleys, Hondas, Kawasakis, etc.) long before it became fashionable, was the Latin American Motorcycle Association, LAMA.

They started in 1980 at Division Street and California Avenue before moving to their current site of 2619 W. Division St. in 1989.

Actively involved in the community they throw parties for area children like bicycle shows at the Humbolt Park Boathouse and Halloween parties with candy-filled piñatas.

The recruiting process for LAMA, for those interested, starts with a sponsor. A club member can sponsor you at which time you start a six-month probation period. During this time, you get to know the club and they get to know you. They do have by-laws that members must follow. Membership is open to any nationality.

In addition to sponsoring parties for the kids, LAMA sponsors some of the best parties for adults like a "Toys for Tots" party and parties for the Illinois Harley Owners Group and A Brotherhood Aimed Toward Education (ABATE).

When they do not have a specific party planned, the clubhouse is open to anyone who wants to pull up and have a few drinks. The walls are covered with pictures of camping trips, bike shows and parties sharing the vast history of the association and members past and present. The atmosphere is so laid back, you can't help but find yourself immersed in a conversation about cooling systems or the last Sturgis run. For non-bikers, the Sturgis run is a festival in South Dakota where more than 50,000 bikers from all over the country converge each summer.

— *Paul Barile*

Laschet's Inn
2119 W. Irving Park Road
773-478-7915
Hours: 2 p.m. to 2 a.m. Sunday to Friday,
2 p.m. to 3 a.m. Saturday

It was a beautiful Saturday afternoon when I visited Laschet's Inn, a perfect excuse to drink a lot of weiss beer. I immediately met Franz Kokott, who owns Laschet's with his wife Ursula. He was careful to check my ID and then I prepared myself to drink, which is what the place is all about.

I say that because every sign in the place is inscribed with an old German saying dedicated to the art (or exercise) of drinking. Ursula was my translator. She pointed out her favorite one. Painted on the inside of one of the cabinets behind the bar, there is a picture of hundreds of men with their arms raised and steins up to their mouths. Above it says: Freiubung: 1-2-3 Proft, g'fuffa. Which means: exercise, 1,2,3, cheers. I recognized it as part of a song that I've heard my friends sing at least a million times.

"I get a kick out of it every time I dust it," Ursula said.

Barfly Laschet's Inn-Last Act

Everything inside Laschet's is a conversation piece. The bar has been there for about 20 years, and the Kokott's took it over seven years ago. A lot of the old memorabilia stayed with the bar after the previous owner left. There are newspapers from 1916, old German currency, cigarettes, and pictures from Chicago-based German festivals. But the three things that Ursula is most proud of are a piece of the Berlin wall complete with graffiti, a post-World War I map of Germany, and a stein atop the bar that holds 15 liters. She said that everybody always asks about the stein. Laschet's two-liter boot steins go for $15, so you do the math.

The beer selection at Laschet's is phenomenal. There are eight on tap at a cost of $2 for a 1/4 liter, $3.75 for a 1/2 liter. There are also 36 bottle choices. They also seem to have a glass with the logo of every beer they carry. I could have stayed there all day.

They also have landjager available, the German beef jerky sausage. They're $1.50, which comes with mustard. They were so good I had two. Ursula shared that they get them from Joe's Meats on Western Avenue. They don't serve any other food there but I swore I saw some frozen pizza floating around.

The crowd at Laschet's is very mixed. The neighborhood used to be primarily German. Ursula said the yuppies are slowly making their way in.

Enjoying myself so much at Laschet's on my first visit, I tried to come back on a Thursday and the place was packed. I found out why. Thursday is when a big German crowd from Holzhacker finishes the night at Laschet's. People my age started gravitating in around 6 p.m. While I was there I talked to a regular patron who told me a great story.

About three years ago there was a fire on the top floor of the building. The Kokotts live upstairs. There were off-duty firemen in the bar who called in the fire. I guess nobody was hurt, but as the bar downstairs filled with smoke, nobody left their stool and kept on drinking. That's a lot of faith to have in a bar. How cool is that?

— Lee DiVita

The Last Act

1615 N. Wells St.
312-440-4915
Hours: noon to 2 a.m. daily, 11 a.m. to
3 a.m. Saturday, 11 a.m. to 2 a.m. Sunday

On first appearance, the Last Act presents itself as a bright green awning suspended above pedestrian traffic at North Avenue and Wells Street. There's always more meaning to any first appearance.

A step within the front door displays a huge showroom with stained glass lights hanging above handsomely dressed booths and tables. In the back room lies two pool tables. Not too many people know about the beer garden secluded

173

further back from the pool tables; that's why I like it. From afar, the garden appears to be a blinding beacon of truth glowing at the edge of a narrow dark hallway. After hiking through the treacherous terrain of the Honey Brown, Michael Shea's and Guinness taps up at the front bar, the real goal lies in the back bar.

The beacon of truth breathes in the southwest corner of the beer garden. It looks like something straight out of Club Med. Behind the counter of the tropical bar is the world's largest lava lamp. And next to the world's largest lava lamp is one of the largest oceana wave machines complete with surf noises. The galvanizing wave machine rocks back and forth and creates waves in slow motion. Kinda like a water bed while the sheets are being shaken. Sometimes when a big wave rolls across the mid-section of the wave machine, the accompanying surf noise gets real loud, as if it was the noise of the actual wave. I'm not afraid to admit it...I have too much time on my hands.

The south side wall of the garden is embellished with a life size mural of a beach front. The foreground reveals a cafe and the background exhibits a great ocean front. At first I thought it was Lake Michigan, but the water was painted blue. Everybody in the mural is drinking "EX," so I think it might be one of the bottled beers Last Act serves. If you're a little light in the loafers, you'll take a soothing satisfaction in the hanging flowers surrounding the perimeter of the beer garden.

Every night welcomes food and drink specials. Two brothers run the bar. Tom cooks and Chris bartends.

The brothers have a selection of riveting food that will knock your socks off. I was talking with Tom and he told me they have the best steak and chicken fajitas. But I peaked through the menu and found a list of other scrumptious pabulums. Tornadoes Piedmonte is one dish which caught my attention. I'm not sure what that is but if I were able to pronounce it, it would probably sound impressive. The menu ranges from juicy tavern burgers to fabulous filets and exceptional prime rib. Appetizers include baked shrimp scampi and vegetable tempura. More big words; has to be good.

One minor detail often overlooked by the common patron of Last Act is the unique pint glasses. For example, one particular style is a Leinenkugel's Red pint glass. The name is embroidered in thick red writing with a multiple colored logo on it. The glasses are extra thick and are durable for years. Every time I have a party, everyone wants to know where I got my glasses.

The tap is any depressed alcoholic's dream and features Dundee's Honey Brown, Michael Shea's, Bass, Bud Light, Guinness, Harp, Heinekens, Legacy Red Ale, Leinenkugel's and Miller Lite. The usual bottled domestics and imports are available for a timid range of costs.

The Last Act has all the needs of life and more. Visit the hidden beer garden and indulge in surf. Get bombed and bloated then go techno dancing afterwards. I love the Last Act, man.

— *Willy Laszlo*

Barfly Lava Lounge-Lawry's Tavern

Lava Lounge

958 N. Damen Ave.
312-772-3355
Hours: 5 p.m. to 2 a.m. Monday to Friday,
5 p.m. to 3 a.m. Saturday

Lava Lounge opened February 1995 and replaced the Zig Zag Lounge. From its outside, it looks like a regular neighborhood tavern but once inside Lava Lounge is surprisingly large with a bar room up front and couches and pool tables in the back room, a former storeroom at the old Zig Zag.

Lava Lounge is a real comfortable non-pretentious place. It has a great microbrew selection and prices are reasonable. It never seems too crowded. There is usually plenty of room to sit. Lava has a nice old long bar to sit at, booths, and tables. The patrons run the gamut from neighborhood folks to Wicker Park artists and musicians. I've found the staff attentive and friendly. Lava is just a good place to go.

-- Tony Gordon

Lawry's Tavern

1028 W. Diversey Parkway
773-276-9730
Hours: 2 p.m. to 2 a.m. daily

It's early on a Saturday afternoon, and Lawry's Tavern is quiet. The dinner crowd won't be coming until later, hungry for homemade chicken and pork chops.

K.T., the bartender, frowns at the question.

"Is Lawry Price here?" she repeats. "Who's that?"

A few seconds later, she remembers.

"Oh, Price is his last name," she says. "You know, I didn't know that. I just knew him as Lawry. That's what everyone calls him."

Most people get a beer or shot when they finally reach that magical age of 21. Lawry Price got an entire bar.

Price took over Lawry's Tavern in 1959, after his father, who had founded the bar, passed away. And though barely legal, this younger Price was more than ready to run the neighborhood tavern Lawry Price Sr. had opened in the 1930s.

After all, Price lived above the tavern for most of his life.

"I always figured I'd be running it some day," Price said, while adding kernels to the tavern's popping machine. "All the time my father was running it, I could never picture myself doing anything else. There just wasn't anything else I ever wanted to do."

Price has now run the tavern for nearly four decades. The bar celebrated its 60th anniversary in May 1997.

"It's been a good run," Price said. "I've met a lot of people. A lot of nice people. Some real jerks, too. But there's been more nice people than jerks. That's why I'm still in this business."

Price's father opened his first bar across the street from the current Lawry's. He was 25.

"The bar was always a part of our lives," Price said. "All the while growing up, it was there."

As a kid, Price spent little time in his father's bar. Taverns were for adults, a rule his parents enforced. Most of Price's bar time came as he ran through it on the way to the family apartment.

As he got older, Price slowly became involved with the family business. Nothing too glamorous, at first. Mopping, sweeping, hauling cases of beer. But these beginnings convinced Price he'd one day stand behind the same bar as did his father.

For Price, it turned out to be a simple choice.

"I remember a lot of family dinners where my dad would be talking about one of his customers getting let go from their jobs," he said. "I didn't want to be working somewhere 25 years, and one day have someone come up to me and say my services are no longer needed. I heard about that happening too many times at the dinner table."

"Here, you take your own shot. You run things. If you blow it, then it's your fault, no one else's. That's the way I like it."

Despite its long history, Lawry's looks pretty unremarkable. A big screen TV dominates one wall. A jukebox hogs another. A lone pool table sits near the bar's rear. A pair of deer antler poke from above the bar.

Pretty standard stuff. But, Price explains, his bar, years ago, set the trends others still copy.

"We were a sports bar before anyone knew what a sports bar was," he said. "We didn't call ourselves a sports bar because we didn't know that's what we were."

Price points out that Lawry's was the first neighborhood tavern to feature a big screen TV. At one time, it was even the first to provide color sets. And in the 1960s, when the Chicago Bears couldn't win enough games to sell out Soldier Field, Lawry's was one of the few places that televised the blacked-out games.

These days, customers don't come for the big screen. They can get that anywhere. And Bears games? That torture, too, can be found in any other Lake View bar.

Lawry's patrons come for the food.

Bartender K.T. didn't take long to discover Price's kitchen talents. She'd been working at Lawry's less than a week when she realized Price was a magician with pork chops and battered fish.

"He cooks everything himself," she says. "He has his own kitchen. He even puts on his own chef's suit. It's pretty cool."

She disappears in a closet, reappearing seconds later with a bright white out-

Barfly Lawry's Tavern-Lemmings

fit, a Lawry's name tag sewn in its corner.

"See?" she asks, holding up the spotless jacket. "He throws one of these on. He has six of them. Always have to have a clean one ready, I guess."

Price serves his dinners from 6:30 to 10 p.m. three days a week. Chicken and pork chops make their appearances on Wednesdays and Saturdays. The all-you-can-eat fish fry highlights Friday evenings.

All attract a crowd.

"It's great food," said Josh, a Lake View resident. "You could eat it 'till you burst. The fish fry, especially. That's some good stuff."

"It's true," agreed Mark, another recent Lawry's guest. "I'd never eaten here before. But it's the kind of food that can make you gain weight, just from its smell. That's the sign of good food."

Price has seen a lot of changes since October of 1959, when he first started serving drinks at Lawry's. Back then, a crew of regulars filled the bar. Most of those are gone now, passed away or moved on to the suburbs. The new regulars are younger, transplants from other parts of the city.

When pressed, Price says no interesting bar stories jump into his head from his 39 years of tending to Lawry's. That doesn't sound right, though. And when Price reconsiders, he remembers columnist Mike Royko and author Studs Terkel stopping in a few times. Film makers with WTTW-Channel 11's "Image Union" television show even filmed the pair at the tavern, and broadcast it nationally.

Matter of fact, Terkel even put Price and his bar in one of his books, "The Great Divide."

"Off the top of my head, though, I can't think of any specific stories," Price said. "But there's been a lot of good times. That's what I remember. That and all the people I've met. I guess that's just as good."

Lawry's is just a great place and a great Chicago tradition — a must stop for any Barfly.

— Dan Rafter

Lemmings
1850 N. Damen Ave.
773-862-1688
Hours: 4 p.m. to 2 a.m. Sunday to Monday,
4 p.m. to 3 a.m. Saturday

Chicago's Bucktown neighborhood is loaded down with great bars — The Riptide, Lincoln Tavern, Gallery Cabaret, The Map Room, and The Bucktown Pub among others. Each place has its own character and own great attributes. Lemmings is no exception. This is a great bar and has everything I want: laid-back atmosphere, good jukebox, television, special movie nights, good beer selection, groovy decor, lots of free newspapers, pool table, board games, dogs,

177

friendly patrons and friendly bartenders.

Steve, a Chicago bar veteran, manages the place. Lemmings is positive reflection of this great guy. Steve's into the history of beer and at Lemmings he's assembled a fantastic collection of Schlitz memorabilia. Most of which I haven't seen anywhere else. He's also into good beer and brings in the latest microbeers. He loves dogs and lets patrons bring their pets into the bar. He's also really laid back and has created a great mellow atmosphere at Lemmings.

Those who work for Steve are mellow as well. I always see Matt behind the bar. He's a super nice guy with a great wit and high intellect. Then there's old friend Sung Koo, a seasoned bartender who can also be seen behind the bar in other neighborhood haunts. Sung's rather interesting in his own right. He's one of the former publishers of parody newspaper The Planet, a monthly newspaper that was around in the late 1980s. It was a great read, real funny, similar to The Onion (new to Chicago) but much better. Sung also ran Haley's Comics, a former North Side comicbook store that had lots of hard-to-find underground comics.

I can't say enough about Lemmings. It's got Stratego, got God's sake. What more can you ask for?

— *Tony Gordon*

The Levee

4035 W. Fullerton Ave.
773-342-2808
Hours: 11:30 a.m. to 2 a.m. Sunday to Friday, 11:30 a.m. to 3 a.m. Saturday

If, after finishing a few Miller Lites, the decor and ambiance of The Levee begins to seem oddly familiar, there's no need for alarm. For as any true sports couch potato can attest to, it was at this very bar, just a few years ago, that the famous "Da Bulls" Lite Beer commercials were filmed. Any more time spent sharing in The Levee's offerings and it becomes easy to see why Hollywood chose this place as a true representation of the down-to-earth blue-collar ethic so manifest in the Superfans.

In a Chicago bar community where the measure of longevity is often times relegated to months or years, The Levee, and its two same-site predecessor — the big-band haunt Gaity Village and the legendary McDuff's — has maintained this ethic on the corner of West Fullerton for more than six decades. When current owner Warren Johnson bought the place in 1980, he changed the name but kept the age-old spirit of the place intact in its tradition as a neighborhood watering hole built upon the self-evident truths of good food, good friends, good sports and beer.

Thematically, the decor of The Levee resembles any number of Wrigleyville sports bar but without any of the gaudy neon glow or Crate-and-Barrel inspired athletic representations. The dusty walls are almost invisible behind a plethora of sports and other drinking-establishment memorabilia, including one wall in

Barfly The Levee-Liar's Club

the bar's main room covered with what many consider to be the world's largest collection of beer mirrors. The wall opposite this boasts a varied selection of Chicago athletic souvenirs. Many are autographed, many are priceless, and the selection once included the actual Heisman Trophy, on loan, of football legend and Levee regular Johnny Lattimer.

The room adjacent to this one, with its walls tastefully accoutered in early American rusty-tool, is a bit more pastoral. Serving as the game room, here are found the many jocular diversions offered by The Levee including ping-pong, darts, a regulation-size basketball hoop and 50-cent pool tables, which at any given time may be occupied by members of the 38-bar pool league for which The Levee is the headquarters.

n these two rooms is The Levee's most unique feature, the actual bar. Shaped like the pretzel found on the label of Ballantine Beer, the bar is an original design of the original owner back in the 1930s. Large enough to seat 50 or so people at any one time, its unique shape also allows for the comfortable forma-tion of cozy beer klatches at any one of its corners.

Drink and beer prices at The Levee are inexpensive around the $2 range. For lunch, the Levee opens up its kitchen to cook an awesome Chicago-style menu. The daily lunch crowd is made up mostly of workers from neighborhood facto-ries like American Decal, Newlywed Foods and the world's original and only manufacturer of lava lamps. Good stuff to eat like beef and corned beef, pizza, fried chicken and the mysterious Cannibal Sandwich.

Rapt in tradition as old as Fullerton Avenue itself, The Levee stands as a monument to all that is good and right in a Chicago bar. From a wooden phone booth to an ancient cash register to a huge wandering dog "Butkus" to a Cubs World Series pennant on the wall, The Levee hearkens back to a past that was a great deal easier and more relaxed than what is dealt by life these days.

This review is dedicated to, in memoriam, Lady a fine dog (D. 1994), and to the sweet old lady that lives upstairs fro the bar and owns the building.

— Johnny Masiulewicz

Liar's Club
1665 W. Fullerton Ave.
773-665-1110
Hours: 8 p.m. to 2 a.m. Sunday to Friday,
8 p.m. to 3 a.m. Saturday

For those who always wanted to drink at a hip shriner or moose lodge but just couldn't find the right one, well head on over to the Liar's Club.

The Liar's Club opened to a packed house on June 22, 1995, and ever since that day it has had a steady flow of patrons enjoying the bar's fez lamp shades, old-time booths with circa-1973 red-hanging wall cushions, disco room and upstairs lounge.

The overall feel of the place is happy, even humorous, which is a representation of the playful personality of owner Herb Rosen.

"I started bartending when I was (age) 21 at the Cubby Bear," Rosen said. "I actually started working there when I was 20. I sold pins shaped like Wrigley Field and I had to take Polaroid photos of hillbillies (Cub fans), cut their photos out, and place them in these pins."

"When I turned 21 the Cubby Bear was in need of bartenders and they asked me one night if I could bartend. "I said, 'uh, yea, sure (wink, wink), I can bartend.'"

After a short stint at the Cubby Bear he moved up the street to work at the Raw Bar, 3720 N. Clark St., where he stayed until April, 1995, as bar manager.

"I learned to bartend really at Raw Bar," Rosen said.

Opening up his own place was a natural progression for Rosen who had a steady following at Raw Bar and additional following from his days as bass player for Rights of the Accused, a defunct local band that used to put on one hell of a show with lots of beer sprayed into the crowd.

When scouting the building that would later house Liar's Club, Rosen stumbled upon a drunk 1970s legendary guitar player/singer.

"The building was owned by a former landlord of mine," Rosen said. "We went over there and Joe Walsh from the Eagles was living on the second floor. He was out of his mind. He looked like a street person and the place was trashed. The big joke is that we were going to play 'Rocky Mountain Way' over and over upstairs (where Walsh used to live and is now the Liar's Club's lounge)."

The bar itself used to be the River East and was in poor condition in early 1995 when Rosen looked at it. Rosen had to completely overhaul the place and throw out the trash left upstairs by Walsh. They enlisted the expertise of former Medusa's and Foxy's owner Tom Hemingway. Medusa's was a popular juice bar in the 1980s (Editor's note — it used to stay open until 9 a.m.!) located at Sheffield Avenue and School Street. Foxy's, formerly located at Belmont Avenue and Halsted Street recently closed and was known for its Sunday "Raunch-O-Rama," an "out-of-control" dance party, Rosen said.

Hemingway came up with much of the design while Rosen and friends did the actual remodeling during an approximate 5-month period. The rehab included ripping down an old office-type drop ceiling, unveiling a high tin ceiling, replacing electrical wiring and installing lamps, booths, wall padding and cleaning the place up.

"We finished rehabbing 15 minutes before opening," Rosen said.

Forty-five minutes later, the bar was filled to the brim and stayed that way until closing.

"I didn't expect Thursday (opening night)," Rosen said. "We ran out of everything," he said adding that the next few nights saw big crowds as well.

To entertain the crowds, Rosen has a strong DJ line-up and continues the tradition of Foxy's "Raunch-O-Rama" on Sunday nights.

But one of the main components of the bar which Rosen is extremely excited about sits in the upstairs lounge.

Barfly Liar's Club-Lilly's

"If it gets too out of hand downstairs," Rosen said, "you can go upstairs where there will be lounge music, a mellow atmosphere and a Kiss pinball machine!"

Liar's Club is definitely one of the best bar's in Chicago. It is a unique and fun place. The bar is located about 50 yards west of Clybourn of Fullerton Avenue.

— Tony Gordon

Lilly's
2513 N. Lincoln Ave.
773-525-2422
Hours: 5 p.m. to 2 a.m. daily, 5 p.m. to 3 a.m. Saturday

The gentleness of Lilly's is rather immediate. Although Lincoln Avenue is often busy and boisterous, Lilly Vonhodowanic's place stands in calming contrast to all those seemingly endless, frenzied hot spots. There is no large-screen television at Lilly's. It's a place without gimmicks: no pool table, no electronic dart board, no Silly String, no heavy-metal nights, no mirrored fishbowl-like facade, and no dizzying array of regional microbrews.

Instead, Lilly's is a casual oasis in a desert of meat-market mayhem. It's comfortable, warm and friendly. A place that's hip, yet unpretentious, with a weathered charm and an intelligent clientele. The conversation is definitely low-wattage and urbane. This is not a place for post-college types who wear oversized sweatshirts and get unapologetically drunk and messy, or their too-cute blond girlfriends who are still "into" tight tops and acid-washed jeans.

The bar itself is small, but it does have enough depth to allow for a stage and a dozen or so wooden tables that are scattered from front to back. The decor is strictly garage sale. There's also an upstairs with several small rooms, all dark and sparsely furnished. Intimacy is not only a possibility up there, it's a backdrop for romance.

Back downstairs, on most nights, you're likely to find live music, starting at 9:30 p.m. There's usually a cover charge, but it's only a couple of dollars, which is what I paid on a recent Wednesday night. My best bargain of 1997 so far, just ahead of Mama Tish's "Buy One, Get One Free" offer on Italian ice.

Never have I been able to carry a tune and my only formal training was the six weeks of accordion lessons that my mother forced on me disguised as a birthday present. Still, I have always loved the sound and feel of live music, particularly when it's good. The night I was at Lilly's, it was very good. So good, that I stayed for both sets from Waldo Ocana & Friends, a band that certainly should have trademark rights on adult contemporary, Latin-flavored music. Ocana is a mid-forties vocalist who is fronting his first band after 30 years as a house drummer at some of Chicago's classiest cabarets. He has an easy, lilting voice and a confident stage presence.

Because Chicago is a city of neighborhoods, Chicagoans tend to frequent their local bars where they know they'll find their favorite place to sit, and have a chance to connect with other familiar faces. Lilly's has the feel of a cozy, corner tavern. Owner-bartender Vonhodowanic knows most people by name, and she's as cordial as she is attractive. She also makes a jumbo Long Island Iced Tea to dream of; one of which almost landed me on file at the Missings Persons Bureau. As we had a drink together, I mentioned to her that at one time my uncle owned the Biograph Theater, just a block down the street from her place. I found out, then, that she's been in business for 15 years. Her father bought her the bar because she was twenty-one years old, unemployed and not too concerned with her future. Lilly turned out to be a sure-bet for success.

In Lincoln Park, bars open and close like matchbook covers. Rents are high and it's not easy to turn a profit. Gentrification has chased away some of my favorite hangouts. Although Lilly's is in no imminent danger, I'm always bothered when I hear that yet another coffeehouse is about to open, because it may be replacing one more small piece of my nightlife. The entire North Side, in fact has been inundated with cafes and espresso bars.

WAKE UP! This AIN'T the West Coast. We are not effete, sun-kissed, bon vivants who don't know a ward committee from Sam Sianis. Not only are we the "City of Big Shoulders," we are the city of Studs Terkel, Gwendolyn Brooks, Buddy Guy and Koko Taylor. No chance of a cappuccino drinker in that group. The point is, we had better take care of places like Lilly's, or, like the unicorn and Jimmy Hoffa, they'll disappear.

— *George Rawlinson*

Lincoln Tap Room
3010 N. Lincoln Ave.
312-868-0060.
Hours: 3 p.m. to 2 a.m. weekdays, 3 p.m. to 3 a.m.
Saturdays, 1 p.m. to 2 a.m. Sundays.

Lincoln Tap Room is a great hangout. There's always cool people, great beer prices, friendly bartenders, and good across-the-board music.

Since its transition from featuring live music, they've redecorated and created a relaxed atmosphere with non-pretentious artsy/slacker furniture, two pool tables, a pinball machine, rotating artwork, two meaty televisions on which they show local indie movies and/or videos. They're working on some type of Sunday matinee. Talk to the bartenders about showing your stuff there. The music is DJ'd or played through the jukebox. There's room galore to sit, stand, dance, or do cartwheels. And, best of all, they've got air conditioning.

Treat yourself to a cozy cab ride there, and even tip the cabbie, because you won't need to penny pinch to drink. Starting with Hamm's in a can for one buck (prices may have changed), they serve 1/2 pints ranging from $1 Berghoff to $1.75 Bass Ale. In between are Sierra Nevada Pale, Legacy, Big Shoulders,

Barfly Lincoln Tap-Lincoln Tavern

Porter and Bell's Amber Ale. Pints are $2 to $3, pitchers start at $6. Heartland Weiss on tap is $3.50 for 16 ounces, $4 for 20 ounces or a pitcher for $13. Bottled beers range from $1.75 to $5.

Lincoln Tavern and Restaurant
1858 W. Wabansia Ave.
773-342-7778
Hours: 10 a.m. to 10 p.m. daily

Lincoln Tavern, owned and operated by the Folak family for 45 years, possesses a certain coziness and warmth that I have not experienced anywhere else. On a recent Friday night, Bill Folak Jr. was more than gracious about showing me around the place which consists of a unique dining room and a bar.

The dining room, was built to look just like a log cabin. Inside one feels as though they are trespassing into someone's hunting quarters. A massive stone fireplace stands in the center of the room, and on the walls hang heads from deer, javelina and wild boar. One thing that must not go unmentioned is a large diorama encased in glass depicting a placid scene of geese flying over a body of water and real vegetation.

The dining room is open for lunch from 11 a.m. to 2 p.m. every day except Saturdays, and the room is open for dinner from 5 to 9:30 p.m. Wednesdays and Fridays. Wednesday nights features spaghetti and Western-style beef tips. Friday nights are geared more for the carnivore with steaks, chicken, ribs and the Lincoln's signature Roast Duck. The Lincoln Tavern is also well known for its homemade chili, served at lunch and dinner.

The bar room has as much personality as the dining room. The walls are busy with many photos and collectable beer mirrors. I sat under an autographed photo of Bill Curtis (famed Chicago television news anchorman) with a young woman in formal attire.

The bar sells Illinois Lottery tickets making it the only tavern I have ever seen with an Illinois Lottery machine (Bill said no one has bought a winning ticket there yet). But what I loved most about the bar was its deer antler changeliers, they're quite unique.

Lincoln Tavern has a rich history and is a collector's item in itself. I was surprised to learn from Bill that Wolcott Avenue, which borders the tavern on its west side, used to be named Lincoln Street. When Bill's grandparents Albert and Sophie Folak started the business in 1950 they named the place after Lincoln Street and decided not to change the bar's name when the city changed the street's name.

So even though the street which borders Lincoln Tavern has changed, the bar itself has maintained its Folak identity. Bill's sister is the chef and Bill's mom and dad help out in just about every area. To drink with the Folaks, beers cost only $1.75 for bottles and draughts. On draught is Pabst, Honey Brown Ale and Augsburger. Draughts change periodically. Bottles consist of Strohs, Special

The North Side Lincoln Tavern-Little Rascal's

Export, Becks, Lite, Black Dog, Point and Michelob.

With a barrage of new flashy bars, some complete with dress codes, opening over the past few years just blocks away in Wicker Park, the area has lost many of its neighborhood gems. However, the Folaks, in a quiet consistent manner, have remained steadfast and plan to be around a long time. Bill quoted his father by saying, "It's Chicago's best kept secret."

— *Lisa Gulotta*

Little Rascal's Bar and Grill
4356 W. Belmont Ave.
773-545-1416
Hours: 11 a.m. to 2 a.m. Monday to Sunday,
11 a.m. to 3 a.m. Saturday

I drove by Little Rascal's one night in a desperate search for some place to review. I don't recommend this, especially when you're not familiar with the neighborhood. But a look down Kostner made me feel like I was in the suburbs, complete with the identical-looking bungalows lining the street.

I expected the place to be a total dive, the kind of place that serves Old Style and Schlitz only. But Little Rascal's surprised me.

It does carry Old Style, but it also features a decent selection of imported bottles such as Murphy's, Julius Echter Weiss and Zweic. Draft beer is domestic. Every Tuesday you can get pitchers for $3.50.

On Thursdays, you can get a daiquiri, piña colada or margarita for only $2. I couldn't pass up a deal like that. My margarita was very rich, as was my friend's piña colada. I think we were the first ones to order that type of drink here, because the blender was spotless and the look from the bartender was priceless. But don't shy away from ordering mixed drinks. Little Rascal's has a good selection of hard liquor. And I did see the bartender pour a lot of vodkas.

Little Rascal's is open early for lunch and late for munchies. They have a small but cheap menu. All sandwiches come with free fries and soda. Pizza and appetizers are also available.

The inside of the bar resembles your average sports bar, with a pool table, a couple of TVs and walls covered with posters of sports stars and half-naked chicks. I didn't get a good look at the selections in the jukebox, but I do know it's well stocked with Metallica. I think someone played the band's entire self-titled CD while I was there.

Little Rascal's seems like the kind of place people go to bullshit about the news and whatever game is playing on the TVs. But that's what everybody goes to bars for, isn't it?

— *Lee DiVita*

Lizzie McNeil's Irish Pub
400 N. McClurg Court
312-467-1992
Hours: 3 p.m. to 1:30 a.m. weekdays,
noon to 2 a.m. Saturday, noon to 1:30 a.m. Sunday.

There is a famous exchange between noted British politician Benjamin Disraeli and one of his adversaries in the House of Parliament that goes something like this:

Disraeli was creating some kind of chaos on the floor of Parliament when one of his opponents accosted him. "You, sir, shall die either by the hangman's noose or by a venereal disease."

Calmly yet quickly, Disraeli returned fire, "That, my good sir, depends of whether I embrace your politics or your mistress."

I relate this anecdote, not because it has anything to do with the Irish bar I was to review, but because the Irish bar I was to review was so void of character there's not a whole hell of a lot to write about and I need to take up some space. Whiskey Boy told me this story about Disraeli as we sat at the bar at Lizzie McNeil's Irish Pub, drank our snakebites and fruitlessly took in its vapid decor searching for any hind of Irishness.

Lizzie McNeil's, to be fair, is the bottom floor of one of those huge residential towers on the north side of the river — not a lot you can do about character. The bar is new-looking and feels a little bit plastic. The word we kept tripping over was "faux." There are faux street lamps built into the bar top, faux old bookshelves, faux dart bards, a faux fireplace and faux Leprechauns running around the place. The bartender explained these small people were actually children there with their parents. I didn't buy it.

The room is open with very high ceilings painted black with pipes and vents exposed, strangely reminiscent of a techno dance club. A nice feature is one entire wall is made of windows overlooking the river. When night fell, the Christmas lights on the trees lining the river made for quite a pretty mural-like feel. Toward the back is a cozy little corner with couches and bookshelves containing old books with titles like, "The Autocrat of the Breakfast Table" by Oliver Wendell Holmes, "Burr" by Gore Vidal and a biography of the aforementioned Prime Minister Disraeli by D.L. Murray. I'm sure no one has ever read these books, they are present only to add more faux character.

The bar itself is very long, stretching almost the entire length of the wall opposite the windows. Behind the bar are situated 17 taps and a very helpful, friendly barkeep. There are two TVs, two pool tables and three dart boards (one real, two faux).

Two things that got me off to a bad start with Lizzie's were the smell and the sounds. We walked in to the sounds of ABBA and the arresting stench of popcorn. Popcorn, and especially the smell of popcorn, belongs in the movie theater, period. When I walk into an Irish bar, I don't want to think I've made a wrong turn and ended up in the refreshment barracks at Target.

You'll notice in my description of the Irish bar, my failure to relate anything Irish about it. That is mainly because, when designing this particular Irish bar, the "Irish" part must have slipped the owner's mind. Following is the total sum of things Irish at Lizzie McNeill's Irish Pub: many Guinness mirrors and posters and a Bud Light neon shamrock; Harp and Guinness on tap; Jameson, Blackbush and John Power and Son whiskies on tap; The Pogues, The Cranberries, U2 and Van Morrison on the jukebox; one drunk guy at the end of the bar with a semi-coherent brogue.

My Aunt Patty's kitchen is more Irish than Lizzie McNeill's Irish Pub. The big difference is the drunk guy on the end of the bar. Lizzie McNeill's has to keep him around for faux authenticity. Aunt Patty has to keep him around because it's in her wedding vows.

— T. Wright Townsend

The Local Option
1102 W. Webster Ave.
773-348-2008
Hours: 5 p.m. to 2 a.m. Sunday to Friday,
5 p.m. to 3 a.m. Saturday

When Hugh Haller and his five silent partners rolled their investments from a small real-estate developing company into a building at 1102 W. Webster in 1986, they were expecting the normal rehab challenges. This location, however, was the former site of the Chessman bar, a rough biker joint also known as Fred & Tiny's for more than 17 years.

Because the building contained the bar, they bought the entire package and decided to remodel and reopen it. The rehab continued for about a month when an envelope was slipped under the bar door from "concerned neighbors;" they wanted to know in what direction the owners were planning to take the reborn tavern.

Hugh and one of his partners went to a meeting with about 25 middle-aged and elderly neighborhood residents who made it abundantly clear that they were fed up with motorcycles, fights, and the general ruckus of The Chessman. Hugh, in turn, made it clear that he wanted to improve the tavern.

"We could see the disbelief on their faces, and I looked at my partner, thinking these people don't care what kind of beer we want to serve," Hugh said.

The partners listened to the locals, seeking compromise. Near the end of the meeting, the neighborhood spokesman said, "as long as I live here, there will never be another bar on that spot."

Soon after, a registered letter arrived informing the partners that the locals were going to exercise a precinct option to keep the bar closed. This "local option" is an ordinance that can vote a precinct dry, Hugh said. If the organizing group can get 25 percent of the voters in their precinct to sign a petition endorsing the option, the group can file a public record with City Hall. Bar

Barfly Local Option

owners then have 30 days to attempt a reversal by getting the percentage of local voters endorsing the option back under 25. If the bar owners fail, the issue goes to general election.

"You have to realize the risk an owner faces if this gets on a ballot," said Hugh. "We would be shut down."

The partners obtained legal counsel and initiated a lengthy door-to-door campaign urging people to reverse their opinions about their establishment.

"People were sympathetic, and gave us a chance," continued Hugh. "We found out that people were told that we planned on making the bar a gay punk-rock club with a 1,000 square-foot deck. The misinformation was amazing."

A few days later, Hugh was approached by the spokesman of the local anti-bar group. He handed Hugh an envelope with $1,000 hoping it would keep the bar from being opened. "Are you kidding me?" was Hugh's response.

Two days before the bar's grand opening, Hugh placed a neon sign in the window — THE LOCAL OPTION — his bar's new name. Two month's later, that bribing anti-bar spokesman moved out of the neighborhood, Hugh said.

With the bar up and running, Hugh looked for ways to make his bar distinctive. Sipping a cold Corona one day, he had an inspiration. Corona's bottle was silkscreened, not labeled with paper like so many other beers. He bet that like Corona, Rolling Rock beer has similar appeal because its bottle had intriguing silkscreen labeling. Rolling Rock was the beer he'd known growing up in Cincinnati, and the silkscreened bottle, he thought, would provide the identifier he was looking for.

"Nowhere in Chicago could I find it on draught or in the 12-ounce bottles, only the 7-ouncers with paper labels."

With that, Hugh's mission to bring 12-ounce, silkscreen label Rolling Rocks was on. He called the brewer direct and explained his idea. Brushed off at first, he called every week and finally won over the folks at the Pennsylvania company. They were indeed looking for Midwest exposure.

An administrator from local liquor distributor Louis Glunz was skeptical. "As long as I work here," he told Hugh, "you will never get it. It won't sell."

Hugh, undaunted, called Rolling Rock again. They convinced Glunz directly to obtain a few barrels and a few cases of the 12 ouncers. After a month, the beer was selling so well at The Local Option that the bar was a virtual sea of green. Rolling Rock began to get requests at other bars.

"We were," said Hugh proudly, "the bar that brought Rolling Rock to Chicago."

After a year, The Local Option became involved with the Sheffield Garden Walk, with Hugh taking charge of replacing former sponsor Old Style with Rolling Rock. That year, the formerly skeptical Glunz sent out 50 kegs for the first day of the festival. By day's end, 47 kegs were dried. Rolling Rock was on the map in Chicago, thanks to the Local Option.

— *Dave Carmody*

The Lodge

21 W Division St.
312-642-4406
Hours: 2 p.m. to 4 a.m. weekdays,
noon to 5 a.m. Saturday noon to 4 a.m. Sunday

Down on the Division bar strip is this little bar. The name is fitting as there is a pleasant 'lodgy' feel to this establishment accentuated by an abundance of wood, 19th Century prints of Civil War soldiers, miscellaneous wall plaques, and amber -colored lighting.

The Lodge has been around since 1957 and is often a destination for celebrities. There are a few tables, as the space is needed to fit the crowds. Yet there is still space to plop down your drink on a long shelf along one of the main walls. Underneath the shelf are coat hooks for lack of any place to put a jacket. Towards the back is an old stand-up jukebox containing the best of Frank, Elvis, Aretha Franklin, and the Eagles to name a few . There is also a bowling machine to waste some quarters on with a TV hanging overhead. Another pleasant feature is the shelled peanuts offered at the bar and the empty shells which litter the whole floor. It's a neat little feature for the paranoid, as no one can sneak up on you.

Whether it is Division Street law or a wise move with the amount of rowdies on the weekend, tap beer is the only choice, no bottles. The tap includes McEwan's, Killians, MGD, Lite, Amstel light, and good old Bud. Surprisingly, there is plenty of vodka and whiskey, (who would have guessed?) and the Lodge even has a Jager tap. Rounding out the drink list is wine and Champagne including Dom Perion for the spendthrift.

As with the territory, make sure to bring the I.D. and a couple of bucks for parking.

Luney Tunes Saloon

2744 N. Laramie Ave.
773-237-0456
Hours: 9 a.m. to 2 a.m. Mondays to Friday,
7 a.m. to 3 a.m. Saturday, 11 a.m. to 7 p.m. Sunday

I have often driven past the Luney Tunes Saloon and wondered what was this unassuming drinking hole like. To my surprise, walking into the bar with a friend recently, we found the clientele as low key as the bar itself, in fact, not one patron was present. This was a Saturday night at 8:30 p.m.

The bartender was friendly, and while she talked to my friend, I walked into the other room. There was a pool table and a stage at the front with miscellaneous musical equipment, but no musicians (while there are usually bands at Luney Tunes, this night was an exception).

Returning to the bar, I took note of three video games, a jukebox, and a row

Barfly Luney Tunes-Lottie's

of booths along the wall. During the next hour, several gentlemen of apparently Southern extraction entered, the regulars no doubt. As for women, a poster by the bar proclaimed that Wednesday is ladies night.

The prices for bottle beer caught me by surprise. Shunning the hard stuff, I ordered a Miller, paying the $2.75 in disbelief. A more economical option, Red Dog, was on tap for a buck special. Miller and Icehouse are also available on tap, completing the Miller-product trio of tap brew.

This is definitely not a bar for swinging times, but rather a place to swig a couple drinks down after work. At Luney Tunes, it's possible you'll have the entire bar to yourself, and drink in solitude.

— Pete Schmugge

Lottie's
1925 W. Cortland St.
773-489-0738
Hours: 4 p.m. to 2 a.m. weekdays,
11 a.m. to 3 a.m. Saturday, 11 a.m. to midnight Sunday

Lottie Virginia Zagorski opened Zagorski's Rathskeller, at 1925 W. Cortland St., in 1934, just after Prohibition ended. From then until her death in 1974, at the age of 67, she was the most notorious hermaphrodite bar owner in all of Chicago. It seems that she was loved, respected or feared by those who knew her.

Zagorski's Rathskeller has since been renamed Lottie's after its former owner and her legacy lives on. According to a long-time regular, Lottie served many people at her bar from an assortment of friends, neighboring families and boilermaker-drinking workers, policemen, politicians and "other" clients — all of them came to this spot for drink and relaxation. The fact that some of them entered at the front door and others took a lower side door entryway was overlooked.

The side door did not lead to the barroom. It was a private entrance leading to a cellar bar where much more than liquor was provided. Gambling, prostitution and other vices preferred were available. Here visitors bet on the horses or gambled amongst themselves, a bookie ran a wire room and various forms of entertainment were enjoyed — dancing girls, strip tease and "talent shows."

North Side aldermen and ranking policemen rubbed shoulders with all sorts of Chicago's gangster population. Some of these included Joseph "Joe Gags" Gagliano, who ran a syndicate controlled network of wirerooms; Andy "The Greek" Louchious, a payoff man and gambling boss, and William "Smokes" Aloisis, a mob gambling overseer. Supposedly, Al Capone stopped in once, too.

Lottie's gambling network was established early in her career and carried on through the years. As late as 1972, police were compiling a rap sheet against her, attempting to indict her for gambling on premises.

The bar today still features its original maple, oak and walnut bar. The coolers behind the bar holding bottles of Old Style and Leinenkugel's once held dairy products when Lottie's also served as a local grocery store during World War II. The back of the barroom, once Lottie's living quarters, now contains two pool tables and the legendary cellar is available for private parties.

Lotties also serves food including deluxe grilled cheese sandwiches and half-pound burgers. Lottie's is a friendly neighborhood tavern, a place to come and enjoy the legitimate pleasures of the new century...and don't worry..."Smokes" Aloisis doesn't stop in much anymore.

— Michael Cotter

Lounge Ax (closed Jan. 2000)
2438 N. Lincoln Ave.
773-525-6620
Hours: bands take the stage between 8 and 9 p.m. and closing is around 2 a.m. depending on how many people are there

So... this is Lounge Ax. It's the same bar that I've read about in all of the local publications that refer to its liquor license disputes and some neighbors behind the place complaining about the noise from all the damn rock 'n' roll music. It seems that Lounge Ax is violating the PPA (Public Place of Amusement) license, which it doesn't have anyway, and has been operating with a music and dance license... what's the difference? I don't know! Nothing official to report as of yet regarding the rumors that Lounge Ax is moving to a new location in response to the aforementioned controversies.

On Lincoln Avenue, across from the Biograph Theater, Lounge Ax has hosted more than its share of nationally recognized bands. Some of them can contribute their acclaimed status as a result of playing at this bar. I don't know what it is about Lounge Ax, but it has a reputation around the nation that it is a place to be seen if you're a musician from (or just passing through) Chicago.

If you walk by, Lounge Ax is obviously not your run of the mill watering hole. Promotional posters for upcoming shows decorate the front window and any space available to hang a poster. Once in the bar, you'll notice things like; minimal seating — better to mingle if you're not there to experience the band. There is "used furniture from the alley couches" near the bar, a few bar stools and the plywood perimeter seating/table/whatever near the front of the room. The smell of beer still fills the air from the night before, but most patrons thrive on the "lived-in odors" of the room. If you are only here to see the band anyway, you can shun the bar's shortcomings and head to the stage, where you'll be standing and watching the band play. Bring your own earplugs or purchase them at the bar for 50 cents a pair.

As far as the beer selection is concerned, it's a pretty good selection, from $1 Huber draft to a $3.75 pint of an import or microbrew. The bartenders look quite competent enough to mix your favorite libation, if you prefer. I just stayed with one of the tasty beers they had on tap and had one when the band went on stage. Wandering to the back room, I checked the set up and although

Barfly Lounge Ax-Lucille's Tavern and Tapas

the sound system was good, I wished I had taken them up on the earplugs. The stage is set up along the back wall of the bar and the tinsel hanging on the walls on either side adds a cheesy touch. Once again, plan on standing for a long period of time while the band plays, as there is no seating at all near the stage. If you need to use the restrooms, they are downstairs. I hope you walk into the right bathroom, (I came close to walking in the ladies room — just too many doors down there.)

I am really glad to see a bar that is so dedicated to supplying a venue for locals to showcase their talent. Not a lot of bars are committed to the music aspect of the lounge scene. Come to Lounge Ax for the original music, interesting bar paraphernalia and a chance to rub up against some new people.

— Jon Hermansen

Lucille's Tavern and Tapas
2470 N. Lincoln Ave.
773-929-0660
Hours: 4 p.m. to 2 a.m. daily. Kitchen open
from 4 p.m. to 1 a.m. daily

This last weekend a friend and I decided to push ourselves to the limit and attempt the impossible. Our mission was to find a decent parking spot on Lincoln Avenue in the DePaul area. After much driving we finally found a spot just next to the Fullerton Street "el" stop. After getting out of the car and scoffing at the "lazy, spoiled" train riders who didn't have the guts to attempt parking, we went searching for a pub in which to celebrate and wandered into Lucille's Tavern and Tapas.

We entered the pub and found ourselves in the middle of a wedding party. Before I could think I was staring down the lace of a flying garter headed straight for my chest. I evaded the projectile with a move that would have made Batman jealous, and the garter slammed into the poor sap behind me.

Although the wedding party began to file out, the tavern was still very crowded and we had to push our way to the bar. When we got there we were confronted with eight beer taps and a bartender shakin' up the mixed drinks above his head to the rock rhythms blaring over the bar's speakers. The tap beers were of high quality and included Harp, Sierra Nevada, and, the beer of beers, Guinness Stout. All of these were served up for $3.50 a pint. The shelves behind the bar were stacked with a seemingly infinite number of liquors including a selection of 33 different vodkas, any of which had the potential of screw driving me to the floor.

After getting our beers we turned from the bar and found ourselves very lucky as one of the many crowded booths cleared out, allowing us a place to rest our bottoms. Soon after we sat down, a waitress came to our table and asked if we would like some tapas-style food from the kitchen before it closed at 1 a.m. After perusing the menu I ordered myself a hot pacetta wrapped shrimp for $5.95 and my bar hopping partner, "Fat Adam," ordered several cold

The North Side Lucille's Tavern and Tapas-Lucky Strike

dishes including a meat and cheese platter for $5.25 and a potato salad for $2.95. I sampled all the tapas and was quite impressed. When the waitress came back I ordered a couple more Guinness Stouts and sent my compliments to the chef.

We were then approached by a woman in her late twenties who had been a part of the wedding party. A few of the newlyweds' friends had returned to the bar to find the bachelor who had caught the garter. They wanted to invite him to join their traveling party. Adam saw an opportunity and grasped at it, claiming he was the bachelor. But, of course, when asked to produce the garter, Adam came up short. I helped one of the women in the wedding party ask around the pub for the garter keeper and found the clientele to be a mixed group of people mainly in their twenties and thirties (age).

My questioning eventually led me back to the bar where I raised my hand to hail another pint. But as my arm came into view, I couldn't help but notice my watch and remembered that I was scheduled to work early Sunday morning. I certainly didn't want to leave. It was 1:40 a.m. and the bar was still packed, but I was forced to cut my fun short so I could get up and go to work for "The Man." As we exited the pub, Adam pointed out that Lucille's mellow and friendly atmosphere and crowd could easily put it at the top of our list of regular haunting grounds. I agreed.

-- Pete Axelrad

Lucky Strike

2747 N. Lincoln Ave.
773-549-2695
Hours: 4 p.m. to 2 a.m. Monday to Friday,
noon to 3 a.m. Saturday, noon to 2 a.m. Sunday

In August, 1995, a cruel hoax was played on Chicago area smokers when a large, well-lit Lucky Strike sign went up on North Lincoln Avenue in Lincoln Park. Many folks were initially paralyzed with excitement until the cold, hard slap of reality hit them when they discovered that Lucky Strike was actually a new bowling bar and restaurant from the same owners as the Corner Pocket, 2610 N. Halsted St., and Southport Lanes & Billiards, 3332 N. Southport Ave., and not a shrine and communal smoking den sponsored by a brand of cigarettes.

As any smoker or non-smoker suffering from the delusion entered the bar, they found any disappointment fleeting. Looking like a cross between the movie Citizen Kane and Top Pin, (the high budget, low profile sequel to Top Gun) Lucky Strike allows its patrons an exciting glimpse of art deco posters from the 1920s and 1930s which adorn several rooms and bathrooms. Almost all of the artifacts collected from the establishment are authentic, creating an atmosphere so realistic you almost want to reach into your dinner jacket for a cigarette case, tap a single smoke on its silver lid and call the bartender for a dry martini. I would venture to guess that many of the patrons will opt for the

Barfly Lucky Strike-Luna Lounge

wide selection of domestic and imported beers.

This joint does however have a much more relaxed dress code than this little fantasy may lead you to believe and caters to those bar goers who like to knock down a few pins as well as pints. Part owner Howard Natinsky admits to only bowling one or two complete games a year but noticed with the success of Southport Lanes that people like to do something while they enjoy a cocktail. And, although sitting at the bar burning match after match until the flames just reach your thumb can be fun for a while, it comes nowhere near the enjoyment of bowling a few frames or playing a game of pool on one of the many tables.

Natinsky and his partners admit that creating Lucky Strike was just as much fun for them as it is for their patrons. They came up with the art deco theme and developed it for their own enjoyment, buying the old benches, scorer's tables and even the very wood of the lanes from an old, abandoned bowling alley outside of Kansas City and procuring many of the posters from vintage poster shops. Rumor has it that even authentic foot sweat was imported from a United Auto Workers league outside of Pontiac Michigan.

But regardless of the efforts put into the building of Lucky Strike, you'll find that the decor will please your eyes just as much as the beer will please your throat.

— Tim Dryer

Luna Lounge
4759 W. Belmont

After a long work day, I decided to visit a local tap just for a quick beer. Being very thirsty for a cold brew, I made a stop at the Luna Lounge on the corner of Belmont and Cicero avenues. The immediate reaction I felt was one of uneasiness because the bartender gave me one cold stare. While looking at the tap selection, I noticed the variety of selections. There were three Old Style taps. I asked for Old Style and received a bottle, not a draft.

For some reason, the bartender again looked at me. For some reason, it gave me the impression that he was hiding something. The bartender probably thought I was a undercover police officer because of my beer belly. This brought a sense of worry to me, especially after a long day of work. There seems to be shadows looming throughout the bar, but there were only three or four patrons in this establishment. I felt not welcome by any means with this uneasy atmosphere here.

This is a bar where I have no intention of visiting again. It just seems dangerous and unsafe. The bar is sparsely decorated. There are four video poker games and a pool table in the back.

Shortly before leaving, there was a yelling match between the bartender and an older patron. With my beer gone, I felt the time was right to run out of this scary drinking hole in the wall.

There is no listing for this bar in the telephone book. It might of been just a bad dream. If you like bars that seem unsafe, the Luna Lounge might be your

The North Side Luna Lounge-Lyons Den

new hangout in the Belmont-Cragin neighborhood.

— Whiskeyhead

Lyons Den
1934 W. Irving Park Road
773-871-3757
Hours: 3 p.m. to 2 a.m. Monday to Thursday,
11 a.m. to 2 a.m. Friday, 11 a.m. to 3 a.m. Saturday,
11:30 a.m. to 2 a.m. Sunday

Visiting this establishment brought back old memories, the site used to be Buffoons, one of my favorite drinking holes when I was in my early twenties. But Buffoons switched owners and went down in a spiral decline.

The Lyons Den is now turning over a new page in history at this site. The bar is split in two rooms. The front room features a long bar with six booths along the opposite wall and a photo display of college basketball players and coaches. There's six TVs placed perfectly throughout the room which makes it easy and enjoyable to watch football, basketball, hockey or baseball without having to shift in your seat or peek over somebody's shoulder.

The second room is used for private parties, playing pool and the occasional band. I didn't get a chance to visit the back room because there was a function in progress during my three-hour stay. While visiting the washroom, I did notice a pool table and some tables set up.

For beer drinkers, there is a good selection of tap beers including Guinness, Harp, Red Hook, Samuel Adams, Miller Lite and Lienenkugel's Red. The domestics go for $2 to $2.50 a pint while imports and specialty beers are $3. There are clean filters at this joint, so the beer is cold and tasty without the nasty aftertaste.

The atmosphere is laid back. There are no hyper, screaming, sports fans to deal with. The patrons who visit this tap are mostly in their twenties. This is a comfortable and clean establishment with good service.

Though it's off the beaten path, I wonder if I observed a new trend on the bar scene and the women's fashion style or simply an abbreviation. On this particular night, I noticed a third of the women wearing platform shoes a la 1970s. Are these shoes comfortable or what?

Back to the Lyons Den, it is a good place to relax and enjoy a beer without a hassle. If you actually wanted to talk to your date, you can do it here.

Check out the Den!

— Pete Schmugge

Mad Bar

1640 N. Damen Ave.
773-227-2277
Hours: 7 a.m. to 2 a.m. weekdays,
8 a.m. to 3 a.m. Saturday and Sunday

For those who can't get enough of the bar scene before running off to work, here's the place to go. Healthies can wake up with a cup of java, espresso or mineral water. Drinkers can head to the bar and grab a brew since the best cure for a hangover is...or just eat a muffin and watch the shuffle to work.

Candles and halogen lights illuminate the fine woodwork of the bar. Patrons can sit at tables along wall-size windows, or belly up to the bar, or sit in the back elevated room lined with comfortable couches.

Drinks from the tap cost $3 a pint for micros, Guinness and Harp. Wines run from $14 to $21 per bottle, cognac is $4.75 to $12, port is $4 to $5 and sherry is $2.50 to $3 and shots cost $3.

A pool table intervenes a direct route from the main bar to the couch area. A game of pool costs $1 and there is a sign-up board for busy nights. There is a jukebox on a wall just off of the main bar which contains the latest hits, Rainbow and Frank Sinatra.

Magoo's

954 W. Newport Ave.
773-327-2739
Hours: 8 p.m. to 2 a.m. Sunday to Friday,
8 p.m. to 3 a.m. Saturday

Nine fifty-four Newport Avenue has been around for a long time under a number of different manifestations. I myself knew it best as Club Lower Links, a dimly lit basement bar that offered a wildly off-beat roster of poets, performance artists, benefits, and cabaret acts for an eclectic crowd. When I entered its newest incarnation, I didn't know what to expect, but I certainly was surprised. A transformation had taken place. I had to catch my breath as the scent of raw lumber overwhelmed my bar-hopping partner and I. The bar and stage had switched places. Formerly devoid of television sets and there were now several to accommodate sporting events.

Managing owners Scott Wendorf, Don Ridge, and Wally Nasser, the same owners of Wicker Park's Subterranean, are intent on rising above the location's bad reputation. While there are many factors involved in the frequent change of ownership in that ill-fated space beneath Links Hall, it did not discourage the present owners one bit as they saw it as, not only a commercially viable venture, but a necessary one. The location is central to the local music scene that only has such bigger venues like The Vic to the south and Cubby Bear and Metro to the north, mostly billing the more established bands to fill the greater capacities. Bands that are just starting out don't have many options in that area. The response seems positive as people from the neighborhood wander by and wonder what's happening there now. People are always looking for just a plain nice place to hang out, and Magoo's is just that. Opened in spring 1996, I was there on just the second night of business. They were ready for the crowds with a nice pool table and drinks that are reasonably priced for the Wrigleyville area. Magoo's has a dozen taps that pour many popular imports and micros and another dozen beers in the bottle. There are enough seats and smiles to make one feel comfortable, but a busy night with a killer band could fill the place up fast, so get there early. Ask Wendy to fix you a snakebite, relax and enjoy the show.

— Arunas Ingaunis

Mangi's
3801 N. Lincoln Ave.
773-477-0406
Hours 8 a.m. to 8 p.m. Monday to Saturday,
11 a.m. to 5 p.m. Sunday

I hate it. Mangi's, a hot dog stand that sells beer, is *mangy* but for some reason I go there all the time. I don't know why I go there so much. Possibly because the place has a weird aura about it. There's this guy I work with who has some sort of mental telepathy when it comes to Mangi's. He can tell, well before you enter a room he's in, that you're walking with a greasy bag of Mangi's gook. He never says a thing when I walk in with McDonald's, Wendy's or Burger King; just Mangi's. It's really uncanny and when he shouts "Aahh somebody has Mangi's," it sends a shiver up my spine and gunk to my arteries.

Maybe I don't like it because it's called Mangi's and that name may send some preconceived notions to my bowels. Anyway, I'm just not sure why I go there.

It's small, hot, smoky, unfriendly and serves slop. Although I must give credit where credit is due and the place is kept fairly clean. However, I have been eating at hot dog stands since I could walk. The hot dog stands I grew up with had a familiar Chicago feel with a huge menu of hot dogs, sausages, burgers, and corned beef sandwiches. These places had boisterous "Chicago Guys" who'd get in your face if you didn't tell them what you want to eat within 30 seconds.

Mangi's, on the other hand, has boisterous "Chicago Guys" who come in and pound down $1.25 cans of Old Style and rarely eat hot dogs. Also, the guys who run Mangi's rarely utter a word. They just stare at you like they want to watch your head spontaneously combust or something. I mean, I go there almost every day and they've never once comped me a Pepsi or even said hello. When I was a kid the guys at the corner stand used to give me fries by the bushel even after I kicked their asses in Asteroids.

It's not just me who feels this way about Mangi's. Most everybody I work

196

Barfly Mangi's-Map Room

with has eaten there. They all have said they hate it. When I see them eating Mangi's they always have this beaten look in their eyes. I think Mangi's steals your soul.

But still, I go to Mangi's, seemingly day after day. Its hot dogs and fries taste okay and cost only a buck forty. Its Polish sausage ain't so good. Nor are its hamburgers. Mangi's Italian beef is alright and they have sweet peppers. Surprisingly, Mangi's has pretty decent chili. The chili is definitely above average.

My telepathic friend only eats Mangi's grilled cheese but I don't really like it. I just don't like a whole lot there but I'll probably be slopping down a gyro at Mangi's tomorrow. Oh happy day.

— Leinenkugel's

The Map Room
1949 N. Hoyne Ave.
773-252-7636
Hours: 6:30 a.m. to 2 a.m. weekdays, 6:30 a.m. to 3 a.m. Saturday, 6:30 a.m. to 2 a.m. Sunday

With 26 draft beers, more than 60 bottled beers representing about 40 brewing styles, The Map Room is one of Chicago's premier beer bars. The staff is friendly and knowledgeable. In addition, brewmasters from local breweries hold tastings and the bar is a popular meeting ground for homebrewers.

The atmosphere is comfortable, much like the hip pubs in London's Camdentown neighborhood. The layout consists of two rooms with a bar in each. The room closest to the entrance has a long bar with stools and several tall tables with stools and a coat rack by each one. This room is very dark with candles lighting each table and many maps on the walls. The second room is about a foot lower and has couches and blue walls with the continents painted on them. The painting feels three-dimensional with blacklights making the continents glow.

Having lived two blocks from the bar, I can attest that this is one of the most popular bars in the Bucktown neighborhood. Each night of the week has fairly large crowds, most of which of are in their mid-20s in age. However, bar patrons of all age groups visit The Map Room.

The bar also brings in crowds in the early morning. Cappuccino, espresso, coffee and baked goodies are available for the early crowd. In my opinion, afternoon is the best time to enjoy The Map Room. Crowds are sparse and beer is cold and there's no waiting. In addition, the folks who run the bar don't mind if you bring your lunch in with ya.

Other amenities are live music on weekends with no cover, free international buffets every Tuesday evening, daily $2.50 drink specials, and many special events each month like beer tastings and discussions of brewing techniques.

— Tony Gordon

Nowhere in Chicago is the bond between customer and owner as strong as at Marie's Riptide Lounge, 1745 W. Armitage Ave. Pictured above is Chicago treasure Marie Wuczynski, owner of the Riptide Lounge.

Marie's Riptide Lounge

1745 W. Armitage Ave.
773-278-7317
Hours: 5 p.m. to 4 a.m. Monday to Sunday,
5 p.m. to 5 a.m. Saturday

The Riptide is the pride of Barfly Newspaper. Owner Marie Wuczynski took a chance on advertising in Barfly in late 1993 when me and Phil Brandt approached her with our random idea for a newspaper. Without her support, this book and every issue of Barfly would never have existed. Barfly is forever in her debt.

We are not the only ones indebted to her, however. Hundreds of thousands of patrons have come and gone at the Riptide since Marie opened the place in 1961. On any given evening at the bar, one may find Vietnam War veterans who grew up in the neighborhood and received almost daily letters of support from Marie while serving in Asia. Or the likes of Little Richard, Chicago's Polka General, who used to perform regularly at the bar in the 1960s when Marie had a stage up front. Marie used to grab the microphone herself and sing along with the bands.

Many celebrities have somehow found their way to the old Riptide, nestled right next to the Kennedy Expressway and Armitage Avenue. Some of those include John F. Kennedy, Jr., Davey Jones, Conan O'Brien, and Andy Richter.

For more than 30 years, Marie has played host at the Riptide. She has enter-

Barfly Marie's Riptide Lounge-Marquee Lounge

tained her patrons with song, jokes, tricks and her own amazing charm. Now in her mid-70s in age, Marie continues to bring smiles to new and old patrons. Age hasn't slowed her down one bit. She has more spunk than any other bartender in the city. She's extremely careful that patrons leave with a smile. Birthdays are best at Marie's.

On any given evening, one gets a cozy atmosphere during the p.m. hours and a youthful drinking utopia during the a.m. hours. Its winter decor is difficult to match anywhere with a cool white cotton lining hanging along shelves and a fish tank behind the bar decorated special for each holiday.

Marie's features an antique electronic skeet shoot for customers to play on its north wall. Booths line its east wall, a banquet room to the south and the greatest jukebox in Chicago sits by the front door with ample Elvis Presley, Dean Martin, Frank Sinatra and other mid-1960s stars.

In addition to Marie, three other special people work the bar. On most nights, Marie's faithful employee Shirley is bartender. She's worked the bar for more than 25 years and has tons of great stories about the place. Shirley is from the old school. She actually talks to you and asks sincerely about your well being. Also, when you become a regular, she makes it a point to remember your favorite drink and have it ready for you before you can take your coat off.

Shirley is joined by Ralph and Tina on weekends. Ralph is a super nice guy who's from the neighborhood. A pile of his friends are always in to see him. They're all really great and have some good embarrassing stories about Ralph. Tina, who lives down the street, is an old family friend of Marie's. She's also a kind person who likes to smile and sing along with the jukebox. These are special people and this is a special place.

Some folks might be wondering what happened to Marie's daughter Sharon who regularly worked weekends at the Riptide. Sharon recently joined one of her sons who lives in Florida. She said she misses all the folks in Chicago but is really enjoying the beach and warm weather of Florida. Well, regulars like myself miss her contagious smile and goofy tales.

Over the years, the Riptide Lounge has experienced crowds into everything from Polka to Punk Rock. Yet, the bar has maintained an air of honesty and good times. We at Barfly, are truly "hooked on that feeling." Thank you Marie, we love you!

— *Tony Gordon*

The Marquee Lounge
1973 N. Halsted St.
773-988-7427
Hours: 5 p.m. to 2 a.m. weekdays, noon to 2 a.m.
Saturday, noon to midnight Sunday

Can a phoenix rise from the ashes of a Lincoln Park institution? If the institution is Nick's (now located in Wicker Park) and the phoenix is the Marquee Lounge, the answer is yes.

The North Side Marquee Lounge-Martini Ranch

Owned by the son of the original Nick's, The Marquee Lounge is distinguished from other Halsted Street bars in the DePaul neighborhood by its sophistication and lack of reliance on the sports bar cliché.

A cozy enclave on the corner of Halsted and Armitage, the Marquee Lounge features a long, heavily lacquered bar (a remnant from Nick's early days), and several tables in the back. The tables look ordinary on first glance, but upon closer examination, reveal humorous takes on several classic pieces of art, like "Nighthawks" and Grant Wood's "American Gothic," featuring an aging pair of hipsters complete with shades and earrings. The tables were painted by "Sass," a local artist. Other decorative notes include unusual glass fixtures which cast an indirect, warm light on the place, faux-marbleized walls and distinctive purple "Marquee Lounge" neon signs in the windows. And for those concerned about comfort, all the bar stools have backs, something that this reviewer appreciates.

The atmosphere at The Marquee Lounge is relaxed and laid back, or at least that's how it was on the Monday evening I stopped by. Jonathan, the bartender, told me that typically, The Marquee attracts an after-work crowd early in the evenings, followed by more of a club-going crowd later on. And despite the presence of three televisions in strategic locations, it does not attract a larger contingent of sports-bar types. They did, however, have both Monday Night Football and the Bulls game on when I was there.

Along with complimentary pretzels and spicy mustard, The Marquee Lounge offers drink specials Monday through Thursday. Jonathan told me that they do a mean bunch of coffee drinks, something hard to find in some neighborhood taverns. Might have something to do with the crowd, which tends to be late 20s up to 40s. They seem hospitable to dogs, the night I was there, there was a very friendly Labrador roaming around. And for those not content to just sit still and nurse a drink, The Marquee Lounge offers darts and a Jurassic Park pinball machine.

— *Alexis*

Martini Ranch
311 W. Chicago Ave.
312-335-9500
Hours: 5 p.m. to 4 a.m. Sunday to Friday,
5 p.m. to 5 a.m. Saturday

Tie up the horse and grab a brew at the Martini Ranch. Far from being a country/western bar, this six-year old tavern is donned in dark red and black ceilings and a short bar in front.

It's a hip joint with, of course, killer martinis. Folks at the ranch are laid-back. It's motto is "Hold the Attitude." Gotta like that. This is just a great place to relax. There's comfortable couches on a raised platform and a fireplace to warm up by for those cold winter nights.

There's also a food menu at Martini Ranch the features stuff like burgers and sandwiches.

The bar has a pool table which is sometimes free during the week or $1 on busy nights. The bar's jukebox features alternative rock, soul and the disco sounds of the band the Brand New Heavies.

Marty's
4210 N. Lincoln Ave.
773-871-2666
Hours: 9 a.m. to 2 a.m. Monday to Saturday,
9 a.m. to 3 a.m. Saturday, 11 a.m. to 2 a.m. Sunday

When your day job, Newt or just the shiny-happy people on the tube start getting you down, head on down to Marty's on Lincoln. Now I know what your thinking; here we go another run-of-the-gin-mill yuppie bar review...not exactly. Marty's is a hole-in-the-wall hillbilly dive that serves up brutally cheap drinks, down to earth camaraderie and double shots of reality. Sure there are times when you want to go elbows to assholes with the beautiful people just a little further south on Lincoln where you'll pay way too much for drinks (admittedly better booze), not find parking and probably not get laid anyway (this means you). Then there are the times when what's needed is the dreary, teary, workday troubles of the crew at Marty's, which should leave you with a monster hangover and a fresh perspective on your own small troubles.

Marty's amounts to a couple of poker machines, a country & western jukebox, a pool table, and a long spacious bar littered with two dozen barstools. A humble television sits behind the bar (they take their "Wheel of Fortune" pretty seriously here). On my first visit after a rousing round of "The Wheel," I was treated to a grab bag of overheard conversation that is one of the unintentional live entertainment aspects of the joint. With the exception of an occasional racial epithet, or homophobic joke, some of it is choice stuff. Overheard: a cool chain smoking old lady says to her rumpled companion, "Yup, you can still get opossum (pronounced possem) on the South Side."

And from a seasoned knight of the road from points south: "I sure wish they'd finish up that info-superhighway deal 'cause it took me nine days to hitchhike from Louisville." To be fair I've also observed some uncommon wisdom and have great respect for these soulful, hardworking people.

Marty's is "decorated" with fake wood paneling, strips of red carpet tacked to the back of the bar, and those stick 'em up etched mirror squares that have been off the market since the late 1970s. The only thing missing sadly, is the *de ri gueur* velvet painting depicting dogs playing poker. There isn't much variety here in terms of ones choice of elixir. They got Jack Daniel's and they got beer. Domestic beer, that's right not a single import in the whole of Marty's (no pun intended) these people are not amateurs, they have all been drinking professionally as long as they can remember. Ice cold bottles of beer cost an incredible $1.50, shot o' Jack $2.25, mixed drinks $1.50. Anything I've missed they probably don't have and you definitely don't need.

The North Side Marty's-Martyr's

Longtime night bartender, Truman Frost sums it up like this: "Well...we have a good time. We got good people come in here and if anyone gets too squirrely, there's three, four guys who'll send 'em home before I gotta even say anything." Truman elaborates: "We ain't had a fight in here in over five years!" Allllrrrighty then. Marty's is proudly owned by Truman's brother-in-law, Frank Galloway. If your looking for a place to dance and show off your new suit this ain't it; but if your looking for some country music, a good pool game, a shot and a beer or someone to paint your garage, I give Marty's a heartfelt, double-fisted, two-mugs-up!

—Tom Luplow

Martyr's
3855 N. Lincoln Ave.
773-404-9494.
Hours: 5 p.m. to 2 a.m. Sunday to Friday,
5 p.m. to 3 a.m. Saturday

Crazy Great Aunt Julit nearly keeled over a few years back when she learned that her nephew had moved into an apartment near the corner of Halsted and Armitage. Back in her day, not more than 25 years ago, that intersection swam in poverty and crime. She found it incomprehensible that the once-feared area had since grown into a hotbed of trendy bars, restaurants and retail stores. And there must be plenty of other elders shuddering at thoughts of Bucktown, Wicker Park and Clybourn Corridor.

The North Center neighborhood hardly resembles the post-apocalypse nightmares from which those now-respectable 'hoods rose. But the stretch of Lincoln Avenue that runs through it — from Addison to Montrose — has looked a bit shoddy for the past decade or so. Recently, though, it's shown subtle signs of rebirth, led by Grizzly's Lodge.

Now, Martyr's, 3855 N. Lincoln Ave., hopes to attract the kind of attention that could put North Center on the map as the next risen-from-the-ashes hot spot. Officially serving up its first beer July 22, 1995, Martyr's is a phoenix in itself. In an exclusive Barfly interview, co-owner Dave Andersen outlined the bar's history and future plans.

"The name is really an inside joke on all the time and hard work we put into this place," says Andersen, who along with partners Ray Quinn, Greg Textrun and Dan Salvans, labored for eight months to get it off the ground. The building was originally constructed as a U.S. Post Office facility and has since housed a greeting card factory, coffee house and another bar Andersen prefers not to name.

"It was a rough place and we don't want anyone to think we run the same kind of bar," he says. To erase any confusion, the four owners gutted the entire site and rebuilt it from scratch. The huge 5,000-square-foot main room features two hand-made wooden bars, floor-to-ceiling windows along Lincoln and seating for 90.

202

Barfly Martyr's-Maryla Polanaise Night Club

The tables themselves are worth the trip. "They're part of our 'deceased rock stars' theme," Andersen says cheerfully. "We had various local artists create table tops featuring dead musicians."

Wander throughout the room and you'll spot Frank Zappa, Billie Holiday and, yes, Kurt Cobain. The Elvis table is a particular treasure. A large mural of Joplin, Lennon, Hendrix, Marley and Coltrane hangs near the front bar.

Since September, 1995, Martyr's has been hosting shows by an eclectic line-up of rock bands. Booking agent owner Ray Quinn, who started a successful music scene at Schuba's, he has done the same here. Martyr's has an ample stage with good sight lines, a state-of-the-art sound system and a ticket booth for advance sales. In addition, the building's second story sports a recording studio used to tape live shows as bands wish.

To drink, domestic, imported and micro brews are available in bottles and on tap for between $2.25 and $3.50; wine is $3 a glass. To eat, the menu offers a good choice of appetizers, salads, sandwiches and hand-made pizzas. The vesuvio chicken sandwich was good and the vegetarian sandwich was outstanding.

— Pat McAuley

Maryla Polanaise Night Club
3192 N. Milwaukee Ave.
773-545-4152
Hours: 9 a.m. to 2 a.m. daily

I drive down Milwaukee Avenue often. There is a lot of commercial activity along this road that stretches from the city to deep into the 'burbs. The activity I enjoy most along Milwaukee Avenue is its many drinking houses. I've been in most of 'em. Some of the best ones are in the Polish Village, also known as the Avondale neighborhood.

I recently made a stop at Maryla Polanaise near the corner of Belmont and Milwaukee avenues. The Polanaise, a large venue, is nestled among several Polish restaurants and taverns as well as some commercial American stuff like Kentucky Fried Chicken and Taco Bell.

The layout is simple; two rooms. The first room is the closest to their parking lot. The layout is spacious. The walls are mostly black. This room contains the main bar which is very comfortable. It is easy to find a seat here. There are plenty of seats at the bar and tables along the wall.

For the younger crowd, the second room in this establishment is open only weekends. It's for folks under age 21 and dance music is the theme here. It doesn't open until 9 p.m. There is a security guard or a bouncer who watches their parking lot very closely, so nobody gets blocked in.

But for us older drinking folks, the Polanaise main room is the place to be. The customer base is mostly local neighborhood residents who are Polish. The atmosphere is laid back where locals drink and talk about the issues of the day. If you are hungry, there is some fine Polish food which can consist of anything from Pierogi to Kawa. The prices are quite reasonable from $1 to $4.

The North Side Maryla Polanaise Night Club-Match Box

For recreation purposes, there are two pool tables towards the back. The watching of TV is a popular item here. While I was there, a new cable station that just shows old shows was on.

To drink, the selection of the tap is fine and includes Pilsner Urquell from Czechoslovakia for 2 bucks, Beck's, Heineken for $2.25, and Bud for $1.75. All draft beers are served in a frosty mug which seems less and less common. There are also more than 50 types of hard liquors to choose from.

Overall, the Polanaise offers two options. First, if you are older than 21, you can relax with a drink and fine food in one room. In the other room, if you are near 21, but would like to go out and mingle, there is place where you can go to do some dancing and talking on weekends.

So next time you're driving down Milwaukee Avenue on the city's Northwest Side and you need a place to stop, check out the Polanaise.

— Pete Schmuge

The Match Box
770 N. Milwaukee Ave.
312-666-9292
Hours: 7 a.m. to 2 a.m. Monday to Friday,
noon to 3 a.m. Saturday

During a 1992 rehabbing of the Kennedy Expressway, many drivers were forced to find alternate routes to avoid the traffic. David Gevercer was just one of the many commuters who had to find an alternate route from the Northern Suburbs. Following an alternate route, Gevercer passed a small bar on the corner of Milwaukee and Chicago avenues known as the Match Box. Never stopping too long as the area at that time was quite unsurly, Gevercer said, he put the Match Box in the back of his mind not knowing he would be reopening that bar on June 2, 1995.

Gevercer has been in the restaurant/bar business since 1973 when he first opened a restaurant called Gare St. Lazare on Clybourn Avenue. Later, he said, he moved on and opened a restaurant called Bistro Europa in Skokie for two investors.

After quitting Bistro Europa, Gevercer and a friend decided to get into renovating buildings and were looking at an apartment building near Division Street and Western Avenue, he said. Again, Gevercer traveled by the Match Box where he saw a realty sign on the building. So instead of starting in on renovations of apartments, Gevercer decided to do what he knew, run a bar.

By the time Gevercer was in touch with the realtor, the bar had already been sold. A few weeks later, however, the realtor called him and explained that the deal had fallen through. He jumped at the opening and bought the building, he said.

As he began renovating the 48-year-old bar, he found many pleasant originals still in good shape after almost 50 years of use.

Barfly Match Box

Local musician Tranquility Bass calls The Match Box, 770 N. Milwaukee Ave., his home away from home. The Match Box is the smallest bar in Chicago.

"We sandblasted this wall (pointing to the western wall) and the brick was in really good shape," Gevercer said. "So then we decided, 'Hey, let's try that wall!'"

The barback and the bar itself are the originals that had been in the bar over its almost half-century stint. The barback just needed some new stain as it had been covered by signs and pictures over the years and the bar was still in good condition only needing a good sanding and refinishing. Since he could, he wanted to save as much of the original bar as possible, he said.

"The trick is to try and get as much effect out of every square inch," Gevercer said. "And with a place this size, it is really important to do just that."

The Match Box is not your average small bar, it's really small. The capacity for the room is about 25 patrons. No joke. The shape of the bar is that of a book of matches turned on its side, with the room getting thinner the further in one goes. And Gevercer has no complaints about the size saying that the bartender as well as the patrons have a chance to speak to everyone. All of this gives way to Gevercer's title of the bar as "Chicago's Most Intimate Bar." The Match Box can't help but be just that.

During the sale of the bar, Gevercer had a chance to talk with the original owner, Israel Siegel, who was 94 years old at the time. Siegel's accountant needed to translate for him as most of his English had reverted back to Yiddish.

"I think when he named the bar, his English was not very good and that's why he called it the Match Box not knowing the difference between a match box and a book of matches," Gevercer said. Instead of racking his brain to consider another name for the bar, Gevercer decided to keep the name.

"I figured why change the name when it was called the Match Box for the past 48 years?" Gevercer commented.

To give the bar even more charm, Gevercer went through much tasting to decide which liquors, liqueurs, wines and beers he would serve. He wanted to find fun and unknown drinks to serve. And that's what he did, serving no well drinks but mainly top shelf drinks and even some fun wines. For example, he pulled out a bottle of wine called *Cigare Volant*, meaning "Flying Cigar" which has a flying saucer on the label with a red beam of light shining from it down to a vineyard. But with the foreign choice of drinks, Gevercer has hired a team of bartenders with good pallets to help one make the right selection.

Though many of the drinks are better selections, the prices are not outrageous. Since they are unknowns, there are no advertising mark ups to drive the price up. He wanted the effect of offering choice drinks without "the effect of ripping you off."

Also included in the sale of the bar was the adjoining open lot. So will Gevercer expand his small, intimate bar to include more patrons in the future?

"I don't want to expand," he said. "When you expand a place, you loose the original charm and that's exactly what would happen here."

— Phil Brandt

Mayor's Office Lounge
3506 W. Irving Park Road
773-588-1471
Hours: 7 a.m. to 2 a.m. Monday to Friday,
7 a.m. to 3 a.m. Saturday, 11 a.m. to 11 p.m. Sunday

An anything but politically correct place on Irving Park Road, the Mayor's Office Lounge is a working class crowd who could care less about world politics, and most of them don't give a hoot about domestic politics either.

This is a place you go to after working the graveyard shift to have a few drinks and some laughs. The patrons either work or live in the immediate area and have known each other for years. The camaraderie of this neighborhood tap should not, however, discourage new arrivals. Unlike most places where the bond is usually too strong among the regulars for a newcomer to fit in, one is welcomed as if they have always been there. And that's what makes this a good watering hole, the crowd really makes this a fun place. Everyone is different and there is always something different going on.

The crowd ranges in age from early 20s to late 30s and the jukebox is filled with 70s and 80s rock 'n' roll, but not that Top 40 stuff. There's plenty of Black Sabbath to choose from.

Some readers may have known of this place when it was O'Grady's, which contained mainly an older crowd. But management changed over in 1992, and so has the crowd and feel of the place.

The beer prices are a great deal ranging from $1.50 for domestics up to $2.25 for imports.

Barfly Mayor's Office Lounge-Mirabell Restaurant

Does Mayor Daley come there as the name suggests. Well don't bother asking where the mayor is, it's just like his office downtown, he's never in.

— Derek Scholl

Michael's Sports Bar and Grill
4091 N. Broadway St.
773-929-4149
Hours: 4 p.m. to 2 a.m. weekdays, 11:30 a.m. to 3 a.m. Saturday, 11:30 a.m. to 2 a.m. Sunday

Michael's Sports Grill & Pub stands alone, literally. It's the only bar on a block filled with other types of businesses.

Located just north of the much busier Lake View area, Michael's is filled with people, not bar hoppers, who want to be there and that makes a difference. On a Friday night when I visited, the bar was buzzing by 9 p.m. but it wasn't overly crowded. What impressed me were the people who sat alone at the bar and looked perfectly comfortable doing so, which is something that can not be done at just any bar. They ate, drank and watched TV while others clustered around tables talking and visiting with friends. This is definitely not a pick-up bar.

I stopped counting the televisions after 15. However, if TV isn't your thing, they have basketball hoops mounted on the wall and a dart board in the back. They also have video games and pinball machines. There's something for everyone.

They have a full service menu, too, that includes appetizers, burgers, chili and salads. Their prices are cheap and the food is good.

Michael's is a bar with a friendly atmosphere and definitely a place to try.

— TM Kornelsen

Mirabell Restaurant and Lounge
3454 W. Addison St.
773-463-1962
Hours: 11:30 a.m. to 2:30 p.m. and 5 to 11 p.m. Monday to Saturday, closed Sunday

Ever been in one of those German moods? If your answer is yes, strap on the Lederhosen kids and come on down to Mirabell Restaurant and Lounge.

The lounge area is directly in front where it should be and the walls in this room as well as the restaurant area are packed with German paraphernalia. There's loads of cool beer steins and Weiss glasses with German beer labels on them that line the wall behind the bar. Some of the glasses are so big, if you get one, that will be enough for the whole evening. German flags and signs are everywhere as well. The barroom is small, yet cozy with bar seating as well as wooden booths.

The clientele consists largely of neighborhoods folks and those who greatly

The North Side Mirabell Restaurant and Lounge

Patrons often raise their liter glasses to the German sounds of the Phenix Band at Mirabell Restaurant and Lounge, 3454 W. Addison St.

enjoy Mirabell's German cuisine. This is one of the most friendly places to drink. It's easy to get caught up in energetic German toasts. In addition, Mirabell is very family oriented so don't be surprised if you see a couple of well-behaved kids hanging with the parents at the bar.

But enough with drink, the food is the main reason to come to Mirabell. There's two dining rooms decorated with traditional German paintings. With a large selection of German delicacies, there is something for everyone on the menu. Entrees are overflowing and hearty. My favorite is the thick bratwurst which is served atop saur kraut and includes German-style vegetables.

If you like German food and beer, the Mirabell is a must. And if you happen to go there in the fall you'll probably be treated to a full Oktoberfest house, hoisting steins and singing along with the Phenix band.

The Mirabell is located just eat of the Kennedy Expressway on Addison Street.

— *Tony Gordon*

Mondelli's Lounge
7 E. Oak St.
312-266-7362
Hours: 4 p.m. to 2 a.m. daily

Mondelli's is located next door to Papa Milano's restaurant. The bar and restaurant share an intercom phone as Mondelli's is the waiting area for Papa Milano's patrons. After dinner it is a common practice for Papa Milano's customers to stop at Mondelli's for an after dinner drink.

One of Mondelli's most popular regulars is a patron named Gino. When Gino enters Mondelli's, a group cry of "Gino" is deafening.

Mondelli's is a great place to stop in for a quiet cocktail after work or to join in for a lively time in the later evening. The television at the end of the bar is normally kept mute in favor to a CD player with a wide range of selections. Many of the customers like to hear Frank Sinatra, though a number favor the classic rock and Tina Turner offerings.

When you're hungry you can order a nice meal from Papa Milano's. Columnar and pizza bread are among the favorite dishes among bar patrons. I highly recommend the "Supreme Pizza."

Mondelli's first opened in 1984 by Johnny Mondelli (1936-1997). Johnny, a native of Italy, brought a special atmosphere to his place. When Johnny passed away recently and the loyal patrons and friends gathered from all around to honor his memory.

John was a member of the Screen Actor's Guild and had established in his lounge an actor-friendly environment. A copy of Newsweek hangs on the wall to the left side of the bar. On the cover is a photo of Robert DeNiro as Al Capone with Johnny Mondelli to his right from the movie Untouchables. Johnny worked and became friends with actor Danny Aiello. During one movie Johnny and Danny escaped injury when an elevator being used in a film fell four stories to a dusty, sudden crash. Johnny used to love sharing this story. When Bill Forsooth was playing Al Capone in a new television series we had a ball. Johnny was acting and we all enjoyed Bill's frequent visits. Mondelli's was like a small version of the Beverly Hills Hotel's Polo Lounge.

"That was a special time," recalls former bartender, Tamara.

Presently serving as a bartender, Lisa, remembers being Johnny's first bartender. "He will be missed," Lisa commented.

Now Mondelli's continues operating under the ownership of former patrons, John Sochacz and Mike Mokri. The clientele has changed little. Mondelli's has its own unique flavor. Among the reasons that Mondelli's is a favorite is the friendly atmosphere, the fun customers whose ages cover a wide range and its ambiance. During the warm months, Mondelli's has one of the most pleasant outdoor areas in the Gold Coast. What a great place.

— J. Quillian

The Monkey Bar
1157 W. Wrightwood Ave.
773-935-3760
Hours: 6 p.m. to 2 a.m. Sunday to Friday,
6 p.m. to 3 a.m. Saturday

Lincoln Park bar-goers went bananas when The Monkey Bar opened its shrubs in September, 1996.

"It's a new place to hang," said Monkey Bar general manager Jim Maahs. "It's a fun bar that's pretty eclectic."

With tropical-leaf wallpaper, a bamboo-looking type of wood, tropical trees from Florida, a great mural by Chicago artist Bill Kirby depicting cartoon female and male hip monkeys embracing mugs of beer, and more of Kirby's giant cartoon monkeys playfully lining the back bar, this place has created one of the most unique atmosphere's in Chicago.

"All the customers have given me positive feedback," said Maahs who has been in the bar business for 19 years. "It's a good feeling, people are coming in here."

Maahs said that this site located on the southeast corner of Wrightwood and Racine avenues has housed a bar for the past 40 years. Barfly was able to track down the history of the place from the last 25 years. According to "The Great Chicago Bar and Saloon Guide," written by legendary Chicago Barfly Dennis B. McCarthy in 1979, in the early 1970s, the bar was called The Straight Arrow, a dirty pool joint. In the late 1970s, John Wright purchased the place, cleaned it up, and dubbed it Papa John's.

In the 1980s, the place became a popular punk rock club called The Roxy, Maahs said adding that The Roxy had nightly live bands. The Roxy gave way to Hitchcock's in 1989. Hitchcock's was a shrine to suspense thriller author, movie and television producer Alfred Hitchcock.

Today, the site has all but erased its past except for Hitchcock's wildly popular Wednesday night open-mike comedy. The Monkey Bar name came about during a brain-storming session by the folks who own the place, Maahs said, and the theme has been beautifully captured.

"When you walk in, we wanted people to know that we just didn't paint the walls and clean the place up," Maahs said. "It was a lot of time and a lot of work."

Cushions are everywhere. Hitchock's uncomfortable tables and chairs have been replaced with cushioned booths and the bar rail is even cushioned. All this new decor creates a real comfortable atmosphere.

To drink, Maahs has stocked the place with 12 taps featuring eight micro-brews, two domestics, and two imports. Microbrew lovers should note Thursday nights when The Monkey Bar's micros such as Sierra Nevada, Goose Island, and Oregon Ale, are priced at $2.50 a pint. The bar is also stocked with top-of-the-line liquors and sports nine different types of martinis such as the

Barfly Monkey Bar-Monsignor Murphy's

Bananatini made with the patron's choice of vodka and garnished with fresh bananas or the Dean Martini made with Absolute, Sky, Stoli and served with a cigarette.

And speaking of smoking, cigars are sold at The Monkey Bar and Maahs has installed a good fan-circulation system to increase airflow so the place isn't engulfed in cigar and cigarette smoke.

Another feature unique to The Monkey Bar is free Nintendo 64 and Sony Playstation games.

"I thought it would be something different to do in the bar," Maahs said. "People sit in the booths for hours playing these games."

Game selection includes John Madden Football, NBA Live, hockey, Golf, Jeopardy and Monopoly.

Other entertainment at The Monkey Bar consists of a pool table, a solid CD jukebox with selections ranging from Bach to Bush, and Monday nights are an acoustical Musicians Showcase.

— Tony Gordon

Monsignor Murphy's
3019 N. Broadway St.
773-348-7285
Hours: 2 p.m. to 2 a.m. Sunday to Friday, noon to 3 a.m. Saturday

The first time I discovered Monsignor Murphy's was a few years back on a hot July evening after a full exhausting day of moving into an apartment a few streets down. I was at the Dominick's across the street stocking up on cleaning supplies and food when I saw Monsignor's across the street and felt particularly parched.

I remember as I was walking up the few steps to the front-decked entrance, I wasn't too sure of what I'd find. I was pleasantly surprised.

The front of the bar has a fire place and a large window overlooking Broadway Street. The walls are exposed brick covered with many sport memorabilia pictures and artifacts. My personal favorite is the picture of a triple-dead-heat horse race (three horses coming in first in the same race).

The floor is black and white checkered tiles which I once became up close and personal with after a couple of rounds of Jagermeister.

Along one wall are several tables with gems like chess, backgammon and checkers painted on the woodwork with the game pieces available. The bar is long and sits many people at a time. There are four TVs so you always have a good view no matter where you sit.

On tap they have Miller Light, Guinness and Harp, to name a few. There is also a large variety or bottle beers. In the back are two dart boards with plenty of room to play. The bathrooms are always clean and there are never any lines to wait in.

The bar food is really good, anything from brats to nachos. Also on the menu

The North Side Monsignor Murphy's-Moody's

are ostrich burgers, although who would want to eat a bird that can outrun you or me? I don't know.

The atmosphere is relaxed and friendly. The patrons who frequent Monsignor's are anywhere from age 21 to 75. The bartender Steve looks just like Woody from "Cheers." I keep waiting for everyone to run around and say "Norm!"

In the summer, the front deck is a great place to sit. Towards the evening the sun directly faces the deck right up until sundown. I have spent many nights and a pitcher too many sitting out front people watching which can be quite interesting on Broadway. Also in the back is a beer garden with a TV and bar where the bartenders make an assortment of frozen drinks. A piña colada goes rather nicely on a hot summer day with the tropical fish painted on the fence and a pink flamingo decoy. Tacky, maybe, but if you use your imagination you can envision yourself on a tropical island.

Another reason Monsignor's has become like an old friend are the little unexpected surprises. Like the time the bartender bought a round of pizzas for everyone in the bar because the Bulls won. Or the time I went to Monsignor's to watch a Bears game and found them serving free spaghetti and bread. What a nice surprise! To think I use to go to bars where I had to wait in line to get in, pay a cover charge, then push and shove my way up to the bar.

I have long since moved away from the neighborhood, but I always find time to revisit Monsignor Murphy's and even do some people watching.

— Christy K. Rizzo

Moody's Pub
5910 N. Broadway St.
773-275-2696
Hours: 2 p.m. to 3 a.m. daily

Upon mentioning a beer garden quest to an old friend of mine, his eyes lit up and he said, "I've got a place for you." We were off, and before I knew it, I was at Moody's Pub located on North Broadway. The inside is funky. Without a doubt the darkest bar I've ever been to. The jukebox was delivered straight from the 1970s. An hour of Steely Dan, REO Speedwagon and Gerry Rafferty (you know, Baker Street) drove us out to where I wanted to be. You guessed it, the beer garden.

Hands down, the best garden in the city as far as the ambiance goes. Man, I'm a sucker for ambiance. The walls are covered with ivy ala Wrigley Field for those jocks among us. There are also a couple of well-positioned trees guaranteeing a leafy green surrounding wherever you choose to sit. Let's talk about seating shall we? A double-tiered garden offers 15 tables per section. Thirty wooden and iron tables with occasional stone statues thrown in for effect. Imagine sipping brew amongst the lions, tigers and bears. Oh my!

My friends, I was almost in heaven. This place was aesthetically pleasing and the trendy crowd hasn't found the place yet. All I needed now was a golden ale.

Barfly Moody's Pub-Moretti's

When the waitress informed me that Lite, Michelob and Lowenbrau were on tap, I realized heaven was not a place on Earth. But the food and drinks are priced right and I would recommend the fries. In addition, Moody's burgers and onion rings are legendary.

So if you're looking for summer fun, this garden beats the rest, as far as beauty and atmosphere goes. For you winter fans, there are two nice working fireplaces and the jukebox is not that bad. Who amongst us can't dig the 1970s for at least an hour or two. I'm game, how about you?

— Brian Diebold

Moretti's Pizza and BBQ Pit
6727 N. Olmsted Ave.
773-631-1223
Hours: 11 a.m. to 2 a.m. weekdays,
11 a.m. to 3 a.m. Saturday

Moretti's Pizza and BBQ Pit has done just fine since taking over from the Snuggery in 1992, thank you. Located just off of Northwest Highway in Edison Park, the restaurant/bar does all it can to market itself in a variety of ways. First and foremost, Moretti's has one of the most spacious beer gardens on the Northwest Side. When it's nice outside, there are few places better to have a few drinks under the stars. Second, the bar goes above and beyond the call of duty with its reasonably priced Bennigan's-style menu. Food selections include pizza, sandwiches and even a few traditional Italian dishes. The pizza and sandwiches are the real specialty.

Inside, Morretti's features several large-screen televisions, interactive television games and a disk jockey on the weekends. Music played ranges from Top 40 to slightly alternative to the trashiest of 1980s rock.

And while the old Snuggery catered mostly to Northwest Siders, Moretti's seems to draw a more diverse crowd. Patrons seem to be generally friendly and get along and best of all, no one dances.

Morseland

1218 W. Morse Ave.
773-764-6401
Hours: 8 p.m. to 2 a.m. weekdays,
8 p.m. to 3 a.m. Saturday

Chicago's Far North Side suffered with the closing in early 1997 of Morseland, an eclectic, intimate venue that gave Rogers Park a club comparable to any in Wicker Park or Wrigleyville. Musicians and lovers of live music alike recalled its performance-friendly disposition and discriminating booking policy, as well as its massive beer selection.

Newlyweds Bridget Duggan and Brendan Cunningham, both of whom tended bar and worked the door as far back as when the place was called The Dao, refused to let Morseland crumble. After more than five months of 70-hour work-weeks, they've painted, plastered, sawed and sanded Morseland into The Morseland Music Room. The reincarnation preserves the most positive elements of the old club, while adding numerous improvements.

"It may sound corny, but I believe this building has a certain spirituality," said Bridget during a conversation in the expanded main room. "It's just such a great space, this free-standing building, full of history. I've been associated with it for more than five years, so I had to do something."

Her husband Brendan put pursuing a job with his just-earned Masters in Urban Planning on hold and instead used his mastery of carpentry to make and manage extensive interior renovations. The most dramatic include the removal of a large wall that separated the bar area from the performance area; the room has effectively expanded by almost a third and people seated at the bar can now see the bands.

"That doesn't mean they'll be knocked over by the sound however," added assistant manager Mike Duggan, Bridget's brother. "The sound system was designed to project in such a way that people at the bar can still have a conversation."

Sound engineer Martin Foys, said the new Morseland has all the top sound equipment.

"This is by far one of the best sound systems of any small room in the city," said Martin, who is at the board on Sundays and Wednesdays. "It's all top equipment, and there are four monitor mixes."

Foys explained that most small rooms have only two monitor mixes, on-stage speaker setups designed to provide musicians with ideal sound. Improved sound for the bands improves what the audience hears, so the more monitor mixes, the better.

Both bands and audience will be pleased with Morseland's expanded stage. Brendan reconfigured the kitchen so the stage could be enlarged. He removed a wall separating the kitchen and main room, dropping it back about six feet. The stage also projects back a few more feet, and includes an on-stage door leading

Barfly Morseland-Mother's Too

through the kitchen to the club's back entrance.

"We really wanted to design the space to be band-friendly," said Mike. "Loading in is a lot easier now, and the bigger stage gives even large bands plenty of breathing room."

The Morseland Music Room still has plenty of its original appointments: the marble staircase leading upstairs, the pool tables, pinball, a smaller lounge and bar area on the second floor and an old upright piano near the stage. Additional improvements are on the horizon. Mike suggested that there may be a rooftop beer garden in the future, and several of the upstairs rooms are currently being re-modeled into a private lounge for musicians. Bridget felt that performers would appreciate having a private space to warm up and cool down before and after gigs.

"Morseland has always had a reputation for catering to musicians," she explained. "I want to improve that reputation, even so far as to start attracting national acts."

While she didn't give specifics, Bridget hinted that the Morseland Music Room is negotiating with some noteworthy bands.

All the effort that has gone into re-opening The Morseland Music Room has been paying off. A corps of old regulars have returned to the bar, and several familiar bands are booked. If Bridget, Brendan and company maintain the momentum they've built, The Morseland Music Room should soon re-claim its place among the area's best live-music venues.

— Jay Ferrari

Mother's Too
14 W. Division St.
312-266-7444
Hours: 11 a.m. to 2 a.m. Sunday to Friday,
11 a.m. to 3 a.m. Saturday

I like Mother's Too. If She-nannigan's is an oasis in the midst of the high-pitched bachelorette party, Mother's Too is an anachronism, as jarring as cyber-porn in Shakespeare... and I like it! It's cozy and comfortable and cute. Whenever I take a stroll down Division Street, I'm always amazed at how out of place Mother's Too is. It looks like it should be nestled on some quaint little corner in Evanston, peopled by bearded gentlemen in tweed jackets discussing Jean Paul Sartre and the efficacy of U.S. Savings bonds. Mother's Too, it seems, should be somewhere with trees and with parking.

It has pool tables and a few TVs and a jukebox. It's got a big island bar in the middle and a few tables scattered here and there. It features a trivia game perched on its well stocked bar. There are generally a few people shooting pool, and often some guy playing the trivia game. But mainly it's one of those bars where conversation comes easily. You go to Mother's Too to talk.

Yeah right...

Mother's Too may not seem like a "Party 'til you puke" kind of place. But,

The North Side Mother's Too-Mulligan's

let me tell you, Mother's Too is the place that lures you back to Division Street. It acts like it's for grown-ups. It sends its siren's call to all of us who, while we remember Division Street fondly from our wilder college years, are now way too cool for that whole scene. We go to Mother's Too, enjoy a lager and watch the youngsters out on the street carousing and acting stupid. We sip on our beers and laugh and say, "Oh I remember those days..." And then, an hour or so later, something happens...

The last time I was there, I sat at the bar with my boyfriend and we chatted with the bartender (Angela). We were swapping stories about old high school drinking games (I was fairly waxing rhapsodic over Thumper) when, suddenly, an overwhelming urge for a kamikaze came over me.

The kamikaze is the sweet elixir of Division Street. Vodka, Triple Sec and lime juice, (and, often, a healthy dose of water). There are those who say that watermelon tastes like summer. Well, a kamikaze tastes like Division Street. And I caved...I gave in to the call of Division Street.

And so I had another kamikaze. And then another. By the end of the night, I'd had enough kamikaze's to tell my boyfriend that he just didn't love me enough (attention any men reading this review: all girls do that when they've had too much to drink, it's not just your girlfriend). And, by the very end of the night, I started noticing that those pool tables are just as good for dancing on as they are for shooting pool on.

The next day, I thought about being embarrassed. I'd kind of made an ass out of myself. But you know what, I'd had a good time and I had been encouraged to have a good time. I confess: I partied on Division Street when I was drunk on kamikaze's. And I don't care, because what I learned that evening, what I learned from all the conversation and all the kamikaze's, is that it's okay to have fun on Division Street. And Mother's Too is a fun place to be. A whole hell of a lot more fun that it would be if it were nestled on that quaint corner in Evanston.

— *Meg Rhem*

Mulligan's Public House
2000 W. Roscoe St.
773-549-4225
Hours: open until 2 a.m. weekdays (opening times vary), noon to 3 a.m. Saturday, noon to 2 a.m. Sunday

In golf, the term "mulligan" refers to a free shot. According to the Irish, it means "fucking cheater."

In Roscoe Village, Mulligan's is a fairly new bar "that wants to be your neighborhood tavern, a place where everyone feels comfortable," says owner Bob Nelson.

In 1994, Nelson wanted to move beyond working at John Barley-corn's in Lincoln Park and get his own bar. Like the westward-bound Mormons, Nelson searched fruitlessly until his buddy Pete Schau, a realtor,

Barfly Mulligan's

Mulligan's, 2000 W. Roscoe St., is the best bar in the Roscoe Village Neighborhood. Don't miss its "Clown Crawls" where patrons dress as clowns for a night of bar-hopping.

told him about the Lucky Lady at 2000 W. Roscoe St. The owner had been shut down for the prior 9 out of 10 months (for reasons best left unexplained) and was willing to sell. The offer was made and after nine more months of total gut rehabbing, "We stripped it down to the two by fours and filled seven dumpsters," Mulligan's officially opened April 21, 1996.

What a swell interior they unveiled. Everything is brand new, including the bar, which runs 3/4 of the inside. Nelson asked that hosannas be tossed toward Mike Olin for his work on the cabinet, bar, and humidor. And it was clean as opposed to the eyesore that was the Lady Luck.

Right hand man Tim Schau gave me the lowdown on Mulligan's and what they're all about. Mulligan's patrons like Jameson Irish Whiskey. On St. Pat's Day, patrons can find the city's only Jameson fountain at Mulligan's. As for music, it's kept relatively low, so as to allow conversation.

"We've noticed a spill over from the other bars in the neighborhood, because they get too loud," Schau said. "We will not become a sports bar. Unless the Bulls or the Bears are on, the jukebox will always supersede the TV. We want this to be a place that appeals to everybody."

To emphasize that, Schau pointed out that Mulligan's has two women's bathrooms. But even more outstanding, he and Nelson want to convert one of them into a handicap-accessible lavatory.

The North Side Mulligan's-New England Inn

In addition to the "Freshest Jameson's in town," they strive to be known as a good place to get a Guinness. Nelson pours a great priest's collar. To ensure that, Nelson bought the top of the line Goliath 16 head tap system. He was adamant about sparing no expense for this system. Mulligan's carries 19 different taps and only five bottled brands because they want to establish a reputation for their taps. All taps go for $3.50 (except Bud Light) and all bottles are $2.50.

One of the things I liked was the satellite music system. You can request reggae, jazz, classical, big bands, R & B, and even hip hop. The older crowd in the afternoon favors show tunes and standards, and blues is what is usually playing. The only thing they won't play is heavy metal.

Mulligan's is starting to get a reputation for its clown parties where dozens of patrons dress up as clowns and go on a pub crawl. It's a sight to see.

Other fun and games at Mulligan's include three cork dart boards and the ever-popular Golden Tee 3-D Golf video game.

So step into Mulligan's to get your Jamesons, a kick-ass Guinness, hear music and enjoy conversation.

— Dan Tucci

New England Inn
6859 W. Irving Park Road
773-685-7155
Hours: 11 a.m. to 2 a.m. Sunday to Friday, 11 a.m. to 3 a.m. Saturday

I love bars. Not just drinking establishments, but the bars themselves. The New England Inn gets four stars in this category. The bar is a beautiful dark wood that runs just about the length of the place. The barback matches. It is mirrored, and the pillars supporting the shelves that hold the hard liquor show gorgeous women sporting cleavage. Ironic, isn't it? Taverns and spirits companies use exotic, scantily-clad creations to get me to consume more. But more often than not, I wake up with a woman that looks more like Vic Tayback than anything off a light beer poster.

The rest of the place, I can tell had been remodeled recently. Wood paneling goes about four feet up the walls, and the rest of them are painted an eerie slate gray. Perhaps the color of the walls is one of the reasons why.

Track lighting runs the length of the bar, and is wound with Christmas lights. The place looks modern and maybe that's why the wonderful bar and barback look so out of place. With the rest of the decor, you would expect a Formica bar. Instead, this bar looks like it should be in a much older establishment. Nit-picking? Probably.

Three tables with checkerboards in the laminate are lined up along one wall. My friend asked the bartender if anyone ever plays checkers on them. She replied, "Not really, but you can if you want...some other time." Whatever that meant.

Barfly New England Inn-New Polonia

The New England Inn also has a full menu. On a chalkboard behind the bar, they had the special listed. Beef Barley soup was $1.50, meat loaf was $4.25, pork shank was $7.95 and the roast duck had no price next to it. That's right, I said roast duck. I had never been to a neighborhood bar that served roast duck before, so I asked to see the menu. They have regular stuff, too. Burgers, beefs and the like are reasonably priced, as is the more exotic stuff. This includes filet mignon, stuffed cabbage, some Hungarian fare, and herring in sour cream or oil. Since I didn't see a cook on duty (actually the word "chef" would be more appropriate), I asked the bartender how one would indulge in one of these delicacies if one were so inclined. She informed me that she would call the guy and he would come over and cook up whatever I wanted. It turns out that he lives upstairs, thank God. If he lived much further away this would be a very inconvenient arrangement for him. We decided to leave him alone to watch cable.

The New England Inn also has another room. Apparently some sort of night-club-type behavior goes on here. This room has its own bar, a stage, and about 40 tables. I was unclear if this was only for banquets (which they do hold — talk to Ted), if they opened this room every Saturday night, or if you could just sit down back there and order food. Either way, it's a nice room.

Overall, the place looks regular enough; beer signs, a pool table, video poker machines, three televisions, good jukebox, and a pretty bartender.

The bartender said they get a neighborhood crowd, mostly, and since it is the only place around, I can see why. The clientele that night was odd to say the least. Two girls talked amongst themselves, and an older, self-proclaimed pool hustler kept talking about doing what it takes to feed your face. Two 20-something jerk-offs who couldn't handle their liquor were harassing the bartender. I'm a 20-something jerk-off, but I can handle my liquor, and I treat the person who brings me drinks with respect and admiration. That is most likely because I am also a 20-something alcoholic. Aside from Jeff, the world's greatest drinking companion, and I, there was one normal, well-spoken patron. He was a nice guy, and he had a cute, friendly little bitch with him. She was a white lap dog, but I couldn't tell what breed.

All the macabre stuff aside, the New England Inn is a nice enough place, with plenty of attributes.

— Bud

New Polonia
6101 W. Belmont
773-237-0571
Hours: 10 a.m. to 2 a.m. Monday to Friday,
10 a.m. to 3 a.m. Saturday, 11 a.m. to 2 a.m. Sunday

The strangers felt the gaze of every patron as they stepped through the saloon door that evening — sound like a scene from an old Western? It could have been, but in our case it wasn't a Western saloon but rather a Midwestern

New Polonia, 6101 W. Belmont Ave., is predominantly a bar for recent Polish immigrants to Chicago. However, patrons such as these guys don't mind an occasional conversation in English.

bar known as New Polonia where this scene played itself out.

Situated on the 6000 block of West Belmont Avenue, New Polonia is a Polish bar in the heart of a Polish community. Although it is true that we were scrutinized at first as we entered the bar, once we sat down and ordered a couple of beers, everything was "hunky-dory."

New Polonia is the quintessential corner bar. It is a small, one room establishment where the bar runs the length of the room. There are no tables at New Polonia, only bar stools. There is also a noticeable lack of English spoken at New Polonia. Go figure. A Polish bar in a Polish community with predominantly Polish speaking patrons.

What we did find at New Polonia was a birthday board announcing the birthdays of local patrons Headzin, Wojtek and Czesiu among others. We also found a jukebox with a wide selection of ABBA-esque tunes sung in, what else, Polish. Finally we stumbled upon a few Polish beers that we'd never seen before which was kind of a nice treat. Of the two Polish beers available, I recommend the Zywiec over the Okocim. Somewhat surprisingly, you wouldn't have been able to guess which Polish beer was best by looking around at what other people were drinking. While we were trying different Polish beers and

Barfly New Polonia-Nick's

finding them to be quite good, most of the other patrons were drinking Bud and Corona. Curious...

In the end we decided that New Polonia is a local's bar. Which is not to say that it is an unfriendly place, but rather it is a place "where everybody knows your name" as long as you live around the corner. If you are a stranger they look at you kind of funny. Of course you might argue that wherever I go people look at me kind of funny, but that's another issue entirely.

At New Polonia it's Polish ABBA, birthday boys and well priced imports ($2.15 per bottle) with very little in the way of conversation unless you're fluent in Polish, which can make for a very interesting night out.

— *Bill Stephenson*

Nick's

1516 N. Milwaukee Ave.
773-252-1155
Hours: 4 p.m. to 4 a.m. Sunday to Friday,
4 p.m. to 5 a.m. Saturday

Peaches has had a rough time. She has spent year after year hanging on a wall, naked, a spectacle for all to see. She has been moved from her home. She has even been shot — three times.

Peaches is a painting at Nick's. A large, curvy European woman — I think many would call her Reubenesque — she has been at the Milwaukee Avenue bar since 1994. And while no one I talked to knew the painting's artist or proper name, many knew about the bullet holes in the canvas.

"In the evening people would line up around the block to get into Nick's," said long-time regular Guy Kendler. "At the old Nick's (on Armitage and Halsted where the bar began in 1977) a couple of thousand people could come through the bar a night."

"One evening someone who had been drinking a lot took offense at being shut off from the bar," Kendler said. "He pulled out a gun. Fortunately, someone grabbed his arm before he could start firing. I don't think the guy wanted to hurt anyone. He just wanted to make a loud statement. Before someone took the gun from his hand, he fired three shots into our beloved Peaches."

Crazy incidents like that were very rare at the old Nick's and non-existent at the new location in Wicker Park. Now the wildest, loudest sounds usually come from the jukebox, which has an impressive collection of soul and blues, and from the R&B bands that play there on the weekends.

Don't get the wrong impression. Nick's is by no means boring or quiet. The place buzzes with conversation and laughter. It's just that many people who enter the bar get a strong desire to sit down, relax and just hang out. From the looks of things at Nick's, a large, diverse crowd gets that desire every night.

The site that houses the new Nick's was the original spot for the Artful Dodger now located at 1734 W. Wabansia. After the Artful Dodger it became Dreamerz, a legendary punk rock/industrial dance club.

The North Side Nick's

It's hard to pin a single label on Nick's. People from all walks of life and economic classes, with different creeds and ways of dress drink at Nick's. On any given night, the young hang out with the old; blue collar with the white collar; the tattooed, bearded and pierced with the clean-cut and shaven.

The diversity of the crowd is complemented by the eccentric look of the bar. In addition to peaches, there are pink flamingoes, pineapples, graffiti art, a striped surfboard and a Bullwinkle pinball machine, all covered by a soft red light that pervades the bar.

Just as there is plenty to see at Nick's, there is plenty to drink. The bar offers single-malt Scotches, small-batch bourbons like Booker's and Baker's and some top notch tequila's (Patron for $3.50 a-shot is excellent). There is also a fairly large beer selection with all the typical, but still good tasting brews you'd find at most bars in the area — stuff like Bell's, Goose Island and Newcastle Ale. I tried for the first time a beer called Celis White, a wheat beer that is one of the sweetest, tangiest beers I have ever tasted. If you like beer, Nick's has beer specials on Sunday, Monday and Tuesday.

There are two high quality pool tables in the back area. They are a buck-a-game and run pretty well even on more crowded nights. They do however get replaced for the stage area when bands come in to jam.

There is a variety of musical groups stopping in at Nick's on the weekends. Big Sweaty Men, a local band, is often making an appearance and always get the weekend crowd going. Surprisingly, Nick's does not offer a cover when bands are playing which is rare in Chicago, but nice for those who continue to play the "bad date" game with little cash in the pocket.

During Chicago's warmer months, Nick's opens its beer garden. Seven days a week from four to midnight, you can drink outdoors in the small patio out back. Even though the beer garden is interesting to look at, drinking there can be uncomfortable. A lack of breeze and air circulation made me sweat even though I was drinking ice-cold beverages and not moving anything but my drinking hand.

Nick's beer garden is a sight, though. It is decorated in the same eccentric fashion as the inside. A Radio Flyer, school desks, mannequins and tombstones litter the patio. The tombstones were used with other rocks to cobble the garden's floor. Some date back as early as 1887.

The man who runs this whole complex is Nick Novich. A former school teacher, he also has interests in two other bars — Toons and The Note. He can usually be seen at Nick's with his patrons, many of whom he knows by name. He has done a good job staffing his bar. The bartenders that served me were friendly and attentive. Like Nick, they knew many of their customers on a first-name basis.

If you want a diverse, friendly crowd in an interesting atmosphere that stays open very late (on many nights it can get slammed after the two o'clock bars shut down), I would suggest Nick's. If you go, say hi to Peaches.

— Joe Schweizer

Nisei Lounge
3439 N. Sheffield Ave.
773-525-0557
Hours: 4 p.m. to 2 a.m. Monday,
11 a.m. to 2 a.m. Sunday and Tuesday to Friday,
11 a.m. to 3 a.m. Saturday

Nisei (pronounced "knee-say") feels like a friendly, neighborhood bar with a cool name. And while both of those facts are true, ask a few more questions and it becomes a lot more interesting than that.

I defy anyone to name another bar in this town that combines Japanese heritage, a Swedish specialty liquor, Gypsy Kings on the jukebox, New Orleans-based theme parties and an elderly man named Kenny who comes into the bar every other day for 12-hour drinking stints.

"Kenny sits under the ceiling fan at the end of the bar and orders one beer every hour," says bartender Dana. "He doesn't speak — it's part of his self-proclaimed persona."

Kenny is, in fact, a nisei, which translates as "U.S.-born children of Japanese immigrants." The original Nisei Lounge was established post-World War II at Clark and Division streets. It moved north about 30 years ago to its present location on Sheffield and was purchased in 1992 by current owner Scott Martin.

"I used to call this place my living room," says bartender James P. Smith. "When Scott first bought Nisei, we had a very small group of regulars who hung out here and that was about it. We've grown a lot since then, but we've really tried to preserve the neighborhood feeling."

And preserve they have. On a Monday night at about 9 p.m. bartender Dana is holding down the fort. Bartender James is in as a patron. His roommate and her boyfriend have just brought him carry-out dinner. They leave, but not before the boyfriend asks Dana to serve him up a "shot for the road." I am impressed by this.

Anthony, a Nisei regular, is sitting next to James shooting the breeze when his buddy David comes in with his greyhound, Trax. Trax is the ideal bar dog who strikes just the right balance between trotting around and nosing people so they'll pet him and laying quietly on the floor when he senses he might be pushing it a bit.

"This is the best bar in the neighborhood," proclaimed Anthony and David. "And we've really tried to find some other good ones. It's a city bar with a small-town feeling."

Nisei carries a range of domestic bottles which go for $2.50 a piece. Imports are $3 and mixed drinks range from $2.50 to $6.75 for top shelf brands. Make sure you check out that Swedish liquor. It's called Malort and is made from "an unusual species of herb which grows wild on northern European mountainsides."

223

The North Side Nisei Lounge-The Note

According to a brochure attached to each bottle of Malort, "only 1 out of 49 men will drink Malort after the first 'shock-glass.'" It didn't say anything about how many women made it past the first "shock-glass." Maybe I'm the only one.

Because of its close proximity to Wrigley Field, Nisei gets a lot of pre- and post-game Cubs traffic during the season. Regulars even leave game-related messages, tickets for friends, and other communiqués with the bartenders. And of course, the game is always tuned in for those who aren't lucky enough to be inside the Friendly Confines.

Bartender James explains that Nisei caters to a diverse crowd, spanning a wide range of ethnicity and age.

"It doesn't matter what you're like the rest of the time," says James. "When you walk into this bar, you have to interact with lots of different types of people. If you don't want to do that, this probably isn't the bar for you."

James grew up in Louisiana and makes it a point to bring southern traditions into the bar. He sometimes holds Crayfish Boils which include fish, corn, potatoes and specialty beers. He has the crayfish flown in from the French Quarter.

James and the boys go on to tell me that Nisei has a "sister" bar in New Orleans' French Quarter called O'Toone's Saloon.

"It's amazing — the place looks just like this. And the people that own it and hang out there are the nicest people you'll ever meet. The bar is in the middle of the French Quarter, but it's the most un-touristy place you could find. And they're huge Cubs fans there."

As if all this isn't enough diversion for you, Nisei has two pool tables, foosball, a pinball machine, a jukebox rated second best in Chicago by "Spin Magazine" and a big screen TV frequently tuned into sports (though James and Dana are always willing to accommodate customer requests). They also make it a point to show Jeopardy, The Simpsons and, of course, Must-See TV.

Check it out. If you're in the mood to hang out and have a few beers, catch a game on TV or down a shot of Malort, Nisei is the place for you. If nothing else, stop by to say hi to Kenny. Just don't expect him too answer.

— Lisa Kueng

The Note

1565 N. Milwaukee Ave.
773-489-0011
Hours: 4 p.m. to 4 a.m. Sunday to Friday,
4 p.m. to 5 a.m. Saturday

When the original Blue Note on Armitage Avenue shuttered in mid-1996, there was a distinct sigh of lament. Industry workers, jazz aficionados and others who appreciate mellow comfort were deprived of an ideal spot to converse, consume and shoot pool while slipping singles into arguably the city's best jukebox.

Their sorrow was short lived however, as Blue Note owner Nick Novich

Barfly The Note

reopened his popular spot a few blocks to the south on Milwaukee Avenue and renamed it The Note. The current bar occupies the former Hothouse space. What's more, it's bringing live jazz once again to West Town's principal intersection.

This migration is especially significant for Novich, who has realized a lifelong dream — to open an intimate live jazz room with a setting tailored to optimal music enjoyment. And while he has done a praise-worthy job setting up this new venue, he has also taken care to preserve the appeal of the original Blue Note. Third shifters will be glad to know that The Note is still perfect for post 2 a.m. heel-coolings.

Sitting at one of The Note's high-top tables while tag teaming a cigarette and a cup of coffee, Novich elaborated on the satisfaction of bringing the old and new together.

"This place needed to expand," he began, waving a curl of smoke through the room. "I always intended to make it a room ideal for playing jazz. We have such a thriving, yet underappreciated scene, and this city doesn't need another blues club or fern bar."

The Note is certainly neither. Novich has projected the history of the old Blue Note onto the new location, preserving the 1940s nightclub elements and art-deco accents. The signature illuminated glass-black bar has been built anew and the room itself is painted with sophisticated subtle lighting.

Improvements include a second bar near the entrance, a separate room for pool, and a large space in the main room to accommodate those content to sit and listen, as well as those who have to dance. When the stage is silent, a half-dozen more high-tip tables are put up, so there's always enough room to relax.

"I wanted to create a place not so fanatic," Novich added. "Jazz music calls for this kind of atmosphere, which is a preservation of our original space."

Tall and silver-hairdo, Novich has almost two decades of experience in the bar industry (his namesake bar, Nick's, has survived a move from Lincoln Park to Wicker Park without a tick in popularity). When building the new Note, he drew on every aspect of his expertise to create a room that caters to musicians as well as customers.

"We went to plenty of expense to create a solid sound environment," Nick said.

Since its opening in the fall of 1996, The Note has featured some of Chicago's best jazz acts as well as those from around the country. Jazz lovers should definitely visit The Note.

— Jay Ferrari

O'Brien's Restaurant

1528 N. Wells St.
312-787-3131
Hours: 11 a.m. to 1 a.m. weekdays,
11 a.m. to 2 a.m. Saturday, 11 a.m. to 7 p.m. Sunday

It's "erin go brah" all over the freakin' place at O'Brien's Restaurant. Let me just say that this is a beautiful bar. O'Brien's may have been around for some 20 years now, but from its grand piano to its copper-clad bar top, it looks brand new.

O'Brien's is not to be mistaken for "Pat O'Brian's" out of New Orleans where "Hurricanes" were made famous. Chicago's O'Brien's, owned by a guy named Dan, is better known for its good beer, good wine and good food than its alcoholic slurpees.

We made the mistake of associating O'Brien's with the New Orleans bar of similar name and thus decided to show up on Fat Tuesday expecting a party. We were prepared for a big crowded bar of drunken revelers. We got a big beautiful bar with a few gentleman sipping drinks, discussing the finer points of life and listening to a player on the grand piano. All together opposite of what we expected, and at the same time you couldn't help but love the place.

The light fixtures, the beer garden, all the decoration at O'Brien's speaks of big money. You'd expect in this Old Town bar to find only big spenders and the upper crust of the North Side's pub crawlers. Instead, the crowd is mixed. So much so in fact that even a Barfly writer could feel welcome (don't laugh, we're not a pretty crowd).

Amidst several Irish stouts and increasing (proportionately) admiration for the bar, we asked to see a menu from the restaurant. Rest assured, the menu does not fall short of the decoration at O'Brien's. The usual items such as potato skins, chicken wings, burgers and sandwiches are mixed in with items such as Oysters Rockefeller and big, juicy steaks. Prices are typical with appetizers at about $4, sandwiches and burgers at $5 and steaks at about $20. Our bar tab for the evening was $15 for four stouts. That puts imports at between three and four dollars, again pretty typical.

If, like me, you've walked by O'Brien's Restaurant a dozen times without ever stopping in, do so. If you're not sure where it is on Wells Street, I'll give you a hint: look for the large four-sided clock in the middle of the sidewalk that says O'Brien's on each clock face. It's not Big Ben, but it's pretty good for Irish Chicago.

— *Bill Stephenson*

Barfly O'Callahan's

O'Callaghan's
29 W. Hubbard St.
312-527-1180
Hours: 11 a.m. to 4 a.m. Monday to Saturday

When you first walk into O'Callaghan's, looking at the bar, you think you're about to step into a space full of yuppie pseudo-intellectuals in Armani suits. The actual decor is so ornate and classy, I thought for sure the drinks would be way expensive and that I would be very much out of place. In all actuality, I couldn't have been more wrong. The old saying goes, "don't judge a book by its cover."

I walked into O'Callaghan's through a very weird back entrance on Kinzie Street, which looked like I was about to enter someone's apartment building. (A friend told me once that 'the cool' and the regulars always enter a bar through the back entrance.)

Once inside, the first thing I noticed was very dim lighting, a perfect compliment to this classy but rustic looking bar. The actual bar was surely a sight to behold with giant mirrors all along the back of it. The back bar is at least five-feet tall, with humongous wood carved statues of maidens acting as pillars to hold up the bar. The place reminded me of one of those hotel bars you see in the old black and white movies. Very aesthetically pleasing.

As for the bartenders themselves, well, let's just say they their land of origin couldn't be further away from Ireland.

The choices in beer selections and prices are very good. The bottled beers in domestics are the usual favorites, as well as the imports. Such domestic draft beers are Sam Adams and Leinie's Red. Import drafts feature Pilsner Urquell and Guinness. Import drafts are $3.75, domestic drafts $3.50. They also feature a beer of the month, and June is Molson bottles for $2.50, which seemed to me quite the bargain.

They also have a plethora of liqueurs (very cheap ones), but for what reason I'm not sure, since just about everyone in the bar was drinking beer.

Another nice feature is that they have "bar pizza," usually not very tasty when sober, but always good when drinking heavily and the munchies kick in before you're ready to go.

The only negative attribute about O'Callaghan's is that they have too many TV sets, showing such luscious sports as boxing and drag racing. It totally took away from the classy ambiance of the room.

The owners of the bar definitely have a sense of humor. There is a large poster in the middle of the bar which reads, "The floggings will continue unti-morale improves." I'm thinking that this little saying keeps the bartenders productive and chipper, because they were both very productive and very chipper while serving me. No slackers here.

So next time you're Downtown and would like to try something different, check out O'Callaghan's. You'll definitely be happy you checked it out. And if you get lost trying to find the bar just look for a four-foot neon lavender wolf in the front window.

— *Nicole Engebretson*

Drinking at O'Hare Airport

There are 90 bars at O'Hare. Ninety bars and they are all operated by the Marriott Corporation. Ninety bars and they all maintain the same personality of a stale hotel Bible. Only one bar, inbetween terminals 2 and 3 and next to the Chicago Neon Skyline rotunda, is slightly modified. The Chicago Bar and Grill has a wood bar, brass railings and tables.

"You pamper them, you do what we call "Kiss Ass" in the biz," said Trish when I asked if she gets sick of hearing people's stories of air-travel trauma. Trish, who works at both The Chicago Bar and Grill and other station bars, seems to have the monopoly on personality in comparison to the other servers who have to share their stations with doughnut shops, piles of shaved ham and hot-dog carousels.

Being really bored at O'Hare while waiting for my sister's flight to finally arrive, I decided to use this time effectively by exploring my propensity for being annoying. While drinks are expensive, beers are $3.50 for domestic, $3.80 for imports and cocktails are $4.50, asking answers to inane questions are free. Trish told me she has heard every story imaginable. This created quite a challenge.

Except for a few individuals, most of the employees of the Marriott bar stations seem to enjoy their positions with the same verve as fast-food employees. Ask anything out of the ordinary and you're back asking for a vegetarian Whopper in 1983.

"Oh, I get it," I said in response to Mark, a very insightful bartender. "You're saying when the weather is bad and flights are delayed, people kill time in the bar....that's so odd." As I ceased scratching my chin in earnest contemplation, I asked, "The day after a major plane crash, do you notice people drinking more?"

"I've never noticed," Mark replied.

I soon realized the only people I could get straight answers out of were the airport personnel wearing red blazers, the quasi-security and customer service types just waiting around to give directions. I asked one particular young man if he had ever seen a pilot drunk at one of the bars.

"The pilots drink at the private clubs," he said. "Who are you?"

"Merely curious," I said and then asked, "How can I get to Terminal 4?" This questioned stumped him as I thanked him and left.

One of the biggest mysteries at O'Hare is the scam with those private clubs. Each major airline, United, American, Continental have a private club with a regal name such as: The Red Carpet Club, Admiral's Club or the President's Club. Membership for frequent flyers is anywhere between $200 and $300

228

Barfly O'Hare Airport

annually. Which breaks down to roughly under twenty bucks a month. The real scam is targeted towards smokers. These clubs are the only places you can smoke in the airport. As legend goes, these places are a veritable oasis, some have showers, some have free coffee, some have free peanuts — all of them have couches. I tried to get in, but the door person did not believe that my dad was in there.

If you ever find yourself beyond bored at O'Hare and decide to take the train over to the International Terminal, you may want to reconsider. People of European persuasion, begotten of lands full of fjords and Alps, who work at an airport bar surrounded by flatness, have absolutely no sense of humor. There are two bars in the International Terminal and drinks are a little bit more expensive: domestic beer is $3.75, imports $4.25, and cocktails are $5.25. Moreover, security does not take kindly to persons wandering aimlessly carrying cardboard suitcases decorated with Christmas birds who unfortunately happen to have scrap hardware in their pockets and made the unfortunate mistake of neglecting to remove various screwdrivers and pliers from their back-packs. Moreover, if you ever find yourself really bored, and go to a foreign land, perhaps a group of islands in the far Northern Pacific, here is a discretionary note to recall when going through customs:

If your officer's lack-of-English-skills limits him to blatantly asking, "Do you have any marijuana or firearms?" Don't smirk. While you may do many things to cure boredom, conducting a cavity search probably isn't considered one of your prime options.

Back to the job at hand, drinking at O'Hare, I found out that drinking at airports isn't as celebrated as it used to be. Alcohol consumption compounds the effects of jet-lag and adds to that dehydrated feeling caused by flying. Moreover, smoking at most airports is restricted to out of the way spots or prohibited. So, the question may be raised, why even bother?

"People use flying as an excuse to drink," is what Trish the bartender said. Why not? Quite simply, your plane may go down. Maintaining a middle ground may save your life. You need to be buzzed enough so all your muscles are relaxed to avoid the bodily trauma incurred on impact. Although, you need to be cognitive enough to operate your oxygen mask, find your floatation device and maneuver yourself down the escape slide. If you can avoid reaching the inebriated target zone at the airport bar, do so. If you are having a send-off party, or are traveling with a group, it is perfectly acceptable to drink a bottle of wine or enjoy cocktails you brought at the gates.

Therefore, I must recommend that you bring your own because the bars at O'Hare are truly boring. But preparing yourself for the worse is often the best way to be surprised. Airline travel defies the laws of nature, so take this into account, next time your flight is delayed. You may need the time to reflect and wonder where are the Hare Krishna's?

-- Margy Stover

O'Lanagan's Bar and Grill

2335 W. Montrose Ave.
773-583-2252
Hours: noon to 2 a.m. Sunday to Friday,
noon to 3 a.m. Saturday

"The best lunches around," according to bartender Lisa Weinstein. Lunch is served from noon to 3:30 p.m. and menu items include 2-pound burritos, Italian beef sandwiches, burgers, pork chops and other goodies.

O'Lanagan's has been around since 1990 and is much like a typical neighborhood bar where everybody knows everybody. Yet, if the regulars don't know you, they don't hold it against you. Folks there are really nice. It's almost like being in someone's living room, watching TV and drinking a few beers.

Weinstein said a whole variety of people venture into the place from millionaires to those with just enough dough for a pint.

The place is small, featuring a long wood bar and two worn pool tables. It's decorated in typical bar fashion with beer sings and posters. The best piece of decoration is an old ship made out of Miller Lite cans; a bit dusty but pretty cool.

O'Lanagan's has billiard leagues Tuesdays through Thursdays. Shelves behind the bar are filled with trophies and plaques won by O'Lanagan's pool players in league play.

To drink, there's Bud and Miller and they have the standard assortment of Scotch and whiskey. Specials are 75-cent Bud on Mondays and Wednesdays, and 75-cent Miller's on Tuesdays and Thursdays.

O'Lanagan's usually celebrates St. Patrick's Day with a corned beef and cabbage party.

— *Tony Gordon*

O'Malley's Pub

6345 W. Belmont Ave.
773-327-5454
Hours: 4 p.m. to 2 a.m. weekdays,
4 p.m. to 3 a.m. Saturday, 6 p.m. to 2 a.m. Sunday

In the world of neighborhood pubs, this is one damn good joint. It is one of the few bars that has weekend drink specials and that gives complimentary rounds. Without to say, the service at this local pub is courteous and quick. You will not wait long for a cold brew.

What does O'Malley's have to offer? There is a dart league from Mondays through Thursdays, on Fridays there is karaoke (though be careful, there are some bad singers that audition their aching voices), and on Saturdays there are live bands ranging from Irish folk music to alternative rock. There is never a

Barfly O'Malley's Pub-Off The Line

cover charge.

For a small bar, there is plenty to do here. In the front room there are two television sets, a fine jukebox, a stage at the front of the bar and a fireplace. There are two electronic dart boards, eight cork dart boards, a foosball table and two video games. In addition, the bar will soon start serving meals to its patrons.

The prices on the beer are quite reasonable and chilled. Domestic bottled beers are $1.75 and include Rolling Rock, Old Style, Michelob, Miller products, and Rock Bock. The imports are $2.25 and include Heineken, Woodpecker Cider and Weiss beer. On tap there is Harp, Guinness, Bud Light and Red Wolf. Domestic pitchers cost $3.75 and import pitchers are $9.

O'Malley's opened in 1991 and in my book the place is a lot more fun than its predecessor Zigfields. So if you are ever driving on the Northwest Side of the city and are wondering where to go for a cold beer — from one beer drinker to another — you should head west on Belmont until you reach O'Malley's.

— Pete Schmugge

Off The Line
1829 W. Montrose Ave.
773-528-3253
Hours: 5 p.m. to 2 a.m. weekdays,
3 p.m. to 3 a.m. Saturday, noon to 2 a.m. Sunday

As soon as I spilled out of the cab I had commissioned to bring myself to the 1800 block of Montrose, my eyes were greeted by a glowing neon pink triangle; a beacon in the night. I, like many other I'm sure, have grown too accustomed to the disappointment which goes hand in hand with usual gay haunts this city has to offer. A new bar and hopeful change of faces and scenery are always welcomed and embraced.

Arriving at the door, I was greeted by a small fence which barely cleared my knees; to any older and wiser lesbian, this is a sure sign that animals abound. And sure enough, there is a resident pup, whose name eludes me, but take comfort, it's a friendly and adorable beast...so please, watch where you step.

The bar itself is quaint and comfy. The walls are donned with ever-changing murals, painted by the bar owners themselves. But perhaps what distinguishes Off The Line from other lesbian bars is its spectacular selection of bottled beers. I counted 33, along with five beers on tap! Other boons that Off The Line can boast: cable TV, beef jerky, and usually The Barfly. What more can one possibly require?

I couldn't dream of reviewing this bar without commending them on their wonderful restrooms — a joy and a privilege to use. They're fresh and clean, and not only do they supply ample rolls of toilet paper but towelettes for one's hands as well. Both of these at a single bar are indeed a luxury. Also, there is an erasable billboard in each stall for one to write down his or her neurotic

231

drunken ramblings. I don't know about you, but some of my most profound thoughts come to me in the bathroom, and often I've wished I had a place to write them down.

Although I've described the bar as being "quaint," don't assume the place doesn't fill up; on a week night it is usually reasonably full.

Oinkers

3471 N. Elston Ave.
773-463-4222
Hours: 11 a.m. to 2 a.m. Monday to Friday,
11 a.m. to 3 a.m. Saturday, 11 a.m. to 1 a.m. Sunday

If you are ever driving on Elston Avenue near Addison Street, it's not hard to miss a large pig logo; this is Oinkers Bar and Restaurant. When you walk in, it is hard to believe how big this bar really is. The bar has two rooms and one of the largest beer gardens in the city.

The first room has a large screen for sports and movies, a long narrow bar starting near the entrance way, a jukebox including songs from Pearl Jam to Thin Lizzy, and a display of Oinkers merchandise like T-shirts, mugs, bumper stickers, and hats.

In the second room, there is another bar, more tables with a stage at the front of the room in the corner. There is live music every Friday which is mostly oldies-type bands and on Saturday there is Karaoke.

When the sun warms up the city, Oinkers' beer garden has a cooling atmosphere with plenty of shade trees looming over drinkers heads. It is a good place to check out after a ballgame.

One of Oinkers best qualities is the size of the bar. This is especially true of the washrooms. There is plenty of room. What really is unique about the washrooms are that there are large chalkboards in them. There are no markings on the stalls nor the walls in the washroom. Rather the clientele write their feelings of the band playing or their political ideology.

On the night of the review, Johnny Star and the Meteors were playing. They were playing tunes from the Beatles, Herman and the Hermits, and Elvis. The bar was packed in both rooms. The crowd mix was from the 20s and well into the 40s. There were groupings of white collar, neighborhood regulars and blue-collar workers. The crowd really enjoyed the band and didn't hide the fact by dancing to almost every song.

The beers on tap are all domestics. The beers are mostly Bud and Miller products, except for Killian's and Old Style. A pitcher of beer runs the customer $5.50, a mug costs $1.50, and bottles cost $2.25 for domestics, Beck's and Heineken costs $3, Pschou Brau Weiss which goes for $3.75 for a 17 ounce bottle. There is also wine on tap but many of the patrons were drinking mix drinks.

In addition to a comfortable and interesting atmosphere, the bar serves up

Barfly Oinkers-Old Town Ale House

tasty meals and appetizers. Oinkers starts serving food at lunch and serves until midnight. There are daily specials which include anything from meat loaf to perch. Some of the appetizers are mushrooms, shrimp, cheese sticks, and fish and chips. Also, there is free popcorn.

Oinkers is well worth a visit to watch a band or simply getting a meal. It is located a block south of Addison at Elston and Albany.

— *Pete Schmugge*

Old Town Ale House
219 W. North Ave.
312-944-7020
Hours: 11 a.m. to 4 a.m. Sunday to Friday,
11 a.m. to 5 a.m. Saturday

Jump jazz, polynesian Tiki masks, $3 Guinness pints — first impressions of a drink joint often stick, only to be further submerged into memory by such things as a hospitable bartendress and fellow drinkers who half eavesdrop only to gain the context of a conversation they can later jump into.

I know not where it came from but the Ale House, according to persistent Old Town dwellers, is a gift from gods who used to rule the foolish mortal world of social drinking. Opened in 1958, The Old Town Ale House had quietly breathed the air of a much smaller North Avenue location until 1971 when a fire ravaged the original place. According to a bartendress, "after the fire, they just picked up the old bar and moved it across the street through these doors."

Through the 1970s, a local artist rendered portraits of the regulars on the bar's west interior wall. Faces of patrons through the years have thrown their gaze toward the backs of current elbow tippers.

"You can tell which people she (the artist) liked more than others," the bartendress said. "Some (drawings) aren't very flattering."

The bartendress knows about half of the names of the folks on the wall and her portrait is on the end.

"See that guy," she said pointing to the portrait of a man with a parrot on his shoulder. "He just had a stroke."

On my second visit to the bar, I was imbibed enough to let a friend convince me to run a wind-up alligator, I carry with me, down the length of the bar. Though the heavy wood was well-populated by people discussing life, luxury and the pursuit of the ultimate improv comedy skit, the alligator ran unimpeded but was jovially noticed by the patrons. Passing the myriad doll figures, Tiki heads, head shots of semi-celebrities (including one taken of Roger Daltrey while shooting a not-even-video-bound movie on location in the bar), and Toulouse-Lautrec reproductions, the alligator arrived at the end of the bar. This leads to the bar's three state-of-the-art pinball machines which lie next to a reading area stocked to the gills with semi-best-sellers, forgotten titles and true-

233

The North Side Old Town Ale House-Ole St. Andrews Inn

crime pulp. From there, the observant patron can see all corners of the cozy wood-brown, well-worn bar while listening to the coolest of jazz, soul, ballads and showtunes on a CD jukebox so eccentric in its range of choices that you can swing the whole mood of the bar for a mere pittance of $1.

The beer prices are reasonable enough to keep you drinking. Pints of draft run between $2 for Old Style to about $3 for imports while bottles fall into a gray area of two bills and change for most brands. The bar has a typical and adequate selection of whiskeys, rums, gins and spirits that don't stray far toward the exotic but are enough to please most gullets.

This eclectic, cluttered landmark of truly local continuity is alternately busy with first-time visitors and die-hard Old Towners, Second City students, press folk and musicians. At any given moment, the bar can be jovial, mellow, cool, talkative, quiet, a little forbidding and reflective. But, for all its eccentricities, or rather because of them, it is an anomaly of the rarest sort, a place out of time where you lose all sense of geography until you step back out on the corner of North Avenue and Wieland Street.

— *Chris Handyside*

Ole St. Andrews Inn
5938 N. Broadway
773-748-5540
Hours: 11 a.m. 2 a.m. Sunday to Friday,
10 a.m. to 3 a.m. Saturday

My interest in Scotch whiskey has been growing. So as it were, my mission was to find someplace which would accommodate me. I consulted with some top advisors to help me find, what else, a Scottish bar that has not yet been reviewed by any of Barfly's drunken staff. It was the Ole St. Andrews Inn that was suggested to me. The tavern was formerly known as the Edinburgh Castle Pub which was Scottish.

The nature of the pub's current national status was in question. One had contested that it had to be Scottish because of the name, while another who had actually visited the establishment, claimed it was Irish. Well, they were neither right nor wrong, as I had gotten the proper information from the source, barmaid and manager Margaret Dillard. It is in fact, an English-style pub, with the flavor, or should I say flavors, of Scotland and Ireland. Margaret, a long time customer of the Edinburgh, was born and raised in Glasgow, Scotland. She was the perfect candidate to assist owners Dave Jenkins and Kay Whipple, whose establishment, opened in the fall of 1994, as a tribute to Jenkins true love (apart from his fiancee, of course), the game of golf. Named after the place where golf was invented, where he travels often and acquires in the process the imported decor that lends to the authenticity of the pub. People will come from miles around who are seeking a comfortable place to socialize and drink.

While it's not a very dimly lit place, and includes some of your typical pub fanfare; darts; juke, televisions, etc., you can look at the surroundings and

Barfly Ole St. Andrews Inn

absorb yourself in the wide variety of whiskies and imported/domestic beers. There are 11 beers on tap including standards Guinness, Woodpecker Cider, and Old Style. There are more than 50 different bottles.

The night I visited, the bar was busy, not packed, not typical for a Saturday night there. The service was very polite and at a comfortable pace, the kind of pace where you have to relax and wait patiently (there are many regulars who attend the bar, so whoever is tending has to, not only pour drinks, but do a lot of listening and talking as well).

Margaret imparted as much information as she could with me about the different kinds of Scotch they had and let me inspect the bottles so that I might, with my limited knowledge, make educated guesses of the samples that were going to best represent the wide spectrum of characteristics. There were a couple dozen bottles to choose from, but I got lucky and picked out what was collectively decided on as one that was uncommonly smooth (Cragganmore), one that was smoother than most (Glenkinchie), and one that was undoubtedly not as smooth as the other two (Knockando).

When those were finished, we ordered again so that we might relax in one of the huge booths that line the walls around the lounge area, that included tables and a small stage where live music had played on in the back-ground. In celebration of the weekend, they hired singer/guitarist Sheila O'Donell, who sang holiday and traditional songs. Acts on the mellow side that range from folk to jazz (such as that which has been performed by the Charles Williamson Band) are a part of the live entertainment that they are trying to feature on the weekends. For performance information you can contact Margaret (heavy rock bands need not apply).

The lounge area is also a dining room that serves up a British-American menu including, but not limited to, such stick-to-your-bones dishes like lamb or Guinness stew (the recipe belongs to the legendary Mrs. Conolly) and chicken or shepherd's pie. Kitchen's open until 10 p.m. Mondays through Thursdays, until 11 p.m. Fridays and Saturday and until 8 p.m. on Sundays.

While the prices have not been scaled down for the starving artist, you won't spend anymore than you would at anyone of the many over-hyped Chicago theme restaurants that sprout like weeds across Chicago's culinary lawn. This food is grassroots.

On a final note is one last bit of advice, beware if you grab the first booth by the bowling machine, you may be joined by an unexpected guest, a regular who goes by the name of "Frank," who might move the glasses or bottles around in the table, or put a "cold" hand on your girlfriend's thigh. Not to worry, though, he is harmless and you really wouldn't notice him anyway, because "Frank" is the resident ghost (how can you have an English pub without one). He was rumored to have been a heavy vodka drinker and ladies man who had died accidentally at the spot, where unexplained phenomena prevails.

What more could you want; there's nothing fancy about the Ole St. Andrews Inn, and that's the way everyone seems to like it...

— *Arunas Ingaunis*

Orso's Restaurant

1401 N. Wells St.
773-787-6604
Hours: 11 a.m. to 11 p.m. weekdays,
4 p.m. to midnight Saturday, 4 p.m. to 10 p.m. Sunday

Orso's Restaurant has a great outdoor patio in a neighborhood where eclectic galleries, shops, and nightspots crowd gentrified streets. The courtyard patio is of first rate and exhibits the romantic ambiance of a cafe rather than that of a beer garden.

On the particular hot May night I visited Orso's Restaurant, the patio was abuzz with action. Renee, the friendly face behind the bar, told us "the patio is very popular" and suggested that reservations were a good idea for Thursday through Sunday night.

Sitting at the bar, I was reminded of the many outdoor cafes I visited while traveling throughout Italy. While I did not eat, many people at the bar told me the food was good. The presentation, preparation, and loving consumption of food are all close to the core of Italian culture and the patrons of this establishment appeared to be thoroughly enjoying Orso's authentic Italian cuisine.

On an excursion into the restaurant, I couldn't help but notice that the walls were lined with autographed pictures of famous Chicago politicians and celebrities, as well as stained glass windows and other interesting works of art. I found the atmosphere inside to be as friendly and inviting as it was outside. A pianist played soft, soothing music that provided a nice background to the sounds of the restaurant. Renee said that Orso's Restaurant has been a family run operation for 25 years and that Bob, the pianist, came with the place.

The atmosphere, service and friendly employees at Orso's Restaurant left a lasting impression. It was most definitely an experience you will enjoy.

— Craig Greenfield

Paris Dance Club

1122 W. Montrose Ave.
773-769-0602
Hours: 5 p.m. to 2 a.m. weekdays,
7 p.m. to 2 a.m. Saturday, noon to 2 a.m. Sunday

For years Paris Dance has been a staple amongst the lesbian bar scene; perhaps more than a staple, but rather a Mecca itself as far as bars catering to women are concerned.

During the week, Paris has more of a homey feel to it; the mood is mellow...it's a nice place to unwind after work. The crowd is naturally smaller...but still friendly nonetheless. I invited myself in on a conversation between a patron and the bartender regarding gin. Seagram's lost the alcohol content contest by far; my vote went with Booth's, and I was wrong as well. It comes

Barfly Paris Dance Club-Payton Place

with little surprise that I would suppose if I had a burning desire to know I could easily enough find out — but, like I said, no one ever really asked me. I invited myself into the conversation, and so I would just like to comment on the friendly and patient cliental.

If there still exists a lesbian who has not been to Paris Dance on a Friday or Saturday night, I will say here and now, "WHERE THE HELL HAVE YOU BEEN?" Okay, if you're one of those types that doesn't care for dancing or loud music, go ahead, stay inside, live in your parents' basement the rest of your life fantasizing about Dr. Crusher on Star Trek (No offense to Trekkies!) All I'm saying is that at the very least, give this place a try. It's quite an experience.

Payton Place
5624 N. Broadway
773-878-4052
Hours: 11 a.m. to 4 a.m. daily

Feeling a bit apprehensive about walking into a desolate and dark looking bar, I was soon surprised and found the interior just the opposite. The bar had few customers but was loud with laughter and jokes.

"Everybody knows everybody," said one patron.

The bar has been in business for more than 15 years. And their business is to provide quick, courteous service with a smile at no extra charge.

Payton Place has established itself as an Edgewater neighborhood bar catering to locals and passerbys.

Along with the bar, the folks who own the bar operate as a type of convenience store, having a cooler in the back selling six-packs so customers can take a beer home. Equipped with the cooler, a cigarette machine, and entertainment, a customer does not have to travel far for anything nor do they have to bring anything. Well, maybe some money.

Payton Place has two mini-pool tables, a couple of poker machines, and a jukebox. It's a different, little place to have a few beers and play pool to some great tunes.

The bartender, Linda, who was on duty while I was visiting, was helpful and friendly. Prices are reasonable to cheap. A domestic runs $1.75 a bottle and there's no cover. Linda let me in on a little secret while I was there. On the weekends come early because it gets really crazy. They bring in extra staff solely for the overflow.

Before leaving you get a good piece of advice too. Over the register hangs an oversized bumper sticker which reads, "I love sober drivers."

Payton Place is open seven days a week from 11 a.m. until 4 a.m. so there is no reason for you not to stop by and say hello.

— T.M. Kornelsen

Peabody's Pub

4933 N. Milwaukee Ave.

773-777-8298

Hours: 3 p.m. to 2 a.m. weekdays,
4 p.m. to 3 a.m. Saturday, 8 p.m. to 2 a.m. Sunday

A name like Peabody's could make many people think of that geeky cartoon dog that wore glasses and spoke like a college professor while at the same time transported his trusty, although equally as geeky, sidekick (Sherman) through time.

Peabody's Pub, however, certainly does not give any indication of the cartoon, it doesn't transport you through time, it holds you there, kind of in a "what decade is this anyway" mode.

It must always be the holiday season at Peabody's, although no gifts were being handed out, because multicolored Christmas lights were still glowing behind the bar in many shapes and colors even though the season was edging into late spring when I visited the bar.

The bar itself is a relatively nice carved wood model complete with glass built cases and shelves, but it is never going to realize its full potential with the gaudy Christmas lights strewn madly up, over and through it.

The rest of the decor also leaves room for wondering. The walls are covered half way down from the ceiling with fake-brick siding-type of material and the other half to the floor is covered with paneling. Fake plants in hanging baskets are hung in uneven intervals from the ceiling, where one can also see the exposed air conditioning and heating vents and a dark ceiling with missing tiles. The feeling that I was spending time in someone's fixed-up 1970s basement was coming on me too strong, so I had to focus my attention on the crowd, or rather, lack of there of.

My date was the only female in the bar besides the bartender. The bartender was wrapped up in a white cotton halter top and tight jeans. She ruled the bar like the Queen of England and didn't let you forget it.

With empty beer bottles, cocktail glasses and day-old newspapers still lying about, even though the bar was practically empty, I wondered if it was closing time even though it was 10 p.m.

Besides young men at the bar hoping to snag a date with the Gloria Estevan-like bartender the rest of the 20 or so patrons busied themselves watching the two televisions screens on either side of the bar while others played a dart game in the rear of the bar. A big screen television, although not turned on, loomed eerily over the rear hallway to the bathroom, sort of like a guillotine for an unsuspecting customer as a punishment for an offending comment to the diva-of-the-minute bartender.

Seeing Peabody's Pub from Milwaukee Avenue, you might be semi-enticed by seeing the "Tommy" pinball game right up front, which lured my date and I in, but after a good look around you'll wonder just how fast you can finish your beer and make tracks. As my date said, "I was ready to go the minute we walked in."

— *Dennis Mahoney*

Peacock Lounge
3394 N. Milwaukee Ave.
773-286-4482
Hours: 5 p.m. to 4 a.m. Sunday to Friday,
5 p.m to 5 a.m. Saturday

A seven-foot guy walks up and down the bar offering beef jerky, then says to the bartender, "This sells for $15 full, I'll give it to ya for five bucks." Coupled with the name "Stosh" being thrown around, I didn't need to remind myself that I was in one of the many Polish neighborhood bars of Milwaukee Avenue.

Something should be said for neighborhood bars. Everyone knows one another and it's just a cool night hanging out with friends from down the street, buddies from high school or new neighbors looking to meet more people. Or, it's a night in a foreign bar where one can be incognito and no one cares who you are except when you get too drunk. The Peacock Lounge is such a place.

The Peacock Lounge offers no real frills. Wood paneling, a couple pool tables with ample lighting, two electronic casino machines, and a jukebox with 1980s dance/pop and 1960s to 1980s rock.

Any night of the week brings in the regulars of the neighborhood and then a few more with the late-night 4 a.m. license. The crowd, as usual sticks to the neighborhood tap feel: shooting pool, talking with friends or the bartender, whatever their forte. So if you're an outsider, there is no apprehension and you can sit and talk with your friends.

The big bonus of the Peacock Lounge is that 4 a.m. license. It is rare to go to a 4 a.m. bar that continues to have the feel of just a neighborhood crowd and not the usual "not from around here, want to start trouble with everyone, way too drunk" late night crowd.

Since the barroom has no true jump to it, one should not expect the drinks to as well. They have Gösser and Old Style on tap, a few imports such as Beck's and Heineken, and a good amount of hard liquor. The selection is bland, but the prices are excellent — $1.50 for a 12-ounce glass (which looks smaller but is 12-ounces) of Gösser or $1 for 12-ounces of Old Style. Beck's and Heineken in bottles for $2 and $2.50 for shots. Please keep in mind also that these are the prices at four in morning. Out of the wide selection of hard liquor, I highly recommend downing a couple of Arctic's Vodka and Melon or Arctic's Vodka and Peach. Quality stuff that does what you want it to.

So if you wish your local tap stayed open a little later, head to Milwaukee Avenue and Roscoe Street and sit back with the neighbors and down a few. Don't worry about understanding Polish, if you're still drinking Arctic shots at 4 a.m., you'll probably speak it fluently.

— *Phil Brandt*

Pequod's Pizza

2207 N. Clybourn Ave.
773-327-1512
Hours: 11 a.m. to 2 a.m. weekdays,
noon to 2 a.m. Saturday, noon to midnight Sunday

Across the street from the Webster Place Theater lies one of Chicago's most prized possessions. Established in 1970 in Morton Grove, Pequod's Pizza's location on Clybourn is definitely one of the best and most unique pizza places anywhere in the country. The bar itself only seats about ten people but there are tables galore for those who wish to have possibly the best pizza experience of their life.

This establishment is so comfortable that you could write on the walls — literally. Owner Keith Jackson said, "We originally started that for younger kids, but..."

Yes, indeed, for if the creative side of yourself should rear its head during your visit, it would be a challenge to find an area of plaster untouched by magic marker. "Connie," the mannequin, who co-manager Cindy keeps in fashion, stands watch over the restaurant as folks eat, drink, and of course, write on the walls. It is, however, B.Y.O.M. (bring your own marker, and no gang writing, please).

Miller Lite and Leinenkugel's flow from just two tappers, but there are plenty of bottles to satisfy the beer drinker, as well as a limited selection of hard liquor. They also carry Tucher Weizen in three different varieties, and it makes an excellent after dinner drink in each. The one thing that stands out in my mind is how cold the beer is. That is a good thing because, let's face it, warm beer sucks.

Well, I hate to stray from talking about booze to all of you barflies, but forgive me, I have to tell you about the pizza. Because this is not just pizza, I believe it is crafted by the gods. I have my favorite places that deliver in my area, such as Durango on Laramie, and Father and Son on Milwaukee, as I'm sure you do, but this pizza is not only great it is unique.

If you don't care how bad pork is for you, order the sausage, it's the leanest around. The vegetables are always fresh, and the pie is consistently tasty. The pan pizza has a ring of what they call "caramelized cheese" around it, and although it may look burnt, it is the best part of the pizza. There is also a menu of pasta and sandwiches, as if you would want anything other than the pizza. Food is available during all open hours, as well as delivery if you live within their area. Let it suffice to say that I've never had a bad meal or drink there. So, enough said...

Pequod's definitely has a refreshing approach to a restaurant. Two whales in a 69 position with the slogan "eat out," a topless mermaid, and of course, just plain whales are printed on their T-shirts. The sign advertising that they have slices says, "two if you're hungry, one of you're not," in blatantly honest form.

Barfly Pequod's-Pinewood

Hand written signs on the walls say, "for your safety, please do not: stick your fork in your eye, drink the candle wax, French kiss the electric outlet," and several others. It's just nice to see a place that takes the food, drinks and service seriously, but lets the business approach of it be laid-back and humorous.

By the way, in case you were not paying attention in American Lit, The Pequod was the ship from Moby Dick.

— Bud

Pinewood
2310 W. Touhy Ave.
773-973-4443
Hours: 11 a.m. to 1 a.m. Sunday to Thursday, 11 a.m. to 2 a.m. Friday, 11 a.m. to 3 a.m. Saturday

Search this place out and, among many other delights, you'll discover a solution to many of life's troubles. As soon as you see Pinewood's rustic log-cabin facade, your head will throb a little less, your pulse will slow and you'll know that sleep will be yours tonight. Just think: Cousin Otis, though still hundreds of miles from his Canadian home, stops his constant sniveling about missing the Great White North; a photo of ex-roommate Bernie in front of the place convinces his parole officer that he never left Minnesota; your Lincoln-enthusiast girlfriend agrees to put off the trek to Springfield and down a few pitchers in the "Bar that Abe built" (wink).

Inside the Pinewood, you'll find many other reasons to return . . . not the least of which is the fact that the bar refused to serve WXRT jock Terri Hemmert. Seems she demanded steak and eggs one summer Saturday. The reply came in the form of a record — her rare copy of the "Yesterday and Today" (Butcher cover no less!) being busted over her head before she was tossed out Beatle boots first. Though that yarn has a nearly inaudible ring of truth to it, it's something to contemplate as you sit in Pinewood's beer garden, which stretches 50 yards beneath tall mulberry trees and a protective canopy. A dozen picnic tables provide a perfect spot for taking in warm nights and sunny days. Owner Jim Brockhagen built the large wood deck after buying Pinewood about 11 years ago. Today, families, softball teams and other outdoor fans mingle in this Roger's Park Eden.

Back inside, Larry, the main man behind the bar, and Ellie serve up $5.50 pitchers of domestic beer, and five types of wine at 2 bucks a glass. The juke pumps out new and old, and Irish favorites on 45s.

Food at Pinewood is the real showstopper. Cooks Lucy and Kirk provide a broad menu of appetizers, soups and no-bullshit meals. I've devoured, and heartily recommend the meatloaf, spicy gumbo, cheeseburger, chicken sandwich and stuffed pepper. Also, count on the Friday-night Fish Fry, Sunday-Night Prime Rib dinner and a host of other daily specials to satisfy the munchies or give you the sustenance to get you through a long night.

While we eat and drink at Pinewood, the establishment has set its sights on bigger things. Plans have the bar expanding to three times its current size. The 75-year-old building will be joined by a restaurant room and private party room, served by an expanded kitchen. Before then, however, Otis, Bernie, and especially friends of Old Abe will have a great time at Pinewood.

—Patrick McAuley

Pippins Tavern
806 N. Rush St.
312-787-5435
Hours: 11 a.m. to 4 a.m. Sunday to Friday,
11 a.m. to 5 a.m. Saturday

Pippins (not affiliated with former Bull Scottie) is the kind of bar in which you can lose all track of time. It is, by far, one of the best spots to be at if you're in the neighborhood. There is just enough commotion around to remind you that you're on Rush Street: big-time clubs standing around the corner, horse-drawn carriages rolling by. But inside, everything is just right.

Let me warn you, though, the place is small, with only about 12 to 13 tables surrounding the bar. But there is so much to look at. The walls, ceilings and bar posts are absolutely cluttered with neon beer signs, foreign money, framed mirrors, business cards, memorabilia and so on.

Under the pretense that I wanted to check out how clean it was, I went into the men's bathroom. The truth was, a friend of mine told me that they sold fun stuff in there. I wanted to see what that meant. For 50 cents you can get yourself a fake tattoo and a variety of condoms, including ones that glow in the dark. (The bathrooms were clean, by the way.)

When I spoke with Jay Jingst, the manager, I was referred to the bar's marketing department, which surprised me. The place was so laid-back, I couldn't picture someone sitting at a desk pondering how to get more butts in the seats. Nevertheless, the place is owned by Lodge Management, and the space has been occupied by bars since the 1950s. Next door sit Downtown Dogs (also owned by Lodge Management), which features a very appropriate "munchies menu," where everything from nachos to fried calamari is under $5. On nice nights, you can enjoy your dog and your beer outside on the three available tables.

Speaking of beer, there is something for everybody. Pippins selection is huge. It carries all major domestic bottles and nine import bottles. There are 11 beers on tap, including a very tasty Widmer Hefeweizen. Prices are very reasonable. Most domestic bottles are $2, and domestic pitchers start at $6.

This is not just a beer place, though. Just recently, Pippins has made four small batch bourbons and five single-malt Scotches available, including an 18-year-old Macallan for $5.50 a glass. Jingst said that the Scotches are doing well, thanks to the surrounding hotels and a different drinking attitude.

"People might not be drinking as much, but they are taking the time to drink

Barfly Pippins Tavern-The Players Club

well," he said.

Drinking well is what you can expect at Pippins. It is an honest, neighborhood place, where the patrons leave their money on the bar and keep the drinks coming. There's nothing fancy, no free pours, no drink specials. There doesn't need to be. It's all good.

— Lee DiVita

The Players Club
2500 N. Ashland Ave.
773-477-7769
Hours: 4 p.m. to 2 a.m. weekdays, noon to 3 a.m.
Saturday, noon to 2 a.m. on Sunday

Forget the guillotine. Sure, Mark has one and he'll gladly let you use it. But why not try his "v cutter" for an elegant v-shaped tip? Or his bullet cutter for a simple, clean hole?

And don't think of lighting that cigar with a Bic. Mark has a lighter with an extra-strong flame for the $5 to $14 cigars he keeps behind the bar.

Such attention to detail is what Mark's wife, Mary, hopes will make The Players Club, "a nicer bar than anyone else's — a bar with just the right feeling."

When the Jurczyks bought the building on the northwest corner of Altgeld and Ashland, the bar space came as part of the package. At the time, it was Manny's Place, a tavern with a reputation so nasty that cops were afraid to enter.

"We saw a lot of potential," Mary explains.

The Lincoln Park West bar marks the first retail-type real estate investment for the Jurczyks, who had previously limited their purchases to apartment buildings.

To reach the space's potential, the couple had to dig deep, literally. To build bathrooms adults could stand in, they had to lower the basement floor another 4 feet. The rest of the bar was gutted.

"All that is left (of Manny's) is the bricks," Mary says.

The wood floor is new. The bar is new. The blades of the white ceiling fans are white.

Mark, also owns the MAJ Construction Company (he's averaging four to five hours of sleep), and his crew spent a little over five months remodeling the bar, which opened in November, 1996.

"I don't know what you would call that?" Mark asks Mary as he tries to describe the monolithic wood poles placed at 90-degree angles to frame the bar. The effect might be Lincoln-Loggish, except that the wood is highly polished and the pieces are separated by much tinier, evenly-spaced wooden rectangles that add a dash of Frank Lloyd Wright.

The wood came from Menard's. The design came from Mark.

"We do it ourselves," Mary explains as casually as Mark describes the race

243

The Player's Club is one of Chicago's best new sports bars. Pictured here are owners Mark and Mary Jurczyks with former Bear linebacker Joe Cain.

car hanging from the back room ceiling as "a good conversation piece."

Legendary driver Rick Mears won the 1984 Indy 500 behind the wheel of No. 6. Now you can play pool underneath the bright yellow car.

Checkered flags from the Michigan 500 and driver-autographed posters hang by the entrance.

"Everything is shaking, it's so beautiful," says Mary, describing the beginning seconds of a race. "That a human being could control a machine at that speed..."

"You make a mistake, you're in another zip code," Mark says.

The Greg Moore Martini and the Michael Andretti Stoli Cocktail are among the special mixes named for famous drivers. The martini menu also includes a fresh raspberry martini and home-made blue cheese olives.

In addition to its selection of martinis and Stoli mixes, The Players Club offers 13 Scotches, 13 vodkas and 13 draught beers.

It was the first Chicago bar to offer Fiddler, an imported vodka. In fact, Players started serving it the day it arrived in Chicago. Bartender Martin knows this because he works days for the distributor, Stawski Distributing Co., Inc. In addition to vodkas, Stawski supplies the bar with a variety of European alcoholic beers, wines and liquors.

Barfly The Players Club

With their shiny white bodies and brass accents, three tappers stand proudly in the middle of the bar. The black hand of the Left Hand Ale pull is life-size.

But the number one choice of the largely yuppie clientele?

"Lite," says Martin with a smile.

Domestic bottles are $2.50; imports $3. Imported draught selections run from $3 to $4.

The Players Club offers a special every night. The week begins with all Miller products priced at $2 for Monday Night Football and ends with a Build-Your-Own Bloody Mary bar on Sunday ($3 well, $4 call).

Each night a different draught beer is on special: 16 ounces for $3.

To advertise the cigar part of The Players Club experience, Mark plans to place a 6-foot wooden sculpture of an American Indian holding a handful of cigars at the entrance. Until then, a doll-sized version stands on the bar. Mark picked up the carved piece while in the Virgin Islands on a recent construction job.

On the night I visited, Mary and Mark arrived straight from the airport. He had just flown in from the Virgin Islands.

From his pile of bags, Mark pulled out several boxes of Brazilian cigars that Chicago has yet to discover. He offered everyone at the bar a sample.

"This is the way you smoke a cigar," announced a thirty-ish woman as she dipped her's in cognac. She smoked a vanilla-scented, cigarette-size Dannemann's, a cigar Mark described as a "lady's cigar."

"The idea," Mark said, "is that this be a bar anyone can come to for a good beer and a good cigar."

In May 1997, they opened their kitchen and serve a variety of finger foods — from veggie burgers to cheeseburgers, from classic chicken wings to a brie-with-almond dish. Mary, who, like Mark and Martin, emigrated from Poland, plans to add some European dishes to the menu.

— Alice Bendig

Podhale

2924 N. Central Park
Won't give out phone number
Hours: 2 p.m. to 2 a.m. Sunday to Friday,
3 p.m. to 5 a.m. Saturday

Set smack dab in the Polish community centered along North Milwaukee Avenue, this place is quite a find.

Everyone seems to be Polish. When I visited they all spoke Polish and listened to Polish pop music on the jukebox. There is a pool table in the back which hosts a friendly game here and there. Even a couple of older guys were playing a game of chess with nice handmade pieces.

I sat at the bar with the majority of after-work lushes like myself. This gave me a chance to enjoy the nice art deco bar along with all these weird decorations covering it, of which I couldn't figure out what they were.

The North Side Podhale-Polly Esther's

The place has an all around classic bar feel with a Formica covered bar, a fine tin ceiling, and plenty of beer mirrors. However, the best feature of the bar is the velvet Elvis which hangs triumphantly over the jukebox. It's a choice painting. Usually I see velvet Elvis depicted with the trade mark shiny studded lapels and twisted grin. This one has Elvis in the same lapels but this time screaming into a microphone.

I thought that alone was worth the trip until I found out that they have Okocim in bottles for only $2. This is going to make the work day just a little bit longer.

— Phil Brandt

Polly Esther's
213 W. Institute Place
312-664-0777
Hours: 8 p.m. to 4 a.m. Wednesday to Saturday, closed Sunday to Tuesday

Hang on to your Hawaiian shirt Steve Dahl...DISCO is back! Looks like there were some wax survivors from one of the greatest radio "commotion promotions" of all time: Disco Demolition. I know this because the disco records that were not blown up along with the outfield at the old Comiskey Park are being played loud and proud at Polly Esther's here in Chicago.

They're baaaaaack. Leisure suits, bell bottoms, bean bag chairs, go-go boots (I think my mom still has a pair leftover from the early 70s), platform shoes (they made my cousin Jeffrey look 10 feet tall), and the dyn-o-mite music that everybody claimed to never want to hear again. Well boys and girls, it's all back, alive and doin' well at Polly Esther's.

Far Out! Polly Esther's is virtually a 70s shrine worshipping retro. On the main level, 1970s icons surround you. On one side of the room, you've got a replica of the Partridge Family school bus, while on the other side, Herbie the Luv Bug rides again. Display cases showcasing collectors lunch boxes and other 70s collectibles are sprinkled throughout the room.

In addition, Polly Esther's features Chicago's only authentic illuminated "Saturday Night Fever" dance floor where you can strut your disco moves. Also, the nightclub offers a Twister game board built right into the floor along with an interactive Brady Bunch Wall featuring Mike, Carol and all of the kids. Put your head through Alice's spot and it's a Kodak moment.

The club proudly displays a plethora of Chicago 1970s memorabilia. Momentos from the Bozo Circus TV Show are featured as well as some stuff from "Disco Demolition." They even have one of Ray Rayner's jump suits (just kidding). Does anybody remember "TV POW!"??? Anyway, you get the picture.

The club carries the 70s shrine in its bar menu, with drink specials like the Brady Punch, The Captain, The Tenile, Jaws!, and their very own version of Tang which will surely take you to the moon. Somewhat apprehensive, I went

Barfly Polly Esther's-Pop's for Champagne

with a Heineken at the Lava Lamp Bar.

On the evening I checked out the club, the DJ was cranking "The Hustle." And believe it or not, everybody was out on that dance floor. Even I got into the fun, and for a brief moment, thought I was John Travolta. Then, I realized I wasn't. Nevertheless, Polly Esther's is all about fun...so not too many people laughed at me. I think I need to get my "Do the Hustle" record out and brush up...problem is, I don't have a turntable.

Polly Esther's Chicago is the ninth club in a chain of clubs. The others are all out east. General manager Ty Neal game me the nickel tour and explained that quite a few of his customers were too young to even remember the 70s. Even so, it seemed to me that there was an even mix of people born in the 70s as well as people who remember when John Travolta was first a star. Neal went on to say that it's the solid 70s dance music that brings people back for more.

Polly Esther's also features a lower level dedicated to the 80s. The "Culture Club" basement features games including the original Pac Man, Ms. Pac Man, Donkey Kong, and Defender. Of course, all games are retro-priced at a quarter per play. Make sure you check out the lamp shades made out of Devo's hats. On Thursday nights, the lower level really goes, with a new-wave dance party featuring no cover and drink specials.

Polly Esther's offers the space for corporate events and private parties. I'm thinking this place would be pretty cool for a holiday party. So, if you're devoted to the sounds of the smooth 70s or an 80s rocker, Polly Esther's is a must see.

— Greg Dellinger

Pops for Champagne/The Star Bar
2934 N. Sheffield
773-472-1000
Hours: 8 p.m. to midnight Sunday and Monday,
8:30 p.m. to 12:30 a.m. Tuesday to Thursday,
9 p.m. to 1 a.m. Friday and Saturday

Do you scrub up well? The next time you want to leave your grubby weekend uniform of T-shirts and jeans behind, dress up and head for Pops for Champagne. An elegant twinkle of a place, it literally shines in the night with warm inviting live jazz, an outdoor garden, and a cozy fireplace. They have 140 types of Champagne to choose from by the bottle and 12 selections by the glass. Bring a major credit card when you treat yourself and a special someone to an evening at Pops. By the bottle, Champagnes range in price from $16 to $400. By the glass $4 to $11 dollars. No full course meals are served, but appetizers and desserts are offered.

This is the perfect place to "make a memory." Want to "pop" the question? This is the place. Want to show mom and dad how well you're doing? This is the place. Want to have a real creative solution to the age-old question "What can we do that's new and different? This definitely is the place. Want to have a quiet conversation where you can actually hear what your companion is saying? You get the idea.

Pop's is also a place for events. They hold champagne tastings at least six times a year. Next on the schedule will be a Cognac tasting. I ask you, where else in Chicagoland can you go for a Cognac tasting? In July they sponsor a La Bastille Day Fest with live music, food and, of course, champagne.

Located in the same building as Pops is the Star Bar. It offers the same selection of Champagnes, appetizers and desserts. What, you say, makes this place any different than Pops? No live jazz, less formal and a slightly younger crowd. Three television monitors surround the bar for game watching or other musical performances. The Star Bar also sports a fireplace and outdoor garden. The drink coasters have a quote from Dom Perignon that seems to fit the whole atmosphere of sipping Champagne in an elegant, comfortable atmosphere; Dom Perignon said, "I'm drinking stars." And so will you when you visit this little place.

Pop's On Chicago
2053 W. Chicago Ave.
773-633-0828
Hours: 3 p.m. to 2 a.m. weekdays,
11 a.m. to 3 a.m. Saturday, 11 a.m. to 2 a.m. Sunday

In visiting all the new establishments in the Chicago area, I have to admit that it's a little hard to find a place with personality. But after stepping into a little place called Pop's on Chicago, I guess I need to take that back.

Manager Tom Burton informs me that the place used to be called the E & J Club and has been a bar since 1953. In fact, Burton went on to say that both his family and the bar are steeped in tavern history.

"The place is named after my father," Burton said. "He was known all around the South and West Side. Anyone in the paint and construction business just knew him as pops."

Pop's On Chicago's owner is actually Burton's sister, Bonnie Biddulph. Bonnie also owns The Whistle Stop, 4200 W. Irving Park Road. Emphasizing his family's tavern roots, Burton said, even his grandmother once owned a tavern in Chicago. But let's get back to a little Pop's on Chicago history.

"This place is full of stories," Burton said. "I remember one guy who used to come in when the place was E & J. He'd sit himself at the bar dressed only in his boxer shorts. The bartender would tell him to get out and get dressed. So old man Harry would go and about 20 minutes later, Harry would be back, dressed. Dressed in nothing but the boxers and a tie."

The transition from E & J to Pop's wasn't much of a hassle, according to Burton.

Barfly Pop's On Chicago

These folks at Pop's On Chicago, 2053 W. Chicago Ave., know how to keep a down-home friendly place in the middle of the big city.

"We just put in some new windows and covered the place with new paint."

Speaking of paint, the decor in this place is something to see. In the front room, great flaming notes line the wall near the ceiling, as they trail off into a painted rendition of Jerry Lee Lewis' famous flame infested piano. Burton said that an 18-year-old artist named Robert Myers from Uptown is responsible.

In the bar's back room, an intimate setting has been created for live music. A double run ceiling, which looks like an intricate grid system replaces normal acoustic tiles, and Burton said it provides for a great sound.

Pop's On Chicago prides itself on music selection.

"You gotta give the people what they want," Burton said. "There's something here for everyone."

Hard rock, country to jazz, Pop's offers acoustic nights on Thursdays and live bands every Friday and Saturday nights. Along with the variety of live music, Pop's boasts a 90-disk jukebox with everything from the Stone Temple Pilots to country classics and classic rock mainstays.

Other folks on the Pop's staff include Ramona, Roberta and ace bartender Maggie who threatened to sue me if I told how long she'd been in the business, but I can suffice it to say that she knows the job well.

"My father owned a couple of bars up and down Clark Street for years, and got me behind the bar at an early age," Maggie said.

I learned that her best drink is a Margarita and that Maggie also has a flair for song. A singer of both jazz and contemporary music, she's pushing Burton

The North Side Pop's On Chicago-The Pour House

to buy a piano for her right in the bar. No pressure, Tom!

As far as a philosophy goes for Pop's On Chicago, the staff and patrons agree that it's a classic neighborhood tavern. A little something is provided for everyone, all at decent prices.

Pop's is also giving out a call to all artists. Any and all bands are encouraged to drop off demo tapes, but that's not all. They are also looking for artists to claim a space on their walls. Anyone interested would be given their own space to display completed projects or even to create a new piece right there on the wall. Give Pop's a call for the details.

So, if you are looking for a new place with a little "old school" history, Pop's is the place to be.

— *Brian Diebold*

The Pour House

2559 N. Southport Ave.
773-248-0002
Hours: 4:30 p.m. to 2 a.m. weekdays,
5 p.m. to 3 a.m. Saturday, 11 a.m. to 2 p.m. Sunday

Peanuts and popcorn everywhere but not a bottled beer to drink. Whatever meaning of the Pour House you choose to accept, you won't be far off. Whether it's the old, tattered Bungee cord keeping the front door open, or the fact that the only beers they have flow from a keg, the place definitely lives up to its name. No you won't find any 12-ounce brown or green glass containers, just five beers on tap and a moderate assortment of hard liquors.

"It's the Pour House," bartender Greg Cavitt said, in response to my surprised look when I learned there were only five different kinds of beer. Beers range from Bud Light to Berghoff, and the pitcher prices range from $7 to $10.

Along the bar are bottomless baskets of peanuts and popcorn. And the Popcorn tastes better than what most Chicagoland movie theaters serve.

A word to the wise though, when you do frequent this bar, I highly recommend you don't put your used peanut shells in the ash trays. Rumor has it that the owner, Al Dyal, will question whether you were "born in a barn," or just don't have any common sense. Used peanut shells should be thrown on the floor. "It's the Pour House."

Unfortunately I was there on a night when Dyal took the day off. Thankfully the bartender and clientele were able to clue me in.

"People come in from all over the area to see Dyal and are disappointed if he's not here," Greg Cavitt said. "He's got a ton of jokes and can keep you going all night."

But be sure and let Dyal do all the talking or he might tell you, "If you want to tell jokes, get your own fucking saloon."

Dyal has run the bar at the same address for 15 years and has created something rare in Chicago Tavern history. He's a no-nonsense owner that will tell you how he feels. Sometimes he'll sarcastically snap at you if your bar eti-

250

Barfly The Pour House

quette isn't up to par. Then two weeks later, he'll remember your name when you return to the bar, a Pour House patron said.

Along with the alluring owner, the bar itself has all the fundamentals: a juke-box, cigarette machine, basketball game and a smaller than regulation-size pool table Billy Barty would find diminutive.

It also has the atmosphere that makes you want to keep coming back. It doesn't try to live up to anything it's not. It has an assortment of hard liquor and five beers on tap, and that's it. "It's the Pour House."

The bartenders are friendly as they pour your pitchers for you, light your cigarettes and tell you "it ain't time to leave if you still got money."

Women have the benefit of two bathrooms opposed to just one for the males, and they even come equipped with hand lotion.

The crowd is made up of locals, freeloading peanut and popcorn junkies, and bar cruisers who choose to start and end there.

With a big screen television and five other televisions scattered throughout the bar, it's nearly impossible to miss a big sporting event. Although there's no satellite dish, the screens are always showing something relating to sports.

While inside watching a game, you can't help but notice the similarity of the interior of the bar with that of a winter weekend get-away cabin in Wisconsin. And what weekend cabin wouldn't be complete without various memorabilia lining the shelves and walls?

"People just bring things in and leave them here and they end up being our decorations," Cavitt said.

The Pour House is definitely worth checking out for both its decor and free food, but most importantly, you've got to meet Al.

— *Kevin Toomajian*

The Pumping Company
6157 N. Broadway St.
773-743-7994
Hours: 2 p.m. to 2 a.m. Sunday to Friday,
3 p.m. to 3 a.m. Saturday

The Pumping Company located in Edgewater, around the corner from the Granville 'el' stop, has its own unique feel. Exposed brick, wood railings, and old firemen paraphernalia lend to the feeling of being transported to a different era. One can almost conjure up the image of firemen from a bygone time meeting at the bar to swill beer and swap stories after a brutal 24-hour shift of sleeping and playing cards.

The layout of the bar is that of a cozy neighborhood tavern. After walking up a few steps to enter, one is presented with several options; grab a stool and belly up for a hard night, settle at a table in the corner to catch up with friends, flee downstairs to avoid the crowd, or outside to the beer garden. The beer garden offers, what I enjoy most about beer gardens, the sense of entering a secret hideaway where faithful beer drinkers commune to enjoy the great outdoors.

The North Side The Pumping Company-Quencher's

Plenty of lush green provided by vines and hidden nooks makes it a great place to enjoy your favorite libation.

The Pumping Company has great drink specials. They change every few months, so check up on them. On the entertainment side there are the standards, electronic dartboards and television sets. The bonus is a live DJ three days a week, Friday theme parties and monthly pool tournaments.

The Pumping Company is an enjoyable place to land. Whether enjoying a beer with a colorful local or a Loyola coed, the Pumping Company always allows one to feel right at home.

— Bob Schertler

Quencher's Saloon
2401 N. Western Ave.
773-276-9730
Hours: 11 a.m. to 2 a.m. Sunday to Friday,
11 a.m. to 3 a.m. Saturday

I was having a dream. A good one. I was on a pub crawl, but not your typical neighborhood jaunt. In this dream, it was an international pub crawl — England for a Double Diamond, Scotland for a McEwans, Germany for a Holsten, Denmark for a Carlsberg...then I woke up. Good thing, too, because I made it just in time for Quencher's 18th annual European Beer Tour.

Initially, a one day event featuring eight beers, but popularity and demand have escalated it into a 10 day fest with 44 beers from 18 countries. Its purpose? (Do we really need one?) To highlight the best of Quencher's vast stock of European brews, maybe discovering a new favorite along the way.

Standard imports, like Heineken from the Netherlands and Guinness from Ireland are on the tour list. The more adventurous might try Cirstal .51 from the Czech Republic, Moretti's de la Rossa from Italy or Pripps from Sweden.

European beers are just one aspect of Quencher's appeal to the true beer connoisseur. Since 1979, proprietor Earle Johnson and his tavern have been building a solid reputation among beer lovers in Chicago. Considered by many to be the best beer bar in the city, Quencher's boasts a selection of imports from Australia to Venezuela, and domestics from regional favorites to craft and microbreweries.

More than 200 bottled brands are in stock and 15 taps make some of the best stuff available on draft. If you have not yet tried some of Chicago's own, sample a Baderbrau Pilsner, Heartland Weiss or Golden Prairie Maple Stout. I think you'll be impressed. Being locally brewed, these brands are not only of exceptional quality, but taste very fresh, which is a statement even some of the best imports cannot make.

The bar is also stocked with a wide assortment of fine liquors — bourbon and Scotch whiskies, Cognacs and premium tequilas. (If I ever make my way through the entire beer list, I'll have yet another selection to contend with.)

Barfly Quencher's

Quencher's, 2401 N. Western Ave., has one of the best
beer selections in the city as well as a good selections of
cigars.

The building itself has been associated with the liquor trade since 1946, when
it opened as Jug-Full Liquors, operating until 1979 when it reopened as
Quencher's. Earle signed on as bar manager and part owner, taking full ownership in the early 1980s. He brought with him an extensive knowledge of the bar
industry and a taste for good beer, having worked on the management staff at
the Downtown Berghoff's.

The main bar room is a spacious delight with high ceilings and an open comfortable feel. A long wood bar wraps around the far corner, with plenty of
stools on hand. Several tables situated around the room give the casual drinker
a choice of perspectives in the bar. In 1989, Earle expanded the bar, opening a
back room that added almost 150 percent of floor space overall. He set this
room up with more tables, a piano, some pinball machines and a basketball
free-throw game. Two large screen TVs and a CD jukebox with everything
from Sinatra to the Neville Brothers are also on hand.

After marvelling at the blackboards listing all the beers in the house, don't
miss Earle's collection of breweriana displayed around the bar. These include
drink trays, neon signs and other beer memorabilia dating as far back as the
earlier part of this century.

Basically, Quencher's is a special place and Earle is a special guy. Try some
of his famous chili or if you're there in April join in Quencher's annual "Walk
to Wrigley" where for a nominal fee, patrons meet at the bar at 9 a.m. and walk
to Cubs' park stopping in at 11 taverns along the way. It's a three-mile walk
and a heck of a lot of fun. Tickets to the game and T-shirts are included in the
fee.

Rainbo Roller Rink

4836 N. Clark St.

773-271-6200

Adult skate hours: 8:30 p.m. to 12:30 a.m. Wednesday, must be age 25 or older; 9 p.m. to 2 a.m. Thursday for ages 18 and older, midnight to 4 a.m. Friday for ages 18 and older, 11:30 to 3:30 a.m. Saturday for age 18 and older, 8 p.m. to 1:30 a.m. for ages 25 and older

There is not much of a difference at Rainbo since I was last there. Unfortunately, the last time I was there I was in the eighth grade. It was a field trip for school, and I think the last song they played was "Purple Rain" by the artist formerly known as Prince.

Not much, but yes there is a difference. A shining difference. A stellar difference. A difference not to be forgotten. Yes my friends Rainbo has opened a bar! Or was it always there and nobody ever noticed? Anyway, yes there is the bar. Located over the roller rink where you can sit and watch people fall on their butts. You can now sit and *get drunk* and watch people fall on their butts. It is much funnier when you are drunk.

Don't expect many surprises at the bar. The prices are a tad high, but I guess we have all come to expect that by now. Other than that, all I can really say is that the normal fare is on tap as well as in bottles. But hey, where else can you go with a bunch of friends and skate around to disco while being drunk? Besides the park, you got me.

The backdrop over the roller rink is very cool. A night-time view of the city's skyline gives you the feel of swishing around outside. Of course, the only thing I was feeling all night was the wood hitting my behind. I can barely skate sober let alone drunk.

Another cool feature to Rainbo is its private party room. Well, it is not so private. It is located right off of the arcade and anyone can look inside but let's not argue shall we? If you are planning a special party and want something a little different, I'd give Rainbo a try.

Let's be serious, it's a nice concept in an otherwise mundane world. But I'd call well in advance to set up all the arrangements. The number to call for party info is 773-271-5668. As for the other info you need to know, two sessions are held daily. Afternoons usually from 4 to 6 p.m. for families where kids skate for $1.50, adults for $2.50. Evening sessions run generally from 8:30 to 12:30 a.m. You must be 18 or older or 25 or older, depending on the night, to get in and skating is $4.75 for everyone. There are theme nights at Rainbo as well. I've heard of special gay league nights, and special skate nights for divorcees, but don't quote me on that. Oh yeah, skate rental is $2 for everyone.

-- Brian Diebold

Ranalli's Off Rush
24 W. Elm St.
312-440-7000
Hours: 11 a.m. to 2 a.m. daily

Visitors to Chicago, and those newly arrived, would be well-advised to make their way to Ranalli's Off Rush. A regular, irregular schedule of bus trips to the Bears, Bulls and Blackhawk games helps bring patrons into their own social circle.

When I moved to Chicago five years ago, I was pleasantly amazed at all the activities planned for the customers. People in Dallas and the South, in general, may claim to be the nation's most friendly, but Jerry Ranalli cannot be beat for making people feel welcome.

Unfortunately, I don't get down to the Gold Coast as much as I would like, but it really is nice to see Steve and Joe and other loyal employees when I walk into the Victorian mansion that exudes the warmth of greeting that is Ranalli's.

The Ranalli's at Elm Street and Dearborn is one of seven. This red rock mansion is tied to Ranalli's 4 a.m. bar, Late Night, a few doors down on Dearborn.

When you sit at the bar, you have to wonder what's up with all the silver-finished mugs hanging from the ceiling. These belong to members of Ranalli's Beer Club. Membership is simple, and the reward great for the adventurous beer drinker. The requirement is to sign up for $25, and drink 100 different imported beers. At the conclusion of the liquid journey, you receive a case of imported beer, a $25 gift certificate, a Ranalli's T-shirt and $1 off the price of any imported beer on Sundays.

If this does not appeal to you, then the various trips are a must on the humor scale. My first trip was to a White Sox game in a school bus. I never heard such a rendition of "Yellow Submarine" in my life. Another trip took me to the Empress Casino in Joliet. We rode in pure comfort on a plush tour bus. Each of the trips, whether they be to the Cubs, Bears or Blackhawks games, or to a casino, starts with a private party at Late Night. It continues with beer on the bus, and concludes with everyone having a last shout at Late Night on their return. I was most proud of the group when they didn't scorn me for winning a Blackhawks jersey signed by Chris Chelios. I was completely unaware of the drawing until the announcement.

When you enter Ranalli's, you see a room of pool tables on the right and a large "L"-shaped bar to the left. If you happen in after work, a buffet stands between the rooms. It has a large selection of hot and cold pizza slices, cracker nibbles, fruits and veggies. Upstairs is a large dining room, where intimate tables for two, and larger tables await diners reading the extensive menu of American, Italian and ethnic food.

If you are in the mood for a long evening, and don't want to be bothered by the 2 a.m. close, you can venture a few steps down Dearborn to Late Night. There, you can resume playing pool, or just enjoy the lively conversations that take place at the long bar. You can even make yourself comfortable on a soft, comfy sofa.

Ranalli's is an especially fun place to go, whether alone or with a group that likes a wide selection of drinks and food. I'm glad I had the opportunity to get well acquainted with Ranalli's. I strongly recommend this Chicago mainstay.

— J. Quillian

Red Dog

1589 N. Damen Ave.
773-278-5138
Hours: 7 p.m. to 4 a.m. Sunday to Friday,
7 p.m. to 5 a.m. Saturday

One of the hippest night spots in Chicago is guarded by a ten-foot high red dog. His home? The corner of Milwaukee and Damen avenues, in front of a bar called, not surprisingly, Red Dog. This soul- and house-music dance bar in the heart of Wicker Park remains one of the few clubs in Chicago where funk reigns supreme.

Of course, in order to find funk nirvana, you've got to find Red Dog first, and that's no easy task, even considering the aforementioned huge animal painted on the side of the building. The place is located on top of Cafe Absinthe. Neither establishment has a visible-from-the-street sign, and only if you're approaching from the north can you see the big canine. It doesn't help that the entrance to the place is on the side of the building, too. Look too quickly, and the bouncers milling around by the door look like your typical shady dudes waiting for some action.

The real action, however, starts one floor up. Fork over the $5 cover charge and the bouncers will show you to the creaky stairs that lead up to the main dance space. Red Dog has been converted from an industrial building, so there is lots of large space abound. The sunken barroom has lots of private booths, all pushed against the walls in case the dancing gets out of hand (not an unusual occurrence) patrons spill over from the dance floor.

Mellow times can be had at Red Dog, providing you arrive before 10 p.m. The wraparound bar features five beers at an average (slightly steep) price of $3.50, and seats are easily obtainable. An upstairs lounge, which is occasionally closed off, overlooks the dance floor and has pool tables. The place starts to kick around 10:30-11, when the trippy, multicolored light projections start flashing on the main room's brick walls and the music picks up speed and volume.

Customers respond in kind by packing the main room. Dancing at Red Dog is not for the fainthearted; sweaty bodies abound and often bump into each other. The crowd (one of the most diverse groups ever to be found in a Chicago bar — a mix of African-Americans, Hispanics and Caucasians) doesn't seem to notice or care.

Even the fastidiously hygienic bar-goer should give this club a try, though. In

Barfly Red Dog-Red Lion Pub

spite of the less than spic-and-span dancing conditions, the bathrooms at the place are without a doubt some of the cleanest in any bar. Apparently, the big Red Dog is house trained.

— Lisa Hofbauer

Red Lion Pub
2446 N. Lincoln Ave.
773-348-2695
Hours: noon to 2 a.m. daily

Since the 1934 gunning-down of John Dillinger in front of the Biograph Theater, the supposed antics of his ghost (or what most people say is his ghost) have become one of the most popular draws of those apostles of the macabre to this strip of Lincoln Avenue. But if the management and the patrons of one nearby drinking establishment are true to their word, Dillinger's ghost isn't the only denizen of the undead realm who has taken up residence in this neighborhood.

For right across the street from the theater, nestled among a multitude of shop fronts and liquor stores in this hip stretch of Lincoln Avenue which houses the likes of the Three Penny Theatre and Lounge Ax, sits the Red Lion Pub, one of Chicago's most authentic English pubs. At the Red Lion one can enjoy the most true-to-life empirical experience possible in a Midwestern American city, including an indulgence in one or more of a multitude of imported English beers and ales. It is also here that one doesn't have to sample even a small amount of any of these brews to bear witness to the cold chills, telekinetic activity and eerie whisperings that would normally occur only after incurring an extremely high blood alcohol level.

The Red Lion was designed by its founder and original owner, English native John Cordwell, who brought over from England a definite sense of the charm and ambiance of the pubs in which he grew up. A brightly lit facade which opens up onto the sidewalk cheerfully illuminates red-brick floors and wainscoted walls, the upper portions of which are adorned with a cornucopia of Anglo-American memorabilia; from maps of the London metro and the 17th Century Thames River skyline to caricature mugs of English literary heroes such as Robin Hood, Sherlock Holmes and Shakespeare.

Another import from the British Isles found at the Red Lion is the knowledge and appreciation of hearty English pub food. Red Lion's kitchen is open until 11 p.m. during the week, midnight on weekends and 10 p.m. on Sundays and offers a full menu consisting of both typical American fare and such traditional English selections as fish'n'chips and steak and kidney pie, all of which are served in abundant portions for five to seven (pounds?) dollars.

There is one more thing that accompanied Red Lion's founder over the Atlantic from his native England. Something that, above the sense of decor and the beers and the food, lends itself to the true ambiance of the Red Lion. That something is the ghost of Mister Cordwell's dearly-departed father. Keeping true to a promise that he made before he passed away to "be with his son always," the benevolent spirit has manifested itself on various occasions, most notably making his presence known when a person plays the upright piano on the second floor.

In addition to the piano, this second level currently holds another amply stocked bar which serves as the centerpiece for a spacious area of low-slung tables and a cozy wooden-beamed outdoor patio.

Before it was turned into the pub's adjunct, however, this space, like most of the similar spaces above the street level along this strip of Lincoln, was comprised of apartments. It was in one of these apartments, on June 4th in the early 1950s that a young girl, known now only as Jane, died of the measles on the anniversary of her twentieth birthday. Witnesses, including a recently-visiting cousin of the deceased, have attested to the exact spot against the wall where Jane's deathbed was set. The bed is now gone, but on that spot sits the southernmost bar stool of the second floor, a barstool on which numerous people have felt sudden cold chills and ensuing dizziness that many attribute to Jane's ghost's lingering presence.

This presence is also accredited to other mysterious activities on the second floor including a cricket bat that mysteriously hurled itself across the room and barstools reportedly being dragged about by an unseen force.

Further adding to the mystery of the second floor is a tale of another former tenant, a Mister Dan Danforth, or "Dirty" Dan as current owner Colin Cordwell likes to call him, "a man with not one redeeming defect." Malicious and unctuous in life, the obstinate and eventually evicted Danforth has apparently returned and is just as malicious in death.

It was just last year, after customers and employees alike began to tell of strange and rude whisperings in a voice that sounded like Danforth's, that John Cordwell was on his way upstairs when he was violently shoved by some mysterious invisible force and fell backwards onto the brick floor.

Although the fall did send Mr. Cordwell to the hospital, the management is confident that this was an isolated incident, and that potential patrons should not be scared away by any supposed presence of spectral activity. "In fact," maintains Colin, "many people come into the Red Lion for the sole purpose of getting to see something of this nature."

Whatever the reason for going: the English ambiance; the wide selection of English brews ($3 to $4.25 a pint); the hearty food; or the inhabitants of the spiritual world, the Red Lion is a convivial stop in which to party or relax or both. There is never any cover to get in and the doors open for lunch (liquid or otherwise) every day at 11:30 a.m. except on Sundays when they open at 10 a.m. and Mondays at 2 p.m.

(Author's note: after talking to the Red Lion staff regarding these eerie occurrences, I ventured up the to the second floor to sit in the afore mentioned bar stool that lay on the site of Jane's death. Bracing myself stoically against any ensuing chills or feelings, I was suddenly startled at the sight of a small swarm of fruit flies buzzing my naked forearm. I leapt up with a shout with my

Barfly Red Lion Pub-Redfish Restaurant/Voodoo Lounge

stomach retching and gruesome images from the movie "Amityville Horror" flashing through my mind. It was only from this standing position that I could see a small pool of sweet, sugary grenadine that was spilled on the bar underneath the spot where I had rested my arm. I had interrupted the fly's lunch, and they had caused me to almost lose mine.)

— *Johnny Masiulewicz*

Redfish Restaurant
Voodoo Lounge
400 N. State St.
312-467-1600
Hours: 11:30 a.m. to 1:30 a.m. weekdays,
5 p.m. to 1:30 a.m. Saturday, 5 p.m. to 11 p.m. Sunday

New Orleans is a mess. People sweep the clutter from the streets. The city's head is once more calm. Normal. It sleeps after the night of howling, speaking in tongues, dancing to drums; watching strange lights streak across the sky...But if the Jes Grew which shot up a trail balloon in the 1890s was then endemic, it is now epidemic, crossing state lines and heading for Chicago.

—Ishmael Reed, Mumbo Jumbo

But for those who cannot make it down to the land of Hoodoo Voodoo for Mardi Gras, not to fret. Chicago has its own answer to those nasty winter blues. On Aug. 24, 1995, the corner of State and Kinzie saw the opening of the Redfish Restaurant and Voodoo Lounge. Located near the newly established "House of Blues" and "Rock Bottom Brewery," general manager Doug Clements seems extremely confident in what Redfish has to offer.

"The neighborhood is fantastic," Clements said. "One of the hottest new areas," he said adding that owners Roger Greenfield and Ted Kasemir went down to New Orleans with a designer to capture the unique New Orleans atmosphere right here in Chicago. Upon their return, Greenfield and Kasemir found they had loaded up a semi-truck full of authentic New Orleans paraphernalia, Clements said. Art pieces, photographs and genuine portions from Mardi Gras floats make Redfish's decor feel as though you'd stepped through the door of a Bourbon Street Voodoo parlour.

"A real life down and dirty Bourbon Street feel," according to Clements.

Along with all the artifacts, the owners also brought along chef Keith Mahoney. Mahoney's job is to showcase New Orleans' fine cuisine while Clements takes care of the Voodoo Lounge. Mahoney seemed perfect for the job as he was taken from the Commander's Palace, a five star restaurant in New Orleans.

A major plus at Redfish is that the food is served until midnight. Gumbo, Blackened Redfish and BBQ Shrimp are just a few of the specialty dishes on

The North Side Redfish Restaurant/Red Head Piano Bar

tap. Clements said that at Redfish, "We cater to the Chicago palate. If you're not used to Cajun, it may be too much to handle."

But not here. Of course, if you think you can handle the Creole, they will be more than happy to suit your taste.

As for the Voodoo Lounge, located inside the Redfish Restaurant, its specialty is the specialty drink. Hurricanes, Cajun Martinis, Daiquiris and Real Bloody Marys are always par for the course. Garnished with chili peppers or crawfish, the Voodoo leaves nothing to the imagination. The Lounge also serves up 45 different beers. Blackened Voodoos along with many other microbrews are another draw to the lounge.

For the musically inclined, you can expect a fine mix of Southern rock to jazz. A wide range of classics from John Lee Hooker to the Black Crowes are usually heard.

So come on down to the New Orleans roadhouse for a whole lot of fun. This is Chicago's Mardi Gras headquarters. I garauntee.

— Brian Diebold

The Red Head Piano Bar
16 W. Ontario St.
312-640-1000
Hours: 4 p.m. to 4 a.m. weekdays,
6 p.m. to 5 a.m. Saturday, 6 p.m. to 4 a.m. Sunday

"You'll see a lot of 50-ish men with their 'nieces.'" I heard this warning time and time again whenever I mentioned that I had never been to the Red Head. Imagine my disappointment when I walked into the rather tony establishment around eight o'clock on a Tuesday and saw nothing of the sort.

A few couples. Several groups of 40 to 50 year-old men. A few thirty-something men. More than one pot belly. Some women here and there who looked as though they had come straight from work. A relaxed, mellow crowd — certainly not the scandal I had been hoping for.

I even checked with Bob, the manager.

"Aren't there supposed to be lots of men here with their 'nieces.'" I asked, smiling knowingly.

"Well, that's what they say, but this really isn't the meat market people think it is," said Bob, who went on to tell a story about how he had teased a middle-aged patron about being in with his beautiful "daughter," and ended up being embarrassed because the woman turned out to be, well, his daughter.

"You know this is like any bar," continued Bob. "Sure, sometimes guys get drunk and start talking to women, but we're very sensitive to that. If a single woman feels she is being bothered, all she has to do is tell one of the bartenders or floor people and we'll make sure she's okay. This is a very comfortable bar — we want people to be able to relax here."

And comfortable it is. Low-lighting, russet-colored walls, cushy seats and

Barfly Red Head Piano Bar

The Red Head Piano Bar, 16 W. Ontario St., is a great place to meet the fellas for a cocktail after work.

framed sheet music combine to create a relaxed, polished atmosphere. There is, as you might expect, live piano music being played almost constantly. The wait staff is friendly, attentive and clad in provocative Las Vegas-style, low-cut bustier uniforms. A small bowl of very tasty Chex-mix type snacks (which ended up being my dinner that evening) was placed on our table as soon as we walked in and constantly replenished.

Domestic beers are $3, imports are $4 and mixed drinks are $5.50. Their biggest sellers, you guessed it, martinis at $7 a pop. Cigars and cigarettes are also sold.

By about 9:30 or 10:00, the place started filling up, and Bob assured me that it gets very crowded on weekends. He recommends getting there close to opening time on Fridays and Saturdays to get a seat.

"This is a great place to go right after work if you just want to get away from it all — it's like walking into another world," said Julian Howell, a 30ish advertising professional who was sipping an imported beer. "It's also a good date bar — a perfect place to go if you want to impress someone."

And impressed I was. Even if I didn't see any nieces.

— Lisa Kueng

Regina and Joe's Tap
2988 N. Milwaukee Ave.
773-276-6777
Hours: 7 a.m. to 2 a.m. daily

My girlfriend and I drove down North Milwaukee Avenue in search of a Polish bar. It was a chilly Saturday night, but not cold enough to keep the door of Regina and Joe's Tap from swinging open. As we entered the cold, dank tavern, all eyes (all male except the petite barkeep) turned toward my girlfriend, Jennifer. Regina and Joe's is apparently a male dominated bar, sort of a Polish "sausage-fest" if you will.

One guy, seated at the bar, had a small crowd around him singing along while he kicked out some jams on his accordion. Toward the back of the bar, pool was being played, but for the most part the patrons, about 15 tops, were belly-up at the bar.

We ordered two Heinekens, only $2.25 each, and tried to sit at the bar. An old, quite-tanked Polish fellow, asked/slurred us about 20 times if we spoke Polish. As he tried to get off his barstool to get closer to us, he swayed back a few steps, lunged toward me and fell into my lap. Jennifer backed away from the bar to give this man some room when another Polish guy came on to her. His concern went beyond that of the Polish guy in my lap when he placed his hand on her behind.

After prying the drunk off my lap and helping him to a barstool, we just kind of smiled at the non-English speaking patrons and sat over by the pool tables where we could absorb the atmosphere from a safe distance. The walls (wood paneled) were covered with posters of bikini clad women lying on cars, maps of the world and Illinois and surprisingly an "In Utero" Nirvana poster. Behind the bar were the customary deer antlers strategically placed around more posters of babes in bikinis.

The jukebox was filled with Polish artists but, surprise, scattered about were classics from Madonna, the Beach Boys and ABBA. Since the jukebox was a disappointment and the accordion player wasn't playing regular sets, we decided to entertain ourselves with some billiards. It was one of those small tables, but at 50-cents-a-game who cares.

After playing a lousy game with Jennifer, I was invited to a doubles game of pool by some of the buzzed Polish guys. My skills continued to slide as I missed easy shot after easy shot, and any chance of getting in good with these guys was fading fast. I luckily knocked in the 8-ball for the win and kind of redeemed myself. It was after that game we decided to bid farewell to Regina and Joe's Tap. I shook hands with my competitors (Jennifer kept behind me) and my partner slapped me on the back and smiled. I smiled too, in relief that he slapped me on the back instead of my behind.

— *Chris Olvera*

Relax Sports Bar
2935 N. Milwaukee Ave.
No phone — Hours vary

Do you like to drink Old Style? I really don't either, but if someone's willing to give me a glass of it on tap for only 75 cents, hell, I'll drink it and enjoy it. You can find just such a deal at Relax Sports Bar. Across the street from the Orbit Restaurant and Banquet Hall, it's a classic no-frills, neighborhood tavern with a Polish flavor.

Not much on decor, the Relax Sports Bar kind of resembles a V.F.W. hall that underwent a little remodeling back in the 1970s. With a tile floor and a bar that could double for a lengthy stretch of kitchen counter, it's certainly not for the aesthetically-minded. But then any tavern that exclusively features Old Style as its only beer on tap probably isn't trying to win any interior-design points in the first place. Its main priority is to provide a cheerful getaway for the neighborhood regulars, who are always clustered about the two pool tables. It doesn't seem to matter if there's only five people in the bar or 15; any time I've been here both tables were being played. Three video poker machines are installed as well, with two TVs and jukebox containing a heavy selection of Polish "big band" music comprising the rest of the gadgets.

From what I've seen, however, the main source of entertainment here is the customers, themselves. It's a true intergenerational mix, and I get the impression that most of them have known each other their entire lives. Good-natured jibes flow back and forth between young and old.

"What kind of a shot (pool) was that? You better have your eyes checked," laughed an old man with a Polish accent.

The person he ribbed, a large twenty-something youth in a Blackhawks jersey, had just scratched a shot, joked back in a heavy Chicago accent, "Oh, yeah? Well I'll be the one laughing when your old lady comes down here and drags your ass home."

So it goes, the customers giving the impression that they're one big, happy family. Which leads me to mention that outsiders probably won't be privy to the same treatment. Not that you'll be treated rudely or impolitely, but I do get the feeling that it's a rather close-knit society in here and that's how the customers would like to keep it. The fact that you have to be buzzed-in from the sidewalk tends to bear me out.

This is fine with me, though. An acquaintance and I stumbled upon the Old Style deal almost by accident, and since then I'll drop in only when I'm in the neighborhood and hankering for some cheap brew. Then I simply hop on a barstool, exchange an occasional pleasantry with the person next to me, quaff my drinks, and leave. The atmosphere of the bar remains unchanged and my presence goes largely unnoticed, unlike a variety of similar places where it seems as if every eye is focused on you. I mean, even though little taverns with strong, neighborhood character are usually the cheapest places to drink, it's sometimes hard for outsiders to feel welcome or even comfortable in some of them. Yet, at Relax Sports Bar you're simply treated with polite, friendly indifference. Which is plenty fine with me as long as those 75-cent Old Styles keep coming.

Next time you're caught up in the notorious traffic clogging Milwaukee Avenue on weekend afternoons, stop in for an hour or so. I guarantee you'll resume your start-and-stop journey up north in a much better mood. Your wallet will be pleased as well.

—Bill Franz

Resi's Bierstube
2034 W. Irving Park Road
773-472-1749
Hours: 3 p.m. to 2 a.m. weekdays, 3 p.m. to 3 a.m.
Saturday, and 3 p.m. to 2 a.m. Sunday

Resi's is something one would expect if bar hopping in Germany. The features of the indoor bar include a very unique post card collection hanging over the bar, an international coaster collection, a clock that is built backwards, and German beer drinking songs played in the background.

It's a wonderful place. Patrons and matrons are warm and friendly and Resi's kitchen cooks up some of the finest German treats in Chicago.

During the summer, Resi's opens its outdoor beer garden. With trees and hanging lights watching over 10 picnic-style benches, this is one of the best settings to drink down a stein of thick German beer. A full picket fence provides an area separated from the neighborhood and adds an intimate effect.

The bar has more than 130 imported beers and 12 German beers on tap. Some of the tap selections offered are Pshorr, BBK, DAB and Warsteiner. The choice of servings are half and liter mugs. Weiss beers are served in towering glasses with a slice of lemon.

During the winter of 1995, TVs Conan O'Brien stopped by and put Resi's and several other area bars and national television. If you ever catch a rerun, you'll see Conan and Andy drinking and singing German beer songs with a pile of Resi's colorful regulars.

The Stober family has been running Resi's for decades. Rich Stober is usually tending bar. He's a super nice guy and can inform interested patrons on a variety of neighborhood and German history.

Overall, Resi's is a real treasure. It was one of the best taverns in Chicago.

Reza's Restaurant and Brewery
432 W. Ontario St.
312-664-4500
Hours: 10 a.m. to midnight daily

Barfly Reza's Restaurant

In 1992, Reza's opened a second restaurant in what was formerly Berghoff's Restaurant and Brewery. Back then, I just happened to be in the area and watched workers install Reza's name on the massive Berghoff's neon sign that hangs down in front of this beautiful old warehouse-type building. The workers deleted Berghoff's but skipped the part that still reads "Brewery." And upon entering this large restaurant, the first image that comes in view is of two large brewing kettles. But bartender Lupe Aguirre told me that the kettles are used as show pieces and Reza's does not brew beer.

However, Lupe said Reza's has a large selection of beers on draft and bottles and I was to discover that a pint of Goose Island Honker's Ale, brewed just down the street, is a fine compliment to Reza's delicious Persian food.

Both of Reza's restaurants are extremely popular. The other restaurant is at 5255 N. Clark St. and is compact and borders on swank. The Ontario Street restaurant is a huge lofty place with an almost cafeteria-type feel.

I prefer the Ontario Street restaurant. It is casual and caters a bit more to drinkers. The bar area is set up in front of the brew kettles. Unlike the Clark Street location, there is a nice long bar, comfortable stools and several cocktail tables. The Clark Street restaurant has a tiny bar area.

On my recent visit, I sampled several micros such as Sierra Nevada Pale Ale at $3.50 a pint. For wine drinkers, Reza's has an extensive wine list in addition to large decorative wine racks outlining huge windows facing Ontario Street. Lupe said some of the wines customers prefer most include merlot Colos du Boi and cabernet Cotes du Rohn. He said Reza's also carries Sangria — Spanish wine. Lupe said Spanish folks get thrown off when they come to Reza's for Persian food and see Sangria on the wine list. Reza's also serves mixed and tropical drinks. Lupe claims to make the best Mai Tai around. And for coffee lovers, Reza's stocks a large selection of international coffees.

But no matter what Reza's serves to drink, the refreshments are merely a side show to the restaurant's fine assortment of Persian, vegetarian and Mediterranean cuisine. With a choice of 27 different appetizers, it is hard to make it through to the entrees, let alone pick a few of these dishes.

I started with the appetizer sampler plate made up of hummus, tabbouli, baba ghannouj, dolmeh, and felafel. Each was excellent, especially the hummus which was extra creamy and the felafel covered in a dark sour sauce.

For the main course, I went with the chicken kabob on the bone. Although the name doesn't sound all that appetizing, this dish included mouth-watering char-broiled pieces of chicken marinated in a sweet lemon sauce. It was so good — almost like eating candy. Complimenting the chicken was a nice big pile of Persian dill rice.

After a few beers and all that food, I just couldn't do dessert. But Reza's is one of those places that brings out a dessert tray. With my sweet tooth, it was sheer pain turning down thick raspberry cheese cake, tiramisu, baklava or bameih which is a tender deep-fried pastry, sweetened with syrup.

The price of this feast was reasonable for fine dining. For two people, my visit cost around $30.

The North Side Reza's-River West Brewing Company

Lastly, I must mention the great service I received at Reza's. I've found that so many of Chicago's finer restaurants greet and treat patrons with a sneer; but not at Reza's on Ontario. Folks there are kind and considerate — an extreme pleasure.

— Tony Gordon

River West Brewing Company
925 W. Chicago Ave.
312-226-3200
Hours: 11 a.m. to 1 a.m. Monday to Thursday, 11 a.m. to 2 a.m. Friday and Saturday, noon to midnight Sunday

Open in winter 1996, it completes a triumvirate of brewpubs owned and operated by Udo and Marguerite Harttung. Their two Weinkeller brewpubs have earned acclaim in Berwyn and Westmont.

An impressive facility, River West is housed on the first two floors of a 100-year-old former wood-working shop in the neighborhood of the same name. The 16-foot ceilings, abundant windows and original timber throughout make it a distinctive, and distinct location. The ground floor hosts a 220-seat restaurant, brewing equipment and bar. Upstairs is a spacious, loft area with five regulation pool tables, another bar and a cigar lounge. General manager Harvey Turner also noted that expansion plans are already in the works to open the third floor, with similar lounge amenities and private banquet areas.

"We've created a very comfortable, clubby space here," Turner said. "The decor is elegant, but not overdone."

Turner's description is accurate, as River West is decked out in warm wood and brick top to bottom. Save a few vintage beer posters and some brass, the accents are kept to a minimum. Seating is comfortable, encouraging people to stay a while as they sip a beer and smoke a premium cigar (sold at either the upstairs or downstairs bar). That second-floor cigar lounge, with its wingback chairs and cocktail tables, looks like it's right out of some British executives club. So any smoker should feel like they're in the old boy or old girl network. Another nice touch is that televisions are strategically and economically placed. If people want to catch the game, the single upstairs big-screen is ideal. Around the downstairs bar, there are a couple more sets as well, but the bar is not a wall-to-wall video monitor nightmare.

While an extremely beautiful place, River West serves up some terrible food. Quite airline-like. Definitely skip eating here. The beers however, are excellent.

The particular beer drinker should have a good time working his or her way along the taps at River West. There are usually about six taps and a seasonal selection or two to sample. The Red Fox Amber Ale is a great start. It is a smooth, tremendously flavorful drink, not so cold or crisp that your tongue

Barfly River West Brewing Co.-Rock Bottom Brewery

curls up, but rather, very drinkable. There's also a delicious weiss beer, which, according to brewmaster Andrew Cummings, is one of the few traditionally made weiss beers in the area.

Harttung lured Cummings from Davis, Calif., where he was working as an apprentice brewmaster for a renowned West Coast brewpub. Having been an official brewmaster for almost two years, Cummings is performing quite capably for Harttung's operation here in the Midwest.

"The key to River West's process," Cummings explained, "is that we use the German three-vessel brew house style. As opposed to infusion mash, this method gives more beer, and more flavor, per amount of grain."

Cummings also noted that River West also obtains select ingredients, even strains of yeast, from the oldest beer institute in the world, the Weihenstephan Institute in Freising, Germany. As he blends malt, hops and water, Cummings looks after the huge, stainless steel tanks and jumble of tubes like a brain surgeon, carefully monitoring pressure, temperature and time to get the best possible beer. Some of his other offerings include Windy City Pilsner, Bullfrog Bitter, and a Doppelbock.

"Response has been excellent," Cummings said.

Good news to fans of good beer.

Rock Bottom
Restaurant and Brewery
1 W. Grand Ave.
312-755-9339
Hours: 11:30 a.m. to midnight Sunday to Thursday, 11:30 a.m. to 2 a.m. Friday and Saturday

Rock Bottom Restaurant and Brewery opened in October, 1995, at the corner of State Street and Grand Avenue.

Being one of Chicago's precious few brewpubs, Rock Bottom offers local beer lovers a cozy place to warm up and experience the art of brewing beer first hand.

Like a fine winery, Rock Bottom Brewery has a wide but simple range of finely brewed ales. From a clean and crisp Grand Slam Gold Ale as the Pinot Grigio to the perfect complement to red meat Terminal Stout as the Merlot; all six of Rock Bottom's ales can be compared to finely crafted wines.

The process of brewing beer takes place in two rooms situated inbetween the restaurant and bar. Patrons can peak through the glass walls at the large serving tanks that contain thousands of gallons of mouth watering ale. If the friendly staff isn't too busy they are always willing to give tours to the avid beer-lover's appetite with a wide range of choices. Old standbys such as buffalo wings and

The North Side Rock Bottom-Rosa's Blues Lounge

burgers are complemented by unusuals such as grilled portobello and buffalo fajitas made with real buffalo meat.

Another attraction to Rock Bottom Brewery is the decor itself. Along with the large scenic pictures lining the walls, big wooden booths and comfortable bar stools add to the coziness. Plenty of professional pool tables and televisions makes Rock Bottom's bar into a friend's den on a Saturday afternoon.

In the summer of 1996, Rock Bottom opened up its second floor for catered parties and events. It also opened a roof-top beer garden.

In all, Rock Bottom Restaurant and Brewery has all the essential ingredients to brew a fine future and beer for all of Chicago's beer lovers.

— Brendan O'Brien

Rosa's Blues Lounge
3420 W. Armitage Ave.
773-342-0452
Hours: 8 p.m. to 2 a.m. Tuesday to Friday, 8 p.m. to 3 a.m. Saturday, closed on Sunday and Monday

Do you want to hear some classic Chicago Blues in a neighborhood setting without any out-of-town tourist? The place to go is Rosa's Blues Lounge in the Logan Square neighborhood near the corner of Armitage and Kimball. While portions of this neighborhood have been going through some gentrification, it has not reached this block of the city. This block seems to be very urban and not for trend setters.

From the outside, Rosa's seems very mysterious with its small windows on its front facade. While walking into this establishment, I was greeted by Momma Rosa, a very friendly lady who also is the owner and bartender of this fine music club. This was my first visit to this bar, and by the way, I did have a good old time.

Blues music has been blaring out of this joint since 1985. Most of the walls are blue, just right to get you into the mood of the live sounds. There is a wall of who who's in the blues world of who have played here including Junior Wells, Son Seals, Sugar Blue, Melvin Taylor, and even the Rolling Stones.

On the night of my visit, the legendary Pinetop Perkins was playing some great piano licks. He has had a long career that includes performances in the Muddy Waters Band, Johnny Winter, the Nighthawks, and the Legendary Blues Band. He was very professional looking with his suit and hat. Even after all these years, Pinetop still has all the magic.

The stage is at the front and views are unobstructed throughout the bar. It is also a clean and comfortable establishment.

If you're feeling a little thirsty, there are four beers on tap. There are two beers that are quite good which include Honey Brown Lager and Michael O'Sheas. A pint of one of these fine brews is a reasonable $2.50.

Barfly Rosa's-Rose & Crown London Pub

The slogan of this bar is Chicago's friendliest blues lounge which is not false advertising, but quite true. If you like blues music, check out Rosa's without the hype of other blues bars in Chicago.

— *Pete Schmugge*

Rose & Crown London Pub
420 W. Belmont Ave.
773-248-6654
Hours: 4:30 p.m. to 1 a.m. weekdays,
noon to 2 a.m. Saturday, noon to 1 a.m. Sunday

A welcome addition to Lake View is the Rose & Crown London Pub, located at the downstairs entrance of the 30-floor high-rise at 420 W. Belmont Ave. When Rose & Crown opened in September of 1995, this English style pub became an instant favorite of those experiencing its charm.

The atmosphere is light and warm, enhanced by the floor-to-ceiling windows along the Belmont wall. This relaxed restaurant and bar offers top-quality food; an extensive selection of canned, bottled and tap beers; as well as liquor and quality wines. The staff is among the best. Quick like bunnies, they feature smiles like the Cheshire cat and an extraordinary attentiveness that is usually found in restaurants counting their stars.

The owners, Chris and Randy Funk, demonstrate a great dedication to immaculate housekeeping and customer satisfaction. From that first adventurous step into the Rose & Crown, you can choose your own social preference. You feel comfortable whether seeking a solitary drink at the bar or a meal in the restaurant. You feel comfortable, too, in joining in with the regulars who line the 12-seat "I"-shaped bar. A common sight is people reading, studying or watching a sporting event on one of the televisions. During big game days, a large screen TV is available in the dining room to sports fans cheering their teams to victory.

Hungry? The Rose & Crown has the best fish and chips I've tasted outside of Newcastle, England. Another recommendation is the ale-battered fried chicken, and chips and sandwiches. For those looking for a more dietetic, healthy meal, there's a fine selection of salads, a veggie burger or gilled items. Eating at the Rose & Crown is made more entertaining by the countless items of British memorabilia decorating the walls and shelves.

A full suit of armor stands guard at the back of the dining room, between the path to the clean restrooms and an area equipped with pool table, darts, jukebox and two video games. Randy and Chris' mother found the suit of armor in a suburban flower shop. The owner agreed to sell the suit that was later named Wally (an English term meaning idiot) by two British waitresses.

A regular face at Rose & Crown is that of the building's condo association president, Matt Williams. As an opening-day gift, Matt presented an aged copy of an Emily Post etiquette book. During the fall of 1996, three transplanted New Yorkers, Chris, Doug and Alex, became regulars. On one occasion, Alex, who is prone to philosophical discussions, contended that broccoli is alive, and that if you listen real close, you can hear a little scream when a stalk is broken. During the same evening, Alex proposed that I be tagged like a bird to monitor my migratory bar path on the flyway. Since that evening, "I was out on the flyway last night," has become a familiar expression for bar hopping. Thanks, Alex, this is a classic.

Around midnight, a handsome couple, George and Lori (the Amstel Light twins) usually make their appearance. George is another transplanted New Yorker, who is quite interesting to converse with.

I recommend that you get your feathers flapping, get out on the flyway, and look for adventure in the Rose & Crown. On a scale of five, I give the Rose & Crown five wings.

— J. Quillian

Rosie O'Brien's
5734 N. Elston Ave.
773-594-7258
Hours: noon to 2 a.m. Monday to Friday, noon to 3 a.m. Saturday

What does a large gristly slab of bacon, a burning mule and a wall mirror have in common? Unless you are demented .. nothing. Does a neon leprechaun on the wall constitute an Irish bar? I think not, although I was trying not to think too much as I sat at Rosie O'Brien's. Admittedly, I was intrigued when I walked in and Danzig was bellowing from the jukebox. I darted fellow patrons' glances as I retreated to the bathroom. Upon exiting, the next musical selection was kicking in — Billy Joel. As though all the other patrons were possessed leprechauns coming after me in a blinding frenzy whose glances were as subtle as being smacked repeatedly with a shillelagh, I tried to keep my composure. I drank some sort of variety of tepid generic beer. I noticed that the number of gambling machines in the bar was double the number of women, lending to notions if I was longitudinally a little lower, perhaps a setting for a Jodie Foster movie would come to pass.

As Rosie O'Brien's is on a corner, it has a triangular interior. With the illusions of mirrors and diagonal paneling, you may feel truly trapped in some form of Bermuda-isosceles vortex. However, you may deduct, the money is probably put to better use with the quality of drink. Well, the bar is stocked with those big daddy economo-size bottles and they have four beers on tap. Four beers that if you switched the taps around, nobody, except a discerning connoisseur, would notice.

So, Rosie O'Brien's is a corner bar that probably expects, like a negligent step parent, her patrons intermittently go elsewhere for a more nurturing environment but keep coming back similar to how hostages start to empathize with

Barfly Rosie O'Brien's-Rossi's

their captors theory. Located past blocks of bulk salt shops/warehouses, depending on where you live, you really have to go some distance to get there. There is an impressive coat rack and piston system so weekends must get packed or perhaps the regulars all wear puffy down coats.

The jukebox with its impressive diversity: Neil Diamond "Hot August Night Live" (both discs!) to Frank Zappa, "The Bodyguard" movie soundtrack to Nirvana, Garth Brooks to Danzig — is an unexpected wonder.

I did learn some humbling things that evening: 1) If you put a glass of ice in your pitcher, it stays cold — duh. 2) Hockey hair never goes out of style — it accentuates the neck. 3) Ruth Westheimer is a midget. 4) Just because a man wears a shirt that states "Try burning this one (picture of the flag) Maggot," does not mean he is not a friendly guy who likes happy music.

— Crumpey

Rossi's
414 N. State St.
312-644-5775
Hours: 7 a.m. to 2 a.m. Monday to Saturday,
11 a.m. to 2 a.m. Sunday

What appears to be a hole-in-the wall just north of the State Street bridge is actually a den of iniquity, a haven of debauchery and a site of unbridled sin. Around mid-day, a pair of young women parade around the bar in lingerie, describing their attire to a crowd of seedy business men in for some lunch-time thrills.

Apart from the floor-show, Rossi's is a comfortable, quiet establishment. A semicircular bar on the north wall offers plenty of seating, and there are more than 30 bottled beers available. Specials include $1.50 Bud drafts, and the Sticky Fingers (a shot of XO Cafe and Sambuca served chilled). With the entertainment, it's likely that some of the patrons leave with sticky fingers of their own. Other bottled specials change monthly, but are around two bucks.

Rossi's generous hours make it ideal for a breakfast beer. A cooler near the back offers package-good sales, so you can take the party on the road if needed. There's also a dart board, and televisions for catching a game. Of course, if knocking a few back while flirting with the entertainment gets your juices going, Rossi's fits the bill.

The girls do a tremendous job of keeping their composure and always smile back despite blue comments from the leering, potbellied corporate types getting their jollies.

In the morning or evening, Rossi's is like any well-appointed neighborhood bar. When the sun is high, however, be prepared to drink in an atmosphere saturated with white-collar sexual frustration. Beers and rears for all.

— bird-dog

There's nothing like the fine conversation at Sak's
Ukrainian Village Restaurant & Lounge, 2301 W. Chicago.

Sak's Ukrainian Village
Restaurant & Lounge

2301 W. Chicago Ave.
773-278-4445
Restaurant Hours: 11 a.m. to 11 p.m. Tuesday to
Sunday. Closed Monday. Bar Hours: 11 a.m. to 2 a.m.
Sunday to Friday, 11 a.m. to 3 a.m. Saturday

Nothing ever seems to stay the same, the town is always changing.
Sometimes for the better, sometimes not.

You've got a favorite bar to go to for a cold brew and maybe something good
to eat. It's a friendly, sometimes even quiet place where you can contemplate
your troubles or plan your strategy for improving the rest of your life. You're
comfortable with the bartenders, the customers, even some of the women who
come into the place lookin' for company.

Then one day they newspaper over the windows and lock the doors. A sign
says "Closed for Remodeling." Below that heart-rendering notice it says (in
very small lettering) "open soon."

For nearly three goddamn months you drive by the place and see the damn
newspaper on the windows. You see workmen going in and out. You stop the
owner on the street and ask, "Hey, Roman, when ya' openin' up?"

He shakes his head and smiles. "Soon, we're still remodeling the place. I
wanna make it look good. Be patient, you'll love what we're doing."

Yeah, except I liked it the way it was.

Barfly Sak's Ukrainian Village Restaurant

It was old, but nice old, the joint's been there for 80 years and I'd spent a lot of hours there — took my first adult date there (I was 21 and she was 17 — but so what, she looked older). The bar was long and dark and there was a solid wood wall panel like in the cowboy movies. They had this ancient telephone booth with its own fan inside so you didn't fall over in the summertime if you shut the door to make a personal call.

It was my kind of place, and I liked it.

Roman's gonna make it into one of those soulless sports bars with phony beer signs (instead of real ones) on the walls, high prices, tasteless food, and new bartenders who put more head into the glass than beer.

It was the end of the goddamn world as I knew it.

Shit, was I surprised!

Sak's Ukrainian Village Restaurant & Lounge, located in the heart of the hustle-and-bustle Ukrainian Village, re-opened on June 23, 1996, with a bang! Hell, man, a double-bang!

They kept the antique bar and the wall panel. And, they kept the goddamn phone booth, fan and all! Yes, they remodeled the place, and it's really, really sharp. But, more importantly, they kept the Heineken on tap, along with Miller, and both are deliciously COLD.

Owners Roman (the son), Nadia and John (parents) Sacharewyca — don't even try to pronounce it — believe in offering their customers a comfortable atmosphere in which to bend their elbows. The bar stools are new (the booths too), new air conditioning ducts are all over the place, new lighting and a great sound system. God, just like home.

The place, there's two rooms, is contemporary, clean, well thought out and comfortable. The bar is in the front with seating for about 60 and three large screen TVs hanging from the ceiling. Two electronic dart boards, a 100 CD jukebox and a pinball machine.

The backroom is where you eat, and what a treat it is! A dozen tables and booths provide you with a place to enjoy fantastic Ukrainian and American food at prices that'll make you cry — not because they're high, either.

You can get everything from authentic Borsht (with or without beets), potato pancakes with sour cream, delicious Ukrainian sausage sandwiches on rye, to steaks, hamburgers, salads and ribs. All of it at half the price you'll pay three miles east in River North.

Let's get back to the bar. Heineken tap is $2.25. Imported bottles are $3.25, and there are about 15 types to choose from. Domestic bottles are $2, draft $1.75. Mixed drinks are $3.

Sak's has a number of very good bartenders, but Anna "Sunshine" and Luba are probably as friendly and professional as you'll find anywhere. Roman, big, walrus mustache and all, is good company and willing to talk about just about everything you'd care too, especially the neighborhood.

"Hell, my family has owned this place for 15 years," Roman said. "I was raised here. Except for fixing it up and making it more efficient, I wasn't going to change anything. A good honest drink, great food, and a safe place where

273

The North Side Sak's-Saxony Liquor Lounge

you and your friends can come and not find any trouble."

There's plenty of free parking all over the place and the neighborhood is quiet and safe to bring your date to.

Shit, to think I allowed my imagination to run wild while those goddamn windows were covered over. It's the some old new place, only better.

Check it out, and be damn sure you order something to eat: the beer is great, but beer is beer, the chow is the something extra.

— Roy Koz

Saxony Liquor Lounge
1136 W. Lawrence Ave.
773-334-4464
Hours: 7 a.m. to 4 a.m. weekdays,
7 a.m. to 5 a.m. Saturday, 11 a.m. to 4 a.m. Sunday

Chilling comfortably between the Aragon Ballroom, the Green Mill, and the Riviera, is arguably Uptown Chicago's most "authentic" gin mill: The Saxony Liquor Lounge. To enter the Saxony you must first be buzzed in the security door. This quaint notion alone has kept out many a slumming yuppie.

If you pass muster (which amounts to you not being one of the dangerous criminals that have been barred out for the general safety of the rest of us) you will walk into a dark, smoky paradise which I can best describe as looking like Henry Hill's bar in "Good Fellas" where Joe Pesci's character whacks the unwise gangster who calls him a shoeshine boy. Well-appointed with over-stuffed black pleated booths, a jukebox, Formica bar top, and a handy riser for your feet, the Saxony is *the* perfect place to mull over some bad news with a quiet drink. With domestic bottles at $1.50, draught Hamms and Bud at 75 cents, and most shots, including Jagermiester, at only $2, your mood is sure to improve.

According to Mr. St. Claire, a 90 year-old man and 30-year Saxony regular, who sits regally in his corner stool by the window, and speaks with unerring authority: "This place has been here 55 years, young man, 55 years way before your time." Ten-year evening bartender Laura Castro reminds me to mention the famous people who have visited the Lounge. "Like who?" I ask, thinking she means me.

"John Goodman," she responds, "came in here for a six-pack and a pint of Jack Daniel's when they were filming that movie (The Babe) across the street." Laura also names "That guy who played Pauly in the Rocky movies." After several $2 Jager shots and a nice Weiss, (even served in a Weiss glass), at $3, we figure out that Burt Young was Pauly in the Rocky movies.

"So Laura," I invite, "tell the readers who else comes in here."

"Working people, hopefully," she answers, laughing at her own joke. "Let's break it down like this: you got your daytime 7 a.m. regulars from the hood who might have a $1.50 breakfast shot of Malort, then sip Pabst Blue Ribbons from a can over a glass of ice all day. If there are three of these early morning

Barfly Saxony-O'Malley's Schoolyard Tavern

patrons, they are most likely to have over 200 years between them. Then you've got your Uptown characters straight out of a Bukowski story; cops, cabbies, prostitutes, thieves, junkies, and general working class drunks. But remember, they must get past the buzzer, so if they're in here they probably want the same thing you do; an honest drink at an honest price.

"In six years of drinking in this gin joint," she continues, "I've never witnessed a single physical hassle. Sometimes after concerts at the Aragon or the Riv or the Green Mill, the trendy kids come in *en mass*, spend good money, and play Sinatra, Elvis or Billy Holliday on the jukebox, and they seem to get a big kick out of it. The proud owner of the Saxony is Dave Jemmillo, who also owns the nearby Green Mill and formerly Lincoln Park's Deja Vu.

Being a pretty serious barfly myself, I unreservedly recommend this world class joint for first dates to see if your potential mate can handle his/her booze. The Saxony Liquor Lounge also has an attached packaged goods store so when Laura calls last call at 3:45 a.m., don't forget that pack of GPC's and a pint of Richard's Wild Irish Rose 'cause it's a long way 'till 7 a.m. The Saxony, it's not just a bar, it's an adventure.

— Tom Luplow

Schoolyard Tavern
3258 N. Southport Ave.
773-528-8226

In 1994, Southport Avenue's new kid on the block was O'Malley's Schoolyard Tavern. It's an indoor playground where old school friends, neighborhood drinking pals and curious newcomers can meet, greet and drink.

Owners Matt O'Malley and Paula Riggins have created a local tavern that may win the "most likely to succeed" award.

Although the partners' high school yearbooks have barely 10 years of dust on them, they have had crash-course lessons on the inner workings of the food and beverage industry. Their many intense years in the business compensate for their young ages.

Both O'Malley and Riggins are alum of Deacon Brodie's, 2515 N. Halsted St., where O'Malley was a former manager and Riggins was a bartender. Prior to Deacon Brodie's, O'Malley was Leona Helmsly's lackey in Beverly Hills while Riggins was bartending at Otis'.

"We've both had a lot of people teaching us things," O'Malley said. "We've always treated places like they were our own."

Riggins explained that she and O'Malley act like nervous parents. "We're always checking up on it. It's like calling the baby-sitter," Riggins jokingly admitted. "I'll call the bar and ask, 'How's everything? Do you need anything? The limes are downstairs if you're out.'" Even her parents get a kick out of the newest member of the family. Her parents will tease her at dinner by asking, "How's the grandchild?" Anyone wanna see pictures?

The duo said they hope O'Malley's becomes popular with folks who live

The North Side O'Malley's Schoolyard Tavern

around the bar as well as those who venture to this popular North Side neighborhood for its outstanding entertainment.

"It might sound corny, but we want to create a Cheers-like place," Riggins said, "where there are a lot of regulars and you can come here by yourself and you'll see someone you know."

Besides recreating a live Cheers set, the owners hope to distinguish their bar from other taverns by providing a different bar experience.

"We each have our own niche," O'Malley said.

The Schoolyard has a pool table, an electronic dart board and four televisions that air sports and late night shows such as Letterman. While these amenities are similar to those offered at other taverns, the unique appeal at this neighborhood bar is its atmosphere.

O'Malley described the Schoolyard as an upscale bar. The sparse yet tasteful decor reflects O'Malley's interior-decorating side. The floor is made of a light tan-colored wood, the tables are of a worn yet polished mahogany wood, and the seats are black-leather stools. O'Malley is going for the subdued minimalist look, with a peppering of art here and there. The walls are decorated with sailboat and equestrian paintings, which look as if they were found in the attic of a stately mansion. To add to the refined ambiance, the staff wears white shirts and ties.

The exterior also emulates class and care. The building has a Cape Cod appearance with a deliciously lazy yet intellectual appeal. Flower boxes popping with clashing pinks and reds line the expansive windows. Striped awnings with the colors of a prep-school boy's uniform create the impression of a drinking club for the local erudites and sages. As a whole, the bar has a well-worn feel to it, somewhat like your favorite threadbare cashmere cardigan with its peeling leather buttons and moth-made holes.

Besides the Schoolyard's style, the owners offer a balance of practical and innovative entertainment features. The bar will always play University of Illinois and University of Arizona games (the latter being O'Malley's alma mater) and has fun field trips to see these games. To quench the thirst of rooting crowds, the bar serves 14 drafts, 10 bottled beers and mixed drinks. The beer menu boasts Pete's Wicked Ale, Sierra Nevada Pale Ale, Tenants of Scotland and Newcastle Brown Ale. The bar also highlights microbrewed beer.

There are also other specials that go beyond a full glass of beer. On Wednesday nights, a guest bartender gets to play Bacchus for a few hours. The substitute can be a regular customer, a drinking pal or any friendly face. The hourly wage that normally goes to the bartender is donated to a neighborhood charity.

O'Malley and Riggins believe that giving to the neighborhood is as important as being a part of this close-knit community. "Our goal is not to hit a zenith and crash," O'Malley said. "We're long term and our goal is longevity."

If O'Malley and Riggins are correct, then the Schoolyard Tavern will become more than just one short recess period in a long school year. Rather, they hope the neighborhood bar will become an extension of Southport Avenue's family and an active member from the Class of '94.

— Andrea Sachs

Schuba's
Harmony Grill

3159 N. Southport Ave.
773-525-2508
Bar Hours: 11 a.m. to 2 a.m. Sunday to Friday,
11 a.m. to 3 a.m. Saturday. Restaurant Hours: 11 a.m.
to 2 a.m. weekdays, 24 hours on weekends

This corner of Southport and Belmont avenues has housed a tavern since 1900. Back then, many breweries used to build their own taverns. Eventually, small bar owners complained that they couldn't compete fairly with brewery-owned taverns and lawmakers forbade breweries from owning bars. Yet, in cities like Chicago, remnants of these pieces of history exist in abundance. Schubas is one of these treasures and one of the best kept.

Schlitz Brewing Co. originally built the bar, inside and outside, and the old Schlitz sign sits proudly on the outside of the building. Some of the interior of Schuba's is similar to the original Schlitz design.

The bar is now owned by Schuba Brothers Chris and Mike. Chris ran the successful Everleigh Club in Lincoln Park during the Reagan era. The brothers opened Schuba's in 1989 replacing Gaspar's, a long-time music club. Today, with the addition of Harmony Grill, the site is at its most unique point in its history. Schuba's is not only a shot and beer place but a great bar to relax, hang out in, eat a good meal or listen to live music. And you can do all of these things without knowledge of the other going on.

Three separate rooms make up Schuba's. A walk through the bar's front door leads to a long newly refinished wood bar with smiling bartenders. It has more than 70 bottles of hard liquor including a special selection of bourbons. Schuba's carries 16 bottled beers and has 12 taps ranging from Guinness to Sierra Nevada to Bud Light. Cost ranges from $2.75 to $3.75 and there are all day beer specials Monday to Wednesday.

As you continue walking down the bar, past a photo booth, Millipede video game and a pinball machine, you come to a crossroads. You can either go left into a concert hall that doubles as a brunch room on Saturday and Sunday, or right into the adjacent Harmony Grill.

Make a left into the concert hall and you'll catch a rock band from the area or a nationally touring new country or folk band. Depending on who is playing, dictates who shows up to listen. Although the bar has its steady flow of locals, the concert room attracts anyone from the flower-baring Joan Baez fan to the body-surfing Zack De La Rocha wannabe. If you were lucky enough to be at Schuba's in 1995, you may have caught the Dave Matthews band.

The North Side Schuba's-Second Time Around

Bands usually play six nights a week and covers range from $3 to $15. The room can hold up to 150 people. When the music begins, the doors are shut from the concert hall to the main bar. If you're relaxing in the bar with a glass of Chianti, you wont' be able to tell that a concert is going on just 25 feet from your stool.

However, if hunger supersedes live music, then make a right into the Harmony Grill. With many types of appetizers and menu items like southern-style fried chicken and an assortment of sandwiches like tasty grilled vegetable pita (get it with feta cheese), there's something for everybody. At 11 p.m. on Friday and Saturday nights, the Harmony Grill dinner menu changes to a late night supper that's served until the next morning. Just a smaller version of the dinner menu, but now with several breakfast items to choose from including the often ordered breakfast burrito.

If you haven't checked out Schuba's and the Harmony Grill, you've been missing out. The staff is friendly, the food is tasty, the atmosphere is relaxing and it is an important page in Chicago's tavern history.

— Kevin Toomajian

The Second Time Around
8303 W. Irving Park Road
773-589-9040
Hours: 7 a.m. to 2 a.m. daily

It's cold, windy, rainy and a Friday night. You missed the bus. The next bus is in 45 minutes. Across the street you spot a small bar. Anything has to be better than sitting out in the rain waiting 45 minutes for the bus. You open the screen door, and then the wood door. As you enter the bar, the smell of stale beer and whiskey, and cigarettes flatten your senses.

The bar is full of people you don't know. Most of this crowd is in the late 30 to early 40 age group, mostly men. There are Christmas lights hanging from the wall. There is a pool table with darts, a new jukebox, and the monitory cigarette machine. The place has one main bar with about three tables opposite the bar. After sitting at the main bar you notice two small color TVs hanging on the wall. The bar has Old Style on tap, that is about it.

After waiting about five minutes the barmaid notices you. After waiting another five minutes, she asks you what you want to drink. In asking the price of the drinks, the barmaid totally ignores you. A guy next to you answers, tap 75 cents a-glass, bottles $1.75, mixed $2.50.

You order a beer. The beer comes warm, stale, flat, and in a small glass. Annoyed at the fact that the barmaid would not answer your questions, you notice that most of the people in the bar know each other. It seems that this place is a close-knit neighborhood bar. While drinking the beer you notice advertisements on the ceiling. Just what you needed, more exposure to advertising. Nothing happens of any interest in this place. In this place, outsiders are ignored.

278

Barfly Second Time Around-Sertano's

If a boring, uninteresting place is your thing, then the Second Time Around is the place you want to be.

—E. Marsh

Sertano's

200 N. LaSalle St.
312-726-3511
Hours: 10:30 a.m. to 10 p.m. Monday to Thursday, 10:30 a.m. to 11 p.m. Friday, closed Saturday and Sunday

One of the best dining deals in the Loop, Sertano's is an oasis of inexpensive, delicious home-made Italian sandwiches, pastas and specialties. Sertano's two stories are tucked back behind an office building on Lake Street. The kitchen, salad bar and dining area are on the ground floor. Up a broad staircase next to the entrance is Sertano's bar. Complete with pool table, jukebox and plenty of additional seating, upstairs is where people chase their sausage, spaghetti and salad with pints of Bass or a bottle of their favorite domestic, and work off the meal with a game or two.

Sertano's two-story set-up is more than adequate for a quick, well-above-average workday lunch anytime of the year. When the weather cooperates however, Sertano's adds an outdoor dining area, filling the courtyard in front of the Lake Street entrance with tables and chairs, as well as the occasional noon-time jazz combo for ambiance.

Under the rattling Lake Street el tracks, Sertano's patrons sit soaking up the ample sunshine, devouring huge sandwiches smothered in mozzarella, red sauce and hot peppers. People bring out bottles of beer or a mixed drink to accompany their lunches. Daily specials tend to be a big plate of pasta with a meat side such as sausage or meat balls, and fresh bread. A full salad bar is also available.

Sertano's is a noteworthy member of Chicago's legion of Italian restaurants because it has combined two of the most desirable restaurant features: authenticity and value. While Chicago is jammed with Italian establishments, many concentrate on regional dishes or create an eclectic menu loosely based on Italian cuisine. Sertano's concentrates on the fundamentals: spicy, hearty dishes priced to make fast-food fans look twice. For around five dollars, diners can enjoy a fully dressed sandwich. For around seven dollars, the selections rival the best Taylor Street has to offer. And after the meal, many folks knock off early to spend the rest of the day shooting pool or shooting the breeze upstairs, or working on their face tans outside. That might be the restaurant's most delightful (albeit dangerous) attraction. It has to be hard to return to work after the head-clearing, belly filling excursion Sertano's provides.

— Jay Ferrari

Sharon's Hillbilly Heaven

1113 W. Lawrence Ave.
Won't release phone number
Hours: 9 a.m. to 4 a.m. Sunday to Friday,
9 a.m. to 5 a.m. Saturday

Overwhelmed by a grim prospect of another evening spent in the company of my generational cohorts (you know: liberal arts degree, decorative tattoos from a salon not a stint on the U.S.S. Nimitz, recitations on the Tarantino *oeuvre*, frappaccino breath, endless in-the-know jokestering...), I sought relief.

Gratefully, I found a sweet tonic for conversational blandness in Sharon's Hillbilly Heaven — smack dab in the heart of Uptown under the Lawrence el stop.

This is a saloon with a selective clientele. To enter, you must first ring the doorbell and be buzzed in by one of several life-loving bartenders. Once within its cozy confines, belly on up to the bar and prepare to talk. Strangers might get a cautious glance or two, but after a short while, one of the regulars will undoubtedly seek you out as an audience to outlandish stories or as a referee to an ongoing debate.

The bar is dark, long, and narrow, brightened by tiny Christmas lights and countless signs touting tavern advice: "If you came in here to bitch, you've just wasted 98 percent of your time. We suggest using the other 2 percent to find the door."

Sharon's doesn't have much in the way of table seating: 20 bar stools in various styles bring you close to the party. Fine specimens of taxidermy line the walls, and a nifty old faux-stained-glass Schlitz dome illuminates. Along with the poker and pinball machines, Sharon's offers an amazing jukebox that boasts more than the expected Hank William's Jr. and James Brown classics. Sharon's customers know their Ike & Tina b-sides and sing along accordingly.

Drinks are cheap and plentiful with domestic bottles of beer going for $1.75 and call brand cocktails running $1.75 to $2.25. Thanks to co-owner (and Sharon's husband) Werner's German upbringing, the bar also offers a nice selection of imported beers for $2.50 and giant Weissbier for $3.50. Try getting those prices at your next concert across the street at the Aragon Ballroom.

Friends ask, "Aren't you afraid to go in there by yourself?" Hell, no.

The unknown truth about supposedly tough bars in low-income neighborhoods is that chivalry and unpretentious friendliness thrives in them. I, as a rather petite female, feel safer alone in Sharon's than I would in, say, a thick-necked-mutual-fund-swapping bar a la Dave & Buster's. The men in Sharon's are exceedingly polite, offering their high-backed chairs to women customers and watching them get safely into a cab or bus upon departing. These are the kind of men that leap to their feet and toss out any cad who puts the hard moves on a lady.

Yes, the folks who frequent Sharon's may not find themselves on any USA

Barfly Sharon's- Sidelines

Today chart of upwardly mobile consumer trends. However, many of them are quite well-read and self-educated in the school of life despite adversity. These are not people who mark significant personal events by whether they occurred before or after "Smells Like Teen Spirit" hit big.

By not visiting Sharon's and bars like it, you cheat yourself of unique perspectives and good gab. Muster up some guts and stop by next time you take in an alterna-hype show at the Aragon or Riviera. You might just learn something about real alternatives.

— ms. joy

Sheffield's

3258 N. Sheffield Ave.
773-281-2989
Hours: 2 p.m. to 2 a.m. weekdays,
noon to 3 a.m. Saturday, noon to 2 a.m. Sunday

Sheffield's is my corner bar. I take it for granted and go there on occasion for core reasons like it's close and safe and I like the employees.

Weeknights and weekend afternoons are the best times to visit; your own barstool or table and personal attention from the bartenders enables you to see what's really there. You can choose from almost 100 different beers ranging from obscure imports to regional microbrews. They've got a menu with full descriptions, explanations and even a glossary to guide and educate those interested which might lead to joining their Beer Society.

Beer of the Month/Bad Beer of the Month specials are posted and, in addition, they serve wine and some interesting homemade mixed drinks like the Kalua Swish, made with chocolate syrup or the Blomo Bloody Mary with a Guinness base.

Their beer garden features two bars, a pool table, a grill, and climate control. (It's always about 10 degrees warmer in there because the buildings on either side block the wind.) They don't mind you ordering food in or bringing your own to grill out while you drink.

Fang may be there as well. He's the indestructible cat on his third life. I heard he's survived a fall from a balcony, a hit by a car, and is currently on the prowl with three pins in one of his legs.

Sidelines

2843 N. Halsted St.
773-528-7569
Hours: 5 p.m. to 2 a.m. weekdays, 11 a.m. to 3 a.m.
Saturday, 11 a.m. to 2 a.m. Sunday

Sidelines deserves a lot of breathing room right now. It changed ownership in August, and a grand re-opening occurred the first week of September. This offers nothing but good news to both its established patrons and neighborhood passersby, for there is ample opportunity to add input to the development of a supreme local watering hole.

The new owner, Al, is an amicable, energetic guy trying to implement many ideas in a short period of time while still keeping the doors open. Any transitional period is difficult and hectic, but he appears committed to transforming his new business into a tavern for the ages. He is completely revamping the menu, maintaining pub fare but embracing both his Italian heritage and his love of food to expand beyond the norm. The temporary dish list comprises sandwiches, burgers, and munchies, but his plans include numerous pasta specialties and an extensive selection of innovative items which would satisfy gastronomes.

He is currently updating the kitchen equipment and enlisting his brother, a food critic, to reach his level of perfection. As for drink specials, at the moment he has Honkers Ale for $2.75 a pint on Mondays and Wednesdays, but as with the menu, give it time. The man has plans, I tell you.

The space itself is split into two rooms with a hallway and small outdoor patio connecting. The front room has an area by the window set aside as a makeshift stage for singer/songwriter-types, numerous tables hugging the walls, and seven televisions, including a big screen in need of some repairs. Until it's repaired, patrons will figuratively and literally see red while watching the Bears play. The backroom is more expansive and has a significantly larger stage. Al has three to four bands playing every Friday and Saturday, generally each with an hour-long set, and this variety assures that the room reaches its full capacity on weekends.

The clientele is hard to figure. The evening I stopped by, there was a crowd of folks in their twenties and thirties, some listening to a performer doing Marley covers, both eternal optimists and looking-for-a-reason suicidals watching the tail end of the Bears game, and packs huddled in self-absorbed private conversations. I guess, a place for everyone, and everyone in his place.

Al needs about two months to put his mark on this bar and secure its position in the neighborhood. He has wondrous ideas and genuine passion. This is a perfect time for the calling of all locals: don't pass up the chance to observe and contribute to the metamorphosis of Sidelines. It might just become your ideal hang-out.

— *Deborah Hamilton*

The Signature Room
96th Floor of the John Hancock Building
875 N. Michigan Ave.
312-787-9596
Hours: 11:30 a.m. to 1:30 a.m. daily

Sure it's packed full of tourists. And sure, they want $4 for a domestic beer. But, who cares, look at that view!

The Signature Room is the kind of place your regular Joe doesn't frequent. It

Barfly Signature Room-Simon's Tavern

has a reputation for being snooty, overpriced, geared toward the other half. But it's really for everyone. You can go in jeans and a T-shirt, or you can go in your Sunday finest. Bud or Champagne. Swisher Sweets or Macanudos. All are welcome to sit down, have a glass of something and look out the window.

The lighting is soothing, the service is smooth, the selection is expensive, but extensive. But all these things pale next to the Signature Room's reason for existence: the view.

There are days when you fight traffic for an hour coming home only to spend 45 minutes looking for a parking place. There are days when the packed subway train stops between Grand and Chicago for 10 minutes and you never know why! There are days when you get your purse snatched and you have to wait in line at the Secretary of State's office for two hours, and all those damn people just got in your way and you HATE living in a city.

Spend half an hour on "Top of the 'Cock" sipping a glass of wine and looking out the window. You'll remember why you love Chicago.

— Meg Rhem

Simon's Tavern
5210 N. Clark St.
773-878-0894
Hours: open at 9 a.m. daily,
close depends on crowd

Simon's Tavern is a living history of the Andersonville neighborhood on the city's Far North Side. The bar, the oldest in Andersonville, is one of the few remaining Swedish bars in this once predominantly Swedish neighborhood.

Simon's opened in 1934 by Swedish immigrant Simon Lundberg who has since passed away. However, the bar stayed in the family until 1995 when Mr. Lundberg's son Roy and his wife Rose sold the bar to regular Scott Martin.

"This is all I've ever wanted to do," Martin said. "I grew up in this neighborhood, started working at Alice's Tap when I was 14 and I've been in the bar business ever since."

Martin's bartending stints have also included the Wild Hare and Deja Vu where he hooked up with partner and mentor, Dave Jemilo.

According to Martin, Simon's will continue to be a shrine to the Lundberg's. Simon's stern portrait hangs just inside the bar and Martin insists there it will stay. Formerly a cafe owner, Lundberg was inspired to set up shop by gangster Al Capone, Lundberg's son Roy said. Apparently, one sunny day Capone walked into Lundberg's cafe amidst the Prohibition years and coolly asked Lundberg, "You want to make money. I'll make you money. I'm going to sell you whiskey and make sure to put a shot of it in that coffee over there."

"Pretty soon," Roy said, "My Dad is making more money selling coffee than food."

Six months after the appeal of Prohibition in November of 1934, Simon's Tavern was open for business.

283

The North Side Simon's Tavern-Simply Ray's

Over the decades, Simon's Tavern has offered more than just local hospitality and the annual warm, spicy, and wickedly potent Christmas glögg. Martin explains that Lundberg also served as neighborhood banker, often cashing up to $18,000 in weekly paychecks for neighbors still leery of local banks from the stock market crash of 1929. Foregoing any service charge, Lundberg would simply suggest a cold beer to go along with his neighbor's recently-filled wallets.

Martin promises to highlight Lundberg's former cashier's booth complete with 18-gauge steel and a special ceiling trap door where Mrs. Lundberg would secretly pass money down through the floor of the family's upstairs home to the bar. Martin is also preserving the bar's art deco ocean-liner design, while planning additions like a CD jukebox, tables, and a long bench just below the tavern's signature "Deer Hunt Ball" wall mural.

The new owners, along with Martin's wife Angela, and parents Tom and Delores are all working hard to bring fresh vigor into this old landmark while painstakingly preserving its historical significance and charm. Roy Lundberg, who has known Martin since that very first drink, had this to say when passing his father's legacy into new, but still at least one-half Swedish hands, "He's doing things the way I'd be doing things if I was a lot younger."

— *Cynthia Grows*

Simply Ray's

4709 N. Damen Ave.
773-561-1757
Hours: 11 a.m. to 2 a.m. daily, 11 a.m. to 3 a.m. Saturday. Kitchen hours: 11 a.m. to midnight daily.

Ray Pate always knew that he wanted to incorporate "Ray" into the name of his first solo venture in the bar business. Not satisfied with the name variations that he and his friends were coming up with during a Sox game at Comiskey, Ray finally suggested, "How about 'Simply Ray's'?"

"My wife Cassandra said 'stupid' and I took that as an endorsement," Pate said.

Simply Ray's opened on July 1, 1996.

Opening Simply Ray's (previously Fox's Pub), by himself was a logical next step for Pate. He has been gradually advancing in the bar business since his first bartending job at the former Bottle Necks on Broadway in 1978. Four years later he was managing his first bar, Spooners formerly at 3912 N. Clark St., where he stayed until 1987. In 1990, he bought his first bar, Players on Clark near Wrigley Field with two partners. After selling that in 1993, he bought the former Third Base Inn at 3458 N. Lincoln Ave. with Kenny Miller of Yak-Zies and turned it into Ray's Chili & Suds.

Ray and his chili were replaced within a year, however, with the Yak-Zies name and its signature spicy chicken wings. When he got out of that venture in April of 1996, he knew he "didn't want to do the partner thing anymore."

Barfly Simply Ray's

Owning his own place solo has rejuvenated him. He said he loves "the challenge, all the competition. It's so much fun."

It's a good thing he feels that way. The first day of solo bar ownership brought a broken cooler and ice machine. On day two, the air conditioning went. A few days later, the roof began leaking. With no partner handling this crises and a landlord vacationing in Greece, it was simply up to Ray.

These unanticipated repairs were all in addition to the changes Pate knew he wanted to make.

"The last owners admitted they lost interest in the place the last few years and let it deteriorate," Pate said.

Feeling that he could only afford to close the bar for two days, he called up his uncle, an electrician and carpenter.

"Can you make this place beautiful in two days?" Pate asked and recalled his uncle's response, "Not beautiful, but cute maybe."

Together with a team of 8 to 10 workers, Pate and his uncle worked to turn a "dark, dingy, pit" into something more like the sports bars in Wrigleyville and Lake View that Pate was used to.

One of his main objectives, he said, was to open up the place, tear down a front wall that had only two tiny windows for light, tear down a back wall that divided the bar, and unclutter the space in general (poorly placed phones, ice machine, and pinball games all got in the way).

Three coats of white paint over the dark paneling also helped. Other aesthetic and safety concerns taken care of include a nicotine-stained suspended ceiling refitted with white fire-proof panels, the electrical work was redone, new refrigeration units were bought, and the floor was re-tiled. Pate's uncle built a dozen high wooden bar tables to extend the seating. Though neither "beautiful" nor "cute," the result is simply a nice-looking sports bar.

One thing that Pate wisely chose to keep the same was the enormous old bar. It takes up about 3/4 of the main room and seats people on all four sides. As far as bar amenities go, Simply Ray's already has two TVs, four dart boards, and a bowling game. The CD jukebox contains a mix that includes Julio Iglesias, Bob Dylan, Patti LaBelle, the Talking Heads, the Beatles, Glen Miller, and the Andrew Sisters.

"The days of selling booze without food are gone," he proclaimed. His last three years with chili and chicken wings provided him with valuable experience in food and made him realize that he enjoys that aspect of the business. During the early weeks of operation, Ray experimented with various pizza recipes until he found a combination he was proud of and could go public with. He hopes to make pizza a cornerstone of his kitchen and already has plans to delivery.

Along with pizza, the kitchen churns out fried appetizers, sandwiches, salads, and chili at reasonable prices. Chicken fingers, jalapeño poppers, fried shrimp, breaded zucchini, etc. served with your favorite dipping sauce run $2 to $4.25. Burgers, turkey burgers, beefs, brats, Italian sausages, hot dogs, and BLTs all come with fries, chips, or potato salad and range from $2 to $5.25.

Simply Ray's beer menu is basic but contains a few surprises. Bottles include

The North Side Simply Ray's-Six Penny Bit

Miller and Bud products, Heineken, Beck's, Legacy Lager, and Hacker Pschorr Weiss. On tap, Miller Lite, Leinenkugel's, and Leine's Berry Weiss.

While immersed in the countless daily details involved in running a bar, Pate is also tending to the future. He selected Simply Ray's location because he liked the neighborhood and thinks that it's on its way up. By making his place "the nicest bar in the neighborhood," Ray believes he has paved the way for other "nice bars" to join him in the area.

To continue with his improvements, he would like to make his non-affiliation with the adjacent liquor store more obvious, perhaps by erecting an outdoor divider, he said. His goal is to attract a more upscale clientele without losing the loyal customers from previous owners.

"I already have one customer that's a lawyer," he joked.

If it's up to Pate, Simply Ray's will simply be Ray's forever.

"I plan to pass this on to my kids (his young daughters, Lisa and Olivia) and go on opening other bars," he said.

Find it 1/2 block north of the Damen stop of the Ravenswood El line.

— Sharon Woodhouse

Six Penny Bit
5800 W. Montrose Ave.
773-544-2033
8 a.m. to 2 a.m. Monday through Friday,
8 a.m. to 3 a.m. Saturday, 11 a.m. to 2 a.m. Sunday

With a long family history of operating pubs here and in Ireland, the Birt family's Six Penny Bit has become a home away from home for its dedicated regulars up on the Northwest Side.

"We are always willing to help out our patrons and have done so many times," said Ronnie Birt, who's dad Thomas owns the place. "I think our customers realize this and feel more at home here. It's a family atmosphere that I don't think you get at many other places."

The Six Penny Bit is without clannish trappings and maintains a friendliness that is so typical of the Irish people. Of all the attractions boasted by the Six Penny, I guarantee this will be the most apparent when you come on down.

If it's entertainment you are looking for, you can't compete with the Six Penny. Live bands, both local and from as far away as Ireland, play Thursday through Sunday nights. THERE NEVER IS A COVER CHARGE! Music selection is a combination of your typical traditional Irish folk music and the top hits from both here and from Europe. Stop by and check out the jukebox and you will see what I mean.

Besides music, the Six Penny has a satellite dish that brings all of the popular sporting events from Ireland that a homesick puppy demands. Bus trips are always being arranged to such events as Summer Fest in Milwaukee, as well as ski outings and trips to Las Vegas. The Six Penny sponsors many extra-curricula activities from darts to softball and pool. There are numerous dart boards to

Barfly Six Penny Bit-Sluggers

keep your beer going down smoothly, plus all the snacks you desire.

"We try to keep a good stock of all the goodies you would find at a pub back in Ireland," Ronnie said.

Most importantly, I suggest you visit the Six Penny Bit for the Guinness. There is no doubt it is the best ever poured in this great city of ours. I challenge anyone who ever had the real thing in Ireland to suggest it is not one and the same. No more will you have to put up with a stale pint that some bartenders can't even take the time to pour correctly.

This is the place, but I must warn you, unless you like beautiful Irish lasses brushing up against you with the throb of live music playing, don't show up on the weekend. But if you do, don't worry about getting a beer from the bar. The Six Penny has the sweetest, most dedicated waitresses that have ever served anybody anything. So stop buy and have a Guinness, you will not regret it, in fact you owe me one.

P.S. Say hello to Maggie.

— Scott Sisco

Sluggers
3540 N. Clark St.
773-248-0055
Hours: opening times vary, close 2 a.m.

Sluggers is the epitome of sports bars in Chicago. Expect a packed and noisy house during any playoff sporting event and all Cub home games. Large, medium and small televisions fill the bar. However, viewing and hearing the event/game is still challenging. Audience reaction and participation brings the sights, smells, and sounds of the game/event to any ticketless sports fan. However, expect an early close if no one is around drinking in the bar. During Cub home games Sluggers opens extra early wetting the whistles of Cub junkies. Chicago's favorite sports team T-shirts are displayed in cases. Pictures and autographs of famous sports figures wallpaper the interior. An outdoor cafe offers white plastic chairs and tables for patrons wanting to watch the traffic. What really distinguishes Sluggers from any other sports bar is the Upper Deck, hidden on the second floor. The Upper Deck is loaded with amusement park entertainment like baseball and softball batting cages, air hockey, modern pinball, video games, volley basketball, and bowling for prizes.

The basic premise of the sports bar is a good one: bring the game to the people if the people can't go to the game. Some future improvements to sports bars may be in-house scoreboards to keep the viewer up to date in case a broadcasted scoring update was not seen or heard. Editing out the commercials has been frowned upon by the networks and sports bars should offer some method of getting around the commercial part of televised sporting events. One method could be to turn off the audio of a broadcasted event and hire an in-bar announcer for play-by-play for an additional realistic effect.

287

Smiler Coogan's

5637 W. Grand Ave.
773-889-0601
Hours: 2 p.m. to 4 a.m. daily

Chicago is a city of great traditions, the Everleigh Sisters, Al Capone's vaults and quarter beer night at Smiler Coogan's (under the bridge at Central and Grand Avenues).

For the last 15 years, every Tuesday evening, hordes of serious beer drinkers have taken their laundry money here and left (crawled out) sweaty from dancing with their ears ringing from the music spun until 4 a.m. (this is the voice of experience talking).

Smiler Coogan's is the brainchild of Sabu Gabhawla. A man truly dedicated to offering (literally) something for everyone. He purchased the bar 13 years ago and, for reasons of familiarity, he retained the name and the Tuesday night tradition as well as adding a few new events to round out the week.

There are actually two separate rooms, each with a fully stocked bar. On one side they have the standard issue video games and popcorn machine. They also offer free darts (real darts — not those silly plastic things). The jukebox has more than a hundred compact discs catering to the diverse crowd that you will find there on any night of the week.

On the other side is the stage area, where live music is featured every weekend. National acts like the "Dead Fly Boys" and local acts like the "Bulldogs" recently played there. Every Friday is "Rock-n-Roll Night" (is one night really enough?). Every Saturday night is "Heavy Metal Night" (One night is more than enough!)

On Wednesday nights they have an open mike with $1 well drinks and free food for all. Thursday nights offers $1 bottles, that's any beer for one dollar a bottle. This is also booking night for bands. So you can get a date (for your band) and celebrate with great priced beer.

As far as decor, which can often enhance the drinking experience for the serious drinker, the first room mixes the standard corner bar look, a lot of paneling and gratuitously prurient cheesecake beer posters with the decadence of some castle on the coast of Wales around the Turn of the Century.

The stage area resembles just about every roadhouse that I have ever been in, complete with thick heavy wooden tables. Having been in more roadhouses than I care to remember (or can remember) I can only say that you have not been to a rock-n-roll show until you have been to one in a road house. Everything else is just a pale substitute.

So, whether you want to see some of the area's best bands or you just want to drink yourself silly, shake yourself down to Smiler Coogan's. I'll catch you on the bounce around.

— Barile

Snuggles Pub
5856 N. Milwaukee Ave.
773-631-3351
Hours: 11 a.m. to 2 a.m. weekdays,
11 a.m. to 3 a.m. Saturday, noon to 2 a.m. Sunday

In bar hopping, I have been into a place called Snuggles. Snuggles is in Chicago's Gladstone Park neighborhood on the Northwest Side. There are about three burbs that border the area. The place is a city/suburbanite kind of place.

The marquee on the outside of the bar displays the weekly specials. There are sports team awards on the windowsill. I think that the bar sponsors several neighborhood sports teams like softball and bowling teams. While the bar is billing itself as a sports bar, I would not consider it to be a jock, or muscle head place to show off.

The music in the place is loud enough to where you cannot hear conversations from across the bar. I would consider the music to be rock: mostly medium, not the heavy stuff like Krokus or Megadeath. I was quite happy with what was playing.

My only peeve about the place is that it was smokey, but that is more a personal preference. If cigarette smoke does not bother you, then skip the criticism.

Many of those who hang out at Snuggles are in the late twenty something, or early thirty something age range. As a sports bar, there are several color televisions, no large screens, however. The early opening time on Sunday suggests that there are specials for game times.

The decor of the place is not shooting for any gold medals in Architectural Digest, but I would not gut the place and try and make it into some yuppified watering hole.

Going into some bar lore, I believe a long time ago the place use to be called "The Bag" or "The Nickel Bag." I guess that in the early 1970s the place was a good hang out to cop a bag, and watch local music talent. The bar has changed its name, and image.

— alt Ex gen

Southport City Saloon
2548 N. Southport Ave.
773-975-6110
Hours: dining 11 a.m. to 10 p.m. during the week,
11 a.m. to midnight on weekends
The bar is open from 11 a.m. to 2 a.m. weekdays,
11 a.m. to 3 a.m. weekends

The Southport City Saloon has an abundance of space with an eclectic atmosphere in each of its three rooms. The dining room has a mellow mood, so patrons can relax and enjoy a fabulous repast along with a tasty cocktail. Hanging from the dining room ceiling are 25 flags from around the world. White brick walls give the place a pristine look decorated with toy parrots and a few televisions are available for viewing delight. The ceiling is an intricate lattice design, creating a patio feeling.

Adjacent to the dining room is a sunken room called "The Cellar." In this room, there are an array of objects to gaze at. A huge fireplace is the center-piece for this exciting room. Among some of the objects hanging on the wall: a large slide ruler, a deer's head that is placed at the top of the fireplace, a weather vane, and three antique sleds. This room is also used for private parties or banquets for 25 people or more.

Most important is the outdoor patio. This is equipped with its own bar, which people can unwind or take in the warm evening air at a table while enjoying dinner.

Bartender Susan Suarez says the food is great and the patio area is really popular for dining. She said the patio should be open around June 1.

The building itself is 100 years old and throughout the years it has had many different personalities. In 1885, it was a dry goods business owned and operated by the Hilbrund family, who lived upstairs. In 1923, the business became the Southport Wetwash Co. The back part of the building ("The Cellar") was added to house a boiler room and a commercial laundry while the front stayed a public entrance. Sometime in 1940, the business changed hands and became the White Bunny Laundry. During this time sources say that this was allegedly a front for the largest bookmaking establishment on the North Side. In the 1960s it became a barbershop and a Vienna hotdog stand. In 1976, Larry Price bought the building from the Maria Harbeck estate. On Nov. 11, 1979, the doors opened to the public fulfilling Price's dream to make a hospitable environment for everyone to enjoy.

My dining experience was memorable. The burgers are not for shy people. They are succulent and the onion rings are perfect. Entrees run from at $7.95 to $15.95 and include a variety of sandwiches, salads, chicken dishes, steaks and ribs. Food specials are offered Sundays through Thursdays from 5 p.m. to 7 p.m.

Barfly Southport City Saloon-Spike's Rat Bar

In the bar area, they have four beers on draught; Rolling Rock, Leinenkugel's, Southport Lager Pale and Dark. The latter two are brewed in Wisconsin. To round the place out, the bar itself features two pool tables, a jukebox, and televisions surround the room along with video slot machines.

— *Lisa Gulotta*

Spike's Rat Bar
12 W. Elm St.
312-337-3200
Hours: 5 p.m. to 2 a.m. Sunday to Friday,
5 p.m. to 3 a.m. Saturday

Spike's Rat Bar is comfortably hidden off to the side of the Hangge Uppe's sign on Elm Street. But that's OK, it's always the better bars that are harder to find. Walking in, I immediately noticed a diverse crowd ranging from young attractive women to some old guy wearing a blue down coat, red down gloves and a red hunting hat. I guess that explained the 12-point buck tied up to the parking meter in front of the bar.

The interior is long and narrow. A pool table and a foosball table sit at the back.

Sue, the bartender, informed me on Thursdays they have $1.50 Special Exports, Special Ex Light, Michelob and Michelob Light. Not bad for a high-priced tourist-infested area.

No sooner had I written, "Spike's Rat Bar," on a piece of paper, then some dude approached me and asked:

Dude: Is this seat taken?

Me: No.

Friend of Dude: Willy!

I looked over my shoulder and recognized "Bill," an old neighbor. I usually bump into Bill about twice a year. For the record, Bill is doing fine. He's working at Great Ace. Bill's friend, Lyle, also works at Great Ace and is living with his Swedish girlfriend above the "Rat Bar." The building, he said, used to be owned by Al Capone.

According to Bill and Lyle, Spike used to be a Navy Seal and is a martial arts expert. He recently installed a glass cigar cabinet in back of the bar with temperature control and two humidifiers in it. On Fridays and Saturdays, the bar follows a strict policy: if a girl dances on the bar for three songs in a row, Spike buys a round of Kamikaze shots for every person in the bar.

On Sundays and Mondays, all food is half off. Bill suggested the 8-ounce New York strip sandwich, but I was not that hungry. Instead, I ordered the nachos. Fortunately, all food was half off because the bar was celebrating its Christmas party. I ordered the nachos with ground beef and Lyle bought beers

The North Side Spike's Rat Bar

for all of us.

The setting became the beginning of an Elvis concert. The lights dimmed and the theme song from "A Space Odyssey" began to play. A spot light illuminated a hot, wiggling plate of nachos on the bar in front of us.

Now, this just wasn't any normal nacho plate. These were the best nachos I have ever eaten in my life (picture a canyon echoing the last sentence three more times). A mound of culinary enigma with at least 16 different cheeses existed before our eyes. Rumor has it, a small town in Wisconsin (Milwaukee) is employed solely for the purpose of producing cheeses for Spike's nachos. Chunks of tomatoes glistened in the spotlight while marinated ground beef as big as hamburger patties rested atop a mound of killer, artery-clogging food. You couldn't even see the nachos. Plus, the cheese was layered so not one nacho was picked without a quarter pound of delicatessen hanging from it. The three of us ate. Lyle left halfway through. I got so full, I felt like an Oompa from Willy Wonka. Bill and I waxed off the rest of the cheese with just a couple chunks of ground beef left. I put them in my pocket and went home and threw them in the freezer. I'll use them for a BBQ on the first day of spring.

To sum it all up, "Spike's Rat Bar" is a rarity on the Rush and Division circuit. It's a great neighborhood bar to hang out at. Sue and Spike create a chemistry capturing the obvious, which is often overlooked: having fun.

— *Willy Laszlo*

Sports Corner
952 W. Addison Ave.
773-929-1441
Hours: 11 a.m. to 2 a.m. Sunday to Friday,
11 a.m. to 3 a.m. Saturday

Describing what it's like to attend the friendly confines of Sports Corner is a pretty tall order. An accurate assessment of this Wrigleyville staple depends largely on what the calendar says. When the Cubs are out of town it is a real Chicago kind of place. Small, upbeat crowds of locals and sponsored softball and volleyball teams dot the canvas during the week.

Sports Corner brandishes an ample sized bar and offers plenty of round table seating, including a sprawling outdoor patio complete with awning and a 60-foot maple tree. But when the Cubs are in town, all its small neighborhood appeal dissipates into a throng of tourists. On one day at least I saw a Cub fan beg a waitress to bite him. Another asked her if she had some friends that they could "conversate with," wink, wink.

It's true, when the Cubbies are the home team people seem to think that their mere presence is an automatic license to act like a laboratory monkey injected with an aging frat-boy virus. So, if you would rather get to a bathroom in less than four minutes, be heard without screaming and not pay $3.50 for a beer

Barfly Sport's Corner

(ouch), it is in a better interest to attend these services when the Cubs are visiting other quarters. If not for reduced beer prices then for untraditional munching.

One outstanding facet about Sports Corner is, not so much its location, but that it is getting a reputation among the neighbors for having the most eclectic bar menu in the city. Where else can you order a hot dog and brat as easily as (insert double-take here) blackened salmon and fresh grilled halibut in a mango pesto?

Behind this unusual fare is Lou, who in addition to concocting gourmet meals, also fires up a world-class chili that is developing a near cultish following. Breakfast is also available for harried yuppies who have gone unfed in their haste to make it to the "el" on time. If you are in the mood for something that is not on the menu, don't panic, Lou also takes requests for meals. One patron who told me he had a "hankerin' for Chinese food," was promptly served a plate of sweet and sour chicken. Undoubtedly by one of "the Corner's" impossibly gorgeous waitresses.

O.K. it's no secret that sports bars have an eye on the bottom line and, unless you were absent that day in Marketing 101, a beautiful waitstaff will sell beer. But Sports Corner seems to have a Ph.D. in winsome females, who possess enough charisma and electricity to light the bulbs in Wrigley for one of the night games.

Once you snap out of the effects from this estrogen bomb, there are seven TV sets crowning the main floor that, during football season, will have several different games on. An unscientific vote dictates which image gets the volume. There is also an upstairs bar with more TVs when it gets too crowded. Psst, go up there during Cubs games for a breather, you'll actually be able to sit down.

Cigars are available to the elite drunkards but for lesser complicated folk, the usual bar toys are there: pop-a-shot, video golf, darts and pool table.

The very accommodating waitstaff (even the bouncers are nice) and the old worldly charm of its chef is slightly tarnished by the rather chilly and brusque decision to have computerized, regulated pours and scanners that read beer bottles. Blechh!!

— Blair Cooke

293

Sporty's

5920 W. Fullerton Ave.
773-745-7756
Hours: 2 p.m. to 2 a.m. daily

As a lingerie fashion model, I find there are some bars I like to work at because the people are pretty nice and the money's OK, and there are some bars where I grit my teeth as I walk through the door because I know the money's no good and the people are assholes, and then there are the bars that I just put up with because the money is so good I can sorta overlook that all the people are assholes.

Sporty's is none of the above. It's one of the rare places I look forward to working and I don't even care about the money (much) because every time I go in there I have a blast. Sometimes I even forget that I'm there to do a job at all. Every time I visit Sporty's, something fun happens.

Like many places, the saloon itself is long and narrow, with a bar to the front and the pool table at the back. A couple of gaming machines and a jukebox make the decor complete. As in many places, there is an official bar cat who likes to make herself at home in my duffel bag. And as in many place, the clientele is working-class, and overwhelmingly male on fashion show nights (Fridays, 9-11). But the big difference at Sporty's is that unlike in most other bars (not to mention most other groups of humans, with or without alcohol), I seldom encounter that one rotten apple who spoils the bunch.

Once I had a couple of young Hispanic guys with limited English skills try to get out of line. Using my limited Spanish, I let them know that I was in no way pleased, and stomped off. Within a few minutes, another guy came over and told me his friends didn't understand why I was angry with them. When I explained (again) that I am a model, not a whore, the go-between went off and spelled it out to his friends. Soon all three of them came back, and the two offenders apologized! Turns out, in these guy's homeland, the prostitutes walk around bars in their underwear looking for customers. Well, I thought, that explained the confusion.

Another time, I broke up a frustrating slow evening by dancing the jitterbug and the East Coast swing with a guy named Vinnie. Now, mind you, this wasn't some guy pretending to dance and trying to hold me so close I could've gotten pregnant if I hadn't had nylons on. Vinnie was actually a really good dancer who could do everything from a polka to a waltz to a jig. I laughed so much that night my sides hurt, and I actually forgot I was wearing lingerie.

So, like I say, for good fun and good laughs, check out Sporty's. If the Friday fashion shows are any indication, just about any night of the week ought to be damn well entertaining.

Colleen's weekly schedule is available form the Sheer Madness office, 773-792-1293.

— Colleen O'Reilly

St. Pauli Bar
5109 N. Lincoln Ave.
773-769-1922
Hours: 8 p.m. to 4 a.m. Monday to Thursday,
4 p.m. to 5 a.m. Friday and Saturday, closed Sunday

St. Pauli's could be considered a home away from home to the regulars. At first glance, it really does appear to be the place "where everybody knows your name." If you ever find yourself this far north, St. Pauli's should be a spot to visit.

St. Pauli's is of German origin, but the inside features a kind of '70s-era bowling alley motif. A dim orange glow illuminates a central oval bar, a pool table, jukebox, Elvis tapestry and several video slot and poker machines, "for entertainment only," of course.

St. Pauli's has been around for 18 years. Margaret, its owner, just celebrated her 60th birthday, and still works behind the bar. The first time I showed up, I immediately liked the place. I met Anna, the bartender, who was sitting at the bar smoking and watching the "The Simpsons" on TV. She told me that she and the patrons have a lot of fun here.

The regulars, just like the neighborhood, are a blend of different ethnic backgrounds. You probably won't find a lot of college kids or trendsetters here. What you will find are regular folks there to drink or hang out with friends. The beer selection is limited to Old Style, Dab and Pschorr Brau Weiss on tap, and only seven bottle choices. But the tap beers aren't any more than $2, and the bottles $2.75. Mixed drinks aren't very popular, but Anna told me anything asked for can be made. I recommend her "ass-kicking" margarita for just $3.

On the second visit I made to St. Pauli's, Anna made me feel like I was a guest in her own home. Before she took her seat to watch "The Simpsons" again, she took money out of her own pocket and bought me a beer. She let me snoop around and ask stupid questions. And right before I left, she told me to come back. I think she really meant it.

St. Pauli's is a great place for a change from the busy Chicago scene. Show up late so you can enjoy your Jagermeister and play some old German standards for some drunken, stein-swaying sing-a-longs. Parking is a breeze, the bathrooms are immaculate, and I've never seen a cheaper cigarette machine in the city ($2.75). It might be worth the jog up north to find some good-hearted people and another home away from home.

— *Lee DiVita*

Stanley's Kitchen & Tap

1970 N. Lincoln Ave.

773-642-0007

Hours: 5 p.m. to 2 a.m. weekdays,

noon to 3 a.m. Saturday, noon to 2 a.m. Sunday

How could any self-respecting bar patron give a bad review to a bar that leaves a bottle of whiskey on the bar surrounded by shot glasses? At Stanley's, the bottle is there, wearing a label that says Kessler's and meant as a gesture of "appreciation" to visitors, according to one Stanley's staffer.

Whiskey for the taking is only one plus for Stanley's, located at Lincoln and Armitage avenues roughly equidistant from both Gamekeeper's and Sedgewick's. How many other bars do you know that have peanuts? Popcorn is everywhere, sure, and a few bars have pretzels. But peanuts? In baskets on the tables and in a barrel next to the jukebox, and yes, the shells are the things making that crunching noise as you meander around the bar.

The jukebox only has a couple of Clapton discs, but it's rich in other areas, with plenty of great country tunes and a terrific selection of Elvis Presley classics. One patron, his breath still smelling faintly of Kessler's, said it was a jukebox of "massive potential."

Four screens, a 30-foot bar well-stocked with bartenders, a few booths and some tables filling up the empty space make the tavern a tavern, though the swinging bench toward the back (liberated, I'd wager, from a suburban porch) makes for a Southern touch.

The menu, wearing the motto, "Home Cooking Always Pleases," only adds to the down-home ambiance. Though the bar portion of Stanley's could hardly be called dive-like, it still seems somewhat beneath the quiet, tasteful dining room located in the back. Served with such staples as hamburgers, cheeseburgers and steaks are macaroni and cheese, Southern-style fried chicken, catfish and "The Meatloaf." Desserts are apple pie, cherry popsicles and "Chocolate Something," and nothing on the menu breaks $9.

The meager tap offering is offset by the 17 different bottled beers. Want to hear about the nonalcoholic beers? I don't think so.

For the record, at least one November patron who said her name was Julie, called Stanley's a "cheesy meat market" and a "pickup bar."

This reviewer will be back to Stanley's, and not just to prove Julie right or wrong. Personal policy: when you know there's a bottle of whiskey waiting on the bar, go back until they take it away.

—*Kev Smith*

The Store

2419 N. Clybourn Ave.
773-871-6599
Hours: 2 p.m. to 2 a.m. weekdays,
2 p.m. to 3 a.m. Saturday, noon to 2 a.m. Sunday

If The Store on Halsted does not have enough space for you then try The Store on Clybourn. This bar generally has more of a blue-collar clientele than its Halsted Street sibling. During the week on Wednesdays nights, the bar has a Saturday night atmosphere when Volleyball teams sponsored by The Store pile in the bar.

One of the great things about this place is that the whole bar, including the upstairs back room with the pool table and the downstairs back room with the dart board, can be rented out. Operating in three-hour increments, the bar offers draft beer and well drinks for around $20-a-head and a full open bar for around $25-a-head.

Truth be told, neither of this bar or its sister on Halsted are the flashiest taverns in Chicago. There may be bigger bars, cheaper bars, louder bars and bars with live animals (Lincoln Avenue saucehounds will know what I'm taking about). But for the serious drinker, the person who knows how to get everything possible out of the Chicago drinking environment, The Store on Halsted and The Store on Clybourn are well worth knowing about.

— Kev Smith

The Store

2002 N. Halsted St.
773-327-7766
Hours: 3 p.m. to 4 a.m. weekdays,
11 a.m.to 5 a.m. Saturday, 11 a.m. to 4 a.m. Sunday

If you make them longer, they will come.

This is not necessarily sexual advice; instead, it's the key reason The Store maintains such popularity in a region well populated by fine taverns. It's tough to escape the logic that says an open bar at 3 a.m. is more inviting than a closed bar at 3 a.m. And with hours keeping the doors open until 5 a.m. every Sunday morning and 4 a.m. every morning after that, it should be clear why The Store is very inviting.

Of course, its hours are hardly the tavern's only attractive trait. It's got a prime location (Halsted Street and Armitage Avenue) that makes it perfect for either beginning or ending an evening, and while other regions of the city can be tough places to flag down a cab, taxis travel up and down Halsted right up until closing time.

Inside, The Store is split into two areas, with the narrow front room wrapped around more than 30 feet of classic bar, highlighted by a Jagermeister dispenser

297

that's likely dropped more people than former Bears' defensive back Doug Plank. The bar features six bottled import and 12 bottled domestic (14 if you count the non-alcoholic beers, which I don't). The Miller standards (Lite and Genuine Draft) are on tap, along with Bass Ale, Leinie's Red, Guinness and Molsen Ice. A multi-colored chalkboard just inside the door lists the specials.

The Store isn't the worst place in the world to watch a ball game, it's well short of being the best, as the placement of the screens in the front room will lead some patrons to watch through a mirror or at a distance of 30 feet or more.

Having dropped dollars at the bar, coins will be accepted by the wall-mounted jukebox, the dart and basketball games and two video gambling machines.

The backroom, serviced by one relatively small bar, would at first glance seem to make a good coatroom. But its dimensions, combined with furniture located only along the wall, allow it to accept a surprising number of drinkers. The same could be said of the rear third of the front bar: roomier than one might think. In truth, The Store itself has room, it's just that entering the bar on a crowded night is a battle and a half for the first 20 feet.

— Kev Smith

Subterranean

2011 W. North Ave.
773-278-6600
Hours: 4 p.m. to 2 a.m. daily.
Dinner served until 10 p.m. Sunday to Thursday,
until 1 a.m. Friday, 2 a.m. Saturday

With such a name, you'd think Subterranean is going to be underground, literally or figuratively, but it's actually three stories high, housed in an old banquet hall near Wicker Park's ground zero intersection. Subterranean bills itself as a cafe and cabaret, offering a full kitchen and live music, There seems to be a proliferation of establishments cropping up that offer the food/drinks/music trio, so each tries valiantly to distinguish itself. There's no question that Subterranean is in an excellent space and an enviable location, and it's been designed with an artisans touch that both creates a comfortable contemporary energy (pay attention to the sherbet-colored wall murals) while highlighting all the warmth of this vintage building (double-check the old chandelier upstairs).

The menu offers an interesting variety of eclectic American food, including St. Louis-style fried ravioli, sandwiches, pastas, risotto (a specialty that changes frequently and has been consistently good), Cajun dishes and a tremendous blackbean chili. All the entrees I sampled were well-cooked and tasty, the shrimp and sausage jambalaya earned a special personal mention.

The bar boasts an even dozen taps, with import and micro favorites getting

Barfly Subterranean-T&A Two

the limelight. Pricing was surprisingly reasonable for draughts and mixed drinks as well, preserving the generally economic beverage costs of the neighborhood. The main bar, to the right as you enter, offers lengthy accommodation for the social drinker, The reminder of the first floor, with the exception of a pool table, is devoted to dining space, with high tables, booths and banquet style furnishings. There is, in fact, a noteworthy amount of red velvet furnishing in Subterranean, which should bring out the Bela Lugosi in anyone.

The second floor houses the performance area, which has been showcasing familiar local talent like Underwater People, Bedbugs, Rockin' Billy etc. — fairly safe and reliable stuff that should suit the weekend "party band" crowd. The space is really well-suited for live music, offering good sight lines acceptable acoustics, especially from the third-floor balcony area. There's also another bar upstairs, more pool, and some bizarre phone booth/personal-sauna looking contraption that nobody can define, so make it what you will. Add to that plenty of crash corners and miscellaneous places to kick back. Overall, you can get fed very well at Subterranean and have plenty of room to relax, shoot a game or catch a background band afterward.

— Jay Ferrari

T & A Two

Southwest corner of St. Louis and Berteau
Hours: 3 p.m. to 2 a.m. weekdays, noon to 3 a.m.
Saturday, noon to 2 a.m. Sunday

In that 1976 made-for-TV classic, "Nightmare in Badham County," Deborah Raffin and Lynne Moody star as two UCLA students whose car breaks down in a small town. The evil sheriff Chuck Connors arrests them and the evil screw Tina Louise makes their lives a living hell on the prison farm. One of the coeds, if I remember correctly, dies during the big escape. My best friend, Kathleen, insists that similar peril awaits the pair of women who walk into a corner tavern called the T & A Two. All the more perfect, I thought, to fill Barfly's request for a "scary bar review."

The T & A Two is one of those side street corner bars that looks oddly inviting on a cold night. It's the type of tavern where you probably won't find the future spouse or even a one-night-stand. You imagine, however, that this kind of bar would be the perfect place to wrap up a romantically lonely evening — the perfect follow up for, say, a Swanson turkey dinner on Thanksgiving. The only problem is that you're too chicken to go in because it's probably packed with locals who wouldn't make you feel welcome. And you'd be right.

Like many corner taverns, the T & A Two's windows are just large enough to hold a neon beer sign. When you enter, the patrons glance at the unfamiliar form, but they don't sneer, jeer, or leer. They return to their conversations, and you are thereafter ignored. Which is fine, if that's what you want.

If you want to go even more unnoticed, don't wear anything bohemian, goth-

299

ic, or collegiate. This is a working class bar of middle-aged or near middle-aged security guards, construction workers, cops, and movers. They dress down in industrial-strength flannel over work pants and jogging shoes.

I've asked my friend Brian, a patron of the "theater real" as played out in the seediest Chicago taverns, to escort me. We get the standard once-over upon our entering. In our leather jackets, black boots and faded black jeans, we look like a couple of artsy-fartsy Michigan transplants exploring the city west of Western Avenue. We are carded. We clench our Miller High Lifes. We retreat to the far end of the bar.

Miller High Life is as good a choice as any at the T & A Two. The tap is long dry, so you choose among the bottles of Miller, Budweiser, and Old Style. At $1.75, a beer is cheap enough to occasionally lure in a younger neighborhood crowd on their way to a disco. Looking like he'd be more at ease at a disco, the young bartender, Sasha, explained that he used to tend bar in a 250-capacity dance club in his native Yugoslavia. He came to the United States a year and a half ago to help his Aunt, who bought the bar nine years ago. No, not even she knows what the "T & A" stands for and if there is a T & A One somewhere. As far as anyone can remember, it's been the T & A Two since it opened some 60 years ago.

T & A is in short supply at the T & A Two. I was one of three women of childbearing years in a crowd of about 25. Sasha said that this is basically a man's bar, kept alive by a family of seven brothers and their friends. The seven brides sometimes drop in, but will leave around 8 or 9 o'clock.

"When their kids turn 21, they start coming here," Sasha says. On cue, the telephone rings and the flannel-clad young man talking to the woman in the credit union T-shirt grumbles, "Oh, that's my ma calling."

The regulars are crucial to the T & A Two. Even those patrons who have escaped to the suburbs regularly return. The bar empties when a big family event, like a recent fishing trip, takes the group out of town.

Once back in town, it's back to the bar, which could easily pass for someone's clean, yet run-down rec room. Not only does duct tape hold together a few of the few stools, it keeps strips of carpeting wound around a pole near the entrance. A spare role sits behind the bar, ready for emergencies.

The decor is a mixture of Bud, Old Style, and Miller promotional paraphernalia, oversized posters with the local teams' schedules, and items honoring Vietnam veterans. Scan the room and you'll see a framed picture of Dennis Rodman, an "I wasn't there, but I care" bumper sticker, a Northwestern pennant, and a "you are not forgotten" banner. There's the requisite cigarette machine, pool table, electronic darts game, and jukebox filled with the standard discs as well as Dean Martin for the patriarchs.

The main draw, however, is sports television. When the satellite went out during a hockey game last season, the crowd went elsewhere for the duration of the game. Sasha makes another mental note to get that fixed before the football season gets serious.

During the big game, Sasha's aunt offers hot dogs or pizza, but hot food is

Barfly T&A Two-Tai's Lounge

otherwise not available. In addition to chips and Rolaids, you can nosh on beef jerky/cheese combination packs. To my left, someone buys two packs for a dollar. This is the first time I've seen jerky pass hands.

I'm able to stare at the exchange without a problem because I'm invisible in this bar. No one pays attention to the stranger once he's past the carpet pole. Sasha explains that he has seen the occasional stranger try to cozy up to the regulars by attempting to buy a round. The regulars refuse such offers. They don't take drinks from strangers.

I'm startled by someone saying "excuse me" as he moves toward the bar to order a beer. He takes it to a duct taped stool on the far side of the pool table. Sasha's eyes follow him and the bartender remarks, "He's never been in here before. Once he finishes that Icehouse, he'll leave." Sasha is almost right: the guy doesn't even finish one before bolting. My friend and I shake Sasha's hand, thank him, and follow the other stranger's tracks.

— Alice Bendig

Tai's Lounge
3611 N. Ashland Ave.
773-348-8923
Hours: 7 p.m. to 4 a.m. Sunday to Friday, 8 p.m. to 5 a.m. Saturday

Trends come and go in the bar business, but the popularity of a comfortable neighborhood tavern is timeless and enduring. Since 1961, Tai's Lounge has been such a place. Located one half block north of Addison on Ashland, Tai's is family owned and operated by the father and son team of Thomas "Thai" and Blake Itagaki.

"The neighborhood has changed over the years," said Thai, "but we still know 90 percent of our customers."

When the bar first opened, the crowd bellying up to the bar was predominately Irish and German locals. Today the area boasts a wide range of ethnic groups and a recent younger clientele has made Tai's a popular late-night stomping ground.

Arrive at 7 p.m. when Thai flicks on the pink neon sign and the regulars begin to wander in. The mood is friendly, relaxed and low-key. Thai greets everyone with a cheery hello and serves up an assortment of libations. Bottled beers are prominently displayed above slushy machines boasting Mai Tais from famed Chicago area restaurateur and family friend, Bob Chinn.

From opening until midnight, the regulars swap stories and kick back. After midnight, Blake takes over. He comes complete with his dad's friendliness and his own customer base. Just after his shift begins, new and younger faces fill the lounge.

Both the regulars and the younger crowd drift from the bar's front room, that also has a pool table, to a small hallway leading to a back room complete with ample seating and standing room. This is where the game of darts is given appropriate space to be played by both individuals and leagues. Dart teams gather to compete on Mondays, Tuesdays and Thursdays. Tai's has also sponsored softball and hockey teams.

In November of each year, Tai's usually celebrates its anniversary with complimentary buffet and raffle. Thai always has a few memories to share as the younger generation looks forward to another 35 years of a good family business.

— Cynthia Grows and Michael Cotter

Tailgators

2263 N. Lincoln Ave.
773-348-7200
Hours: 4 p.m. to 2 a.m. weekdays,
11 a.m. to 3 a.m. Saturday, and 11 a.m. to 2 a.m. Sunday

So, you got your big-screen TVs showing every possible sport being played in the United States, and probably some parts of Europe. You got your satellite dishes and your microbrews. And, as all things in bars and nature follow a certain course, you also got your baseball-hat-wearing patrons, your Alanis Morissette piped in during commercial breaks and lots of chicken wings and stuff.

On a pleasant Sunday evening, Tailgators is serving about 20 people. The huge front windows are thrown all the way open, and a pleasant breeze comes in. The large, nicely decorated room has tons of sports memorabilia adorning the walls. It also features a huge, gleaming bar.

Opie, a Tailgators regular, is earnestly trying to persuade someone named Paul to stay and play another round of video golf.

"Paul, just stay and play another 18."

"I'm out. I can't do it. Got too much work to do."

"Paul, it only takes 20 minutes."

"I don't got it."

Paul walks away. Opie shouts his name, one last time.

"Pauuuul ..."

And so it goes at Tailgators. I ask Opie why he spends so much time here.

"Look around," he says, pointing to seven 10-foot TV screens and more than a dozen smaller sets. "They've got every (satellite) package available here. I really love sports, and I can see anything I want at this bar."

Gregg Weinstein, Tailgators' general manager, confirms that his bar has the ability to pick up any sporting event in the country.

"We try to accommodate our customers and put on the games they want to watch," he says. "And the great thing is that we have so many TVs in here, that you can always see what's going on, even if it's something like a packed playoff game. We have the best TV definition around, too. Look at the quality of that picture. It's beautiful."

As Tailgators patrons gaze at the beautiful picture, they can choose from a

Barfly Tailgators-Teasers

larger than normal selection of beer, including Newcastle, Bells, Sierra Nevada, Guinness, Red Hook and Harp on tap. Bottled beers include Sam Smith and Hacker Pschorr Weiss. You can get Bud Light and Miller Lite on tap, too. (This is Lincoln Park, after all.) Beer prices range from $3 to $4. Mixed drinks start at $3.50.

If you work up an appetite, you're in better shape at Tailgators than you would be at most bars. Choose from a wide selection of starters, including the chicken wings and mozzarella sticks, but also some unexpected options such as hummus and a selection of salads. Heartier fare includes beef, turkey and veggie burgers with an assortment of toppers. Prices are reasonable, with appetizers starting at $1.75, burgers at $3.75 and sandwiches and other entrees between $5 and $7.

Opie recommends the fries. "They're incredible. Just like McDonald's."

As if we needed that extra encouragement.

The bar runs specials that change monthly. At press time, the lineup included $5.50 domestic pitchers on Mondays, $3 martinis on Thursdays and $3 bloodies on Sundays.

There are some other bells and whistles you should know:

You can buy cigars stored in a humidor behind the bar. Opie, who has been smoking cigars for about two years now, appreciates this special touch.

Tailgators brings in a deejay to spin on weekends, and hopes to offer dancing this summer. Tailgators is available for private parties. They're flexible on size and terms.

So, there you go. Good beer, nice space and access to any sporting event known to man. Check out Tailgators the next time the Bulls or the Chattanooga Lookouts are playing at home.

— Lisa Kueng

Teasers

7123 W. Higgins Ave.
773-775-7975
Hours: 1:30 p.m. to 2 a.m. Sunday to Thursday,
1 p.m. to 4 a.m. Friday, 3 p.m. to 5 a.m. Saturday

Teasers, set on Higgins by Harlem, is basically a pick up joint. It has a real nice interior with good sturdy bar stools and a nice bar counter. There is a huge TV screen for sports viewing, as well as many others sets inside the place to keep people entertained by video. Teasers has a very unique video presentation late nights. Sports videos can be seen, clips from games as well as other video presentations. I have spent many nights just looking at the TV screens and being very mused by the vid's. The place can accommodate quite a few people, and Teasers does attract a huge crowd on late Friday and Saturday nights when a DJ spins records for folks doing the twist on the dance floor.

An assortment of booze will keep any drinking soul going. On tap selections include Miller Genuine, Miller Lite, Michael O'Shea, Red Dog, Ice House, and Sam Adams. Pint taps will run $2, except Sam Adams which runs $3. There are about 10 different bottled beers. Domestics will run $2.25, imports $2.75. Mixed drinks start at $2.75 for well, $3 for call and $3.25 for top shelf. Mondays and Wednesdays are mug nights — you can buy a mug (35oz) for $3.50 and keep the mug. Refills are $1.75 after that. Only regular tap beers! It's a deal.

I've been to Teaser's quite a few times and failed miserably picking up women each time. Actually it is the place where one of the most embarrassing moments in my life occurred. I was power drinking T&T's for about four hours and I was soused beyond belief. It was about 11 p.m. — I scoped out a woman sitting down. I was tired of not saying anything to anyone so I got a spine and went up to her and introduced myself. I was slurring my words, and teetering just a tad. I can't remember her name, but we seemed to hit it off. We talked for about an hour. This woman was a bit on the muscular side. I would not classify her as dainty.

During our conversation it came up that she was a police officer. I freaked. Couldn't believe it. We started telling some jokes. She laughed at couple I told. I laughed at a couple she told. I figured that she was the type of chick who could take a joke so I asked her, "Hey on the job have you ever been mounted" I saw stars. Wow! What a right cross. My glasses went one way, I landed on the floor, and she ran out of the bar. I was shocked and humiliated. After shaking it off, I left. Believe it or not, few people saw what happened, and to my surprise, just one guy asked me if I was okay.

Yup, Teaser's.

— Gen eX alt

Ten 56
1056 N. Damen Ave.
773-227-4906
Hours: 4 p.m. to 2 a.m. weekdays,
4 p.m. to 3 a.m. Saturday, 6 p.m. to 2 a.m. Sunday

It was 5 p.m. on a Wednesday when I headed to my local health club with the best of intentions. Just then, I passed a bar on Damen Avenue, "Ten 56." I thought to myself, "I'll just stop in for one cold beer, then be on my way."

As I walked through the red padded vinyl door, though, I knew I was in for a unique experience.

Red lighting shimmered throughout the place, while white candles lined the bar. I caught a glimpse of the CD collection. It counted well into the hundreds.

The atmosphere was hip and kind of funky. As I scanned the list of cigars, I began to feel like Uma Thurman from "Pulp Fiction." I usually don't smoke cigars, but this place seemed to call for it. The one cold beer turned into three. And my resolve to achieve tight abs and lose five pounds fizzled away like the head on my beer.

Barfly Ten 56-Ten Cat Lounge

This bar is well stocked and serves excellent martinis. Three TVs dot the bar, although the music clearly dominates. More red padded vinyl coats the wall behind the bar, reminding me of the old drinking lounges populated by the old men from the neighborhood.

A disco ball hangs from the ceiling, and a pool table stands in back. A medieval-looking chandelier casts an orange glow over everything. The bathrooms are extremely clean and tidy, with a touch of potpourri.

Ten 56 opened in March 1997 and was formerly Sweet Alice. If you want to be part of a new hip bar in Wicker Park, free from big-haired suburbanites, straight-collared yuppies or your uncle, check out Ten 56.

Personally, I love the place, and will make it a regular stop.

— Christy K. Rizzo

Ten Cat Lounge
3931 N. Ashland Ave.
773-935-5377
Hours: 3 p.m. to 2 a.m. Sunday to Friday,
3 p.m. to 3 a.m. Saturday

Let's take a look. Napoleon was scared to death of them. Hitler hated them. On the other hand, the ever-hip Egyptians deified them, treated them as family members, and went so far as to execute anyone caught harming one of them. I'm speaking of course about your friendly domesticated housecat, which in recent years has usurped the dog's position as the favorite national animal. And why not? Cats are cool. Cats got style. Ever see a cat fetch your copy of Barfly 'cause you were too lazy to do it yourself? I think not. So, it's only appropriate that the Ten Cat Lounge, located on Ashland Avenue, be as diverse and individual as the species of its namesake.

Which brings me to the name. It's not Tin Cat as I've heard numerous times, or Ten Cats (plural) for that matter, but simply Ten Cat. Its name stems from the fact that the owners of the bar, Richard and Connie Vonachen, did at one point have 10 felines living with them in the apartment upstairs. Since opening the bar in 1991 (it was previously a vintage clothing store), the loft-style setting has attracted quite a loyal following. Locals speak of it almost reverently, and value its eclectic mix of customers and accoutrements. In fact, you could spend half the night just looking around.

This is just a sampling of what Ten Cat offers the attentive eye: mermaid lamps, one mounted sailfish, an extensive collection of plaster ashtrays, three games (including Asteroids), one dilapidated skylight, a back room for larger groups (possibly furnished by my grandmother), a number of easy chairs (the cardinal-on-tree-branches print has to be seen), local art which changes on a monthly basis, one church pew, and Ten Cat's centerpieces: two beautiful, regulation-sized Brunswick pool tables. Show up between 3 and 8 p.m. and pool is free every day. But be forewarned — bring your A-game, or you'll be swept under the proverbial rug.

Otherwise, check out the jukebox which offers a fine selection of blues and jazz and tap your feet on the hardwood floors. Chances are pretty good someone will strike up a conversation with you before long, whether it's a World War II vet drinking Scotch on the rocks or an art student with a Nutbrown Ale. And that's the thing. For every cat you can think of — be it a neighborhood tabby or a cultured Siamese — you can expect to find a person to match the description. And if you can wrestle a spot at the bar, you'll be dizzied by the overwhelming selection of bottled beers and top shelf liquors. So put this place on your must-see list. Who said curiosity killed the cat?

— Mike Curtin

Tequila Roadhouse
1635 N. Wells St.
312-440-0535
Hours: 10:30 a.m. to 4 a.m. Sunday to Friday,
10:30 a.m. to 5 a.m. Saturday

Look hard for this place on Wells as a 'Used Cars' old sign takes up most of the space on the sign board. But, with the large wall-sized windows in the front, it's difficult to miss the people quaffing a few.

In the front area lies a small wooden bar, tables, a long line of old vinyl car seats, probably taken from the same junkyard as the front sign, which add additional seating along the wall. Old car dealer, repair shops, and gas signs hang from the wall; even a 1950s gas pump stands at the end of the vinyl double seaters, as a cigar indian found in most ghost towns of the Old West is propped up at the other end. There's also a nice metal, shanty-type ceiling to finish off the garage feel. However, the bar offers a contrast to those.

The front bar is an old and wooden stand with a nice, rustic, cowboyesque theme. Longhorns are placed in the middle of the bar display with cows' skulls at each end. The wood is well worn, and the bar seems shorter than normal; I'm pretty sure it is.

Heading to the back, the semi-open kitchen stands out with a canopy over it with the front resembling that of a chuck wagon. This kitchen area also has a register for just shots and beers which is handy on busy weekend nights.

In the middle room is a slanted bar which rises up to the seating wrapped up and around it. And the TVs! There is plenty in this room along with a projection screen. Not a bad seat is found here to watch a game.

Finally, there is a small back room with a small bar, brighter lighting, and more wall-sized windows. Two pool tables take up the majority of this room. And, a DJ cage is located in the corner for requests.

The crowd is mainly young, sporty, Lincoln Park/Old Town types huddled in groups on weeknights, but Friday and Saturday brings packs in for a free for

Barfly Tequila Roadhouse-Texas Star Fajita Bar

all. Thursdays draws the best sized crowds and offers a good night to try out this place. It is mainly a misplaced Division Street bar.

The music is a mixture of 1950s through 1990s pop, but stuff not normally played on the turntable.

There are a lot of specials throughout the week consisting of food and drink.

Texas Star Fajita Bar
2259 N. Lincoln Ave.
773-871-7788
Hours: 11:30 a.m. to midnight daily

When you walk into the Texas Star, it is kind of like walking into an old watering hole in Texas. There is a very-southwestern feel to it. It isn't very trendy though. There is nothing really "Chili's" about it. Old wood floors and miscellaneous wall hangings give it a very rustic and friendly atmosphere. We sat at a table right next to their huge front windows, which were open. It was very nice to sit in a place that was virtually outdoors. I was sitting inside feeling the breeze, feeling the sun, watching walkers pass by and just feeling good.

I ordered by first Dos Equis and was a little disappointed with myself. I did not properly peruse the menu. I found out that the main drink special at Texas Star is a cold bucket of four Lone Star bottles for seven bucks. This is a great deal. My drink was already at my table and opened by the time I could have changed my order; what a sad, sad state of events.

My girlfriend got a margarita, she claimed it was specifically for my review but I am actually not that slow. When she ordered her third round I knew she was no longer taste testing the concoction they created but she was actually getting buzzed. There is a wide range of drinks at Texas Star and they have specials on their shots of Tequila. It is a fun room to drink in. This is especially because of the windows; open air really makes the alcohol pour down fast.

The two of us ordered entrees and were knocked out by the punch this place has to offer. This is not average bar food. Their food is fantastic. I had fajitas (must have been subliminally seduced by the bar name) and loved them. Good portions at a good price. Steak smothered in peppers and onions put on some tortillas with rice and beans makes a happy stomach. Emily had a veggie burrito and she hardly touched it. It was so damn big! The waitress asked her, "Did you not enjoy this?" She explained she loved it, it was just so overwhelmingly big. I admired her attempt to take down the monster and must admit, I don't know if I could have done it. It is quite a feast.

Afterwards, we got ready to leave. I asked the waitress if I could go through the large open window instead of th door. She let me. I hopped out the window and Emily did the same. As soon as she saw me acting like a child, I guess she had to follow suite. Texas Star Fajita Bar is a great place to hang out and eat. I guarantee a good time and who knows, maybe you'll get to jump out of a window too.

— *Scott Tipping*

The North Side Thatch Pub-The Big Horse
Thatch Pub
5707 N. Milwaukee Ave.
773-774-9868
Hours: 10 a.m. to 2 a.m. weekdays,
10 a.m. to 3 a.m. Saturday, 11 a.m. to 2 a.m. Sunday

One of Chicago's greatest gifts is the variety that it offers its residents. Besides the wide range of delicious foods, there are a great number of interesting drinking establishments that grace this city. In my latest journey, I visited the Gladstone neighborhood on the Northwest Side and its Thatch Pub.

When walking into this pub, you will first notice its small size. This drinking establishment quickly fills up on weekend nights and sometimes you will feel a bit cramped. In spite of this drawback, this is a cozy pub. There is Harp and Guinness on tap for $3 a pint. Why go overseas when you can enjoy the Irish culture right here in Chicago.

In addition, every Friday and Saturday there are live Irish and folk players with no cover charge. The stage is very small so don't expect U2 or the Pogues to play here. Besides musical entertainment, there are two dart boards, a jukebox and two television sets.

The decor of this pub is quite comfortable. It has the classic Irish setting. It sits about 40 people and has panel walls that give you the home feeling.

Being an Irish pub, the crowd that visits here is generally 90 percent Irish. Being an ethnic bar, there is a wide age group that visits this establishment as well.

If you are in the Gladstone neighborhood, the Thatch Pub is well worth the stop.

— *Pete Schmugge*

The Big Horse
1556 N. Milwaukee Ave.
773-384-0043
Hours: 6 p.m. to midnight weekdays,
5 p.m. to 2 a.m. Saturday, 5 p.m. to 1 a.m. Sunday

Like the children's book "The Lion the Witch and the Wardrobe," where a rip in the fabric of time leads to a mythical other dimension hidden within an unassuming closet full of clothes, here too lies a dark and smoky land of mystery, intrigue and occasionally diseased puppet shows concealed behind a deceptive store front called The Big Horse.

Being that I live in the general neighborhood, I must have walked by the place at least a hundred times before realizing this bar ever existed. Big Horse is camouflaged from the prying eyes of anyone passing by on the street.

Were you even specifically looking for it, it would still call for some pretty tough detective work to track it down. From a cursory glance at the outside

Barfly The Big Horse

shell, it looks to be just an ordinary take-out burrito joint, imperceptibly blending in with the dozens of other Mexican restaurants that line Milwaukee Avenue. But one must dig deeper to discover the true heart and soul of this treasure. Dig deep past the fiery gusts of sticky, jalapeño flavored heat streaming out through the entrance. As you walk in the door feel the suffocating aroma of burrito grease billowing from the beanery's kitchen and assaulting your senses as you make your way inside and then finally out the back exit for the location of your destination, The Big Horse Bar.

Its atmosphere is not unlike that of your local, old-man type bar (in a good way, though) with a pool table and a jukebox greeting you at the door. Shadowy, cavernous lighting hides the lines in the hardened faces of its patronage. A murky stillness lingers in the air, broken only by occasional clouds of nicotine-laden fog rolling overhead.

Surveying the decor of the place, I was struck by an amazing collection of cartoon-like advertisements for Budweiser stuck up and down the wall leading to the bathroom/stage area in the front. A remnant from some banned ad campaign geared towards bringing 10-year-old boys into the Anheuser-Busch fold, the comic-book-style posters depict mainly scenes of flashy stock cars whipping around a dream-like race track and cowboys riding atop neck-snapping bulls at a rodeo (both of which activities, whether as a spectator or a participant, are best experienced when totally ripped on the "King of Beers," by the way). Each advertisement contained the omnipresent logo and refreshing bottle of Bud hovering over the rugged action.

Gazing upon these mighty testimonials to the indisputable link between beer consumption and increased virility and testosterone levels, I was filled with an overwhelming urge to go off, slam down a six-pack of brew and either climb Mount Everest with my barehands or head to the zoo and sucker-punch a rhinoceros. Cooler heads prevailed, however, when my friend reminded me that all the beer in the world wouldn't make me any more of a man (especially in light of that sex-change operation I had last fall). We decided to stay and see the band that the waitress told us was coming on soon (local music can be heard there every Thursday, Friday and Saturday night).

We then bellied up to the bar, ordered ourselves some local anesthetic (bottles of Bud were $2 a piece and is their best deal since they have no beer on tap), snagged a table for ourselves and watched as the homey little bar filled up with people and rapidly took on the air of a cool, little underground nightclub. We sat and drank for an hour 'cause the group was late (a tardy band? Blasphemous!) and when they finally did get onstage, they decided to put on a performance art piece with some puppets instead of playing a set.

What could've been an interesting change of pace, however, turned into an uninspired, 90s-update of the old Punch and Judy routine with musical accompaniment by some soulless guitar cretin who played nothing but bad retreads of Led Zepplin and AC/DC riffs over puppeteering that was about as entertaining as watching sausages hanging in a butcher's window. I refuse to let this one dark cloud sully my opinion of this bar, however, and would definitely return to this swell groggery in a second if not for the fact that I lost my I.D. that night. If anyone happens to run across it, I'm begging you to please send it to me care of the Barfly as soon as possible. Without my Driver's License, I'll be shut out of virtually every bar in town and forced to give up my new job as a driver for Renoir's Pet Taxi and Poodle Limo Service.

— Brian Farrelly

The Montrose Saloon
2933 W. Montrose Ave.
773-463-7663
Hours: 2 p.m. to 2 a.m. weekdays,
noon to 3 a.m. Saturday, and noon to 2 a.m. Sunday

The Montrose Saloon, is a place where you can go to drink, talk and shoot pool. It ain't about anything else but that.

It's a small bar on a corner in a working class neighborhood with a friendly down-to-earth atmosphere. It feels like being welcomed into someone's home when you first enter.

The owner Barbara has had the place for 14 years and has won herself a loyal clientele. Once a year she sponsors a family outing with grilled food and free soda for the kids. She'll throw the occasional bash for a major sporting event and even sponsors athletic teams.

So it should surprise no one that, following her husband's death in 1992, the regulars got together and poured the concrete for her new beer garden at no charge.

The beer garden is small and simple in design, with five sizeable picnic tables and a heavy wooden fence to muffle the sound of traffic. No, the garden is not tree-lined, but I've spent a few hot summer nights there with good friends and cold beer. Besides, all the tree-lined beer gardens I've been to in my days come equipped with loutish yuppie-boys who just discovered cigars.

Just off the beer garden are horseshoe pits, where the regulars like to play but is open to everyone. Never played the game myself, but I'll learn this summer. Unlike the nightmare bars in Lincoln Park, beer is priced right. Old Style and Lite Beer taps are 75 cents Monday through Thursday and pitchers of the same are $4.

Four dollars! Try finding that around Wrigley Field. Also on tap is Weinhard's Boars Head Red, a beer with a bit of a kick to it. The Montrose Saloon features specials Monday through Thursday on their bottled beers. Monday-Miller, Tuesday-Bud, and Wednesday-Old Style, all for $1.25, on Thursday, imports are $2.

So if you're looking for a place that is easy on the wallet and easy on the attitude, park yourself at the Montrose. And make sure behave yourself when leaving, it's a quiet neighborhood.

— Dan Tucci

The Sea of Happiness
640 N. Wabash Ave.
312-787-2721
Hours: 11 a.m. to 2 a.m. daily

Three years ago The Sea of Happiness, a cozy little Downtown lounge at the foot of the Hotel Cass, was really great place. The jukebox had 45s in it, and there was a Pac-Man machine in the corner. You could order a can of beer from the transvestite bartender (well, some people thought she was) and listen to old Prince singles (from when he was still Prince).

Imagine my disappointment when I rediscovered The Sea of Happiness. The old jukebox is now full of CDs; Pac-Man is gone, and three video slot-machines are in its place. A sign above reads: *No Gambling or Cussing or Spitting.*

I sat down at the bar and ordered a can of Bud. The bar also has Bud Light, Coors Light, Old Style and Miller Lite. Sure, you could get a bottle if you wanted, but where's the novelty? Besides, no glass is allowed at the beach.

I sipped my beer and looked around, noting the prominent nautical theme. Life preservers, giant fish and tiny ships hang throughout the room (after too many, they begin to interact with one another). The clock behind the bar is a porthole.

There are also the few leftover Christmas decorations and a lovely string of red jalepeño lights bordering the room. A sign posted on the mirror behind the bar reads: *No Credit, Please Don't Ask. Thank you, we appreciate your patronage. Captain George and staff.*

"Are you Captain George?" I asked the bartender. At first he denied it, but through a thick Greek accent, he disclosed his identity, saying that he had been the proprietor of the "S of H" for 11 years.

I went to flip through the selection on the CD juke and found, among newer stuff, Elvis and some Greek bouzouki music. I played "Hound Dog" and "The White Rose of Athens."

There is a minimal amount of Chicago sports paraphernalia. George likes the Bulls, but he really loves the sea. Three TVs line the back wall to ensure you don't miss the big game.

"I like this place," I thought, finishing my beer. Pac Man or no Pac Man, The Sea of Happiness is still great. I crumpled my beer can, like a good sailor, and said goodnight.

— *Donna Donato*

Theresa's Red Door Inn
3656 W. Fullerton Ave.
773-342-5850
Hours: noon to 2 a.m. daily

In making my first visit to Theresa's Red Door Inn, I was surprised because it is located in the Logan Square neighborhood. The outside decor reminds me of a pub in the Alps. When I walked in, I was greeted by a smiling face. She could have easily been related to one of the St. Pauli Girls.

The size of the bar is small, but welcoming. There are three tables on the west side while two window tables are at the front. There are three video poker games and a pinball machine. Also, there are two televisions on both sides of the bar.

The beer garden seems to be an island off a busy and noisy Fullerton Avenue. There are tall wooden fences and tall maples that help to block off the noise from the street. Also, there is a tall fence that blocks the alley view which makes the outside experience more pleasant. There are many beer signs which include Gosser, Miller, Bud, St. Pauli and Michelob. As a security measure, there were pointing nails sticking out on top of the fence, especially at the front.

Theresa's beer garden is a good place to relax and enjoy a bottle of Dabs for a mere $2 while the special of the month was Ceros Royal from Denmark for $1.75. If you are on Fullerton Avenue near Central Park (3600 W) check out this pleasant neighborhood treat.

— Pete Schmugge

Thurston's is one of the best rock venues in Chicago. Pictured here is Herb Rosen and Mike O'Connell of Beer Nuts, during an October, 1998, performance.

Thurston's

1248 W. George St.
773-472-6900
Hours: 6 p.m. to 2 a.m. weekdays, 6 p.m. to 3 a.m.
Saturday, 2 p.m. to 2 a.m. Sunday

Thurston's is one of Chicago's most unique bars. It is housed in a former meat packing house and owner Mark Romano has converted the place into an exciting two-floor rock 'n roll diner.

The first floor features a marble bar with comfy stools and plenty of tables, chairs and a couch. The ceiling is made up of wood rafters which have various trinkets hanging from them such as chili beans and bells. There's also a pool table, pinball and electronic darts. But what really makes the first floor is the tasty Italian food made special by Romano.

After a hardy meal patrons can wander up swivel stairs to the second floor where some of the best local and national alternative rock bands perform. The upstairs room is rectangular shaped, has a bar, several red couches, tables chairs and a stage which is just at the perfect height so the bands can be viewed without any obstructions. The room has track lighting and the stage has Christmas lights. The acoustics in the room are amazing, usually in small rock clubs the sound gets lost and muddled but at Thurston's the sound is great.

Those who hang out at Thurston's are usually young and hip and include members of Chicago bands such as Smashing Pumpkins, record label people and recording engineers such as Steve Albini.

To drink, the bartenders, who are all involved in the music industry, serve a variety of cocktails and bottled beers such as Miller, Leinenkugel's, Rolling Rock, Becks' and Heineken. On draft there's Ice House and Blackthorn Cider.

And when drinking in Thurston's you may want to be aware of the staff motto, "If you don't drink here, we will."

The bar is named after "Gilligan's Island" character Thurston Howell. The

TV show is a favorite of Romano who used to own a bar called Gilligan's.

Romano is an active owner who always finds new ways to entertain his patrons. He recently purchased an all-ages license from the City of Chicago so patrons of all ages can enjoy some of the hottest live acts and some of the best food in Chicago.

Timothy O'Toole's

622 N. Fairbanks Court
312-622-0700
Hours: 11 a.m. to 3 a.m. Monday to Sunday

Descend to the depths of Timothy O'Toole's located a couple blocks off the "Magnificent Mile." In a smattering of green, there is something for almost every taste. There are raised tables and booths to eat at or slurp those suds. There are plenty of waitresses roaming the bar, whether you are sampling the cuisine or just having a few. There is ample seating at the rectangular bar which fills the middle of the bar.

In the back there is a small room containing two pool tables, funky-colored sofas, and a couple of small, raised tables large enough to rest your pitcher and glasses on as well as a wide screen television. There is really just room enough for the pool players and challengers. There are also three pool tables near the bar, but slightly sectioned off to prevent run-ins. Along the back wall are two pinball machines, a video game, and two draw poker machines. In the south wall there is a niche with two electronic dart boards and the house has darts. The niche helps to keep crowds out, but it can be pretty tight if you have neighbors. More than 20 televisions line the ceiling and a large-screen glows in the back.

O'Toole's has a wide variety of tap and bottled beers and a tasty menu featuring ribs, fajitas and burgers.

T.J. Twisters

7021 W. Higgins
773-775-0036
Hours: 3 p.m. to 2 a.m. weekdays,
3 p.m. to 3 a.m. Saturday, noon to 2 a.m. Sunday

When I first saw Monty across the bar at T.J. Twisters, I thought Dragnet. But what I had mistaken for a dark-suit white-shirt slim-tie ensemble was actually an American Airlines gate agent's uniform.

That makes sense because T.J. Twisters, located on the edge of the Northwest side, is relatively close to O'Hare. Monty is not the only airport employee among the patrons. Maria, one of the owners, likes that.

"It's not a punky crowd — not a problem crowd," she said. People who work all day with the public know how to treat other people in public places. "A

Barfly T.J. Twisters-Tommy's on Higgins

woman can feel safe in this bar."

I felt safe but a little uncomfortable as I entered alone on the early end of a Thursday night. The 'not a regular' sign was blinking over my head. But after the requisite beer, I could relax enough to see that Twisters is in many ways the typical working-class sports bar. The clientele, ranging in age from 21 (the bartender cards) to the late fifties, includes the requisite Tim Allen and David Caruso look-alikes. The Marlboro Red to Marlboro Lights ratio is 2:1. Beers sell for $3; domestic pitchers $6. A "grub and a Bud for a buck" special is offered during Monday night football games. A condiment station sits parallel to the "Cherry" card machines.

Regulars tell tales of shot consumption and about patrons Sweet Cheeks and Snuggles. Things are done "for shits and giggles." People are humble and blunt, with one guy prefacing a statement with, "It sounds stupid — and it is stupid!"

But the bar stands out on a couple of points. Unlike neighbor Teasers, Twisters doesn't charge a cover for Friday and Saturday dancing to a DJ. The menu includes filets and ribs. You can find street parking within steps of the entrance.

If you want more of a meal than a microwaved pizza and don't require a beer better than a Sam Adams, visit Twisters.

— Alice Bendig

Tommy's on Higgins
6954 W. Higgins Ave.
773-631-4451
Hours: 4 p.m. to midnight Sunday to Thursday, 2 p.m. to 2 a.m. Friday and Saturday

The thing I think that makes Tommy's great is the fact that it is packed on a Friday or Saturday night. The crowd that hangs there is mixed in age, but has a tendency toward the early to mid-twenties. To get a seat is often a challenge. The bar is a loud boisterous place teeming with social activities. I recommend going into Tommy's on a busy night only. I have been there on a quiet night, and don't recommend it.

After hanging around a while, most people are easy to talk to and don't really have that bad attitude the goes along with some bars. The place is packed and jockeying for space can be a problem. I found that trying to compete for space and it became almost like a game for me: I would stand in one place and then get bumped around into another spot.

The are several beers on tap (glass $1.75). Bottles start at about $2.25. During the football season there are specials during the week to keep everyone entertained. That's about the only time you can get to the dart boards. I believe the bar sponsors some sports teams. If you are in the area Tommy's is a definite don't miss on packed Friday or Saturday nights.

— Gen eX alt

Pictured here is Tony, the kind proprietor of Tony's Place, 2635 N. Central Ave.

Tony's Place

2635 N. Central Ave
773-889-4175
Hours: opens between 1 and 3 p.m. and closes at 2 a.m.
Sunday to Friday, opens between 3 and 6 p.m.
and closes at 3 a.m. Saturday

If you want a pint of pale ale, a good burger, and the company of ultra-professional patrons, then you want to be somewhere other than Tony's Place. But there's no crime in not wanting these things once in a while, and that's why a trip to Tony's Place might trip your fancy.

Every bar has certain atmospheric attributes, and I think Tony's lack of trying to make his place look special is the exact thing that makes it just a bit special. St. Patrick's Day and Bud Bowl VI pendant are still strewn across the ceiling, and for some reason they do not take away from the charm, they in fact add to it. So does the Christmas wreath that still hangs beside the front door. Even the grammatically incorrect banner behind the bar denoting that on Thursdays, domestic " beer's" are a dollar, doesn't seem out of place at all.

There is one piece of art hanging on Tony's wall that I'm certain is a collectors' item. It is a large, framed landscape scene, and the windows of the cottages depicted light up with an eerie glow. It is above the pool table, and if it is not illuminated when you step in, go ahead and turn it on yourself-no one should mind. Another wall hanging I enjoyed was the Bob Talbot photo of the dolphins (which every yuppie on Lake Shore Drive had in their dining room a few years ago), unframed and stapled askew to the wall behind the bar. It seems almost like inadvertent snub to the aforementioned yuppies.

The single nicest thing about Tony's is the bar itself — heavily lacquered

Barfly Tony's Place-Toons

dark wood that Tony himself rubs with club soda. You can see yourself in it. After a few $2.50 large mugs of Dab or call mixed drinks, you can see several of yourself.

There's the typical pair of video poker machines by the door and pub darts by the pool table. And though you won't find the new Alice In Chains on the CD jukebox, if you leave a note, you may find it the next time you're in, amid the wonderful selection of AC/DC and the like.

Tony himself is a friendly, welcoming Croatian-American man. The crowd he gathers is completely different. At some taverns the regulars are hostile, while at others they are cordial. The regulars at Tony's are neither. They don't seem to care if you're there or not, which in itself is refreshing. This means you will seldom get a second glance unless you are a complete frothing lunatic, and sometimes, I'm sure, not even then.

When I asked Tony what time the bar opened, he said, "I don't know, my wife won't tell me," whatever that means. Tony also said that he's the only one in the neighborhood that serves Weiss beer. But even if he didn't, Tony and his place are just eccentric enough to make this tavern much more comfortable, yet that much more twisted, than the average shot and a beer joint.

— BUD

Toons

3857 N. Southport Ave.
773-935-1919
Hours: 3 p.m. to 2 a.m. Monday to Friday, 11:30 a.m. to 3 a.m. Saturday, 11:30 a.m. to 2 a.m. Sunday

What can I say about Toons after 200 visits? OK, so I exaggerate. When I lived near this neighborhood bar a couple years ago, I was a weekend regular. I can't say exactly how many times I ate and drank there, but it was often. Returning, my first impression was that it just wasn't the same. But as I watched the World Series, I compared this trip to some of my early drinking experiments and remembered that Toons is the kind of place where repeated visits breed a kind pleasant familiarity and a sense of ownership. What can I say? The more you go there, the more you want to go there.

One of the first things you notice when you walk into Toons is surreal lighting that shows up around the bar in colors of yellow, red and blue. The theme seems to be a kind of cartoonist effect that highlight brightly colored everyday objects grouped in paintings on the walls. There is a fairly average bar-type menu that has shrunk noticeably over the years, along with your usual selection of beer brands and liquor. However, I still heartily recommend the turkey melt — it's on Boboli bread with melted cheese and Thousand Island dressing (I skip the tomato).

My favorite thing about Toons besides the Foosball table and pool table is (this will sound weird until you go there at night) the hallway leading to the bathrooms. It's very dark except for tiny glow-in-the-dark stars and planets

317

sprinkled on the walls and ceiling. There's a black light effect going on, making your white clothes glow eerily. I don't know about you, but my wait becomes more interesting when I'm staring at other peoples' clothes in the psychedelic spirit of the early 1970s.

You may have gathered from the black light remark that Toons tends to be a late twenties/early thirties crowd. They're a fairly diverse lot for the area, and every once in a while you'll run into a middle-aged couple or a bunch of college students.

Toons is located at the northern tip of the West Wrigleyville area on Southport Avenue that extends south to Belmont and beyond with trendy new and not-so-new restaurants and bars. Yet, it's slightly west, so you see elements of the artsy-crowd that moved away from the lake. All in all, Toons is a satisfying experience that is remarkably down-to-earth and relaxing. And oh yeah, it's a good place to watch a Bulls game, too.

—Stephanie Behne

Top Hat Lounge
1414 W. Morse Ave.
773-465-8255
Hours: 7 a.m. to 4 a.m. daily

The Top Hat Lounge, snuggled between restaurants and liquor stores on Morse Avenue, looks more like a half-seedy motel than a workday watering hole. The closed venetian blinds that hide the 11 a.m. subterranean drinkers from the sun's dangerous ultraviolet rays also close out all but the devoted seeker of suds and spirits.

I first stumbled into the Top Hat one fine evening when my personal stash of brew had run dry. Searching for any pool-tabled, jukeboxed port in a quick sobering storm, I had to knock twice before the bar matron unlocked the door. What I found was pure drinking simplicity. The bartendress, a stout, ageless, white-haired woman was more than happy to inform me that they had no beers on draft, and that the three varieties of Miller they sold were all $2 (I believe they also had Heineken for $3, but...).

The long linoleumed bar runs just far enough toward the back of the bar to allow one six-foot pool table with ample room for strangers-to-the-scene to shoot stick comfortably. Along the bar, and in the several booths sit the real stars in the Top Hat stable: steadfast drinkers who have conditioned their innards sufficiently to make the bar's bathroom seem obsolete.

It is 2:30 a.m. Hanging on for squatter's rights on the front stools of the bar are the same two or three grizzled old men who were there at 11 a.m. They don't say anything and their beers are always half full. Hiding under their mesh of baseball hats, they just stare in various directions for long periods of time, occasionally tipping their elbows. The earth does not move for these men. At the other end of the slab are the two upstarts, old men in practice. One of the

Barfly Top Hat Lounge-Trader Todd's Adventure Bar

two bar matrons spends half her evening tending in some form or another to their needs, be it a fresh beer or a tip-teasing comeback to their flirtation. In a poofy, battered winter coat with fluorescent stripes, caroming along the bar's edge, is a faceless female conglomeration of hair, denim and drink. "Paint It Black" is on the jukebox and the female goes into barely rhythmic, unbalanced contortions, inviting the loudest of the burly, mustached barfly apprentices to dance.

"Aaaw, honey, I'd love to. Believe me. I can't hardly walk," he splurts, spinning his stool to face her and halfheartedly waving his arms to the music. But she won't go away that easily.

"I broke my last leg last month. I can't even walk. I'm sorry honey."

She doesn't care anymore. She does a half-solo-tango back to her stool. "Takin' Care of Business" continues the nightly classic rock ritual. It is followed by the Stones' "Time Is On My Side" and Seger's "Like a Rock." All of this is to the sing-along joy of "the man who couldn't dance," who now rises from his perch and strides fluidly to the bathroom without the hint of a limp.

In the meantime, I order another. While waiting at the bar, I notice a 50ish year-old woman who alternately looks over her shoulder, muttering something to someone I'm sure she can see. Behind her, enjoying each other's loud company is a group of four grumpy, rumpled businessmen with their dates. The old men still haven't moved, but now they're staring at football highlights on television.

What ended up as a desperation attempt at further libation turned out to be as close to fraternal company as one can get without breaking the solace of a lonely night's drinking. This is the just reward for spending a late night in a bar that has no exterior invitation, but puts its name only on the coasters under the cold and strong drinks that it serves.

— *Chris Handyside*

Traders Todd's Adventure Bar
1157 N. Dearborn St.
312-943-3944
Hours: 4 p.m. to 4 a.m. daily

At the end of August 1997, after 28 years, owner Nick Loane sold O'Leary's to make way for Trader Todd's Adventure Bar, which continues as a 4 a.m. bar.

"I intend for this to be a true adventure bar in every way," owner Todd Hyatt said. "The employees each have adventuresome interests and backgrounds. We interviewed as many as 200 people for each of the positions."

Todd then introduced some of the people working Friday evening: Brian Yehl, rock climber and former Chippendale dancer; Boyena, former Yugoslavian pilot; Michelle Lacy, commercial and theater actress (Michelle worked recently on IBM and Ivory Snow commercials); Joe, a stand-up and television comedian; and Jennifer Davis, a surfing champion bored with her numerous jumps into volcanoes.

319

The North Side Trader Todd's Adventure Bar-Tres Amigos

Davis has now elected to spend more of her time surfing and hang gliding. Another hang glider is Patrick Fegan, who has worked as a "spotter" for the U.S. Forestry and Agricultural bureaus.

"A 'spotter' is one who, either by airplane or hang gliding, spots for forest fire fighting and for pollutants in the water," Patrick explained. "It's great to combine something that you enjoy with something occupationally useful."

Each one of the employees could easily be magazine or television models. When you combine their attractive appearances with their winning personalities and interesting pastimes, you can't help but be intrigued.

"We're going to have a lot of adventures for the enjoyment of the customers and staff," Todd says. "We have a number of trips planned like skydiving, ski trips, scuba diving in the Caribbean and a bus trip to the Bears game in Detroit. We want to make Trader Todd's a continually changing and interesting place to come. This is a neighborhood corner bar with an emphasis on adventure."

Todd is the name sake of his great, great grandfather Todd, an explorer and treasure hunter in the Caribbean Islands.

"Everything in here is for sale," Todd says. "A lot of this stuff is from my forefather Todd's collection."

Beginning in September, Todd's will be the location for a cable access comedy talk show hosted by Joe "The Bartender" Guse. Among Joe's adventures is that he attended school in Las Vegas. When I told him that I was born in Las Vegas, N.M., he told me that he had been there and that this Sande de Cristo Mountain village had quite an interesting history. Las Vegas, N.M., is where Doc Holiday and Wyatt Earp met before locating in Tombstone, Ariz.

In the later hours on Friday evening the pool table was busy, the bar and tables became crowded and the mood was fairly bar typical. Then an overpowering bullhorn announcement blasted, "Attention! Attention! We are going to auction off this bottle of Heineken beer. Who will give me one cent?"

Joe held several auctions for everything from bottles of imported beer, which sold for $2, to a bottle of Champaign, which sold for $14.

When you come down to the Gold Coast, keep Trader Todd's in mind. It's an experience and an adventure I think you'll thoroughly enjoy.

Don't expect the bar to be the same every time you visit, though. This Gold Coast bar is a constantly evolving place to party.

— J. Quillian

Tres Amigos
3625 N. Harlem Ave.
773-736-1484
Hours: 11 a.m. to 10 p.m. Tuesday to Thursday, 11 a.m. to 11 p.m. Friday and Saturday, noon to 9 p.m. Sunday

I'm going to share a secret with you. If you have started your partying on the Northwest Side somewhere other than Tres Amigos, you have made a grave error. Though not much more than a store-front upon first glance, it will quick-

Barfly Tres Amigos

ly become one of your favorite stops. Okay-technically it is not a bar (in fact this restaurant can't even boast a lounge), but any place with this warning printed right on the menu, "Our margaritas are wonderful but wicked. More than two can be hazardous," deserves a review in Barfly, as well as continued patronage.

During the summer months Tres Amigos opens up its beer garden. It is small in size but large in atmosphere. Street lamps illuminate the view, and a few beer signs give the indication that you are somewhere that serves alcohol. This is a place where you cannot forget the city. You can hear busy Harlem Avenue and its bustling droves. It is close enough to O'Hare to watch the planes, and an abundance of power lines give the garden an even more urbanesque feel. I liken it to partying in a friend's backyard, but there are no annoyed neighbors, and your plastic is good there.

Though the portions are substantial, this is not a place where you'll get a burrito as big as your arm filled with a bunch of shit you wouldn't feed your dog. The food is fantastic, and the prices reasonable. The owner Teri said everything is made from scratch with no preservatives, and it shows. They cut their own steak, and I strongly recommend that as a taco or burrito filler.

The margaritas are out of this world and served on the rocks as margaritas should be. They do creep up on you, however, so beginners may want to adhere to the "no more than two" rule, unless you like falling down. If your evening in the garden is cool, try a "Cafe De Amigos" for dessert. When Cuervu, Kahlua, whipped cream, and coffee come in the same glass, good things happen such as loss of judgment and stumbling. And though they have only a few domestic swills on tap, there is a fair selection of bottles (the imports are mostly Mexican, of course), and a full liquor bar.

The service is just like the establishment — friendly, but real, with no pretensions. Atmosphere is key, both inside and out. The decor is eclectic with a Southwestern flair, and the tables are close enough together that if you don't have a conversation with the table next to you by the time you leave, you probably have a personality disorder-especially if you are unfortunate enough to be seated next to a long-haired regular named Jeff.

Perhaps the best thing about Tres Amigos is that it's a great place to start a drinking extravaganza on the Northwest Side (Mom always said, "eat first!"). A lot of folks seem to know this, so you'll need reservations most weekend nights. Many bars are close, and you'll be well primed for them after starting at Tres Amigos, but you might want to walk after the margaritas. And if the bartender at your second or third stop asks why you're on the floor, just flash a peace sign and say, "I'm the fourth amigo."

— *Bud*

Tuman's Alcohol Abuse Center, 2159 W. Chicago Ave., bartender Colleen can handle orders from many patrons at once. Pictured center is Bill, who owns da place.

Tuman's Alcohol Abuse Center
2159 W. Chicago Ave.
No Phone

MENTAL DISTURBANCES
1. _The victim may NOT TALK, even to give his name._
2. _He may be COMPLETELY CONFUSED or SEEM STUPOROUS._
3. _He may show complete disregard for a SERIOUS INJURY, YET COMPLAIN LOUDLY of some minor CUT or BRUISE. BE REASSURING, and do not ARGUE WITH HIM. Do not IMPLY that YOU THINK he is MENTALLY DISTURBED._

The ALCOHOL ABUSE CENTER is located on the corner of Chicago and Leavitt. Inside the foyer is an ancient humidor showcasing a startling display of

Barfly Tuman's Alcohol Abuse Center

shotgun and pistol shells, golf balls, books on guns, including THE STORY OF THE FBI. Stony faces caught on a photo acetone of the Soviet's livelier sock-hops infect the cover of an album entitled MOSCOW'S GREATEST HITS. Or something like that. More shotgun shells merrily beat a path around the album. Smaller shells sprinkled like confetti collect near golf balls, and finally, like tiny explosive infants, several shells nurse on a random can of SPAM. Behind the humidor is a stained glass bar cabinet containing shiny bottles of bourbon, vodka, and gin. Half pints of Skol vodka wink promiscuously next to a propped book entitled THE BOOK OF KNOWLEDGE.

FOREIGN BODY IN THE FOOD PASSAGES

If foreign objects are swallowed, they most often PASS HARMLESSLY ALONG and are excreted. Other objects sometimes requiring extraction include: COINS AND DISCS, FOOD, PINS, BUTTONS, SHELLS and TOYS. Persons should TAKE CARE when EATING FOOD containing BONES and REMEMBER NOT TO TALK while FOREIGN OBJECTS are IN THE MOUTH.

The bar housing the ALCOHOL ABUSE CENTER is more than 100 years old. Old poker tables set against a white tin wall. Yellow light floods a painting of Bela Lugosi hanging over a tunneled hallway leading to the LADIES' ROOM. A stench hangs over the MEN'S ROOM. A suspended pot-bellied man exits the MEN'S ROOM shouting "I AM THE LONE RANGER, I AM THE LONE RANGER." A lush painting of a naked lady hangs from a Tiffany fixture crowning the top of the towering back bar.

TRANSPORTATION

OBJECTIVE; TO AVOID subjecting the patient to UNNECESSARY DISTURBANCE during PLANNING, PREPARATION, AND TRANSFER: TO PREVENT INJURED BODY PARTS from TWISTING, BENDING, and SHAKING. The TIME for GOOD TRANSPORTATION is PRECISELY when the victim is in BAD CONDITION.

The ALCOHOL ABUSE CENTER does not speak vain gloriously about its Wisconsin-like prices. Neither does it BLUBBER, BOOHOO, or SOB OR WAIL about having to maintain low prices in order to bleed other taverns of business.

WHAT CLAPTRAP JAZZY NONSENSE

Prices for most BOTTLED DOMESTIC BEERS begin at $1.25 AND STAY THERE. FOREIGN BEERS ARE TWO BUCKS. Mostly. TAP BEER IS USUALLY ONE OR TWO BUCKS. BIG DEAL.

THERE IS WINE. BOOZE PRICES ARE MILES BELOW SEA LEVEL of the tired, sagging dive bars of the Wicker area. COME TO THE UKRAINIAN VILLAGE!!!

HOURS ARE DAYTIME AND NIGHTTIME. Closed on SUNDAYS.

— Gladys Kravitz

The Twisted Spoke
501 N. Ogden Ave.
312-666-1500
Hours: 11 a.m. to 2 a.m. Sunday to Friday,
10 a.m. to 3 a.m. Saturday

In this mass-media world, sloughing off an unwanted public image, whether founded in fact or not, is difficult if not damn near impossible. This is a fact that people in the limelight such as Michael Jackson, Roseanne and Clarence Thomas can readily attest to. But even on a lesser, homefront scale, such an image can loom over a person or a venture with all the unrelenting animosity of a Midwest thunderhead. For proof, just ask Laurie Pighini, co-owner and co-partner of The Twisted Spoke.

"We knew that the motif on which we planned the Twisted Spoke might cause an image problem at first," she said during a recent conversation, "but we didn't think it would cause this much trouble."

The motif stirring up such trouble at The Twisted Spoke includes, among other things, a genuine Harley fatboy revolving atop a 20-foot pole serves as the place's signpost, walls festooned with motorcycle parts and memorabilia, a wall mural featuring a bevy of weathered leather jackets painted across the wall of the pool room, menu items with names like "sidecars," "choppers" and "flat-head," and a phone number that begins with the digits "666." This glut of two-wheeling atmosphere had led, not surprisingly, to the buzz on the street and among Chicago's nightlife community that The Twisted Spoke is a biker bar. But this label, like a Michael Jackson marriage, is misleading. For whereas the stereotypic biker bar so portrayed in the movies and in Hunter S. Thompson books is an unruly, dirty, brash manifestation of some unwritten, misogynist "code of the West," the Spoke stands as one of the warmest, friendliest and most family and fun-oriented new eateries and drinkeries in the city.

Open since April, 1995, the Spoke has morphed comfortably into a space that was first built in the 1940s and which originally house a vehicle service station. Situated by new housing developments and rehabs, the Spoke seems to have gotten in on the ground floor of a blossoming neighborhood.

Passing through the tabled and umbrella-ed outdoor seating area and into the building proper, one is immediately struck by the size of the interior in relation to what is definitely a diminutive exterior appearance. Months of gutting the original building, exposed a monumentally high-lofted ceiling and that, combined with a myriad of windows on all sides gives the Spoke an airy and spacious feel. A handsome granite styling of the tables and fixtures provides a solid and industrialized anchor to this spaciousness throughout, most noticeably in the custom-built bar to the right of the entrance and the high-topped kitchen counter to the left.

It's from behind this counter that the Spoke's eclectic yet down-home menu is served throughout the day and up to one hour before closing every night. A

324

Barfly Twisted Spoke

full menu of appetizers, salads, entrees and desserts is available.

At the bar, no single libation really takes the center stage here, but true to the biker image of the bar, beer does hold a place of prominence. With more than 27 different brands to choose from, most everyone's taste is sure to be satisfied. Selections run from Busch and the various manifestations of the Miller company, to those whose tastebuds savor the more eclectic brews like Sam Adams Oatmeal Stout, Indiana's Blue Ridge Beer and even the hard-to-find Chimay's. Priced as serenely as the food, beers range from $2.50 to $3.50, tap and/or bottle, and are supplemented at any given time by an ambiguous and unpredictable "Butch's Beer Special" at a constant $1.25.

The Spoke also offers a full selection of call, well and premium liquors, noticeably displayed on an array of shelves behind the bar and most noticeably used in their two signature libations: the Bloody Mary and the martini. The Bloody Mary (or "Road Rash Mary" as they like to call it here) was created and developed by bartender Jason and stands as a glorious monument to mixological science. Almost more of a liquid antipasto than a drink, it consists of a heavily-guarded secret blend of juices, spices and vodkas and is garnished with a veritable smorgasbord of olives, peppers, salami, onions and parmesan cheese.

Even more creative is the Spoke's martini list, which is made up of a dozen pieces of bartending artwork including those with the self-descriptive monikers "Chocolate Kiss" and "Honey-Nut Cheerio." Martini affectionados also have the opportunity to join The Twisted Spoke's elitist Martini Club, which includes a membership card, the chance to indulge in the full menu of martinis, and the officious initiation rite of a free party when that menu has been conquered.

One other attraction that most often doesn't get brought up in a typical bar review but which merits a mention here is the women's bathroom. Now for years and years journalists and pollsters alike have deemed the women's bathroom in the Drake Hotel's Palm Court as the city's finest. One visit to the Spoke's ladies room is enough, however, to know that the Palm Court's bathroom is soon going to get a run for its money. Tastefully decorated in postmodern "biker-hunk," the bathroom not only boasts the comfort and spaciousness of the rest of the establishment, but even offers, among its other accouterments, one of the few condom machines ever seen in Chicago that's politically correct by being located in a women's washroom, but also an up-to-date selection of "Harley Man" and "Harley Woman" magazines for the patrons' reading pleasure.

And pleasure seems to be job one at the Twisted Spoke, from these bathrooms to the food and drink and even to the ease with which one can find a parking space outside. The Spoke's attitude and atmosphere does nothing but provide for a comfortable and thoroughly enjoyable visit, and although it is located at a place that many people, especially those who think that anything west of Wells is "too far" or a "bad neighborhood," may consider an out-of-the-way place, one visit with the staff and the food and the drink and any number

The North Side Twisted Spoke-U.S. Beer Co.

of people who make it past the biker bar image makes it well worth the trip. Even if you are one of those people that travels on four wheels.

— Johnny Masiulewicz

The U.S. Beer Co.

1801 N. Clybourn Ave.
773-871-7799
Hours: 11 a.m. to 2 a.m. Sunday to Friday,
11 a.m. to 3 a.m. Saturday

The building which houses the U.S. Beer Co. was built in the late 1800s and first housed Mattick Printing Co. from 1898 to 1912, according to a U.S. Beer Co. spokesperson. Monarch Brewery bought the building in 1912 and converted it into a bar. Monarch owned buildings all over the city and would lease the space to bars with the agreement that they would sell Monarch beer. In 1913 times were good and the bar was opened and deemed Sheffield Tap with the upstairs units used as medical and legal offices.

During Prohibition and the Great Depression (1920 to 1933) the bar was converted into a sandwich shop and the back room, which was called the "Family Room," was conveted into a secret parlor which was used for gambling. The building remained the Sheffield Tap until 1939 when the business was purchased by Charles and Eleanor Bunge for $30,000. The new owners renamed the place Bunge's Triangle Inn. This was appropriate since the building and lot are both triangular in shape. The clientel back then was mainly houligans and blue collar workers, according the spokesperson.

In the 1950s the "Family Room" was converted into Mac's Grill to accomadate the booming industries thriving on the riverfront. The 1960s saw a downturn with race riots and crime engulfing the neighborhood. The professionals took to higher ground and the upstairs had to be used as a bowery type rooming housing daily and weekly rate tenants. Yet the Bunge's survived thanks to loyal hardnose clientel. When the 1970s and 1980s came along the neighborhood underwent a gentrification similar to what is occurring in the Wicker Park area and the clientele became more upscale.

The U.S. Beer Co. replaced the Triangle Inn at the end of 1994. The U.S. Beer Co. completely renovated the place and is more sports oriented and viewer friendly with 10 televisions and a big screen, two satellite dishes, two cable feeds, and VCR's for replays and presentations. The bar's sound system is state of the art and includes a 100-CD jukebox with a diverse selection. The new place has a 1950s-era bar and more than 100 micro-brews, imports and domestic beers. The decor includes exposed brick walls, sandblasted wood ceiling rafters, antique light fixtures and original rose petal-stain glass windows.

The bar is home to the Lincoln Park Rugby Club, the Lincoln Park Social Club and sponsors a variety of league sports teams. In addition, The U.S. Beer Co. has its own pool and dart leagues.

Vaughan's Pub
2917 N. Sheffield Ave.
773-281-8188
Hours: 1 p.m. to 2 a.m. Sunday to Friday,
1 p.m. to 3 a.m. Saturday

From points North and South, the Vaughan clan has converged towards the center.

In November 1996, owners of Vaughan's Pub, 2917 N. Sheffield Ave., Eamonn and Kevin Vaughan, brought the family's pub legacy to Lake View. An uncharted territory for a family whose other pubs are located at 6462 S. Central Ave. on the South Side and 5105 N. Milwaukee Ave. on the Northwest Side. Yet this new area mixing brings out the best in these boys. While both went in on the new business, Kevin remains a more silent partner while Eamonn takes the reigns, a position the 26 year-old is very pleased to hold. He began in the hospitality industry when he was 14 years old, a year after arriving in the United States from Ireland.

"I lied about my age and told (my employers) I was 16," Eamonn said. "I enjoyed working more than going to school!"

His father would later open the first Vaughan's bar on the Northwest Side and Eamonn went to work for him, he said. With the later arrival of a South Side Vaughan's location, Eamonn had his work cut out for him.

"I worked at the North and South Side locations," Eamonn said. "Between the two places, I learned a lot."

With his knowledge of the industry ingrained, Eamonn, along with Kevin, decided to get their own place independent of their father.

"This was a thing I was looking for, for about a year," Eamonn said. "This place happened to be the right place."

The Sheffield Avenue bar was formerly known as Redmond's, a classy neighborhood bar. Much of the beauty of Redmond's remains as the Vaughans saw no reason to change anything.

"I was never in the place until I knew it was up for sale," Eamonn admitted. "There was nothing I had to do. All I had to do was put up a new sign."

According to Eamonn, there was little work to be done because much of Redmond's barroom was left intact when the former owner vacated the premises. The barroom is that of a beautifully kept old-fashioned pub with deep, dark wood abounding throughout in wood slats halfway up the walls, wooden framed windows, a cherry wood back bar, all complimented by a dark-colored tin ceiling. At night, Eamonn uses candlelight to give the room even more spark.

The new location has enabled them to hone in on skills left to the side at the other Vaughan pubs. Cigars and martinis are important staples in the area and Eamonn is getting his knowledge extended of the two.

Eamonn Vaughan, owner of Vaughan's Pub, 2917 N. Sheffield Ave., pours one of the best pints of Guinness in the city.

"We make the chocolate ones and everything," said Eamonn about the martinis. "One night one person asked for one and everyone right in a line all asked for a martini."

Though not trying to push himself as a martini and cigar bar, neither does he try to push the bar as an Irish pub. However, a bit of the green shows through the dark wood.

"I wanted an Irish theme, but not to the extreme," said Eamonn who only brought a couple staples of the family's other pubs. One such staple was the traditional Irish music which he placed on the CD jukebox. He said he hopes to feature live musical performers in the near future. And the other important staple, especially in this reporter's viewpoint, is Guinness Stout.

"I'm selling a lot of Guinness," Eamonn said. "I know that a lot of bars are carrying it now, but I have guys coming in because I'm serving a good pint of Guinness."

And that he is, especially since he installed a $1,000 special system in order to blend the gases together as well as his extensive experience in pouring a good Guinness.

"You gotta hold the glass up to the spout," stressed Eamonn.

The system formerly used for the Guinness was just run through a cold plate system where the beer was pumped through a tube and cooled by a metal sheet packed with ice. With these changes in the way it is served, patrons are responding.

Barfly Vaughan's

"Redmond's went through a keg (of Guinness) every three to four weeks," Eamonn said. "I now go through seven to ten a week. (However) I would like to be selling 20 a week like at my father's place!"

To get more people interested in Guinness, Eamonn offers pints with a splash of black currant flavoring to give it a fruity taste. He said he has found this too has been a big seller. Though pushing the Guinness, Eamonn said that he likes to offer a wide variety of beers.

"There's always going to be someone in the group who wants something different," said Eamonn about his selection of domestic, imported, microbrew and cider beers.

Also with other neighboring places such as Pops for Champagne, 2934 N. Sheffield Ave., offering fine wines and spirits, Eamonn said he is stocking quality wines and single-malt Scotches as well since he gets some of Pops overflow.

"Pops attracts a finer crowd, but we're less stuffy and sometimes that's what people want," Eamonn said.

So far he has found that his clientele has been enjoying the little changes and additions to the bar as crowds continue to gather, particularly on weekends. Yet, he has received one complaint.

"The worst complaint is that I took the pool table out," Eamonn said with a shrug. "I took the pool table out for more tables. I just don't want to be squeezing them in and squeezing them out. I do (however) get a lot of comments that I've done good with this."

In addition, so patrons can enjoy the bar more often, Eamonn is opening the bar earlier in the day, a point he wishes to push for obvious reasons.

"Nobody's open before four (p.m.) in the area," Eamonn noted. "If (people) get off work early and want to know of a place to go..."

Though the early hours are not popular as of yet, Eamonn does not mind waiting until it catches on. Everything is going so smoothly so far, being in the bar just brings a smile to his face.

"I'm happy with it," Eamonn said. "The place speaks for itself. What more can a person ask for than an atmosphere that's right there?"

— Phil Brandt

Village Tap

2055 W. Roscoe St.
773-883-0817
Hours: 5 p.m. to 2 a.m. Monday to Thursday,
3 p.m. to 2 a.m. Friday, 2 p.m. to 3 a.m. Saturday,
2 p.m. to 2 a.m. Sunday

Outside appearances of the Village Tap in Roscoe Village may lead one to believe that it is a typical run-of-the-mill neighborhood bar. However, this bar is far more special. This is one of those places that's just very comfortable to go to, with a bit of an edge over its neighborhood counterparts. Aside from the psychedelic artwork, which changes every month, the Village Tap is famous for an unusual jukebox music selection, and the 31 beers they keep on tap.

Entertainment-wise they have board games, such as chess, checkers, Battleship and backgammon. Entertainment is not a big issue at the bar, but it doesn't need to be. According to assistant manager James Krogh, the bar sustains itself on the fact that it is simply "not pretentious, and one of Chicago's authentic neighborhood bars." The beer garden is probably one of the most comfortable I've been in, and you can talk to each other without having to shout. It has high walls with ivy crawling all the way up for an English garden feeling, and a small waterfall and soothing Christmas-type lights also make for a nice effect.

The menu consists of "American-eclectic" cuisine, including vegetarian entrees, as well as "typical bar grub," and Krogh particularly recommends the vegetarian burrito.

The crowd ranges from young artist types and theater people to yuppies and families on the weekend.

The Village Tap has only four bottled beers: two non-alcoholics, Rolling Rock and Amstel Light. The thing that sets the Village Tap apart really is the huge selection of draught beers. These run from $2.50 to $4.75 and include imports, domestics and micro-brewed beers. They run specials every night, and I recommend trying a new beer each time. This will provide all the entertainment you need for a long time.

— *Paris*

"W" Cut Rate Liquors & Package Goods

1690 W. Division St.
773-227-8857
Hours: 7 a.m. to 2 a.m. weekdays,
7 a.m. to 3 a.m. Saturday and Sunday

Whatever you think of the actual establishment, you gotta respect a bar that opens up at 7 a.m. every day. For those of us reeling and ready to keep on drinking from a night-long bender or just looking for a quiet place to pour some whiskey on our corn flakes in the morning for a semi-liquid breakfast, "W" Cut Rate Liquors provides an invaluable service to the community and should be commended as such right off the bat.

Situated right across the street from Cut Rate Liquors, and where most of the hard-core drinkers go when Cut Rate closes its doors. "W" Cut Rate Liquors is an unassumingly cheerful watering hole, that upon first glance might put off any passersby because of its dark and shadowy interior. Once past the black-tinted windows, though, your fears of having your throat slit are slightly way-laid by the smiling Polish woman tending to the libations behind the bar and the festive Christmas lights strung from wall to wall. Saddling up to the bar, I asked the bartender what kind of beer they had and she answered "What kind of beer do you want?" Then and there I knew I was in the right place.

Much like Cut Rate Liquors, nearly every beer under the sun (except for your more pricey yuppie-style beers) are available to you. Going for economy, my friends and I went for the $1 drafts of Old Style, but soon drifted into liquor country because shots of all kinds were so insanely cheap ($1.50 - $2 each).

Where else, besides maybe drinking with the riff-raff in the park can you get your fill of rum and rye for under $5 while still getting your daily quotient of drunken psycho-babble. Though the general clientele of black-eyed, white trash yokels in cowboy hats and loopy Mexican guys hepped up on the latest cock fight scores might put you off at first, the bar is really something to be experienced. With a cross-section of society like this, a pool table, Tom Jones' Greatest Hits on the jukebox and a built-in liquor store to boot, this place may soon become my favorite drinking establishment or at least the one I'll go to first thing in the morning and right before I pass out for the night.

Cheap alcohol and good company. On most nights "W" Cut Rate can satisfy both of these needs and if the belligerent conversation isn't up to your snuff, you can always liven things up with a cheap round of beers. It doesn't always help, but it definitely couldn't hurt.

— *Brian Farrelly*

Walsh's Schubert Inn

1301 W. Schubert Ave.
773-472-7738
Hours: 11 a.m. to 2 a.m. Sunday to Friday,
11 a.m. to 3 a.m. Saturday

Tucked back from major strips like Lincoln Avenue and Halsted Street, the Schubert Inn is a safe haven from the smattering of sports and highbrow bars that congest this area. This is the neighborhood tap desperately needed in this area.

A harmonious bar where one can quaff a few with friends or by oneself where there is no attitude problem. Patrons of the Schubert Inn are a blend of blue-collar workers and white-collar workers creating a nice light-blue mixed clientele which makes this place a friendly hangout to relax and toss a couple back directly after work or later in the evening.

Still, even at this safe-haven, sports continue to play a role, but it is uncharacteristic of surrounding bars. It's rare to hear, "Where's the Hawks game?!" That phrase becomes more of a kind question such as, "Can we turn on the Hawks? I think it's on Sports Channel." And there's less tension from the watching patrons concerning the game at hand. If one is interested, the tension about winning stays within that group and rarely gets wild.

For a quick rundown on Schubert's, the barroom itself is a good size for a neighborhood tap. The bar covers one wall and projecting tables cover the opposite. A bowling machine and electronic darts are stationed in the back. The jukebox has good tunes, including Country/Western and some good oldies. Tap beers include Dab, Harp, Guinness, Miller Genuine Draft and Miller Lite. Tap beers are served in either glasses or pints, so one can get the amount they need. MGD and Lite run $1 for a glass and $1.50 per pint. Dab goes for $1.75 per glass, $2.75 per pint. And Harp and Guinness top off the price range at $3.25 for a pint. Bottles of domestics go for $2 and Imports are $2.50. The range for bottles is good for the drinking, not so much expert beer tasting, palate. Owner Tim Walsh makes his own pizzas for $6, offering no reason to stop at home first for a quick snack before getting hammered.

Head past the bowling machine and one will find what we all look for in a summer bar, the beer garden. Hanging out at a bar, yet still having the feeling of being in a city backyard doesn't get any closer than this. The garden is walled off by the bar's building, two wooden fences and a garage, yet the grass has been poured over with concrete. The major plus at this beer garden, which I have yet to see with any other beer gardens, is tent-like screens over the open area. No bugs at night, even when mosquito season hits. What a prime idea. Though small in size, the beer garden continues with that relaxed feel found inside. An escape, an island, a safe haven: call it what you will, Walsh's Schubert Inn should be put on anyone's plan for outdoor summer fun.

— Phil Brandt

Webster's Wine Bar
1480 W. Webster Ave.
773-868-0608
Hours: 5 p.m. to 2 a.m. weekdays,
4 p.m. to 3 a.m. Saturday,
4 p.m. to 1 a.m. Sunday

Although the Webster's dictionary on the bookshelf probably serves more for witty decor than for reference, customers can't help but learn from Webster's Wine Bar. Webster's boasts an enormous and informative menu including both usual and unusual reds, whites, and Champagnes, as well as beer, brandies, whiskies, cordials, and mixed drinks — not to mention pizzas, salads, flourless chocolate cake, and an exquisite cheese plate. If you can think of it, Webster's probably has it, and with monthly specials which currently include South African reds and zinfandels, you'll find pages and pages of new discoveries available by the bottle, glass, or in tasting portions.

The staff, too, is quite friendly and ready to answer questions and offer advice. Our server, Randy, introduced me to a stunning Clos du Bois Flintwood Vineyards Chardonnay which had been part of the Names Project fundraiser, with participating groups (including Webster's and Clos du Bois) donating part of the proceeds to the AIDS Memorial Quilt.

Webster's, aside from its service to the curious and the connoisseur, is a place where you can go for comfort and conversation. Elegant yet soothing atmosphere and design extend through all three rooms. Non-smoking and smoking sections are spacious and well-divided downstairs, and upstairs another smaller bar serves additional tables. Even the music fits, ranging from jazz to funk to classical, but never overpowering. It's an excellent spot for a date, or a relaxing evening alone or with friends.

Although a bit hidden (across from the Webster Place Theatre), any night, on any budget in any mood, Webster's is well worth a visit.

— Jennifer Shook

Weeds
1555 N. Dayton St.
312-943-7815
Hours: 3 p.m. to 2 a.m. daily

If you have been looking for a bar with brassieres, panties and (unused) condoms hanging from the ceiling as well as a beer garden within sniper range of Cabrini Green, then look no further than Weeds pub.

I paid a visit to Weeds on a recent Thursday not only because the guys at Barfly asked me to review the pub, but also because on Thursdays Weeds has live jazz until two in the morning. Mondays and Saturdays they have open mic, and on Fridays they have live blues. When I turned off North Avenue to get to Weeds I thought I was going to be entering a shady neighborhood. But much to my surprise I backed my sorry automobile into a spot across the street from the pub and was able to box in a convertible Mercedes with its top down. When I got out of my car I heard swingin' rhythms and social chatter echoing from the bar, so I shuffled through the front door.

There were people packed wall to wall inside the pub so I had my bar partner, "Fat Adam," use his girth to run blocking for me and get us to the bartender. I was upset to find that they had only three beers on tap, none of which was a brand of stout. As Adam admired a pair of black lace panties on the ceiling I leaned over the bar and asked for a couple of Guinness Stouts. I may not have had the pleasure of watching the thick head pulled from a tap but I did receive cans and pint glasses for $3.25 each, which more than satisfied my beer needs.

I found an empty stool next to the dance floor, placed my butt on its surface, and socialized with the bar's clientele. I was surprised by the diversity of the crowd. When I first sat down, I began speaking with a 46-year-old insurance underwriter and by the end of the band's set I was chatting with a 22-year-old DePaul student named Stephanie.

She and I decided that the bar was a little crowded and hot so we went outside to the beer garden which turned out to be as big as the indoor portion of the bar itself. The garden was crowded with tables, antique chairs, small sculptures and an old weather torn piano. In the back of the garden we found a sheltered area with couches, end tables and a small unit fireplace. As we sat on a couch and sipped our beers the band began their last set of the evening. And, fortunately, in the comfort of the outdoor garden we were still well within range of the band's swing.

At the end of the set I went back into the bar and found my bar hopping partner playing the "Popeye" pinball machine in the corner of the pub. After joining him in a game the bar was closing and it was time to go. So while no one was looking I snaked a pair of panties from the ceiling and then we hit the road.

—Pete Axelrad

WhirlyBall

1880 W. Fullerton Ave.
773-486-7777
Hours: 10 a.m. to 2 a.m. Monday to Saturday,
noon to 2 a.m. Sunday

I always say...there's nothin' better than getting a group of people together, having some cocktails, and then jumping into some bumper cars in order to whip whiffleballs at each other. Actually, what I've just described rather simply is — WhirlyBall.

WhirlyBall is a combination of lacrosse, hockey, and basketball, along with a

Barfly WhirlyBall

good dose of demolition derby. It involves normally sane adults driving bumper cars while using hand-held open scoops to pass and propel whiffleballs at a scoring target. According to owner Sam Elias, everybody is at the same skill level (or lack thereof).

"WhirlyBall is the world's only mechanized sport, and anyone can be competitive, whether you're an all-star ball player or an out-of-shape channel surfer," Elias said.

Elias originally saw the WhirlyBall concept in Florida and then brought it out to Chicago by opening a location in Lombard. Well received by the public, he opened the Chicago store January 1996. Based on the crowd during my visit, this location is a true success. Lots of people having fun. The three WhirlyBall courts were in use with a couple of groups enjoying some beers while waiting their turns. Now the big thing is, you do not have to play WhirlyBall in order to have a good time.

First off, the place is huge. I'd say there's at least 24,000 square feet of party room. In addition to the three WhirlyBall courts, the place has three 10-foot video walls along with 10, 27-inch monitors placed throughout the location. Da' Bulls were playing the night I checked out WhirlyBall, so just about anywhere you went, you could see and hear the action.

A full service bar is located smack dab in the middle of the place. It seemed to me that most of the patrons were drinking beers. As far as beer selection-goes, WhirlyBall features your standard domestics including Rolling Rock, along with a nice selection of imports. The barkeep mentioned to me that Bass and Murphy's Irish Amber move pretty well.

WhirlyBall offers some great menu items to keep your energy up. Munchies include chicken wings, cheese styx, and poppers, just to name a few. I went with an order of wings. My order was delivered quickly and the food went just as fast. Ten wings in about five minutes. Also, WhirlyBall features pizza which I'll have to try on my next visit. The N.Y. style cheese looked and smelled really good.

Bar decor consists of beer signage along with sports themed banners sprinkled into the mix. Four nice pool tables will keep you busy before and after your WhirlyBall game. Other amusements included the tried and true pinball machines, a couple of electronic dart games, some video games, and a few sports games-of-skill thrown in. WhirlyBall even has an air hockey table. The table is not just one of those small ones you played with in the basement but a real regulation table with lots of air power. This game alone mandates a visit.

The tunes at WhirlyBall are handled by a CD jukebox. The sound system is killer. On the weekend, WhirlyBall offers up some live music like Dick Holliday & The Bamboo Gang.

One final thing...WhirlyBall is super clean. From the restrooms to the entrance. The place is ready for your business. Looking for fun? Check out WhirlyBall!

— Greg Dellinger

Wild Goose

4265 N. Lincoln Ave.
773-281-7112
Hours: 6 p.m. to 2 a.m. Sunday to Friday,
6 p.m. to 3 a.m. Saturday

If you've ever been here, you've never been here. Come today and you won't be able to say you've been tomorrow. By the time you get here, it won't be the same here.

I know what you're thinking: philosophy by Goldschlager. But although Wild Goose certainly serves up its share of cinnamon brain damage, the above truths add up: this is a place in transition.

For instance, the bar's most glaring blemish was removed in August, 1995. An eight-line draft system now offers Guinness, Bass, Sam Adams, a weiss and a few big-brewery domestics where previously only Lite, Leine Red and Old Style were available. So drinkers of reasonable taste have no excuse to turn away.

Boldly breaking from Lincoln Avenue bar-naming tradition (i.e. Clancy's, Marty's, Margies, Billie Lu's, etc.), Wild Goose opened in 1990 in a space the size of a large cheese wedge. Some time later, an inside wall of the triangular building was knocked down and the bar's area more than doubled. The dark, comfortable space includes a pool table, CD jukebox, some couches and a scattershot arrangement of tables. History buffs can appreciate the vintage cigarette machine and antique water closets in the bathrooms.

In 1998, new management came in and really fixed the place up nice. It is a new sleak, well-oiled machine, Wild Goose is. In addition to beers, a classier selection of cocktails are available. And the food menu has been upgraded as well, and is still reasonable. Wednesday is $2.99 All-U-Can-Eat spaghetti. Great lunches and dinners are offered and Sundays offer an awesome brunch featuring a Bloody Mary bar.

Football fans will love the new Wild Goose with college games on ESPN Game Plan, Monday Night Football 10-cent wings specials and all Bears games. Wild Goose has satellite and will show what ever game you like. Games are shown an a 12-foot by 10-foot big screen TV.

Pop in, check out the new draft selections and monitor a work in progress. You probably won't recognize the place the next time you're there.

— Pat McAuley

Will's Northwoods Inn
3032 N. Racine Ave.
773-528-4400
Hours: noon to 2 a.m. Sunday to Friday,
11 a.m. to 3 a.m. Saturday

It would be hard to find a cozier place in the Lake View area than Will's. It evokes images of that Wisconsin cabin on Lake Manywhiteman you rented with your roommates a few summers ago, forgoing the fishing to put away the Point. On Sunday's, however, Will's can become terrifying if you grew up south of Kenosha. That's when the Lambeau Field homesickness gene of more than a few Packer fans kicks in. These folks are inarguably the NFL's most ardent. Bear fans, with all their beer-swilling, brat-belching charm, have nothing on the fanaticism of The Pack.

On Sunday's, they swarm to Will's to back the Pack, cheering with the elongated "oos" and clipped "ths" that characterize Green Bay vernacular. "Hey der," said one fan as his Dairyland peer strolled in wearing the 66 jersey of Ray Nitzsche. "It's aboot time ya shooed oop."

Recently, Will's Pack had to endure a struggle against the surprisingly strong Minnesota Vikings. Packer intensity was at full tilt. This was one green-and-yellow organism that takes team support to the absolute. It's something to behold because everyone knows the specifics of each player, from the all-stars to the third-stringers. And their Packer regalia is also most impressive; one fan was even proudly displaying her game socks, taken, she maintained, from former Pack receiver Sterling Sharpe. How she got Mr. Sharpe's socks is probably best left unsaid, but it may well typify Packer loyalty.

Apart from the Sunday Pack maniacs, Will's is the kind of comfortable, friendly bar that belongs on the corner of every neighborhood. The lodge-like interior immediately mellows even the most overwrought urbanite, and an array of fish, both stuffed and live, invites every struggling Babe Winkleman to reel off a few fish stories. Will's selection of beers runs from refined to Racine, so every taste and every budget will be pleased. There are also plenty of ways to pass the time at Will's if there's no Green Bay game to follow. A stack of board games by the front-window aquarium are available for the asking, as well as pool and pinball.

Will's also frequently features live entertainment in its spacious second room, and its neighborhood-appreciation summer cookouts (held on the stretch of yard outside the back door) are legendary. While this summer's has passed, look to next year for another afternoon of free beer and bratwurst to draw a smiling crowd.

— *Jay Ferrari*

Windy City Tavern
2257 Irving Park Road
773-588-0788
Hours: 11 a.m. to 2 a.m., weekdays, 11 a.m. to 3 a.m., Saturday, 11 a.m. to midnight Sunday

It's been a long day. After picking up your car at the Windy City Automotive and your laundry at the Windy City Cleaners, you had to race over to Windy City Investments to make a last minute adjustment to your portfolio. Now the only thing on your mind is where you can go to wash down the Windy City Pizza you just ate.

Yes, you guessed it, the perfect place to sip on some suds and watch your favorite Windy City sports team is none other than the Windy City Tavern. Where else can one get liquored-up beneath a wall-sized mug shot of the late Richard J. Daley? There's even a separate pool room for you and your friends to shoot some stick and reminisce about your favorite Windy City experiences. If that's not enough, they have a well-stocked jukebox, with an excellent selection of Bob Seger hits. The TVs are arranged throughout the tavern so that from whatever direction you are facing there is always a clear sight of the local and national sports shows. There are also several good beers on tap served in Windy City Tavern's own engraved glasses. The kitchen provides a variety of delicious edibles with service that is friendly and efficient, just like you would expect here in the Windy City.

However, if the high fivin', ball cap and docker wearin' crowd ails you, then you probably should look elsewhere for those suds. If this sounds good though, or you just feel like having some drinks at a fun, distinctive Chicago bar, then give the Windy City Tavern a test. After all, you can always take a Windy City taxi home if you have had one too many.

The Underground Wonder Bar
10 E. Walton St.
312-266-7761
Hours: 4 p.m. to 4 a.m. Sunday to Friday, 4 p.m. to 5 a.m. Saturday

The glorious freak-fest at the Underground Wonder Bar rages on in the face of the high-volume, low-brain world of the Gold Coast — and to some, freak isn't such a bad thing to be called — a badge of honor — a way to be distinguished from the brutes in Armani suits sucking cocktails with hookers down the street.

It's like the difference between plastic and flesh, the pale and the psychedelic, rich bastards with deep pockets of blow and the weird subculture of musicians with...well, not all things are different.

Barfly Underground Wonder Bar

But, this is neither the time nor the place for such rantings...as the name indicates, the Wonder Bar is underground, a gaudy neon sign hovers in the window, four steps down and you're in where you'll be met by Glen. Hand over a few bucks and you get your mojo on, work it for all it's worth, this is a place conducive to drunkenness.

A small bar bathed in green light stands to the right. To the left is a row of stools, beneath red track lighting, hugging the wall with a narrow ledge to rest your martini, gin and tonic or whatever the hell is your choice. Straight back is an intimate section of tables leading to a stage where Lonie Walker, co-owner of the Wonder Bar, wails and whispers her heart's jazz-stirrings.

The 'roid-boys are nowhere to be found — inside is a collection of societal outsiders and fringe Americans — men in rubber suits, Mafioso jackals, blinded flappers of old, tormented souls of beauty, long-legged models and hip young kiddies with their one-hitters and dilated pupils. Not exactly the type of bar Kerouac and his cronies hopped around during the Chicago fifties.

The Wonder Bar is more of a time capsule of 20th Century America — ultimately weird, but musically fanatical. Guest performers have included Tiny Tim, the Commitments, Steve Winwood and Herbie Hancock. Music begins at 10 p.m. on weeknights and 7:30 p.m. on Saturdays.

For those with an insatiable appetite for alcohol and chaos, the Wonder Bar, open until 4 a.m. on weeknights and 5 a.m. on Saturdays, is a constant. When the lights of all the other local night spots are dim, this place is only getting warmed up. It's jammed until closing when the bartenders have to shove the glorious barflies out the door with a cattle prod.

I was introduced to the hole at 10 E. Walton by a poet who has since moved to Dallas — it was like having sex for the very first time — to continue the analogy — I crawled back on a weekly basis moaning for a repeat performance.

Sometimes, she's cruel and others she wraps her arms around me and it's love all over again. I've dragged many a friend to the Wonder Bar. Some dig it, and others don't get it. I've been kicked out with a fiendish grin on my face and hazy eyes, have lost consciousness in Technicolor lights and have been moved by random artists hunched in dark corners.

Every night has been different. Take the good with the evil and know that whatever happens, however far the brain wanders, there will be Lonie perched on the stage holding you tight with her soulful and tormented voice.

— Rich Webster

Workingman's Palace

4400 W. Diversey Ave.
773-736-4830
Hours: 10 a.m. to 2 a.m. Sunday to Friday,
10 a.m. to 3 a.m. Saturday

Workingman's Palace and that's what it is. Locals hanging out in their neighborhood tap, enjoying the finest of domestics and common liquors to finish off the working day or to pass the weekend by.

A great facade to fit the name, with gray-colored brick and cut-outs on the roof that well-resemble a castle. The inside is filled with wood paneling, an island bar and plenty of dart boards, eight in all.

The best thing about playing darts here, as opposed to other watering holes I've been at that feature darts, is that many of the boards come equipped with an electronic scorekeeper. No, the boards are cork, but the scoreboards are electronic. Though I'm a math major by choice in college, there is something about crunching numbers while drinking. It just never works.

The bar is stocked with the usual favorites and there's plenty of bottle choices as well as the big domestics lining the taps. Icehouse, Miller Lite, Special Export, and of course, Old Style are on tap. Prices are plenty reasonable.

What's nice about this bar is the neighborhood feel. No gimmicks here. Just drinkin', playing darts, video poker or "Golden Tee Golf" video game. The patrons mainly flock to one of two places, the bar or dart boards. Age ranges mainly mid-30s plus. All pleasant. And the music of choice is Country/Western which can bring out a dancer or two in the crowd.

One big bonus is the beer garden. Bordered by a high wood fence and a neighboring apartment building, the beer garden is an all-wood deck with plenty of plastic chairs with umbrellas to enjoy. There are also two gas grills for those late-summer BBQs or private parties. It's a nice place to relax without losing a bit of the neighborhood feel.

Workingman's Palace is a worthwhile stop for those who enjoy a good, real Chicago bar without any gimmicks. Saturday afternoons is the prime time to enjoy this place. And, even if that dart game goes into the dinner hour, no biggy. The Palace serves up fine diner-style meals which are, just like their beer prices, plenty reasonable. The only thing truly above $3 are the dinners, which can range up to $10.50 for a full slab of ribs.

— Phil Brandt

Wrigleyville Tap (closed October, 1999)
3724 N. Clark St.
773-528-4422
Hours: 3 p.m. to 2 a.m. weekdays,
noon to 3 a.m. Saturday, noon to 2 a.m. Sunday

Wrigleyville Tap — Cub fans by day — North Side band scenesters by night. For the Cub fan, the bar has some great old photos of the '69 team and 1980s favorites like Jody Davis and Rick Sutcliffe. Be sure to check out the old baseball cards inside the cigarette machine. For the scenesters, Wrigleyville Tap has one of the best jukeboxes around from rap to old punk rock to Kiss.

There's two rooms at this bar, one with a bar and tables and the other with two pool tables, two dart boards and a free throw shooting game and tables.

Drink prices are $2 for domestic bottles and $1.50 for drafts.

Zack's
Elk Grove Avenue and Honore Street
Hours: 3 p.m. to 2 a.m. Monday to Thursday,
11 a.m. to 2 a.m. Friday, 11 a.m. to 3 a.m. Saturday,
noon to 2 a.m. Sunday

Whoa, wait a minute, where am I? I thought I was in Bucktown or close to it but this bar looks and feels like the South Side. There's bad scary bar snacks like Blind Robbins or those over-salted slimy pieces of smoked herring. I'll have a Jager and a beer. Good, they have Jager but who are those creepy-looking guys playing pool. The table is really close to the bar.

Any specials? Who cares? The specials are the people who come into this place. This bar is cool, it has a lot of real flies. If you're searching for a bar where no one looks like you and you know who you are, then check out this "Ye Olde Tavern." This place is untouched by the gimmie mimmie '80s and the politically correct '90s. It's a place where men smack women just for looking the wrong way. I mean THEIR women.

It's located on the corner of Elk Grove and Honore if you dare. There's no sign.

Zakopane
1734 W. Division St.
773-486-1559
Hours: 8 a.m. to 2 a.m. Sunday to Friday,
8 a.m. to 3 a.m. Saturday

Zakopane (pronounced Zock-oh-ponnie) is a throwback to the days when Division Street was known as the "Polish Broadway." This area was once the heart of Chicago's Polish community until the 1960s when Chicago Poles moved Northwest and Southwest. At one time, Division Street from Ashland to Damen avenues had dozens of Polish bars. Yet Zakopane is one of the last true Polish bars on the street. Actually, Zakopane is relatively new and wasn't around during the days of the "Polish Broadway" but on Saturday nights it recaptures the ghost of Polish past.

With performances by Polish pop bands, many recent Polish immigrants flock to Zakopane on Saturday nights to dance and drink vodka. The bar opens up its back room where there is a stage, dance floor and tables with a bottle of vodka on each. The bar is decorated for a party and the evening has a festival feel.

Any other day or night at Zakopane is slow and typical of a neighborhood bar. But what separates Zakopane from a typical neighborhood tap is that many of those who work and drink there are recent Polish immigrants and the language of choice is Polish.

In addition, the friendliness factor here varies. Some nights or days folks are quite nice but on other occasions they can make you feel like an outsider if you're not a regular or don't speak Polish. However, there was one night when I was in there and people were rather friendly and explained some Polish drinking traditions to me such as putting a little bit of cherry juice in a beer.

I've been going to Zakopane since 1990 and one of the main reasons I go there is that there is rarely anyone using its single pool table. So I drink a few cherry beers, play pool and sometimes watch a movie shown on a large screen. It's a nice change of pace.

— *Tony Gordon*

Zum Deutschen Eck (closed Jan. 2000)
2924 N. Southport Ave.
773-525-8390
Hours: 11:30 a.m. to 10:30 p.m. Monday to Thursday, 11:30 a.m. to midnight Friday, noon to midnight Saturday, noon to 10 p.m. Sunday

It was a very atypical Monday night. We found ourselves at Zum Deutschen Eck in the Lakeview neighborhood for an evening of food, drink, football and revelry...German style! Well, all except for the football anyway.

"Zum Deutschen Eck," it doesn't exactly roll off the tongue. The phrase means "The German Corner" and it is just that. The large Tudor building that houses Zum Deutschen Eck spans much of the block of Southport between Oakdale and George streets. German is written all over the building, literally.

Once a corner bar, Zum Deutschen Eck, has been transformed by the Wirth family into a facility that houses three banquet rooms, two dining rooms, and a comfortable bar, otherwise known as "Zum's Lounge." Between the three banquet rooms, Zum Deutschen Eck can accommodate parties of 25 to 400 people. That's a lot of schweinebraten. It may not be large enough to accommodate

Barfly Zum Deutschen Eck

quite as many people, but the lounge does have the same beautiful decor as the banquet and dining rooms. Murals, stained glass and finished wood decorate the interior. This may lead you to believe they cater only to an elegant dining crowd. However, I am pleased to say that this is not the case. Although, it is not uncommon to see patrons wearing a coat and tie or Leiderhosen if there's a party in one of the banquet rooms. Primarily, Zum Deutschen Eck is a casual dining facility that specializes in traditional German dishes at fair prices.

The most important thing to keep in mind is the full menu is available in the bar, as well as the dining room. The lunch menu basically consists of sandwich plates ranging from $6 to $8. The dinner menu offers a wide variety of German specialties in the $12 to $16 range; though both menus are available throughout the day.

"Zum's Lounge" is one of the smallest rooms in the Zum complex. It is also one of the most comfortable; especially if you, like me, define comfort by a well-stocked bar with several German beers on tap. A half liter of beer at Zum Deutschen Eck is a bit pricey at $4.25. However, if you wish to economize order a boot of beer for $9.50. What is a boot of beer you ask? It is essentially a boot-shaped glass pitcher containing a liter and a half of beer. Its sole intention, I am convinced, is making those who partake in the boot ill. It's truly an amazing thing and it's influence should be documented. Once you order a boot of beer for your group, the novelty of drinking out of this tall, goofy looking glass is irresistible. Before you know it, boots keep coming and coming until finally the next trip to the bathroom isn't for routine service.

Don't let this mislead you into thinking that "Zum's Lounge" is a beer-soaked Oktoberfest tent. The food is way to good for that. On top of the great menu offerings, great atmosphere, and of course, the boots; this is a neighborhood bar with regular customers who just like too hang-out. The TVs aren't always on and the music isn't overbearing. However, if you happen to catch the sing-a-long with "The Hans Rager Duo" you may be overwhelmed.

At Zum Deutschen Eck, the beer is cold and the food is great, but beware, Joey the bartender claims in his first few weeks working he put on about 20 pounds. Okay, so it's not exactly heart-smart cuisine, but who goes to a German restaurant to eat tofu anyway?

— *Bill Stephenson*

Chapter Two
The South Side

Buddy Guy's Legends, 754 S. Wabash Ave., is one of Chicago's biggest and best blues bars.

The South Side is the largest section of Chicago running south from Madison Street all the way to the Indiana state border. The South Side unfairly gets a bad rap as being a dangerous area. While there are some unsafe sections there are far more good neighborhoods than bad and worth exploration.

The 44 neighborhoods on the South Side are South Lawndale, Lower West Side, Near South Side, Armour Square, Douglas, Oakland, Fuller Park, Grand Boulevard, Kenwood, Washington Park, Hyde Park, Woodlawn, South Shore, Chatham, Avalon Park, South Chicago, Burnside, Calumet Heights, Pullman, South Deering, East Side, West Pullman, Riverdale, Hegewisch, Garfield Park, Archer Heights, Brighton Park McKinley Park, Bridgeport, New City, West Elsdon, Gage Park, Clearing, West Lawn, Chicago Lawn, West Englewood, Englewood, Greater Grand Crossing, Ashburn, Auburn Gresham, Beverly, Washington Heights, Mount Greenwood, and Morgan Park.

Except for the Near South Side with its old warehouses turned into loft living space, new restaurants, bars and condos, the South Side neighborhoods run closer along ethnic lines than on the North Side. In Armour Square is the city's wonderful China Town with great restaurants and shops, Grand Boulevard is predominantly African-American and the birthplace of Chicago Jazz, Hyde Park contains the University of Chicago, the Lower West Side contains the Little Village Mexican enclave with many restaurants, taverns and shops, Brighton Park is mostly Polish with many Polish taverns, and Bridgeport and Beverly are known as Irish enclaves and for great Irish bars.

Go and enjoy these great communities and its taverns.

Alcock's

411 S. Wells St.
312-922-1778
Hours: 11 a.m. to midnight Monday to Thursday,
11 a.m. to 2 a.m. Friday and Saturday,
open Sundays for Bears games

Alcock's "We Rock" sits on Wells in close proximity to the Board of Trade. Alcock's is the first bar I set foot in after my move here in 1990 from the East Coast. I was working as a runner on the Grain Floor at the Board of Trade. When the bell tolled at 1:15 p.m., we would head over to Alcock's to knock back a few. This schedule often played some havoc because by 5 p.m. I was blitzed and headed home with the 9 to 5 crowd. And by the time I went out with my non-Board of Trade friends, I was in the thrones of a hangover.

Entering Alcock's there is a small wooden deck that serves as a beer garden facing onto Wells (my favorite place to sit). Once inside is a pool table to the left with glass doors for a view and a breeze from the outside beer garden. To the right is a large screen TV for all the sporting events along with two other TVs placed along the wall opposite the bar, while the bar itself has two TVs and can sit 20 to 25 people at a time. Alcock's also features a hoop shot machine, a 3D golf game and a cigarette vending machine.

The walls of Alcock's pay tribute to the Rolling Stones, Carlos Santana, The Who, Pink Floyd and Stevie Ray Vaughn. Also on the walls are pictures of Frank Martello (the owner of Alcock's) with Keith Richards and another picture of Frank with Robert Plant. If you appreciate rock 'n roll, this place demands respect. "I'm not worthy," as Garth from Wayne's World would say.

Alcock's also features a kitchen where "Chef Arnay" will serve you up an assortment of Polish dogs, chili dogs, nachos, steak, chili or pizza. No beers on tap but cans of Bud, Miller Lite and Miller High Life are $2.25, bottles of Bud Light, Miller Genuine Draft and Rolling Rock are $3 and bottles of Amstel Light, Heineken, Molson and Sam Adams are $3.50. Bartenders Susie and Craig will be more than happy to fill you in on any daily drink specials.

I also recommend asking about Alcock's outings and summer parties such as its annual golf outing, a WCKG 105.9 FM outdoor summer party, Bulls shuttle trips and my all-time favorite, Bears bus trips to and from the game. Alcock's is a true Chicago bar that believes in local camaraderie, supporting Chicago teams and flat out having a good time with a little rock 'n roll thrown in for good measure.

So whether you come to Alcock's for fellow sports companionship, classic rock 'n roll music or you call in sick to work (even though you're not sick) and you want to knock back a few in the middle of the day with other party-goers, Alcock's wins hands down.

— *Christy K. Rizzo*

It's just shocking all the good times had by all at Artis',
1249 E. 87th St.

Artis'

1249 E. 87th St.
773-734-0491
Hours: 10 a.m. to 2 a.m. Sunday to Friday,
10 a.m. to 3 a.m. Saturday

If you really want to see what happens when professionals, business owners, and middle to upper income patrons let their hair down, come to Artis'. This place is so smooth and so well run, it is hard to tell that you are in a bar.

The evening that I visited there, Big Mack, the manager told me, "First a stranger, never a stranger," and I believe it. You are greeted like you have been there several times, and the staff knows you well. Well dressed and well groomed seems to be the topic of decor, for both the bar as well as the clientele. (Not spoken, as more ambiance)

There is something going on here almost every night. Unless you have been living under a rock, the name Herb Kent should not be a strange one. This legendary DJ is at Artis' on Tuesday at 8 p.m., and is well worth the visit. Along with the theme of entertainment, Sunday at 9 p.m. J.W. Williams & the Chi-Town Hustlers rock the house. On Monday, Billy Branch & the Sons of the Blues jam at 9 p.m. This is a must for the Blues and R&B crowd on either night.

You will find lots of off street and patrolled parking, it is also well lit. Inside you will find an oval shaped bar, which gives credence to see as well as to be seen. On Friday there is an after work set, and by any definition it is just that.

A relaxed, comfortable atmosphere settles in on you the minute that you enter. There is a DJ on every night of the week, and they do requests. The DJs

Barfly Alcock's-Baby Doll Polka Club

at Artis' are J.R. and Sweetback. They play adult music, meaning Blues, R&B, and Jazz so if you want hip-hop or rap, this ain't the place.

The staff can plan a party for almost any event that you have in mind, and deliver on that event. After being at this location for over 11 years, they have been a cornerstone of the South Side bar scene. At any given time you might get a chance to see Chicago celebrities passing through, just to say hello to the owner and many of the clientele (they seem to know each other).

So if you want to be well treated, have a good time, park your car in a well lit and secured lot, meet others of your status, this place must not be missed. Rated at 2 1/2 stars and do not forget that they take Visa, Amex, and Master Card.

— John W. Singer

Baby Doll Polka Club
6102 S. Central Ave.
773-582-9706
Hours: 5 p.m. to 2 a.m. weekdays, 2 p.m. to 3 a.m. Saturday, 3 p.m. to 2 a.m. Sunday, live music starts 9:30 p.m. Friday and Saturday and at 5:30 p.m. on Sunday

It was just about twelve midnight when some fellow barflies and I stumbled into the world famous Baby Doll Polka Club. Stories from friends who had gone 10 years ago seemed impressive, and enticed me to investigate this legendary club.

Believe the hype, the Baby Doll is a name that speaks for itself. I'm willing to bet my weekly beer money that someone in your extended family has been there at one time in their life. Although it is not primarily a Polish bar, it is a polka bar (one of the very few left that still provide some live music) and has kept the tradition alive for more than 40 years. The reason for that success is bar owner Irene D. Korosa, who is no stranger to the polka scene. The club's namesake was a number one polka hit that was written for Irene's daughters. Her dedication to her life's calling has earned her countless awards and worldwide recognition in newspapers, magazines and television segments.

"Polka music is happiness," she says sincerely, "...(it's) for everybody."

She does mean everybody — young and old have been frequenting her establishment since 1954, when polka was hot and beaded sweat clung to the brow of those who came to dance the night away. The club moved from its original location at 73rd Street and Western Avenue in 1982, to its presently downscaled Central Avenue address.

Although polka is not quite as popular as it was, Irene keeps busy tending to regular customers as well as the out-of-town clientele that have discovered it or had been searching. For Irene, the Baby Doll has always been a place where people can make a friend or meet a lover.

Irene, a humble celebrity, is an outstanding outgoing hostess who greets everyone that comes through her door and sets the mood for an evening that can't possibly go bad.

"Why stay at home?" Irene says.

There's a cozy den-like feel to the Baby Doll with its exposed rafters and dark brown paneling. The bar itself is very long, curving around in an L-shape at one end to accommodate a large crowd. Patrons seated at the front picture window are afforded an impressive view of Midway Airport.

The fully stocked bar has a variety of bottled domestic and tap beers (including the classic Old Style, an avert of mine). Import bottles include a popular Polish beer Zyweic (pronounced *Shiv Yets*). If you have the taste for a cocktail of exotic nature, they can most likely make it for you — all of the drinks are moderately priced considering the city location.

In the back of the bar is a ballroom, preceded by a small cabaret-style cocktail area that comfortably seats patrons who are waiting to dance or taking a short breather. It's a modest, raised wooden dance floor, complete with mirrored ball, where the dancers share their space with the band. This stage has hosted many polka legends, including her own son, Eddie Korosa Jr. The best night of the week, according to Irene, is Sunday night, for two reasons. First, there is usually some sort of celebration going on (a birthday, the occasional wedding anniversary, etc...) and secondly, the music starts earlier for those who don't or won't come out late on weekend evenings.

In between band breaks, or on the nights that the band isn't playing, there is a jukebox with a wide selection of Polka classics, crooners, country and even a little rock n' roll that keeps everyone dancing. Even if you don't know how to dance a polka you don't have to worry as there is someone who would be more than willing to show you how. There is never a cover charge and the dress is casual. No video games, no pool tables, and no darts; just drinking, dancing and romancing. We had a good time, and as I was relieving myself for the last time that evening, a gentleman asked me if it was our first time. I replied, "yes."

He looked up at me in the mirror and said, "I bet you'll be back." He was right, but I kind of knew I would all along.

— Arunas Ingaunis

BJ's Pub

7023 S. Harlem Ave.
773-586-2929
Hours: 7 p.m. to 2 a.m. Monday to Saturday, closed Sunday

BJ's Pub, located on Archer and Harlem avenues, does not necessarily offer anything new to the bar-going experience. What it does offer, however, is, "A warm smile and good service," according to bartender Cindy. One regular refers to Cindy as the best bartender on the South Side.

Another regular, Brian, who said he's been coming to BJ's for the past 10 years, was very quick to point out a friendly atmosphere in what he calls a typi-

Barfly BJ's Pub-Bohica Bar and Grill

cal neighborhood bar.

BJ's Pub is, in fact, a typical neighborhood bar. The pool table is well worn but in good condition. The dart board was lit up the entire time that I was in (and it was a Monday night).

Eager hockey fans watched the Hawks play on two TV screens behind the bar while they ate peanuts and drank Miller High Life (the only beer on tap).

They are also becoming increasingly popular for their food. BJ's Pub serves Chicago-style hot dogs that are so good, people come in just for the hot dogs, but most end up staying or at least returning often.

The average age of the people that come into the bar is 30ish, Cindy said adding that there is always room for new people to drop by and become regulars.

"Especially women," Brian added. "There are a lot of good looking single men here."

I noticed, from my comfortable barstool, that no one bought just one drink at a time. Every time someone ordered a beer, they told Cindy to make sure that she got this guy and that guy a drink.

The bar itself is very modest, with the necessities well within the reach of the bartender. It looks like it may have been the original bar dating back to when BJ's first opened its doors in the mid-1970s.

Actually, not much appears to have changed in the 20-plus years that Bobby has owned BJ's Pub. Not much has to when you have a successful operation like this one. You don't need to have 27 different beers on tap if you know that your patrons will be drinking just the one.

You don't need crazy trends or promotions to get people to come in and drink in a place that people want to come into anyway because they enjoy the company.

BJ's has the perfect blend of all the right ingredients to make a successful bar on the South Side or anywhere. They serve cold beer and good food.

So stop in, drink some beers, throw darts, and ask Cindy why the lights on the ceiling are shaped in an Italian flag. See ya there.

— Paul Barile

Bohica Bar and Grill
5518 S. Archer Ave.
773-581-0397
Hours: 3 p.m. to 2 a.m. weekdays, 11 a.m. to 3 a.m. Saturday, noon to 2 a.m. Sunday

Most bars these days seem to have a gimmick or cater to one specific group of people. Places like these do not allow "outsiders" to come in, sit down and be comfortable. Luckily there is Bohica where a diverse crowd can congregate, be comfortable and have no problems.

With an eclectic aura that absorbs everyone, Bohica seems to have everything to keep a diverse crowd happy. An inside that is constantly pouring out sounds

349

The South Side Bohica Bar and Grill-Boston's

via a band, DJ or jukebox. Televisions located in convenient spots throughout the bar and the place offers a comfortable outdoor patio.

Bohica has a quality that shows no bias of age, race, or sex; everyone is welcome here. This bar is a melting-pot that allows everyone to mingle and interact. Bohica has taken the challenge of allowing every type of person in and allows them to have a good time. The winners are the patrons.

The bar itself (closed off by a railing) has ample seating, and the main room is roomy enough so no one feels crowded. There's enough space for people to walk around and not have to worry about knocking into someone. Surprisingly, there is even enough room to walk around the pool table and not interrupt the game or the players.

Another Bohica extra is the "outdoor patio" or beer garden. A spacious garden-like spot where a person can sit back and enjoy the outside. With quick service, the patron is not forgotten and does not have to wait long to be taken care of.

The only few down sides of the Bohica is the actual size of the building. The building being long and narrow and made out of brick allows, unfortunately, all sounds to echo through the bar. With music and other usual bar noise, it could become very wearisome. Also, the front wall is retractable to let people roam freely into the beer garden. But, with the wall not there, all the noise of the bar escapes into the garden; so the tranquillity is lost.

All for all, though, Bohica is a good place to go for a good time. Good prices and nice people. What else could someone ask for in a bar?

— *William Gleich*

Boston's
451 W. 26th St.
312-842-9253
Hours: 1 p.m. to 2 a.m. Monday to Saturday, closed Sunday

One wouldn't expect the bar closest to Chinatown being titled Boston's, but it is. Chinatown has a wide variety of restaurants which serve various tropical drinks but there just isn't a place to pull up a stool and sit down for a drink and a cigarette.

Boston's is located southwest of the main Chinatown drag and is a typical neighborhood tavern. There is not much flash, not much of a drink variety, and nothing to eat. But there's plenty of stools and the beer is cold.

The layout is paneling, most everything in the place is paneled. The patrons are all local folks who know each other and stare rudely at visitors from outside the neighborhood. However, the bar does have cable television and I caught "Raiders of the Lost Ark" on the screen. So if you are in Chinatown and in dire need of a bar, drop by this place, but don't forget your copy of TV Guide.

— *Tony Gordon*

Brewskee's

11836 S. Western Ave.
773-238-2302
Hours: 4 p.m. to 2 a.m. Sunday to Friday,
4 p.m. to 3 a.m. Saturday

The sign across the street read, "Brewskee's Drinking Emporium," and featured an arrow pointing to this South Side tavern. It was a hot June night, and that sign just screamed, "Cold beer!" As I entered, in fact, the air conditioner above the door dripped moisture on my head.

Once in, another sign greeted me. This one, scrawled in black marker on a wall, read, "No hypocrites allowed, from Andy." This was written by the owner, I found out later, and not some vandal.

Andy is a nice guy, and a dynamic character. When I mentioned how different the temperature was inside the bar as compared to outside, he replied, "I don't care. I'll bring it down to 60 degrees in here if it keeps people happy."

What made me happy? The prices.

To Andy's credit, he charges just $2 for a bottle of Sam Adams. He charges the same for Michelob. Mickey's Big Mouth is only $1.75.

The bar features black wood and seats about 30. Tap selections include Bud, Old Style, Woodpecker and, as Andy is quick to point out, the best Guinness in town. They clean the lines on a regular basis, and have them changed every six months. This tap also has a machine that cools the Jagermeister to about 0 degrees Fahrenheit, the only tolerable temperature for cough medicine.

The rest of the decor is cool, sports-oriented stuff that isn't tacky. Anyone can put up a poster of O.J., but Brewskee's has very classy (and probably very expensive) pictures of sports stars, including one of Ditka in uniform.

The only amusement Brewskee's lacks is a pool table. The bar has video golf, pub darts, real darts, video poker and a card machine that baffles Andy himself. The jukebox is fantastic and very up to date. It includes the newest releases by Aerosmith, Counting Crows and, unfortunately, Seal. And I didn't have to crank my head around to see the game. The four TVs were all angled to make sure there isn't a bad seat in the house. Brewskee's shows all the games, too.

Brewskee's isn't overpriced or overdone. It makes one feel right at home. The bar still has ladies night on Fridays, drink specials and bands on most Fridays and Saturdays. And though the place is small, I know it rocks. The most important feature is up to par — the attitude (or lack thereof). I never once felt uncomfortable at this bar.

I walked in as a patron, not a writer. The bartender didn't know I was going to express my opinion to 24,000 people. Yet I was treated with kindness and respect. This place really cares about the patrons. Hell, they'll even rent it out to your for special occasions. Brewskee's caters to all — sports fans, music

The South Side Brewskee's-Buddy Guy's Legends

lovers, there was even a Harley parked in front.

I will go to Brewskee's again, whether I drive or take the bus. I give it my dad's highest rating: "It's a good joint." And, as his son would add, "Cleaner than a motherfucker, too."

— Bud

Buddy Guy's Legends
754 S. Wabash Ave.
312-427-0333
Hours: 5 p.m. to 2 a.m. Monday to Friday,
5 p.m. to 3 a.m. Saturday, 6 p.m. to 2 a.m. Sunday

This is one of the biggest blues bars in the Chicago area. The bill the night I stopped by featured Larry Coryell and Jimmy Johnson. Coryell is one of the founding fathers of jazz rock who has 60 releases. Johnson, one of Chicago's very own, has been playing for nearly 40 years.

I have visited this club a few times, but had not been here for the last two years. To my surprise, there were many improvements. Before the change, the bar kind of looked like a soup kitchen. The new look includes all blue walls just right to get you in the mood for the blues. About two years ago, Buddy Guy bought his partner's share and became the principal owner of this joint. There have been obvious changes for the better. There is a lot of memorabilia that hangs on much of the walls and includes many blues greats like Muddy Waters, Willie Dixon, Buddy Guy, Jimi Hendrix and many others. Also, there are guitars that hang behind the bar which adds class to any establishment.

There is a wide range of clientele. The customers could be tourists, college students, blues freaks, or yuppies. On my night there I didn't notice heavy drinking going on probably because there are no beer specials here. This is not a place where one comes to solely drink because the price for domestic bottles is about $2.75. The purpose of this club is to see and watch top-notch blues players. The bands can range anywhere from the Fabulous Thunderbirds to Luther Allison.

Besides music, there are four pool tables on the side which are away from the front of the stage. Also, if you are hungry, the kitchen is open from 5 p.m. to midnight Mondays through Fridays, 5 p.m. to 1 a.m. Saturdays and 6 p.m. to midnight Sundays.

If you are in the mood for some good blues or if you got the blues, turn south off of Congress Parkway on Wabash, head down about three blocks and be ready for some cookin' tunes.

— Pete Schmugge

Cal's Bar
488 S. Wells St.
312-922-6392
Hours: 9 a.m. to 7 p.m. Monday to Thursday,
9 a.m. to 8 p.m. Friday

Where's a booze hound to go for a relaxing cheap drink in the Downtown area and to escape the every-day pressures of getting up and going to work? Well, there's a place on Wells you've probably seen dozens of times and never really noticed it. Hidden behind beer banners and neatly tucked away between Cal's Liquors and Peppers fast food is Cal's Bar.

"Eat, Drink, & Get the Fuck Out!" is the motto at Cal's, and that's pretty much how things go around there. The clientele ranges from the buzzed board of trade worker, to blotto business men, to sauced Streetwise vendors. All races, religions, and creeds unite for the sole purpose of catching a buzz. God bless Cal's Bar!

The wall behind the bar is a huge mirror so you can actually watch yourself get drunk. Taped to the mirror are catchy phrases like, "If assholes could fly, this place would be an airport." The bar itself is an original from 1958 and somewhere under someone's ass is an original bar stool. If you can't sit at the bar, there's plenty of table seating between the makeshift garbage cans. They're really just empty beer boxes.

Cal's fabulous selection of ales, lager and swill is wide and affordable. On tap, they have Michael Shea's, JW Dundee's and Honey Brown. Domestic bottles start at $1.50 and imports at $2.25. Cal's also has a deal with Peppers. This is available for lunch or if you need something to cover up your breath. The food is burgers, hot dogs, beef and sausage all with fries for under $4.

Cal's Bar opens at 9 a.m., but if you need to start your day earlier, Cal's Liquors opens at 7:30. Sure you might have to drink it in the alley or under your desk, but it's better than being sober. Cal's Bar closes at 7 p.m. (8 p.m. on Friday) and then it's really time to get the fuck out. No weekends either.

Cal's is a great place for many reasons (and seasons) and is rich in history, but Cal's should be known and recognized for keeping Chicago drunk. Cheers to Cal's.

— *Chris Olvera*

Carol's Archer Pub
5978 S. Archer Ave.
Hours: 11 a.m. to 2 a.m. weekdays,
11 a.m. to 3 a.m. Saturday, hours on Sunday vary

Guided by voices and the smell of a cold beer, I found myself down on Archer Avenue once again. I am quickly becoming enamored with the scene in that section of the city. At Carol's Archer Pub, they truly emphasize the "relax and have a beer" attitude of the South Side of our fair city.

The South Side Carol's Archer Avenue Pub

As with most bars in the area, Carol's (named for Carol the owner) bypasses trendy names and decor and settles in with the traditional beer signs and astro-turf coasters. Everything about this bar, from Cathy, a genial bartender, to a vibrating fish pinball game, speaks of comfort for the travel-weary drinker.

Carol's offers a couple of drink specials that are sure to tempt even the jaded barfly. Every Tuesday they offer 50-cent tap beer and on Friday (a drink special on Friday you ask?) they have all shots $1. Did I mention that they have free pool and darts on Wednesday nights from 8 p.m. until midnight?

The music from the CD player is at a perfect level. When you are drinking you don't want to have to yell your incoherences to your friends. Here you can talk to your friends without being embarrassed because the jukebox cuts off while you were still yelling about your last hangover.

Family-owned and operated was never as evident as it is here, where they keep personalized shot glasses behind the bar with the names of all of the regulars painted on them.

There is also time and energy spent raising money and holding food drives for local families that are in need. I, for one, feel better knowing that the money I am spending is going to people who are interested in putting it back into the neighborhood, not some Loop corporate office.

Carol and her family have been in this location since 1992 and have developed an acute sense for what the clientele is looking for — an established South Side trend that I am finding more and more often.

While Lincoln Avenue bars offer the latest popular food (hummus in a bar? P-U-H-L-E-A-S-E...) Carol's offers such culinary delights as Sloppy Joes with chips or cheeseburgers. The kind of food that belongs in a bar because it was designed to have a less negative affect on your condition.

When asked about a typical night, Cathy told us this, "Basically, we have a mixed crowd. You can't say that they are mostly old or mostly young, and if women want to meet men, this is the place. Lawyers, laborers, we have all types coming here."

Another South Side trend, one that I am having a bit of trouble with, is that they seem to think that Corona and Molson are the premium imported beers. This is not really a problem, per se, more like an adjustment one has to make. Everything else about these places makes it well worth the trip.

So, when you have had enough bars that change their name with every season, take I-55 south to Central, go south to Archer, west to the front door of Carol's Archer Pub and tell Cathy we said hello. And remember...Drink now...it may be later than you think.

—Paul Barile

Chateau Lounge and Liquors

3904 W. 47th Street
Hours: 10 a.m. to 2 a.m. Sunday, Monday,
Wednesday, Friday and Saturday,
7 a.m. to 2 a.m. Tuesday and Thursday

It is early Saturday evening at the Chateau Lounge and Liquors on 47th Street on Chicago's Southwest Side. Angie, the bartender is waiting to train two new bartenders who are already a half hour late.

To call Angie a bartender is a gross understatement. She is currently serving drinks, cooking in the kitchen, serving the food she cooks, and running package goods out of the front of the building. She does all of this with a smile on her face and a joke for the customers.

The Chateau Lounge and Liquors is the archetypal Chicago corner bar. The bar itself is a big square in the middle of the next room. There is no room for a pool table although there is a dart board on the wall. Two televisions showing football (when every other bar we went into was showing some bullshit stock car race) and a jukebox with everything from NIN to Frankie Yankovic add to the ambiance.

For tap beer drinkers, the selection is limited to Red Dog (No thanks), Old Style (No way) and MGD, with a really cool Bulls Basketball tapper complete with rim and net.

Above the bar hangs the Budweiser globe with the motorized Clydesdales rotating pulling the mini-wagon of Budweiser. This is in addition to the beercap clocks, cheesecake posters and neon animals with a beer name tattooed onto their neon backs.

Across the bar from us, a large headed marine-looking guy is sharing a laugh and toasting something that the long-haired biker next to him just said. A few beers later, it looked like Bill Clinton drinking beer with Carlos Santana.

The trainees have still not shown up but Angie continues to move through the bar and the front register with agility and grace not seen since Number 34 (Bear's legend Walter Payton) in the early 1980s.

Food is served at the Chateau from 11 a.m. to 1 a.m. daily. With the standard variety of hamburgers and chili. They offer an incredible variety of Beef Jerky products as well. This is the type of food that really only belongs in bars and gas stations.

As we get ready to leave, we stop at the cash register to buy cigarettes ($2.50 a pack in a bar is unheard of) and out pops Angie from behind the bar. She grins happily and greets us as if we are new customers and she wants to welcome us. She gives me my smokes and we walk out the door and back into the summer heat. My partner and I look at each other and laugh. We'll be back. We will definitely be back.

— Paul Barile

The Checkerboard Lounge

423 E. 43rd St.
773-624-3240
Hours: noon to 2 a.m. Sunday to Friday,
noon to 3 a.m. Saturday

Pick up any local guidebook and somewhere in it you're sure to find Chicago proclaimed as the "Blues Capitol of the World." We are so established as such that even the mighty conglomeration known as House of Blues has recently arrived to pay homage to our city with its river-front megamall. It's ironic, though, that only a handful of successful blues clubs still exist on the South Side, where it all really began and where in the late 1950s it was all but impossible to walk through the Bronzeville area without finding live blues in one club after another.

By the 1970s, the blues in Chicago was becoming a North Side way of life for a new audience of white, upper-middle-class fans. Most of you have been to at least one or two of the more popular blues clubs on the right-side-of-the-tracks: B.L.U.E.S., Kingston Mines, Blue Chicago, or B.L.U.E.S. Etcetera. Few of you, however, have ventured down to 423 E. 43rd St., where the legendary Checkerboard Lounge still lives as the hottest club in town.

You don't have to be a musicologist to know that the blues is more than chords, bent notes, guitars, and amplifiers. It's also attitude and ambiance. The Checkerboard Lounge has plenty of both. The first time I went there was in 1979. I hadn't been back again until this past January, on one of those middle-of-the-month sub-zero afternoons. The building that houses the lounge is still as run down as I remember it, but the hand-painted block letters telling you where you are seem cleaner and more colorful. The neighborhood is somewhat threatening, but once inside, the atmosphere is friendly and color-blind. I was the only white person out of the nine customers. Of the other eight, there were five woman and three men. For the entire two hours that I was there, the jukebox never stopped cranking out music from Koko Taylor, Willie Dixon, Sonny Boy Williamson, Muddy Waters, John Lee Hooker, and other blues artists; some cornerstone, some from just around the corner. In fact, the bartender told me that the lounge is a regular hangout for a lot of South Side bluesman. He didn't say who; not wanting to seem too much like a tourist, I didn't ask.

Before leaving that afternoon, I had a lengthy conversation with two new friends: Linda and Keisha. Over shots of Martel and bottles of Budweiser, we talked about the Taste of Chicago, Dennis Rodman, restaurants, riding the el, O.J., blues music, and, of course, the weather: a great conversation starter anywhere. I danced with Keisha to what I think was a Valerie Wellington song, during which I noticed a sign behind the bar which prohibited using profanity while inside the lounge. Unusual, I thought, for a place so decrepit to the eye, but not at all unusual for a place so warm to the soul.

I returned to the Checkerboard Lounge on a recent Friday night. The music

Barfly Checkerboard Lounge-Ciral's House of Tiki

begins nightly at 9:30 p.m. Cover charges vary, but average around $6. At night, the lounge uses its own off-street parking lot, which is located nearby, and has a security guard on duty. You can, on request be escorted back to your car. Don't worry, though, even with all these precautions, a visit to the Checkerboard Lounge is still a fairly deep plunge into the world of real, urban blues.

After spending part of an afternoon with Linda, Keisha, and six other patrons, give or take a few stragglers, I was surprised to discover this time at how small the lounge actually is. It seats about 100, with standing room for a couple of hundred more, but it only takes half that to make the place feel really crowded.

I was lucky enough to catch the great Vance Kelly, whose music hit the ground running. The front of the stage was jammed with people, both white and black, dancing, clapping, and singing along. In between songs, there was more than a little handshaking between musicians and the audience. There were shouts of approval, also. Three extremely pretty woman wearing pulled down fedoras made there way to the front and danced in such a slow, surging, sexual way that the word tentative was given a seat in the back for the rest of that evening.

In between one of his sets, I was able to have a few words with Vance Kelly. He was sincerely touched that someone from northwestern suburbia would cross over so much "foreign" territory just to hear him play. Someone chirped in, "There's nothing foreign about the blues." As insipid as that remark seemed then, it does carry with it a great deal of accuracy.

— *George Rawlinson*

Ciral's House of Tiki
1612 E. 53rd St.
773-684-1221
Hours: 2 p.m. to 4 a.m. Monday to Friday,
2 p.m. to 5 a.m. Saturday

There is so much to love about this Hyde Park tavern, where should I begin?

The House of Tiki is not too hard to find being just blocks from the lake and having one of the most amazing neon signs the city has to offer. Walking into the House of Tiki, one can not help but to gawk at this beautiful shrine to those Polynesian gods. Tiki statuettes honor the walls with their weapons, glowing blowfish swim underneath bamboo rafters as wicker monkeys hang from the same and all the while incredibly designed zombie glasses overwhelm the coconut cups and Tiki god porcelain glasses. There is so much in the decoration, it's too numerous to mention it all.

One of my new drinking companions, Keith, the self-proclaimed "Mayor of Hyde Park" said it best referring to the decor, "If this place ever closes down, I want to buy just six things." Knowing so many others would want to get their hands on a few of the decorations.

Sitting at the bar while checking out the decor, it's hard for the curious to not

The South Side Ciral's House of Tiki-Cork and Kerry

bend the ear of Bea and Ted, the best hosts in Chicago. "There's an old story in everything in here," said Bea who told us some of them as we continued to quiz her on the particulars of the decorations, which they have been collecting for the bar since 1968. Also, in that same year, the House of Tiki was a regular spot for many important players in the 1968 Democratic National Convention like Abbie Hoffman.

Today, one of the main attractions of the bar is its jukebox. Stocked with 78 rpm records of various songs from the 1930s, 1940s and 1950s, it adds to the post-WW II feel of the place.

The room is large because the House of Tiki is also a restaurant. The dining room exemplifies the Tiki decor more than the bar, making the dining experience a quality one. The food is delicious with a recommended choice being the fish and chips. The menu consists of many classic tavern meals, not the usual fare of quick-fried stuffs or sandwiches. The prices are reasonable, starting around $5. The kitchen stays open until the odd hour of 3:15 a.m. So for any late-night starving bar patron, this establishment should be put on anyone's list.

What's a Tiki bar without tropical drinks? The House of Tiki is the place to go for those rum-based fruity drinks. They carry the traditional as well as some of their own personal recipes that are very intriguing. For the record, Bea and Ted know everyone who lives within walking distance of the House, so if you want to try a "zombie" (six shots of five different rums in a 20-ounce glass) you better prove you have a designated driver. There is large choice of Polynesian specialties, so don't be afraid to be a little finicky. Beers include a selection of Beck's, Miller products, Old Style, etc., all in bottles.

Typical in Hyde Park, the crowd is very mixed due to University of Chicago's students and professors, neighborhood folks and the lack of drinking establishments in the area. The mood is always laid back and there are plenty of people throughout the week, Friday night is the big night and the place is packed to the gills.

— *Phil Brandt*

Cork and Kerry
10614 S. Western Ave.
312-445-2675
Hours: 11 a.m. to 2 a.m. Sunday to Friday,
noon to 3 a.m. Saturday

Among the slew of bars in this section of the Southwest Side, the Cork and Kerry stands out as one of the more popular places, especially on the weekends. Though it may seem as though this bar jumped from Wrigleyville to the South Side, it remains true to its South Side Irish form and flare.

During the day, the bar fills with regulars of an older stature with their noticeable Irish accents, but on weekend nights a younger crowd takes over with their mass numbers and few accents. The Cork and Kerry, however, still prevails as another definitive Chicago neighborhood tavern.

Barfly Cork and Kerry-Exchequer Pub

The bar is beautiful with wood and glass used to decorate throughout. There is ample seating and plenty of room where one can stand and chat with friends during drinking sessions. For the hot summer months, the Cork and Kerry is one of the few bars in this locale to have a large beer garden to escape into the heat. The area which encompasses the beer garden is enclosed between the Cork and Kerry building and a neighboring business. There is a wooden fence which closes off the garden from the street, but it reportedly still takes in a fair amount of breeze when the wind is blowing.

Similar to North Side bars is the amount of sports stuff that hogs the patrons heads. There is a (what seems standard in this section of the city) sports constantly on the televisions so the boys in baseball caps can release their sporting event testosterone. The jukebox unfortunately does not have the Clancy Brothers or other great Irish bands to relieve one from the drone of sporting events, but does have the latest in pop rock hits with a few classic rock discs on the list.

The beer selection is good and consistent with the Irish neighborhood featuring, of course, Bass, Guinness, Harp as well as a few microbrews. Though many patrons order domestic products, the biggest selling imported beer is Guinness, so sometimes the kegs run out faster than any of the other tap beer. The list of shots and cocktails is high with an excellent choice of gin, vodka and whiskey. Again, the prices are reasonable.

— Phil Brandt

Exchequer Pub
226 S. Wabash Ave.
312-939-5633
Hours: 11 a.m. to midnight Monday to Saturday, noon to 9 p.m. Sunday

The name, Exchequer Pub, seems to suggest that this is a place worthy of consideration by Chicago's more tasteful inebriates. And a tasteful place it is, without question. However, the "Pub" portion of the Exchequer makes up a relatively small share of business itself.

Located under the shadow of the Wabash Avenue El tracks, the Exchequer is a deep three-room facility, with a 20-foot bar (appearing exceptionally well-stocked) lining one side of the first room. Two rooms beyond that are strewn with tables and chairs for that portion of the population that uses silverware rather than a straw when having lunch.

There is a jukebox, of course, and a serve-yourself popcorn maker along one wall, with four screens generally tuned to ESPN. Exchequer lists nine beers by the bottle and nine on tap. Clientele, according to the manager, tends towards Loop business people, with a solid share of theater traffic before and after nearby performances at the Shubert on Monroe. DePaul University's Loop campus is even closer, so faculty and grad students are regular visitors.

Not a place to bring the softball team or watch a Bulls' game, the Exchequer

The South Side Exchequer Pub-50 Yard Line Sports Bar

is better suited to a quiet drink after work, with dinner an option if the beer is going down more smoothly than usual. The menu ranges from appetizers and seafoods to shish-kabob and fillet mignon, with standard sandwiches, Italian specialities and thick and thin crust pizza rounding out an impressive bill of fare. Entrees start around $6 and go no higher than $11.95 for the New York sirloin, with pizzas topping out at $15.

The Exchequer is a museum of Chicago culture, an above version of the Billy Goat Tavern lacking only the stilted Chicago speech patterns. The walls feature photos of past mayors and presidents, as well as front pages from the days when three newspapers fought for the Windy City's readers. A relatively modern Bears poster featuring the Black and Blues Brothers (Anyone else remember Stephan Humphries?) fits in well with the black and white memorabilia.

Not a classic bar in itself, but the Exchequer serves its purpose well. If you want to see Chicago in one hour, with the roar of the El train putting ripples in the beer pitcher that's next to the pizza, then use the door under the green awning, and you won't be disappointed.

50 Yard Line Sports Bar and Grill
69 E. 75th St.
773-846-0005
Hours: 10 a.m. to 2 a.m. Sunday through Friday,
10 a.m. to 3 a.m. Saturday

Has any other Barfly reader noticed that civility is disappearing faster than Twinkies at George Foreman's house?

There is a national epidemic of disintegrating manners. Even in Chicago, churlish boors push cartloads of cheese curls and fig bars through the line clearly marked for 10 items or less. Others clip their fingernails in restaurants, while still other barbarians try to force themselves into elevators before well-behaved passengers are allowed to exit.

Fortunately, there are places in which the basic rules of courtesy are still followed. One is the 50 Yard Line Sports Bar and Grill, located a block or two east of the Dan Ryan Speedway on 75th Street. Here, patrons and staff realize that rude behavior, screaming and in-your-face conflict belongs only in the world of daytime talk shows.

Manager Zack Blasingame runs a place that is chiseled in class. His clientele is predominately African-American, but most noticed just for a moment that I was the lone white in a sea of color. During the day, the 50 Yard Line is a relaxed sports bar with enough television screens that your vision is never blocked. Bar stools are comfortable, and upholstered with material that features sports logos on each seat.

Reproductions of famous black athletes line the walls. Muhammed Ali is

Barfly Fifty Yard Line

50 Yard Line Sports Bar and Grill, 69 E. 75th St., is one of the classiest sports bars in Chicago.

awarded the most space. My favorite, though, is an action shot of the great Sugar Ray Robinson landing a hook square to the jaw of the raging bull, Jake LaMotta.

On weekends, the bar features a moderately priced brunch that is terrific and has it all, including the regular soul dishes you'd expect.

At night, the club becomes a hot-hot-hot spot. Large, but friendly, doormen enforce a dress code. Fashion faux paus include gym shoes, ripped jeans, baseball caps and anything hinting at gang affiliation. You must be at least 25 to enter, something that reduces the dog collar and satanic tattoo crowd to zero. It also disqualifies those youngbloods who are easily dissed and immediately bold. On Fridays and Saturdays there is a $5 cover charge; a small price to pay, I thought, to be in the company of many of our city's most beautiful women.

Weekend nights also feature a disc jockey who plays hits by Babyface, Blackstreet, Brandy, En Vogue, Luther Vandross and other soulful performers. A cluster of colored, overhead lights illuminate the mixing and matching of well-dressed men and women. I almost expected to see Lonetta McKee and Billy Dee Williams slip onto the floor.

Bartenders wear black ties. Not only are they attentive, but they pour drinks and converse with equipoise. Mixed drinks aren't cheap ($3.50), but every third or fourth one came "on the house," compliments of Teddy, just about the 327th bartender that I know by name. Teddy was quite gracious, even refusing to chastise a Wesley Snipes stand-in who knocked over a drink while taking notice of a Chanel-scented diva.

There is an adjacent room, more for conversation than introduction. Glass partitions separate the two rooms.

The bar's owners spent a lot of money on the decor, and it shows. Polished wood tables and pillars ooze sophistication. Perhaps the sound system could use a slight update, but that's only because the music gets such worshipful attention.

The Fifty Yard Line has been in its current location for eight years. Business is good, with crowds growing to near capacity on weekends after 11 p.m. The club rests on a residential street, and Blasingame and his employees work hard to make sure order and respect is enforced for their neighbors. As with everything else, security is carried out with aplomb.

I realize that for many of you, a trip down to 75th Street is as likely as a weekend in Rio de Janeiro. Don't forget, though, that Chicago is more than Lincoln Park, pulled-over cabs that snarl traffic and young preppy boys and girls. What's more, there's chic night life across the river; there's even Armani, Calvin Klein and Gucci. So, if you want to get a sense of how urbane the South Side can get after dark, a night at the Fifty Yard Line is a must.

— George Rawlinson

The Fireside Beverly
10730 S. Western Ave.
773-779-3606
Hours: 4 p.m. to 2 a.m. Tuesday to Sunday.
The kitchen is open until midnight.
The Fireside is closed on Monday

After years of traveling across the country, living and working in the suburbs and the North Side — South Side native Bob Jones has returned to his childhood neighborhood and opened up the Fireside Restaurant Beverly.

"You have a lot of ups and downs in your life and this has been an up," said Jones who along with his wife Beth and investors Rich Wohn and John Lydon opened up the Fireside Restaurant Beverly in November, 1996.

In August, 1996, the group purchased the building, that had housed the Maple Tree Inn, from Charlie Orr. The Maple Tree Inn has moved to 13301 S. Old Western Ave., in Blue Island.

"I used to come here 15 years ago," Jones said of the Maple Tree. "I ate here, drank here, went to White Sox games from here. I grew up here."

Jones, age 42, has been in the restaurant business off and on for the last 27 years. His first restaurant job, at age 15, was in 1970 at a Burger King located at 87th Street and Cicero Avenue.

In college at Western Illinois University he continued working in restaurants. After college, he went on a six-year restaurant hiatus to work as an engineer.

"I was sitting at a desk with a calculator, bored and reading the Wall Street

Barfly Fireside Beverly

Journal," Jones said.

So he quit his engineering job, stayed in Chicago long enough to watch the Cubs blow the 1984 division playoffs to the Padres and hopped on his motorcycle and drove cross-country.

He went down to Jacksonville, Florida, and up to Alaska, stopping long enough to work in a few restaurants and bars.

"I worked in a honkey tonk in Jacksonville," Jones said. "I even wore a cowboy hat."

He later returned to Chicago and worked in a Downtown night club, then a North Side Tavern and for 4 1/2 years he worked for Rich Wohn and his Fireside Restaurant at 5739 N. Ravenswood Ave.

The events that led to the creation of the Fireside Beverly were random.

"Things just fell together," said Jones looking around at his newly opened restaurant. "I had my 40th birthday here two years ago."

Jones and his wife moved from the North Side and now live above the restaurant.

"Neither of us have ever been happier," Jones said.

The restaurant business is a new field for Beth. She had been working as a dental hygienist and seems pleased with the change.

"I love it so far," Beth said. "It's a totally new thing for me but I am liking it a lot."

The pair enlisted their large legion of friends to rehab and redecorate the 74 year-old building which was once the Orr family home. The result is a beautiful, warm, cozy establishment that beckons one to relax with a fine meal and a drink.

The bar area is long and narrow. The room has an exposed-brick wall and lots of windows. The most interesting of these, are the windows behind the bar that enable bar patrons to peak at the dining room located a half-level above the bar.

To drink, Jones has 16 different beers on tap like Breckenridge IPA, Schell Pils, Goose Island Honkers Ale and Golden Prairie.

"I've always been a beer person," said Jones. "All my faves are here."

Jones is responsible for the Ravenswood Fireside Restaurant's brewmaster dinners that are widely popular.

He also serves a great deal of wine in Beverly. He said he has trained his staff on the stock of wines and beers that he carries. So they are able to help patrons in selecting a wine or beer.

The dining room has a country-feel to it. Jones knocked down several walls and opened the room up. He put in textured walls and brightened the room.

A small room adjacent to the dining area is a former bedroom which Jones now calls the library. It has several tables and booths.

"This was Charlie's mother's bedroom," Jones said. "This was Charlie's grandparent's home. I'm the only owner outside of his family."

The bulk of the work Jones did on the building was centered in the kitchen.

The South Side Fireside Beverly-Galloway's Mystic

Most of what is now the kitchen was a part of the bar area at the Maple Tree. During a walk through of the kitchen, Jones pointed out a section which used to have a dart board and tables. The area now has stoves and refrigerators.

Heading the kitchen is chef Joe Miller who formerly worked at the Maple Tree as well as the Hyatt and Marriott corporations.

"The guy's just unbelievable," Jones said. "We tell him he can never leave."

Miller created much of the menu which in pricing is similar to the Ravenswood Fireside but many of the dishes are different.

For starters, Miller's Artichoke Fritters are very popular. The dish features tender artichoke hearts stuffed with fresh herbed goat cheese and fried in a tempura beer batter until golden brown.

"Everything is made from scratch," Jones said. "Our Artichoke Fritters are unbelievable."

The menu features nine other starters, five different salads and an extensive entree list of specialties, meat dishes, seafood dishes, light dishes, pastas, desserts and a kids' menu.

A dish Jones is especially excited about is Cajun Meatloaf made moist and hearty, laced with Cajun spices and Miller's homemade smoked andouille sausage and served with natural juices on the side.

The portion his so huge that most people have to take much of the meal home. And for those who take the meatloaf home, Jones recommends melting Monterey jack or provolone cheese on top with green olives.

One of the best days to stop by the Fireside Beverly is St. Patrick's Day when the infamous South Side parade marches right in front of the Fireside. Windows in the restaurant are open for parade viewing and a beer stand is set up outside.

Jones smiles when asked how it feels to have his own place.

"I've never been happier in my life," Jones said. "It's just awesome except for my car, we both have shitty cars."

— Tony Gordon

Galloway's Mystic
10649 S. Pulaski Road
773-239-2626
Hours: noon to 2 a.m. Sunday to Friday,
noon to 3 a.m. Saturday

Mystic is not a mystical place. It seems that the sole purpose is to cater to the just-turned-twenty-one group. The bar offers darts, and a small, but sufficient, beer garden.

Mystic is a local bar that put in neon, mirrors, and a few lithographs; so that they could set themselves apart from the other local bars. Yet, after accomplishing the task of setting itself apart, the bar does not offer anything different. The service is good, prices are all right, offering monthly specials.

Barfly Galloway's Mystic-Groucho's Bar and Grill

Inside the bar the constant sound from the jukebox is a good companion — if you're into newer music, with a mix of Sinatra and other crooners. Also with several televisions well placed, a patron can easily watch some sporting events.

The actual bar nearly runs the entire length of the building — allowing enough room for everyone to be comfortable. Sadly though, the bar's two dart boards rest close to the bar. If someone does not tread carefully, the expected can happen.

On the outside on the right night, the outdoors can be enjoyed in the beer garden. With no bar in the garden, you have to walk back and forth inside to the bar. Small, but secluded, the garden is the best kept secret of Mystic. Few wander into the garden — that is good for there are not many tables to sit at.

Regrettably, the main problem with Mystic is the lack of parking. Unless you were willing to walk from the side streets, which proves to be the only legal parking in the area, the lack of parking can only hinder business. This is a local spot — definitely a nice place to go to if you live nearby.

— *Bill Gleich*

Groucho's Bar and Grill
8355 S. Pulaski Road
773-767-4838
Hours: 3 p.m. to 4 a.m. weekdays,
noon to 5 a.m. Saturday, 11 a.m. to 4 p.m. Sunday

In making a voyage of 25 miles from the North Side to this long standing South Side drinking establishment, I wondered if I was in for a surprise? To my recollection, the journey was well worth it. Groucho's has much to offer its patrons.

There is plenty of choices in their beer selection. There are more than 25 bottled beers. The prices range anything from $1.75 for Miller to $2.50 for Dab. On tap, there are four beers choices which includes Miller, Killians, Honey Brown Lager, and Lite. Also, there are drink specials every day.

On Tuesday, Miller bottles are only a buck. On Wednesday, pitchers of beer are a mere $1.75. On Friday, Amstel Lite is $1.25. There are two specials where you get to keep the pint glasses with the logos. For $2.25, you can get a Killian's and refills for $2. Also, Honey Brown Lager is $2 for the first one and refills for $1.75. These are two tasty brews and you get to keep the glass not bad for a Barfly.

Groucho's is a long narrow bar. In the back, there are two pool tables and two dart boards which are used the entire night. There is a very long bar that goes form the front to the back. There are plenty of seats available, if you are not playing pool or darts. A few nights a week, there is a DJ. On Saturday, there is live bands that range from tribute bands to local blues heroes. If you are hungry, there is a kitchen where you can get a delicious meal at a reasonable price.

The crowd at this local bar is mixed. The age ranges anything from 21 to 50.

365

The South Side Groucho's Bar and Grill-Guide's Sports

For those looking for a babe, there are some good looking ladies at this drinking hole who are not married. This a comfortable bar where you can have a good time that isn't restricted with dress codes and high prices. Also, the bar is kind of dark which is good for your wrinkles.

If you are on the Southwest Side of Chicago, I highly recommend you to make a stop at this comfortable drinking establishment. You will get friendly service from bartenders and the waitresses. Don't worry about parking, Groucho's has its own parking lot.

— Pete Schmugge

Guide's Sports Club
5544 S. Archer Ave.
773-284-0634
Hours: 9 a.m. to 2 a.m. Sunday to Friday,
9 a.m. to 3 a.m. Saturday

You gotta get down to Guide's Sports Club right now. This spacious 50 year-old Chicago landmark bar should not be missed by anyone who likes to drink beer or eat Buffalo Wings. (Forget Hooters, Guide's has meatier wings and prettier waitresses). Joe Guide, who has owned the bar for the past 18 years has established such a friendly relaxed atmosphere that he nurtures even to the point of noticing that I had left my car lights on which probably saved me a dead battery.

On the night that I stopped at Guide's, a lucky guy named Bob Thomas was having his bachelor party. He and his friends Sue Wilkinson and Marge Markoff have been coming to the bar for the last 15 years and decided that it would be the perfect place to celebrate his upcoming nuptials.

"It's a neighborhood melting pot," Wilkinson offers. "People from the neighborhood come in after work for a beer and to see their friends."

"We know the owner," said Markoff. "He's a real good guy who does a lot for the local sports teams."

"I come for the De Lisa Pizza," Thomas says. "I grew up on De Lisa Pizza and this is the last place that has it."

I tried the De Lisa pizza and it is a good reason to come into any bar. The crust was so thin and the cheese was so perfectly seasoned that I ate almost an entire pizza myself, after devouring the order of Buffalo Wings that will often be imitated but never duplicated, as they say.

As for the bar itself, it is very spacious and comfortable. The back bar is the original from nearly 50 years ago. It is mostly crafted wood and a lot of mirrors and is very well maintained and stocked.

"The crowd varies," Guide said. "The weekday crowd is a little older than the weekend crowd. But generally everyone who comes in has fun and enjoys themselves."

They have a different special Monday through Thursday including $3 pitchers on Thursday nights. This complements the extensive menu which includes a variety of sandwiches as well as the pizza and Buffalo Wings.

The bar also sponsors many trips to sporting events as well as golf outings, Myrtle Beach vacation trips and an annual Las Vegas trip.

So you see that this is not some "passing fancy" that will come and go as quickly as Green Day. This is a bar with staying power more akin to the Rolling Stones.

This is also a bar that you should visit as often as possible. You work hard for your money so you should get the most from every dollar you spend. You will if you spend it at Guide's Sports Club on Archer Avenue.

— *Paul Barile*

Illinois Bar and Grill
4135 W. 47th St.
773-847-8218
Hours: 7 a.m. to 2 a.m. Monday to Friday,
9 a.m. to 3 a.m. Saturday, 11 a.m. to 2 a.m. Sunday

Walking into the Illinois Bar and Gill, I was hit by a rush of moist cold air courtesy of a brand new air conditioning unit. The only thing that cheered me more was to see that they offered Rolling Rock longnecks for $1.50.

Pulling myself up onto the barstool, I noticed that everyone around me appeared to be happy. That theme runs pretty solid on the South Side (most North Siders seem to have this sullener-than-thou attitude).

The atmosphere was like a summer party on the beach back when you could do that without fear of police intervention. Michelle, behind the bar, was moving from patron to patron dispensing drinks and taking orders for the people working the six-foot-long grill.

They maintain a menu ranging from chili to lemon pepper chicken sandwich, and prices are so reasonable I thought that the menu was left over from the Reagan era. The big attraction (pun intended) though is the "Famous Illinois Burger." In all of my years of hedonistic excess, I have never seen a slab of red meat that large that wasn't still standing in a pasture.

What started out in 1985 as a little place to get a sandwich and a beer, has turned into one of Chicago's drinking and dining treasures.

While giving me a little history on the bar, Kathy James said she still likes to refer to it as a "regular corner bar." It is easy to see, however, that with the continuous expansion, it won't be long before it is a major competitor on the Chicago club and restaurant scene.

Owner Frank Vrchota personally guarantees quality and comfort at a time when, frankly, those are not priorities for businesses anymore. He even printed his personal beeper number on the menu for unhappy customers. There have been none yet.

For the true Chicago sports buff, there are two of the most unique plaques that I have ever seen anywhere. The Bears' plaque glares menacingly down from the bar with (what looks like) real bear claws imbedded in the fingers.

The North Side Illinois Bar and Grill-Joe Bailly's

The Bulls' plaque boasts real bull's horns mounted onto the wooden Bull's head. It's almost enough to make me a fan of Chicago sports. Nah!

There is plenty of parking around the building for cars as well as motorcycles. Kathy is very quick to point out that everyone is welcome all of the time. Did I mention that they serve Green River?

Take the time to make it down to Illinois Bar and Grill. Try the burgers and a cold beer (or two). Wherever you are, it'll be worth the ride.

And in the meantime...try to stay cool....

— Paul Barile

Joe Bailly's

10854 S. Western Ave.
773-238-1313
Hours: 11 a.m. to 2 a.m. Monday to Saturday,
9 a.m. to 1 a.m. Sunday

Joe Bailly's is a fun, upscale, Irish sports bar. My first impression of Joe Bailly's was that it was too 'dressy' to just get a beer and sit around in after work but that wasn't true. The indoor/outdoor bar area is great for after hours plus the establishment provides a separate tablecloth dining area for dinner.

The outdoor tables seem to be the spot of choice. They are set back a short distance from the main road, Western Avenue. The noise level is surprisingly low, probably due to the large number of potted trees and plants that enclose the area. The garden look gives the outdoor area a very "Euro" feel.

I sat inside at the bar on a wooden stool and had a draft beer. They have a full service menu with different appetizers. I opted for the chicken wings. Joe Bailly's has an excellent system for ordering chicken wings. Instead of ordering a pre-arranged number, you can order how ever many you like for 25 cents a piece.

Chicken wings, beer and watching sports are nearly synonymous. The bar has several televisions hanging from the ceiling, all conveniently located. While I was there, beach soccer was the program of choice. It is an entertaining sport.

The crowd at the bar was in their late 20s to early 30s, with a few exceptions. The patrons and employees were very friendly and it was easy to make conversation.

Parking is available in the front. It's convenient because your car is safely parked in a lot and not on the street. Plus you don't have to drive in circles for half an hour to find a spot.

Joe Bailly's is a great spot if you should find yourself on the far Southwest Side.

— T.M. Kornelsen

Julie's Place

5237 S. Cicero Ave.
773-582-8209
Hours: 11 a.m. to 2 a.m. Monday to Saturday, hours vary Sunday

God I love the South Side. I love the cheap beer and the friendly people and the shameless cheesecake posters on every wall. Julie's Place, on South Cicero Avenue, is no exception.

From the time that I walked into Julie's Place, Gino and Rafael, two of the regulars, made me feel like I was part of their extended family. They shared stories about the bar and some of the more colorful characters who inhabit it on a regular basis.

There is nothing trendy about Julie's Place. They don't employ gimmicks to bring patrons in. They employ two simple concepts that are steeped in South Side Bar frame-of-mind.

The first is low prices. On Mondays, you can get a 16-ounce Budweiser for a buck. On Wednesdays, a pitcher of Bud is only $3.50. All pints of draft beer are only $1.50 all the time.

While they don't have anything exotic on tap, it is still good to know that you can get a good buzz at a good price.

The second concept is a clean and friendly atmosphere. Throughout most of my experiences, the one most single annoying feature in most bars, is frat rats with their Hootie and the Blowhards concert T-shirts standing in groups blocking the bathroom.

These guys are less prevalent in the South Side bars which makes the experience more enjoyable. The guys like Gino and Rafael who will shake hands with you and buy you a drink are much more conducive to a pleasant bar experience.

As far as the cleanliness part, Julie keeps a very clean bar. While cleanliness may not be important to everyone, I have always believed that a clean bar is a happy bar. This is a very happy bar.

For eats they have (what else) Big Al's pizza. Another South Side staple is anything relating to Big Al. At Julie's Place it is the pizza.

I have to admit, I was kind of perplexed by the sign on the women's bathroom door that read "Women only please." But I think that some things are better left unasked.

The pool table is in a small alcove next to the bar, so that the players won't bother the drinkers and vice versa. On the south wall is the familiar tapestry of the "Dogs playing pool" which helps lend a certain familiarity to the bar.

The jukebox is full of "everything from Zeppelin to country music," Gino says.

Rafael concurs and adds that it has the best selection that he knows of a jukebox. I would agree that there is a nice cross-section of music which would

The South Side Julie's Place-Juniper Club

make me wonder why "Rhinestone Cowboy" is the most popular selection.

In addition to the standard bar decor and cheesecake posters on the walls, they do have a bleacher seat from the original Comiskey Park mounted above the freezer for all to see. The Sox are the obvious heroes here.

So if it is cheap beer and good company you want, go to Julie's Place on south Cicero Avenue.

"It's the best bar on the South Side," Rafael says. He just may be right. See ya' there.

— Paul Barile

Juniper Club
3825 S. Morgan St.
312-767-4677
Hours: 3 p.m. to 1 a.m. Sunday to Friday,
3 p.m. to 2 a.m. Saturday

A fellow bar-goer told me about this bar on the South Side and said it was a great place to dance the "traditional way" and meet singles, as if bars in my own neighborhood didn't already have this. Nevertheless, one night while desiring to meet a "dancing partner" I hopped in my rusted-out Ford Escort and headed south.

A quick word to the wise, I found that it would have been better to just take the Dan Ryan Expressway and bypass most of the unsavory neighborhoods and the family of rats I saw in a viaduct. Even though I have often debated about meeting the dancing partner of my dreams via a drive-by shooting, I continued on. Also, the place is really hard to find if you are not familiar with the area as there is nothing but fields of warehouses throughout and Morgan and Racine both cut off at railroad tracks and then start up again.

Once at the bar, I noticed that it was quiet until about 10:30 p.m. or so when the dancing groupies rolled in. Otherwise, the place was filled with local patrons, many from the trucking warehouses nearby and they were there to get good and plowed. Many them on this night slurred wildly and clumsily leaving before the small handful of dancers. The dancers were composed of a truly all-ages crowd trying to look sharp and lookin' for love. They did old-way-style dancing to maybe five or six different songs by Frank Sinatra and some other oldie artists. It was fun for about five songs but then the small selection on the jukebox became a redundancy and made sitting and drinking tiring.

Surprisingly, the young left early (most likely to go to another bar), then it was just oldies and drunks. I was glad they closed earlier than usual bars, so I said a prayer to St. Arnulf, patron saint of brewers, that I may get home with only this place as a scar for my evening.

— Phil Brandt

Just Joey's
4455 W. 55th St.
773-735-8647
Hours: 5 p.m. to 2 a.m. Sunday to Friday,
5 p.m. to 3 a.m. Saturday

If Frank Sinatra had opened a bar on the Southwest Side of the city, it would be exactly like Just Joey's at 4455 W. 55th St.

Initially, the red brick of the interior doorway is a bit foreboding but once in, you are transported to a secret society meeting of the original Rat Pack. Is that Dean Martin in the corner sipping a martini?

The bar has been in existence since the 1930s and has probably had 10 different owners. It's clear, from where we sat, that they knew exactly what they were doing when it came to preserving the building and its integrity.

The walls are covered with pictures of everyone from Marilyn Monroe to Bogie. There are pictures of Richard Daley and Al Capone on the wall behind the bar. Famous historical newspapers front pages are framed and hung throughout the building. They include the blizzard of 1967 and the heat wave of 1995. Decorations on the walls behind the bar also include antique sports items and posters of musical instruments and three Mardi Gras masks.

They only have two beers on tap: Lite and MGD. This much can be said for South Side bars, they don't deluge their customers with choices nor do they subscribe to flights of fancy. They know what sells and they make sure they have plenty of it.

An unnamed patron next to me told me to mention that they have "damn good food" including beef sandwiches, hot dogs and pizza. He went on to explain that Just Joey's is a great place to unwind after work. You can sit and relax, have a beer and some good conversation without having your back against a wall.

There is no pool table in Just Joey's, just an electric dart board. It is my belief the light hanging over a pool table would destroy the dark dim atmosphere the owners worked so hard to create. Even the wood on the bar and the tables is dark and highly polished.

I would be neglectful if I didn't mention that the bathroom was very much like the WCs found in England; high ceilings and little leg room.

My designated driver, Buzz (isn't that ironic? My DD is named Buzz...), said that the cola tasted like bar 7-up. He was not pleased at all. Neither of us were happy with the stock car races on the three television sets.

In general, if I wanted to impress a date, I might take her here because it is quiet enough that she could hear all of my lines and the place would help to charm the pants off her. Since I am a married man, I'll have to take my wife there and we can sit in the corner drinking wine, waiting for old blue eyes to show up. Maybe we'll even see you there.

— *Paul Barile*

Keegan's Pub

10618 S. Western Ave.
773-233-6829
Hours: 2 p.m. to 2 a.m. Sunday to Thursday,
noon to 2 a.m. Friday, noon to 3 a.m. Saturday

Dwarfed by a neighboring beer garden, this dimly-lit place offers plenty of the Irish pub feel. Definitely a neighborhood bar, attracting young and old alike for some down and out drinking. This is more of a bar to sit and drink and shoot the poop with your neighbor, whether friends or not. The bar wraps around in a horseshoe shape covering the front of the two rooms with tables, both raised and normal size, forming the outside semi-circle. The Irish bartenders are really fast and cover everyone's needs in a timely fashion. Their speed is great, unless craving a slowly-poured Guinness.

The place is nicely dimmed all around, except for in the back hallway inbetween the two rooms. The bathrooms are in an odd spot, next to the cooler and a wash tub sink. So just look for the well-lit area of the bar for relief.

There is a jukebox for musical entertainment, which plays the latest hits and some Irish songs, as well as some 1960s stuff. The main entertainment is just the drinking aspect. This is a bonus, as it forces conversation and good times. There is not much room to mingle, so not much of that occurs. The crowd, again ranges from just-turned-21 on up. More males frequent the bar, but the females don't seem to get crowded with an abundance of unwanted attention. Everyone is pretty much stuck with their group and remains there, so relations are fairly cool.

Keegan's offers a good number of taps, from Bass, Harp, Woodpecker, and Guinness. There is also Bud and Miller Lite on tap. Pitchers are available, and they make a good black and tan, though they don't have the "official" black & tan spoon. Prices are moderate.

Kiko's Sports Bar & Grill

312-254-8342
3503 S. Halsted St.
Hours: 11 a.m. to 2 a.m. Sunday to Friday,
11 a.m. to 3 a.m. Saturday

One afternoon, my drinking partner and I were walking down Halsted Street when we paused in front of a sports bar. I was not in the mood, believe it or not, for an afternoon snort nor for going to a sports bar, one of the few types of bars I least enjoy. But my partner, already with a few belts working in his system, seemed ready to take on any sort of place for another drink. Only a few seconds passed when a regular of the bar walked in front of our puzzled view and said, "Comin' in? We'll shoot some pool." In we went.

Barfly Kiko's Sports Bar and Grill-Kitty O'Sheas

The bar room was nicely done with wood planks encasing it all. A pool table sat in the back with a dart board by its side. Plenty of commemorative plaques of Chicago sports heroes and teams filled the walls as Sox banners floated overhead. It was not the biggest place I've ever been in, resembling more of a nice neighborhood tap.

My partner made his way to the pool table to take up the initial offer while I headed straight for the bar. Looking through the numerous bottles of imports and domestics I grabbed a couple Old Styles from the tap, only because they were out of Guinness, and I sat down at a table to watch the pool match.

The crowd here ranges through all age groups and with very little attitude, it makes for a great mix. On the weekends, however, there is more of a younger crowd. And with a location just a hop, skip and a jump from Comiskey Park, there are plenty of after-the-game drinkers stopping in.

The one thing that overwhelmed me so much about this place was how friendly everyone was. I can't recall any place where everyone treated one so nicely. I felt like a regular within 15 minutes. Even dogs are welcome. It was quite ironic as my partner and I were talking about the number of bars I've been in just a few minutes before we walked into this place. I guessed near a few hundred or so. A few hundred and here I was, finally, in such a wonderful crowd, I had to question if it were pay day or something. The bartender, Steve, was high quality too. Even as we were easily coaxed into the bar, others looking through the windows were coaxed in as well to tip back a few. Strangely, for some reason, their attitude was so laid-back it seemed so foreign to me.

While my partner played pool, I just sat back and drank my Style like it was some sort of nectar enjoying the pure bliss of a great crowd in a neighborhood tap. I have found my new home and it is a sports bar.

— *Phil Brandt*

Kitty O'Sheas
720 S. Michigan Ave.
312-922-4400.
Hours: 11 a.m. to 1:30ish a.m. daily

Hotel bars are universally expensive and cryptically sterile. Often times than not, if you are sitting in one you either have no idea where you are. If you know where you are, you would be wondering why you are there or at least, hopefully, be a) questioning your unadventurous spirit; b) maximizing the benefits of your expense account; or c) waiting for a hotel employee to get off work.

So, sitting in Kitty O'Sheas, located in the lobby of the Chicago Hilton and Towers, I was clueless. Kitty O'Sheas has been oddly canonized by two friends of mine. I have, by these two pure-bred Irish-Americans, often been used as the sound board for their pro-nationalist/pro-organized union ranting that echo the sentiment, "Brits get out" and "God made unions on the eighth day." As a nationality mutt, I know a casserole when I see one, therefore, I was confused as to how this typical "thematic" hotel bar had been inflated to such epic proportions by my Sinead O' Norma Rae friends. Baffled by their glorification, I resigned to discover what made this pub different from other hotel bars.

While it matters little, it is interesting to note the history-laden name of Kitty O'Sheas. Kitty O'Shea was the mistress/wife of Charles Steward Parnell. By some people, Parnell is considered to be the 'uncrowned King' of Ireland or the Irish Caesar. In 1880, when Kitty and Parnell met, their passions were not tempered by the fact she was married and he held public office. Parnell was only the second Irish man to be elected to British Parliament. Parnell headed the Irish home rule and land reform movement — also known by the ancient term, Fenians. Britain controlled all of Ireland at this time. As a selfish landlord, Britain gave no land rights to the Irish and could raise rent or evict any one they pleased. Ireland's population, especially the countryside, was devastatingly low due to effects of the famine and extensive immigration to the U.S. As an oppressed people with a stark population, Ireland had no power. Parnell by giving a voice to tenants' rights in British Parliament played an essential role in unifying the Irish people to seek self-determination and gain home-rule.

Obviously, Parnell's politics did not make him especially popular in Britain. Moreover, the media did not look fondly upon Parnell's involvement in a 10-year affair that bore three kids with a married woman. He was slated for destruction by the press in both his homeland and England. Kitty eventually got a divorce from her husband and married Parnell in 1891. However, Parnell's political battles and his diminishing popularity, a result of tabloid exploitation had made him a geezer at age 45. Parnell died a few months after their marriage and Kitty was left to live 30 more years with her bittersweet memories.

This tid-bit of a history lesson seemingly inconsequential, except for the fact Kitty O'Sheas is popular with some members of the Hotel Employee Restaurant Employee Union. Depending on your politics, you may see the poetic parallels between the notion of organized unions and Parnell. Although they all are in hotels, the infamous Kitty O'Shea in Dublin, Paris and Brussels, has no technical relation to Chicago's Kitty O'Sheas (because of the 's').

So for the non-union, apolitical, lay-person, what does this have to do with whether or not Kitty O'Sheas is an entertaining place? Nothing really. While it is the typical hotel bar, Kitty O'Sheas has a little more to offer than other hotel lobby franchises. They have more than three beers on tap and the bartenders are Irish. They have State Street and Goose Island on tap as well as Bud/Bud light and the typical Irish inspired varieties — Michael Sheas, Harp and of course, Guinness. The Guinness is not poured with timed precision. There is also one of those ice drink machines, the Island Oasis, so you could order a "Bailey's shaky type of drink" if you want.

The bar itself is very large oval with a partition in the middle as well as cross section glass dividers. The front of the bar is open with tables and counters with stools. There's a small stage where six nights a week they have some sort of Irish variety type of music. I was taken back, one particular week night, that there was live music and people were dancing about the bar. Because there are

Barfly Kitty O'Shea's-Lee's Unleaded Blues

so many partitions, you can either be in the midst of action or removed in more a private, quiet area. Supposedly these 'sections' are allusions to the penal days of Ireland, when women were not served in bars. They had to sit in private rooms separated from the men folk, and be served through a window door. Then when they began to drink in the big boys' areas, women realized they preferred what was called these 'ante-rooms' or 'snug rooms' for privacy on dates. This information was extracted from a paper handout. There is also a ditto about Cladagh rings. The T-shirts, the Shillelagh Club on the wall dedicated to union guys and aldermen with brass plaques, the Parnell Gift Shop in the lobby, the dittos — it's all done with a little more subtlety than perhaps, Planet Hollywood, but it makes Kitty O'Sheas kind of the Hardrock Cafe of Irish pubs.

The prices are more expensive than regular bars, but you're Downtown in a hotel — no big surprise. The bartenders are friendly. They are impervious to being annoyed by incessant questions about their homeland and other overly zealous yada yada bantering. Given the choice, Kitty O'Sheas is more appealing than other Michigan Avenue places i.e. Bennigans. They serve bar food. Plus, the lobby of the Hilton Towers is especially enticing with its quasi-Japanese, semi-Persian, mauve-ala-Liberace decor.

— Crumpey

Lee's Unleaded Blues
7401 S. Chicago Ave.
312-493-3477
Hours: noon to 2 a.m. Sunday to Friday,
noon to 3 a.m. Saturday

When you walk into this place, you get an immediate sense that you have been there before and it feels like a pair of jeans that you know will fit perfectly every time. This is a real club for the blues, and it shows.

Service is very good and the atmosphere is laid back with that welcome feeling. The customers at Lee's Unleaded Blues, a 13 year-old club, are varied and interesting: most of whom seem to know each other, and seem to belong in this throw-back to a time of open fun with no hint of false hope.

My observations were that singles as well as couples fare very well at Lee's. Take a look around and you will see two large and generously stocked bars that run the length of the room. In the back is a jukebox filled with all the classic R&B and blues that befits a place like this. Low and mellow lighting set off the feel and respond to your senses.

If you want live, real, back-woods, bare-to-the-bone blues, a stop here will satisfy that craving in fine fashion. In the back, a small stage hosts the big sound of vocals and instruments each Friday, Saturday, Sunday, and Monday (with Monday being "Blue Monday"). Live shows start at 9 p.m. and jam well into the early morning hours. Lee herself helps at the bar when it's crowded. The night that I was there, the barmaid was Kimberly, a charming and very

375

The South Side Lee's Unleaded Blues

Lee's Unleaded Blues, 7401 S. Chicago Ave., is a hidden gem on the Southeast Side. And, hey, you can even ride your bike there.

attractive young woman who kept tabs on the steady stream of customers.

Along with her was a patron, Darrell, who gave me his account of Lee's Unleaded Blues. According to him, Lee's has a number of different personalities: the Friday and Saturday nights are memorable; holidays, you get a very close feeling among the gathered; a good place to be with someone special or that new date you want to show a special time to; or to be alone to gather your thoughts.

If being inside on a warm summer night isn't you, there's the outdoor patio at the back of the club. There you will find fish fry, barbecue and more entertainment. As a bonus, you will see some noted music personalities that are regulars at Lee's; Johnny Drummer, Vance Kelly, Ray Scott, T.J. the King Kong Rocker, Gaylord the Arkansas Belly Roller, Johnny Laws —there are just too many others to name.

To give Lee's Unleaded Blues a rating is not justified, but as I always do, this one is truly BB1/2, out of a four B (bar) scale, just on the strength of atmosphere alone.

— John W. Singer

McDuffy's Lodge
3300 W. 111th St.
773-779-3033
Hours: 7 p.m. to 2 a.m. Sunday, Thursday, Friday,
7 p.m. to 3 a.m. Saturday

McDuffy's is strange at first entrance. It's almost like being in the Northwest Territory of Canada but with the South Side Irish as your drinking companions. The bar is fairly big. The street entrance is a glass revolving door, where you are immediately greeted by a bouncer checking IDs. If you just turned 21 and thought you had all the bars at your finger tips, think again. The age limit to get into the bar is 23, and they will card. The men's bathroom is straight ahead while the bar is to the left. Be careful to move away from the revolving door when the red-haired guy is checking your ID or you'll get popped.

In the center of the first room is a rectangular bar, with plenty of beers to choose from. The tap has Bass, Harp, Guinness, and domestics. Bottled beer has a wide range of brands including German Weiss beers. They carry plenty of popular and not so popular domestics too. Pints of domestics are at $3, and bottled beer prices will vary greatly with the wide selection.

Seating and decor in McDuffy's is most unique to Chicago. There's seats under a moose, a metal owl, a bear's head plaque, and plenty of hanging fish. There is a nice, happy historical picture of a 19th Century hunter trying to scramble away in the snow from two angry bears who have started ripping the man's leg off while the hunter's two buddies and faithful hunting dog try to hold the beasts at bay with a musket, tomahawk, and barking respectively.

There is a lower room where the pool table and jukebox are. The tables get filled and stay that way, so it is necessary to wait to play. Electronic dart boards are all over, and players usually have their own darts. The competition is not shabby, either.

There is a small booth where they sell nachos, hot dogs, chili dogs, and pizza. If the whole group is getting something to snack on, it can become crowded at the tables since they slightly resemble a very large fraternity paddle.

McDuffy's is a hot-spot with those in their 20s. Everyone's well dressed and well groomed, though the rare long-haired person will stumble in. The music is classics from Steve Miller, Billy Joel, Bruce Springsteen; typical party music that everyone at this bar seems to enjoy.

There's lots of guys and girls lookin' for love, or just being jealous. Although I saw no visible confrontations, some patrons showed attitudes.

McDuffy's offers daily specials of drinks and entertainment. The one to definitely check out is Thursday nights when they have SUMO WRESTLING! But call first, specials and entertainment may change.

McNally's

11136 S. Western Ave.
773-779-6202
Hours: noon to 2 a.m. Sunday to Friday,
noon to 3 a.m. Saturday

Walking into McNally's for the first time is like walking into a party given by someone you don't know. Most of the people seem to know each other, and even though you're a stranger, you sense that you're welcome.

If you take the initiative to strike up a conversation with any of the many groups of regulars, they'll be more than happy to shoot the breeze, talk about their softball team, and point out a few of their cronies around the bar, most of whom they've hung out with since they were old enough to walk to school by themselves.

"I play for the Fitz's Gas softball team," said Tom McCann (dubbed "Shoes" as a child because his name matches that of the nationwide shoe retailer). "McNally's has sponsored our softball team for years, so we come here after the games. I tried not to come in tonight, but I did anyway, and now I can't leave. That's what's great about this place, you know about half the bar."

Shoes drifts away to check on the results of a neighborhood game with a man named "Fish" who had just walked in.

"I'd say I know about 80 percent of the bar," said another McNally's patron. "When my girlfriend comes in here, she's always surprised at how many people come up and say hi to me."

On a Wednesday night, almost every stool in the relatively spacious bar is filled mostly with men. A friendly Irish theme pervades, with bright green walls, framed photographs of the current and former mayors Daley, a smiling red-headed bartender named Mary, and more than one patron sporting Irish flag T-shirts. Near the door is a bulletin board with notices advertising neighborhood functions. A jukebox contains a range of contemporary music.

McNally's offers a selection of domestic and imported beers, including Bud, Bud Light, Old Style, Killian's, and Moosehead. Domestic draught beer is a bargain at $1 a glass and $5 a pitcher. Popcorn is free for revelers who get the munchies. Anyone celebrating a birthday can get a "bottomless" McNally's glass and drink all night.

Apparently the scene changes on weekend nights to a more eclectic group of people and a more balanced mix of men and women. McNally's also offers a large, private room upstairs which can be rented out for group events, bachelor parties, and the like.

If you're in the hood, McNally's is definitely worth the stop. You're sure to get a smile, a bargain-priced beer, and, if you're interested, a play-by-play recap of the bottom of somebody's ninth.

— *Lisa Kueng*

O'Malley's Pub
3617 S. Archer Ave.
312-376-2124
Hours: 11 a.m. to 2 a.m. Sunday to Friday,
11 a.m. to 3 a.m. Saturday

Eddie O'Malley, the owner and genial host of O'Malley's Pub, rules his roost from a stool at the end of the bar. This lumbering second generation Irishman, who seems constantly surrounded by family, is every bit of what we have come to expect in a bar owner on the South Side (you should hear him sing Patsy Cline's "Crazy").

The building which houses the bar was built in 1873 and maintains much of the original architecture within. The back bar is a Brunswick circa 1917 and it is, to say the least, a beautiful vision for those weary of neon lights and Chicago sports figures.

The reds and browns in the wood, blend into a high glossed finish that accents a large spotless mirror where just about every customer sitting at the bar can check their hair or the creases in their Notre Dame sweater.

Presiding over everything, including O'Malley himself, is a hand-carved leprechaun named LASOB (Little Asshole Sitting On a Board) who came here directly from Ireland. He is a feisty little guy who has been known to cause trouble in and around the bar especially as St. Patty's Day draws near.

Speaking of St. Patty's Day, O'Malley's Pub usually hosts a proper Irish party. With Guinness and Harp beer on tap, they often compliment the celebration with authentic Irish buffet (bangers, anyone?) and performances from "The Moonshine Band" playing traditional Irish music (Dexy's Midnight Runners?)

We had the good fortune to be in the bar on karaoke night. For the uninitiated, this is the night where people drink enough to think that they can sing but not enough to hear themselves. The result is loud bad singing...but a good time is had by all.

Local favorites blend with karaoke enthusiasts and neophytes for a competition where the winner gets a gift certificate to spend at the bar or the adjoining restaurant. (Note: The fact that this writer won the contest has no bearing on his feelings about the bar. This is a very cool bar and the writer thought so, long before the karaoke contest.)

They do, like most good South Side bars, sponsor a baseball team. Their team has a great name, Bulldogs. They play at McKinley Park and typically make it to the final four. They agree that, aside from the sponsoring connection, this is a great bar to relax in after a game.

"The atmosphere is laid back and the service is excellent," said Mick Lopresti (team member). "I just think it's a great bar."

I have to agree with him, from the little green shamrock lights that run around the bar, to the "Irish Only" parking sign, this is one place that an Irishman (for life or for a night) can feel at home drinking and laughing and

379

meeting people.

So, if you can't make the St. Patty's Day Party or the St. Patty's Day Preview Party (call for details), you should still plan to come out to O'Malley's Pub to drink heavily and meet LASOB. I know I'll see you there. Until then...drink now...it may be later than you think.

-- Paul Barile

The Palm Tavern
446 E. 47th St.
312-373-6292
Hours: 10 a.m. to 2 a.m. daily

One of the problems with the unending march of progress is that it often leaves the past in its wake. Take for example The Palm Tavern, opened in 1933 across the street from the original Regal Theater. The club soon became an outgrowth of the Regal, the place to unwind for countless jazz and R&B artists who passed through the South Side. Such luminaries as Duke Ellington, Sarah Vaughn, Count Basie and Ella Fitzgerald did their share of time on these hallowed barstools. I thought it logical, then, to expect that The Palm would now be a virtual treasure trove of legend and lore.

I arrived there on a Thursday night, at an hour late enough for me to expect a minor crowd. I approached the front door, only to find a man urinating in the alley; I suspected that the current legends of music had long since taken to congregating elsewhere. This was

The last remnant of E. 47th Street's historic jazz past is The Palm Tavern, 446 E. 47th St. Pictured here is owner Gerri Oliver.

380

Barfly Palm Tavern-Phyllis-Up

confirmed when I entered the lobby, a hand-written sign read "KNOCK ON DOOR WITH KEY OR COIN."

An old man with a weather-beaten face let me inside. I scanned the room, and quickly realized that, as humans, the old man and I were in the minority. At least eight cats frolicked about the place, trotting across the bar and tables. They were the only other inhabitants. On a whole, the interior bore the fragrance of a litter box filled with Beefeater gin. The "manager" explained that the owner was resting at home tonight, but she may be in tomorrow. He seemed genuinely surprised that I had heard of the place. Given the state of things, I thought he should welcome the business.

Looking around, I couldn't help but feel a twinge of sadness over the Palm's demise. The foundation of a really interesting historical site remains. Yellowing photographs and various pieces of memorabilia cover the walls. A "wall of fame" next to the bar lists famous customers on what resembles a train station time schedule. And a distinct sense of the swinging past permeates the room. You can almost hear the be-bop playing in the background, the crowds of musicians and well-wishers squeezed into booths, the owners proudly looking upon their thriving business. But that time is now past, as this once-great hall has faded with the neighborhood, its proprietors too old or too financially strapped to maintain the upkeep.

In an age of copycat bars and homogenized entertainment, places offering something truly different and enlightening must be kept alive. The problems of The Palm Tavern are nothing that an influx of curiosity-seekers and jazz enthusiasts cannot cure. It's far too rare to find a place that actually has a past. Now all the Palm needs is a future.

— David Dayen

Phyllis-Up
5716 S. Archer Ave.
773-585-2012
Hours: noon to 2 a.m. weekdays,
noon to 3 a.m. Saturday, 6 p.m. to 2 a.m. Sunday

Archer Avenue, east of Central, has at least one gin mill on each block. I believe that this is in compliance with a city or county entertainment code.

It would seem like people with names like Dolly, Sam or Charlie are mandated to open these small shot-and-beer joints, usually on the corner of the block.

If Phyllis-Up is any indication of what you will find down there, I will be hard-pressed to darken the doorways of the "clubs" on the North Side of our fair city. From the well-worn bar with the friendly homespun atmosphere, to Nanook, the high-fiving Alaskan Malamute, this bar offers a good time in a hassle-free environment.

Schmed, who has owned this bar since 1987, named the club for his mother Phyllis, although the regulars refer to it as "Club Schmed."

While other bars focus on fans and "alternative" passing fancies, Phyllis-Up puts all of its energy on all of the important necessities that guarantee success. They have drink specials every night except for Fridays and Saturdays.

As you spin on the high stools listening to the Firebird II jukebox (with such rarities as the soundtrack for "Reservoir Dogs") you come eye to eye with the greatest modern sports legends with a heavy emphasis on Chicago sports. There are posters, plaques and autographed pictures of everyone from Magic Johnson to Cold Steel on Ice. They even have quite a collection of pictures of Michael Jordan as a baseball player.

If there is a downside to this bar, it is that the nearest thing that they offer to imported beer is Heineken or Corona. The only thing on tap is Bud, Bud Light, and Old Style. That being said, we take into consideration that Schmed knows exactly what his clientele wants and he gives it to them.

So, next time you find yourself south of Interstate 55 and you are looking for someplace to have a drink, remember that just about all roads cross Archer Avenue at some point. Make your way over to Phyllis-Up and have a couple of their special "Green Monsters" and say hello to Nanook. If you're lucky, Jennifer will get him to do his high-five trick. I'm sure I'll see you there soon.

— *Paul Barile*

Puffer's

3356 S. Halsted St.
312-927-6073
Hours: noon to 2 a.m. daily

Chuck and Bruce Puffer have put their name on an inviting bar that seems, if anything, a bit displaced. In a community where nondescript pubs are the norm, Puffer's gives off an almost (dare we say it) North Side vibe. Instead of the minimalist decor common to many South Side bars, Puffer's is warmly appointed with plenty of wood and soft lighting. Patrons are quick to pick up the welcoming mood, which obviously radiates from the namesake brothers, who are frequently on-site, working the tap handles and the clientele with plenty of good-natured brotherly ribbing.

It's a refreshing change of tack as anyone who has ever stumbled unknown into a South Side bar knows they can be a touch exclusive at times. "We don't want nobody dat don't know nobody," is a popular refrain when you're on the low side of Roosevelt Road.

Puffer's displaces that notion, extending true South Side hospitality to residents of every appellation, be they blue collar, professional or artistic. Two-dozen bar seats and 30 table seats give the bar plenty of space to kick back and tip back, and a diverse microbrew and wine selection keeps everyone nice and juicy. In fact, Puffer's is a real find for the non-beer drinker as it makes a rare effort to provide some excellent high-quality wines. The selection changes from week to week, so frequent visits are to the benefit of any South Side sommelier. For the inventive and adventurous beer drinker, Puffer's also hosts an area home-brew club. It meets monthly to compare efforts. Of course, requisite

Barfly Puffer's-Drinking in Pullman

domestic selections are available, although Puffer's encourages everyone to stretch their horizons and sample something new. Like the rotating wine list, Puffer's changes its tap-beer selections frequently; try an Old Rasputin Russian Stout one month, or an Anchor Steam the next.

While keeping palates pleased, Puffer's also offers excellent entertainment. On Thursday evenings, a house band led by bassist Lou Marini lays down jazz, while rock and blues bands are in the spotlight on Saturday. If you need to work up a thirst, Puffer's provides pinball, darts and (dig it) foosball.

— Jay Ferrari

Drinking in Pullman
by Jay Ferrari

Pullman is one of the South Side's richest neighborhoods. Its wealth, however, is not measured in dollars, but in history, personality and legacy. Simultaneously a tribute to the indomitable spirit of the American laborer, and a reminder of industry's manipulative greed, Pullman embodies Chicago's working-class origins; it helped put the "Works" in our oft-quoted motto.

Pullman, named for rail-car baron George M. Pullman's Palace Car Company, was conceived in April, 1880, as an ideal worker community. It provided residence, shopping, entertainment and recreation for Pullman's employees, who built the famous Pullman luxury rail cars. At the time, these rail cars and sleepers were a primary source of transportation, and among the most opulent.

To build the community, Pullman purchased 3,000 acres of land west of Lake Calumet for about $800,000. After only four years, the land was criss-crossed with streets (Florence Boulevard, now 111th Street, was the community's north border), and hosted more than 531 houses. The common Pullman house was a five-room, two-story cottage, and while Pullman workers were not required to live there, the reasonable rent ($14 per month) made moving in an attractive option. In addition to the houses, there were more luxurious homes for managers, company doctors and executives, as well as inexpensive flats for single employees.

The buildings, designed by architect Solon Spencer Berman, are still in exquisite condition. The Historic Pullman Foundation keeps the community history alive, and conducts frequent walking tours. The guides present the history — warts and all, for Pullman himself was no saint. A popular story is how Pullman, who paid his workers in "Pullman Dollars," instead of U.S. currency, was able to get striking workers back to the factories for less than they were getting before the strike. Since his workers couldn't shop anywhere else, they would either starve or return to work. This incident prompted legislation that made payment in anything other than U.S. money illegal, and it proved corporate greed has deep, diabolical roots.

Today, Pullman is less a center of struggle than it is a shrine to history. Filled with excellent restaurants, shops and buildings, it may be one of Chicago's most under-appreciated attractions.

For those who like a little refreshment with their history, Pullman does not disappoint. As it is still home to a hard-working community, Pullman is peppered with places to quench a thirst that allow one to have a soak, and soak up the history.

PUBS IN PULLMAN

The Hotel Florence & The Brass Tapper Bar
11111 South Forestville Ave., 773-785-8900. Hours: 11 a.m. to 2 p.m. weekdays, 10 a.m. to 2 p.m. Saturday, 10 a.m. to 3 p.m. Sunday

Pullman visitors looking for an ideal launching pad will

Although rail-car baron George M. Pullman's model town for his workers failed, it left a legacy of beautiful 1880s buildings that can still be enjoyed today like Hotel Florence, 11111 S. Forestville Ave.

want to visit the Hotel Florence, (about 4 blocks west of I-94 off the 111th Street exit). This ornate Victorian hotel was built in the Queen Anne style, and is now a museum and restaurant. It serves a generous Sunday brunch that is fine fuel for day's hacking around. The Brass Tapper Bar is within the hotel and has perfectly preserved the feel of a late 1880s Chicago pub while keeping the drink selection contemporary. Lots of dark wood, tin ceilings and walls, and ornate stained glass put you right back in the "naughty nineties." Check out the various now-outdated structural appointments, such as the gambler's lookout in the main dining room. This trapdoor in the ceiling let poker players upstairs keep an eye below. After a beer or brunch, walk up to the second floor and see the suite where George Pullman stayed.

Barfly Drinking in Pullman

A bartender at Pulllman's Pub, 611 E. 113 St., models a T-shirt made when a scene from the film "The Fugitive" with Harrison Ford was filmed in the bar.

Pullman's Pub
611 E. 113th St., 773-568-0264
Hours: 9 a.m. to 2 a.m. Sunday to Friday, 9 a.m. to 3 a.m. Saturday

This is a timeless Chicago pub built of brick and glass block. Constructed in the 1920s, Pullman's Pub embodies classic bar simplicity, offering essential Chicago beers (think Old Style) and a full selection of snacks, pizza and miscellaneous munchies. It's a clean, comfortable and quiet place, and its light, polished wood bar gleam with antique pride. The hard working, hard-playing clientele work off their after-work energy with pool and darts, or cheer the White Sox (as any authentic South Side pub goer would). The interior of Pullman's Pub was also featured in the film "The Fugitive." Harrison Ford makes a quick call from the corner pay phone before he hurries out the door and down the alley in pursuit of the infamous "one-armed man."

Lucky Lady Pub
580 E. 115th St., 773-785-4597. Hours: 10 a.m. to 2 a.m.
Sunday to Friday, 10 a.m. to 3 a.m. Saturday

Indicative of South Side drinking-establishment endurance, the Lucky Lady Pub has been around since 1909. Don't let the fact that you have to be buzzed in intimidate you, for upon entering you'll find a spacious, inviting tavern. There are plenty of seats available, either at the long bar or at the many high tables throughout the room. Pullman neighborhood history and plenty of Chicago pride adorn the falls, with photos of the 1985 Super Bowl Champion

The South Side Drinking in Pullman-Romantic Club

Chicago Bears proudly hanging next to the bar. To keep busy, play video poker or pool. To set the musical mood, the jukebox has plenty of contemporary and classic rock and pop favorites. And if you work up an appetite, you're in luck at the Lucky Lady. Their bar food menu is great, offering plenty of inexpensive, hearty sandwiches and specials. Italian sausage, chili, and pasta dishes will fill you up without emptying your wallet. Sandwiches with all the trimmings will set you back around $5. To quench your thirst, enjoy an Old Style. If you must break with tradition, however, there's other domestics and a few imports available, but don't say you weren't warned.

The Romantic Club
4818 S. Pulaski Road
773-247-1229
Hours: 2 p.m. to 8 p.m. weekdays, 2 p.m. to 4 a.m. Friday and Sunday, 2 p.m. to 5 a.m. Saturdays

If you hang plastic flowers...they will come.

Casey Wrobel's Romantic Club is more than just another South Side shot and beer joint. From the canopy of plastic flowers that cover the bar and beyond to the Godfather-sized red leather booths, this club must be seen to be appreciated. Martin Scorsese could have shot the first half of his career within these walls.

This club is so cool that after 22 years, the late crowd still comes in to listen to KRAK, the Polish lounge act who plays all night. For those inclined, there is a monster-sized mirror on the wall so that you can watch yourself dance to "Help Me Make It Through the Night" sung in Polish. This band is not to be missed.

There is a certain element of nostalgia that begins to creep in when you look around at the cheesecake posters advertising Jamaica and the little boy in bell-bottoms looking up the older woman's mini-skirt.

The second level holds a foosball table as well as the necessary video games for a bar. That's right, I said foosball. The fond memories of blowing off classes to play in the game room came rushing back to me as I fingered the quarter in my pocket.

As far as offerings, they serve the standards in bottled beer. That would make Heinekens their import beer, but the experience of this club is worth switching to a nice iced Polish vodka and saving the beer for another time.

This is not a week-night bar, along this South Side strip of Pulaski Road there are so many bars and clubs that it would not be worth it to be open late. This also makes the hours that they are open all the more special.

Casey, the owner, is a cordial hostess who appeared to enjoy talking to the patrons about the bar scene from her perspective. She makes it a point to dispel the rumor that there are fights in her club.

Judging by her crowd on the night I was there, I couldn't even see how a rumor like that could have started. She talked for a moment about some historic incident that seems to have attached itself to the bar. We were there late on a Friday night and there were none of the typical signs that a fight would break out.

If you are ready for a couple of drinks on what looks like the set of an old Scorsese film, take Interstate 55 south to the Pulaski exit. Head south until you see a bright green candy-striped building on the west side of the street.

Give Casey our regards before sliding into one of the large leather booths to listen to KRAK. See ya there!

— Paul Barile

Rudy and Ann's Lounge
5788 S. Archer Ave.
773-284-9808
Hours: 11:30 a.m. to 1:30 a.m. daily

If there is a museum dedicated to generations of beer advertising, it must be Rudy and Ann's lounge on Archer Avenue. Rudy, who has owned the bar for 18 years, would be the perfect congenial host.

Rudy bought the bar in 1979 from a family who had owned the bar for approximately 35 years. He has since been an Archer Avenue staple providing live music on Saturday nights and great prices every night of the week.

Upon walking into Rudy and Ann's, the first thing that you see is a beautiful mahogany back bar with the leaded-glass windows. As if this was not impressive enough, the back bar has a second section around the corner that looks like something out of the Chicago Historical Society's overpriced picture galley.

The atmosphere is completed by unusually high ceilings and amber lighting. The amber lighting gives a dreamlike quality which is so relaxing, you just stand back and soak it all in, no worries.

You step up to the bar and order a draft beer. The large one (12 oz.) will be 75 cents, please. This is not a drink special, that is the price all of the time. A small beer (10 oz.) is 50 cents — all the time. Rudy says that he likes to keep the prices down for the old-timers.

So grab your seat in one of the high barstools and gaze at the wonders from the past. The mid-1970s Miller High Life clock which has surely logged a lot of hours does not appear to be out of place next to a late 1980s faux neon sign of Budman.

The beer and alcohol industry has generated many wonderful advertising tools over the years. Rudy seems to have gotten the best of them and arranged them throughout the room in a way that they compliment each other. The Jim Thorpe V.O. mirror is worth the trip in itself.

Now you are probably reading this and shaking your head. You are saying that this place is utopia and you're Sir Thomas Moore, so what more could you possibly ask for?

You are from Chicago so you are used to (and you deserve) the best. That is why Rudy and Ann's Lounge features polka parties with the likes of "Mr.

The South Side Rudy and Ann's Lounge-Septembers

Happiness" himself. That's right Lil' Richard (not the one you're thinking of) and his Polka All-Stars perform occasionally at Rudy and Ann's Lounge.

There is a dance room attached to the main bar which has a stage for the band and enough room to polka with your sweetie or just watch and listen to the happy music.

There might be other places in Chicago where you can get a Zywiec beer or listen to polka music amongst an impressive collection of bar memorabilia. You might even find an older, more beautiful back bar. What I don't think, though, is that you will find many places that can combine all of these things under one roof.

When you add in the draft beer prices, you have a place that needs to be visited time and time again.

Septembers
649 S. Clark St.
312-427-7007
Hours: 11 a.m. to 2 a.m. Monday to Saturday,
noon to 8 p.m. Sunday

The game is on, but so is the computer screen in your high-rise Downtown cubicle. Quick, think of an excuse to tell the boss, and head out for a brew and a little tie loosening down at Septembers.

The bar is good and long, so bring your favorite sports buddy. There are six TVs, to check out the game on, placed well throughout the bar, so no seat is a neck twister. If there is a couple different sporting events going on at the same time, there will be no problem catching them all. Whether you're partial to the North- or South-Side sluggers, or still enjoying the end of the hoops and ice season, they are on. There's even a dart board, two poker machines, pool table, and a golf video game to make your own little competition.

Wipe the day's dust off the face, and chill with a tall, cool one. There are three tap beers to choose from. Miller Lite, Genuine Draft, and Leinekugel. (Relief) Pitchers are tossed out at a good price. Domestic bottles include Bud, Michelob, Miller, Killian's, Rolling Rock, and, of course, what is Chicago without Old Style. But beware, the ice beers are moving in. Or, shoot for a Guinness, Harp, St. Pauli Girl, Beck's, or Dos Equis.

There's food until midnight, so no need to head home in that late afternoon traffic and catch the end of the game on the local AM station. There's a large selection to choose from, and prices are mainly in the $4-5 range. Throughout the week there is a 14" pizza special with choice of two toppings and a pitcher of suds.

Sheehan's Lounge
3801 S. Union Ave.
312-523-9812
Hours: 9am to 2am Sunday to Friday,
9 a.m. to 3 a.m. Saturday

You know you're in a South Side bar when you walk in the door and one of the first bits of decor that you see is a poster of Chicago legend Richard J. Daley with the caption, "Our Friend...In Our Hearts and Minds Forever."

Sheehan's is certainly no stranger to the South Side, and you're certainly not a stranger for long upon entering this historic pub. There is, in fact, three Sheehan's pubs within blocks of each other. Although they don't have the same owner, they are all owned by the same family. The original location, which was at 3707 S. Halsted St. (across the street from Schaller's Pump and the Ambrosia Brewing Co.), was established in 1890 by John Sheehan who had come from Ireland. The bar was handed down to John Jr. , who was succeeded by Patrick and stayed open until 1990.

"Everybody in the family, at least all the men, because women didn't work in saloons at that time, worked at 3707 (Halsted) at one time," said Jack Sheehan, who is John's grandson and owns the third Sheehan's located on Halsted just off 35th Street. Dan Sheehan, who is John Sr.'s son, opened at 38th and Union about forty years ago in a 100 year-old building that had been a saloon probably as long under a number of different owners.

"This neighborhood used to be packed with bars," said Mike, a younger guy who happened to know quite a bit of the area's history. He seemed to think the reason that many closed down was because of, "people becoming health-conscious, the closing of the stockyards, city sanctions...."

Sheehan's, however, has persevered. The reasons for this seem to be obvious. It's just a simple saloon with people from the neighborhood whose families have grown up there, and that's just the way they like it. During the day, the bar is sparsely occupied with older folks, chatting with the bartender, studying the daily racing form, or just watching the afternoon game with an Old Style. The evening brings in the younger crowd as either a gathering before a big night out, or just to hang out and soothe the day's stress with buddies and fellow barflies. Not uncommon for the business, the weekends fill the small bar pretty quick and Sundays bring everyone of all ages together, usually for the football games. Sheehan' s also seems to attract Sox fans and can end up quite crowded after a game. Word of mouth is the only advertising that they rely on, it's worked for almost 40 years.

There are no martini menus, they do not have a dozen micros on tap, and their classic Scotch collection includes J&B. On draught they have EX and in bottles you can get one of most Miller products (they don't have the new Miller red), Old Style, or Heineken. They do have a modest assortment of spirits for your typical mixed drinks, but I wouldn't count on any fancy blender drinks or sickly sweet shots. This is a whiskey and beer joint.

"That's all they have ever been," Mike spoke candidly, "and all they will always be."

The decor consists mostly of family memorabilia; a picture of John Sr. above the bar, an old autographed snapshot of Dan with a young state Sen. Richard M. Daley, painted renditions of the original Sheehan's and Comiskey Park when trolley cars were still the only mode of public transportation, and a friendly "Welcome To Bridgeport" sign. There are snacks in sacks available; popcorn, peanuts, chips, etc... and half-pints of whiskey or brandy to take home as a souvenir, well at least for the evening.

Apart from the television sets, the only means of distraction come in the form of two video poker machines and a jukebox, unless the daily paper is laying around. Service is straight-forward; no special attention for that extra big tip, but you are not ignored. The pace is casual there, so if you feel you need white-glove, butler service, go to the Hilton. So after the Sox game or if you are just plain tired of the regular haunts on your own stomping grounds, take a little field trip to Sheehan's Lounge and meet some different and friendly people.

— *The Iguana*

Sheehy's
6546 S Archer Ave.
773-229-1512
Hours: noon to 2 a.m. Sunday to Friday,
noon to 3 a.m. Saturday.

Visiting Sheehy's in the Garfield Ridge neighborhood was a pleasant surprise. It's been in business since November of 1995. Though a local neighborhood bar, I didn't get the impression of being the stranger in this Irish drinking hole. There's an abundance of seating arrangements at this tap, offering a comfortable and relaxed atmosphere. Taking into account this review was done on a Sunday night, I still feel you will get quick and courteous service from the bartenders any time of the week.

The tap selection is a bit limited, with only three beers: Old Style, Miller Genuine Draft, and Killian's Red, but the cost for a pint is only $1.25. Domestic bottles are $1.75, while imports like Beck's and Heineken are $2.25. Also, there are specials, which include $1 domestic bottles every Wednesday and Thursday and $1 house shots.

The age group that visits Sheehy's according to bartender Heidi is a good mix. The crowd here can range any where between 21 to 35 and some older patrons that visit regularly. The busiest nights are Friday and Saturday.

What are upcoming events at this pub? A dart league is forming. In addition, there will be Bears parties that include free food. There are future specials to be announced at a later date.

Is Sheehy's worth visiting? The answer is a definite yes. It is a comfortable bar with good service. Where can you go on the North Side and receive a cold

Barfly Sheehy's-Studio 31

pint of Killian's Red for only $1.25? So the next time, you are near Midway Airport take a spin down Archer Avenue near Narragansett and stop in for a cold brew.

— Pete Schmugge

Studio 31

5870 S. Archer Ave.
773-284-8903
Hours: noon to 2 a.m. weekdays, 8 a.m. to 3 a.m.
Saturday, 11 a.m. to 2 a.m. Sunday

"Let's do it again!" is the theme at this hot South Side dance club located on Archer and Central avenues. While that could mean a lot of different things to a lot of different people, it means one thing to the Orlando brothers who own and operate Studio 31.

It means that people who loved the original Studio 31 (in Bridgeport) can expect the same high energy good time and party atmosphere at the new location, where they have been for the last three years.

"Tony 'O' is the greatest host in the world," says a patron speaking of Tony Orlando, who is one of the owners of the club.

"The hot dog stand connected to the bar doesn't hurt either," says another patron referring to the fast food venue which is also owned by the brothers.

Tony "O" and his brother Santo have created a full service party atmosphere for anyone interested in having a few drinks while they dance their asses off. When they get hungry, they don't even have to leave the bar for something to eat.

They have also created a neighborhood bar where generations of beer drinkers can gather to drink and listen to music and have a great time. On this Wednesday, a brave couple or two even made their way to the dance floor for a quick spin.

The dance floor occupies a good portion of the back of the room, including movable dance blocks for those who want their every move to be seen. The walls are lined with mirrors for those who want to see their every move.

Above the mirrors are black and white airbrushed images of everyone from the Stooges to Elvis and all cultural points in between.

Studio 31 is on the site that formerly housed "Fast Eddie's" ("warm beer and lousy service" was their motto). They maintained Fast Eddie's original back bar which provides a nice contrast to the more modern decor that exists throughout the bar.

"We have a Downtown atmosphere without the Downtown hassles," Tony "O" told me. "That includes no cover charge."

As far as the weekends, the couples who hesitate may have trouble getting out onto the floor. One of the patrons told me this about the weekend revelry:

"Friday and Saturday nights the place gets packed with people who come out to dance and party. The music is great. My friends and I haven't missed a

These ladies like to hang out at Studio 31, 5870 S. Archer Ave., one of the funnest dance clubs on the South Side.

weekend since they opened the doors."

On the weekends, ripped jeans and baseball hats are not permitted. That means that you will not only have a packed dance floor, but everyone will look good doing it.

For those who want to enjoy a summer evening under the stars, they have a beer garden complete with horseshoes and picnic tables.

So if you love to dance, boogie on down to Studio 31. You'll want to do it again and again.

— Paul Barile

Ted's Place

5030 S. Archer Ave.
773-735-1819
Hours: noon to 2 a.m. Sunday to Friday,
noon to 3 a.m. Saturday

Go to Ted's Place and lose your hat. Drink the "fisherman's" drink or two and you will certainly lose your hat. Drink your beer through a straw and share sports trivia with some of the friendliest people on Archer Avenue and...well you know the rest.

Ted's Place has been serving up cherry beers and vodka drinks for almost seven years. They take great pride in their service as well as their soccer team "Royal Wawel." This team boasts a collection of trophies that are displayed in glass cases.

On the night that we made our way down to Ted's, we found the hostess,

Barfly Ted's Place

Barbara, very accommodating. She was kind enough to translate our banter from English to Polish so we could be more at home and converse with the regulars. Everyone seemed to agree on one thing; *zimne piwo ya dobzre!* (Cold beer is good!)

Hanging above the bar and throughout the room, is an impressive collection of baseball hats and other caps. Ted has been collecting them from customers who offer them up willingly, and some who where less willing. They almost got my Steeler hat but that wasn't going anywhere.

They did share some exciting new drinks that I have never heard of in all of my bar experience (that's a long time). The "fisherman's" drink for example is an enticing mix of honey and vodka. Later we were treated to a vodka with cherry cordial which was also called a "fisherman's" drink.

Don't let that confuse you, just remember that fishermen love vodka and you'll be alright. Barbara also drew up an Old Style (gag) on tap and tossed in a shot of cherry juice which we drank through a straw.

Looking around the bar, we saw that most of the people were drinking beer with cherry through a straw. They also offer the three main Polish beers in a bottle including, Okocim, Zywiec, and Lezajsk.

As for vodka, a serious staple in Polish bars, they advertise ZYTNIA whose ad boasts, "From Poland... Where vodka was born!" We drank two or three different brands that night with the different drinks (and shots).

Barbara likes to think of Ted's as a neighborhood bar where people can get together and drink and share stories and plan their fishing trips. These people are very serious about fishing. Could it be the "fisherman's" drink?

It really is a neighborhood place. The back bar is well stocked and organized but purely functional. This is not a fancy "get-your-best-dress" place. This is definitely a jeans and T-shirt place. For my money, I'd rather drink with friendly people than some of the snobs in the "flavor-of-the-month" bars elsewhere in the city.

So leave your hat at home and jump into the car and get on down to Ted's Place. It's just off of Pulaski Road on Archer Avenue and the trip is well worth the ride. Order something unusual and challenge anyone at the bar to name the goalie for the Yugoslavian soccer team. Maybe you can go with them to the Pulaski Day Parade.

— *Paul Barile*

Jimmy's Woodlawn Tap

1172 E. 55th St.
773-643-5516
Hours: 10:30 a.m. to 2 a.m. weekdays,
10:30 a.m. to 3 a.m. Saturday,
11:30 a.m. to 2 a.m. Sunday

(Note -- Owner Jimmy Wilson died in February 1999 and the bar is closed as of press time. However, word is former employees are fixing the place up and attempting to re-open. Please call first before going to make sure the bar is open. The following review was written before Jimmy passed away.)

A trip to The Woodlawn Tap is a must for any Barfly spending an evening in Hyde Park for some reason or another. Whether attending an event at the University of Chicago, a night of theatre at Court or having a bite to eat at one of the various restaurants in the Hyde Park/Woodlawn microcosm, The Woodlawn Tap opens its arms welcomingly. "Jimmy's," as it is affectionately called by regulars, is a haven for all types: big or small, short or tall, of any class, creed or color. I myself have spent more than a few nights drinking in Jimmy Wilson's neighborhood tavern, and will attest to the diversity of the crowd.

I was originally introduced to Jimmy's in 1991, the year I moved to Chicago. More directly, I had moved to Hyde Park to study at the University of Chicago and it wasn't long before I was looking for a neighborhood bar to call my own. The Woodlawn Tap lends itself easily to Hyde Parkers for the simple fact that it is the only bar open to the general public in a 10-block radius. The only other public (read Non-University affiliated) bars in Hyde Park are the House of Tiki, The Cove and the Falcon Inn. These three are a bit out of the way, set on the far east side of the neighborhood and, in my opinion, leave a bit to be desired. The lack of drinking establishments in Hyde Park, and the fact that The Woodlawn Tap remains open to this day, is really quite interesting when considering the history of the bar scene in the area.

For all of you who don't know your Chicago history, the Gold Coast of Chicago wasn't always centered around what we now know as Downtown Chicago. In fact, the real swingers lived in the South Side, and more importantly, in and around Kenwood/Hyde Park. Back then, the draw to Hyde Park wasn't so singularly the University (although the U. of C. did boast the original "Monsters of the Midway" and the first Heisman Trophy winner). What brought people in droves to Hyde Park was the fantastic social scene: fine restaurants, the best accommodations, fine clothes, clubs and bars by the dozens. The likes of Mae West, Al Capone and others all strolled along 55th Street looking for a good place to have a drink and see some live music. Jazz and blues phenoms played to small crowds in smoky clubs before they were ever known to be phenomenal.

Unfortunately, as it seems with most things, the social wonder of Hyde Park

Barfly Jimmy's Woodlawn Tap

had come to an end. It was a combination of many factors, i.e. the focus on the "Loop" as Chicago's city center, the flight to the suburbs by the middle-class, the flight to the north by the city's upper-class, the encroachment of the ghettos, just to name a few. Not to mention that as soon as things started getting bad, the University took it upon themselves to close every bar on 55th except for The Woodlawn Tap. In fact, there are rumors going around that Jimmy's too will close as soon as Jimmy himself leaves this world (every year he has signed a one-year lease for his space and some doubt if that lease will be renewed when it's someone other than Jimmy coming to sign it). Today, the culture and economy revolves largely around the University of Chicago and its varied but fully academic brand of living.

It has forced Jimmy's to be far more accepting than your average neighborhood tap. In most of Chicago there is a bar to be found on any given neighborhood corner and the bar itself is filled with a relatively homogenous crowd representative of that particular neighborhood. Not to say that Jimmy's isn't representative of the Hyde Park neighborhood. In fact, it's probably as representative of Hyde Park's diversity than anything. On any given night, you can see a Nobel Prize winner sitting beside a neighborhood homeboy, a former Secretary of State with a group of current students, two grizzled old men playing chess or checkers, and all manner of Asian, white and black races. There simply is no other place to go out to have a drink within easy walking distance, so people of all types must come together.

Personally, the diversity in and of itself is enough to get me to Jimmy's. For those of you that are looking for something more, it probably has what you're looking for too. The bar itself is great to look at. It has something of an English pub-type feel with its fair share of authentic bar memorabilia. Jimmy's serves good and greasy bar food at reasonable prices. It's downright excellent if you've had a pitcher or two.

If you're looking for live entertainment, look no further. On Wednesday nights at 9 p.m. The Woodlawn Tap presents Sheila, a multi-member improv group that on any given night can really stink it up or be the funniest thing you've ever seen. The line-up comes from a larger and more famous group on the North Side and members seem to revolve every couple of weeks. On Sunday nights there is often a free blues or jazz band playing in the University Room, with South Side players of note sometimes sitting in.

The only bad thing I could possibly think of saying about Jimmy's is its lack of a tap beer selection. I myself enjoy draught far more than bottled beer and only four beers available, Miller Genuine Draft, Miller Lite, Lienie's Red, and Heineken. The bottle beer selection is more than adequate though, especially when considering most North Side bars are far more expensive.

So, if you're in Hyde Park and looking for a drink and some cheer, head to The Woodlawn Tap. If you want to catch a glimpse of Jimmy himself though, you better go in the afternoon when it's not so crowded and noisy.

— *Zach Paradis*

Chapter Three
Downtown

The Big Brassiere and Bar, 151 E. Wacker Drive, contains enough cognac, brandy and port to keep a gaggle of elder statesmen blurry for months.

Our Downtown section of this book is made up of the central business district which doesn't have a whole lot of bars. Very few people live in this area and most of those who work Downtown high-tail it out after the 5 p.m. bell tolls. As a result there are few bars and the ones that do exist usually close around 8 p.m. Downtown (also known as the Loop) workers usually drink in the bars at the southern end of the Loop (listed in Chapter Two), at those in the River North neighborhood (listed in Chapter One), or bars in Greek Town and Little Italy located just west of Downtown (listed in Chapter Four).

While lacking in watering holes, the Loop is rich in history, architecture, museums, art, personality and should definitely be explored. It took its name, the Loop, in the 1880s from a recently constructed cable-car system which ran two lines south from Downtown, one along State Street, the other along Cottage Grove Avenue. The lines converged near Marshall Field's Department Store on State Street and created a loop where the trains turned around to head back south. So ever since those first South Side passengers dubbed Downtown "The Loop," succeeding generations have followed suit. Now then, go forth, explore, be safe and enjoy. Incidently, don't look for a cable car while Downtown. What was once the largest cable car system in the world, closed down in 1958. Take a cab.

The Berghoff Cafe
17 W. Adams St.
312-427-3170
Hours: 11 a.m. to 9:30 p.m. Monday to Saturday, closed on Sunday

The Berghoff Cafe sits one door east of the renowned German restaurant of the same name. Incurably inviting, it oozes Chicago tradition from every panel of its wood-clad interior. The cafe designation will mislead folks expecting biscotti and Perrier, for this is a bar in the most absolute sense of the word, and a living example of Chicago's Turn-of-the-Century establishments.

The bar itself runs just about the length of the east wall, and the Berghoff's after-work popularity forces the traders who frequent it to keep their elbowing skills honed. It gets crowded, and getting a bartender's attention can be cutthroat, especially when you're competing against guys who spend all day shoving and shouting.

On the plus side, you don't have to worry about finding a seat here because the Berghoff is not equipped with such luxuries. To explain: The Berghoff was, for many years, a man's bar. Women challenged this exclusivity and earned admittance, but the crafty guard countered by simply removing all chairs and stools. Ladies, so they maintained, do not like to drink standing up. The strategy has worked for the most part, as the Berghoff is almost always packed with cigar-chomping, shot-swigging types either reveling in old-school spirit, or trying to recapture it.

For refreshment, the Berghoff offers four varieties of its namesake beer, the red being especially tasty. And there are two excellent house bourbons; the 10-year-old is outstanding, and the 14-year-old, when you can get it, is incomprehensibly smooth. The Berghoff also offers an excellent lunch buffet of sausages, fish sandwiches and miscellaneous Germanic grub, all products of the restaurant's reliable kitchen, and all to be had for just a couple of bucks. If you'd rather spend all your allowance on beer, however, you can raid the pretzel baskets generously placed throughout.

If you're ever in the Loop and you have an itch to drink in a cloud of capitalistic chaos, or you simply want to enjoy good beer and cheap eats in Chicago fixture, the Berghoff will fit the bill.

— Jay Ferrari

Big Brassiere and Bar
Hyatt Regency Chicago
151 E. Wacker Drive
312-565-1234 ext. BIG
Hours: 11 a.m. to 1:30 a.m. daily

Big lives up to its name. It's immense. The bar itself is more than 175 feet long, stretching the length of the lounge's north wall. Behind the bar, a score of shelves holds almost every liquor humanity has created — there are as many as 1,500 varieties at any time, including enough cognac, brandy and port to keep a gaggle of elder statesmen blurry for months. The back bar is essentially one enormous window, giving everyone a nice panoramic view of the city skyline and the Chicago River.

Big's colorful clientele makes for great people watching. When a convention is in town, the accents and foreign languages drown out any local lingo, and events such as Mr. Leather International, Science Fiction/Fantasy Enthusiasts or Miss Ethnic Hair provide a great free floor show. This often contrasts with Big's conservative decor; the high ceilings and prominent marble fixtures are very impressive, if somewhat straight-ahead. In addition to PLENTY of bar seating, there are a couple dozen tables around the bar, each accommodating parties of hotel guests, conventioneers and, often, their new "friends."

Naturally, since it relies on folks with crazy expense accounts, Big ain't cheap. The old maxim that you get what you pay for, however, is evident. Drinks are sizable and strong. The Kettle One martini is about $7, but should be served with a life preserver. The bar also has a fine selection of cigars, as well as a good menu of munchies including pizza, gourmet nachos and sandwiches.

Overall, Big is a very civilized, comfortable spot for drinking and conversation. Live music played at the piano in the hotel's downstairs lobby drifts up to Big, giving a soft soundtrack to conversation. And if you're lucky, some crazy convention will be in town, and you'll get to drink among impressive crossdressers, Klingons and coiffures.

— Jay Ferrari

Govnor's Pub
207 N. State St.
312-236-3696
Hours: 11 a.m. to 2 a.m. weekdays,
11 a.m. to 9 p.m. Saturday, closed Sunday

A solid location can make or break any business. In addition, catering to the needs and wants of your customers is almost equally important. At Govnor's Pub, I can fully guarantee that your food and drink needs will be met, and you'll have no trouble finding this tap room.

Barfly Govnor's Pub

With the Chicago Theatre directly to the south and the Leo Burnett Building right across the street, Govnor's Pub draws a wide range of people to its tables. Celebrating its 10-year anniversary in 1997, Govnor's has attained a solid group of regulars, according to manager Steve Carlson.

"Everybody is made to feel welcome" Carlson said. "We work hard at creating a friendly and hospitable atmosphere."

He's right. I'm sure everybody has walked into one bar or another, and as soon as you enter, everybody turns around from the bar to check you out. After a once over, they quickly return to their beverage, not wanting to make any kind of eye contact. That kind of reaction always makes me feel like I don't belong...like I've invaded their clubhouse. You won't get that kind of reaction at Govnor's. In fact, my server was table side within 30 seconds of me choosing my location, with a smile and a verbal greeting.

Because of its location, Govnor's is a popular meeting spot. I'd say it's just plain popular. In fact, during my two-hour stay, I watched the place fill up quickly, as the after-work crowd rolled in. Up at the bar, the concentration is on beers. Offering a wide range of domestics, as well as, imports....let's just put it this way, you won't go home thirsty. In addition, Govnor's offers my favorite beer from the tap — Murphy's Irish Amber. Darn good stuff. Give it a go the next time you're out. A nice selection of single malts and bourbons are in place along with a really cool martini list. Moreover, Govnor's takes full advantage of the harsh Chicago weather by serving up some tasty hot drinks. Try the spiced rum cider.

The music at Govnor's is taken care of by a jukebox playing CDs. It features something for everybody, although it seemed like it was stuck in the 80s. When I heard Raspberry Beret by Prince, I got up to check out the restroom. One word describes it...CLEAN. Now I didn't poke my head into the ladies room, yet if the men's room is clean, I can report that the ladies room was immaculate.

Bar decor consists of framed pictures including some great shots of fun seekers from past St. Patrick's Day celebrations at Govnor's.

If you're hungry, Govnor's offers some super kitchen items including a "Five Way Grilled Cheese" sandwich which I tried and recommend. My server Lisa, stated that Govnor's does a nice lunch time business with quite a few carry-outs. Even though I didn't get a chance to sample the burgers, the couple seated at the next table over, were really goin' to town on a couple of cheeseburgers. One thing I'll try during my next visit will be the "Caveman Chili." It just sounds good.

Govnor's is indeed for everybody. With a solid location that gives customers what they want, I'm confident Govnor's Pub will remain as popular during its second decade of business. Check the place out the next time you're in the Loop.

— Greg Dellinger

Knuckles

Hyatt Regency Hotel
151 E. Wacker Drive
312-565-1234
Hours: 5:30 p.m. to midnight weekdays,
11 a.m. to midnight weekends

With more than 2,000 moderately furnished rooms in twin towers, five restaurants, 24-hour room service, a health club and an intoxicating city view, the Hyatt Regency is extremely popular with conventioneers and tourists.

This largest of all Hyatts also has a glass-enclosed lobby that is luxurious without being overpowering. Italian granite floors surround a 4,000 square-foot reflecting pool with fountains. Impressive landscaping includes 27-foot double-trunk palm trees, 14-foot ficus trees, seasonal plants and prairie grasses. Still, there is enough open space to beat back that swallowed-up feeling.

In the southeast corner of the East Tower sits Knuckles, a sports bar developed jointly by Hyatt and the Chicago Bears. Not surprisingly, then, the place is loaded with Bears memorabilia. Autographed footballs, pictures, posters and jerseys from such greats as Dick Butkus, Gale Sayers, Jim McMahon and Walter Payton line the walls. Several Bear forgettables (Thomas Sanders and Trace Armstrong, among others) are there, too. Celebrities from Chicago's other major sports are also honored, with his Airness, Michael Jordan, given the most reverence. His number 23 hangs at the entrance, its drawing power mightier than that of any mere Monster of the Midway.

Knuckles has a cozy, full-service bar that conveys an unpretentious "neighborhood" atmosphere. It is intentionally down-scale, sort of a well-worn back-room where friends meet after work. The main room, however, is large, noisy and often filled with people not interesting enough to get better acquainted with.

This area is well-stocked with pool tables, electronic darts, air hockey and two dozen or so TV monitors: a giant large-screen is centered to offer state-of-the-art sports coverage. A jukebox is there to liven things up between games. It has pretty much what you'd expect: Elvis, Frank, Tony Bennett and Neil Diamond. Keep selecting, though, and you'll uncover cuts by the Eurythmics, Melissa Ethridge and Natalie Merchant.

Each night at Knuckles features a different special. Tuesday's is probably the best, since you can get up to 22 tasty buffalo wings for 22 cents a-piece with any purchase of a jumbo Miller Bomber. You can also choose from burgers, chicken, hot dogs, pizza, potato skins, salads, tacos and other standard bar food.

Other than daily specials, don't go looking for street-level prices. A bottle of domestic beer is priced at $4, and even a small lunch or dinner will cost you more than $10. Be patient, too. Main room service, which is always friendly, is usually painfully slow. Waitresses are forever delayed by topsider- and Polo-

400

Barfly Knuckles-Monk's Pub

shirt-wearing yuppies who act as if the singles scene is their moveable feast. Boys will be boys, I suppose.

But this is definitely not a place for "guys" to meet members of the opposite sex. On a recent Sunday night, I counted only 10 women in a crowd of at least 80; none were unattached. So for all you Rob Lowe types, pay close attention: when the Bears are playing, bring your act to Rush Street, look for your own private Demi Moore and leave the rest of us alone with our blitzing linebackers, nickel backs and tight ends.

Those interested in watching the Bear's this season should venture to Knuckles at least once or twice. Go with a bunch of friends, avoiding the hotel-bar feeling of isolation that is common in this particular stretch of the Magnificent Mile. Whenever you leave Chicago's neighborhoods, after all, you lose a major part of the city's charm. Nevertheless, the Hyatt has been pretty successful in gearing their bar to locals instead of guys wearing name tags on their lapels.

The Hyatt has also done a good job providing entertainment at the bar on nights when our home teams are idle. Definitely check out the regularly scheduled Sports Trivia nights. Pop-a-shot basketball tournaments can also be a lot of fun.

As with other Downtown bars, parking for knuckles can be tough if you're not willing to pay. There are several city-operated lots nearby. Otherwise, you'll have to depend on your parking karma to divine a spot.

— *George Rawlinson*

Monk's Pub

203 W. Lake St.
312-357-6665
Hours: 11 a.m. to midnight weekdays

If you want the world to beat a path to your door, design a better-looking beer cooler.

Why are so many coolers aesthetic nightmares? There you are, in a nice, dark, womblike bar — its once shiny surfaces pleasantly dimmed by a sticky film of beer and smoke, and its floor buffed by hundreds of staggering feet — looking at this heartless glass and steel box beaming hostile fluorescent light through its doors.

"I wasn't made for this," sniffs the box. "I would be just as happy filled with flowers or milk."

Well, speak for yourself, pal. I'd like to start seeing coolers that, like me, were designed to be filled with beer.

The cooler at Monk's Pub features a particularly rude-lighted top panel. Despite an attempt to dampen its glare with dabs of spray paint, regulars warn that you'd better not sit in front of it unless you want your head to throb before its time.

Just take the simple precaution of sliding down a few stools, though, and

Downtown Monk's-Old Timers Restaurant and Lounge

you'll find Monk's to be a friendly place where a rainbow coalition of yuppies, slackers and trades people find common ground over a cold one.

The bar is a large, "L"-shaped room. Lighting ranges from murky to nonexistent, with the exception of the rabbit-stunning glare given off by the aforementioned beer cooler. The orange stucco walls would be startling with the lights on. But in the dark, they work with the heavy wooden beams and furniture to provide a cozy psychedelic glow.

Near the Wells Street entrance, black-and-white cheesecake stills of dead starlets frolic across a big-tit wall of fame. On busy nights, the lines form outside the single-stall bathrooms, allowing patrons plenty of time to figure out whether they should be using the room marked "monks" or the one marked "nuns." Believe it or not, this causes confusion.

The place was packed on the Friday night when I stopped in. Regulars congregated at the bar or around the pool table. The tables were crowded with suit-and-tie types unwinding after a hard day of shouting "Show me the money!" at each other.

The clientele leans heavily toward guys in their 30s and 40s. This demographic was reflected by the vaguely retro selections playing on the jukebox. I'll tell ya', a body just can't have too much "Rock Lobster."

With two bartenders and two waitresses working the floor, the crowd was efficiently served. The bartenders were even nice to the moron with the laser pointer who kept tagging them with his beam.

This is definitely a beer-drinking establishment. Along with the usual domestic standbys, there are Bass and Michael O'Shea's on tap, and weissbeir in bottles. There's also, inexplicably, O'Doul's not-even-near beer. For variety, have a shot of Cuervo or Jagermeister. I think I glimpsed a box of white zinfandel at the bottom of the cooler, but I'll bet it's there for when somebody's mother is in town.

Monk's also serves a full menu of bar food, including half-pound burgers, chili and fish and chips. The kitchen is open from noon to 8 p.m. Tombstone pizzas are available until closing.

— June Hathaway Vigor

Old Timers Restaurant & Lounge
75 E. Lake St.
312-332-3561
Hours: 6 a.m. to 2 a.m. weekdays,
7 a.m. to 1 a.m. Saturday, closed Sunday

Hey harried Loop worker, an idyllic rest stop is right under your nose. Just off Michigan Avenue at the bottom of a typical office building sits Old Timers. Stop in for a club sandwich or an omelet if hunger is the driving appetite. If it's thirst, however, duck through the doorway between the cash register and the revolving pie case. Within is Old Timers Lounge. A dozen or so stools surround a horse-shoe shaped bar, which is ringed with padding so thick, you'll want to

Barfly Old Timers Restaurant and Lounge

drop your head and take a nap.

This sleep-inducing vibe dominates at Old Timers. The lighting is soothing and dim, perfect contrast to the harsh work-day glare so many patrons are escaping from. Stained-glass windows and small ceiling lamps (which look like they were made in a grade-school art class from tin cans and yarn) provide enough illumination to order. A pair of televisions behind the bar will show whatever game is on, but the sound is appropriately soft.

If the action at the bar is too hot to handle, there are several small booths along the back wall. The adjacent restaurant can send any menu item to the lounge. Ever wonder what draft goes best with a francheezie? Here's the place to find out. There are four taps including Miller and Guinness, along with familiar domestic bottles, and a commendable selection of call-brand and top-shelf liquors. The bar back is worth noting as well, a kind of kaleidoscopic, two-tiered shelf that echoes the stained-glass windows. The fidgety will find two video poker machines to play if necessary; noisier diversions like darts or pinball are unavailable.

The Old Timers crowd tends to the friendly type of municipal workers and tradesmen who service the surrounding office buildings. It's appropriate that this bar is at street level because patrons are similarly down-to-earth. Sit back and sip a pint while eavesdropping on the days events at the Daley Center or Prudential Plaza. Chime in if you have an observation about a local team (the acquisition of Albert Bell by the Sox caused quite a positive stir). In an area where bars can be dense with extra-loud middle managers romancing interns, Old Timers is an oasis of unpretention. Ease in for a cold one. And keep it down.

— *Jay Ferrari*

Chapter Four
The West Side

The West Side of Chicago has undergone an amazing amount of change throughout its history. During the early 19th Century, beautiful mansions were scattered throughout. By the end of the 19th Century, the mansions were swallowed up by waves of immigrants who densely populating this area located west of Downtown. Jews, Italians, Greeks, Irish, Bohemians, Poles, English, Scots, German, and French each called portions of the West Side home. Most of the immigrants were poor. Yet, they had a savior in Jane Adams whose Hull House at 800 S. Halsted St. provided jobs, education and entertainment. Hull House grew into a huge complex of buildings on the Near West Side. However, just one building remains and is now a museum. Actually, very little of the old West Side remains. In the 1950s two highways, the Dan Ryan and the Eisenhower expressways, were constructed and cut through the area, displacing residents. A decade later, the city condemned about 60 acres and built the University of Illinois at Chicago. Generations of family histories, including most of Littly Italy, were wiped out. In addition, the city built several housing projects and white ethnics fled to the suburbs. New immigrants to the area include hispanics and blacks. Although their numbers are a fraction of what once was there before, their poverty is similar to previous residents.

A few remnants of the area's past still remain such as a few buildings on Maxwell Street at Halsted, the city's first Jewish ghetto. A thriving open-air market existed here for more than 100 years until officials tore town many of the buildings and moved the market east to Canal Street just a few years ago. In the 1950s and 1960s, the market became predominantly black and known for its talented street performers playing wonderful Chicago blues music.

To the north of Maxwell Street is Greek Town. While today it has fantastic Greek restaurants, scarcely nothing else remains of a once-vibrant Greek community. Same goes for Little Italy just south on Taylor Street.

Another West Side neighborhood is Austin, which spans the largest area of any neighborhood in Chicago. Not much of a drinking neighborhood, it's named after an 1870s state legislator who was an early prohibitionist. Also, it's pretty run down as is are other West Side neighborhoods like East Garfield Park and West Garfield Park. Other than the United Center (UC), home of the Bulls and Blackhawks, safest drinking areas on the West Side of Chicago are located along Halsted and Taylor streets.

However, since the Democratic National Convention was held at the UC in 1996, the area has shown signs of improvement and may once again become of vibrant section of Chicago.

Hawkeyes
1458 W. Taylor St.
312-226-3951
Hours: 11 a.m. to 2 a.m. weekdays,
noon to 3 a.m. Saturday, noon to 2 a.m. Sunday

Upon entering Hawkeyes, one is greeted by a plethora of smiling young faces and heavy drink specials. This is not your typical sports bar. Cubs fans, BEWARE! This is a South Side bar. In the theme of your finest sports bars, Hawkeyes provides shuttle buses to and from Bear, Bulls, and Blackhawks games.

One may think that the entire bar is filled with noisy, young adults. The fact of the matter is that, during the day, it is a business persons' eating arena (located separately from the main bar area). There are also two additional rooms, a private party room and an outdoor cafe.

The music is typically classic rock, as the sign states, "105.9 WCKG." There is also a jukebox in case this music doesn't suit your taste.

Asked where most UIC students hang out, the manager Kevin said, "This is where they come." He also stated that the busiest nights are Wednesdays, Thursdays, and Fridays. Wear what most college students wear: shorts, T-shirts, and sneakers.

Get ready to drink. Amstel Light is $1.75 per bottle and a 22-ounce Leinenkugel's Honey Weiss is $2.75 daily. Miller beer will run you a measly $1.75 per bottle on Fridays.

DON'T let the neighborhood put you off. Kevin has been working there for eight years, and is also from the neighborhood. He said that there have been only a couple of minor altercations since he's been there.

Eat, drink, and be merry! Hawkeyes is the place to be for an entertaining evening.

— *Scott Terry*

The Illinois Bar and Grill
1421 W. Taylor St.
312-666-6666
Hours: 10 a.m. to 2 a.m. Sunday to Friday,
10 a.m. to 3 a.m. Saturday

In Jan. 1997, The Illinois Bar and Grill on 47th Street spawned a new location on Taylor Street. Never having been to the original, I can judge this place without any comparisons to the former. So I am here to tell you that this is an excellent establishment, one of the finest I've been to in a long time.

Glass cinderblocks greet you as you enter. The rest of the place is decorated with an elegant mixture of steel and wood. I know not what previously occupied this address, but I guarantee that a lot of work went into rehabbing it.

405

The West Side Illinois Bar and Grill

Wood booths, floors, and paneling make this tavern a beaver's paradise. Oddly enough, the one thing that is devoid of wood is the bar. Rippled sheet metal with what appears to be something that was once a liquid poured over it, holds the drinks. Stainless steel around the edges help make it one of the most unique I've seen.

More sheet metal and some wood made into a roof-type structure over hang the bar. This gives a wonderful illusion that you're drinking in a shed. It is awesome.

Beer signs hang everywhere and they seem to match the selection available. A moose's head hangs opposite a picture of Mayor Daley Sr. and it could scare the shit out of you. The moose's head, I mean.

The rear holds more tables, a video golf game, an electronic dart board, old baseball photographs, and a sign that reads, "No Condo, No MBA and No BMW."

Although there are about half-a-dozen TVs throughout the establishment, it doesn't seem to sports-barish.

We were there on a Sunday and the crowd was light. As I expected, it seems that they get quite a few college drinkers from the university and cops. Good God, I thought the joint was getting raided. Two uniformed officers entered first, then what seemed like the entire police force joined them. But is was cool, they were just there to eat. By the way, they were all drinking Cokes, Mister Commissioner.

A regular named Jose, who works down the street at Hawkeyes, said, "It's a nice, cozy place. It mixes up the neighborhood."

Try the Blue Moon Belgian Wit Ale. At $3 a pint, served with lemon, it is a good beer. The Illinois Bar and Grill Lager is also decent at the same price. They have some domestics on tap for the not-so-rolling-in-dough college as well as more premiums and a good selection of bottles.

Hacker Pschorr Weiss also holds a tapper. Yum yum. The hard liquor selection had everything I could possibly have wanted but they do not clutter the bar back with a bunch of unnecessary bottles.

The food is OUTSTANDING, especially because I just expected bar food. I had an excellent bowl of chili and some freshly made onion rings. My buddy Jeff had a cheeseburger that was about the size of a wheel from a 1971 Monte Carlo. He said that it was one of the best he's ever had. For only $3.50 it is probably the best bargain around.

On the bottom of the menu it reads, "If you like the service, please tip your server. If not, please tip me. Please call me..." Then Frank proceeded to leave his pager number. I was really impressed that someone cares so much about their business in a world where service is just another word.

The bathroom was one of the coolest things I have ever seen. The urinal looks almost like a trough, but the stainless steel goes all the way to the ceiling, and water constantly trickles down. The stall is made of more of that flanged sheet metal, and the door slides on a track. I tried to go into the ladies' room, but I was bombarded by words like "pervert" and "creep." That really insulted

Barfly Illinois Bar and Grill-Kallisto

by journalistic integrity.

I don't know why I've gone on about this place so much. I could have saved a lot of ink and just wrote, "Get your ass over here or you are a complete waste of human flesh," and that would have summed it up. There are times that reviewing bars is the best job on the planet and going to the Illinois Bar and Grill and Taylor Street was one of those times. This place is the very epitome of what a bar and grill should be. Not too bad for an establishment that was, "Piled to the ceiling with shit," as the bartender said before the renovations began. I'll be there again.

— Bud

Kallisto

232 S. Halsted St.
312-454-1227
Hours: 4 p.m. to 2 a.m. Sunday,
11 a.m. to 2 a.m. Monday and Tuesday,
11 a.m. to 4 a.m. Wednesday and Friday,
11 a.m. to 3 a.m. Thursday, 4 p.m. to 5 a.m. Saturday

Kallisto is a popular night spot in Greek Town. My Greek girlfriend, Patty, introduced me to it during her bachelorette party.

On a recent trip back there, the doors to Kallisto were open wide to the summer air, letting a combination of American and Greek music drift toward the street. Entering the bar, I saw a seating area to my left that featured a plush velvet couch the length of one wall. In the same direction are glass doors that allow for a scenic view of Halsted Street.

A quick look to my right provided another nice view, this one through a brick wall missing its mid-section that offered a glimpse of the stone-tiled dance floor and outside verandah.

Kallisto has two bars for your drinking pleasure. One long bar sits eight to nine. You can have a glass of wine or some good cognac here. The second bar waits beyond the dance floor.

There are no beers on tap, yet I spotted a Miller Lite bottle displayed among the many rows of liquors behind the bar. I also saw an Amstel Light, Sam Adams, Heineken's, Beck's and others. That's not a bad bottle selection. Before I had the chance to order a beer, though, someone asked for a round of Ouzo shots. Shortly afterward, the dancing began. Granted, I'm not a very coordinated person, but after so many Ouzo shots, I was convinced to join a Greek "line" dance.

If the munchies sneak up on you, the kitchen is open until 2 a.m. I suggest the saganaki or souvlaki sandwich. Menu items are moderately priced.

Leaving Kallisto, I gleefully repeated the three Greek words I had learned to the bartender, cocktail waitress and cab driver. "Tha Ta Spasoume," refers to an old custom of breaking dishes, meaning, "Let's celebrate and have a hell of a good time!" So stop by Kallisto and "Tha Ta Spasoume!"

— Christy K. Rizzo

The Parthenon
314 S. Halsted St.
312-726-2407
Hours: 11 a.m. to 1 a.m. daily

Greek immigrants began to settle in Chicago's Near West Side in the 1800s. At one time, so many resided in this triangle-shaped neighborhood that it became known as the Delta, after the triangular Greek letter. The Greek restaurants packed in along Halsted Street, between Monroe and Van Buren, are virtually all that's left of Greektown. A few shops like the Athenian Candle Company, Pan Hellenic Bakery and Athens Grocery remain, but the residential community has long since scattered.

In restaurants with names like Athena, Costa's, Estia, Hellas Cafe, Greek Islands, Pegasus, Roditys, Santorini and Zorba's, cries of "Oohhppa" are as sacred as an Orthodox chant. It's a celebration of food and theater in which customers and waiters consecrate the joys of eating and good company.

The Parthenon is my choice whenever I'm in Greektown. After almost 29 years, Chris Liakouras still runs the restaurant, along with Peter, his nephew and partner. Not too long ago, the Parthenon underwent an extensive facelift. The oak-trimmed dining rooms are simple, yet very attractive. Everything is bright and airy. Murals emphasize the importance of ancient Greece on western civilization. Even the outside was redone. The owners added a striking Greek classical facade. The five columns in front evoke the restaurant's namesake in Athens.

Because of its almost mythological reputation, the Parthenon attracts a lot of tourists. T-shirts and other souvenirs are available at the door. Once at your table, though, these Planet Hollywood touches disappear.

The Parthenon has an enormous menu, with the majority of entrees priced under $10. Check the daily specials insert for interesting additions. One Thursday night, I had a flavorful lentil soup, broiled skinless chicken breasts and a dish of Greek pasta for $8.75.

Like the best Greek restaurants, the Parthenon has a way with chicken. Even better, is their lamb. Rotisserie-roasted lamb served with rice pilaf and roasted potatoes is my favorite selection, but there are at least a dozen additional lamb dishes to consider.

The gyros is a Parthenon specialty. It is split-roasted and made right on the premises. It is, without question, the best I've had anywhere. In fact, it was Chris Liakouras who introduced the gyros to the United States.

Incidentally, saganaki (flaming cheese) was also born at the Parthenon. It proved popular enough to actually make its way back to Greece.

The best deal for those dining in a group is the family-style dinner, a multi-course extravaganza that takes you from saganaki to gyros to Greek salad to

Barfly Parthenon

mousska to pastido to rotisserie lamb. You can also go from chicken breast kebob, pork tenderloin kebob, and dolmades to rice pilaf, roasted potatoes, baklava, galaktobouriko and coffee. This breathtaking journey is only $13.50 a person.

Baklava and galaktobouriko should be of special interest to anyone with a sweet tooth. Baklava has layers of phyllo and a crushed walnut spread saturated with honey. Galaktobouriko is filled with custard and baked in syrup.

Other desserts not to be missed are the cream caramele and the homemade yogurt with honey and walnuts.

For those of you with at least a dozen friends, the Parthenon offers a split-roasted whole suckling pig for $7.95 a person for groups of 12 or more. This has to be ordered at least one day in advance. You'll see it turning in the window as you enter. The pig dinner comes with sesame bread, rice pilaf and roasted potatoes. The waiters bring the finished product to your table before taking it back to the kitchen for disassembly. It returns on platters for your feast. The head shows up, too, but only as a centerpiece for your table.

Throughout my many dining experiences at the Parthenon, the service has always been good. Waiters take their time to explain how certain dishes are made. They are energetic, fun and at least slightly louder than the family or the college friends who will invariably be at the table next to yours.

Expect Greek wines to flow. Bottles of Roditys ($11.50) help spark the spirit of celebration that is natural to a good Greek restaurant. There is an almost endless wine list to choose from if Roditys is not your preference. My favorite is St. Pandeleimon ($14.95), a semi-sweet wine that is exceptionally quick at fulfilling its destiny.

There is no dress code at the Parthenon. Reservations are recommended for parties of six or more. There are inexpensive city parking lots a block north, but there is also free valet parking available.

Chicago is a city of great restaurants. The Parthenon not only offers great food at reasonable prices, it brings a real adventure in an original big-shoulders setting.

— George Rawlinson

Chapter Five
Breakfast in Bars

It doesn't get much better than Sunday brunch at J.T. Collins Pub, 3358 N. Lincoln Ave.

Weekday Breakfast

The Garage, 730 N. Green St., is a fine place for a early morning drink and a few pastries. The Garage opens at 7 a.m. and if your not in the mood for alcohol, you can get some tasty coffee. For more information, call 312-633-0911.

Watch **The Map Room,** 1949 N. Hoyne Ave., transform from one busy bar at night to an early morning coffee house. Opening at 6:30 a.m., one can stop in for a cup o' joe to go or stay a while and nurse down $1.50 bottomless cups along with some 50-cent scones or muffins. Espresso and cappuccino are also featured. What makes this place a worthwhile stop for coffee in the morning is that the bar keeps that neighborhood feel from the night before so there is no reason to travel to any of those stale, corporate coffeehouses in the area. Read, watch CNN, listen to some jazz or talk with your neighbor. We suggest drinking a cup with "coffee master" Greg who is excellent company to start your day. For more information, call 773-252-7636.

Mad Bar, 1640 N. Damen Ave., is another nice coffee and pastry stop if you are on the way to the el or waiting to catch a bus. Positioned about a block

410

Barfly Breakfast in Bars

from the Damen, North and Milwaukee intersection to take one in almost any direction necessary to get to work. Choose from 12- to 16-ounce cups of various coffees, espresso or cappuccino to subdue that hangover on the way to work or relax and listen to some good jazz. Plenty of seating at tables and a few at the coffee bar. For more information, call 773-227-2277.

Pamela's Haymarket Restaurant and Saloon, 615 W. Randolph St. This place rules! It's located just across the street from the site of the famed Haymarket riot and it is quite a relic. The place oozes with Chicago history. Its walls are dotted with old Chicago photos, knick knacks and German bier steins. On the morning we ventured in, there was even a couple of guys drinking and complaining about their union. No worker riots though, just plenty of good drinks and fine food. The place is run by a nice old couple and their two-egg breakfast with bacon, toast and potatoes is quite tasty and affordable at $2.55. Also on the menu is French toast, pancakes, and an assortment of omelets like Denver, ham and cheese, and Greek all served with toast and potatoes and ranging in price from $3 to $4. The Haymarket opens at 6 a.m. After 11 a.m. tack on $1 for all breakfast prices. There's also a full lunch and dinner menu. For more information, call 312-648-9330.

If your heading further into Downtown, the **LaSalle-Wacker Bar & Grille,** 221 N. LaSalle St., is an optimal spot to break your fast. The room is large and cozy with ample seating available including window seats to check out the hustle and bustle of city workers. The menu is limited, but in some ways exotic. We've never heard of a lox omelet, but if you've ever craved one, this is the place to go. Chunks of potatoes accompany any of the omelets which are plenty tasty. Other items to choose from are eggs and bacon or sausage, pancakes or cereal. Although slim in the pickings, the rates for a meal are extremely reasonable. It's hard to believe that this place co-exists Downtown with those outrageously priced food stops nearby. The average price of a nice breakfast is around $3. However, that lox omelet tops the prices at $4.50. For more information, call 312-641-6400.

Sports Corner, 959 W. Addison Ave., has the perfect decor for a spring breakfast. Its comfortable booths line walls painted like the ivy-laden outfield of neighboring Wrigley Field. To eat, there are various egg offerings all including toast, choice of meat (yes, meat!) and potatoes made with onions. Tony rather liked the onion addition but Phil disliked such an intrusion to his hash-browns. There's also omelets with your choice of filling, French Toast, biscuits and gravy, all reasonably priced between $3.50 to $5.50. The staff when we were there was only a cook who sidelined as a waiter and he was extremely pleasant offering up a choice of a Tribune or Sun-Times to look over while dining. And this being the Sports Corner, there are plenty of sports to view, even in the morning, on the televisions scattered throughout the place. To drink, there's a full bar with Bloody Mary's costing $2.75. For more information, call 773-929-1441.

Oooohhpah! How 'bout a little Saganaki Flaming Cheese for breakfast. Well, Saganaki and a glass of Rodity's is available near sunrise at **Zorba's Lounge,**

301 S. Halsted St., in Greektown. Zorba's is open 24 hours and is a veritable eating and drinking complex. It features a take out area, bakery, restaurant and lounge. Zorba's menu is packed with a variety of Greek favorites available at any time. We stopped by in the morning and were rather tempted by sparkling red slabs of barbecued ribs residing safely behind a glass counter in the take-out area of Zorba's. So we settled for a couple of gyro omelet's which were excellent and highly recommended. Other breakfast items include eggs served any style, about a dozen different types of omelets, and Zorba's Super Breakfast which is two eggs, sausage, hash browns, toast or pancakes. The prices are reasonable, most dishes cost under $4. University of Illinois at Chicago students and police officers get discounts. For more information, call 312-454-1397.

Weekend Brunch

Deacon Brodie's, 2512 N. Halsted St., serves breakfast from 11 a.m. to 2 p.m. on Saturdays and Sundays. You can dine in the bar area or Deacon Brodie's no-smoking room which has a movie screen-size television excellent for watching sports. When you sit down to eat, make sure you bring your appetite because the portions are large and tasty. The breakfast menu features two eggs with sausage or bacon, English muffin, and hashbrowns for $3.25; a croissant sandwich filled with scrambled eggs and your choice of cheese and served with hashbrowns for $3.50; Scottish Breakfast with two eggs, sausage, bacon, tomato and sautéed mushrooms served with an English muffin and hashbrowns for $5.95; steak and eggs with an 8-ounce steak with two eggs, English muffin and hashbrowns for $5.95; Scottish toast — Tony had this and said it was awesome — Deacon Brodie's version of the French and better with Texas toast battered and grilled and served with bacon or sausage, syrup and powdered sugar for $4.95. There's also a variety of omelets like Mexican with chunks of avocado, Denver, veggie, and ham and cheese. There's a full bar featuring a fine array of Scottish, Irish and English brews on tap, perfect for a Scottish breakfast. For more information, call 773-296-9700.

After a long weekend of power drinking, stop by **The Beaumont,** 2020 N. Halsted St., between 11 a.m. and 3 a.m. for their "Power Breakfast" to regain your strength for the up-coming work week. The Beaumont's Sunday breakfast really lives up to its name with all you can eat for only $3.95, which includes bottomless cups of coffee or tea! Hard to beat with quality food at such a deal of a price. For more information, call 773-281-0177.

Jack Sullivan's, 2142 N. Clybourn Ave., offers a nice weekend brunch with plenty of food. For example, where else can one get a plate of steak AND Eggs Benedict? Now that's a meal to last you through a long sports Sunday! Or choose from other items on the menu which include Belgium waffles, pancakes, eggs and choices of meats. What makes this a great brunch place as well is the "build your own Bloody Mary bar" with so many selections to make your signature Bloody Mary even better. Even if the weather is still on the chilly side, Jack Sullivan's offers plenty of warming sunlight with their sky light over the bar and a front wall of nothing but windows. For more information, call

Barfly Breakfast in Bars

773-549-9009.

For those with a wee-bit of the Irish still in the blood from St. Pat's Day, definitely go to **The Abbey Pub & Restaurant,** 3420 W. Grace Ave., and get their Irish Breakfast #1. Phil couldn't get enough of this platter of food, even though it was plenty to fill his gut. Two eggs, two Irish sausages, two Irish bacon, potatoes, with two black and white puddings. Skip the coffee and head straight for a Guinness with this breakfast. Phil also recommends a little malt vinegar on the potatoes. For those wanting to stay with the traditional American breakfast, but still want plenty of food, try the "Hearty Man's Breakfast." This comes with two eggs, potatoes, meat and pancakes. Prices range from $3.50 to $5.75, but are well worth it. For more information, call 773-478-4408.

Clancy's Pub & Grub, 4264 N. Lincoln Ave., is another place to have a good Irish or American breakfast. Starting at 8 a.m. and continuing until 2 p.m., one can choose from an Irish breakfast similar to the Abbey Pub's or go for a create-your-own omelet with about eight different ingredients. Go for the coffee here as they give you a large coffee thermos full of coffee with free refills. The great thing about Clancy's is the homey feel this place offers with a carpeted floor, place mats, and plenty of friendly folks getting started on their drinking weekend. For more information, call 773-252-6297.

McGee's, 950 W. Webster Ave., currently serves Saturday and Sunday brunch from 11 a.m. to 3 a.m. However, due to such fine breakfast items that McGee's chef Phil Piazza serves up, rumor has it that brunch will be starting an hour earlier to calm the crowds. One can choose from Piazza's special omelets with plenty of veggies and/or meats added in, biscuits and gravy, or piles of pancakes. The main item, however is "Phil's steak & eggs benedict" which is a nice skirt steak marinated overnight then cooked to perfection. Prices range from around $3 to the "Phil's steak & eggs benedict" at $9.95. For more information, call 773-549-8200.

Also, for eggs benedict lovers, stop in at **Charlie's Ale House,** 1224 W. Webster Ave., for their Sunday brunch from 9 a.m. to 3 p.m. What the Ale House does to make their eggs benedict so "eggseptional" we couldn't figure out, but it didn't seem to cross our minds while we were chomping them down. There are other quality items including a chili omelet and a lox plate. Delicious muffins accompany almost every meal. Prices range from about $6.95 to $8.95 and are well worth the price. For more information, call 773-871-1440.

The Fireside, 5739 N. Ravenswood Ave., has one of the best build your own Bloody Mary bar's around on Sundays from 11 a.m. to 3 p.m. The Fireside offers patrons 110 different ingredients to toss into their Bloody Marys. We personally enjoyed this extremely and made spicy thick drinks from such items as Carolina Swamp Sauce, Sylvia's Queen of Soul Food Spicy and Sassy Sauce, and Endorphin Rush Beyond Hot Sauce. To eat, Fireside has some excellent breakfasts. We ate the Eggs Benedict with chicken breast which was delicious. Other Eggs Benedict-type meals include swordfish steak raspberry hollandaise sauce and petite filet mignon hollandaise sauce. Portions are large and include O'Brien potatoes and cost around $8. For those who like omelets,

413

Sunday at the Fireside Ravenswood, 5739 N. Ravenswood Ave., is Bloody Mary heaven with more than 100 spices to concoct the perfect drink.

there are several types including Cajun-Andouille sausage with bronzed red and yellow peppers and red onions; seafood with shrimp, catfish, baby clams, sautéed first in garlic and white wine; Fireside's famous meatloaf with Monterey Jack cheese; The Fireside omelet featuring Brie, walnuts with lemon hollandaise sauce; and a spinach omelet with fresh spinach and goat cheese. Omelets cost around $7. There's also a variety of two egg or egg beater combinations such as London broil steak and eggs, grilled or blackened catfish and eggs, and stuffed pork chop spinach and garlic bread stuffing and eggs all costing about $8 and served with O'Brien potatoes. Basically Fireside's brunch menu is thorough and excellent, there's even a kids menu. For more information, call 773-561-7433.

J.T. Collins Pub, 3358 N. Paulina St., serves weekend brunch from 10 a.m. to 3 p.m. on Saturdays and Sundays. Eggs Benedict is one of J.T. Collins' most popular brunch dishes as well as its multi-grain pancakes with blueberries and gingered maple syrup. Eggs Benedict cost $6.25 and the pancakes cost $4.25. Other breakfast goodies at J.T. Collins include an open faced omelet with ham, peppers, onions, tomatoes, cheddar and home fries for $5.50; brandied French toast with blueberry compote for $4.25; steak and eggs with hollandaise and home fries for $7.25; J.T.'s half pound chuck burger with French fries for $5.25; grilled chicken sandwich with chipotle mayo and french fries for $5.25; and quesadillas with grilled chicken, Chihuahua cheese, jalapeño peppers in a flour tortilla served with tomatillo sauce. This place is an excellent place to dine, with its large windows facing Roscoe Street, Lincoln Avenue and Paulina

Barfly Breakfast in Bars

Street, there's plenty of morning sunshine. Also, J.T. Collins makes Bloody Marys any way you want them. They also serve a variety of morning drinks including mimosas. For more information, call 773-327-7467.

Lakeview Links, 3206 N. Wilton Ave., serves hangover food from 11 a.m. to 3 p.m. on Saturdays and Sundays. According to the folks at Lakeview Links, fat and grease are the perfect cure for a hangover. This place is really laid back. Brunch patrons are encouraged to come wearing the same clothes worn the night before. At Lakeview Links there's no lines, no-nonsense and plenty of sports to be viewed on large-screen televisions everywhere in this huge bar. To start that hangover cure, Lakeview Links has $5 pitchers of Bud and Bud Light and $3 Bloody Marys. To soak up the suds, there's egg sandwiches, French toast, breakfast burritos, huevos rancheros, three eggs any style, a variety of omelets and everything costs $3.75 each and includes bacon or sausage and potatoes. The breakfast burritos are pretty big and really popular. For more information, call 773-975-0505.

Yet another excellent place to enjoy a Sunday brunch and a "Build Your Own Bloody Mary Bar" is **Hog Head McDunna's**, 1505 W. Fullerton Ave. Brunch is served 11 a.m. to 3 a.m. while the Bloody Mary bar lasts the whole day through. One can even purchase an "Unlimited" Bloody Mary for $7.75 just to prove that point. For the brunch there is an awesome selection of pancakes to choose from including walnut and blueberry, butter pecan, whole wheat raisin, apple and cinnamon. Even their French toast has its own little kick of some orange liqueur thrown in the recipe. There is also a couple different omelets on the list. The Bloody Mary bar is the main feature with more than 100 different sauces and garnishes filling a whole table. Other features are plenty of large screens for sports and free darts and pool. For more information, call 773-929-0944.

— Tony Gordon and Phil Brandt

Chapter Six
Lunch in Bars

The McCauley and Bodziak families enjoy lunch at
Lincoln Tavern, 1858 W. Wabansia Ave.

Lunch at **Lincoln Tavern and Restaurant**, 1858 W. Wabansia Ave., is as
comfortable as the soft fabric of a well-worn lazy-boy. It's Matt, Vince, Henry
and Rich, coming in every day for lunch and sitting in the same barstools.

"To bad the service isn't as good as we are prompt," Rich joked on a recent
afternoon.

The service from the Folak family is excellent and the chow is affordable. A
bowl of chili costs 2 bucks, an Italian beef sandwich is $3.50, a thickly-piled
corned beef sandwich is $4.25.

Other tasty delights include Polish sausage, liver sausage, ham, hot dogs,
chili dogs, tamales, salads and daily specials.

The Monday afternoon we stopped in, the specials were chicken soup, barbecued beef, and beef stew. Tony had the barbecued beef sandwich that featured a
hearty portion of beef dripping in sauce on a French roll and served with potato
chips. Phil went with the Polish sausage, also served on a French roll with lettuce, relish, onions, tomato, pickle and chips. Both sandwiches were excellent.

This is one of our favorite places for lunch and we have eaten here many
times. Other recommendations are the corned beef sandwich which is the best

Barfly Lunch in Bars

around and Friday's tuna fish sandwich special. The tuna is great and served piled high on toast. And to top it off, we recommend a cool Pabst on tap. For some reason Pabst taste better at Lincoln Tavern than anywhere else. Maybe it's because they have been serving it since 1934.

For a serious Chicago lunch experience, the **Golden Ox**, 1578 N. Clybourn Ave., is the place. This part of the Near North Side was once a German neighborhood and the Golden Ox, opened in 1921, is the last remnant from the old neighborhood. The interior is beautiful. Old wood carvings and paintings help make the dining experience special.

But what is really special — the food. We stopped in on a Tuesday and Tony ate the pork and veal special. The entree included slices of pork and veal smothered in a delicious mushroom sauce with potato pancakes and apple sauce. The meal also came with oxtail soup which was fresh and creamy and included tender beef on the bone. Phil dined on a hearty plate of sauerbraten that came with potato salad and sauerkraut. When the waitress mentioned dessert we didn't hesitate and assaulted some German chocolate cake.

The Golden Ox menu includes many German dishes like Bavarian Bratwurst and Smoked Thueringer as well as stews, seafood, sandwiches and low-calorie dishes. Prices range from $8 to $12. The Golden Ox has a full bar with many fine German beers on tap. Service is excellent and friendly. Lunch begins at 11 a.m. daily. For more information, call 312-664-0780.

In the South Loop, one of the best stops for lunch is the **South Loop Club**, 701 S. State St. It's a mellow place where Loop workers and Columbia College students dine amongst a 70-inch television, a long bar, lots of liquor signs, promo stuff and large windows facing either State Street or Balbo, perfect for people watching.

Nick the owner says his burger is the best in town. After inhaling a huge charbroiled burger with grilled onions, mushrooms and cheddar cheese, we have to say that Nick's burger is definitely one of the best. It's tough to say whose burger is best, but South Loop Club's burger is in the top three for sure.

South Loop Club offers much more than burgers though. There's rotisserie chicken served in half or whole, either barbecued, Grecian or original style. There's barbecued ribs, tacos, veggie burgers, salads, pizza, sandwiches and a variety of appetizers. Prices go from $3.50 to $11.50.

To drink, SLC has 12 beers on tap and about 50 varieties of bottled beers. There's daily food and drink specials and take-out is ok. Lunch starts at 11 a.m. For more information, call 312-427-2787.

Whoops! Sports Bar and Grill, 2853 N. Kedzie Ave., is an excellent place for lunch in Logan Square. Whoops! features two rooms, one is a restaurant and the other is a bar. The bar area isn't open until evening, leaving the restaurant area a pleasant place for some Mexican food. This clean room features a variety of Mexican dishes like burritos, tacos, tortas, enchiladas, bistec, pollo and vegetarian. They also serve American dishes like tuna sandwiches, ham sandwiches, grilled cheese, BLTs, and burgers.

Tony dined on a chicken torta and a vegi taco. The torta is served on a fresh bun with spiced chicken, lettuce, tomatoes, cheese, refried beans and sour cream. The sandwich is pretty large. The vegi taco is served on a soft tortilla, with lettuce, tomatoes, rice, corn and refried beans.

Phil ate a vegetarian burrito which was hearty and excellent.

Lunch at Whoops! begins at 11 a.m. There are daily food specials and the Orchata is always fresh. For more information, call 773-267-2672.

There's nothin' like home cookin' in a neighborhood tavern. One of the best neighborhood joints is the **Candlelite**, 7452 N. Western Ave., located in the Far North Side's West Ridge neighborhood. The Candlelite is an old place laid out in two rooms; one room has a long bar, the other has wood booths. We stopped in at about 1 p.m. and there were a few guys at the bar and a couple dining in a booth. The Candlelite has daily food specials and a pretty good menu with soups, salads, sandwiches, entrees and pizza. The menu boasted that the Chicago Tribune had rated the pizza four-star, so that's what we ate.

The pizza was cooked from scratch and was delicious. It has an amazingly thin crust, creamy cheese and lotsa sauce. Needless to say, we wolfed that sucker down pretty quick. Our waitress/bartender Julie, who's from the neighborhood, said she's been going to the Candlelite for the pizza since she was a little sprout. She also said customers crave the other menu items as well.

"A lot of people like the Italian beef served on garlic bread with mozzarella cheese," said Julie adding that the barbecued ribs are also excellent.

Well, we enjoyed our afternoon at the Candlelite. Lunch is served from 11 a.m. to 2 p.m. For more information, call 772-761-8070.

The food at **Wrong's Tap**, 10014 S. Western Ave., is amazing. Located in the South Side's Beverly neighborhood, this regular place serves excellent lunch. The guy responsible is cook George Savaglio who has run the kitchen for about two years. Everything George cooks is made from scratch.

We both ate the Italian Beef sandwich. Phil says this is the best Italian Beef he's ever had. The beef is piled thick and covered in George's own au jus sauce, sweet peppers stored in olive oil before they are cooked, and topped with mozzarella cheese.

George also cooks up some Italian sausages, meatballs, barbecued beef, burgers and in the winter months chili. He has specials every day. He said in the summer the specials are usually lighter fare. Some regular specials are Prince Spaghetti Day on Wednesday featuring homemade lasagna, baked mostaccioli, and ravioli.

Thursday is pork chops and Friday is pepper and egg sandwiches.

All of George's items are old family recipes.

"It all comes back to my grandmother," George said. "All the sauces are homemade. Nothin' comes out of a can in here."

George takes great pride in his cooking and he likes to see a pleased customer.

"It's something here where you can't get anywhere," George said. "I want to be different and a little special."

George's food and all the folks at Wrong's are definitely special. Lunch is

Barfly Lunch in Bars

served from 11 a.m. to 2 p.m. For more information, call 773-238-5534.

Quenchers, 2400 N. Western Ave., is a nice, relaxing place to stop in for lunch. Owner Earle Johnson is always a treat to discuss the day's events or whatever.

The best part about Quenchers is its selection of beers from across the world, including some local favorites. Though Earle's lunch menu only consists of just a few items which include Earle's Famous Chili, a Wisconsin bratwurst, Polish sausage, a smoked ham sandwich, corned beef, a hot dog with chili, cheese or both, it is easy to find a complimenting beer specified to one's taste.

We're very partial to the chili with good reason. Earle said he has been cooking up his chili for close to 10 years and his time put into it shines through. Chock full of tomatoes, beans, beef and perfectly seasoned. The best part about the chili is that Earle serves up just enough for either a light lunch or to go along well with one of his sandwiches or sausages. At $2 a bowl for chili, it's beyond a bargain.

Phil also loves the bratwurst with the chili. It is a nice compliment on its nice, big toasted roll. Plenty of space for condiments such as relish, onions, jalapeños, mustard, brown or yellow and ketchup.

Earle's chili and sandwiches are served daily from noon to 6 p.m. For more information, call 773-276-9730.

Slippin' up Elston Avenue near noon? Stop in at **Oinker's**, 3471 N. Elston Ave., a popular lunchtime stop which offers a great menu.

Oinker's has a large selection on their lunch menu. Choose from Tony's favorite of a barbecue beef sandwich, to Italian beef and sausage, fish sandwiches with cod and/or perch fish, or a jumbo shrimp basket; Reubens, salads and of course a BBQ pork sandwich.

To add to this large selection sandwich are Oinker's fries. Fresh cut with the skins still on part of them and good 'n greasy. Yum! Or stay on a healthier note and pick soup in place of the fries. But don't get the hamburgers -- way undercooked! Food prices range any where from $4.50 to $7.

Beer selections are mainly domestics, however one can get import bottles of Heineken, Beck's, Corona, or Hacker-Pschorr Weiss.

This is an great place to stop for lunch, just look at the number of people stopping in on any given day. Plenty of tables, and not those 10 feet-off-the-ground ones, or enjoy the bar and watch TV news on the big screen.

Lunch is starts at 11 a.m. Monday through Thursday, at 10:30 a.m. Friday and at noon on the weekends. For more information, call 773-463-4222.

A great pick for lunch is **Tavern On The Pier**, 435 E. Illinois St. It is a prime spot near the lake to eat and drink.

Though inside the North Pier building, this place has the charm of a good ole neighborhood tap, and even offers patio seating at the dock side. The beauty of the tavern is that it keeps the neighborhood feel even when it comes to the food.

Tavern on the Pier offers a variety of sandwiches, salads and appetizers, but the daily lunch specials are the best picks here. Choose from items such as

419

Yankee Pot Roast on Tuesdays and meatloaf on Thursdays, both are served with great mashed potatoes. All in all the menu is wide-ranging from very hearty to a lighter side so everyone can find something they like.

Prices run about $5 up to $9 for Tavern On The Pier's steak sandwich, which Phil really had a hard time turning down.

Tavern on the Pier is open daily for lunch at 11 a.m. For more information, call 312-321-8090.

A word of warning before heading to **Mirabell Restaurant & Lounge**, 3454 W. Addison St. for lunch: don't plan on returning for the afternoon shift!

Mirabell is a very friendly place to enjoy great German food and fine German beers. And one can enjoy the feast in their colorful "Biergarten" room and even at the bar. The best part is that the waitresses wear traditional German dress. Quite a visual experience even before the food hits the table.

Another extensive menu can be found here which features German specialties such as a wurst plate, poached salmon sandwiches or choose the house specialty (and Phil's favorite) weiner schnitzel. Side dishes vary from spatzle, German potato salad to sauerkraut. Either way, all are a great treat. And, to start off the entrees, we both recommend the Goulash soup. A wonderful mix of veggies and meat in a meat broth, quite excellent.

And dessert...Mirabell has cakes, like German chocolate cake which Tony couldn't say no to, and a variety of pastries as well.

Prices range from about $8 to $13 for entrees. Mirabell is open for lunch from 11:30 a.m. to 2:30 p.m. For more information, call 773-463-1962

For fresh beer and tasty tavern food, **Goose Island Brewpub**, 1800 N. Clybourn Ave., offers plenty of both.

The first choice one needs to make here is the beer. Any are a sure bet, especially the seasonals, like Summertime. The beer list offers nice descriptions of each to make the choice a bit easier.

There's plenty of choices on the food menu too. From entrees of ale-marinated grilled chicken to sandwiches of beer braised brisket of beef. Go grilled with items such as grilled vegetables and goat cheese or blackened catfish poorboy. Various salads, personal pizzas, and even a special section for two types of Wisconsin-style brats. Phil is partial to the Carolina pulled pork barbecue sandwich which he puts up there in the top BBQ sandwiches in the city. Smothered in a great, spicy barbecue sauce and covered with fabulous cole slaw makes this one a tough choice over the rest.

However, one big complaint about this place is that they give lunch customers complimentary homemade chips. These things are so delicious that they can easily spoil someone's appetite. Tony almost lost a couple fingers as Phil kept diving for these.

Prices on the average range in the $7 range, but can go higher for items like the entrees.

Goose Island brewpub is open daily for lunch at 11:30 a.m. For more information, call 312-915-0071.

Step away from the ordinary and try a bit of wild game at **Grizzly's Lodge**,

Barfly Lunch in Bars

3830 N. Lincoln Ave.

We were both leery on the whole Ostrich/Buffalo burger sensation, but after chompin' one down at Grizzly's we now understand. The meat is tender and flavorful. If you are going to try these specialty items, then Grizzly's is the place to do it. A knowledgeable staff goes a long way when ordering something like wild game and the folks here are happy to help out.

Otherwise, Grizzly's offers plenty choices of regular beef burgers, sandwiches, salads and pasta dishes. Sides can include fries or a salad which is a nice option. And with the summer here, Grizzly's beer garden is great for enjoying a lunch and the sun. Especially with their choice of microbrews.

Prices for lunch items are about $5 to $8.

Grizzly's is open daily for lunch at 11 a.m. For more information, call 773-281-5118.

Hog Head McDunna's, 1505 W. Fullerton Ave., is a definite stop for the burger lover.

This place offers some of the most exquisite items to top their burger like cheeses -- Jalapeño Jack, Port Wine Cheddar or Oak Smoked Gouda. Also, top it with portabello mushrooms, bacon, roasted garlic or onions.

Tony went with the burger while Phil tried out the vegetarian burger. Phil was really impressed that there was no meat in his and Tony couldn't stop to respond about his burger he just gave the thumbs up sign.

Hog Head McDunna's also offers other great pub items like pizza, pasta, chicken sandwiches and baked potatoes. Prices ranged from $6 to about $8.

The tavern is open daily for lunch at 11 a.m. For more information, call 773-929-0944.

Celebrating Irish heritage through food and drink is easy to do at **The Abbey Pub**, 3420 W. Grace Ave.

Appetizers top off the menu with a large selection of favorites like cheese sticks, potato skins, veggies and dip, but also a few Irish favorites like mini-Irish meat pies and The Abbey's own special fries. Food specials include salads, burgers, fish and chips, Shepherd's Pie and a Barfly favorite, Irish breakfast.

The Irish breakfast, which is good at any time and especially with a pint of Guinness, includes a couple eggs, Irish bacon, Irish sausage, potatoes, some black and white puddings, and a slice of fried tomato. It is quite a taste sensation and a definite must for one who has never had it.

The fish and chips (Tony's favorite) is always a great standby. Tony likes to douse it with malt vinegar. The chips are really good too.

Prices for the Abbey's lunch range from about $6 to $8.

The Abbey Pub is open daily for lunch from 11 a.m. And their sidewalk cafe is now open for the summer. For more information, call 773-478-4408.

Another great place for fish and ships is **The Red Lion Pub,** 2446 N. Lincoln Ave.

This pub is a great place to try English lunch fare. Specialty items such as cornish pasties, bangers and mash and again, fish and chips. Other, more common, items like burgers, sandwiches, soups and salads are also on the menu.

Cornish pasties are meat filled pies with plenty of vegetables in a pastry crust. The bangers and mash are English sausages (bangers) and mashed potatoes with peas cover the plate. Phil had the bangers and mash and enjoyed himself to the full. Tony went with the fish and chips, his main choice when visiting this place.

Prices are in the $7 to $10 range.

The Red Lion also has a beautiful patio in the back on the second floor. What is great about this is that although the pub is located on busy Lincoln Avenue, not a sound is heard from the street creating a very relaxing place to enjoy lunch.

The Red Lion is open for lunch at noon. For more information, call 773-348-2695.

For a great Chicago tavern experience, head to **Miller's Pub**, 134 S. Wabash Ave., where Chicago's legends come alive.

This pub is filled with photographs of all the political, sports and entertainment greats that have graced its large dining room from Gov. Jim Edgar to comedian George Burns. Sitting in there brings on a sense that everyone in the room may be an important official or celebrity.

Miller's has one of the largest lunch menus in town. They offer a variety of appetizers, salads, seafood, Italian dishes, steak and chops or go with something from the list of lunch specials.

Tony chose Miller's "World famous" Canadian baby back ribs while Phil went with a basic turkey club. Both meals came with cole slaw and fries, with the rib meal having slightly larger helpings of each.

Tony was impressed with the quality of the long row of ribs and was not at all surprised they were deemed world famous. Phil highly enjoyed the turkey club with its great mix of crisp bacon and lettuce and tender turkey breast and tomato.

Prices are fairly reasonable, especially involving the lunch specials. The Canadian baby back ribs ran only $8.95. The service is incredibly quick and very friendly.

To drink there are a few beers on tap, but plenty in bottle. Miller's also offers an extensive wine list.

Miller's Pub is open daily for lunch at 11 a.m. For more information, call 312-645-5377.

In keeping with legendary places to go for lunch, we stopped by **Alexander's**, 3010 E. 79th St., on Chicago's South Shore. This place goes back 80 years and is known for its live jazz shows in the evening.

Alexander's originally was located at 63rd and Dorchester. The one thing that always remained a constant is its popularity, especially as a political place to be seen.

"Ed Vrydolyak had the first table reserved for him," Eli said pointing to a corner booth. "Harold Washington, when he was alive, had meetings in the back."

Barfly Lunch in Bars

However the area has taken a blow with some of major businesses moving out and Alexander's has felt some of the fallout. But Eli said he has plans to renew interest in the bar with some renovation and he will open again for lunch.

For now, one can still enjoy the 1960s style room with a beautiful curved wood bar and booths throughout the floor. Candles adorn each of the cloth-covered tables.

The menu consists of a variety chicken dishes like fried, barbecue and Southern-style smothered. There is seafood like shrimp, filets, and catfish. There is also lamb and pork chops and Alexander's famous steaks.

Phil went with the barbecue chicken, while Tony ordered a turkey sandwich. The barbecue chicken came with a leg, thigh, wing and a breast. The barbecue sauce was tangy, sweet and had a little kick of spice to it. The chicken was served up with a platter of fries, but you can have a baked potato instead. Tony's sandwich was pretty straight forward and was also served with fries.

Prices range in the $10 to $20 for entrees and $5 to $7 for sandwiches. The service is very formal (bow ties) and very friendly.

Alexander's opens at 3 p.m. Tuesday through Friday. For more information, call 773-768-6555.

Special Mention

Streeter's, 50 E. Chicago, 312-944-5206 — The only item on the list here is Streeter's chili and it is served up fresh and good. Streeters offers plenty of containers of items to make the chili just the way you like it. Choose from cheese, oyster crackers, hot peppers, Tobasco sauce, sour cream and much more. They even have hot dogs a-roastin' to create the best chili dogs in town. A great place to either escape the summer sun in this basement bar or soak it up and sit out in the sidewalk seating.

Beat Kitchen, 2100 W. Belmont Ave., 773-281-4444, this place offers up the usual name stuff, but they like to put twist on the old standbys. Now take for example Tony and Phil's favorite Thai pizza with a variety of veggies and a nice coating of peanut sauce. One may also find a hummus plate, a couple different types of chicken sandwiches, burgers, brats, beefs. If food could be considered clean, this would be the place to find it. Prices range in the $6-$9 range. We have yet to find something we don't like here.

The results of our investigation through Chicago's lunch-time taverns, proved what we knew all along — the best food in the city is served in the bars. Now where's that stairmaster?

— Phil Brandt and Tony Gordon

423

Chapter Seven
Chicago Suburbs

Smilin' faces abound at Alonzi's Villa, 8828 Brookfield Road, Brookfield. But those smiles change quickley when strange phenomenon begin to happen -- Alonzi's Villa is haunted!

The main focus of Barfly Newspaper is taverns within the city limits of Chicago. However, there are a great many excellent bars in the vast suburbs of Chicago which span from southern Wisconsin to northern Indiana. So occasionally we write about watering holes in the 'burbs. Many of the following bars were written about for special Halloween issues of Barfly Newspaper and are known to be haunted. Others were written about for their old-time gangster history and used to serve the likes of Al Capone, Machinegun Jack McGurn and the like. So check them out.

Alonzi's Villa
8828 W. Brookfield Ave., Brookfield
708-485-5443
Hours: 3 p.m. to 3 a.m. Monday to Thursday,
3 p.m. to 4 a.m. Friday and Saturday, closed Sunday

I grew up in Brookfield. While I was living there, the place that is now Alonzi's, used to be Sir Gerald's Pub. I remember that Sir Gerald's served minors and thirsty commuters from Burlington Station, located right across the street. But I never heard any rumors about any spiritual happenings in the building.

Still nestled in a quiet untouched area is Alonzi's Villa. The owners are the first to go public about what has been seen and heard in the early morning hours. Owners Mike and Pat Alonzi bought the place around Thanksgiving, 1989, and Pat experienced something almost immediately.

The Alonzi's began using the upstairs apartment as a storage space and dressing room for their entertainers. Pat's daughter Tricia had gone upstairs to get some decorations for the holidays and heard a young girl's voice say, "hello there." Tricia then yelled downstairs to her cousin to stop trying to scare her. But her cousin was not around and could not have said anything. So Pat decided to investigate.

"I went upstairs and it was like mother's intuition, I just knew. I could feel it, something was different about the upstairs atmosphere," Pat said.

The very next day, she called Father Mike and asked to have the place blessed. Although the priest was apprehensive about blessing a bar, the request was carried out.

On the second incident, the Alonzi's son heard a dog growling at him while on the second floor. The family dog, Dutchess, a regular at the bar, was not in the building at the time. Pat decided to do more investigating, yet she could not find any documentation at surrounding libraries about the circa-1930s building. She learned more from elderly folks who used to frequent the place when it had different names and was under different owners.

She found out that the building first opened as a three-lane bowling alley in 1936. The lanes are still underneath the carpeting in the dining room. It then became a suburban nightclub frequented by commuters from Chicago. In addition to entertainment downstairs at the bar, entertainment was offered upstairs as well. Both Pat and professional ghost hunter Richard Crowe, speculate that the little girl's voice could have been from a daughter of one of the ladies upstairs, who might have been left alone while her mother worked.

Crowe himself, brought his crew in several years ago to see what they could find. He felt several hot and cold spots on the second floor and described sensations of walking through cobwebs when there weren't any. He experienced something while he was there also. He heard a ball being thrown down a bowling lane and crashing into a set of pins.

425

The Suburbs Alonzi's Villa-Brat Stop

Other incidents have included seeing dark shadows whizzing past, the girl's voice calling employees' names, finding lit cigarettes and hearing voices from people in the bar when the bar was definitely empty. Pat has told everybody who cares to know that the spirit is probably a lonely soul. She is not frightened of the poor little girl. Pat follows the advice of her grandfather: you should never fear the dead, you should fear the living.

Pat's husband Mike might think she, their children, and Richard Crowe are crazy. He has never seen or heard one peep from their resident spook.

In addition to a friendly bar that offers karaoke Wednesday and Friday, improv on Saturday, the Alonzi's personally cook from old Italian recipes for banquets and private parties. The bar offers drink and munchie specials daily. But if you're anything like me, you'll be jazzed enough just to sit and listen to the stories about the bar's patron who has been there since 1936.

— *Lee DiVita*

Brat Stop

12304 75th St., Kenosha, Wisc.
414-857-2011
Hours: 8 a.m. to between midnight and 2 a.m. daily

"Brats as big as your forearm and beer so cold it'll freeze the piss in ya!"

Though I highly doubt anyone ever actually said this to me, the above statement perfectly sums up the image I've always pictured whenever someone happened to mention the Brat Stop. I've known of the place for years, but only through the foggy ruminations of others, who never failed to speak of it with beer-drenched nostalgia.

"If you're ever heading to Milwaukee," they'd tell me, "make sure you stop by. It's right off 94 — you can't miss it."

Having a reason to be in Kenosha the other week, I made a visit to the Brat Stop a top priority. Physically, it is pretty much what I expected. A huge, cozy brick and wood barn of a place. It houses a large bar, many tables and booths, and a massive stage for bands. In practically every nook and cranny a mute TV sits up amid the pillars, and a variety of pinball machines and video poker games fill an entire corner. One end of the building even sports a little shop and delicatessen where you can buy anything from cheese, sausage, and gourmet mustards to liquor and souvenirs.

Back out at the bar, drink prices are nice and cheap. Domestics on tap — and they've got pretty much each and every variation of Miller and Anheuser-Busch Beer products you can imagine — ring in at only a buck and a quarter. They've also got Heineken, Beck's and a couple of weiss and amber beers as well. And it is indeed, served ice-cold in a frosted mug.

The menu is not exactly extensive, just your typical sandwiches and a few beef and chicken "entrees," but it is reasonably priced. Plus, of course, they have bratwurst...

Ah, we finally get to the nitty gritty. Bratwursts as big as your forearm?

Barfly Brat Stop-Chet's Melody Lounge

Bratwursts to make even the most red-faced, leiderhosened, feather-hatted Fritz hold his belly and belch contentedly?

What I had expected was a fat, hulking length of white sausage that had been simmered long in beer, sauerkraut, onions and green peppers before being tossed on the grill. One that had then been stuffed into a soft, pumpernickel bun, smothered in brown mustard, and topped with a heap of kraut, onion and pepper. What I received was a skinny length of a brat direct form the grill and the grill only, served on a hot dog bun. Sure they called it a "brat bun," but believe me, a dinky little Oscar Meyer weenie would be more at home in this thing than a brat. Sauerkraut came in a little paper cup alongside. Mustard was on the table, as well as a little bowl of cold, chopped onion.

Now I suppose my expectations might have been a little high. When it comes to bratwurst I have my own ideas about how it should be prepared and served. I pretty much say the hell with everyone else's notions — especially those "traveled" folk that like to tell me that back in der Fatherland brats are usually eaten sans the bun in a puddle of onion sauce. All the same though, when eating in someone else's "house" you can't expect everything to go your way; I accept that. But for a place to call itself the Brat Stop and then pay no more attention to its namesake entree than you would a simple hot dog, is damn-near sacrilegious!

Other than this, the place is alright. Definitely drop in next time you're in the area. It's a nice, comfortable joint. Enjoy the beer and take home some cheese, sausage and pepper jelly from the shop. But if you too harbor an intolerant, strident, bratwurst ideology like me, order something else from the menu.

— Bill Franz

Chet's Melody Lounge

7400 S. Archer Road, Justice
708-496-9202
Hours: 11 a.m. to 2 a.m. Monday to Saturday,
11 a.m. to 8 p.m. Sunday

Spooky, spooky, spooky, is about the best way to describe Chet's Melody Lounge. The drive out to this 94 year-old bar from the city is eerie, eerie, eerie. The route, which runs along the Stevenson Expressway to Harlem Avenue then to Archer, is a trail through the city's Southwest Side and its gargantuan factories that emit putrid odors over poorly lit streets. The path heads through the aging suburbs of Summit and Bridgeview, which are filled with small-town buildings, cold in appearance. These towns appear like forgotten industrial villages. Once on Archer in Justice, the trail to Chet's hugs Resurrection Cemetery, a vast burial ground with few lights and hordes of fading tombstones viewable through a chain-link fence. The area is dark and Chet's, an old roadhouse surrounded only by the wind, is located directly across from the cemetery. Graves lie less than 100 feet from the bar's front door.

The Melody Lounge has a gravel parking lot where on most evenings a cou-

427

The Suburbs Chet's Melody Lounge

ple old Buicks and some old Fords are parked. Once inside Chet's, patrons are bombarded by fish, yes fish. There's fish everywhere in the place but not a lake or a moat nearby. Apparently, the Prusinski family, which owns and runs the Melody Lounge, are avid fishermen and large fish from past outings are stuffed and hanging up all over the place. Regulars at the bar even spend much of their time discussing fish and various angling styles.

However, those who visit Chet's and aren't regulars, usually venture into the bar in search of one of the area's most popular ghosts — "Resurrection Mary." A Chet's bartender, who goes by the name of Donna, said the ghost allegedly is a young woman who died in a car wreck just up the street from the bar on Halloween Eve, 1931. The woman spent that fateful evening at a Halloween dance at the nearby Willowbrook Ballroom, which still exists and even holds weekly dances.

Donna said the legend began in 1932 when a man reported he picked up a hitchhiker along Archer and dropped her off at an unspecified destination. He reported that the hitchhiker was a woman who gave him her address and the next day he went to the house to call on her and the woman's mother told him that she had died a year earlier. Since then, many folks have reported picking up a hitchhiker who disappears after being dropped off. Through the years, the ghostly hitchhiker had been dubbed "Resurrection Mary."

According to the legend, Mary is buried right across from Chet's Melody Lounge in Resurrection Cemetery and her handprints can be seen on the front gates of the cemetery. Throughout the years, many of Chet's patrons have reported seeing "Resurrection Mary." Donna said on one occasion a cab driver said he dropped off a woman at Chet's who told him she'd just run in for a few minutes. After waiting awhile for the woman to return, the cab driver went into the bar to look for her but he did not see the woman nor did anyone else who was in the bar. In actuality, very few bar patrons have ever seen the ghost and most don't care to see her.

"I've never seen her," Donna said. "The first time I do see her, I quit. Fuck that shit!"

Yet, Chet's Melody Lounge is sort of a celebration of "Resurrection Mary," with T-shirts bearing a skeletal caricature for sale and an oft-played song on its jukebox by Guy Gilbert entitled "The Ballad of Resurrection Mary" which sounds like a piece for the old "Munsters" television show.

For those who wish to see "Resurrection Mary," Donna said, they should head out to the bar on Halloween when the ghost supposedly lurks about. Yikes!

— *Tony Gordon*

Country House, 241 W. 55th St., Clarendon Hills, where 'Too many things cannot be explained.' Haunted, perhaps?

Country House

241 W. 55th St., Clarendon Hills
708-485-5443
Hours: 11 a.m. to 1 a.m. Monday to Thursday, 11 a.m. to 2 a.m. Friday and Saturday, noon to 1 a.m. Sunday

You may find yourself out on the road driving for no particular reason, with no particular destination. You may take a wrong turn somewhere along the way to your appointed rounds. Or you may just be in search of something decidedly different and find yourself in the sleepy Southwestern suburb of Clarendon Hills, poised on 55th Street and entranced by the traffic light that flashes yellow at all hours like a lighthouse beacon. Guided by a rather strange impulse, you may choose to investigate further the old farmhouse that lingers nearby, nestled in the stealth of towering oak trees like an unforgettable childhood dream. On this evening, you've come to Country House.

Flashback to 1957: A woman named Marion enters the bar with her daughter. She's in her mid-twenties. She's beautiful. People at the Country House know her, especially the bartender who, perhaps, knows her all too well. And it's true that people are beginning to talk. But why, why now, she asks herself. How can he be so cold?

Marion asks to leave her daughter at the bar, if only for a few minutes. You see, she has a simple errand to run. But already the bartender can feel that latent fear choking off his breath, the inquiring glances of locals who know him and know his wife. And this woman at the bar, well, she does not resemble his wife. So he tells her she must leave, and take her daughter with her. It's for the best, he says.

According to accounts, it was just moments later that her car went speeding head on into the same tree that had stood for more than a hundred years at the end of the block, the same tree that ended her life in one brief flash. Her daughter was unharmed.

Back to the present...Stanley the bartender, an affable fellow with a lightning quick draw for your empty stein, told me to go upstairs. It's a narrow hallway, dimly lit, and graced with the occasional idle bathroom. I passed a milieu of small rooms and wooden chairs stacked to the ceiling and found Liz Grogan at the farthest most point of the second floor, besieged behind a desk of invoices and scattered paper. The kitchen manager at the Country House for the last nine years, Liz believes with everything in her that the bar is, indeed, haunted.

"Too many things cannot be explained away," she said. "I still won't close alone. Nobody will."

She lead me into each room. Some are stark and empty, others are stocked with food items like jars of olives or beer glasses and cookware. At some point it strikes me how odd the entire floor is, all these small 8 by 8 rooms, and for what?

"In the twenties this place was a speakeasy," she says. "What with all these upstairs rooms, one can only imagine the things that used to go on." I walked the creaking floorboards behind her and thought about the photographs lining the entrance way downstairs: old pictures from the 1930s and 1940s when there was little else around here besides a tossing sea of corn and the Fords and Lincolns parked out front, just yards away from where we are now, in the front of this gabled and storied building which goes on seemingly unchanged, seemingly welcoming back the former lives that once embraced it.

I followed her into one particular room at the end of the hall, a room that seems to draw attention to itself. There's one window facing 55th, but it's covered with tarp, or what appears to be plastic garbage bag material, and the walls are imitation wood paneling.

"If you ask me, this is Marion's hang out," Liz said as she surveyed the room with more than a little trepidation. "This is where she's usually seen. In fact, on the day when the current owner reopened the place in the early 1970s, an older couple came into the bar and said 'What are you running here, a brothel? There's a woman in the upstairs window, all dressed in white, waving people in off the street.'"

She says that just talking about it gives her the chills.

"Oddly enough," Liz continued, "she usually appears to young men. I remember one of our stock boys coming down the stairs one day, pale as a ghost himself. He was Spanish and couldn't speak much English, and after someone translated what he was saying, it confirmed what we already suspected. He'd seen Marion upstairs, in the same white dress. He quit the next day."

Barfly Country House-Edwin's

Liz does not claim to have seen anything personally, but firmly believes that something is at work which cannot be explained rationally. She talked of a loud thumping noise on the walls just feet away from her. Customers over the years, seated at one table in particular, spoke of hearing a sound similar to a weeping baby, always at the same time of night, and always at that same table in the downstairs dining room. Moreover, dozens of people, employees and customers alike, have noted that on certain evenings and during any season, there is sometimes an overwhelming and unmistakable scent of fresh flowers in the bar.

"Mediums have been here to study the upstairs and people from various universities hang around all night long taking infrared photographs," Liz said and showed me some of the photographs taken. And although I am by no means a photography expert and am well aware that pictures are easily manipulated, but there is most definitely something there. Never did I once feel she has been anything less than a truthful guide.

"Something keeps her here. Maybe the knowledge that she died before it was her time. Or maybe she's still hopelessly in love," Liz says, stressing that this spirit, however lost or melancholy, is intrinsically good. Otherwise, she would not still be working there.

With that, I walked back downstairs where other good spirits have been flowing all during my tour. A large man at the bar hugs and even larger man in jest, claiming his unrequited love, as the stuffed boar over the fire place looks on approvingly. Part English pub, part hometown restaurant, part gathering place, Country House is unique and familiar, kind of like the den in the house of an old and long since separated friend. The truth is, Country House is less a bar than it is an experience, a place where history blurs at its edges and time is briefly suspended. Bring only yourself, and maybe a good story or two. Grab one of their tasty burgers and admire the fishnet-table candles and the fact that there is nary a window to dispense any natural light. Ask Stanley for another nip. Is it 2 p.m. or 2 a.m.? Who knows.

Take a seat at the bar and think about all the people who have sat there before you and the ones that will follow in your wake. Maybe even Marion.

Beer: Killian's, Berghoff, Andech's on tap.

— Mike Curtin

Edwin's
31851 South Route 50, Peotone
708-258-3393
Hours: 7 a.m. to 2 a.m. Sunday to Friday,
7 a.m. to 3 a.m. Saturday

Edwin's — Al Capone's resort.

When the "heat was on" in Chicago, he headed south to a roadhouse he supplied with illegal liquor called Miami Gardens Restaurant. In 1987 Miami Gardens was purchased by Janice Teuscher and a partner.

According to Teuscher the bar was built in 1929 and Edwin's was once a

431

"resort" for Capone where he and his henchmen would come out for a day or two. It was a prime location. Edwin's still stands almost independently from other businesses and homes and is surrounded mainly by open fields so Capone and his boys could see if police or a rival gang was approaching.

To ensure security for the members of Capone's gang, albeit from the police or a rival gang, there were ways to go unnoticed. Teuscher said that if a particular member, or maybe even Capone himself, wanted to make sure their car was not seen by police, or anybody for that matter, a garage where deliveries were made had a ramp upon which one could drive a car and park it in the basement so it would not be seen.

Teuscher showed how one could travel from the basement through a stairway which led to a kitchen, and then through the kitchen to another set of stairs which led to the second floor. There was a side entrance as well which immediately led to the second floor.

The second floor was styled with 11 small hotel rooms. One of the rooms at the top of the stairs was rumored to be Capone's, Teuscher said. Though most of Capone's room has been renovated since that time, the bathroom remains, for the most part, still intact. The bathroom tiles are the color "Nile Green" which is said to be Capone's favorite color. There is one bathtub which even has a light over the tub, something rarely seen today. Across from the tub is a shower stall containing a total of seven shower heads, four in the front and three in the back.

Included in each of the rooms was a buzzer button which, during electrical renovation of the bar in 1987, were found to lead to a light panel near the bartender's station.

"If someone wanted room service or a girl, he'd just hit the buzzer," Teuscher said.

There were also dumb waiters from the kitchen to the upstairs, so no one from the staff of the bar needed to go upstairs when someone was in a room, Teuscher added.

A facade addition was installed after Capone's days. An old photo of the roadhouse rests on the barback of Edwin's which shows the establishment before the addition. There used to be gas pumps in front of the building, but they were removed with the installation of the addition. A tunnel was rumored to be below the addition , but there is no evidence in the basement where it actually was. It would not be surprising if one did exist, Capone seemed to always have tunnels.

With the addition, one can see the thickness of the outside walls which are about a foot wide and made of brick. If there was a drive-by shooting, it is doubtful that anyone would have been killed.

According to Teuscher, the room past the bar, now labeled "Gangster Hall," was once a dance hall with large booths so that one could be left alone from other patrons in the place. This room also contains an ornate tin ceiling found in many Chicago bars from that time period. There was also a porch above the dance hall where supposedly the call girls took their work breaks, but has since

Barfly Edwin's-Go to Blases

been enclosed during Teuscher's renovation.

Some mementos are on display on the bar back including an original Miami Gardens Restaurant menu and a key to one of the "hotel" rooms above the bar.

Edwin's is located on Route 50 just outside of Peotone. To get there, take I-57 south to the Peotone exit and follow the signs to Peotone. Head south on Route 50 for about a half of a mile, Edwin's is on the east side of the street. The total trip from Downtown takes about an hour.

—Mint Whisky

Go to Blases

7015 N. Milwaukee Ave., Niles
847-647-9373
Hours: 3 p.m. to 2 a.m. daily

An engraved tombstone on the facade reads: "Erected Sept. 5, 1961. Dedicated to those who GO TO BLASES. Founded 1935 Geo Blase - Wally Blase.

On either side of the door are primary colored, diamond patterned windows that have the blurry texture of shower doors. Across Milwaukee Avenue is St. Adalbert's Cemetery. Fearing I was walking into a chintzy mausoleum, my two friends and I crept into the bar supposedly owned by the Mayor of Niles. Thinking I was going to enter the political hot bed of Northern suburbia, I was shocked to see still bodies situated like corpses around a U-shaped bar. I felt conspicuous moving through a room of such inactivity.

Sitting down at the far curve of the U, I quickly realized this was a place of regulars. Sure enough, as soon as the novelty of looking at unfamiliar people wore off, the regulars returned to their inaudible conversations. Star shaped spotlights dimly lit the bar, accentuating the red-stucco ceiling. The bartender sat at the end of the U. She tended bar like a mom making pancakes, serving everyone else and then herself. Her hair was a high-night maintenance clip-pin-and-net-type of style, and it was as red as her striped sweater. Behind me, a red cinder block hallway led to the bathrooms. As an annoying classic-rock song blared, I envisioned being in the cast of an overplayed Eagles' song.

A bar panders to a specific clientele when a juice glass is a given with a bottled beer. I ordered a Miller High Life. My friends ordered drinks that were proportionally poured to induce a severe bar slump from even an adept drinker. An old man in a stupor was leaving. The bartender called, "Ed, you have cigarettes for tomorrow?" Undoubtedly aware of the potency of her pour, this woman was extremely maternal.

Before I could digest that thought, I realized my friends were deep in conversation with a woman who looked like my 5th grade teacher. Familiar faces were all around; a man across the bar looked like Tip O'Neill, sitting next to him was a roots-o-matic Debbie Harry and two women identical to the thespians in the Eagle Man commercial. After introductions, the conversation leaped to spelling, in particular, the woman, the teacher Mrs. Wojczyk look-a-like, believed I spelled my name phonetically incorrect. Then the fateful moment

433

The Suburbs Go to Blases

arrived that determined we would be talking to Mrs. Wojczyk for the evening. She blurts out "Irregardless is not a word."

"Exactly," I exclaimed and regardless of her bad spelling our fate was sealed.

Mrs. Wojczyk said "Wheel of Fortune" was very popular at Blases and certain bartenders give free drinks to patrons who beat the contestants on TV. Sing-a-longs are also popular. Many songs on the jukebox have new lyrics provided by the regulars. Mrs. Wojczyk, after giving a dance lesson, sang "New York, New York" in a voice I thought only Ethel Merman was blessed with.

After noticing how I poured my beer, she was reminded of her last physical. "My doctor wanted another urine sample," she explained. "I failed my urine test, I knew I should have studied! What? There wasn't enough head on it?"

Soon another woman joined our conversation. After discussing food, especially wild game and pumpkin pie, Mrs. Wojczyk left the forum to play darts. The new conversationalist said her brother-in-law is a chef who makes a lamb-potato lasagna that is good enough to die for. She said she could eat lamb because sheep are dumb and sit in shit all day. However, she did not eat veal or "puppy cows."

The conversation darkened when she began discussing her job. As I learned, in animal testing for cancer and AIDS, there are two choices: beagles or monkeys. Beagles are cheaper and are used more often.

Continuing a conversation appropriate only for a bar across from a cemetery, she said "If you had a choice between a beagle and your friend here, who would you pick?" As if the range of topics could not get any more bleak, she said her boss was the premier expert on necropsy, which she defined as "An autopsy on something that is not your species." She repeated "not your species" a few times and then described the images she had seen in books as graphically as she described how she makes pumpkin pie.

By the time exploding heads were discussed, I felt it was time to go. The air in Niles probably may not carry some odd topic distorter, however, exiting a bar onto the vista of a cemetery is more dramatic if you have been discussing the dynamics of dissection. Topics that you can bet your right arm that nobody else in the state was talking about at that moment in time. Do not ask the bartender about the mayor, he has never had anything to do with the bar. A woman named Sophie has owned Go To Blases for 28 years. However, the identity of Geo or Wally Blase remains a mystery.

— *Crumpy*

Hickey's He's Not Here
1527 S. Harlem Ave., Forest Park
708-366-4728
Hours: 11 a.m. to 2 p.m. Monday to Friday,
8 a.m. to 2 a.m. Saturday, 8 a.m. to 8 p.m. Sunday

So you say you like quiet clean neighborhood bars where you can walk to the corner and be at the mouth of the Waldheim Cemetery? Hickey's He's Not Here is just the place for you. I doubt that you will find a crowd that you could incite into funeral merry-making there but you will find the most beautiful back bar that I have ever seen in my entire life.

It was brought here about 40 years ago from its original site just outside the World's Fair and I am here to tell you that it alone is worth the trip from the cold heartless city.

The Waldheim Cemetery, which is on the south corner of the block, used to be much bigger but they excavated most of it so that they could build a mini-mall complete with Highland (out of business now) and Blockbuster video (corporate assholes). It is still an expansive cemetery that segues into a Jewish cemetery which segues into Woodlawn Cemetery causing for an amazingly populated underground community. Developers are currently working on more strip malls and another Wal-Mart.

Anyway, this working class bar in this working class neighborhood does not offer much in the away of exotic beers or groovy music but they do offer free chili on Saturday afternoon and services by "Monsignor" Hickey on Sunday mornings for the late-night Saturday crowd.

One of the most ignored art forms in our culture is the beer stein. I am not talking about tacky high gloss promotional Pudwiser Clydesdales steins, I am talking about the real item. Delicate, sophisticated steins that tell a story or bare a message.

Throughout Hickey's place, there are some of the most beautiful steins from all over the world. They are displayed as elegantly as the *objet d'art* that they are.

A quick trip through the menu and we see that they offer everything from the "Hickey" burger to a half slab of ribs all at a reasonable price to be consumed in the comfortable seating area or at the bar. All of the soups are made from scratch.

Bernie Hickey purchased the bar in 1979 from a Mr. Magory who had owned the bar for the previous 24 years. When Magory bought the building and they moved the backbar in, the door was on the other side so that when Hickey took over and the location of the door was changed, that left the opening of the bar on the entrance as opposed to the opposite wall where most bars have theirs.

The sight of walking in and feeling like you are walking behind the bar had a strangely psychological feeling that welcomes you and makes you want to sit in and have a few with the regulars.

435

The Suburbs Hickey's He's Not Here-Just Call Moose

So next Saturday night, when you find that even Lincoln Avenue offers nothing new, hop on I-290 and head west. Get off at Harlem Avenue and turn left. Go straight for two lights, it's there on your right. You can celebrate mass, the way it should be celebrated, in a bar. See you there...now go in peace.

— Paul Barile

Just Call Me Moose
3500 S. Laramie St., Cicero
708-222-6667
Hours: 8 a.m. to 2 a.m. Monday to Saturday,
11 a.m. to 2 a.m. Sunday

Often, baseball memories find their way into my consciousness at the strangest times.

Take last month, for example. I was on my way to a friend's birthday party in Hyde Park. The Eisenhower was especially slow, even for a Friday afternoon. After deciding to exit early, I criss-crossed onto Laramie Street. At 35th Street, I was hooked by the sight of old-timer Bill "Moose" Skowron. He was crossing at the light, walking into the corner bar he owns.

All at once, I remembered my father sitting in front of our small black-and-white TV, drinking Old Style and restlessly waiting for Moose to come to bat. Perhaps he liked the Moose's crewcut, or his five-alarm swing, or his Chicago pedigree. I never really found the right time to ask.

Anyhow, I decided to park and go in for a beer. Maybe I would overhear Skowron's retelling of some mythical tale. Or maybe I would go as far as to bother him for a handshake and a chance to disappear back into the innocence of childhood.

Skowron's story began when he was a teen in the 1940s. Talk of his long home runs emerged from the city's Northwest Side. Moose was hitting baseballs out of Hanson Park as if he was swinging with his back to a wind tunnel. Major League scouts took notice. By 1954, Moose stood at first base for the New York Yankees, the dynasty that has served as the backbone of sports for most of this century. From 1955 to 1963, Moose played in eight World Series, seven as a Bronx Bomber, one with the Los Angeles Dodgers. He was an all-star seven times. In 1964, he came back to Chicago and played with the White Sox until 1967, his last year as a big leaguer.

During his career, Moose played on the tip of a luminous diamond, hand-in-glove with Hall of Famers who names roll from the very top of Mount Cooperstown. Hank Aaron, Yogi Berra, Roy Campanella, Roberto Clemente, Don Drysdale, Whitey Ford, Bob Gibson, Harmon Killebrew, Sandy Koufax, Mickey Mantle, Willie Mays, Jackie Robinson and Ted Williams.

These players come from a bygone era. They played before free agency, multi-year contracts, multi-million dollar endorsements and professional autograph dealers. Baseball then was a game of imagination and memory. Even now, the pull of the game's history still exists. There's still an affection toward

Barfly Just Call Me Moose

former heroes that draws passionate fans together like a group of back-porch friends.

Skowron is the most important attraction at his place, Call Me Moose. He's there every day, usually from morning until early evening. He doesn't look much different from other 67-year-old men, except for the World Series ring on his right hand. He's gracious and more approachable than any current star. He talks about team loyalties more than he does the economics of the game. One minute he remembers the way Billy Martin turned the double play, the next being benched by Casey Stengel during the 1956 Fall Classic.

Ask him about Mantle, and the tone of his voice becomes sad, like chamber music. Not only did they stand shoulder-to-shoulder in so many of those great Yankee lineups, they were also close friends. The Mick died at age 63, a victim of his own off-field excesses. Skowron has stored up a lifetime of stories.

His bar is an intimate neighborhood place that sits across from Hawthorne Race Track in Cicero. There's a large-screen TV for sporting events, and a jukebox that has never held anything by Beck, Boyz II Men, Puff Daddy, Spice Girls or Usher. The bar is decorated with baseball memorabilia, mostly from Skowron's playing days. There are many action shots and closeups from his New York years. I was especially taken by the one of Skowron at a banquet with Joe DiMaggio and Roger Maris. Even in a crowd, Joltin' Joe looks larger than life.

Also evident is Skowron's love of horses, the kind you bet on. The bar's centerpiece is a huge blow-up of Churchill Downs on Derby Day, taken in the early 1950s. Because of its proximity to Hawthorne, Call Me Moose is frequented by jockeys and trainers. Pay attention and you just might collect enough inside information to turn a nice profit.

In the back of bar sits a comfortable restaurant with small tables, hardwood floors and folksy ambiance. On my recent visit, I sampled dinner. The room is complemented by a casual and friendly staff. What's more, the food is excellent, prepared with a simplicity that understates the amount of work necessary to put together meals of such quality.

The menu consists of salads, sandwiches and house specialties. Of these, my choice was the teriyaki chicken breast, served with soup or salad, bread basket, rice and vegetables. Dinner was picked-up by my brother, Darrell, who had several winners across the street. He celebrated his good fortune with a full slab of barbecue ribs. With several drinks each, his check for both of us still came in under $35. Other entree selections include broiled chicken breast, rib-eye steak, pork chops and Cajun chicken. Each day, several specials are available.

On-street parking is almost always available. But if you choose to use the race track lot, be sure to tell Moose. He'll refund the $3 charge with a deduction from your bill.

Call Me Moose offers so much good feeling on so many levels, that to capsulize my thoughts in one story is pretty difficult. It's a feeling similar to the one I used to get on opening day, when, for a few moments in Chicago, first

437

place seemed to be ours for the taking.

— George Rawlinson

Mars Cheese Castle
Route 94, Kenosha, Wisc.
414-859-2244
Store hours: 9 a.m. to 9 p.m. daily
Bar hours: 9 a.m. to 9 p.m. daily

You can return from camping, fishing, skiing or visiting the House on the Rock and stop by this famous landmark for your last piece of cheesiana before returning to urban life. The Mars Cheese Castle is synonymous with fresh cheese curds and frosty mugs of Hacker Pschorr Dark.

Just a stones throw off Interstate 94 near a Kenosha exit, there is plenty of road signs to direct you there if you're too blind to see the towering sign. It is said many can travel there by pure instinct without sight or signs.

Once there, patrons can wade through the Cheese Castle's three sections; deli, store, and bar.

The store contains sausages, wines, and cheeses. You can purchase Christmas gift baskets or waxed cheese blocks in the shape of cows or of the State of Wisconsin itself. You can buy anything from here and take it into the bar. Recommended would be a crock of garlic cheddar with sociable crackers and a slab of sausage.

The delicatessen features approximately 20 sandwiches, all available with gobs of a cheese of choice. Highly recommended are the Reuben on dark rye with sauerkraut and cheese, or the chili dog with cheddar. Skip the chips and get the hot German potato salad and you won't be disappointed. You can order any deli item and return to the bar. They will notify you when it is ready.

When you enter the bar you are greeted with a smile and a huge crock of sharp cheddar surrounded by rows of Ritz Crackers on a serving tray. You can feast on this for a while until another bar patron enters. In which case, they will become the new temporary owner of the tray. They will also remove the tray if you make a complete pig out of yourself. The draft beer selection is limited as is the bottled beer. What they lack in quantity they do make up in quality, featuring most common domestics and an impressive, although short, line of imports. The bar has a certain charm only found in Wisconsin that makes you feel immediately comfortable and at home. You know you are in Wisconsin when you see a large drawing of ex-Packer quarterback Bart Starr on the wall next to a smiling JFK.

If you are lucky enough to visit when Jim the bartender is working, order a bloody Mary. He will personally work with you on every detail of the mix to get it to your exact specifications. After which he will remember the recipe for you if you require further Marys.

Barfly Mars Cheese Castle-Ron's Bungalow Inn

One word of caution: once you stop there it will reel you in every time you pass. You may even find yourself driving to Wisconsin for the sole purpose of visiting the Cheese Castle. This is truly a highly recommended slice of Americana and should not be missed. I give the Mars Cheese Castle my highest rating of four stars.

— Dave Carmody

Reilly's Daughter
4010 W. 111th St., Oak Lawn
708-423-1188
Hours: 2 p.m. to 2 a.m. Monday to Thursday, 11 a.m. to 2 a.m. Friday to Sunday

What better location for a suburban bar than a strip mall!

Actually, Reilly's Daughter has a cool layout even with being in a strip mall and it's barely outside the city limits, just kissing the Mount Greenwood neighborhood. With the mall setting, not only is there plenty of parking at night, but one can get those menial purchases out of the way before stopping in for a shot or two.

Also, since there is no room in this concrete corner mall for an outdoorsy feeling beer garden, Reilly's has made up for that by leasing out some of the courtyard for some tables and chairs. This area is much needed as this place is packed pretty much throughout the week, so in warm weather it is a good way to escape the crowd for some fresh air. On any good night, there may be more than 10 bartenders working the crowd with small bars set up outside to take care of that crowd.

The barroom itself is in an "L" shape with plenty of room at the bar. There is a stage in the larger section of the barroom which brings some local acts out to play as well as featuring many sports stars, past and present, who stop by for an appearance and autograph signings.

Reilly's maintains crowds with good-deal beer specials on slower nights and they keep the draughts of Bass and Guinness along with some domestic beers flowing from the taps.

The patrons are mainly sports-oriented and Irish making this is a great place to catch any or all of the Notre Dame football games or any of the pro team games. It's a jolly crowd, something unfamiliar in other sports bars.

— Phil Brandt

Ron's Bungalow Inn
4033 S. Oak Park Ave., Stickney
708-484-5430
Hours: 11 a.m. to 1 a.m. Monday, Wednesday, Thursday; 11 a.m. to 2 a.m. Friday, 6 p.m. to 2 a.m. Saturday,

The Suburbs Ron's Bungalow Inn
noon to 11 p.m. Sunday, closed Tuesday

Dateline: Monday, December 2, 1929, Stickney Ill. — Federal officers raid Stickney "roadhouse" LaRuth's Bungalow, home of Anton Rench, the police chief and president of the village board, seizing five barrels of beer and assorted bottles of gin, whiskey, and wine.

Rench, who last year was indicted in connection with election fraud, was not at home at the time. Also indicted, at that time, were Alphonse ("Scarface") Capone and Ralphie ("Bottles") Capone.

The fraud charges were eventually dismissed against the three.

***

In 1915, the roadhouse, originally called Kral's Palace, opened up at 4035 S. Oak Park Ave. Kral (Bohemian word for King) created the establishment in a sprawling white stucco bungalow to create a business that would be supported by the soldiers building a canal just south of the house. He also provided a buffet for various clubs and organizations throughout the area.

The bar was very popular and its popularity increased when the boys began coming home from World War I. The Kral family had a very prosperous business and little Violet Kral had an indoor bicycle track.

But the prosperity for Kral family ended when President Warren G. Harding passed what some people call the darkest law in history; PROHIBITION. To many, Prohibition was the spark which formed organized crime as we know it today. By outlawing the production and the consumption of alcohol, the doors to organized crime blew wide open.

Al Capone was one of the organized crime bosses who, by the time President Franklin D. Roosevelt put an end to Prohibition in the early 1930s, would amass a large fortune and achieve legendary status in the annals of gang history.

Tired of trying to compete with organized crime, Kral sold his palace to Anton Rench who renamed it LaRuth's Bungalow. Capone did not waste any time setting up shop including beer barrels and bathtub gin. He also supplied girls that could be purchased for sex in little alcoves in a back room.

Although Capone operated many brothels in and around the area, LaRuth's was his suburban entertainment mecca. While the alcohol flowed freely, people (often high school-aged kids) danced and partied and threw money around with little abandon. This was to be a nightly practice until that night in December, 1929, when federal authorities closed the place down.

Chicago and its history are generously peppered with Capone and his associates. Tunnels and vaults and any other proof of his existence is a constant source of intrigue to locals as well as international travelers. One of the last remaining artifacts of Capone and his legacy can be found in the bar that used to be LaRuth's Bungalow now called Ron's Bungalow Inn. The place is a home to rock-n-roll music, an incredible buffet and an eerie set of bullet holes in the wall above the basement stairs. The holes, authenticated by local police officials, are credited to a Tommy gun. While no one knows for sure how they got

Barfly Ron's Bungalow Inn-Round Up

there, it is clear that they were made with small caliber slugs. (Tommy guns used 25 caliber slugs). A common question asked is if the slugs are still imbedded in the wall. No one wants to take a chance on ruining the wall to find out.

Currently, Ron's Bungalow Inn, which is housed in the exact building that Kral built, is more than just another rock-n-roll club in the Near West Suburb of Stickney. These days, Ron's has more (legal) activity than any two people should be able to coordinate but that is what Ron and Donna Safranek have been doing since 1986.

Every weekend they feature a variety of live rock-n-roll bands and patrons can drink and dance until 2 a.m. without fear of federal officers breaking up the party.

On Sunday evening, they have the hottest polka show in town. Dancers of all ages come out and dance to Chicagoland's hottest polka bands including the legendary Eddy Blazoncyk and the Versatones.

The atmosphere, throughout the bar, is that of an entertainment hall of fame. Album covers and 45s cover the walls along with movie posters and photos of movie stars. Every spare bit of shelf space is used to display ceramic busts of everyone from the Stooges to Peter Lorre.

The jukebox plays 45s, not the ones on the walls, when a band isn't playing and Ron and Donna serve up the best Rum Runner in the country.

"It's got a kick," Ron says modestly, "After two you won't be able to say the name."

They have a daily lunch buffet and dinner specials ranging from tacos to roast lemon-herb chicken. This is not standard bar fare nor is it prepared like standard bar fare; we're talking home-cooked meals here! They do maintain the standard "burger-hot dog" menu for those interested. All of which are reasonably priced for anyone on a budget.

Donna and Ron are very welcoming hosts who will gladly share their stories of Capone lore and the fate of one poor marlin with customers over a drink. As hard as they work to keep things exciting, they always seem to find the time to let their patrons know that they have come to the right place.

Ron's Bungalow Inn is a hidden treasure well worth the trip (about 20 minutes from the Loop). So go there right now and drink a couple of Rum Runners or it's cement Nikes for you babe!

— *Paul Barile*

The Round Up

4152 W. Roosevelt Road, Hillside
708-544-0586
Hours: dining room 11 a.m. to 1 a.m. daily,
bar 11 a.m. to 2 a.m. Saturday to Thursday,
11 a.m. to 3 a.m. Friday

The Round Up looms across from Glen Crest Cemetery like a shivering candle flickering softly in a darkened old room. It is housed in a 100-year old structure much like the old road houses of yore. The building is poorly lit and its coarse gravel parking lot is tough on tires.

Inside, the place is a living antique with an old creaky bar room and restaurant. The bar features old cushioned booths, a well-worn bar, televisions, pinball, Miller products and a weathered bartender named Joe. The crowd is surprisingly young, male and sports a suburban tough-guy attitude.

But while the bar is a tad uncomfortable, the restaurant is a cozy gem. Its odd-paneled walls display a strange array of Depression era family photos, portraits, and knick-knacks. It feels almost like a well-decorated barn. The folks sitting in the restaurant are decidedly older than those in the bar. With its smallish room, conversations carry quite well giving travelers a bit of insight into the lives of those who dwell on this end of Roosevelt Road.

To eat, The Round Up is a traditionalist's fantasy with hearty portions of spaghetti, lasagna, mostaccioli, barbecued ribs, chicken, steaks, burgers and pizza all at reasonable prices. I had the half-barbecued chicken and it was succulent, fresh and fulfilling.

However, rather unfulfilling was the lack of ghostly activity at the Round Up which really feels like it is older than old. One would think that being so old and existing just across the street from a large cemetery someone would have had a strange tale to tell. Yet, none were to be found and folks there even laughed at the thought. Oh well, a trip to the Round Up is still worth the time because its food is so good but pass right on through the bar, it is a bit stale.

— *Tony Gordon*

Tiffany's

2120 S. Cicero Ave., Cicero
708-656-2744
Hours: noon to 6 a.m. Sunday to Thursday,
8 a.m. to 6 a.m. Friday and Saturday

When cruising down South Cicero Avenue the yellow billboard sign reading "Tiffany's" is very hard to miss. I arrived under the sign and entered the place at about 11 p.m. The social setting resembles a typical neighborhood stop.

The interior is like older neighborhood bars, not a swanky trendy type place. There are pictures of 1920s-era gangsters Johnny Torrio, Bugs Moran, and Rodger Touhy on the walls of the bar. The pictures are lit up in a shrine-like manner. The bar is rumored to have been a popular hangout for Al Capone's gangsters in the 1920s and 1930s. However, the current owners are quite paranoid and wouldn't talk to me about the bar's history and would not let me take a photo of the bar as well.

Yet, I do have this to report: the bar has a separate section where a patio setting is attempted. An old fashion street light pole stands in an indoor patio-type

Barfly Tiffany's

area and is very impressive, but in need of some work. There is a wood dance floor and a small DJ booth that makes the transition between the bar and patio section. There is another bar in the patio section that serves drinks. This opens when the bar is crowded.

After sitting down at the main bar, I noticed that most people knew each other. The price of drinks breaks down like this: 75 cents for coke, $2 tap beer (Bud, Bud Light), $2.25 domestic-bottled beers, $2.50 imported bottled beers, $1.75 house brands mixed, $2.25 specific brands mixed $2.50 specialty drinks (daiquiris, margaritas, etc.) I am told prices will vary slightly depending upon what is going on at the bar.

However, this bar seems to have a split personality. After 2 a.m. there is a cover charge of $2. It seems this is one of the few after-hours bars in the Chicagoland drinking area. The bar then transforms itself into a dance club. A DJ starts to spin records and the place gets mobbed real quick after 2 a.m. The crowd that hangs there is in the late 30s age group and have gold a-hanging everywhere. Patrons and workers are real cold towards any non-regulars. I'd have to recommend skipping this place even if you're searching for a little gangster history. Hospitality is a foreign art to these folks.

— Gen eX alt

Getting around Chicago by car is nothing short of a nightmare, especially if a bar is the destination. Chicago is a city with very little parking, aggressive metermaids, and high-priced parking lots.

The easiest and safest way to bar-hop is to take a cab. Cabs are easily obtained Downtown and on the Near North Side. In other parts of the city, hailing a cab can be tough. We have found that the most reliable cab company in Chicago is American Cab: 773-248-7600.

The only downfall with cabs (besides psycho cab drivers) is the cost. So for those on a tighter budget, the Chicago Transit Authority (CTA) is the best bet at $1.50 a ride. Bus lines are thorough, however, some lines don't run all night. The elevated train (El) is the other option. These trains are great for people coming from Downtown, but for those starting out elswhere in the city, the El, isn't very thorough. For more information on the CTA, call 312-836-7000.

Also, Chicago is fairly easy to navigate. Most streets are laid out in a grid pattern. On the North Side Milwaukee, Elston, Clybourn, and Lincoln avenues run on an angle northwest from Downtown. On the South Side Archer Avenue cuts through the grid southwest from Downtown.

For those unfamiliar with the city, a map is an important traveling tool. The best Chicago maps are available in bookstores. Our favorite is Rand McNally's "Chicago & Cook County StreetFinder" available for $14.95 in most stores. Maps of Chicago can also be obtained from the Chicago Office of Tourism: 312-744-2400.

In addition, we have provided phone numbers for most of the bars in this book. A simple phone call will more often than not, find a friendly voice to give to give out directions to their bar.

Good luck!

Bar Type

Be Careful
North Side
Cut Rate Liquors & Package Goods
Luna Lounge
Regina & Joe Tap
Saxony Liquor Lounge
"W" Cut Rate Liquors

Bohemian
North Side
Bucktown Pub
Club Foot
Gallery Cabaret
Gold Star
Inner Town Pub
Lakeview East
The Last Act
Lava Lounge
Lemmings
Liar's Club
Lilly's
Lincoln Tap
Lounge Ax
Map Room
Martyr's
Morseland
The Note
Old Town Ale House
Pop's on Chicago
Quenchers
Simon's Tavern
Ten 56
Ten Cat
The Big Horse
Tuman's Alcohol Abuse Center
Weeds
Wonder Bar
Wrigleyville Tap

South Side
Puffer's

Brewpub
North Side
Goose Island
River West
Rock Bottom

Buzzed In
North Side
Beachwood Inn
Edgewater Lounge
Relax Sports Bar
Saxony Liquor Lounge
Sharon's Hillbilly Heaven
South Side
Lucky Lady (Pullman)

Cheers Bar
North Side
Friar Tuck's
Guthrie's
Lakeview East
Schoolyard Tavern
St. Pauli Bar
South Side
McNally's

Corporate Chain
North Side
Banana Joe's
Bw-3
Dick's Last Resort

Barfly Index

Subterranean
Ten Cat
Trader Todd's Adventure Bar
Village Tap
Webster's Wine Bar
Wonder Bar

South Side

Buddy Guy's Legends
Checkerboard Lounge
Ciral's House of Tiki
Lee's Unleaded Blues

Family Owned
North Side

Ed & Jean's
Farragut's
Four Treys
Friar Tuck's
Gio's Sports Bar
Glascott's
Kelly's Pub
Kronies
La Flor De Acapulco
Laschet's Inn
Lawry's Tavern
Lincoln Tavern
Mirabell
Pop's on Chicago
Resi's Bierstube
Sak's Ukranian Village
T & A Two
Tai's Lounge
Vaughan's Pub

South Side

Baby Doll Polka Club
Carol's Archer Pub
Puffer's
Sheehan's Lounge

Downtown

The Berghoff Cafe

Suburbs

Alonzi's Villa

Chet's Melody Lounge
Ron's Bungalow Inn

Hip & Cool
North Side

Empty Bottle
Exit
Frank's
Gold Star
Holiday
The Hudson Club
Iggy's
Joy Blue
Jub Jub Club
Lava Lounge
Lemmings
Liar's Club
Lounge Ax
Mad Bar
Map Room
The Martini Ranch
Red Dog
Ten 56
Thurston's

Hotel Bar
South Side

Kitty O'Shea's
Brass Tapper Bar (Pullman)

Downtown

Big Brassiere and Bar
Knuckles

Mellow
North Side

Lilly's
Lincoln Tap
Lincoln Tavern
Luney Tunes Saloon
Lucille's

Barfly Index

New Orleans Style
North Side

Northwoods Lodge
North Side

South Side

Barfly Index

Gambler's
Gin Mill (anything Michigan)
Gio's Sports Bar
Glascott's
Goofy's Hock Shop
Grizzly's (large screen)
Ham Tree (large screen)
Hidden Shamrock (large screen)
Higgins Tavern
Hob-Nob Tavern
Hoghead McDunna's (large screen)
Irish Wolfhound (soccer)
Jack Sullivan's (18 TV Screens)
Jagiellonia (soccer)
Joe's on Broadway
Justins
Kasey's (Packers)
Kat Klub
Kelly's on the Green
Kelly's Pub (DePaul)
Keysters
Kincades
Konak (large screen, soccer fans)
Kronies (large screen)
Lakeview East
Lawry's Tavern (large screen)
The Levee
Lincoln Tavern
Little Rascal's
Lyons Den
Magoo's
Michael's Sports Bar
Monsignor Murphy's
Moretti's (large screen)
Mulligan's
Nisei Lounge (large screen)
O'Callahan's
Oinkers (large screen)
Peabody's Pub (large screen)
Players Club (auto/motorcycle racing)
Pour House (large screen)
Ranalli's Off Rush (bus trips to games)
Rose & Crown London Pub (large screen)

Sak's Ukrainian Village (3 large screens)
Schoolyard Tavern (UofI, UofA)
Sidelines (large screen)
Simply Ray's
Six Penny Bit (soccer)
Sluggers (batting cages)
Snuggles Pub
Sports Corner
Stanley's (four large screens)
The Store
T & A Two
Tailgators (seven large screens)
Teasers (large screen)
Timothy O'Toole's (20 TVs, large screen)
T.J. Twisters
Tommy's on Higgins
Toons
The U.S. Beer Co. (10 TVs, large screen)
Walsh's Schubert Inn
WhirlyBall (multiple large screens)
Wild Goose (large screen)
Will's Northwoods Lodge (Packers)
Windy City Tavern

South Side

Alcock's (large screen)
Bohica
Brewskee's
Chateau Lounge
Cork & Kerry
50 Yard Line
Galloway's Mystic
Illinois Bar & Grill
Just Joey's
Kiko's Sports Bar
McNally's
Phyllis-Up
Pullman's Pub
Lucky Lady
September's
Sheehan's Lounge
Ted's Place (soccer)

451

Downtown

Knuckles (large screen)

Suburbs

Just Call Me Moose (large screen)
Mars Cheese Castle (Packers)
Reilly's Daughter

Tiki Bar

North Side

Banana Joe's
Holiday (Sundays)

South Side

Ciral's House of Tiki

Undefinable

North Side

Blue Frog
Brew & View at the Vic Theater
Bucktown Pub
The Closet
Club Foot
CND Gyros Lounge
Exit
Friar Tuck's
Gallery Cabaret
The Great Beer Palace
Grizzly's
The Hudson Club
Iggy's
Inner Town Pub
Jagiellonia
Joe's on Broadway
Lakeview East
Liar's Club
Map Room
Marie's Riptide Lounge
Maryla Polanaise
Match Box
Mirabell
Mondelli's

The Monkey Bar
Old Town Ale House
Pop's on Chicago
Pour House
Spike's Rat Bar
The Big Horse
Thurston's
Tony's Place
Top Hat Lounge
Trader Todd's Adventure Bar
Tuman's Alcohol Abuse Center
Village Tap
Weeds
Wonder Bar
Zack's

South Side

Baby Doll Polka Club
McDuffy's Lodge
Romantic Club

Downtown

Monk's Pub

Suburbs

Mars Cheese Castle
The Round Up

Upscale

North Side

Jury's
Lizzy McNeil's
Lucky Strike
Mad Bar
O'Brien's Restaurant
Orso's Restaurant
Pops for Champagne
Red Head Piano Bar
Schoolyard Tavern
Signature Room
Southport City Saloon
Webster's Wine Bar

South Side

50 Yard Line

Barfly Index

Joe Bailly's
Downtown
Big Brassiere and Bar

Very Chicago-ish
North Side
Boss Bar
Cleos
Dublin's
Emerald Isle
Family Bar
Finley Dunne's
Foley's
Gambler's
Glascott's
Ham Tree
Home Tavern
Irish Eyes
Jay's
Kasey's
Kat Klub
Kelly's on the Green
Kelly's Pub
Kronies

Lawry's Tavern
The Levee
Lincoln Tavern
Lyons Den
Mother's Too
Mulligan's
Oinkers
Pippins
Ranalli's Off Rush
Signature Room
The Store
T.J. Twisters
Windy City Tavern
South Side
BJ's Pub
Bohica
Cork & Kerry
Exchequer Pub
Kiko's Sports Bar
Sheehan's Lounge
Downtown
The Berghoff Cafe
West Side
Illinois Bar & Grill

Beer Gardens

Many of these establishments are, unfortunately, not reviewed in this book. Chicago has more than 4,000 bars, we can't get to them all. However, each bar on the list has a city beer garden license. Yet, some of these bars may not use the license but most do. Beer gardens are generally open from May through October. Good luck and enjoy!

Adagio, 923 W. Weed St.
Arco de Cuchilleros, 3445 N. Halsted
Aspen Cafe & Coffee Bar, 2623 N. Halsted St.

Avanzare, 161 E. Huron St.
Bee's Archer Pub, 3327 S. Archer
Bennigan's, 555 W. Madison St.
Bernies, 3664 N. Clark St.
Big John's, 1147 W. Armitage Ave.
Big Shoulders Cafe, 1601 N. Clark
Biggs, 1150 N. Dearborn St.
Bigsby Bar & Grill, 1749 N. Wells St.
Blue Frog, 676 N. La Salle St.
Blue Mesa, 1729 N. Halsted St.
Bogey's, 2725 E. 130th St.
Bohica Bar & Grill, 5518 S. Archer
Brian Boro's, 2830 N. Broadway St.
Bucks Saloon, 3439 N. Halsted St.
Cactus Gold Coast, 1112 N. State St.

Barfly Index

Bring Your Dog

North Side

Farrugut's
Harry's on Elston
Inner Town Pub
Lemmings
Local Option
The Marquee Lounge
New England Inn
Nisei Lounge

South Side

Kiko's Sports Bar

Cigars

North Side

Alumni Club
Clark Street Ale House
Emmit's
Fumatore
Higgins Tavern
The Hudson Club
Jake's Pub
Kronies
Match Box
The Monkey Bar
Players Club
Quenchers
Red Head Piano Bar
Signature Room
Sports Corner
Tailgators
Ten 56
Vaughan's Pub

Downtown

The Berghoff Cafe
Big Brassiere and Bar

Crowd Type

Artsy

North Side

Charleston
Empty Bottle
Exit
Gallery Cabaret
Gold Star
Holiday
Hopleaf

Barfly Index

Hungry Brain
Inner Town Pub
Kerouac Jack's
Lava Lounge
Lemmings
Liar's Club
Lilly's
Lincoln Tap
Lounge Ax
Map Room
Martyr's
Morseland
The Note
Old Town Ale House
Simon's Tavern
Ten Cat
Village Tap

Big Weekend Crowds

North Side

El Jardin
Girlbar
The Green Mill
Hopleaf
J.T. Collins
Joy Blue
Kelly's Pub
Kincades
Kingston Mines
Kronies
Lounge Ax
Mad Bar
Map Room
Marie's Riptide Lounge
Martyr's
Maryla Polanaise
Moretti's
Mother's Too
Nick's
The Note
Payton Place
Red Head Piano Bar

Tai's Lounge
Teasers
Tommy's on Higgins

South Side

Baby Doll Polka Club
Ciral's House of Tiki
Cork & Kerry
50 Yard Line
McDuflfy's Lodge
Studio 31

Suburbs

Reilly's Daughter
Tiffany's

Bikers

North Side

Bucktown Pub
Eva's
Exit
LAMA
Players Club
Smiler Coogan's
Twisted Spoke (yuppie)

Blue Collar

North Side

Goofy's Hock Shop
Irish Wolfhound
Jagiellonia
Jefferson Inn
Kasey's
Kat Klub
Keysters
The Levee
Lincoln Tavern
Little Rascal's
Luney Tunes Saloon
Mangi's
Marty's
Mayor's Office Lounge
New Polonia

Barfly Index

Joy Blue
Justins
Kelly's on the Green
Kelly's Pub (DePaul)
Kincades
Kronies (Loyola, Northwestern)
Local Option
Lucky Strike
Magoo's
Marie's Riptide Lounge
The Monkey Bar
Morseland
Mother's Too
Pequod's Pizza
Pumping Co. (Loyola)
Schoolyard Tavern (Illinois,Arizona)
Sheffield's
Sidelines
Sluggers
Stanley's
The Store, Halsted
Tailgators
Tequila Roadhouse
The U.S. Beer Co.

South Side

Galloway's Mystic
Joe Bailly's
McDuffy's Lodge

West Side

Hawkeyes (UIC)
Illinois Bar & Grill (UIC)

Firefighter Hang-out

North Side

G & L Fire Escape
Goofy's Hock Shop
Griffin's Public House
Laschet's Inn
Pumping Co.

Gay/Lesbian Friendly

North Side

Berlin
Big Chicks
Charlie's Chicago
The Closet
Cocktail
Farragut's
Friend's Pub
Girlbar
Lakeview East
Off The Line
Paris Dance Club

Gothic Scene

North Side

Club 950
Exit

Interesting Characters

North Side

Joe's on Broadway
Lakeview East
Lawry's Tavern
Liar's Club
Lincoln Tavern
Lounge Ax
Mirabell
Nisei Lounge
Old Town Ale House
Quenchers
Regina & Joe Tap
Relax Sports Bar
Saxony Liquor Lounge
Sharon's Hillbilly Heaven
T.J. Twisters
Top Hat Lounge

Barfly Index

La Flor De Acapulco
Lake Breeze Lounge
Lakeview East
Laschet's Inn
The Last Act
Lottie's
Lucille's
The Marquee Lounge
Match Box
Mirabell
Mondelli's
Mulligan's
New England Inn
Nick's
Nisei Lounge
The Note
O'Lanagan's
Oinkers
Old Town Ale House
Ole St. Andrews Inn
Pop's on Chicago
Pour House
Red Dog
Red Lion Pub
Reza's
Rosa's Blues Lounge
Schuba's
Spike's Rat Bar
Tai's Lounge
Ten Cat
Toons
Tuman's Alcohol Abuse Center
Vaughan's Pub
Walsh's Schubert Inn
Webster's Wine Bar
Weeds
WhirleyBall
Wild Goose
Zack's
Zum Deutschen Eck

South Side

Baby Doll Polka Club
Bohica
Buddy Guy's Legends

Cal's Bar
Carol's Archer Pub
Checkerboard Lounge
Ciral's House of Tiki
Cork & Kerry
Grouchos
Juniper Club
Keegan's
Kiko's Sports Bar
Puffer's

Suburbs

The Round Up

Singles

North Side

Bird's Nest
Alumni Club
Banana Joe's
Bootlegger's
Butch McGuire's Tavern
Cro-bar
Cubby Bear
Deja Vu
Dome Room
El Jardin
Eliot's Nesst
Exit
Fieldhouse
Frank's
Gin Mill
Ginger Man
Girlbar
J.T. Collins
Joy Blue
Kelly's Pub
Kincades
Kronies
Local Option
Lucky Strike
Mad Bar
Marie's Riptide Lounge
Morseland
Mother's Too

Barfly Index

Eva's Lounge
Lincoln Tavern
Marty's
South Side
Juniper Club
Suburbs
Mars Cheese Castle

Yuppie
North Side
Hidden Shamrock
Jack Sullivan's
John Barleycorn
Jub Jub Club
Kelly's on the Green

Kincades
Local Option
Magoo's
Monsignor Murphy's
Moretti's
O'Brien's Restaurant
O'Callahan's
Pops for Champagne
Schoolyard Tavern
Southport City Saloon
Tequila Roadhouse
Twisted Spoke
Downtown
Knuckles
Monk's Pub

Decor

1950s Decor
North Side
Frank's
Fumatore
Holiday
Kerouac Jack's
The U.S. Beer Co.

1970s Decor
North Side
Moody's
Polly Esther's
St. Pauli Bar
South Side
Romantic Club
Rudy and Ann's Lounge
Downtown
Old Timers

Bras Hanging

From Ceiling
North Side
El Jardin
Weeds

Cool Sports Memorabilia
North Side
El Jardin
Fieldhouse
The Levee
Sluggers
Tailgators
South Side
Brewskee's
50 Yard Line
Illinois Bar & Grill
Kiko's Sports Bar
Downtown
Knuckles

463

Barfly Index

Players Club
Pour House
Resi's Bierstube
Sharon's Hillbilly Heaven
Signature Room
Simon's Tavern
Southport City Saloon
Ten Cat
Tequila Roadhouse
Thurston's
Toons
Trader Todd's Adventure Bar
Tuman's Alcohol Abuse Center
Twisted Spoke

Zum Deutschen Eck

South Side

Buddy Guy's Legends
Ciral's House of Tiki
Exchequer Pub
McDuffy's Lodge
Romantic Club

West Side

The Parthenon

Suburbs

The Round Up

Drink Selection/Cost

Cheap Drinks

North Side

Babe's
The Brewery
Bucktown Pub
City Limits Pub
Crown Lounge
Cut Rate Liquors & Package Goods
Demo's Pub
Ed & Jeans
El-kees
Extra-Innings Sports Bar
Family Bar
Four Treys
Friends Pub
G&L Fire Escape
Gambler's
Gio's Sports Bar
Goofy's Hock Shop
Home Tavern
Inner Town Pub
Irish Wolfhound
Jagiellonia
Jefferson Inn
Kasey's
Kat Klub

Keysters
Kronies
Lake Breeze Lounge
Lincoln Tap
Lincoln Tavern
Little Rascal's
Lounge Ax
Mangi's
Marty's
Mayor's Office Lounge
O'Lanagan's
Payton Place
Peacock Lounge
Pumping Co.
Relax Sports Bar
Rossi's
Saxony Liquor Lounge
Second Time Around
Sharon's Hillbilly Heaven
Smiler Coogan's
T & A Two
The Montrose Saloon
Tuman's Alcohol Abuse Center
"W" Cut Rate Liquors

South Side

Brewskee's
Cal's Bar

Carol's Archer Pub
Julie's Place
McNally's
Rudy and Ann's Lounge
Sheehy's

Suburbs

Brat Stop

Funky Drinks
North Side

Dick's Last Resort (Condom Cocktail)
Grizzly's (Yukon Slush)
Konak (Dirty Mother)
Liar's Club (PooPooPeePeeKaKa Logger)
Lilly's (Jumbo Long Islands)
Match Box (Cigare Volante wine)
The Monkey Bar (Bananatini)
Nisei Lounge (Malort)
Players Club (Michael Andretti Stoli Cocktail)
Polly Esther's (Brady Punch)
Redfish (Cajun Martini)
Sheffield's (Blomo Bloody Mary)
Tai's Lounge (Bob Chinn Mai Tais)
Tres Amigos (Cafe De Amigos)
Twisted Spoke (Honey Nut Cheerio)

South Side

Ciral's House of Tiki (Zombie)
Phyllis-Up (Green Monster)
Ted's Place (Fisherman's Drink)

Downtown

Govnor's Pub (Spiced Rum Cider)

Glogg
North Side

Gallery Cabaret
Konak
Simon's Tavern

Good Beer Selection
North Side

aliveOne (18 taps)
Alumni Club (12 taps, 21 different bottles)
Bird's Nest (13 taps)
Bluebird Lounge
Bucktown Pub (11 taps)
Butch McGuire's (20 taps)
Clark Street Ale House (24 taps)
Cullen's (12 taps)
Deja Vu (12 taps)
Delilah's (unique selection)
Dick's Last Resort (70 different bottles)
Emerald Isle (12 taps)
Emmit's (11 taps)
Fireside Restaurant (10 taps, 50 different bottles)
Ginger's Ale House (16 taps)
Glascott's (14 taps)
The Great Beer Palace (18 taps)
Ham Tree (101 different bottles)
Hoghead McDunna's (11 taps)
The Hudson Club (20 taps, 50 different bottles)
The Huettenbar (10 taps)
Jake's Pub (10 Taps, 70 different bottles)
Kelly's on the Green (21 taps)
Laschet's Inn (8 taps, 36 different bottles)
Lizzy McNeil's (17 taps)
Magoo's (12 taps)
Map Room (26 taps, 60 different bottles)
The Monkey Bar (12 taps)
Mulligan's (19 taps)
Ole St. Andrews Inn (11 taps, 50 different bottles)
Pippins (11 taps)
Players Club (13 taps)

Barfly Index

Quenchers (15 taps, 200 different bottles)
Redfish (45 different bottles)
Resi's Bierstube (130 imported beers, 12 taps)
Rossi's (30 different bottles)
Schoolyard Tavern (14 taps)
Schuba's (12 taps)
Sheffield's (100 beers)
Subterranean (12 taps)
The U.S. Beer Co. (100 different bottles)
Village Tap (31 taps)

South Side

Fireside Beverly (16 taps)
Puffer's (homebrew club)

Downtown

The Berghoff Cafe (Own beer, brewed in Wisc.)

Good Scotch, Whiskey, Bourbon Selection

North Side

Abbey Pub (Irish Whiskey)
Augenblick (11 single-malt Scotch)
The Duke of Perth (60 different types of Scotch)
Delilah's (wall of booze)
Emmit's (classic Scotch selection)
Exit (40 different bourbons)
Fado' (Irish Whiskey)
The Hudson Club
Irish American Heritage Center (Irish Whiskey)
Mulligan's (freshest Jameson)
Old St. Andrews Inn
Players Club (13 different types of Scotch)

Good Wine Selection

North Side

Brown Dog Tavern (50 Australian wines)
Cy's Steak & Chop House
Fireside Restaurant (30 wines)
The Hudson Club (100 wines)
Pops for Champagne (140 types of Champagne)
Webster's Wine Bar

South Side

Puffer's

West Side

The Parthenon

High End

North Side

Brown Dog Tavern
Cafe Fresco
Corosh
Cro-bar
Cullen's
Cy's Steak & Chop House
Dome Room
Fumatore
The Hudson Club
Joe's on Broadway
O'Brien's Restaurant
Drinking at O'Hare Airport
Pops for Champagne
Rainbo Roller Rink
Red Dog
Signature Room

Downtown

Downtown
Big Brassiere and Bar
Knuckles

Ethnic

Barfly Index
West Side
Kallisto
The Parthenon

Irish
North Side
Abbey Pub (live music, real thing)
Augenblick (Tuesday night live music)
Blarney Stone
Butch McGuire's Tavern
Clancy's Pub and Grill
Clancy's Belmont Saloon
Cullen's
Dublin's
Emerald Isle
Emmit's
Fado'
Foley's
Glascott's
Gunther Muphy's
Harp & Shamrock
Hidden Shamrock
Irish American Heritage Center
Irish Eyes
Irish Village
Irish Wolfhound
Kelly's on the Green
Kelly's Pub
Lizzy McNeil's (faux)
Mulligan's
O'Brien's Restaurant
Six Benny Bit
Thatch Pub (live folk music weekends)
Timothy O'Toole's
Vaughan's Pub
South Side
Cork & Kerry
Joe Bailly's
Keegan's
Kitty O'Shea's
McNally's

O'Malley's Pub
Sheehy's
Suburbs
Reilly's Daughter

Italian
North Side
Fumatore
Orso's Restaurant
Sertano's

Jamaican
North Side
Hollywood East

Japanese
North Side
Nisei Lounge

Latin
North Side
El Jardin
Gio's Sports Bar
Gloria's Sports Bar (live music)
La Cita
LAMA
Lucille's (tapas)

Mexican
North Side
Jagiellonia
La Flor De Acapulco

Persian
North Side
Reza's

Extremely Clean

Barfly Index

Serves Food

Key: MB = more than burgers
TB = typical bar food

North Side

Alumni Club (MB)
Abbey Pub (MB)
Beat Kitchen (MB)
Bird's Nest (MB)
Andy's (MB)
Augies (TB)
Banana Joe's (MB)
Billy Goat (TB)
Boss Bar (TB)
Boston Blackies (MB)
Brown Dog Tavern (MB)
The Bulls (TB)
Butch McGuire's (TB)
BW-3 (TB)
Cafe Fresco (MB)
Carol's Pub (TB)
City Limits Pub (TB)
Clancy's Pub & Grill (MB)
Cleos (MB)
CND Gyros Lounge (TB)
Congress Restaurant & Lounge (MB)
Corosh (MB)
Crystal Inn (TB)
Cubby Bear (TB)
Cullen's (TB)
Cy's Steak & Chop House (MB)
Deja Vu (TB)
Dick's Last Resort (MB)
Don't Worry (MB)
Dublin's (MB)
Duke of Perth (MB)
Edgewater Lounge (TB)
Emerald Isle (TB)
Emmit's (MB)
Fado' (MB)
Family Bar (TB)
Finley Dunne's (MB)

Fireside Restaurant (MB)
Gallagher's (MB)
Ginger's Ale House (TB)
Goose Island (MB)
The Great Beer Palace (TB)
Grizzly's (MB)
Hidden Shamrock (MB)
Higgins Tavern (TB)
Hoghead McDunna's (TB)
Hollywood East (MB)
Howard's Bar & Grill (TB)
The Hudson Club (MB)
Iggy's (MB)
Irish American Heritage Center (TB)
Irish Village (MB)
J.T. Collins (MB)
Jack Sullivan's (MB)
John Barleycorn (MB)
Jury's (MB)
Kelly's Pub (TB)
Kerouac Jack's (MB)
Kincades (TB)
Konak (TB)
La Flor De Acapulco (TB)
Lakeview East (TB)
The Last Act (MB)
Lawry's Tavern (MB)
The Levee (TB)
Lincoln Tavern (MB)
Little Rascal's (TB)
Lottie's (TB)
Lucille's (MB)
Lucky Strike (TB)
Mangi's (TB)
The Martini Ranch (TB)
Martyr's (TB)
Maryla Polanaise (MB)
Michael's Sports Bar (TB)
Mirabell (MB)
Monsignor Murphy's (TB)
Moody's Pub (TB)

Barfly Index

Serves Food Late

North Side

Fireside Restaurant
Iggy's

Lakeview East
Lucille's

South Side

Ciral's House of Tiki

Bars Open Until 4 a.m.

The following is a complete list of all the bars in the City of Chicago open until 4 a.m. Sunday to Friday, 5 a.m. Saturday. Each of these bars has a 4 a.m. license, however some may still close earlier. Also some of these bars may be closed down. City officials are on a campaign to close down the city's taverns and to keep a list like this up to date is extremely difficult. Lastly, only a portion of these bars are reviewed in this book. Still for those who work the late shift or like to stay out all night, this is a valuable list.

North Side

1000 Liquors, 1000 W. Belmont Ave.
1531 Tavern, 1531 N. Kingsbury St.
Aaron's S.L., 5308 N. Lincoln Ave.
Aftermath, 1332 N. Halsted St.
Beaumont, 2020 N. Halsted St.
Berlin, 954 W. Belmont Ave.
Bistro Too, 5015 N. Clark St.
Boondocks River Shanty, 1177 N. Elston Ave.
Borderline Tap, 1958 W. North Ave.
Carol's Pub, 4659 N. Clark St.
Casanova's, 2415 W. Lawrence Ave.
Charlie's, 417 W. Laramie Ave.
Clark's on Clark, 5001 N. Clark St.
Club Continental, 5515 N. Lincoln
Crobar, 1543 N. Kingsbury St.
Deja Vu, 2624 N. Lincoln Ave.
Deni's Deli, 2939 N. Clark St.

Dynasty Club, 5447 N. Lincoln Ave.
El Mekido Nodermo, 1247 N. Ashland Ave.
Estelle's Pub, 2013 W. North Ave.
Exit, 1315 W. North Ave.
Fenik Lounge, 2906 N. Pulaski Road
Fireside Restaurant and Lounge, 5739 N. Ravenswood Ave.
Ginger's Ale House, 3801 N. Ashland
Green Mill Lounge, 4802 N. Broadway St.
Hidden Cove, 5338 N. Lincoln Ave.
Iggy's, 700 N. Milwaukee Ave.
Infinity, 1860 N. Elston Ave.
Joker Pub, 1553 W. Devon Ave.
Kafield's Restaurant, 5035 N. Lincoln
Kimmik Tap Room, 6015 N. Sheridan
Kingston Mines, 2548 N. Halsted St.
Lakeview East Bar & Liquors, 3110 N. Broadway St.
Lakeview Lounge, 5110 N. Broadway
La Pachanga, 2554 N. Halsted St.
Laurie's Pizzeria, 5153 N. Broadway
Little Jim's, 3501 N. Halsted St.
Manhole, 3456 N. Halsted St.
Marie's Riptide Lounge, 1745 W. Armitage Ave.
Mycroft's Pub, 5911 N. Lincoln Ave.
Neo, 2348 N. Clark St.
New Saxony Lounge, 1136 W. Lawrence Ave.
Nick's, 1516 N. Milwaukee Ave.
Number's, 6406 N. Clark St.
O'Lanagan's, 2940 N. Broadway St.
Payton Place, 5624 N. Broadway St.

Northwest Side

South Side

Barfly Index

Downtown

(Many of these bars are in Old Town and River North)

West Side

Games

Board Games
North Side
Beachwood Inn
Blue Frog
Guthrie's
Lemmings
Monsignor Murphy's
Podhale
Village Tap
Will's Northwoods Inn

Bowling
North Side
Diversey River Bowl
Kat Klub (Shuffleboard Bowling)
Lucky Strike
Southport Lanes

Darts
North Side
Abbey Pub
Apple Pub
The Brewery
Brigadoon
Butch McGuire's
Casey's
Charlie's Chicago
Clark Bar
Critters
Emerald Isle
Eva's
Extra Innings Sports Bar
Family Bar
Foley's
Friend's Pub
Gallagher's
Gambler's

Gio's Sports Bar
Griffins Public House
Grizzly's
Ham Tree
Harp & Shamrock
Hob-Nob Tavern
Hoghead McDunna's
Jagiellonia
Jake's Pub
Jefferson Inn
Kasey's
Kat Klub
Keysters
Kincades
Kronies
The Levee
Michael's Sports Bar
Monsignor Murphy's
Mulligan's
O'Malley's Pub (leagues)
Peabody's Pub
Pumping Co.
Rose & Crown London Pub
Rossi's
Sak's Ukrainian Village
Schoolyard Tavern
Second Time Around
Simply Ray's
Six Penny Bit (leagues)
Smiler Coogan's
Snuggles Pub
The Store
T & A Two
Tai's Lounge
Thatch Pub
Thurston's
Timothy O'Toole's
Tommy's on Higgins
Tony's Place
The U.S. Beer Co. (leagues)
Walsh's Schubert Inn

Workingman's Palace
South Side
BJ's Pub
Brewskee's
Carol's Archer Pub
Chateau Lounge
Galloway's Mystic
Groucho's
Just Joey's
McDuffy's Lodge
Puffer's
Pullman's Pub
September's
Downtown
Knuckles
West Side
Illinois Bar & Grill
Suburbs
Go To Blases

Foosball
North Side
Emerald Isle
Gio's Sports Bar
Keysters
Nisei Lounge
O'Malley's Pub
Spike's Rat Bar
Toons
South Side
Puffer's
Romantic Club

Golden Tee
*Note -- most bars seem to have this game now. We recommend giving most any bar a call, they may have it.
North Side
Grizzly's

Mulligan's
Riptide
Kelsey's
South Side
Alcock's
Brewskee's
September's
West Side
Illinois Bar & Grill

Good Video Game Selection
North Side
Diversey River Bowl
Emerald Isle
Finley Dunne's
Michael's Sports Bar
The Monkey Bar
Players Club
Polly Esther's
Schuba's
Sluggers
Ten Cat
WhirlyBall
Wild Goose

Pinball
North Side
Jake's Pub
La Cita
Liar's Club
Lincoln Tap
The Marquee Lounge
Michael's Sports Bar
Morseland
Nick's
Nisei Lounge
Old Town Ale House
Peabody's Pub
Quenchers

Barfly Index

South Side

Downtown

Roller Skating
North Side

480

Ghosts

Haunted

North Side

Billy Goat
Gold Star
Guthrie's
Lincoln Tap
Ole St. Andrews Inn
Red Lion Pub

Suburbs

Alonzi's Villa
Chet's Melody Lounge
Country House

Go To Blases

Located Next To A Cemetery

North Side

Extra Innings Sports Bar
Fireside Restaurant

Suburbs

Chet's Melody Lounge
Go To Blases
Hickey's He's Not Here
The Round Up

Good Place to People Watch

North Side

Joe's on Broadway
Lakeview East
Lounge Ax
Drinking at O'Hare Airport
Red Dog

Texas Star Fajita Bar
Top Hat Lounge

South Side

McDuffy's Lodge

Downtown

Big Brassiere and Bar

History

Been A Bar Since The 1940s

North Side

Fireside Restaurant (not originally
Fireside)
Gallery Cabaret (not originally
Gallery)
Match Box (same name, second
owner)
The Monkey Bar (not originally
Monkey Bar)
Saxony Liquor Lounge
T & A Two (same bar, different own-
ers)

Barfly Index

Magoo's (opened 1996)
The Monkey Bar (opened 1996)
Players Club (opened 1996)

Open Since Repeal of Prohibition

North Side

Billy Goat Tavern, 430 N. Michigan Ave (same family owners since 1933)
Club Foot (former bar on same site)
Deja Vu (former bar on same site)
Emmit's (former bar on same site)
Gold Star (same name since 1933)
Jake's Pub (same name since 1933)
John Barleycorn (former bar on same site)
Lawry's Tavern (same family owners since 1933)
The Levee (third bar since Prohibition on site)
Lottie's (same name since 1933)
Sak's Ukrainian Village
Simon's Tavern (same family until recently)

South Side

Just Joey's (former bar on same site)
Palm Tavern (same bar since 1933)

Suburbs

Tiffany's

Remnant of Old Polish Broadway

North Side

Gold Star

Same Family

Running Bar Since 1800s

North Side

Glascott's (current site since 1937)

South Side

Sheehan's Lounge

Downtown

The Berghoff Cafe

Site Has Housed A Bar Since 1900

North Side

Club Foot
Schuba's

North Side

Lucky Lady (Pullman)

Suburbs

Chet's Melody Lounge
Ron's Bungalow Inn

Site Has Housed A Bar Since 1900

North Side

Delilah's
Glascott's
Gold Star
The Green Mill
Jake's Pub
John Barleycorn
Simon's Tavern

South Side

Pullman's Pub

Suburbs

Country House
Edwin's

Ron's Bungalow Inn

Speakeasy In The 1920s

North Side

Delilah's
Glascott's
Gold Star
The Green Mill

Jake's Pub
John Barleycorn
Simon's Tavern

North Side

Pullman's Pub

Suburbs

Country House
Edwin's
Ron's Bungalow Inn

Lingerie Fashion Shows

North Side

City Limits Pub
Eva's

Jefferson Inn
Rossi's
Sporty's

Located Next To An 'L' Stop

North Side

Jefferson Inn
Kelly's Pub
Kerouac Jack's
The Martini Ranch
Red Dog

Sertano's
Simply Ray's
Sports Corner

North Side

Exchequer Pub

Movie Location

North Side

Emmit's ("Uncle Buck," "Backdraft")
Saxony Liquor Lounge ("Babe"
across street)

South Side

Pullman's Pub ("The Fugitive")

Music

Alternative Rock
North Side
Augenblick (live music)
Beat Kitchen (live music)
Bluebird Lounge (stereo, no jukebox)
Club Foot (DJ)
Club 950 (DJ)
Dome Room (live music/DJ)
Empty Bottle (live music)
Exit (jukebox, industrial)
Farrugut's (jukebox)
Gallery Cabaret (live music)
Gunther Murphy's (live music)
Joy Blue (live accoustic)
Jemmings (jukebox)
Liar's Club (DJ)
Lincoln Tap (DJ, jukebox)
Lounge Ax (live)
Map Room (jukebox)
Martyr's (live)
Morseland (live)
Simon's Tavern (jukebox)
Subterranean (live)
Ten 56
The Big Horse (live)
Thurston's (live, DJ)

Amazing Variety
North Side
Inner Town Pub
Jagiellonia
Kasey's
Lakeview East
Marie's Riptide Lounge
The Martini Ranch
Martyr's (live)
The Monkey Bar
Mulligan's
The Note (live)

Pop's on Chicago (live)
Rosie O'Brien's (jukebox)
Simply Ray's (jukebox)
Stanley's (jukebox)
Tai's Lounge (jukebox)
The U.S. Beer Co. (jukebox)
Village Tap (jukebox)
Weeds (live)
Wonder Bar (live)
South Side
Chateau Lounge (jukebox)
Julie's Place (jukebox)

Bar Bands
North Side
Banana Joe's
Cleos
Cubby Bear
Deja Vu
Emerald Isle
Gambler's
Ginger's Ale House
Grizzly's
Hoghead McDunna's
Lilly's
Luney Tunes Saloon
Lyons Den
Magoo's
Nick's
O'Malley's Pub
Oinker's
Ole St. Andrews Inn
Pop's on Chicago
Schuba's
Sidelines
Six Penny Bit
Sluggers
The U.S. Beer Co.
WhirlyBall

Barfly Index

Mad Bar
Moretti's
Polly Esther's
Pumping Co.
Red Dog
Teasers
Tequila Roadhouse
Thurston's

South Side

Artis'
Bohica
50 Yard Line
Groucho's

Suburbs

Tiffany's

Grateful Dead

North Side

Brother Jimmy's
Martyr's (live bands)
Morseland (live bands)

Hard Rock/Metal

North Side

Aftershocks (jukebox)
Bucktown Pub (jukebox)
The Closet (jukebox)
Diversey River Bowl (stereo)
Exit (jukebox)
Jake's Pub (jukebox)
Little Rascal's (jukebox)
Oinkers (jukebox)
Smiler Coogan's (live)
Tony's Place (jukebox)
Wrigleyville Tap (jukebox)

Irish

North Side

Irish American Heritage Center (live

bands)
Irish Eyes (live music)
Irish Village
Pinewood (jukebox)
Thatch Pub (live)
Vaughan's Pub (jukebox)

Jazz

North Side

Andy's (live)
The Bulls (live)
Deja Vu (live on certain nights)
Empty Bottle (live on certain nights)
Ginger Man (jukebox)
The Green Mill (live)
Jury's (jukebox)
Old Town Ale House (jukebox)
Pops for Champagne (live)
Sertano's (live jazz)

South Side

Palm Tavern (jukebox)

Karaoke

North Side

Friar Tuck's
O'Malley's Pub
Oinkers
The Store, Clybourn
Trader Todd's Adventure Bar

South Side

O'Malley's Pub

Suburbs

Alonzi's Villa

Open Mic

North Side

Bird's Nest
Gallery Cabaret
Inner Town Pub